Nuremberg Principles and Ukraine

Nuremberg Principles and Ukraine

The Contemporary Challenges to Peace, Security, and Justice

Edited by
Marshall J. Breger and Hebert R. Reginbogin

BLOOMSBURY ACADEMIC
NEW YORK • LONDON • OXFORD • NEW DELHI • SYDNEY

BLOOMSBURY ACADEMIC
Bloomsbury Publishing Inc, 1385 Broadway, New York, NY 10018, USA
Bloomsbury Publishing Plc, 50 Bedford Square, London, WC1B 3DP, UK
Bloomsbury Publishing Ireland, 29 Earlsfort Terrace, Dublin 2, D02 AY28, Ireland

BLOOMSBURY, BLOOMSBURY ACADEMIC and the Diana logo are trademarks of Bloomsbury Publishing Plc

First published in the United States of America 2025

A catalog record for this book is available from the Library of Congress.

ISBN: HB: 978-1-6669-6076-1
ePDF: 978-1-6669-6077-8
eBook: 978-1-6669-6077-8

Typeset by Deanta Global Publishing Services, Chennai, India

For product safety related questions contact productsafety@bloomsbury.com.

To find out more about our authors and books visit www.bloomsbury.com and sign up for our newsletters.

Dedication

Marshall J. Breger dedicates this volume to his wife of more than forty-eight years, Jennifer Stern Breger, who has sustained him throughout. She opens her mouth with wisdom; And the law of kindness is on her tongue. *(Proverbs 31:26). And also to his newborn grandchild, Ira Elias—may he go from strength to strength.*

Herbert R. Reginbogin dedicates this volume to his wife, Karin, and son Michael. It is a daily reminder of today and the future of tomorrow.

Contents

Tables and Figures

Tables

Figures

Acknowledgments

Most contributions in this volume stem from papers presented at the 2023 "Nuremberg Principles: Contemporary Challenges" conference, held at the Catholic University of America in Washington, D.C. Gathering a diverse array of highly qualified experts from various disciplines to discuss the Nuremberg principles would not have been possible without the pressing need to address the crime of aggression, often referred to as the "supreme international crime." This crime, regarded as the most severe international offense, embodies the profound evil of war; it stands as the ultimate crime among all others, as the volume deals with the effects of the international world order following the Russian invasion of Ukraine on January 24, 2022. We owe tremendous gratitude to all the contributors who painstakingly underscore the seriousness of writing their chapters to emphasize the evolution of international criminal law from 1945 until today.

The editors would like to express their special thanks to Dean David P. Long of the Institute of Policy Research and Catholic Studies (IPR) for his enormous moral and material support for this project, as well as numerous other Catholic University of America employees.

We thank, as well, Bloomsbury Publishing for their interest in publishing this volume. Thanks to Holly Buchanan, the acquisitions editor, for her continued assistance and feedback. We thank Ambassador Beth Van Schanck for the advice and assistance; Lydia Korostelova (CUA 2023) for her substantive assistance in preparing papers for publication; Chris Morris of the John K. Mullen Memorial Library and Frances M. Brillantine, Head of Access Services, Judge Kathryn J. DuFour Law Library, both at the Catholic University of America, for bibliographical assistance; and Rebecca Riddell for administrative assistance.

We also thank the Federal Ministry of Justice of the Federal Republic of Germany for material support for the conference that led to the writing of this volume, most notably State Secretary Dr. Angelika Schlunck; Professor Christoph Safferling, president of the International Nuremberg Principles Academy, Nuremberg, Germany; and Vice President Viviane Dittrich. We are most grateful to the International Research and Documentation Center for War Crimes Trials at Philipps-University Marburg and Case Western Reserve University School of Law for their assistance. Also, thanks for the advice and support from Counselor Oleksandr Borysenko of the Ukrainian Embassy in the United States and her H.E. Ambassador Oksana Markarova. Also, thanks to former ambassador Anatoly Antonov of the Russian Federation to the United States for expressing his views on the Russian invasion of Ukraine.

We would be remiss if we did not recognize and thank Benjamin Ferencz, whose last public appearance before his death was at the Nuremberg Conference. He was (and is) an inspiration to all those concerned with promoting the rule of law.

Foreword
The Nuremberg Principles Today
Christoph Safferling

On December 11, 1946, Resolution 95 (I) of the United Nations (UN) General Assembly "affirmed" the Nuremberg Principles as principles of international law.[1] Some four years later, on July 29, 1950, acting upon another General Assembly Resolution, a nascent International Law Commission developed a comprehensive version of these seven principles.[2] The Nuremberg Principles represented the main achievements and postulations of international law that had been featured in the charter and the proceedings of the International Military Tribunal (IMT) held in Nuremberg in 1945/46. The visionary prospects and radical amendments of international law that arose out of the IMT's pioneering charter and judgment were thus presented in a principled and approachable way, determined in its language, and easy to comprehend. With the formulation of these Principles, the language and delineations of international law have forever been changed.

In essence, the seven Nuremberg Principles stated the following: No impunity for international crimes (Principle I), no priority of domestic laws (Principle II), no immunity for heads of state or responsible government officials (Principle III), no superior order-excuse (Principle IV), the right to a fair trial (Principle V), the list of core crimes, namely the crime of aggression (then as crimes against peace), war crimes and crimes against humanity (Principle VI, amended in 1948 by the Genocide Convention adding genocide as a fourth core crime), and the criminality of complicity (Principle VII). These propositions compose the core fundamentals of any international criminal justice system that has evolved since the formulation of the Nuremberg Principles.

Of course, the international community sacrificed the ideals and enforcement of these Principles on the altar of political necessity in the following decades. This stalemate fulfilled Justice Jackson's fears that political wrangling and rivalries would prevent the farsighted cooperation that would be required for the meaningful growth of international criminal law.[3] However, the spirit of these principles was still displayed in courageous and groundbreaking domestic initiatives such as the trials of Klaus Barbie in France, Adolf Eichmann in Israel, and the *Trial of the Juntas* in Argentina. The Nuremberg Principles were, however, rediscovered by the international community in the early 1990s with the end of the Cold War. For a short moment in history, the UN system worked the way it had been envisaged, and the Security Council's perennial deadlock vanished. This was the period when the aspirations and hopes connected to the Nuremberg Principles could eventually break through and be truly transformed into peremptory norms of international law. The stony path led through several uniquely shaped *ad hoc* tribunals created for different situations and ultimately to the adoption of the Rome Statute for a permanent international criminal court in 1998. In a way, the International Criminal Court (ICC) is the body competent to execute the promises of the Nuremberg Principles—it is the one international institution which since its setting into practice in 2003 embodies and represents the Nuremberg Principles in international relations.

For several reasons, however, the story does not end here. First, the ICC is not universal per se, but based on membership. Sadly, some seventy-five states are not members of the Rome Statute, among them very powerful states like the USA, China, India, and the Russian Federation. The Court is, however, widely accepted in Africa, Europe, and Latin America. Second, the crime of aggression, even if contained in the original list of crimes under Art. 5 of the Rome Statute, was only defined in 2010. In the so-called Kampala-Compromise, the prosecution of this crime of crimes was put under such procedural restraints that its implementation is highly unlikely. In addition, the ratification rate of the Kampala Amendment is minimal. Third, the International Criminal Court is a complementary institution with acutely limited resources and thus heavily reliant on domestic jurisdictions of both member and non-member states in relation to *inter alia* cooperation and prosecutions. For those non-member states, the Nuremberg Principles remain a singular point of reference when it comes to obligations under international law with regard to international criminal justice.

On February 24, 2022, the Russian Federation conducted a full-scale invasion of Ukraine and thus committed an act of aggression, which is punishable as a crime of aggression within the meaning of the Nuremberg Principles. Whereas Ukraine, not being a member state, has accepted ICC jurisdiction since 2014, accountability for the war in Ukraine is also hindered by the deficiencies described above. Powerful states are not members of the ICC, the crime of aggression cannot be prosecuted by the ICC, and domestic jurisdictions, like in Ukraine itself, are insufficient and heavily overloaded. In such a context, the Nuremberg Principles become all the more relevant. They call for accountability including the prosecution of state officials not only for the commission of war crimes and crimes against humanity but also for orchestrating the crime of aggression. This is sadly ironic as many of the crimes which were committed between 1939 and 1945 during the Second World War and which eventually compelled the international community to create the IMT in the first place were actually committed on Ukrainian and Russian soil. The Nuremberg Principles were thus drafted for nothing less than preventing and deterring this and other regions from ever again suffering from war, occupation, and hatred.

It is thus worthwhile and necessary to call for faithful adherence to the Nuremberg Principles with regard to the aggression against Ukraine. It is critical to find ways forward to prosecute the crime of aggression in perhaps the most blatant breach of the UN Charter that European soil has witnessed since the Nazis unleashed war in 1939. Similarly, domestic jurisdictions need to fulfill their duties in cooperating with the ICC and reinforcing its mandate by prosecuting core crimes like war crimes and crimes against humanity. Many states, whether ICC member states or not, have started to act accordingly and have begun using innovative tools such as by setting up an

International Centre for the Prosecution of the Crime of Aggression and other joint investigation teams through Eurojust. Here, the Nuremberg Principles are pertinent and capable of giving the non-member states of the ICC the necessary legitimacy required to proceed with prosecuting international crimes committed in this context. They can also serve as a reminder to the Russian Federation that, in violating these principles, the country is renouncing a legacy that it had helped to conceive and one that it is legally obliged to uphold.

The war in Ukraine shows that the Nuremberg Principles are the cornerstone of an imperfect international criminal justice system that is in development and in need of constant refinement and augmentation. The struggle of humanity for justice is eternal, and no one is above the laws of humanity. Those who think they are will be held responsible. This is the central and enduring message of the Nuremberg Principles, and it holds true today as much as it did all those years ago.

Notes

1 See International Law Commission, Principles of International Law Recognized in the Charter of the Nürnberg Tribunal and in the Judgment of the Tribunal (1950) https://legal.un.org/ilc/texts/instruments/english/draft_articles/7_1_1950.pdf Also see United Nations General Assembly Resolution 95 (I) of December 11, 1946, Affirmation of the Principles of International Law Recognized by the Charter of the Nuremberg Tribunal (December 11, 1946) https://legal.un.org/avl/pdf/h/ga_95-I/ga_95-I_ph_e.pdf.

2 United Nations General Assembly Resolution 177(II) of November 21, 1947, Formulation of the Principles Recognized in the Charter of the Nürnberg Tribunal and in the Judgment of the Tribunal (November 21, 1947) https://documents.un.org/doc/resolution/gen/nr0/038/84/pdf/nr003884.pdf?token=bwJf3ELe7108hrtU1p&fe=true.

3 Francis Biddle, the principal US representative at the IMT, has elaborated on Justice Jackson's concerns in this regard. See Francis Biddle, *In Brief Authority* (London: Bloomsbury Academic, 1976), 478.

Foreword

Eli M. Rosenbaum

In their landmark decision rendered at Nuremberg in October 1946, the judges of the International Military Tribunal held major surviving leaders of the defeated Nazi regime of Germany accountable for having committed war crimes and crimes against humanity, criminality that cost the lives of many millions of people. For their respective roles in Germany's invasion and subjugation of other European nations, twelve of the defendants were found guilty of committing the crime of aggression. The tribunal declared that waging a war of aggression is "the supreme international crime," for it "contains within itself the accumulated evil of the whole"—that is, it is the crime which most commonly precipitates and makes possible the perpetration of the other major international humanitarian and human rights crimes—war crimes, crimes against humanity, and genocide.

On February 24, 2022, the Russian Federation, under the leadership of its longtime president, Vladimir Putin, launched a full-scale, unprovoked, and unlawful invasion of neighboring Ukraine, aiming to deprive the largest country wholly inside Europe of its sovereignty and independence, destroy its democracy, and gain dominion over all of Ukraine's territory that remained unconquered by Russia following its 2014 invasion and illegal annexation of Crimea.

As in the case of the bloodiest *prior* invasion of Ukraine—namely, the one launched in June 1941 by Nazi Germany—the 2022 Russian invasion was accompanied by the perpetration of war crimes and crimes against humanity on a vast and profoundly shocking scale, as well as, in the opinion of many observers (this writer among them), the commission of genocide. Tragically, Putin's Russia has thereby proved anew the veracity of the IMT judges' portrayal of the crime of aggression as containing "the accumulated evil of the whole." By mid-October 2024, Ukrainian authorities had recorded more than 141,000 war crimes, including notorious mass atrocities committed in Bucha and elsewhere. Like others who have visited Bucha and spoken with massacre survivors there, I found the experience heartbreaking and one that cries out for justice.

It is commonplace, nearly to the point of cliché, for endorsements on book dust jackets and in advertisements to refer to this or that book as being "timely and essential." However, in the case of the present volume, those words are amply warranted, particularly given the continuing refusal of the Russian leadership to desist from their forces' lethal rampage through Ukraine, the failure to date of criminal law mechanisms (or trade or other sanctions) to achieve significant (if any) deterrence of Russia's atrocity crimes, and also given the incisiveness of the analyses presented in the pages that follow. With the world's four most dangerous authoritarian regimes—

those of Russia, China, Iran, and North Korea—now having joined forces to destroy the independence of a peaceful United Nations member state, the credibility of international criminal law principles and enforcement mechanisms is being tested as never before.

Russia's brutal invasion of Ukraine presents the world with the most serious challenge to international humanitarian and human rights law and to international criminal law more generally, since the Nuremberg trial of 1945–46. Indeed, the facts of Ukraine's perilous situation show that the Nuremberg legacy itself is also imperiled.

For many decades after the conclusion of the international Nuremberg trial, it seemed virtually inconceivable that the perpetration of aggressive war and barbaric violations of humanitarian and human rights laws on a colossal scale, such as Russia is now committing, would recur, especially in Europe, where thousands of survivors of the Hitler regime's catastrophic world war continue to live, many of them in Ukraine and, ironically, in Russia as well. That, however, is precisely what has transpired. If anything, the situation has worsened significantly in recent months. Russia continues to record military advances against the vastly outnumbered and outgunned Ukrainian armed forces, all the while committing the most egregious form of aggression, namely aggression to achieve territorial conquest. Moreover, the Putin regime continues to target civilians and civilian structures in Ukraine, including to destroy critical energy infrastructure. Most frighteningly of all, Russia has gained the appalling distinction of becoming the first country in the history of the world whose leadership has threatened to use nuclear weapons in the course of waging a war of aggression.[1] "Life is a living hell for the people of Ukraine," UN Secretary-General Antonio Guterres aptly declared on the first anniversary of Moscow's invasion. That invasion, he added, "has unleashed widespread death, destruction and displacement."

Both international and national law enforcement mechanisms have struggled to respond to Russia's continuing unbridled criminality. The Prosecutor of the International Criminal Court has obtained arrest warrants against President Putin and three other Russian officials for committing war crimes and crimes against humanity. However, the prosecutor cannot charge the "supreme" crime of aggression, as the ICC lacks jurisdiction over aggression committed by non-state Parties absent a UN Security Council referral. Russia, which never ratified the ICC Rome Treaty or endorsed the 2010 ICC Kampala Amendments, would certainly block such a referral attempt with its "P-5" veto. An informal "Core Group" of more than three dozen countries seeking to create a special tribunal to prosecute persons responsible for committing aggression against Ukraine has been meeting since January 2023. But at the time of this writing, no agreement on the form that such a tribunal would take has been announced, with participating nations reportedly continuing to disagree on whether it should be an international or, instead, an "internationalized" tribunal (also termed an "internationalized national tribunal") that is based in Ukraine's judicial system but that also incorporates international elements involving, for example, substantive law, personnel, information sources, and structure.[2]

Meanwhile, the Kremlin has taken the position that it does not "recognize" the ICC arrest warrants that have been issued for Russian officials for the reason that Russia is not an ICC State Party. Russia's contempt for ICC efforts to secure a measure of accountability and deterrence has arguably been eclipsed in cynicism and disrespect for the rule of law by the governments of two ICC States Parties, South Africa and Mongolia, which, despite having a treaty obligation to arrest Putin and deliver him to The Hague, have declined to do so in connection with official visits by the Russian president. (Putin ultimately decided to deliver his August 2023 address in Johannesburg via remote means from abroad, but he did make an official trip to Mongolia in September 2024. He was received warmly there and was never taken into custody.)

National jurisdictions are conducting important investigations, and a few have brought criminal cases. Most notably, under the widely admired leadership of Prosecutor General Andriy Kostin, Ukrainian authorities have indicted more than 500 suspects and obtained 132 convictions for war crimes—including killings, torture, abduction of children, conflict-related sexual violence, and environmental war crimes (the first environmental war crimes prosecutions in world history).[3] They have recorded these extraordinary accomplishments under almost unimaginably difficult circumstances, with their country under continuous attack and, of course, despite receiving no cooperation from the government in Moscow, which has the most extensive access to key evidence. Most of the perpetrators are protected by the Russian government and remain beyond the reach of law enforcement authorities in Ukraine and elsewhere. Ukraine's prosecutors, civilian law enforcement personnel, judges, and the country's military investigators are attempting to do something that no other nation has ever done: pursue comprehensive justice for the large-scale perpetration of atrocity crimes while their nation is in the midst of defending itself in an existential war. In this work, they are receiving substantial assistance from foreign governments, multilateral organizations, and civil society groups.

Some other countries' authorities are conducting their own investigations. The United States was the first of these to bring charges in December 2023, when I headed a special US Justice Department unit set up to pursue justice for victims in Ukraine. The case involved the torture of a US citizen in Russia-occupied Ukraine.[4] In February 2024, Lithuania followed suit, commencing legal action against three persons for murdering a Lithuanian civilian in occupied Mariupol. However, all national efforts are routinely plagued by jurisdictional limitations, evidentiary obstacles, victim-witness issues, and an inability to date, in most instances, to gain custody of suspects.

In sum, the profound challenges to the rule of law and international stability presented by Russia's blatant and continuing violation of the cardinal principle of the UN Charter—its proscription against "the threat or use of force against the territorial integrity or political independence of any state"—requires that creative solutions be found to the myriad problems encountered by those who are laboring against long odds to pursue justice on behalf of Ukraine's victims and that those solutions be implemented as soon as possible. In bringing together so many impressive contributions from experts that address some of these problems and potential strategies for overcoming them, in part by reference to the triumphs and imperfections of Nuremberg, the present volume is not only "timely and essential," it performs an invaluable service to the urgent causes of pursuing justice, protecting human dignity, upholding the rule of law, and promoting peace.

Notes

1 See, for example, Aliss Higham, "Putin Ally Vows Nuclear Strike on Washington If Ukraine Wins," *Newsweek*, February 18, 2024 (quoting Telegram post by Dmitry Medvedev, deputy chairman of Russia's Security Council), at https://www.newsweek.com/vladimir-putin-ally-nuclear-threat-ukraine-win-1871005; and Francesca Ebel, Natalia Abbakumova, Robyn Dixon, and Catherine Belton, "Russia's Nuclear Doctrine to Include Attacks on Nonnuclear States: Russian President Vladimir Putin Said Non-nuclear States Supported by Nuclear Ones Could Face Russia's Nuclear Deterrent in an Expansion of its Policy," *The Washington Post*, September 25, 2024, at https://www.washingtonpost.com/world/2024/09/25/putin-nuclear-deterrent-ukraine-threat/.

2 Extensive public debate continues on the practical differences between these two alternatives in the Russia/Ukraine context. Criticism of the hybrid "internationalized" form has focused primarily on the likelihood that such a tribunal will lack jurisdiction to try Vladimir Putin and the other most senior Russian leaders (who, of course, are the individuals believed most responsible for the aggression, that is, to be prosecuted) while they are in power, because of immunities that are recognized under Ukrainian law. (Those immunities are consistent with international law that generally renders government leaders protected from prosecution in the domestic courts of other countries during their terms in office. Ukrainian authorities have indicted more than 400 lower-level Russian officials and others for committing aggression in violation of Ukrainian criminal statutes, and more than 175 of those individuals have been convicted, generally *in absentia*.) Critics of the international model question whether such a tribunal can be created that gains the support of a broad-based and large enough group of UN member states, as did the ICC, to be considered "sufficiently international"—that is, to be deemed truly reflective of "the will of the international community as a whole" and hence able to overcome immunities as a genuinely international tribunal. See, for example, Emily Mullin and Gregory Stanton, "Prosecuting Putin: Creation of a Special Tribunal for Russian Aggression," *Opinio Juris*, October 1, 2024, at https://opiniojuris.org/2024/10/01/prosecuting-putin-creation-of-a-special-tribunal-for-russian-aggression/; and Gaiane Nuridzhanian, "International Enough? A Council of Europe Special Tribunal for the Crime of Aggression," *Just Security*, June 3, 2024, at https://www.justsecurity.org/96320/council-of-europe-ukraine-tribunal/.

3 Statistics on these indictments and convictions (and on indictments and convictions for the crime of aggression presented in Note 2, *supra*) are as received by the author on October 18, 2024, from Ukraine's Prosecutor General's Office.

4 See the US Department of Justice press release, "Four Russia-Affiliated Military Personnel Charged with War Crimes in Connection with Russia's Invasion of Ukraine," December 6, 2023, at https://www.justice.gov/opa/pr/four-russia-affiliated-military-personnel-charged-war-crimes-connection-russiasinvasion.

Introduction

Marshall J. Breger and Herbert R. Reginbogin

With the outbreak of the Russo-Ukrainian War on February 24, 2022, the international world order once again experienced a watershed in global governance. Many in the international community were reminded of the Nazi German invasion of European countries that led to the prosecution of the German leaders responsible for unimaginable atrocities. It would be in the well-known International Military Tribunal at Nuremberg and subsequent Nuremberg Trials (1945–9), where the Second World War war crimes would be adjudicated. It would also be here that the Nuremberg Principles and legacy would emerge, ushering in a new era of accountability for governmental leaders by reaffirming the Briand-Kellogg Pact (1928), which outlawed the nineteenth-century idea that all wars are legal and instead recognized that aggressive war is criminal.

The Nuremberg Principles embraced a legacy of international justice as reflected by the ad hoc international tribunals designed to provide accountability in the post-Cold War conflicts in the former Yugoslavia and Rwanda, the establishment of a permanent International Criminal Court, and the plethora of international justice mechanisms that have followed since—dealing with crimes against humanity, genocide, war crimes, and the crime of aggression. The Russian invasion of Ukraine tests the principles of Nuremberg front and center in the public consciousness of justice. It raises the question of whether Nuremberg-style justice is even possible, especially when the aggressor nation is a permanent member of the UN Security Council and one of the principal founders of the International Military Tribunal.

The book starts with the historical British, French, Soviet, US, and German perspectives on the International Military Tribunal and their relevance to Ukraine. The authors underscore international criminal law's universal and pivotal development and the ensuing Nuremberg Principles as a landmark achievement regarding a new rules-based international order. The perspectives of the trial are relevant to understanding the developments throughout the Cold War and post-Cold War Era of changing domestic laws in Western society, as well as altering the jurisprudential mindset about the rule of law.

The following section deals with two of the twelve subsequent Nuremberg Trials (1946–9), the Doctors' Trial and the Judges' Trial. The 'Doctors' Trial case was about the lack of medical ethics of the Nazi physicians and the creation of the Nuremberg Code to guide future human experimentation. Despite the condemned unethical experiments in Nazi Germany, similar experiments sadly continued at major academic institutions in the United States. Ordinary physicians did not feel that the Nuremberg

Code applied to them personally, as the Code was a reaction to Mengele's atrocious experiments.

The 'Judges' Trial Trial, also called The Justice Case, involved figures in the Nazi legal establishment. The trial illustrates how lawyers (often leading figures in the Nazi legal establishment) can commit hideous crimes, even mass murder, while going along with their regular duties. Ironically, those US legal scholars justifying forms of torture after 9/11 derived much of their legal thinking from Nazi jurist Carl Schmitt. The post-Nuremberg Trials, a half-century after the first Nuremberg trial, depict the different ad hoc tribunals from Rwanda (ICTR) and the former Yugoslavia (ICTY), among other states as well as proceedings from the International Criminal Court (ICC).

The remainder of this book considers how the laws of war and international humanitarian law impact the current war in Ukraine. It considers complex questions of venue (where the tribunal should be situated, in a domestic site or an international venue), what the organization of the tribunal should be (type of judges, appeals process, laws of procedure), questions about the head of state immunity, the problem of trials in absentia, the possibility of alternative forms of accountability, and so on. The book will further discuss substantive areas such as the destruction of cultural heritage, abduction of children, aggressive war, and war crimes.

Part 1

The Historical and Legal National Perspectives of the Crime of Aggression at the International Military Tribunal (IMT) at Nuremberg, 1945–1946

1

The Soviet Role in the Nuremberg Trials and Why It Matters Today

Francine Hirsch

Since Russia invaded Ukraine on February 24, 2022, there has been much talk about the Nuremberg Trials among international lawyers, journalists, and world leaders. Numerous plans and proposals have circulated for a tribunal that would hold Russian president Vladimir Putin and those in his circle accountable for launching a war of aggression—for committing a crime against peace. It is unclear what such a tribunal might look like; there has been significant debate about the merits of a fully international tribunal versus a hybrid tribunal based on Ukraine's domestic jurisdiction.[1] It is also highly uncertain if such a tribunal will ever be convened. Indeed, even those who advocate for such a tribunal admit that it "would be naïve to think the Russian president or his most senior functionaries are likely to appear as defendants in any court of law anytime soon."[2] Presumably, Ukraine would first have to win the war. But there is general agreement about one thing: waging a war of aggression violates international law and is a punishable criminal act.

This was not always the case. The category of "crimes against peace" category only fully came into being at the Nuremberg Trials after the Second World War. It did so largely thanks to the efforts of the Soviet Union and a Soviet lawyer named Aron Trainin. The Soviets made this significant contribution to the first International Military Tribunal (IMT) and the development of postwar international law even as they envisioned Nuremberg as a show trial—and even though they themselves were responsible. At the same time, they were responsible for significant crimes against peace. This dual role of the Soviet Union in the IMT complicates the usual story of Nuremberg as a Western liberal triumph. But if Nuremberg will continue to be invoked as a model for postwar justice today, we need to know its entire history—in all its complexity.[3]

Soviet Contributions

In popular American books and films about Nuremberg, the US chief prosecutor, Supreme Court Justice Robert H. Jackson, is held up as the driving force behind the entire trial. The British and the French are depicted as playing noble but supporting roles. The Soviets, however, are barely discussed at all.[4] When they are mentioned, it is almost as always the "Achilles' heel" of the endeavor.[5] This is all part of the "Nuremberg myth" that became conventional wisdom about the trials in the United States and other Western countries during the Cold War. In fact, the Soviet Union had a pivotal role in setting the IMT into motion. Without Soviet leaders and lawyers, Nuremberg likely never would have happened.

The Soviets took up the question of Nazi criminality during the darkest days of the war, prompted by the brutality of the Nazi occupation. In April 1942, Soviet Foreign Minister Vyacheslav Molotov published his "Third Note on German Atrocities," citing evidence that the burning of villages and the massacre of civilians were part of a deliberate German plan.[6] Six months later, in October 1942, Soviet leaders publicly called for the convening of a "special international tribunal" and invited all interested governments to cooperate in bringing Adolf Hitler, Hermann Goering, Rudolf Hess, and other Nazi leaders to justice.[7] The Soviets were out in front here; the United States and Great Britain were slow to come on board. The US government worried about reprisals against Allied prisoners of war. British leaders argued that the crimes of the Nazi leaders were far too serious to be dealt with by judicial procedure and pushed instead for punishment by executive decree (without a trial).[8]

The Soviets went down their own path. They rejected an invitation from the British to participate in an Allied war crimes commission—what would become the United Nations War Crimes Commission (the UNWCC)—arguing that the British were not prepared to go far enough. Instead, the Soviets created their own war crimes commission: the Extraordinary State Commission to Investigate German-Fascist Crimes Committed on Soviet Territory.[9] At the same time, the Soviet Ministry of Foreign Affairs turned to the Institute of Law of the Soviet Academy of Sciences in Moscow and asked its lawyers to assess a key question of international law: What was the criminal responsibility of Nazi leaders for invading another country in pursuit of predatory goals and for atrocities committed as part of that invasion?[10]

One of the lawyers who took up this call was Aron Trainin, a criminologist and international law expert who published two books in the mid-1930s on the problem of aggressive war. Trainin's 1935 book *Criminal Intervention* argued that the League of Nations (which the Soviet Union had just joined in 1934) had been so preoccupied with halting the spread of communism that it had ignored "the real problem of preventing aggressive war."[11] Trainin had taken this argument further in his 1937 book, *The Defense of Peace and Criminal Law*. Again, he criticized the League of Nations and its member states for treating the legality of war as a given. He conceded that the Kellogg-Briand Pact of 1928, an ambitious multilateral peacekeeping agreement that the Soviet Union and sixty-one other countries had signed on to, had been a step forward. The signatories had renounced war "as an instrument of national policy." However, they had fallen stopped short of making the waging of war a punishable offense. Warning of the "Nazi threat to peace and humanity," Trainin called for the establishment of an international criminal court to try persons, including leaders, "who violated the peace."[12]

Trainin's ideas about the defense of peace and the criminality of aggressive war took on new significance after the Nazi invasion and occupation of the Soviet Union in the summer of 1941. As the Extraordinary State Commission investigated Nazi war crimes in liberated territories and uncovered evidence of the organized mass murder of civilians, Trainin further developed his arguments. Trainin argued that the scope of the war was so overwhelming and Nazi crimes against civilians so shocking that it would be "unthinkable not to hold the perpetrators to account." He maintained that the German state must face political and economic sanctions for its crimes, arguing that individual perpetrators must bear criminal responsibility at all levels. Trainin rejected the plea of following "superior orders," which was still a standard defense at the time. He argued that soldiers must face punishment for war crimes. But he underscored that the most significant degree of criminal responsibility belonged to Germany's leaders. Here he called out Hitler and his ministers, the leadership of the Nazi Party, Nazi authorities in the occupied territories, the Military High Command, and the German financial and industrial leaders who had bankrolled Hitler.

Trainin further argued that Germany's leaders should be tried not only for "traditional war crimes" as set out in the Hague and Geneva Conventions but also for waging an illegal war in the first place—for committing a "crime against peace." Trainin coined this term and gave it a definition that included: acts of aggression, propaganda of aggression, the conclusion of international agreements with aggressive aims (intent to commit aggression), and terrorism. He also argued that Nazi leaders could and should be tried for participating in a criminal conspiracy.

Trainin set out these ideas in a report for the Ministry of Foreign Affairs.[13] In the late summer and fall of 1943, Soviet leaders disseminated an English-language summary of Trainin's ideas in several publications, including *Information Bulletin*, the English-language newsletter for Soviet embassies.[14] The Ministry of Foreign Affairs also turned Trainin's report into a book, *The Criminal Responsibility of the Hitlerites*, published in Moscow in July 1944.[15]

In the fall of 1944, as British and American forces were advancing across France toward Germany, Trainin's book made its way across Europe to London; it was discussed at meetings of the UNWCC in October 1944. The USSR was not a member of the UNWCC, but the Czechoslovak representative, Dr. Bohuslav Ečer, assumed the role of a middleman. Ečer argued that defining the current war as "criminal" made it possible to see acts like "the extermination of foreign races" not "as simple 'violations of the laws and customs of war' but as instruments of a general criminal policy." Using Trainin's term, he urged that the "preparation and launching of the present war be punished as a crime against peace."[16]

Not all UNWCC members were on board with Trainin's arguments and Ečer's proposal. Some expressed unease about what they saw as the introduction of *ex post facto* or retroactive law. They agreed that a state which violated the Kellogg-Briand had Pact committed a criminal act. But they challenged the idea that criminal responsibility could "attach to those individuals who are responsible for the preparation and launching of a war." [17]

In November 1944, Trainin's book and Ečer's analysis of it crossed the Atlantic and landed at the US State Department.[18] An English translation of the book was sent on to the US War Department and the White House. In January 1945, two lawyers from the War Department, Murray Bernays and D. W. Brown, wrote a secret report for President Franklin Roosevelt on whether starting the current war was a crime for which Nazi leaders could be tried and punished. They answered yes—even as they acknowledged that this opinion broke from current US policy. They maintained that international law evolves with "the public conscience" and that it could no longer "be disputed that the launching of a war of aggression today is condemned by the vast majority of mankind as a crime." Bernays and Brown noted that Polish-British law professor Hersch Lauterpacht and US secretary of war Henry L. Stimson both referred to the idea of a criminal or illegal war. They also referenced the "Soviet view," which held, as they put it, "that the launching of an aggressive war is today a crime in international law." Bernays and Brown gave special attention to Trainin's concept of "crimes against peace."[19]

After the victory, when the other Allied powers came around to the idea of an international tribunal, Trainin helped shape its framework. He was one of two representatives that the Soviets sent to the four-power London Conference in the summer of 1945 to meet with British, French, and American representatives and work out the Nuremberg Charter. "Crimes against peace" was included as one of three main categories of crimes under Article 6 (along with "war crimes" and "crimes against humanity"). A few months later, Trainin headed to Germany, where he would serve as a legal advisor to the Soviet delegation at the Nuremberg Trials. The illegality of a war of aggression would become the crux of the entire case.

Soviet Contradictions and Complications

When the Soviets pushed hard for a "special international tribunal" to try Nazi leaders, they were imagining a short process consisting of nothing but open-and-shut cases. The Soviets took Nazi guilt as a given. The Soviet Union's losses during the war were almost beyond belief. Some 27 million Soviet citizens had perished; two-thirds of the dead were civilians. The whole world had seen the newsreel footage of razed Soviet villages, bombed-out Soviet cities, and slaughtered Soviet civilians. It had heard stories about Auschwitz, Majdanek, and other death camps. The crimes of the Nazis were so abhorrent, the evidence of mass atrocities so extensive, that Stalin and Molotov were sure of guilty verdicts and hangings down the line. They certainly did not expect the defendants to be allowed to take the stand in their own defense or to be allowed to call SS men and German military leaders as witnesses. Nor did they expect the defense to be allowed to dispute official Allied war crimes reports or to challenge the prosecution during cross-examination.

These expectations shaped Stalin's choice of personnel for the Nuremberg Trials. Almost all the key members of the Soviet delegation's legal team were connected to the Soviet show trials of the 1930s. The Soviet judge Iona Nikitchenko had been a judge at the Trials of 1936–8, grand political spectacles whose outcomes were never in dispute. The Soviet chief prosecutor Roman Rudenko had served as the prosecutor for show trials in the 1930s in Ukraine and more recently as the prosecutor for a show trial of the leaders of the Polish Underground State held in Moscow. The Soviet assistant prosecutors at Nuremberg had similar credentials.

To ensure that things went as planned, Soviet leaders created two secret Nuremberg commissions, both based in Moscow, to oversee the Soviet case and Soviet personnel from afar. Stalin appointed Andrei Vyshinsky, who had prosecuted the Moscow Trials and was now Molotov's deputy foreign minister, to head one of these commissions. Stalin made Vyshinsky responsible for all aspects of the Soviet case, including the screening and selection of witnesses and evidence.[20] Vyshinsky, in turn, ordered the Soviet prosecutors and judges to check in with him about all decisions regarding the IMT, no matter how large or small. This required secret long-distance check-ins, usually via back channels and with tight deadlines. Making things even more complicated, even Vyshinsky lacked the authority to give directives about most matters on his own. He had to report to the second secret Nuremberg Commission, which included Molotov and the highest-ranking officials from the worlds of Soviet state security and law.[21] Many decisions required a round-robin of consultations with Soviet leaders—up to and including Stalin.

The Soviets thought that the victors would control the script at Nuremberg, just as the prosecution had done in the Soviet Union's own war crimes trials like the Krasnodar Trial of July 1943 and the Kharkov Trial of December 1943. They carefully compiled extensive documentary evidence of Nazi war crimes, crimes against humanity, and crimes against peace. They interviewed thousands of survivors and prepared affidavits and official reports. They selected eyewitnesses who could testify about the abuse and execution of prisoners of war, communists, and Jews, people who could bear witness before the world about the Nazi concentration camps and the Einsatzgruppen (mobile killing units) and the mass murder of old people, women, and children. The Soviet case was compelling and powerful.

But, Soviet leaders overstepped. They were so confident that the victors would control the script at Nuremberg that they tried to pin one of their own war crimes, the Katyn massacre of thousands of Polish officers, on the Nazis.[22] They did not think the defendants would be allowed to challenge their evidence. Soviet leaders were so confident that they initially did not tell Soviet chief prosecutor Rudenko about the secret protocols to the Soviet-German Non-Aggression Pact of 1939—in which Hitler and Stalin had plotted the division of Poland and the Baltic States of Latvia, Lithuania, and Estonia. They did not see a need for Rudenko to know about these protocols, even though former German Foreign Minister Joachim von Ribbentrop, who had signed the pact, was one of the defendants. Vyshinsky ultimately briefed Rudenko about the secret protocols during a short trip to Nuremberg a week after the start of the trials—and only after Hans Frank's defense attorney, Alfred Seidl, made noise about having "dug up" some documents about Hitler's secret agreement with Stalin. This was the first sign for the Soviets that little would go at Nuremberg as Stalin had planned.

Soviet confidence about controlling the defendants, the narrative about the Second World War, and the course of the trials seems absurd in retrospect. But a closer look at the framing of the trials helps to explain at least some of their misplaced expectations. First, the Nuremberg Charter, written in London in the summer of 1945, had established that the Nuremberg tribunal would address only European Axis crimes. None of the countries of the prosecution wanted to have their own foreign policies and wartime actions scrutinized on the international stage. Second, the Soviet, American, British, and French prosecutors had agreed before the trials started that they would work together to keep awkward topics out of the courtroom. The Soviets referred to this as a "gentlemen's agreement."[23]

This agreement among the prosecutors had come about at Jackson's suggestion back in early November 1945, a couple of weeks before the IMT convened in Nuremberg. Jackson had warned the other chief prosecutors that the defense was planning to launch "political attacks" on the countries of the prosecution during the trials and would likely focus on the actions of Russia and England in connection with the "aggressive war" charge. This, of course, was an area where the Soviets were especially vulnerable, given the secret protocols and the subsequent Soviet invasions of Latvia, Lithuania, Estonia, Finland, and Poland. Jackson had suggested that the United States, "being late to the war and remote from the scene," was immune to these kinds of political attacks and, therefore, in the best position to shut them down. He had then proposed that the prosecutors draw up confidential memoranda enumerating those wartime actions of their governments that could be fodder for the defense's attacks.[24] In effect, he had asked them to come clean about their countries' war crimes.

In Moscow, Soviet leaders had put their own spin on Jackson's request and made a list of "taboo topics" that they wanted kept out of the courtroom. The list included critical items about Soviet-German relations, including: "the relationship of the USSR to the Versailles peace"; "the German-Soviet Non-Aggression Pact of 1939 and all questions relating to it"; "Molotov's visit to Berlin and Ribbentrop's visit to Moscow"; and "the Soviet-German agreement about the exchange of the German population of Lithuania, Latvia, and Estonia with Germany." It also included more general topics concerning Soviet foreign policy on the eve of the war, including "questions about the [Dardanelles] Straits and about the alleged territorial pretensions of the USSR"; "the Balkan question"; and "Soviet-Polish relations." Off limits as well were all questions "connected with the socio-political structure of the USSR" and "the Soviet Baltic republics."[25] Vyshinsky shared this list with Rudenko during his visit to Nuremberg. Notably, Vyshinsky did not permit Rudenko to share a physical copy of the list with anyone. Moscow did not want to lose the shield of plausible deniability. He directed Rudenko to reach a verbal agreement with the Western prosecutors to steer clear of these topics. Vyshinsky left Nuremberg after Rudenko reported success with this critical assignment.

There was something essential, however, that neither Vyshinsky nor Rudenko understood. The British, French, and American judges, unlike the Soviet judges, were operating independently from their governments. They were also operating independently from their countries' prosecutors. These three Western judges were not on board with shutting down the defense to keep "sensitive" topics out of the courtroom. In fact, the Western judges were extremely concerned about allegations of "victors' justice" and were intent on showing the world that the defendants were receiving a fair trial.

To the Soviets' dismay, the Western judges gave significant leeway to the defendants in the Nuremberg courtroom. The defendants, in turn, did what they could to put forward their own narrative about the war—and focused on Soviet war crimes and crimes against peace. Goering, Wilhelm Keitel, and Alfred Jodl all insisted that Germany had launched a "preventive" war against the Soviet Union and not a war of aggression.[26] Ribbentrop riveted the courtroom with his description of the secret protocols of the German-Soviet Non-Aggression Pact, relating how he, Stalin, and Molotov had all talked "frankly" about Poland in August 1939. He confirmed that an agreement had been reached and that soon after, in keeping with its terms, Soviet and German troops had occupied Poland and the Baltic States. He argued that if Germany was guilty of planning and waging an "aggressive war" toward Poland, then surely the Soviets were "guilty of it" too.[27] One Soviet diplomat, Mikhail Kharlamov, writing home after Ribbentrop's testimony, expressed alarm that the Soviet Union, "a country of victors, had gone to Nuremberg to prosecute the fascists and had instead become the object of their provocative attacks."[28] The challenges to the Soviets continued. Goering's attorney petitioned for witnesses to counter Soviet charges about Katyn. The three Western judges, outvoting Nikitchenko, allowed it. In July 1946, three defense witnesses and three Soviet witnesses testified in open court about the massacre. Enough doubt was cast on the Soviet version of events that no mention of Katyn appeared in the judgment.

The Soviets had gotten their "special international tribunal"—but it was a far cry from the one they had been anticipating. Nuremberg looked nothing like Soviet war crimes trials. The Western judges had made sure of this. The Soviets had presented robust evidence of Nazi crimes, including crimes against peace. But the defendants had used the Nuremberg courtroom, as well as the international press, to make all kinds of counter-accusations against the Soviet Union. Stalin blamed the Western powers, especially the "Anglo-Americans," for allowing this to happen. By the time the trials wrapped up and the IMT was ready to render its verdicts, the wartime alliance, which was always tenuous, had frayed entirely.

In the end, Stalin was incredibly disappointed—appalled, really—by the Nuremberg verdicts. Twelve of the twenty-two defendants were sentenced to death by hanging; three were acquitted, and the others received prison sentences. Stalin had been expecting nothing less than a guilty verdict and a death sentence for every single defendant. Here, too, he blamed the "Anglo-Americans" for things not having gone as planned. The Western powers, for their part, wanted to forget about the role of the Soviets in the Nuremberg Trials. They especially wanted to forget about the Soviet effort to use Nuremberg to blame the Katyn massacre on the Nazis. Soviet participation, from their perspective, had threatened the legitimacy of the IMT while it was in session. They worried that too much attention to the Soviet role in the trials after the fact could ruin Nuremberg's legacy. American and British memoirs about Nuremberg thus omitted key details about Soviet participation, instead presenting a simple and uplifting story about victory, justice, and the rule of law.

Legacies

Bringing the Soviets fully into the Nuremberg story upsets the Nuremberg myth—but does not undo or diminish the IMT's remarkable achievements. All tribunals have their politics, and Nuremberg was no exception. Nonetheless, the IMT's contributions were significant. The IMT sparked a revolution in international law. It recognized the "new crimes" of crimes against humanity, genocide, and crimes against peace.[29] It established that the leaders of a state could be held criminally responsible for waging a war of aggression—that leaders did not have immunity from prosecution. Nuremberg served as a precedent for further postwar trials. Furthermore, ideas about justice and human rights that were expressed at the Nuremberg Trials fed into a broader discussion about the role that new international institutions should play in preserving the peace and preventing atrocities. The postwar moment was a time of optimism about "the progressive development of international law" to better serve humanity.

Bringing the Soviets into the history of the Nuremberg Trials reminds us that the Soviet Union was part of this revolution in international law after the Second World War. The Soviet Union had helped establish the illegality of aggressive war—and a Soviet lawyer had introduced the concept of "crimes against peace." We need to know this whole story, especially now. Putin has breached an international legal system that the Soviet Union played a major role in creating.

Given the politics of the present, knowing the complete and complicated history of the Nuremberg Trials matters. We should celebrate Nuremberg's achievements—and we should also discuss Nuremberg's shortcomings or flaws. The fact that the Nuremberg judgment addressed only European Axis crimes has had unexpected long-term consequences. The Nuremberg judgment held Nazi Germany alone responsible for the invasion of Poland in September 1939—allowing Putin to invoke "the Nuremberg verdict" to suppress information about Soviet war crimes and crimes against peace. A 2021 Russian memory law that forbids "any public attempt to equate the aims and actions of the Soviet Union and Nazi Germany during World War II" cites "the findings of Nuremberg" to justify its distortion of history.[30]

Of course, even many who participated in the IMT understood that the Nuremberg model of justice was far from perfect. After the trials, the French judge, Henri Donnedieu de Vabres, revealed that he had been troubled at Nuremberg by allegations of victor's justice: by the concern that a court of victors could never be truly impartial. De Vabres and others argued passionately for creating a permanent international criminal court—which would eliminate the need for ad hoc tribunals of the victors, like the IMT, in the future.[31] Two months after the Nuremberg judgment, in December 1946, the United Nations Codification Committee began work on a new international law code that would include the new international law principles articulated at Nuremberg. Over the following year, it also discussed the creation of a permanent international criminal court. These efforts ran aground during the Cold War. The IMT had "worked" because it was restricted to the investigation and judgment of European Axis crimes. A permanent international criminal court would require all member states and their leaders to cede at least some degree of sovereignty to an international institution. For several powerful states, including the United States, Britain, and the Soviet Union, this was a non-starter.

The end of the Cold War saw the creation of the International Criminal Court (ICC). But concerns about sovereignty have remained. As a result, the ICC has very limited jurisdiction over the crime of aggression—crimes against peace. All ICC member states can opt out of ICC jurisdiction for "aggression crimes," and the majority have done so. Plus, when it comes to the crime of aggression, the ICC has no jurisdiction over non-member states like Russia. The ICC can investigate Russian war crimes and crimes against humanity in Ukraine. However, it cannot investigate Russia for its predatory invasion of Ukraine. This is why there has been so much talk of creating a Nuremberg-like special tribunal: it would fill in where our current international legal system still falls short and would allow Russian leaders to be tried for the crime of aggression.[32] If we do not want ad hoc tribunals in the future, we will need a permanent international criminal court with a much broader mandate. For now, though, the focus will likely remain on Nuremberg—making it imperative that we consider and grapple with all aspects of its legacy.

Notes

1 For example, Jennifer Trahan, "Why a 'Hybrid' Ukrainian Tribunal on the Crime of Aggression Is Not the Answer," *Just Security*, February 6, 2023, https://www.justsecurity.org/85019/why-hybrid-ukrainian-tribunal-on-crime-of-aggression-is-not-the-answer/ and Ambassador Rein Taamsaar, "An International Special Tribunal is the Only Viable Path to a Just and Lasting Peace in Ukraine, *Just Security*, May 9, 2023, https://www.justsecurity.org/86516/an-international-special-tribunal-is-the-only-viable-path-to-a-just-and-lasting-peace-in-ukraine/.

2 For example, Editorial Board, "How to Bring Putin to Justice," *The Washington Post*, January 22, 2023, https://www.washingtonpost.com/opinions/2023/01/22/international-court-putin-ukraine-war-tribunal/.

3 For an elaboration of the arguments made in this article, see Francine Hirsch, *Soviet Judgment at Nuremberg: A New History of the International Military Tribunal After World War II* (New York: Oxford University Press, 2020).

4 See, for example, Joseph E. Persico, *Nuremberg: Infamy on Trial* (New York: Viking, 1994), Whitney R. Harris, *Tyranny on Trial* (Dallas, TX: Texas A&M University Press, 1954), and the PBS American Experience documentary *The Nuremberg Trials*, which aired in 2006.

5 Christopher J. Dodd with Lary Bloom, *Letters from Nuremberg: My Father's Narrative of a Quest for Justice* (New York: Crown Publishing, 2007).

6 Library of Congress, Manuscript Division, Robert H. Jackson Collection (LOC-RHJ) b. 95, f. 3, "Note sent by M. Molotov on April 17, 1942."

7 Archive of the Foreign Policy of the Russian Federation (AVPRF) f. 06, op. 4, p. 4, d. 35, ll. 42–49; p. 6, d. 65, ll. 42–57. The Soviet government broadcast the statement the following day. "Zaiavlenie Sovetskogo pravitel'stva ob otvetstvennosti

gitlerovskikh zakhvatchikov i ikh soobshchnikov za zlodeianiia sovershaemye imi v okkupirovannykh stranakh Evropy," *Pravda*, October 15, 1942, p. 1.

8 For British ambassador Sir Archibald Clark Kerr's discussions with Stalin and Molotov in the Kremlin on this question, see AVPRF f. 06, op. 4, p. 1, d. 14, ll. 57–61. On the UNWCC, see Arieh J. Kochavi, *Prelude to Nuremberg: Allied War Crimes Policy and the Question of Punishment* (Chapel Hill, NC: University of North Carolina Press, 1998).

9 On the creation of the Extraordinary State Commission, see Marina Sorokina, "People and Procedures: Toward a History of the Investigation of Nazi Crimes in the USSR," *Kritika: Explorations in Russian and Eurasian History* 6, no. 4 (2005): 797–831.

10 Archive of the Russian Academy of Sciences (ARAN) f. 586, op. 4, d. 6, ll. 1–3.

11 A. N. Trainin, *Ugolovnaia interventsiia: dvizhenie po unifikatsii ugolovnogo zakonodatel'stva'stva kapitalisticheskikh stran* (Moscow: State Publishing House of Soviet Legislation, 1935).

12 A. N. Trainin, "Iz raboty *Ugolovnaia interventsiia*," in N. F. Kuznetsova ed., *A. N. Trainin: Izbrannye trudy* (St. Petersburg: Juridical Center Press, 2004), 461–551.

13 ARAN f. 499, op. 1, d. 32, ll. 20, 27–50.

14 A. Farrin [Trainin], "The Responsibility for Nazi Crimes," *Information Bulletin* (Embassy of the USSR), October 2, 1943, 5–7; A. Farrin [Trainin], "The Responsibility for Nazi Crimes," *The Central European Observer*, September 17, 1943, pp. 281–2. Also see George Ginsburgs, *Moscow's Road to Nuremberg: The Soviet Background to the Trial* (The Hague: Martinus Nijhoff, 1996).

15 A. N. Trainin, *Ugolovnaia otvetstvennost' gitlerovtsev* (Moscow: Juridical Press of the People's Commissariat of Justice of the USSR, 1944).

16 National Archives and Records Administration (NARA) RG 238, entry 52, b. 7, "UNWCC, Minutes of Thirty-sixth Meeting held on 17th October 1944." Also "UNWCC, Report Made by Dr. Ečer on Professor Trainin's Book *The Criminal Responsibility of the Hitlerites* at the Commission's Meeting of October 31, 1944."

17 NARA RG 238, entry 52, b. 7, "UNWCC, Minutes of Thirty-sixth Meeting held on 17th October 1944."

18 Harry S. Truman Presidential Library and Museum (HSTPLM), Samuel I. Rosenman Papers, War Crimes File, "Memorandum from the United Nations War Crimes Commission, 'Report Made by Dr. Ečer on Professor Trainin's Book', November 11, 1944." The Soviets also had the work translated into English in 1944. A. N. Trainin, *The Criminal Responsibility of the Hitlerites* (Moscow: Juridical Publishing House of the People's Commissariat of Justice of the USSR, 1944). The book was also published in French, Arabic, and other languages.

19 HSTPLM, Samuel I. Rosenman Papers, War Crimes File, "Memorandum from Murray C. Bernays and D. W. Brown," January 4, 1945.

20 AVPRF f. 07, op. 13, p. 41, d. 9, l. 3. This was the Commission for Directing the Work of the Soviet Representatives in the International Tribunal and the Committee of Chief Prosecutors in Nuremberg.

21 State Archive of the Russian Federation (GARF) f. 8131, op. 38, d. 238, ll. 158–9. This was the Politburo Commission for Preparing to Conduct the Nuremberg Trials.

22 Archival documents released in 1992 clearly demonstrate that the Soviets carried out the atrocity. See "Russia Opens Some Katyn Documents to Public," *Radio Free Europe/Radio Liberty*, April 28, 2010, https://www.rferl.org/a/Russia_Opens_Some_Katyn_Documents_To_Public/2026888.html.

23 AVPRF f. 07, op. 13, p. 41, d. 9, ll. 112–16.
24 GARF f. 7445, op. 2, d. 8, l. 394.
25 GARF f. 7445, op. 2, d. 391, ll. 45–16.
26 For example, "147th Day, Wednesday, June 5, 1946," *Nuremberg Trial Proceedings* (*NTP*), Avalon Project at Yale University Law School vol. 15, http://avalon.law.yale.edu/imt/06-05-46.asp.
27 "96th Day, Monday, April 1, 1946," *NTP*, vol. 10, https://avalon.law.yale.edu/imt/04-01-46.asp.
28 AVPRF f. 07, op. 13, p. 41, d. 9, ll. 112–6.
29 Genocide was included in the war crimes section of the Indictment to refer to the intentional destruction of "particular races and classes of people and national, racial, or religious groups."
30 "Duma Adopts in First Reading Ban on Putting Soviet Union, Nazi Germany on Same Footing," *TASS*, May 25, 2021, https://tass.com/society/1293829. On the history of this memory law see Nikolay Koposov, "'The Armored Train of Memory': The Politics of Memory in Post-Soviet Russia," American Historical Society, *Perspectives on History*, January 1, 2011, https://www.historians.org/research-and-publications/perspectives-on-history/january-2011/the-armored-train-of-memory-the-politics-of-history-in-post-soviet-russia. Also see Francine Hirsch, "Putin's Memory Law Sets the Stage for His War in Ukraine," *Lawfare*, February 28, 2022, https://www.lawfaremedia.org/article/putins-memory-laws-set-stage-his-war-ukraine.
31 UN document A/ AC.10/ 21, "Memorandum Submitted by the Delegate of France, Draft Proposal for the Establishment of an International Court of Criminal Jurisdiction," May 13, 1947.
32 For a full discussion of what the ICC can and cannot do see Francine Hirsch, "War Crimes: What Are They? How Can They be Prosecuted?," *Great Decisions*, 2023, pp. 17–28.

Selected Bibliography

Ginsburgs, George. Moscow's Road to Nuremberg: The Soviet Background to the Trial (The Hague: Martinus Nijhoff, 1996).

Hirsch, Francine, *Soviet Judgment at Nuremberg: A New History of the International Military Tribunal after World War II* (Oxford, 2020).

Lebedeva, N. S. (ed.) *SSSR i Niurnbergskii protsess: Neizvestnyi i maloizvestnye stranitsy istorii. Sbornik dokumentov* [The USSR and the Nuremberg Trials: An Unknown and Little-Known History. Document Collection (Moscow: International Foundation for Democracy, 2012).

Lewis, Mark, *The Birth of the New Justice. The Internationalization of Crime and Punishment, 1919–1950* (Oxford, 2016).

Sorokina, Marina, "People and Procedures: Toward a History of the Investigation of Nazi Crimes in the USSR," *Kritika: Explorations in Russian and Eurasian History* 6, no. 4 (2005): 797–831.

Zviagintsev, G., *Glavnyi protsess chelovechestva. Niurnberg: Dokumenty, issledovaniia, vospominaniia* [The Major Trial of Humanity. Nuremberg: Documents, Research, Reminiscences] (Moscow: OLMA Media Group, 2011).

2

The Historical and Legal National Perspectives of the Crime of Aggression at the Nuremberg International Military Tribunal (IMT) Trial 1945–6

The British Perspective

Toby Simpson

On April 12, 1945, "The Manager" of the Wiener Library, Manchester Square, London, received a letter from the recently established United Nations War Crimes Commission (UNWCC), based not far away on the Strand. The letter introduced Mr. E. Schwelb, legal officer for the UNWCC, and enclosed a request "to allow him to use your library in connection with his official work."[1] That same day, Franklin Delano Roosevelt, whose administration had set in train the work of the Commission, died on holiday in Warm Springs, Georgia; Roosevelt's death was not announced in the newspapers until the next morning.

As Francine Hirsch has shown in *Soviet Judgement at Nuremberg*, the death of Roosevelt was a turning point. The dramatic change of leadership on the part of the strongest economic and military power in the world, just as the Allies were emerging victorious from a catastrophic global conflict, put Harry S. Truman in the driving seat of postwar justice. Planning for a postwar trial decisively steered away from the still plausible idea of administering justice behind closed doors. It is worth remembering that by 1945, several bends in the "road to Nuremberg" had already been carefully navigated. On October 7, 1942, Roosevelt and the British Lord Chancellor John Simon had pledged together in public that the Nazi regime would face punishment for their crimes following victory in Europe.[2] Reaching an agreement between the four major Allied powers regarding the trials' purpose and procedure was extremely difficult, and even the momentum injected by a new US administration did not resolve underlying tensions. This essay will consider the role played by the British in establishing the basis and course of the Nuremberg Trials from the point of inception in the Spring of 1942 until the conclusion of the International Military Tribunal in October 1946 and the attempt to elucidate the unique character of the British contribution.

The starting point for this analysis of the British perspective is the appointment of a UNWCC legal officer to work on behalf of the British with evidence of Nazi crimes gathered by a group of German-Jewish refugees (who had been working principally in London and secondarily in New York since 1939). This approach to the subject matter reflects two key points. Firstly, the British perspective on the Nuremberg trials is intimately bound up with the US perspective. Secondly, the British perspective is also closely bound up with the European continental perspective, and particularly the distinctive perspective of Jewish refugees from Nazi persecution. On the first point, it is hardly to be doubted that the Americans played a leading role at Nuremberg due to the political influence and resources they were able to bring to bear on the trials, unmatched by any other state at the time; it is also the case that no other Allies worked so closely together as the Americans and the British, who shared a common language, longstanding diplomatic relations, and similar legal systems.

The importance of the continental perspective in shaping the British perspective on the trials is arguably less obvious but not necessarily less important. Perhaps the best-known example of this transnational effort is the contribution of Hersch Lauterpacht to the preparation work of the British prosecution team, including Hartley Shawcross's famous closing speech. According to Philippe Sands' analysis in *East West Street*, Shawcross "took the essence of Lauterpacht's ideas, with a passing nod to Lemkin's ideas on genocide and groups."[3] Less well known than this, despite recognition given at the time by the UNWCC, is the contribution of Alfred Wiener and his colleagues, particularly Louis Bondy, in providing access to crucial materials as the trials were taking shape. It is tempting to ask what exactly the contribution of the British prosecuting team really was, given the leadership role of the Americans in setting the pace of the trials and the profoundly important supportive role played by continental Europeans, mostly refugees, in preparing the British prosecution's case. This combination of specific transnational entanglements in wartime London, both on a personal and organizational level, created the distinctive British perspective. Arguably, it was this that enabled the British to play such an important role in shaping the IMT. This essay argues, therefore, that it is necessary to avoid thinking in ethnically or culturally exclusive terms to capture the Britishness of the British perspective at Nuremberg.

The British Perspective and the Road to Nuremberg

The British opposed holding a public trial to punish leading Nazis until May 30, 1945. The then foreign secretary, Anthony Eden, had been explicit about his government's stance against such a trial throughout the war. On August 6, 1942, Eden sent a communication to other foreign ministers describing the idea of public proceedings as "undesirable."[4] His reasons included several serious concerns, especially a widely shared fear that a trial of this kind (if conducted according to British legal standards and traditions, as opposed to the show trial that the Soviets had in mind) would be long and unpredictable, granting the Germans the rights routinely afforded to defendants.

The British did not want to create opportunities for leading Nazis to subvert justice and risk alienating public opinion—these concerns by no means disappeared in April 1945. News of Roosevelt's death, however, was followed two weeks later by news of Hitler's suicide, fundamentally altering the dynamic of preparations for postwar justice.

Roosevelt had shared enough of the concerns held by the British government to want to keep the option of punishing Nazi criminals through an executive tribunal open until the last possible moment. This had become, however, an increasingly difficult position to sustain. If it had materialized, a trial behind closed doors would have struggled to do justice to the fact-finding work already undertaken by the UNWCC and the Soviet Extraordinary State Commission since late 1942. Both commissions had come into existence that summer as part of the fallout from the massacre of the inhabitants of the Czechoslovak village of Lidice. At that time, approximately 340 civilians had been murdered, and the entire village was razed in a barbaric act of vengeance. The act being avenged was, in fact, a British-sponsored Special Operations Executive mission, which had successfully assassinated the head of the Nazi security apparatus, Reinhard Heydrich, in May. In June, following the Lidice massacre, the British and Americans began serious discussions about tracking Nazi atrocities. Simultaneously, pressure to act from governments-in-exile, mostly based in London, considerably increased as Nazi methods of repression became more extreme in occupied Europe.

Demands from governments-in-exile and from Jewish groups demanding justice for Nazi racial persecution, deportation, and mass murder could be and were ignored at first. The UNWCC was not initially empowered to determine the shape of any plans for criminal proceedings. Similarly, demands from the Soviets that the British and Americans commit to a public trial fell on deaf ears. The British government was, however, especially vulnerable to allegations of hypocrisy. As Stalin pointedly noted to British Ambassador Sir Archibald Kerr on November 5, 1942, Rudolf Hess had been in British custody since May 1941. Could men like him be seen to escape justice despite the obliteration of Lidice and growing evidence of mass murder?[5] Serious entanglements of this kind were already beginning to exert pressure on the British government, but given that the Americans continued to doubt the value of a public trial, the key issues of how to deal with postwar justice could be deferred for some time, though not indefinitely.

Roosevelt and Churchill shifted their position on postwar justice significantly in February 1945 at Yalta, at which point Stalin held the upper hand, and consensus on the issue was more desirable than ever. The result was a joint commitment to prosecute the Nazi leaders, but even then, flexibility on the specifics was retained.[6] However, Harry Truman's attitude to the prospect of a public trial was quite different from Roosevelt's and Churchill's. As Ann and John Tusa have pointed out, "[Truman] had a profound belief in the beneficent power of law and the wisdom of judges, an abhorrence of summary execution, sensitive antennae to the balance of political forces in Washington and greater drive and disposition to make decisions than his ailing predecessor."[7] As far as the British were concerned, however, despite shifting political sands following Roosevelt's death, Truman's accession in April 1945 merely prompted the Lord Chancellor, Lord Simon, to issue another memorandum restating the government's objections to a public trial.[8]

However, the British had already largely lost the argument against a trial even before Roosevelt's death. Truman's representative in the ongoing discussions, John McCloy, who had arrived in London in mid-April 1945 in his capacity as assistant minister of war, joined a delegation of three judges, Rosenman, Weir, and Cutter. All four were committed to the outline of a paper drafted just before Yalta by the Russian-Jewish émigré lawyer Lieutenant Colonel Murray Bernays. The Bernays plan garnered broad support from Roosevelt's administration regarding the preferability of a public trial to a summary execution, including crucial support from the secretary of war, Henry Stimson. The strength and depth of American commitment to the Bernays plan did not fully sink in for the British until May 30, however. At that point, the Cabinet was forced—following the appointment of Justice Robert H. Jackson and the receipt of a telegram directly from Truman on the May 24—to approve American proposals for a two-stage process, beginning with a four-power International Military Tribunal to try leading Axis war criminals.[9]

It is interesting in this context that the UNWCC arranged for a British legal officer to obtain access to Dr. Alfred Wiener's Library on 19 Manchester Square on April 12, 1945. As outlined above, until the end of the following month, it was not official government policy to prepare for a public trial. Nevertheless, the collections held by Wiener and his colleagues were clearly of growing interest to the British government at this stage. They were, one of the strongest collections of evidence of Nazi crimes, and in particular pre-war anti-Jewish persecution and antisemitic propaganda. The dispatch of a legal officer on April 12 suggests that British preparations via the UNWCC were already starting along the lines set out by the Bernays plan in mid-April. The legal basis of the Nuremberg Trials had a long and complex gestation. The overall result of these debates and political wranglings was the eventual adoption of a plan to prosecute leading Nazis. This plan foresaw prosecuting figures like Göring, Streicher, and Schacht as individuals but charging them with participation in a conspiracy to wage a war of aggression, constituting a crime against peace. Proving the criminality of the Nazi party leadership on this basis, as well as proving the broader involvement of members of crucial Nazi organizations, was the key challenge of this approach. It therefore became crucial to the success of the trials, which were (as the British pointed out) a serious public relations risk, to prove that the Nazis waged war on a criminal basis. This set the stage for the Wiener Library to make a significant contribution. Staffed mainly by German-Jewish refugees, the employees of the Library had been gathering evidence of Nazi activities in Germany, Austria, and occupied Europe since the 1920s. They would subsequently play an important role in the British prosecution at Nuremberg.

The Preparation of the British Prosecution Case: Documents

The Wiener Library is the oldest continuously operating archive of documentation relating to the Nazi party in the world. The British officials who used this resource to prepare the prosecution at Nuremberg referred to the institution as "Dr Wiener's Library." The official name of the Library was the Jewish Central Information Office (JCIO), an anti-Nazi documentation center that first opened its doors to researchers in Amsterdam on February 1, 1934. The origins of the JCIO trace back to the work of its German-Jewish founder, Dr. Alfred Wiener, a pioneer in the struggle against antisemitism, who began monitoring antisemitism in Germany after the First World War. Recognizing the specific danger of the Nazi party at a very early stage, Wiener's efforts built on the work of the Central Association of German Citizens of Jewish Faith (*Centralverein*, CV), founded in the late nineteenth century to combat discrimination and prejudice against Jews in Germany.

On behalf of the CV, Wiener spoke out against the Nazis in public, and helped create a special office in Berlin to counter Nazi misinformation, the *Büro Wilhelmstrasse*. By the time of Hitler's appointment as Chancellor of Germany in January 1933, Wiener and colleagues had amassed a substantial archive. However, this very early material could not be made available to the prosecutors at Nuremberg, because it had remained in situ when Wiener fled to Amsterdam. The *Büro*'s archive was destroyed to protect the identities of CV workers still living and working in Nazi Germany. From October 1933, Wiener worked with leading figures in the Jewish community in Britain and the Netherlands to coordinate documentation and dissemination of evidence that could prove useful in resisting the new Nazi regime. By the start of the Second World War, the material gathered by the JCIO included records from trials such as the Bern trial on the Protocols of the Elders of Zion, detailed reports about the persecution of Jews and opponents of the regime in Germany, and 350 eyewitness accounts of *Kristallnacht*.[10]

As German pressure on the Dutch government increased, the British Foreign Office increasingly recognized the value of JCIO materials for intelligence and propaganda. Throughout the war, Wiener and his colleagues continued to gather reports, books, journals, and other documentation that could (and on several occasions did) prove useful to the effort to defeat Nazi Germany via the Political Warfare Department and Ministry of Information. At this stage, however, the British government was not interested in what Wiener and his colleagues knew about the persecution of the Jews but rather what they knew about the Nazis.

Despite varying levels of interest, a trove of vital documentation accumulated between 1933 and 1945 was made available to the British legal officer who began his work preparing for the prosecution on April 12, 1945. Eighteen months later, the Wiener Library published an assessment of its role at the Nuremberg trials provided by General M. de Baer, the Belgian Commissioner of the United Nations War Crimes Commission. Coming just weeks after the sentences had been handed down, and, in the case of death sentences, executed. Baer's statement must be read with the awareness that it is meant as praise rather than historical analysis, but there is no reason to doubt its fundamental point:

> It may be said that it is thanks to the Wiener Library that the criminal decrees, regulations, orders, and circulars of the Nazi rulers were made known in this country and that from 1942 it has been the center of documentation on German

> matters. Documents that could be found nowhere else were available there. The help it has given has been invaluable in the preparation of charges against the leaders of Nazi Germany.[11]

In late 1944, Wiener's deputy in London, Louis Bondy, made efforts to ensure that the London-based UNWCC was aware of the documentary evidence available at the Library.[12] It is not clear, however, that British officials made any proactive attempts to make use of the Wiener Library's collections for the purpose of preparing for trial prior to mid-April 1945. Thereafter, it served as an important resource, even assisting with translation from Yiddish into English. [13]

The unique value of the Wiener Library to British preparation for Nuremberg rested in the first place on its documents, which were extensive and particularly strong on the issue of the persecution of German and Austrian Jews by the Nazi regime. In the face of resistance from British officials, the persecution of German Jews in Germany and Austria before 1939 became a relevant matter for consideration at the trials following the intervention of Herbert Pell and Henry Morgenthau in late 1944. Subsequently, the adoption of the American-led Bernays plan crystallized the Allied prosecution's overarching legal strategy, which was to charge leading Nazis with conducting a criminal conspiracy to commit crimes against peace. Furthermore, the concept of "crimes against humanity" was incorporated into the Nuremberg Charter in August 1945. This made persecution on political, racial, and religious grounds part of the jurisdiction of the IMT insofar as this persecution was relevant to war crimes or crimes against peace.[14] The most egregious example of such a "crime against humanity," which lent weight to the idea that the Nazi invasion of Poland was a pre-meditated "crime against peace," was the persecution of Jews by the Third Reich. Fortunately for the British prosecution team, the persecution of Jews in Germany and Austria had been carefully documented by Wiener and colleagues between 1933 and 1939 in Amsterdam and in London during the Second World War.

Furthermore, the British and American prosecution teams, led by Robert Jackson and Hartley Shawcross, respectively, built their case on documentation rather than oral testimony. While the Soviets had no concerns about meting out "victor's justice," the British and American teams placed value on gathering accurate information to create a strong foundation of credible evidence. Both hoped to avoid the kind of public relations problems that had occurred after the First World War, when lurid eyewitness accounts of German atrocities had sometimes proven inaccurate or false.[15] Building the case on the German documentary record did present risks and challenges, however, not least due to the sheer scale of written evidence that could theoretically be put before the judges. This problem was only partly solved by the judges' early decision to make only those documents read at the trial part of the official record.

While the documents chosen for the prosecution at the IMT were significant, the political and theatrical dynamics of courtroom procedure did not lose their significance. On the contrary, the decision to build the trial around four languages—by reducing the overall number of eyewitnesses and creating a relatively long-winded, dry, and monotonous courtroom dynamic—arguably focused observers' attention more intensely on those dramatic moments that did occur. These moments of drama sometimes had an undesirable effect from the perspective of the Allies, such as the mishandled cross-examination of Göring, while others helped anchor the moral legitimacy of the trials, such as the reactions of the defendants to the screening of film footage from the concentration camps.[16]

The Preparation of the British Prosecution Case: Expertise

The best-known expert contributor to the British prosecution case at Nuremberg is undoubtedly Hersch Lauterpacht, who created the first draft of Hartley Shawcross's famous closing arguments. The expertise amassed by Wiener and his colleagues was also valuable to the British prosecution team, however, in terms of finding the right document at the right time and navigating potentially risky cross-examinations. The role of Louis Bondy is particularly noteworthy in this respect. As noted, Bondy had already established contact with the UNWCC in late 1944. At this stage of the war, Alfred Wiener was based in New York, where he was better placed to obtain crucial printed materials, leaving Bondy to run the London office as Acting Director. Born in Berlin in 1910 as the son of a German-Jewish literary magazine editor, Bondy was "let go" from his job on a German news desk in Paris when Hitler came to power. After a stint doing photojournalism work in Spain, Bondy began working for Wiener in the late 1930s and became his trusted deputy after assisting with the Library's relocation to London. One of Bondy's areas of specialist knowledge was the international network of antisemites connected to the Nazi party who disseminated antisemitic propaganda and misinformation via the "news" agency *Weltdienst*, which was granted pseudo-respectability in the Third Reich as an office of the Frankfurt-based *Institute for the Study of the Jewish Question* in 1939. Through studying the activities of the Nazi regime's most virulent antisemites, Louis Bondy was able to build a detailed picture of what he called "the Jew Baiter's International."[17]

Specialist knowledge of the kind provided by the Wiener Library staff was potentially useful to the prosecutors at Nuremberg in several ways. However, experts like Louis Bondy could be of particular use whenever their specialists concerned the leading defendants in the dock. In Bondy's case, preparing the case against Julius Streicher gave him a specific opportunity to make use of his expertise. Having been the proprietor and editor of *Der Stürmer*, the most notorious and salacious of Nazi antisemitic publications, and an important patron of international antisemitic conferences prior to his fall from grace in the Nazi movement in February 1940, Streicher had been a focus of Bondy's investigations. Streicher was also, to a degree, emblematic of the "criminal" and premeditated nature of Nazi antisemitism, and therefore the case against him had become an important pillar of the overarching conspiracy charge. Streicher's testimony at Nuremberg had also been the target of delaying tactics on the part of the Soviets, who argued prior to the start of proceedings that he was not fit to stand trial due to insanity.[18] There was certainly potential, therefore, for Streicher's cross-examination to go badly, even though, as Hartley Shawcross observed in his memoirs, his guilt and likely sentencing to death were never seriously in doubt. Assistance from the Wiener Library in preparing documentation implicating Streicher was therefore welcome.

In recognition of its assistance to the British prosecution, Justice Jackson granted the Wiener Library observer status at the IMT. Despite his recent return from the United States, Bondy was chosen to travel to Germany as the Wiener Library's representative at the trials, perhaps because of his established working relationship with UNWCC staff. While there, Bondy developed a working relationship with the British prosecuting lawyer Lieutenant M. Griffiths-Jones, who would eventually be responsible for cross-examining Streicher and helped the Library by dispatching reference material back to London with Bondy.[19] Although he had to return home in February 1946, before Streicher's cross-examination by Griffiths-Jones, Bondy did have the opportunity to see Streicher in the dock, an experience which he wrote about in his book entitled *Racketeers of Hatred: Julius Streicher and the Jew Baiter's International.* Of Streicher, Bondy observed:

> [he] looks an inoffensive and tired old man. He wriggles uncomfortably on the wooden bench, stares unseeingly into the large courtroom, and his jaws move interminably as if he were chewing. Those who watch him often remark that it seems impossible to believe that he has done any harm.[20]

Other eyewitnesses to the trial reported that Streicher had a penchant for American chewing gum.[21] The sensitivity of multiple observers to such fine details attests to the fact that while carefully prepared documentary evidence was certainly important, the confrontation of leading Nazis in the dock with this evidence often made lasting but unpredictable impressions on observers.

If the "British perspective" on Nuremberg is limited only to the government's perspective, then it might be argued that the main aims of the trials were accomplished in October 1946 when the sentences were handed down and the prominent criminals punished. The same might be said of the British legal establishment, whose main representative at the trials, Attorney General Hartley Shawcross, looked back on his memoirs with satisfaction at the success of the British prosecution in terms of the professionalism with which their case materials were presented.[22] Bondy noted, however, that alongside the continuing threat of antisemitism during the trials, a new threat of denial of Nazi crimes had appeared. Claims that the trials were a sham emerged among the very antisemites Bondy had been tracking throughout the war, including Alexander Ratcliffe and Maurice Bardèche, as a defensive reflex against the Nuremberg trials. Although lies denying Nazi crimes were not widely disseminated at the time, the conspiratorial thinking they reflected would have a long afterlife.[23]

From the perspective of British Jews, therefore, and especially those who had reached Britain as refugees from the Nazis, the work of Nuremberg was far from over. Bondy and Wiener were intensely aware of the continuing need to rebut antisemites who were actively seeking to undermine the evidence that underpinned judgments reached at Nuremberg. This explains why Bondy, Wiener, and his colleagues were so eager to secure copies of documentation from the trials; much of the correspondence between the Library and the United Nations War Crimes Commission from 1946 onwards concerns efforts to obtain copies for Wiener's ever-growing reference collection in London.[24] In June 1953, Alfred Wiener wrote to Hartley Shawcross to warn him that he was being misquoted in German newspapers by nationalists wishing to portray the Russians as a renewed threat to Germany and offering to sign him up for the Wiener Library Bulletin, which tracked the activity of antisemites and deniers of Nazi crimes.[25] The meaning and memory of the trials for British nationals after October 1946 depended greatly on who was being asked what question and when.

Conclusion

This essay has made three main points to place the British approach to the Nuremberg trials in a broader perspective. Firstly, the British government reconciled itself to the idea of a full public trial quite late and later than the other powers, namely, after the political turning point that followed Roosevelt's death and Hitler's suicide in April 1945. Secondly, once the key parameters of the trial were established, the British prosecution relied heavily on the documentation gathered by the Jewish Central Information Office, which had become known as "Dr Wiener's Library" since it moved to London in 1939. Thirdly, despite the importance of documentation for presenting a robust case at the IMT, the role played by experts who had more direct experience and more profound knowledge was key to shaping the trials and determining their legacy in Britain and elsewhere.

The contribution of Jewish legal thinkers like Raphael Lemkin and Hersch Lauterpacht is relatively well-known. Less well-known, but arguably not less influential, was the expert guidance provided to the UNWCC and the British prosecution team, specifically by figures like Alfred Wiener and Louis Bondy. By 1942, as Baer pointed out, Wiener and his colleagues had developed the most comprehensive documentary record of the Nazi regime available anywhere in the world. If the British prosecution team were exceptionally well-prepared to present their case at Nuremberg in 1945, it is largely thanks to the assistance provided by the Wiener Library. The Library's contribution was recognized at the time, partly through the granting of observer status at the trials, but also through the provision of copies of documentation for Wiener's Library during and after the trials. This documentation would ensure that the Library became the first port of call for historical researchers seeking to understand the rise of fascism in Germany and Europe.

This is not to say that the tendency to see the British perspective from the point of view of official bodies is incorrect. It is probably still fair to regard Shawcross's closing remarks as the most impactful British contribution to the trial, for example. In fact, the solid documentary underpinning of the legal case as presented to the judges at Nuremberg arguably cleared the space for dramatic interventions, including Shawcross's memorable rhetoric and the shocking film footage gathered by British filmmakers at Belsen. These unforgettable moments, along with the defendants' responses to the case arrayed against them, captured the imagination and shook the world's conscience at Nuremberg.

However, two such contrasting figures as Hartley Shawcross and Alfred Wiener can both reflect different but important aspects of the British contribution to Nuremberg. Hartley Shawcross, very much a British establishment figure despite his progressive political credentials, arrived on the scene relatively late and was able to synthesize the disparate elements of the trial preparations, including most notably the work of Jewish refugees, above all the ideas of Hersch Lauterpacht. Alfred Wiener, by contrast, was culturally German-Jewish and very much an outsider. However, he brought with him a lifetime of anti-antisemitism work and years of active commitment to the British war effort. He created an organization that not only facilitated the preparation of a robust evidence base for the British prosecution at Nuremberg but also safeguarded its records long after the British establishment ceased to be actively interested in the trials and their legacy. In summary, the distinctive British perspective on the Nuremberg International Military Tribunals cannot be adequately captured by focusing exclusively on the perspective of official bodies; the British prosecution was, in fact, a cosmopolitan effort, even if it was never intended to be so.

Notes

1 Letter, April 12, 1945, The Wiener Holocaust Library, 3000/9/1/1049/4.
2 Francine Hirsch, *Soviet Judgment at Nuremberg: A New History of the International Military Tribunal after World War II* (Oxford, 2020), pp. 22–4.
3 Philippe Sands, *East West Street: On the Origins of Genocide and Crimes Against Humanity* (London, 2016), p. 349.
4 Tusa Ann and John Tusa, *The Nuremberg Trial* (New York, 2010).
5 Hirsch, *Soviet Judgment,* p. 26.
6 Ibid., pp. 40–1.
7 Ann and John Tusa, *Nuremberg*, p. 65.
8 Bradley Smith, *American Road to Nuremberg: The Documentary Record* (Stanford, 1982), p. 155.
9 Ann and John Tusa, *Nuremberg*, p. 67.
10 See Barbara Warnock, "Lost Cause? The Wiener Library, its Predecessor Organisations and their Struggle against Antisemitism and Nazism, 1919–1945," in *Anti-Antisemitism: Countering Anti-Jewish Racism in Western Europe, 1890–2022* (London, 2022).
11 Quoted in Ben Barkow, *Alfred Wiener and the Making of the Holocaust Library* (London, 1997), p. 111.
12 Letter, December 2, 1944, Louis Bondy to Colonel Wade, Wiener Holocaust Library Archive, 3000/9/1/1049/1.
13 Letter, November 19, 1945, ibid., 3000/9/1/1049/4.
14 Arieh J. Kochavi, "The Role of Genocide in the Preparation of the Nuremberg Trials," in *Holocaust and Justice: Representation & Historiography of the Holocaust in Post-War Trials*, pp. 71–8.

15 Lawrence Douglas, *The Memory of Judgment: Making Law and History in the Trials of the Holocaust*, p. 17.
16 Ibid., pp. 20–1.
17 See Toby Simpson, "Jew-baiting in Hitler's 'Legacy to the Post-war World': The Significance of the Wiener Library's Anti-antisemitism Work, 1945–1980," in *Anti-Antisemitism: Countering Anti-Jewish Racism in Western Europe, 1890–2022* (London, 2022).
18 See Hirsch, *Soviet Judgement*, p. 285.
19 Letter, February 25, 1946, Louis Bondy to Lieutenant Griffith-Jones, 3000/9/1/1049/12.
20 Louis Bondy, *Racketeers of Hatred: Julius Streicher and the Jew Baiter's International*, cited in Barkow, *Alfred Wiener and the Making of the Holocaust Library*, p. 112.
21 See Hilary Gaskin, *Eyewitnesses at Nuremberg* (London, 1991).
22 Sir Hartley Shawcross, *Life Sentence: The Memoirs of Lord Shawcross*, p. 122.
23 See Simpson, "Jew-baiting in Hitler's 'Legacy to the Post-war World': The Significance of the Wiener Library's Anti-antisemitism Work, 1945–1980," p. 67.
24 See 3000/9/1/1049/.
25 Letter June 10, 1953, Alfred Wiener to Hartley Shawcross, 3000/9/1/1266/1.

Selected Bibliography

Barkow, Ben, *Alfred Wiener and the Making of the Holocaust Library* (London, 1997).
Bondy, Louis, *Racketeers of Hatred: Julius Streicher and the Jew-Baiters' International* (London, 1946).
Finkelstein, Danie, *Hitler, Stalin, Mum and Dad: A Family Memoir of Miraculous Survival* (Glasgow, 2023).
Sands, Philippe, *East West Street: On the Origins of Genocide and Crimes against Humanity* (London, 2016).
Shawcross, Hartley, *Life Sentence: The Memoirs of Hartley Shawcross* (Edinburgh, 1995).
Tusa, Ann and John Tusa, *The Nuremberg Trial* (London, 1983).

3

The Historical and Legal National Perspectives of the Crime of Aggression at the Nuremberg International Military Tribunal (IMT) Trial 1945–6

The French Perspective

Hervé Ascensio

France's presence in the organization for the prosecution of war crimes by the Nazi regime was not guaranteed, given the military collapse of 1940 and the collaboration of Marshal Pétain's regime with the Nazis. The *Comité national français* (French National Committee), the official body of Free France led by General de Gaulle, was one of the signatories of the Declaration of the Governments in Exile of January 13, 1942, adopted at the end of the conference at St. James Palace, placing France among the territories to be liberated and not yet among the powers capable of imagining the post-war period.

The political situation changed with the liberation of the French territory, the formation of a provisional government under the leadership of General de Gaulle, and the rapid takeover of French institutions by the leaders of the *France libre*. At that moment, the French Republic had a clear interest in being present on the international stage restoring France's position as a power in the new international order. France, now seen as one of the victorious Allied Powers, was represented at the London Conference in June and July 1945, where the statutes of the International Military Tribunal were drafted. However, the context of rebuilding a state apparatus remained difficult in France. Its involvement in the prosecution and punishment of major war criminals was a logistical, financial, and human challenge. But it was also an opportunity to highlight the crimes committed by the Nazi regime against the French people during the occupation, the economic plunder of France, and the role of the resistance.

Above the geopolitical context, the perspective of the French jurists involved in the Nuremberg trial was rooted in a long legal tradition with which they tried to reconnect, just as the French provisional government tried to reconnect with the republican tradition by stepping over the authoritarian parenthesis and the complicity of the Vichy regime. It is likely that this concern for continuity extended well beyond

Nuremberg and explains the somewhat paradoxical legacy of Nuremberg in France, although the paradox is not unique to the French perspective. The crimes of the occupation, understood as war crimes, were constantly at the center of the concerns of the French actors involved in the trial. Both the crime of aggression, under the expression "crime against peace," and the crime against humanity appeared to be novelties that risked casting doubt on the entire judicial process. Yet it is the crime against humanity that has progressively emerged as the main legacy of Nuremberg, while the crime of aggression has been entirely cast into the shadows.[1]

This contribution will look at the aspects specifically linked to the role of France and the French actors in the Nuremberg trial, with some remarks about the crime of aggression, in accordance with the request of the editors of the present book. It will first recall the limited French influence on the drafting of the statutes of the International Military Tribunal (2) before examining the awkward French presence at the Nuremberg trial of major nazi criminals (3) and the legacy of Nuremberg in French law and French legal thinking (4). This will lead to concluding remarks from a contemporary perspective (5).

The Limited French Influence on the Drafting of the Statutes of the International Military Tribunal

As we have seen, France's involvement in the project to prosecute German war criminals began with the St. James Palace Declaration of January 13, 1942. The governments in exile wanted to keep this issue high on the agenda of the three powers leading the fight against Nazi Germany, that is, the UK, the USA, and the USSR. In this framework, the French transmitted a first oral note to the Soviet representative in London in July 1942. On October 3, 1942, the English government proposed the creation of a fact-finding commission to the signatories of the St. James Declaration, but the first session of the Commission on War Crimes occurred only on October 20, 1943. There were French representatives in the Commission, notably Professor René Cassin, commissioner for justice and education in the French national committee and the future co-drafter of the Universal Declaration of Human Rights, seconded by Professor André Gros, legal adviser of the French national committee. These steps prepared the Moscow Declaration of November 1, 1943, according to which the Three Allied Powers—and still not Four at that time—"speaking in the interests of the 32 United Nations," condemned the atrocities committed by the Hitlerite forces in Europe and announced the judgment and punishment of the perpetrators.[2]

To contribute to the work of the War Crimes Commission, the French National Committee set up a specific structure, the *Service des crimes de guerre* (War Crimes Department), which evolved over time and was later to become, after the liberation of France and the creation of a provisional government on June 3, 1944, the *Service de recherche des crimes de guerre ennemis* (Enemy War Crimes Investigation Department).[3] This structure encountered many practical difficulties in compiling files, initially calling on the resistance to obtain information and then progressively trying to recover documents as the country was liberated, but many archives had been taken away by the Germans. The first files were submitted to the UN War Crimes Commission in February 1944 to put perpetrators on the inter-allied list of wanted persons. However, the quality of these files was uneven, as the war crimes department only had limited human resources and limited access to evidence. At the same time, the legal services of the French National Committee were also working on the urgent issue of the domestic purge trials against those most compromised in the collaboration.[4]

As for the methods for repression against German war criminals, the French representatives to the War Crimes Commission took a position in favor of prosecution by national courts, supplemented by the creation of an international tribunal responsible for judging the major war criminals, preferably a civilian court, or failing that, an international military tribunal—which was to happen. They also pointed out the role of certain organizations within the Nazi regime and the responsibility of all their members. The repression of war crimes was a constant objective of the French National Committee, which focused on the crimes committed by the occupier on French territory, that is, war crimes under *jus in Bello*.

The issue of repression against major criminals was discussed again at the San Francisco Conference in May and June 1945, during which the French authorities remained in favor of an international tribunal. However, the French delegation to the London conference was set up on an improvised basis. It was initially planned to send Professor Jules Basdevant, the former jurisconsult of the French Ministry of Foreign Affairs. However, Basdevant, skeptical about the process and involved in the negotiations on the creation of the United Nations Organization, refused.[5] Therefore, the Ministry of Justice invited the members of the Court of Cassation, the highest judicial authority in France, to apply for a post in a future international criminal tribunal, with a condition of English proficiency. Robert Falco, a magistrate dismissed by the Vichy government and just reinstated as a counselor at the Court of Cassation, was the only member of the court to respond.[6] He was then considered for the post of public prosecutor and appointed as France's delegate to the London Conference. But Robert Falco had little technical knowledge of international criminal law, no experience of diplomatic negotiations, and received no official instructions before his arrival in London; after the conference, he would finally be appointed deputy judge at Nuremberg.[7] To strengthen the French delegation, the French ambassador in London requested that Robert Falco be assisted during the conference by Professor André Gros. André Gros was at that time legal counsel at the French embassy in London, having previously followed all the discussions within the War Crimes Commission and the difficult process of compiling files on the crimes committed by the Germans in occupied France.[8]

The role of the French delegation, composed of these two persons only, seems to have had a rather limited influence, both in the definition of offenses and in the choice of an almost entirely adversarial procedure. Following the view developed by the Ministry of Foreign Affairs, the delegation expressed skepticism about the crime of aggression, as the Soviet delegation also did, and took the position that prosecution should focus primarily on atrocities committed during the war and so on war crimes and crimes against humanity.[9] The main reason was the fear that the trial would be criticized for violating the principle of the non-retroactivity of criminal law; another reason was a difference in legal culture, especially concerning the concept of "conspiracy."[10] Interestingly, André Gros also pointed out that a practice of humanitarian interventions had also existed until then and that aggression, if it were to be criminalized, had to be differentiated by its purpose, that is, the domination of other nations.[11] These arguments were probably accompanied by a concern for *realpolitik* on the part of the French Ministry of Foreign Affairs: it could not yet be ruled out that France might in future have to use force preventively or occupy certain parts of German territory as a guarantee against a neighbor which had invaded its territory three times in less than a century.

As is well known, the approach proposed by the American delegation, and in particular Robert Jackson, won out, and the Statutes put forward the crime against peace, which was to become the focus of the prosecution at Nuremberg. The small French delegation was probably not in a position to counterbalance this view in any manner. Anyway, the most important result for France was probably to be mentioned as a victorious nation in the London Agreements of August 8, 1945.

The Awkward French Presence at the Nuremberg Trial of Major Nazi Criminals

France's participation in the trial itself was necessary to mark the country's return to the ranks of the great powers and to satisfy public opinion in search of justice after the crimes committed during the years of occupation and when the German troops withdrew.[12] Highlighting the role of resistance fighters was probably also one of the objectives. However, it came up against major material difficulties, as the country's institutions had to be rebuilt, hence the very gradual increase in the number of people and material resources allocated to the French presence at Nuremberg. However, the appointments show a will to send top legal experts who had not been compromised with the Vichy regime and even, for some of them, who had been directly involved in the resistance. This can be seen as a way of reviving the rule of law and a certain tradition of international criminal law while taking into account the political objectives of the French presence at Nuremberg. This also led the French actors in the trial to have hesitations and doubts about some aspects of the indictment, including crime against peace.

On the prosecution side, the French general prosecutor, François de Menthon, was a law professor who joined the resistance in 1940 and after that General de Gaulle in London in 1943. He was a former minister of justice in the provisional government, where he had been in charge of organizing the trials related to the "*épuration*" (purge) policy. However, he was criticized for being overly concerned with respect for the legality principle. He was also a leader of the Christian Democratic Party and resigned during the Nuremberg trial due to the general elections called in France. He was replaced by Auguste Champetier de Ribes, a lawyer and prominent Christian Democrat politician under the Third Republic. He was one of the few members of parliament to refuse full powers to Marshal Pétain in 1940. The team included figures from the Ministry of Justice, such as Charles Dubost, a prosecutor who had also been a prominent member of the resistance, and jurists who had served in the provisional government, such as Edgar Faure, a lawyer, and politician who would go on to become *président du conseil* (prime minister) of the Fourth Republic.

The French prosecution was in charge of the prosecution of crimes committed by the occupying forces in Western Europe, that is, in France, Belgium, Luxembourg, and the Netherlands. This means that it played no part in elaborating and presenting the strategy focusing on crimes against peace, which was to be presented first by the American and then the British prosecutors. The question of aggression did find a place in Menthon's introductory statement but from a political rather than a legal angle. Menthon blamed the aggressiveness of the German nation, German philosophy—including Nietzsche and Hegel—and the moral degradation of Germany under National Socialism,[13] continuing to think of aggression as a collective fault rather than an individual crime. Then, given the division of tasks between the various national teams, the French prosecution focused on war crimes and crimes against humanity committed in Western Europe.

The French prosecution was uncomfortable with the concept of crimes against humanity, which had been the subject of internal discussions centered on the principle of non-retroactivity of criminal law. Therefore, these crimes were not clearly distinguished from war crimes, a much more solid legal ground. The presentation of evidence put stress on the crime of deportation and the crimes committed during internment in concentration camps, both against resistance fighters and Jews, as well as on economic crimes and compulsory labor of French citizens in Germany.

Clearly, the prosecutor and his deputies faced two kinds of difficulties: material problems in supporting the prosecution and a cultural gap in understanding the procedure, which was essentially based on the common law legal tradition. The other delegations, particularly the USA, feared that the French would be unable to present a solid case due to a lack of organization and documentation of their own. Thus, in addition to information from the War Crimes Department, the French prosecution benefited from documents transmitted by the Anglo-Saxons. But this led to a degree of redundancy during the trial, as the documents on the camps had previously been used by the US and English prosecutors to present an overview of the Nazi criminal project in order to support the charge of conspiracy to wage a war of aggression and establish a link—legally required—with crimes against humanity. The boundaries between the various offenses had thus remained blurred, with the search for criminal intent in crimes against peace encompassing not only the outbreak of war but also the subsequent crimes, understood as characteristic of the criminal project.

During the trial, the French prosecution sometimes appeared clumsy and ill-adapted to the procedure. However, it did make a number of contributions, including the persecution of Jews in France and the functioning of concentration camps. One of the French deputy prosecutors, Edgar Faure, received and probably used information gathered by the *Centre de documentation juive contemporaine* (Centre for Contemporary Jewish Documentation), thanks to the work of historians like Leon Poliakov and Joseph Billig.[14] The French prosecution was also notable for calling victims to testify, generally members of the resistance who had been deported to the concentration camps. These testimonies were sometimes considered long by the presiding judge. However, there were some highlights, such as the testimony of Marie-Claude Vaillant-Couturier, a communist resistance fighter who was deported to Auschwitz and who was the only female actor at the trial. On the other hand, the complicity of the Vichy regime was largely ignored, with a few exceptions, such as when Edgar Faure talked about the deportation of the Jews or when Marie-Claude Vaillant-Couturier recounted her arrest by the Vichy police.

On the side of the judges, it has already been explained how Robert Falco, who represented France during the London conference, was appointed deputy judge by a combination of circumstances. The question of the appointment of the French judge, Professor Henri Donnedieu de Vabres, was settled very early on, before the London conference. It can be understood as a way of reviving the pre-war French legal tradition. He was clearly a leading French pre-war international criminal law specialist and a central intellectual figure.[15] He had participated in all the international intellectual networks of the time, notably in the International Association of Penal Law and the Institute of International Law, and his reputation emerged intact after the war.[16] It may also be worth noting that his son was, at the time, a member of the cabinet of General de Gaulle, president of the Provisional Government of the French Republic.

Henri Donnedieu de Vabres was very discreet during the trial and, according to the witnesses, also in his dealings with the other judges and the small Nuremberg society. He, however, came out to support the organization of a meeting of the International Association of Penal Law in parallel with the trial and under the presidency of another prominent intellectual figure of pre-war international criminal law, Vespasian Pella, thus showing a desire to place the trial in a certain intellectual continuity.[17] Moreover, at the start of the deliberations, the French judge suddenly stood out by transmitting a memorandum criticizing certain aspects of the prosecution, beginning with the conspiracy to launch a war of aggression, the first count of the indictment.[18] We also know today that he intervened to oppose the death penalty for some of the accused, including the governors of provinces subject to the Reich. All his positions correspond to a tradition of thinking in criminal law that is suspicious of collective forms of liability and defends the individualization of sentences.[19] He explained this clearly in the course he gave in 1947 at The Hague Academy of International Law.[20]

On several points, Judge Donnedieu de Vabres' vision thus directly opposed the prosecution's strategy, particularly the vision of Prosecutor Robert Jackson. He was pleased that the court was very cautious about the conspiracy charge because it created a form of solidarity between all the defendants and, therefore, did not sufficiently individualize responsibility.[21] For the same reasons, he approved the conditions added by the judgment with regard to the subsequent implementation of the liability of members of organizations declared to be criminal,[22] which corresponded to a request of the French prosecutor Champetier de Ribes in his closing statement. Donnedieu de Vabres also emphasized the near disappearance of crimes against humanity in the judgment, which were confused mainly with war crimes. He felt it was prudent and again in line with the position of the French prosecution.[23]

In so doing, Henri Donnedieu de Vabres sought an acceptable compromise between justice and legal rigour. As a counterpoint, he supported the criminalization of aggression in the form of a crime against peace, admitting the need for flexibility in applying the *nullum crimen sine lege* principle in the context of the unprecedented crimes committed by Nazi Germany. Actually, the acceptance of the function of a judge at Nuremberg presumed such flexibility since it was clear that the crimes against peace would be the main charge.

The cautious approach to the new features of the IMT Statutes remains the central point of the French perspective at Nuremberg. It is part of a historical and sociological understanding of the discipline of international criminal law among French lawyers. French specialists in public international law had played an essential part in the debate on the prosecution of war criminals after the First World War by strongly supporting the idea of individual responsibility for crimes under international law, calling this "new international law."[24] Donnedieu de Vabres used the term again in his lectures in The Hague and continues this tradition,[25] but his ideas were somewhat different. For him, repression is justified more by the idea of a criminal law common to civilized nations.[26] In this sense, the French prosecution also refers to "common international law" and the conscience of humanity as the basis for prosecution. From a theoretical point of view, a justification based on domestic criminal law and the general principles of law seems to us to be more open to the novelty of the crime against humanity since the underlying elements are all punishable under national criminal codes than to the crime of aggression, which is steeped in interstate relations and political considerations.

The Paradoxical Legacy of Nuremberg in French Law and Legal Thinking

The demand for justice was strong in French public opinion. For the French press of the time, the trial was considered long and tedious, and the verdict was decried because of the acquittals. Over time, however, it became a benchmark and a gateway for the repression of crimes against humanity under French law.

In parallel to the Nuremberg trial and in the years that followed, trials for war crimes were held before French military courts against German war criminals based on ordinary offenses as defined by the French criminal code.[27] Such a legal basis, in line with the traditional approach based on criminal law rather than public international law, necessarily ruled out any prosecution for the crime of aggression—which in any case only concerns the highest political decision-makers. The Enemy War Crimes Investigation Department had opened files on around 20,000 war crimes. However, in most cases, the individuals sought could not be identified or were on the run, resulting in around 16,000 dismissals. However, 2345 people were tried, including 1314 in absentia, according to figures from the military justice archives.[28] The proceedings gradually came to a halt in the early 1950s due to the rejection of extradition requests, including those addressed to the command of the US military occupation zone in Germany and in the context of Franco-German reconciliation. Some of those condemned were pardoned and discreetly released.

In the 1960s, public opinion in many countries reacted to Germany's announcement that the statute of limitations would soon prevent the prosecution of war criminals under German law. In France, associations of former members of the resistance and deportees mobilized and found support in Parliament for the adoption of the law of December 26, 1964, which provided for the non-applicability of statutory limitations to crimes against humanity. The law contains a single article which, by express reference to the Nuremberg Statute, makes this crime "*imprescriptible*" (without statute of limitations) for acts relating to the Second World War. This did not extend to war crimes, let alone crimes against peace, for a number of reasons that had to be weighed up: the fact that French public opinion now recognizes the centrality of crimes against humanity among the crimes committed by Nazi Germany, thanks to the work of historians and the testimony of survivors; the legislator's will not to go to far in the exceptions to the traditional principle of the statute of limitations in criminal matters; and also the context of decolonization, since France had adopted or was preparing to adopt amnesty laws for crimes committed during the Indochina War and the Algerian War.[29] However, this law represented a turning point, even if it is limited to a specific historical period: it made it possible to incriminate crimes against humanity in French law by reference to international law.

Until March 1, 1994, the date of entry into force of the new penal code of 1992, the IMT statutes were thus the sole legal basis for prosecuting crimes against humanity before French courts. On this basis, it was then possible, forty years after the end of the war, to prosecute the SS police officer Klaus Barbie, sentenced to life imprisonment in 1987, but also, ten years later, French collaborators like Paul Touvier, René Bousquet, and Maurice Papon, for complicity in crimes against humanity. This is the best part of the heritage: Nuremberg evolved as a German mirror for French duality, that is, French complicity in the crimes against humanity committed in France during the Second World War. The incrimination by reference disappeared with the new 1992 Penal Code, which defines crimes against humanity in general terms, including genocide. War crimes were not included in the penal code until the second law adapting French law to the ICC Statute was passed in 2010.[30]

The Nuremberg statutes and judgment were, and still are, a reference in French law for two other criminal offenses of a lower degree. The first is the denial of crimes against humanity and war crimes, which became criminal offenses in 1990 for denial of the crimes committed during the Second World War as defined in Article 6 of the IMT Statutes—further expanded to crimes as defined in the ICC Statute.[31] The second one is the prohibition to wear insignia or emblems reminiscent of those used by members of an organization declared criminal pursuant to Article 9 of the IMT Statute—except for a film, show, or exhibition involving a historical evocation.[32]

As can be seen, the crime of aggression has disappeared, mainly because the legacy of Nuremberg was understood through the prism of the crimes committed in France during the occupation. The generalization of the definition of international crimes in French criminal law came later, in 1992, and in the twenty-first century, in order to adapt French law to the statute of the International Criminal Court as adopted in 1998. The International Criminal Court has become the main reference point for French legal policy on international crimes. It has also led to the creation of institutions within the French judicial system dedicated to the investigation and prosecution of war crimes and crimes against humanity, including under universal jurisdiction.[33] However, France has not become a party to the amendment defining the crime of aggression, adopted at the Kampala Conference in 2010 and incorporated into the ICC Statute in Article 8bis. The crime of aggression, like the crime against peace, is therefore not reflected at all in French law.

Concluding Remarks

From the French perspective, the impact of the Nuremberg trial was significant, but it had slightly different effects at different times. First, it was a symbol of justice and restoration of the country. Then, the crime against humanity became its main contribution, with effects progressively recognized in French law. Nowadays, the reference is less marked since the statute of the International Criminal Court has become the central reference in the fight against international crimes. But the symbol remains strong as a seminal precedent.

Despite this, the crime of aggression has remained on the sidelines. This situation is paradoxical because the crime against peace stems from a theoretical tradition in which French authors and some French politicians, notably Aristide Briand, played an active part throughout the twentieth century. But its prosecution at Nuremberg appeared as a novelty resulting from extraordinary historical circumstances, namely Nazi Germany's aggressive policy. The generalization of the offense after the Second World War has proved long and challenging at the international level since it cannot be understood simply as the application of ordinary criminal crimes to a specific criminal context. Here, all the offense elements depend on a certain structure of power and international relations. For that reason, the criminalization of aggression raises major issues of security and international politics.

This explains France's contemporary reticence about the crime of aggression, reinforced by the broad and somewhat shadowy definition of Article *8bis* of the Rome Statute following the Kampala revision conference.[34] Hence, there are also contradictory views in French legal literature as to whether or not this definition is customary.[35] It should also be remembered that, in recent times, France has intervened militarily—and with other states—on several occasions abroad without the agreement of the state concerned and without the express authorization of the United Nations Security Council: for example, in Kosovo in 1999, because of a risk of crimes against humanity, and in Syria in 2018, in response to the use of chemical weapons by the Syrian government against its civilian population.

This reluctance is not unique to France: the low number of ratifications of the Kampala amendment bears witness to this. But, in the case of France, it is possible to see some continuity between its cautious attitude toward crimes against peace at the London Conference and then at Nuremberg and its current mistrust of an even broader definition of the crime of aggression. This also echoes the geopolitical vision of a medium-sized power with an army capable of intervening in foreign theaters.

Lastly, and more generally, it reveals the persistence of two distinct concerns stemming from two different ways of thinking about international relations. The first is a realistic view: the use of force remains an instrument of power that may prove necessary, notably under circumstances where collective security is paralyzed. The second one is an idealist view: to stop a crime against humanity being committed by a state's government against its own population, a certain political and moral tradition favors humanitarian intervention, including the use of military means. In such a context, the criminalization of aggression, with a broad and imprecise definition and without reference to a domination intent—which was essential in the Nuremberg and Tokyo judgments—could act as a brake, and eventually protect sovereignty more than humanity. The challenge of an appropriate definition of the crime of aggression and its judicial interpretation will be to navigate these different pitfalls to strengthen the rule of law and its acceptability in international relations.

Notes

1 Annette Wievorka, *Le procès de Nuremberg* (Paris: Éditions Liana Lévi, 2006), 291–2.
2 Interestingly, the judgment is mentioned for war crimes committed in an occupied territory, with trials "on the spot," whereas for major criminals, those whose crimes have no precise geographical location, only the punishment is mentioned, and this should be organized "by a joint decision of the Government of the Allies."
3 On this institutional evolution, see Antonin Tisseron, *La France et le procès de Nuremberg—Inventer le droit international* (Paris: Les Prairies ordinaires, 2014), 73–81.
4 On those efforts, see the classical book of Peter Novick, *The Resistance versus Vichy: the Purge of Collaborators in Liberated France* (London: Chatto and Windus, 1968); see also Association française pour l'histoire de la justice, *La justice de l'épuration à la fin de la Seconde guerre mondiale* (Paris: La Documentation française, 2008).
5 Jules Basdevant had resigned from this position of jurisconsult on May 29, 1941, in disagreement with the policy of the Vichy regime, and returned to university before being compulsorily retired in 1944. He was appointed a judge of the International Court of Justice in 1946.
6 Robert Falco, *Juge à Nuremberg—Souvenirs inédits du procès des criminels nazis* (Nancy: Arbre bleu éditions, 2012), 28.
7 Ibid. At that time, it was already decided that Professor Henri Donnedieu de Vabres would be the French judge.

8 See above. After the war, André Gros became Director of Legal Affairs at the Ministry of Foreign Affairs (1947–64), and then a judge at the International Court of Justice (1964–82).

9 Wievorka, *Le procès de Nuremberg*, 31.

10 See Raphaël Maurel, "André Gros (1908–2004)," https://sfdi.org/internationalistes/gros, and Wievorka, *Le procès de Nuremberg*, 31–8.

11 See Tisseron, *La France et le procès de Nuremberg*, 98–9.

12 As for the crimes committed during the liberation of France, those committed at Oradour-sur-Glane on June 10, 1944 by a Waffen SS division have become the quintessential example in the French collective memory.

13 Tisseron, *La France et le procès de Nuremberg*, 159–67.

14 See Wievorka, *Le procès de Nuremberg*, 171–9; Tisseron, *La France et le procès de Nuremberg*, 195–8.

15 See the intellectual portrait drawn by Frédéric Mégret, "Henri Donnedieu de Vabres—Penal Liberal, Moderate Internationalist and Nuremberg Judge," in *The Dawn of a Discipline International Criminal Justice and Its Early Exponents*, ed. Frédéric Mégret and Immi Tallgren (Cambridge: Cambridge University Press, 2020), 146–73. Among his works, see especially: *Les principes modernes du droit pénal international* (Sirey, 1928, re-published by Editions Panthéon-Assas, 2004).

16 Mégret, "Henri Donnedieu de Vabres—Penal Liberal, Moderate Internationalist and Nuremberg Judge," 160–1.

17 Some Nuremberg commentators reproached him for this support, because of the allegedly problematic conduct of Vespasien Pella during the war, but recent literature is in favor of Pella, who, as an ambassador of Romania to Switzerland, intervened to protect Jewish refugees and protested against his country's policy. See Andrei Mamolea, "Vespasien Pella—International Criminal Justice as a Safeguard of Peace, 1919-1952," in *The Dawn of a Discipline International Criminal Justice and Its Early Exponents*, ed. Frédéric Mégret and Immi Tallgren (Cambridge: Cambridge University Press, 2020), 49–92, and Muriel Ubeda-Saillard, *Vespasien Pella, La justice internationale au service de la paix mondiale—Commentaire* (Dalloz, 2023).

18 Tisseron, *La France et le procès de Nuremberg*, 207–9.

19 This explanation, linked to his convictions as a lawyer, seems more convincing that the fact that he had briefly met one of the accused, Hans Frank, and also probably Julius Streicher, several years before, in the context of conferences in Germany, as suggested by Philippe Sands in his wonderful but romanticized book, *East West Street: On the Origins of "Genocide" and "Crimes against Humanity"* (Knopf Doubleday, 2016).

20 Henri Donnedieu de Vabres, "Le procès de Nuremberg devant les principes modernes du droit pénal international," *Collected Course of The Hague Academy of International Law* 70 (1947): 481–581.

21 Ibid., 528–42.

22 Ibid., 543–58.

23 Ibid., 525–6.

24 See notably Louis Renault, "De l'application du droit pénal aux faits de guerre," *Journal du droit international* 42 (1915): 313–44; Alexandre Mérignhac, "De la sanction des infractions au droit des gens commises, au cours de la guerre européenne, par les Empires du Centre," *Revue générale de droit international public*

24 (1917): 5–56; Ferdinand Larnaude and Albert de La Pradelle, "Examen de la responsabilité de l'empereur Guillaume II d'Allemagne," *Journal du droit international* 46 (1919): 131–59.

25 de Vabres, "Le procès de Nuremberg . . .", 500. He also refers to the thinking of Louis Renault to justify individual liability for war crimes, at 509.

26 His debatable comment about the dualist view in the Nuremberg judgment is revealing (at 511). See also the analysis of Mégret, "Henri Donnedieu de Vabres—Penal Liberal, Moderate Internationalist and Nuremberg Judge."

27 The equivalence between war crimes and ordinary offenses committed in time of war by enemies is clarified by an order of the French provisional governement on the repression of war crimes of August 28, 1944.

28 Claudia Moisel, "Les procès pour crimes de guerre allemands en France après la Seconde Guerre mondiale", *Bulletin de l'Institut d'Histoire du temps présent* 80 (second Semester 2002): 90–101, accessed August 31, 2024, https://www.persee.fr/doc/ihtp_0247-0101_2002_num_80_1_1788.

29 Philippe Kalfayan, *La France et l'imprescriptibilité des crimes internationaux* (Paris: Pedone, 2015).

30 Law n° 2010-930 of August 9, 2010.

31 Law n° 90-615 of July 13, 1990 ("Loi Gayssot"), art. 24bis, modifying the 1881 Press Act.

32 Penal Code, Article R645-1.

33 For investigation, a Central Office for the fight against crimes against humanity, genocides, and war crimes was created by Decree 2013-987 of November 5, 2013. For prosecution, a specialised unit was created in 2012 within the Paris judicial tribunal, and later merged with the antiterrorist unit in 2019; it has jurisdiction for terrorist offenses, offenses relating to the proliferation of weapons of mass destruction, crimes against humanity, war crimes, crimes of torture, and forced disappearances.

34 Criticisms are clearly set out in François Alabrune, "La compétence de la Cour pénale internationale sur le crime d'agression," in *Statut de Rome de la Cour pénale internationale—Commentaire article par article* I, ed. Julian Fernandez, Xavier Pacreau, and Muriel Ubéda-Saillard (Paris: Pedone, 2nd éd., 2019), 401–5.

35 Against its customary status, François Alabrune, "La compétence de la Cour pénale internationale sur le crime d'agression," 402. In favor of it, although as a passing remark, Robert Badinter, Bruno Cotte, and Alain Pellet, *Vladimir Poutine—L'accusation* (Paris: Fayard, 2023), 86.

Selected Bibliography

de Vabres, Henri Donnedieu, "Le procès de Nuremberg devant les principes modernes du droit pénal international," *Collected Course of The Hague Academy of International Law* 70 (1947): 481–581.

Falco, Robert, *Juge à Nuremberg – Souvenirs inédits du procès des criminels nazis* (Nancy: Arbre bleu éditions, 2012).

Kalfayan, Philippe, *La France et l'imprescriptibilité des crimes internationaux* (Paris: Pedone, 2015).

Mégret, Frédéric and Immi Tallgren (eds.), *The Dawn of a Discipline – International Criminal Justice and Its Early Exponents* (Cambridge: Cambridge University Press, 2020).
Mouralis, Guillaume, *Le moment Nuremberg* (Paris: Presses de SciencesPo, 2019).
Tisseron, Antonin, *La France et le procès de Nuremberg – Inventer le droit international* (Paris: Les Prairies ordinaires, 2014).
Wievorka, Annette, *Le procès de Nuremberg* (Paris: Éditions Liana Lévi, 2006).

4

German Perspectives on the Nuremberg Trial

Stefanie Bock

Post-War Germany and the "Monumental Spectacle of Truth and Justice": First Impressions

German perspectives on the Nuremberg Trials naturally differ from those of the Allies. At the end of the Second World War, Germany was a defeated nation, occupied, destroyed, guilty of crimes without parallel in history, and, in a sense, excluded from the international community of civilized states. This outcast position is reflected in some ways in the orchestration and composition of the Nuremberg Trials: The International Military Tribunal (IMT) focused on the Germans as perpetrators and how they were to be blamed and punished. The active involvement of Germans was sparse and essentially limited to the roles of the defendants, the legal defense, and the witnesses.[1] The proceedings were designed as a "monumental spectacle of truth and justice"[2] to educate the (German) public[3] and to make them aware of the full extent of the crimes committed during the Nazi era.[4] The Office of the Military Government of the United States (OMGUS) reports, which tracked the development of public opinion in Germany from 1945 to 1949, indicate that it did work—at least initially. The German public was informed about the proceedings,[5] and by the end of the trial, 85 percent of those surveyed by OMGUS stated that they had learned new facts about war crimes and about the concentration camps (in particular about those located in East Europe).[6] When interviewed in 1945 and 1946, the vast majority of Germans—between 75 and 80 percent—considered the trial to be fair. They agreed that the defendants were guilty and felt by majority that the penalties imposed were appropriate (or at least not overly harsh).[7] However, this may also have to do with the fact that the Nuremberg Main Trial targeted members of the Nazi political, social, and economic elite, who were seen as responsible for the loss of the war and the devastating living conditions in post-war Germany.[8] The Germans almost unanimously saw themselves as victims of the Nazi regime. Ninety-one percent felt that "Hitler and his government were criminals and misled the German people," more than 70 percent rejected the idea of a "collective German guilt,"[9] and about 50 percent believed that "National Socialism was a good idea badly carried out."[10]

The 1950s: Time to Move on—Critical Perspectives on the Nuremberg Trials

At the beginning of the 1950s (and thus after the denazification process had mainly been completed),[11] the Nuremberg Trials came under increasing academic, political, and social scrutiny. From a legal perspective, the most important point of criticism probably concerns the violation of the principle of non-retroactivity, especially with regard to crimes against peace.[12] In a joint motion, the defense counsel stated at Nuremberg that although there might be good moral and ethical reasons for the international community to "call to account the State which wages an unjust war" and even to demand "that not only should the guilty State be condemned [. . .] but that furthermore those men who are responsible for unleashing the unjust war be tried and sentenced by an International Tribunal," this was for the time being "not as yet valid international law." The defense argued that until the establishment of the IMT, the international community had "never thought of" establishing individual criminal responsibility for "statesmen, generals, and industrialists" for waging an aggressive war and concluded that a crime of aggression did not exist at the time of the relevant acts.[13] As is well known, the IMT rejected this motion, referring to the Kellogg-Briand Pact of August 27, 1928, in which the State Parties renounced the use of war as an instrument of national policy in their relations with one another.[14] However, the Court did not explain in detail how and why a violation of these provisions, which were directed against states (and not against individuals), could raise individual criminal liability.[15] It relied on the moral rather than legal argument[16] that it cannot be considered "unjust to punish those who in defiance of treaties and assurances have attacked neighboring states without warning [. . .], for in such circumstances the attacker must know that he is doing wrong, and so far from it being unjust to punish him, it would be unjust if his wrong were allowed to go unpunished."[17]

More important for the public perception of the Nuremberg Trials than abstract legal issues, however, were general judgments of justice based on impressions of consistency, suppression of bias, accuracy, correctability, representativeness, and ethics.[18] In this respect, the reputation of the IMT suffered in the 1950s from the fact that the impartiality and objectivity of the judges were increasingly called into question. They had been appointed exclusively by and from the Allied powers; there were no judges from neutral countries such as Switzerland or Portugal—let alone judges from Germany.[19] This resulted in the feeling that "justice was applied solely by the victors."[20] Moreover, some judges had already been involved in drafting the IMT Statute,[21] which led the defense counsel to conclude that the Allied powers were "all in one: Creator of the court and of the criminal law norms, prosecutor and judge."[22] This arguably contradicted the doctrine of the separation of powers[23] and raised doubts, particularly among the defendants,[24] about the impartiality of the judges.[25] The related accusation that the Nuremberg Trials were victors' justice[26] was reinforced by the limited jurisdiction of the IMT. It was set up for "the trial and punishment of the major war criminals of the European Axis countries" and thus had no jurisdiction to deal with alleged war crimes of the Allied Powers, for example, the bombing of Dresden and Königsberg.[27] The IMT and the Subsequent Nuremberg Military Tribunals also rejected the traditional *tu quoque* defense, which excludes criminal responsibility for international crimes on the grounds that the opposing party has committed similar crimes.[28] In the Ministries case, the Tribunal was unequivocal:

> The defense asserts that Russia, being itself an aggressor and an accomplice to Hitler's aggression, was a party and an accomplice to at least one of the aggressions charged in this indictment [. . .]. The justifications, if any, which the Soviet Union may claim to have had for its actions in this respect were not presented to this Tribunal. But if we assume, arguendo, that Russia's action was wholly untenable and its guilt as deep as that of the Third Reich, nevertheless, this cannot in law avail the defendants or lessen the guilt of those of the Third Reich who were themselves responsible.[29]

This is persuasive in principle: As the ICTY pointed out some 60 years later, the *tu quoque* defense is incompatible with the "absolute nature" of most obligations under international humanitarian law, which are not based on reciprocity.[30] Nevertheless, the restrictive approach of the Nuremberg Tribunals meant they did not hear any evidence of alleged crimes committed by the Allies. The "guilt of the victors" had no place at Nuremberg.[31] In addition, the IMT did not deal with crimes committed by the Nazis against their own people (with the important exception of certain crimes committed against the Jews, which were considered to be part of the preparation of conspiracy for crimes against peace). It remained largely unconsidered "that Nazism began with oppressing the supporters of deviating opinions, religions or races within its own people."[32]

The Nuremberg Subsequent Proceedings, which focused on representatives of the general public rather than Nazi leaders, were met with greater skepticism from the outset.[33] In addition, the prosecutions were highly selective. The American Office of Chief Counsel identified 2,500 major war criminals, but only 177 were brought to trial. At least some of the decisions on whom to prosecute appear to have been arbitrary, influenced by political, financial, or logistical considerations:[34] Karl Wolff, Himmler's Chief of Staff and a key figure in the SS, for example, was granted immunity—apparently as a kind of reward for his involvement in Operation Sunrise, which had led to the earlier surrender of German forces in northern Italy. Only 20 years later, in the aftermath of the Eichmann trial, Wolff was sentenced to life imprisonment by the Regional Court of Munich for his role in the deportation of 300,000 Jews to the Treblinka death camp.[35]

In line with the increasingly critical discourse, public perceptions of the Nuremberg Trials also changed significantly. In the early 1950s, 30 percent of the Germans thought that they were unfair, 40 percent believed the sentences were too harsh, and some 60 percent generally disapproved of the way the Allies dealt with war criminals.[36] The prevailing view was that the Nuremberg proceedings should draw a final line under the Nazi era: Those most responsible had been identified and punished, and this was seen as absolving all others from guilt.[37] As Otto Kranzbuhler, the former counsel for the defense of Grand-Admiral Klaus Dönitz at the Nuremberg Main Trial, put it: "The reaction of the general public in Germany to the allied war crimes trials [. . .] was that one had had enough of it."[38] Overall, the Germans wanted to concentrate on rebuilding the country and restoring its reputation rather than dwelling on the past.[39] This led to a kind of social suppression of the Nazi crimes, which was facilitated by the fact that the Western powers, especially the United States, needed Germany as an ally in the fight against communism and did not want the close political cooperation to be disturbed by the "war-criminals problem."[40]

Reception of the Nuremberg Trials in Western Germany

This general attitude is also reflected in the early case law in West Germany.[41] The courts followed a strictly subjective approach to the attribution of criminal liability, based (primarily or exclusively) on the actor's state of mind rather than on the weight of his or her actual contribution to the criminal result. A person was considered a perpetrator if he or she wanted the offense to be his or her own, that is, acted with *animus auctoris*. If, on the other hand, a person merely wished to assist another in committing a crime (and thus acted with *animus socii*), he or she was punished only as an accomplice.[42] Such a subjective approach gives the courts considerable leeway in attributing criminal liability—especially when it comes to "political crimes."[43] With regard to Nazi crimes, German courts have essentially held that only Hitler and his inner circle can be considered perpetrators. All other persons involved in the Nazi machinery (whether they were members of the administration or concentration camp guards who physically carried out the killings) could typically only be punished for aiding and abetting since their intention was solely to assist the Nazi leaders in carrying out their crimes. This resulted in lighter sentences (if at all).[44] The German judiciary was particularly reluctant to deal with its own profession. It failed to bring to justice the so-called "blood judges" who had handed down tens of thousands of death sentences. In many cases, "Hitler's jurists" were not only spared from prosecution but allowed to continue their careers through the Adenauer era.[45]

The prosecution of Nazi crimes was further restricted by a penal law reform in 1968 which reduced the penalty for aiding and abetting murder in cases where the participant lacked certain unique personal characteristics (e.g., he or she did not act out of base motives). This had the "side-effect" of reducing the statute of limitations to 15 years. As a result of this "cold amnesty," the majority of Nazi crimes were statute-barred by the end of the 1960s.[46]

Despite these obstacles, one of modern German history's most important trials, the Frankfurt Auschwitz Trial, started in 1963. Under the leadership of the General Attorney of the State Hess, Fritz Bauer, a Jewish jurist who had been persecuted by the Nazi regime and forced to flee to Scandinavia, twenty-two defendants were tried for crimes committed at the Auschwitz death camp. After 183 days of trial, seventeen of the remaining twenty defendants were found guilty and sentenced to between three years and three months and life imprisonment. Three defendants were acquitted.[47] More important for the German discourse than the outcome of the trial, however, was the strong involvement of victim-witnesses in the proceedings. This was in sharp contrast to the Nuremberg Trial, which was primarily based on documentary evidence: More than 90 percent of the evidence presented at Nuremberg consisted of the Nazis' own written record.[48] In Frankfurt, some 360 witnesses—including many survivors of Auschwitz—testified to the horrors of a concentration camp. This was the first time that the German public had been directly confronted with live testimony of victims and the enormous suffering they had endured. This left a deep impression on the society.[49]

From a legal perspective, however, the Auschwitz trial is another example of the restrictive approach of the German judiciary. The indictment was based on a broad concept of attribution. Fritz Bauer argued that every member of the concentration camp contributed to the overall functioning of the killing machine and was therefore responsible for all the victims during his stay—at least in terms of psychological complicity.[50] The Federal Court of Justice disagreed, holding that a conviction of aiding and abetting murder required more than mere membership of the concentration camp staff and knowledge of the killings. Rather, criminal liability was limited to cases in which the defendant had actually facilitated concrete killings—for example, by supervising the release of poison gas.[51] In the years following the Auschwitz trial, many investigations against former concentration camp staff were discontinued because it could not be proven that they participated in specific individual killings.[52]

In Remembrance of Nuremberg—Part I: Germany's Role in the Modern International Criminal Justice System

Despite these shortcomings, the Auschwitz Trials were an essential stimulus for Germany's coming to terms with its past and for the emergence of the German culture of remembrance, in which the Nuremberg trials played a crucial role. Today, they are of fundamental importance for German identity. Germany assumes a special, historical responsibility for preventing international crimes and the judicial enforcement of international criminal law. It aims to keep the legacy of Nuremberg alive by promoting international and national prosecutions of serious human rights violations and international humanitarian law.

Accordingly, when the international enforcement of international law experienced a renaissance in the early 1990s, Germany actively supported the creation of international tribunals from the outset. It has worked together closely with the UN Tribunals for the former Yugoslavia (ICTY) and Ruanda (ICTR), providing them with ongoing logistical, personnel, and financial support.[53] In particular, the first suspect to be indicted and tried by the ICTY, *Dusko Tadić*, was arrested in Germany and later extradited to The Hague. This posed considerable difficulties as Article 101 of the German Constitution (German Basic Law—*Grundgesetz*)[54] prohibits the creation of, and (arguably) the cooperation with, extraordinary ad hoc courts.[55] Nevertheless, with impressive speed, the German legislator created a special legal basis for cooperation with the ICTY,[56] clearly demonstrating its commitment to the international criminal justice system.[57]

Moreover, throughout the negotiations on establishing a permanent International Criminal Court, Germany, a member of the so-called group of like-minded states, favored an independent institution with broad powers. Not only did it advocate a strong international prosecutor with the power to initiate proceedings *proprio motu,* but it also suggested that the ICC should have universal jurisdiction—a provocative proposal that was politically unfeasible.[58] However, Germany has introduced the principle of universality at the national level. The *Völkerstrafgesetzbuch* (German Code of Crimes Against International Law—CCAIL),[59] which entered into force on June 30, 2002 (and thus one day before the ICC Statute), allows for the worldwide prosecution of the international core crimes and empowers the German judicial authorities to prosecute genocide, crimes against humanity, and war crimes even when they are committed abroad and have no specific link to Germany.[60] After some initial hesitation, Germany is now playing an active role in the international fight against impunity for core crimes.[61] Prominent examples that have attracted international attention[62] are the Koblenz torture trial against former members of the Assad Regime,[63] the conviction of Taha Al-J for genocide against members of the Yazidi community by the Higher Regional Court of Frankfurt,[64] and the decision of the Federal Court of Justice on the irrelevance of functional immunities.[65] The latter is also an excellent example of the German judiciary's attempt to establish a certain continuity or connection between modern (German) international criminal law and the Nuremberg Trials. The Federal Court of Justice was faced with the question of whether foreign state officials, such as members of the state armed forces, enjoy functional immunity under customary international law in foreign core crimes proceedings. The Court answered it in the negative and referred in its reasoning, among other things, to Article 7 of the Statute of the IMT, which states "[t]he official position of the defendants, whether as Heads of State or responsible officials in Government Departments, shall not be considered as freeing them from responsibility." According to the Court, this provision has evolved into a general rule of international law in which domestic core crimes proceedings are not precluded based on the notion of functional immunity.[66]

In Remembrance of Nuremberg—Part II: Late Prosecution of NS-Crimes

The emergence of what we might call modern "German international criminal law" also marked the beginning of a new phase in the prosecution of Nazi crimes.[67] The generational change among prosecutors and judges brought about a change in attitudes toward dealing with Germany's past through criminal law. The German judiciary now shows a strong interest in bringing the remaining surviving Nazi criminals to justice rather than letting them live (and die) in peace.[68] The starting point for this new area was the prosecution of John Demjanjuk, a former guard of the Sobador concentration and extermination camp, who was found guilty of aiding and abetting murder in 28,060 cases at first instance in 2011 and sentenced to five years in prison by the Regional Court of Munich.[69] Although Demjanjuk died during the appeals process and the judgment has not become final, this trial led to an expanded interpretation of accessory liability in macro-criminal contexts. According to current case law, a conviction for aiding and abetting murder in concentration camp cases does not require proof that the defendant contributed to a specific crime in the sense that he or she has actually facilitated the commission of individual killings. Instead (in line with the original approach of Fritz Bauer), it is deemed sufficient that the defendant contributed generally to the operation of the concentration camp and was part of the overall Nazi killing machine.[70] This is in contrast to the restrictive view of accountability in the Auschwitz Trial. Based on this broad concept, German courts in recent years have convicted, among others, the ninety-three-year-old bookkeeper of Auschwitz, Oskar Gröning,[71] and the ninety-seven-year-old secretary of the Stutthof death camp, Irmgard Furchner,[72] for their role in thousands of murders. This so-called "late prosecution" (*Spätverfolgung*) of Nazi crimes is not beyond criticism. In particular, it is debatable whether these trials, which are taking place after decades of inactivity on the part of the German criminal justice system, are fair and whether the courts have, at least in some cases, overstepped the legitimate boundaries of accessory liability.[73] Nevertheless, they are vivid examples of how Germany is trying to live up to the legacy of Nuremberg.

Notes

1 Susanne Karstedt, "The Nuremberg Tribunal and German Society: International Justice and Local Judgment in Post-Conflict Reconstruction," in *The Legacy of Nuremberg: Civilising Influence or Institutionalised Vengeance?*, ed. David A. Blumenthal and Timothy L. H. McCormack (Leiden: Brill Nijhoff, 2008), 18.

2 Ibid., 17.

3 Christoph Burchard, "The Nuremberg Trial and its Impact on Germany," *Journal of International Criminal Justice* 4, no. 4 (2006): 812; crit. Otto Kranzbuhler, "Nuremberg Eighteen Years Afterwards," *DePaul Law Review* 14, no. 2 (1965): 346. Kranzbuhler was counsel for the defense of Grand-Admiral Klaus Dönitz in the Nuremberg Main Trial.

4 With a particular view to the Nuremberg Subsequent Proceedings, Kevin Jon Heller, *The Nuremberg Military Tribunals and the Origins of International Criminal Law* (Oxford: Oxford University Press, 2011), 572.

5 See Susanne Karstedt, "Coming to Terms with the Past in Germany after 1945 and 1989: Public Judgments on Procedures and Justice," *Law & Policy* 20, no. 1 (1998): 23, and Christoph Safferling, "German Participation in the Nuremberg Trials and Its Implications for Today," in *The Nuremberg War Crimes Trial and its Policy Consequences Today*, ed. Beth A. Griech-Polelle (Baden-Baden: Nomos, 2020), 42,

who, however, also emphasizes that the ability of the media to inform the public was limited due to the destruction of the country.

6 For a detailed evaluation of the OMGUS-Reports, see Karstedt, "Coming to Terms with the Past in Germany after 1945 and 1989: Public Judgments on Procedures and Justice," 24; see also Safferling, "German Participation in the Nuremberg Trials and Its Implications for Today," 42 who, however, points out that the German population was primarily concerned with surviving in post-war environment.

7 Karstedt, "The Nuremberg Tribunal and German Society: International Justice and Local Judgment in Post-Conflict Reconstruction," at 19; Burchard, "The Nuremberg Trial and its Impact on Germany," 812.

8 Safferling, "German Participation in the Nuremberg Trials and Its Implications for Today," 42.

9 Karstedt, "Coming to Terms with the Past in Germany after 1945 and 1989: Public Judgments on Procedures and Justice," 24 et seq.; see also Karstedt, "The Nuremberg Tribunal and German Society: International Justice and Local Judgment in Post-Conflict Reconstruction," 24.

10 Heller, *The Nuremberg Military Tribunals and the Origins of International Criminal Law*," 372.

11 Safferling, "German Participation in the Nuremberg Trials and Its Implications for Today," 42; see also Burchard, "The Nuremberg Trial and its Impact on Germany," 810 et seq.

12 Safferling, "German Participation in the Nuremberg Trials and Its Implications for Today," 44; Burchard, "The Nuremberg Trial and its Impact on Germany," 808 et seq.; also Kranzbuhler, "Nuremberg Eighteen Years Afterwards," 335.

13 "Motion adopted by all Defense Counsel of 19 November 1945" in *Trial of The Major War Criminals before The International Military Tribunal, Nuremberg, –, Volume I. Official Text in the English Language. Official Documents* (1947), 168; see also Otto Pannenbecker, "The Nuremberg War-Crimes Trial," *DePaul Law Review* 14, no. 2 (1965): 350; Herbert Kraus, "The Nuremberg Trial of the Major War Criminals: Reflections after Seventeen Years", *DePaul Law Review* 13, no. 2 (1964): 244 et seq. Pannenbecker was Chief Counsel for Wilhelm Frick, Minister of the Interior of Germany, Kraus Counsel for the defense of Hjlmar Schacht, the former president of the Reichsbank—one of the three defendants who were acquitted by the IMT.

14 IMT, "The United States of America, The French Republic, The United Kingdom of Great Britain and Northern Ireland, and the Union of Soviet Socialist Republics against Hermann Wilhelm Göring and others, Judgment of 1. October 1946," in *Trial of The Major War Criminals before The International Military Tribunal, Nuremberg, 14 November 1945–1 October 1946, Volume I. Official Text in the English Language. Official Documents* (1947), 171, 218, 219 et seq.

15 Cf. Hans Laternser, "Looking Back at the Nuremberg Trials with Special Consideration of the Processes against Military Leaders," *Whittier Law Review* 8, no. 2 (1986): 573 et seq. Laternser was Chief Counsel for the German High Command and the German General Staff. See also Carl Haensel, "The Nuremburg Trial Revisted," *DePaul Law Review* 13, no. 2 (1964): 252 et seq.; Kranzbuhler, "Nuremberg Eighteen Years Afterwards," 340, 343; in more detail on the discussion Burchard, "The Nuremberg Trial and its Impact on Germany," 808.

16 Crit. therefore Kraus, "The Nuremberg Trial of the Major War Criminals: Reflections after Seventeen Years," 245. On the IMT's merging of moral, legal and political aspects see also Burchard, "The Nuremberg Trial and its Impact on Germany," 800.
17 IMT, "Judgment of 1. October 1946," 219.
18 In more detail Karstedt, "Coming to Terms with the Past in Germany after 1945 and 1989: Public Judgments on Procedures and Justice," 18.
19 For example, Haensel, "The Nuremburg Trial Revisted" 258.
20 Burchard, "The Nuremberg Trial and its Impact on Germany," 803; see also Safferling, "German Participation in the Nuremberg Trials and Its Implications for Today," 43.
21 Burchard, "The Nuremberg Trial and its Impact on Germany," 803.
22 "Motion adopted by all Defense Counsel of 19 November 1945," 169 et seq. Cf. also Laternser, "Looking Back at the Nuremberg Trials with Special Consideration of the Processes against Military Leaders," 563 et seq; Kraus, "The Nuremberg Trial of the Major War Criminals: Reflections after Seventeen Years," 245 et seq.; Haensel, "The Nuremburg Trial Revisted" 258.
23 See also Burchard, "The Nuremberg Trial and its Impact on Germany," 803.
24 Cf. Kraus, "The Nuremberg Trial of the Major War Criminals: Reflections after Seventeen Years," 246.
25 Note, that Defense Counsel Kraus stressed nevertheless that the judges were "guided by the idea of administrating law impartially" and have interpreted the IMT-Statute very narrowly in favor of the defendant in several cases, Kraus, "The Nuremberg Trial of the Major War Criminals: Reflections after Seventeen Years," 246. However, this could not change the fact that there was a fear of bias and that the composition of the IMT gave indeed grounds to doubt the impartiality of the judges.
26 For this line of criticism, see, for example, Burchard, "The Nuremberg Trial and its Impact on Germany," 802 et seq.
27 Burchard, "The Nuremberg Trial and its Impact on Germany," 804.
28 Kai Ambos, *Treatise on International Criminal Law—Volume I: Foundations and General Part* (Oxford: Oxford University Press, 2021), 513; see also ICTY, "Trial Chamber II, Prosecutor vs. Kupreskic et al., Judgement of January 14, 2002, IT-95-16," para. 515.
29 US Military Tribunal Nuremberg, "The United States of America vs. Ernst von Weizsäcker et al. (The Ministries Trial), Judgement of 11 April 1949," in *Trials of War Criminals Before the Nuremberg Military Tribunals Under Control Council Law No. 10, Vol. XIV* (1949), at 321.
30 ICTY, "Kupreskic et al., IT-95-16," paras. 517, 518.
31 Also Burchard, "The Nuremberg Trial and its Impact on Germany," 805.
32 Crit. Pannenbecker, "The Nuremberg War-Crimes Trial," 348 et seq.; cf. also Safferling, "German Participation in the Nuremberg Trials and Its Implications for Today," 45; Burchard, "The Nuremberg Trial and its Impact on Germany," 804 et seq.
33 See Karstedt, "Coming to Terms with the Past in Germany after 1945 and 1989: Public Judgments on Procedures and Justice," 26; Karstedt, "The Nuremberg Tribunal and German Society: International Justice and Local Judgment in Post-Conflict Reconstruction," 23, who shows that the general public wanted to exempt members of mass organizations like the SA or the Army from criminal liability, because most German adults were in one way or the other involved in these

organizations; on the widespread notion that members of the military cannot be held liable for following orders as this was demanded by "loyalty and honour" Safferling, "German Participation in the Nuremberg Trials and Its Implications for Today," 44; Karstedt, "The Nuremberg Tribunal and German Society: International Justice and Local Judgment in Post-Conflict Reconstruction," 28.

34 Heller, *The Nuremberg Military Tribunals and the Origins of International Criminal Law*, 370.

35 In more detail on this case Kerstin von Lingen, "Immunitätsversprechen. Wie SS-Obergruppenführer Karl Wolff der Strafverfolgung entging," *Militärgeschichtliche Zeitschrift* 68, no. 2 (2009): 379–421.

36 Safferling, "German Participation in the Nuremberg Trials and Its Implications for Today," 42 et seq.; Burchard, "The Nuremberg Trial and its Impact on Germany," 813; in more detail Karstedt, "The Nuremberg Tribunal and German Society: International Justice and Local Judgment in Post-Conflict Reconstruction," 28.

37 Karstedt, "The Nuremberg Tribunal and German Society: International Justice and Local Judgment in Post-Conflict Reconstruction," 38. The idea, that Hitler as the "Führer" bears all responsibility was already prominent among the high-ranking defendants in Nuremberg, see Pannenbecker, "The Nuremberg War-Crimes Trial," 357.

38 Kranzbuhler, "Nuremberg Eighteen Years Afterwards," 346.

39 Karstedt, "The Nuremberg Tribunal and German Society: International Justice and Local Judgment in Post-Conflict Reconstruction," 26.

40 Heller, *The Nuremberg Military Tribunals and the Origins of International Criminal Law*, 373; also Burchard, "The Nuremberg Trial and its Impact on Germany," 811.

41 On the development in East Germany see Burchard, "The Nuremberg Trial and its Impact on Germany," 816 et seq.; Safferling, "German Participation in the Nuremberg Trials and Its Implications for Today," 49 et seq.

42 The seminal judgement is Supreme Court of the German Reich, "Judgement of February 19, 1940, 3 D 69/40," *RGSt* [Entscheidungen des Reichsgerichts—Official Journal of Reportable Decisions of the Supreme Court of the German Reich] 74 (1941): 84–86; see also Federal Court of Justice, "Judgement of October 19, 1962, 9 StE 4/62," *BGHSt* [Entscheidungen des Bundesgerichtshofs—Official Journal of Reportable Decisions of the Federal Court of Justice] 18 (1963): 87–96.

43 Thomas Weigend, "Problems of Attribution in International Criminal Law: A German Perspective," *Journal of International Criminal Justice* 12, no. 2 (2014): 257.

44 See, for example, Federal Court of Justice, "Judgement of February 13, 1951, 4 StR 32/50," *Neue Juristische Wochenschrift* 4, no. 8 (1951): 323; in more detail Julia von Eitzen, *Rassistische und fremdenfeindliche Gewalttaten in Deutschland vor dem Hintergrund internationaler Vorgaben und Entwicklungen. Die Aufdeckung des NSU als Wendepunkt—Eine Analyse der juristischen Verarbeitung menschenverachtender Motive im Wandel der Zeit* (Berlin: BWV Berliner Wissenschafts-Verlag, 2021), 21 et seq.; see also Safferling, "German Participation in the Nuremberg Trials and Its Implications for Today," 46.

45 See also Burchard, "The Nuremberg Trial and its Impact on Germany," 814; Safferling, "German Participation in the Nuremberg Trials and Its Implications for Today," 47.

46 In more detail Manfred Görtemaker and Christoph Safferling, *Die Akte Rosenburg. Das Bundesministerium der Justiz und die NS-Zeit* (München: C.H. Beck, 2016), 399 et seq.

47 In more detail Devin O. Pendas, *The Frankfurt Auschwitz Trial, 1963–1965. Genocide, History, and the Limits of the Law* (Cambridge: Cambridge University Press, 2006).

48 Kai Ambos and Stefanie Bock, "Procedural Regimes," in, *International Prosecutors*, eds. L. Reydams, J. Wouters, and C. Ryngaert (Oxford: Oxford University Press, 2012), 493.

49 In detail Karstedt, "The Nuremberg Tribunal and German Society: International Justice and Local Judgment in Post-Conflict Reconstruction," 30 et seq.; cf. also Safferling, "German Participation in the Nuremberg Trials and Its Implications for Today," 47 et seq.

50 Fritz Bauer, "Ideal- oder Realkonkurrenz bei nationalsozialistischen Verbrechen," *Juristenzeitung* 22, no. 20 (1967): 628.

51 Federal Court of Justice, "Judgment of February 20, 1969, 4 Ss 238/68," *Neue Juristische Wochenschrift* 22, no. 46 (1969): 2056.

52 Stefanie Bock, "Zurechnung im Völkerstrafrecht", *Zeitschrift für Internationale Strafrechtsdogmatik* 12, no. 7–8 (2017): 421 with further references.

53 Peter Wilkitzki, "The Contribution of the Federal Republic of Germany and the German Laender to the Work of the ICTY," in *Man's Inhumanity to Man—Essays on International Law in Honour of Judge A. Cassese,* eds. L. C. Vohrah and others (The Hague: Kluwer Law International 2003), 923–33.

54 "Official English Translation of the Basic Law," accessed June 1, 2024, https://www.gesetze-im-internet.de/englisch_gg/.

55 In more detail Denis Basak, *Die Zuständigkeitsregeln internationaler Strafgerichte und Art. 101 GG. Zum Verhältnis der deutschen Strafgerichtsbarkeit zu den Internationalen Tribunalen für Jugoslawien und Ruanda sowie zum Ständigen Internationalen Strafgerichtshof* (Frankfurt am Main: Peter Lang, 2005), 85 et seq.; Stefanie Scholz, *Die Zulieferung an den Jugoslawien-Strafgerichtshof. Zugleich ein Beitrag zur internationalen Rechtshilfe in Strafsachen am Beispiel eines Ad-hoc-Völkerstrafgerichtshofes* (Aachen: Shaker, 1998), 89 et seq.

56 "Gesetz über die Zusammenarbeit mit dem Internationalen Strafgerichtshof für das ehemalige Jugoslawien vom 10. April 1995," *Bundesgesetzblatt* I 486 (Act on Cooperation with the International Criminal Tribunal for the former Yugoslavia of April 10, 1995, *Federal Law Gazette* I 486).

57 Safferling, "German Participation in the Nuremberg Trials and Its Implications for Today," 51–2; Tobias Römer, "Scope of National Duties to Cooperate with International Tribunals and the International Criminal Court," in *On the Correlation between National and International Law,* eds. Hans-Detlef Horn and Stefanie Bock (Marburg: Philipps-Universität Marburg—Publikationsserver, 2020), 100–3.

58 Hans-Peter Kaul, "Der Beitrag Deutschlands zum Völkerstrafrecht," in *Völkerstrafrechtspolitik. Praxis des Völkerstrafrechts,* eds. Christoph Safferling and Stefan Kirsch (Berlin: Springer, 2014), 51–84

59 "English translation of the CCIAL," accessed June 1, 2024, https://www.gesetze-im-internet.de/englisch_vstgb/.

60 For an overview of the CCIAL, see Helmut Satzger, "German Criminal Law and the Rome Statute—A Critical Analysis of the New German Code of Crimes against International Law," *International Criminal Law Review* 2, no. 3 (2002): 261–82; Gerhard Werle and Florian Jeßberger, "International Criminal Justice is Coming Home: The New German Code of Crimes Against International Law," *Criminal Law Forum* 13, no. 2 (2002): 191–223.

61 For a more comprehensive analysis, see Stefanie Bock, "The German Code of Crimes Against International Law at Twenty: Overview and Assessment of Modern 'German International Criminal Law,'" *Journal of International Criminal Justice* 21, no. 4 (2023): 793–813; also Christoph Safferling and Gurgen Petrossian, "Universal Jurisdiction and International Crimes in German Courts—Recent Steps Towards Exercising the Principle of Complementarity after the Entry into Force of the Rome Statute," *European Criminal Law Review* 11, no. 2 (2021): 242–63 and the contribution of Angelika Schlunck in this volume.

62 See, for example, "Statement of Germany in the UNGA Sixth Committee 'The Scope and Application of the Principle of Universal Jurisdiction,'" October 12, 2022, https://new-york-un.diplo.de/un-en/news-corner/-/2558190; "UN Panel Welcomes Landmark Guilty Verdict in Germany's Prosecution of Former Syrian Intelligence Officer for Crimes against Humanity," January 13, 2022, www.ohchr.org/en/2022/01/un-panel-welcomes-landmark-guilty-verdict-germanys-prosecution-former-syrian-intelligence; "IIIM-Syria Welcomes German Court's Crimes Against Humanity Verdict," January 14, 2022, https://iiim.un.org/iiim-syria-welcomes-german-courts-crimes-against-humanity-verdict/, all accessed June 1, 2024.

63 In February 2021, the first defendant, Eyad A., was found guilty of aiding and abetting crimes against humanity and sentenced to four and a half years in prison, Higher Regional Court of Koblenz, Judgement of February 24, 2021, 1 StE 3/21 confirmed in Federal Court of Justice, Decision of April 20, 2022, 3 StR 367/21. About one year later, the main defendant, Anwar R., received a life-long sentence for—among other things—murder, torture, severe deprivation of liberty, and sexual violence as crimes against humanity, Higher Regional Court of Koblenz, Judgement of January 13, 2022, 1 StE 9/19. For more information, see the documentation of the Koblenz trial by the Syrian Justice and Accountability Centre and the Marburg International Research and Documentation Centre for War Crimes Trials available at https://syriaaccountability.org/the-trial-of-anwar-raslan-and-eyad-al-gharib (accessed June 1, 2024) and the branch 251 project (https://branch-251.captivate.fm, accessed June 1, 2024).

64 Higher Regional Court of Frankfurt, "Judgement of November 30, 2021, 5–3 StE 1/20 - 4 - 1/20," confirmed in Federal Court of Justice, "Decision of November 30, 2022, 3 StR 230/22," *Neue Juristische Wochenschrift* 76, no. 16 (2023): 1138 et seq. with commentary Stefanie Bock.

65 Federal Court of Justice, "Judgement of January 28, 2021, 3 StR 564/19," *BGHSt* 65 (2022): 286–313, English summary in *International Legal Materials* 61, no. 3 (2022): 483–9; for the position of the Federal Public Prosecutor General see Peter Frank and Christoph Barthe, "Immunity of Foreign State Officials Before National Courts. A Stress Test for Modern International Criminal Law?," *Journal of International Criminal Justice* 19, no. 3 (2021): 700–36; detailed analysis by Aziz Epik, "No Functional Immunity for Crimes under International Law before Foreign Domestic

Courts: An Unequivocal Message from the German Federal Court of Justice," *Journal of International Criminal Justice* 19, no. 5 (2021): 1263–81.

66 Federal Court of Justice, "Judgement of January 28, 2021, 3 StR 564/19," *BGHSt* 65 (2022): 286 paras. 24 et seq. It should be noted, however, that the Court limited its findings to subordinates and did not expressly exclude the possibility that functional immunity might be applicable in proceedings against high-level perpetrators, Claus Kreß, "Functional Immunity of Foreign State Officials Before National Courts. A Legal Opinion by Germany's Federal Public Prosecutor General," *Journal of International Criminal Justice* 19, no. 3 (2021): 698; Epik, "No Functional Immunity for Crimes under International Law before Foreign Domestic Courts: An Unequivocal Message from the German Federal Court of Justice," 1276.

67 In more detail, Boris Burghardt, "Im Ringen mit sich selbst. Die Spätverfolgung von NS-Verbrechen durch die deutsche Strafjustiz," in *Spätverfolgung von NS-Unrecht*, ed. Moritz Vormbaum (Berlin: Springer, 2023), 221–32.

68 See also Sabine Swoboda, "Paying the Debts—Late Nazi Trials before German Courts: The Case of Heinrich Boere," *Journal of International Criminal Justice* 9, no. 1 (2011): 243–69.

69 Regional Court of Munich, "Judgment of May 12, 2011, 1 Ks 115 Js 12496/08," *Justiz und NS-Verbrechen, Sammlung deutscher Strafurteile wegen nationalsozialistischer Tötungsverbrechen* 49 (2012): 227. In more detail on the proceedings Kirsten Goetze, "Das Demjanjuk-Urteil: Eine späte Korrektur," in *Spätverfolgung von NS-Unrecht*, ed. Moritz Vormbaum (Berlin: Springer, 2023), 83–97.

70 The seminal case is Federal Court of Justice, "Decision of September 20 2016, 3 StR 49/16," *Neue Zeitschrift für Strafrecht* 37, no. 3 (2017): 158–63.

71 Regional Court of Lüneburg, "Judgment of July 15, 2015, 27 Ks 9/14, 27 Ks 1191 Js 98402/13 (9/14)"; in more detail on this case Boris Burghardt, "Die Strafsache 'Oskar Gröning' vor dem Bundesgerichtshof. Zugleich Überlegungen zum Begriff der teilnahmefähigen Haupttat i.S.v. § 27 Abs. 1 StGB bei arbeitsteilig organisierten, systemischen Handlungszusammenhängen," *Zeitschrift für Internationale Strafrechtsdogmatik* 14, no. 1 (2019): 21–40.

72 Regional Court of Itzehoe, "Judgment of December 20, 2022, 3 KLs 315 Js 15865/16"; in more detail on this case, Lawrence Douglas, "Der Wachmann und die Sekretärin," in *Spätverfolgung von NS-Unrecht*, ed. Moritz Vormbaum (Berlin: Springer, 2023), 109–18.

73 See, for example, Bettina Weißer, "Grund und Grenzen strafbarer Beihilfe in NS-Vernichtungslagern," in *Spätverfolgung von NS-Unrecht*, ed. Moritz Vormbaum (Berlin: Springer, 2023), 205–20.

Selected Bibliography

Bock, Stefanie, "The German Code of Crimes Against International Law at Twenty: Overview and Assessment of Modern 'German International Criminal Law'," *Journal of International Criminal Justice* 21, no. 4 (2023): 793–813.

Boris, Burghardt, "Im Ringen mit sich selbst. Die Spätverfolgung von NS-Verbrechen durch die deutsche Strafjustiz," in *Spätverfolgung von NS-Unrecht*, ed. Moritz Vormbaum (Berlin: Springer, 2023), 221–32.

Burchard, Christoph, "The Nuremberg Trial and its Impact on Germany," *Journal of International Criminal Justice* 4, no. 4 (2006): 800–29.
Heller, Kevin Jon, *The Nuremberg Military Tribunals and the Origins of International Criminal Law* (Oxford: Oxford University Press, 2011).
Karstedt, Susanne, "The Nuremberg Tribunal and German Society: International Justice and Local Judgment in Post-Conflict Reconstruction," in *The Legacy of Nuremberg: Civilising Influence or Institutionalised Vengeance?*, ed. David A. Blumenthal and Timothy L. H. McCormack (Leiden: Brill Nijhoff, 2008), 13–35.
Safferling, Christoph, "German Participation in the Nuremberg Trials and Its Implications for Today," in *The Nuremberg War Crimes Trial and its Policy Consequences Today*, ed. Beth A. Griech-Polelle (Baden-Baden: Nomos, 2020), 41–54.
Swoboda, Sabine, "Paying the Debts – Late Nazi Trials before German Courts: The Case of Heinrich Boere," *Journal of International Criminal Justice* 9, no. 1 (2011): 243–69.

5

The American Perspective on Nuremberg

Michael Bazyler and Aubrey A. Butler

Nuremberg was both a centerpiece of Nazism during the Third Reich and the birthplace of today's international criminal justice system. An ancient city in Bavaria, it was the home of Jews for hundreds of years. Over that time, Jewish presence in Bavaria was at best tolerated.[1] The Jews opened a synagogue in 1296. Two years later, 728 Jews were victims of a pogrom.[2] And so it went until 1933 when the Nazis consecrated Nuremberg as the most German of all cities. The infamous Nazi Party rallies were staged there. In 1935, it was the site of the announcement of the notorious Nuremberg laws stripping all German Jews of their civil rights. In the Nuremberg courthouse, ironically named the Palace of Justice, German judges readily sentenced Jews to death for violating anti-race laws. On September 10, 1942, the last remnant of 533 Nuremberg Jews was forcibly transported to the *Theresienstadt* concentration camp in German-occupied Czechoslovakia (27 survived), and Nuremberg became *Judenrein* (free of Jews).[3]

In 1945, American jurists came to that same courthouse at Nuremberg to hold the most important international criminal trial in history. *Nuremberg—The City of Evil* was transformed into *Nuremberg—The Birthplace of Modern International Law*. David Pendas explains: "[T]he tendency in the literature, especially in English, has been to tell the story [of the Nuremberg trials] as an essentially *American* one."[4] This is undoubtedly true since the Americans were the first among equals on the quadripartite team of prosecutors and judges. Several studies have explored the American role at Nuremberg.[5] These usually focus on the prominent role of chief prosecutor Justice Robert Jackson, the American focus on procedural fairness, the importance of convicting the leading Nazis for the crime of aggression, and the pedagogical aim of demonstrating, especially to the German people, the superiority of democratic over totalitarian regimes.

This chapter focuses on three less well-known legal personalities, all foreign-born American Jews who advised Jackson, seeking to convince and educate Jackson and the American team on how the International Military Tribunal should be constructed and what, in their view, should be the central focus of this first international criminal court in history. Two are little-known today, and one, though familiar to international legal scholars as the jurist who coined the word genocide, is less known for the role he played at Nuremberg.

This chapter is dedicated to Benjamin Ferencz, another *shetl*-born[6] Jew, who became the last living Nuremberg prosecutor. Ben died at age 103 on April 7, 2023, in Florida.[7] Eleven days earlier, he was given a standing ovation in absentia at the Nuremberg Principles Conference: The Contemporary Challenges at the Catholic University of America (CUA) in Washington, D.C., from which this volume is drawn.

Murray Bernays

Murray Cohen (1894–1970) was born in the Russian Empire but brought to the United States while he was a child. He completed Harvard College, received a law degree from Columbia University, and served with the US Army in France during the Great War. He legally changed his last name to Bernays upon marrying Hella Bernays.[8]

During the interwar years, Bernays had a thriving legal career with a New York City law firm where he was a name partner. Once war broke out, Bernays rejoined the Army and, by 1945, had advanced to Colonel in the US Army General Staff Corps.[9] It was in this capacity that Colonel Bernays became one of the legal architects of the Nuremberg Charter, given "the principal responsibility [of] outlining the procedures for the trials."[10] A 2017 tribute explains: "It seems only fitting that Bernays, a naturalized American Jewish citizen, would be the one responsible for collecting evidence[,] . . . building the case against the Nazis," and devising a legal strategy for collective criminality, now referred to as the "Bernays Plan."[11]

In 1944, Roosevelt asked the War Department and other cabinet bodies to provide a legal map of how to deal with the Nazi leadership after the war. In mid-September, Bernays developed a rough outline based upon three assumptions: (1) "an international tribunal ought to deal with the top Axis leaders," (2) German organizations needed to be prosecuted in such a way as to create "a precedent on which their hundreds of thousands of members could be conveniently dealt with," and (3) "a comprehensive conspiracy charge" was the best method of reaching top Nazi officers for "a wide array of crimes," including those committed before the war began.[12] This paper, entitled "Trial of European War Criminals," became "the fountainhead of the 'conspiracy/criminal organization' postulate."[13]

In January 1945, as lawyers with the War Department's Special Projects Branch, Bernays, and his colleague D. W. Brown wrote a confidential report for Roosevelt detailing whether the Axis powers could be held legally responsible for ushering in the Second World War. Their answer? Yes. However, this did not align with current US policy or international law.[14] In the report, they admit, "It is . . . commonly agreed that the launching of the war itself by the Axis leaders does not constitute a 'war crime' in [its] strict legal sense . . . [and] international law held that the launching of an aggressive war was not a crime."[15]

Yet Bernays and Brown were not dissuaded. American lawyers schooled in the English legal tradition knew that law can be created by legislation, treaties, or judges over time ("common law"). The tribunal about to judge the Nazi leaders had an opportunity to develop such common law norms—what is known in international law as "customary international law." As Bernays said, "[T]here isn't any legislature that can enact international law, but somebody has got to make a start somewhere."[16] And so they concluded that "it will not be disputed that the launching of a war of aggression today is condemned by the vast majority of mankind as a crime."[17] In support, Bernays and Brown cited four international documents that expressly or impliedly denounced aggressive war as a crime: the Geneva Protocol, the Resolution by the Eighth Assembly of the League of Nations, the Resolution of the Sixth Pan American Conference, and the Kellogg-Briand Pact. Each helped to distinguish the "crime of war" (*jus bellum*: starting an illegal war) from a "war crime" (*jus bello*: conduct during the war). Building upon the work of leading British and Soviet authorities, notably Professors Hersch Lauterpacht at Cambridge and Aron Trainin in Moscow (both also native Yiddish-speaking Jewish legal scholars), Bernays and Brown concluded: "[T]he law of today condemns aggressive war as an international crime, triable and punishable as such . . . [and] the launching of the present war was a crime."[18] This memorandum to Roosevelt provided the legal basis for both "why" and "how" to prosecute the Nazi leaders in an international criminal tribunal to be known as the IMT.

The Bernays Plan recommended charging Nazi groups as criminal organizations acting as a criminal conspiracy.[19] The crime of conspiracy was a largely unknown and undeveloped concept in European law but familiar to common law lawyers. Once an organization like the Nazi party was tried by the IMT and found to be criminal in nature, "all of its members could then be tried on a charge of criminal membership."[20] This, in essence, is the common law crime of conspiracy and is separate from the underlying crime (i.e., one person can be found guilty of murder; two or more individuals planning and then committing murder can be found guilty of both murder and conspiracy to murder). Bernays' specific proposal for the IMT consisted of six main components:

a. The Nazi Government and its Party and State agencies, including the SA, SS, and Gestapo, should be charged before an appropriately constituted international court with conspiracy to commit murder, terrorism, and the destruction of peaceful populations in violation of the laws of war.
b. For the purpose of trial before the above court, the prosecuting Nations should bring to the bar only such individual defendants, considered to be representative of the defendant organizations, as they elect.
c. The proceedings should be public and widely publicized, and the evidence should be full enough to prove the guilty intent (Nazi doctrine and policy) as well as the criminal conduct (atrocious acts in violation of the laws of war).
d. The judgement should adjudicate:
    (1) That the Nazi Government and its mentioned agencies are guilty as charged.
    (2) That every member of the Government and organizations on trial is guilty of the same offense. Such adjudication of guilt would require no proof that the individuals affected participated in any overt act other than membership in the conspiracy.

e. Sentence would be passed by the court on the individual defendants before it.
f. Thereafter, every member of the mentioned Government and organization would be subject to arrest, trial and punishment in the national courts of the several United Nations. Proof of membership, without more, would establish guilt of participation in the mentioned conspiracy, and the individual would be punished at the discretion of the court. Proof of the commission of other criminal acts would subject the individual to additional punishments conformably to local law.[21]

At the time, conspiracy crimes and membership in criminal organizations were absent from existing principles of international law. Bernays' proposal was a radical departure from those principles, and its inclusion in the Nuremberg Charter transformed international criminal law. Today, such collective responsibility goes by the name "Joint Criminal Enterprise," but the root of this doctrine in international jurisprudence stems from Bernays' original conspiracy proposal and its first use at Nuremberg.[22]

Traditionally, imputing accomplice liability requires evidence that the alleged accomplice perpetrated the crime, either through an omission or a positive act. In Bernays' definition, no overt act was required to demonstrate guilt—simple knowledge of the conspiracy and an agreement to become a member was enough.[23]

Not everyone agreed with this, and there was pushback from US assistant attorney general Herbert Wechsler, who argued that "mutual participation" in the conspiracy was vital to finding "multiple liability." After much debate, Jackson leaned more toward Wechsler's definition of conspiracy. When explaining the American plan, he "emphasized [that] the accused's conduct and participation . . . [was] an essential prerequisite for finding him guilty of the concerted crime." Though Jackson did not embrace Bernays' full definition of conspiracy, he refused to remove the charge from the Charter entirely as some had proposed, agreeing it would be an important avenue for prosecuting the Nazi regime.[24] Therefore, "[i]f the prosecution . . . could prove that the Nazi program was indeed a conspiracy against humanity, carried out in violation of international law, then the entire Nazi organization would be found guilty."[25]

Bernays' plan remained a central element of his campaign for justice, and Jackson continued to support the overall idea of using the crime of conspiracy despite being met with resistance during the Charter negotiations. The IMT judges did not adopt wholesale the Bernays Plan, and, reaching a compromise, the Nuremberg Judgment narrowed Bernays' conspiracy plan in three main aspects: (1) "it effectively limited the conspiracy to aggressive war" rather than encompassing every possible crime, (2) the start date of the conspiracy was set as the "1937 Hossbach Conference when the intention to wage war had stopped being 'mere talk,'" and (3) the judges altered the definition of conspiracy only to encompass "a small circle of initiated members."[26]

In 1946, the IMT judges convicted "the SS [*Schutzstaffel*, the Nazi party's protection squad], the SD [*Sicherheitsdienst*, the Nazi's security service] and the Gestapo as criminal organizations." The acts of those organizations were imputed to members who were aware of the criminal activity taking place, which was a "relatively soft burden" for the prosecutors to meet.[27]

The success of Bernays' plan did not go without protest. Some questioned the use of traditional trial methods, while others worried that he had established a precedent where any soldier could be convicted for the crimes of their commanders. Bernays stood behind his decision to use "ordinary legal methods," and explained, "Fascist myths would be more likely to spring up if defendants weren't given their day in court, and in any case it goes against the grain to condemn even the lowest criminal without trial." When it came to using criminal conspiracy, Bernays was similarly steadfast:

> They are being prosecuted because they saw fit to play the dual role of soldier and politician, and in the latter role were as deeply implicated as Hitler and Goering themselves in planning and making wars which were aggressive in their intention, treacherous in their inception, and ruthless in their execution. Surely if political government directs a murderous policy of exterminating civilians and prisoners of war, soldiers who carry out that policy are properly liable to punishment.[28]

When the London Conference began, Bernays was briefly present but became ill before its completion and resigned from the military in mid-August 1945.[29] He returned home and continued the practice of law until his death in 1970.[30]

The Bernays Plan became legendary among international law wonks, though largely unknown to the public. In November 1945—the month when the IMT Trial began—*The New Yorker* brought his work into the spotlight with an interview aptly titled "The Man Behind the Gavel."[31] Bernays was awarded the Legion of Merit for his work—a military honor conferred on those "who have distinguished themselves by exceptionally meritorious conduct in the performance of outstanding services."[32]

Jacob Robinson

Jokūbas Robinzonas (1889–1977) is also a product of a Jewish *shetl*, born in the small Lithuanian village of Seirijai (Serej) to a family of seven brothers descended from a long line of rabbis. After completing a traditional Jewish education, Robinson received his law degree from the University of Warsaw. Lithuania was then part of the Czarist Empire, and Robinson was conscripted into the Russian army to fight in the Great War. He was captured and imprisoned in Imperial Germany for three years. Returning to Lithuania after the war, Robinson began a flourishing public law career focusing on ensuring Jewish rights. Robinson saw the new postwar international legal order, with the creation of the League of Nations and treaty guarantees of minority rights, as a bright new start for Jews in Europe. In 1923, Robinson was elected to the Lithuanian parliament as one of seven Jewish parliamentarians and was a legal advisor to the Lithuanian Foreign Ministry. Among other notable achievements, he represented Lithuania at the Permanent Court of International Justice—the League of Nations' judicial arm.[33]

The resurgence of dictatorship regimes in Germany, Italy, and Spain ended the heyday period of liberal democracy in Europe. The minorities of Europe, especially the Jews, again began to face dangerous times. Robinson was among the lucky ones to escape Europe. In 1940, he and his family—a wife and two daughters—fled Europe and settled in New York. Robinson and his brother Nehemiah (who also escaped and became a leading Jewish activist) were public policy lawyers working for Jewish rights. Both brothers took jobs with the World Jewish Congress (WJC), which was then an important voice in the Jewish world. Robinson was a polyglot, and with his legal experience and knowledge of English, he became the first director of the WJC's Institute for Jewish Affairs (IJA) after its formation in 1941 (Nehemiah later replaced him).[34] American Jews were aghast at what was being done to their European brethren. The Robinson brothers' focus was on how Nazi Germany used law specifically to target Jews, and their research led to the publication by the IJA of several works under one or the other's authorship.

The IJA's 1941 report titled *Jews in Nazi Europe* covered the treatment of Jews from the second day of Hitler's chancellorship through the Nazi invasion of the USSR.[35] Jonathan Bush calls Robinson's monograph "the first study to show the scale of the Holocaust [just] as it was about to enter its most murderous phase."[36] Two years later, the publication *Hitler's Ten-Year War on the Jews* utilized the IJA's extensive collection of official law gazettes and newspapers of Axis and Axis-occupied countries, first-hand reports of European diplomats, documents of "governments-in-exile," underground press reports, and eyewitness accounts of the ongoing horrors. In the book's preface, Robinson wrote:

> The full story of what has happened to European Jewry under Hitler and the rule of the Axis cannot be told at this time. Some of its most terrible pages are still being written, from day to day, wherever the power of the Axis has not been broken. An interim balance is possible, however, of the effects of Hitler's war against the Jewish people since January 30, 1933, and, more especially, since September 1, 1939, when his armies invaded Poland. To present that balance sheet is our aim.[37]

By 1944, a new legal and political issue was looming. Germany was on its way to losing the war, and the Allies had to decide how to treat the country and its Nazi leaders. Robinson desired to make the mass murder of the Jews the primary crime for which the Nazis would be charged. In March 1945, Robinson appeared as a witness alongside several other members of the WJC before the US Senate Committee on Foreign Affairs to discuss the "lack of progress in the war crimes question."[38] On June 12, 1945, a month after Justice Jackson's appointment as head of the US prosecution team, Robinson first met with Jackson.[39]

Robinson strongly urged Jackson to spotlight the extermination of the Jews at the upcoming trial. Michael Marrus explains: "Robinson insisted that it was the Jewish *people* that were at issue—not just Jews who happened to be the victims"—and maintained that because the Jewish people were the "greatest sufferer" of the war, it therefore had "a case of its own against the master Nazi criminals and their accomplices." He insisted that Jackson commit to an indictment for the specific crime the Nazis had perpetrated against the Jewish people, emphasizing that "the anti-Jewish objectives of the Hitlerian regime were at the very core of the conspiracy." Jackson was reticent. His vision for the trial aligned with the War Department's view of charging the Nazi leaders first and foremost for starting a world war. He was further concerned that allowing the Jews to have a separate voice would lead to other persecuted groups requesting a similar voice, thereby complicating the already intricate trial. Along with other prosecutors, Jackson was also reluctant to make the mass murder of Jews the central theme of Nuremberg justice.[40]

Jackson ultimately chose to relegate Robinson and the IJA to a merely supportive role in the months leading up to trial,[41] and no IJA representative sat at the counsel table. Robinson helped frame the American argument, worked alongside the Office of Strategic Services, "assembl[ed] reliable Holocaust estimates for presentation at trial," and even participated in the selection of Nazi defendants, writing letters to Jackson urging that Adolf Eichmann be tried *in abstentia* for his role in the Holocaust.[42] "Jackson was happy to use documentary and evidentiary material assembled by Jewish organizations and to draw on . . . Robinson," but he denied requests to "grant Jewish representatives *amicus curiae* status."[43]

Though Jackson was hesitant to accept the entirety of Robinson's proposed strategy and "was not inclined to accept the uniqueness of the Jewish case" within his trial plan, Robinson's ideas influenced the proceedings, and an American prosecution brief contained language written by Robinson himself, including the need to punish the Nazis for their "plan to 'obliterate the Jewish race.'" [44] Robinson's time at Nuremberg was limited; he only came twice to assist prosecutors with strategy, and possibly this near lack of direct involvement led to an overall absence of his and the IJA's most central ideas at the IMT trial.[45] Ultimately, Jackson's framing of the case did not present the mass murder of the Jews as a "crime *sui generis*" but rather one component of the overall Nazi plan for world domination through the launching of aggressive wars and animated by acts of conspiracy, both of which were criminal under international law.[46]

When the Nuremberg Charter was signed in 1945, it included no provision allowing for the separate prosecution of crimes against the Jewish people, and its definition of "crimes against humanity" was highly restrictive, "requiring them to have been committed in connection with or in [the] execution of war crimes or crimes against peace."[47] As Robinson described in 1972, "the Holocaust did not emerge 'as a unit in fact and in law.'"[48]

Yet Robinson did not view Nuremberg as a failure. He praised the American prosecution team, believing they were the only ones to present the Jewish position as a serious issue at trial. "Robinson appreciated . . . the authoritative acknowledgement, from the highest perch of prosecutorial authority, of the comprehensive, murderous, anti-Jewish objective at the core of Nazi criminality—a theme to which all four prosecuting powers were, in the end, formally committed."[49]

The absence of an official Jewish voice at Nuremberg did nothing to lessen Robinson's feeling "that his essential goals were achieved."[50] "[T]he Jewish case was overwhelming, and largely unchallenged. In Robinson's own calculation, more than 800 Nazi documents and the testimony of thirty-three witnesses were devoted, in whole or in part, to the question."[51] At the heart of Robinson's work was his fervent advocacy for addressing the Nazis' persecution and extermination of millions of Jews—a goal that was met in large part by Nuremberg and its legacy. Justice Jackson apparently felt the same. In a letter sent to the IJA in 1946, he thanked Robinson for his "untiring efforts," and stated that "Nazi persecution of the Jews was one of the major phases of the Prosecution's case, and the successful presentation of that aspect . . . was greatly aided by" the IJA.[52]

After the trial, Robinson continued his storied career as the "lawyer for the Jewish people" (along with his brother Nehemiah). Though he did not get a seat at the counsel table at the IMT, that opportunity came at the 1961 Eichmann trial in Israel, where Robinson sat alongside the Israeli prosecution team, strategizing how to best present their case against the man in the glass booth that Robinson originally wanted to prosecute *in abstentia* at Nuremberg.[53]

Raphael Lemkin

Rafał Lemkin (1900–59) was born to a Jewish family of tenant farmers in the small Polish village of Bezwodne, then located in the northwestern part of the Russian Empire. Growing up in a region that would come to be known as the "Bloodlands,"[54] Lemkin was exposed to antisemitism and other precursors to genocide long before he would give the latter its name. Lemkin credits this upbringing as the impetus for his later pursuit of justice at Nuremberg—a pursuit which began at the Jan Kazimierz University in Lwów where he received his law doctorate in 1926.[55]

"In 1933, [Lemkin] proposed some of the most sweeping changes to the structure of international humanitarian law" with a focus on crimes against culture and groups of people for which he initially used the terms "vandalism" and "barbarism."[56] At the International Conference for the Unification of Criminal Law in Madrid, he delivered a paper focusing on "acts of extermination directed against [an] ethnic, religious or special collectivit[y]." Lemkin proposed legislation making "it an 'offense of barbarity' to commit 'an action against the life, the bodily integrity, liberty, dignity or economic existence of a person belonging to such a collectivity.'"[57]

The Second World War upended his life. In 1939, Lemkin left his parents and siblings, fleeing German-occupied Poland and eventually coming to the United States.[58] He taught law at Duke University, then worked for the Board of Economic Warfare and the US War Department. Pursuing his research, he began to collect German occupation laws used by the Nazis to subjugate the local populace in countries they conquered. This research became the subject of his seminal 1944 book *Axis Rule in Occupied Europe,* later a "set text" for Nuremberg prosecutors.[59] Today, this book is universally known as the work where Lemkin first coined the term "genocide."[60]

> This new word . . . is made from the ancient Greek word *genos* (race, tribe) and the Latin *cide* (killing) . . . Generally speaking, genocide does not necessarily mean the immediate destruction of a nation, except when accomplished by mass killings of all members of a nation. It is intended rather to signify a coordinated plan of different actions aiming at the destruction of essential foundations of the life of national groups, with the aim of annihilating the groups themselves . . . Genocide is directed against the national group as an entity, and the actions involved are directed against individuals, not in their individual capacity, but as members of the national group.[61]

The adoption of this new term and its promulgation as a crime under international law became Lemkin's lifelong mission. His insistence on legal terminology defining "genocide" was meant to encapsulate and inscribe into law not only the physical extermination of a victim group but also other measures aimed at eradicating culture, language, and identity. As explained by Lemkin, "genocide" was meant to express "an old practice in its modern development."[62] "As Lemkin wrote these words, the paradigmatic genocide, [what we later came to call] the Holocaust [or 'Shoah' in Hebrew], was raging in Europe."[63] In his definition, genocide had two phases: "the 'destruction of the national pattern of the oppressed group,' and the 'imposition of the national pattern of the oppressor.'" *Axis Rule* proposed that a new international norm be added to the Hague Regulations of 1907—which guide the conduct of war—that would expressly prohibit genocide in warfare, as well as the "creation of an 'international multilateral treaty' [to] provide strong legal protections for minority groups" who are most vulnerable to persecution.[64]

In *Axis Rule*, Lemkin showed how German laws imposed within occupied countries were "bereft of moral content and of respect for human rights." These laws were part of a coordinated attack to establish German hegemony over the peoples of Europe as colonial subjects of the Reich.[65]

Lemkin believed future redress would be "based upon the responsibility of the German people treated as an entirety" for their crimes.[66] With the world recoiling over the industrial mass murder process being uncovered by Allied troops as they began liberating Dachau, Auschwitz, and other death and concentration camps, Lemkin saw an opportunity to establish an international legal precedent that would protect the inviolable sanctity of human dignity—especially for minority groups often targeted for persecution by the majority population within a state.

By 1945, *Axis Rule* was becoming a leading text for US prosecutors who had little documentary evidence elsewhere, and Lemkin secured a meeting with Justice Robert Jackson. On May 4, 1945, Lemkin introduced himself to Jackson via a letter in which he detailed his new crime of genocide and included a copy of his recent article entitled "Genocide—A Modern Crime."[67] Jackson, in turn, hired Lemkin as a consultant for Nuremberg.[68] The Pentagon's War Crimes Office tasked Lemkin with developing a sample trial brief, and Lemkin was assigned to Telford Taylor, one of Jackson's top lieutenants and eventually Jackson's successor as chief US prosecutor.[69]

Lemkin, like Robinson, advised all four prosecution teams, though he never sat at the counsel table nor anywhere else in the courtroom.[70] His theories nevertheless were relevant to the prosecutors, with Jackson even keeping a copy of *Axis Rule* with him for the duration of the trial, and "[a]t a May 16th meeting . . . Jackson and most of his senior lawyers . . . changed Bernays' ['Planning Memorandum'] draft to include . . . 'genocide.'" Lemkin was not "in London during the four-nation Allied negotiations" that culminated in the London Agreement and Nuremberg Charter signed on August 8, 1945, but "his linguistic and conceptual contributions were present." However, each Allied power understood that their authority to prosecute the Nazis derived from the central crime of waging an aggressive war, and at the time, genocide had no legal definition. As such, the Charter did not use the word "genocide," but it "in substance adopted much of Lemkin's insight," particularly when it came to defining crimes against humanity. Later in his life, Jackson would describe the significance of the London Agreement, declaring: "[H]ere was a clear-cut declaration by four of the dominant powers of the world . . . that aggressive war is a crime, and that these crimes against humanity, such as genocide, are crimes."[71]

When it came time to write the IMT indictment in September and October 1945, Lemkin did not contribute to composing the document but was steadfast in his advocacy that genocide be included, "constantly coming" to see American prosecutor Sidney Alderman with his request.[72] When the indictment was issued, the four prosecuting nations listed genocide in Count Three—War Crimes, "marking the first time 'genocide' appeared in international law."[73]

"Genocide" became a fixture of Nuremberg, described by French prosecutor Charles Dubost as "the unique fact of this Trial, the fact that stands out above all others" and a word which was adopted by three out of the four chief prosecutors.[74] This was an incredible feat, considering Lemkin coined the word only a year earlier.

But the inclusion of "genocide" in the IMT indictment did not meet Lemkin's goal of making genocide a stand-alone enumerated crime in international criminal law. In the end, the prosecutors charged the Nazi leaders with the novel offense of "crimes against humanity," but not genocide. This was due to two principal reasons: there was no legal precedent to support the creation and use of genocide as an international crime, and the core charge against the Nazis was the waging of aggressive war.

The IMT indictment listed four substantive crimes for which the Nazi leaders could be convicted: crimes against peace, war crimes, crimes against humanity, and conspiracy. The indictment rather unintuitively listed "genocide" under the category of "war crimes" rather than "crimes against humanity." The term was also used interchangeably with "mass murder" and "annihilation" rather than being given a distinct legal definition.[75] Furthermore, the judges recognized "crimes against humanity" as parasitic crimes, encompassing only acts that occurred during the war. As a result, the Nazi persecution of Jews between 1933 and 1939—before the start of the war—was excluded as a crime against humanity.[76] Lemkin was disappointed, calling the final IMT judgment "wholly insufficient."[77]

Despite the IMT's failure to recognize genocide as a stand-alone crime, Lemkin's ideas did not fade into obscurity—quite the opposite. The twelve subsequent Nuremberg Military Tribunals (the NMTs) held by the Americans continued to use the term and helped to more fully flesh out the concept of genocide as a crime under international law.[78] Our fourth hero, Ben Ferencz, comes into the picture, forever linking these two great legal luminaries. As chief prosecutor of the SS-Einsatzgruppen trial (Case 9), the 27-year-old Ferencz used the word in his opening address.[79]

In Case 4, US prosecutor James McHaney introduced the issue of genocide at trial beneath the heading "Extermination of the Jews," and by doing so, forever identified "Lemkin's term with 'one of the blackest pages in the history of the civilized world.'"[80] While most subsequent cases at Nuremberg involved some reference to genocide, only Case 8 was a "genuine genocide trial" that was "truest to Lemkin's original idea."[81] Previous cases had limited the definition of genocide to encompass only physical extermination, while Lemkin had always envisioned a more expansive application of the crime. Lemkin's "complex understanding" of genocide "translated into the charges and, more significantly, the language which the prosecution used," transforming Case 8 "into a considerably broader, empirically richer case" that went beyond extermination and reached Nazi efforts to control reproduction in a "sinister program" of racialization.[82]

In direct response to Lemkin's "campaign to convince UN delegates to adopt a resolution that would recognize that genocide was a crime in international law,"[83] in 1948, the UN General Assembly adopted the Convention on the Prevention and Punishment of the Crime of Genocide in which state parties "confirm that genocide, whether committed in time of peace or in time of war, is a crime under international law which they undertake to prevent and to punish"—Lemkin's ultimate triumph.[84] Present at the time of the UN's unanimous vote to adopt the Genocide Convention, Lemkin "was numbed by the outcome," which in his eyes "meant a 'new partnership between two worlds: my own world of long, frustrating efforts, hopes, and agonizing fears, and this new official world which now made a solemn pledge to preserve the life of peoples and races of mankind.'"[85] Despite the Convention's powerful sentiment, it "enshrined a heavily redacted version of Raphael Lemkin's original concept, reducing it essentially to national, ethnic, and religious collectives while omitting the political and cultural criteria." It also "lack[ed] any enforcement mechanisms" and suffered from "less than universal endorsement," with the UK not adopting the Convention until 1970 and the United States not until 1989.[86]

Lemkin's idea of genocide continues to live on. The term "has now become synonymous with extreme evil and . . . [is considered] the 'crime of crimes.'"[87] Of the personalities at Nuremberg mentioned in this volume, Lemkin is among those best known.

Conclusion

There was no unified Jewish lobby pressing the case for making the extermination of the Jews the central theme of the IMT trial. Instead, various Jewish jurists from both sides of the Atlantic played important roles in formulating and executing the legal game plan for how the so-called Major War Criminals and other Nazis would be tried from 1945 to 1949. But *Nuremberg—The Birthplace of Modern International Criminal*

Law is not just the province of lawyers. The IMT trial and those that followed have become a critical part of the historiography of the Holocaust. Today, with the entire archives of these trials available online, a new generation of researchers sitting at their desks can mine these records and other critical primary documents to reveal further how Nuremberg became the seat of international justice.

Notes

1 A *Judensau* (Jew pig) statue dating back to the Middle Ages remains at the Church of St. Sebaldus in Nuremberg, but today, the figure is accompanied by an explanatory plaque in German and English titled, "*St. Sebald stellt sich seiner mitschuld* [St. Sebald Faces Up to its Complicity]." For general discussion, see Katherine Clark Walter, "What Should We Do with Hateful Monuments?," *The Public Medievalist,* https://publicmedievalist.com/hateful-medieval-images/.

2 The word "pogrom" is of Russian origin, meaning "to wreak havoc, to demolish violently." The term came to be used in the late nineteenth and early twentieth centuries to describe violent attacks on Jewish communities, often involving looting, destruction of property, and physical violence. The word has since been generalized to refer to similar acts of mob violence against any ethnic, religious, or social group. *See Pogroms*, US Holocaust Memorial Museum.

3 *Nuremberg, Germany*, Jewish Virtual Library; *see also Nuremberg Race Laws*, US Holocaust Mem'l Museum.

4 Devin O. Pendas, 36 Holocaust & Genocide Stud. 102, 103 (reviewing Francine Hirsch, Soviet Judgment at Nuremberg: A New History of the International Military Tribunal After World War II (2020)). Pendas adds: "The German-language literature has included a parallel tendency to interpret the trial through the distinctly German lens of *Vergangenheitsbewältigung* (mastering the past)." *Id.*

5 See, for example, Telford Taylor, The Anatomy of the Nuremberg Trials: A Personal Memoir (2013); Michael R. Marrus, The Nuremberg War Crimes Trial, 1945–46: A Documentary History (1997); Bradley F. Smith, The American Road to Nuremberg: The Documentary Record, 1944–1945 (1981); Arieh J. Kochavi, Prelude to Nuremberg: Allied War Crimes Policy and the Question of Punishment (2005).

6 *Shetl* is a Yiddish word for thousands of small villages or towns in Eastern Europe with significant Jewish populations. Most were eradicated by the Nazis and their collaborators during the Second World War. In modern culture, it was popularized by the fictional *shetl* Anatevka, the setting of *Fiddler on the Roof*—a musical performed in over fifteen languages since its 1964 debut. Another phrase, "Think Yiddish, Dress British," popularized in the 1960s, referred to native Yiddish speakers from *shetls* who become luminaries, many in law. Our subjects here fit this description.

7 *A Former Prosecutor at the Nuremberg War Crimes Trial*, BenFerencz.org.

8 *Murray Bernays, Lawyer, Dead; Set Nuremberg Trials Format*, N.Y. Times, September 22, 1970.

9 *Murray C. Bernays Papers, 1919–1975*, Archives West.

10 *Murray Bernays, Lawyer, Dead*, N.Y. Times.

11 Clint Ide, *Holocaust Remembrance Day (Yom Hashoah)—The Story of Murray C. Bernays*, Am. Heritage Ctr. (April 24, 2017).
12 Kim Christian Priemel, The Betrayal: The Nuremberg Trials and German Divergence 67–68 (2016).
13 J. J. Lador-Lederer, *The Nuremberg Judgment Revisited: The Bernays Postulate*, 30 Neth. Int'l L. Rev. 360, 362 (1983).
14 Francine Hirsch, *How the Soviet Union Helped Establish the Crime of Aggressive War*, Just Sec. (March 9, 2022).
15 *Memorandum from Murray C. Bernays and D.W. Brown, January 4, 1945*, Nat'l Archives.
16 John McCarten, *The Man Behind the Gavel*, The New Yorker (November 9, 1945) ("The Colonel recently returned from London, where he was military adviser to Justice Robert Jackson . . . [He] tried to use ordinary legal methods in making the blueprint for the Allied tribunals . . . International law, he says, like our ordinary common law, has to be based on the enlightened conscience of mankind.").
17 Memorandum from Murray C. Bernays and D. W. Brown, January 4, 1945, at 2.
18 *Id.* at 2–3, 6.
19 Frank Tuerkheimer and Michael Bazyler, *Forgotten Trials of the Holocaust*, NYU Press (2014).
20 Shane Darcy, Collective Responsibility and Accountability Under International Law 257 (2007).
21 *Id.* at 257–8 (quoting Colonel Murray C. Bernays, *Subject: Trial of European War Criminals*, September 15, 1944).
22 *See* Lachezar Yanev, *A Janus-Faced Concept: Nuremberg's Law on Conspiracy Vis-à-Vis the Notion of Joint Criminal Enterprise*, 26 Crim. L. F. 419, 419, 428 (2015); *see also* Darcy, at 257.
23 Yanev, at 427.
24 *Id.* at 431, 437.
25 Ide, *Holocaust Remembrance Day.*
26 Priemel, at 111, 144–5.
27 Tuerkheimer and Bazyler, *Forgotten Trials of the Holocaust.*
28 *Murray Bernays, Lawyer, Dead*, N.Y. Times.
29 Priemel, at 84.
30 Ide, *Holocaust Remembrance Day.*
31 McCarten, *The Man Behind the Gavel.*
32 *Legion of Merit*, Air Force's Pers. Ctr.
33 Jonathan Bush, *Nuremberg and Beyond: Jacob Robinson, International Lawyer*, 39 Loyola L.A. Int'l & Compar. L. Rev. 259, 266–8 (2017).
34 *Id.* at 268; *see also* Michael R. Marrus, *A Jewish Lobby at Nuremberg: Jacob Robinson and the Institute of Jewish Affairs, 1945–1946*, 27 Cardozo L. Rev. 1651, 1653 (2006).
35 Institute of Jewish Affairs, Jews in Nazi Europe, February 1933 to November 1941 (1941).
36 Bush, at 269.
37 Jacob Robinson, *Preface to the First Edition* of Institute of Jewish Affairs, Hitler's Ten-Year War on the Jews (1943).
38 Priemel, at 65, 99 n.30.
39 Marrus, at 1653.

40 *See id.* at 1654–5.
41 *Id.* at 1656.
42 Bush, at 271–3.
43 Priemel, at 117.
44 *Id.*
45 Bush at 272–3.
46 Priemel, at 117.
47 Marrus, at 1659.
48 *Id.*
49 *Id.* at 1660. For further discussion, see Michael Bazyler, *The Holocaust at Nuremberg: What the Record Reveals*, 39 Loyola L.A. Int'l. & Comp. L. Rev. 35 (2017). Only the French and Soviet prosecutors put on stand Jewish and non-Jewish survivors to tell the stories of what the Germans did to the Jews. The British lawyers, like the Americans, stuck to introducing into evidence the plethora of Nazi documents to prove their case with other high-ranking Nazis taking the stand as witnesses for the prosecution. *Id.* at 36, 51.
50 Marrus, at 1660.
51 Michael R. Marrus, *The Holocaust at Nuremberg*, Yad Vashem.
52 John Q. Barrett, *Holocaust Comprehension, Proof, & Remembrance*, The Jackson List (May 6, 2024) (citing Letter from Robert H. Jackson to the Institute of Jewish Affairs (November 1, 1946)), https://thejacksonlist.com/2024/05/06/holocaust-comprehension-proof-remembrance/.
53 For discussions of Robinson's role at the Eichmann trial, see Bush, at 283; Marrus, at 1653. Robinson's star shined again with his publication of *And the Crooked Shall Be Made Straight: A New Look at the Eichmann Trial* (1965) where he confronted head-on Hannah Arendt's two calumnies (in her *Eichmann in Jerusalem* book) that Eichmann was a personification of "the banality of evil" and that Jewish leadership in Nazi-occupied Europe is to blame for what befell the Jews. Recent Holocaust historiography has validated Robinson's views. *See* Bazyler, *Holocaust, Genocide and the Law*, at 128 (discussing Bettina Stangnett's ground-breaking 2014 book *Eichmann Before Jerusalem: The Unexamined Life of a Mass Murderer*).
54 *See* Timothy Snyder, Bloodlands: Europe Between Hitler and Stalin (2016).
55 Douglas Irvin-Erickson, Raphael Lemkin and the Concept of Genocide 17, 34 (2017).
56 *Id.* at 39.
57 David M. Crowe, *Pearl Buck, Raphael Lemkin, and the Struggle for the Genocide Convention*, in Beyond the Good Earth: Transnational Perspectives on Pearl S. Buck 11, 12–13 (Jay Cole and John R. Haddad eds., 2019); *see also* David M. Crowe, Raphael Lemkin: The Life of a Visionary (forthcoming 2025).
58 *Id.* at 12, 16.
59 Priemel, at 44.
60 Marrus, at 1652; *see also* Michael Bazyler, Holocaust, Genocide and the Law xxiii, 61 (2016).
61 Raphael Lemkin, Axis Rule in Occupied Europe: Laws of Occupation, Analysis of Government, Proposals for Redress 79 (1944).
62 *Id.*
63 Michael Bazyler, *In the Footsteps of Raphael Lemkin*, 2 Genocide Stud. & Prevention: Int'l J. 51, 51 (2007).

64 Crowe, at 17–9.
65 Lemkin, at ix–xi.
66 Lemkin, at xiii.
67 John Q. Barrett, *Raphael Lemkin and "Genocide" at Nuremberg, 1945–1946*, in The Genocide Convention Sixty Years After Its Adoption 35, 36 (Christoph Safferling and Eckart Conze eds., 2010).
68 Irvin-Erickson, at 140.
69 Crowe, at 20.
70 *See* Alexa Stiller, *The Mass Murder of the European Jews and the Concept of "Genocide" in the Nuremberg Trials: Reassessing Raphaël Lemkin's Impact*, 13 Genocide Stud. & Prevention: Int'l J. 144, 144 (2019).
71 Barrett, at 38–9, 41–2.
72 *Id.* at 44–5.
73 Irvin-Erickson, at 141.
74 Priemel, at 118.
75 *Id.* at 101.
76 *International Military Tribunal at Nuremberg*, US Holocaust Mem'l Museum.
77 Crowe, at 21.
78 *The Nuremberg Trials*, The Nat'l WWII Museum.
79 Robert H. Jackson Center, *Ben Ferencz Nuremberg Einsatzgruppen Case #9 Opening*, YouTube (May 7, 2018), https://www.youtube.com/watch?v=b67B-MoKG_o ("We ask this Court to affirm by international penal action man's right to live in peace and dignity, regardless of his race or creed. The case we present is a plea of humanity to law . . . Genocide, the extermination of whole categories of human beings, was a foremost instrument of the Nazi doctrine.").
80 Priemel, at 295.
81 *Id.* at 297.
82 *Id.* at 297–8.
83 Crowe, at 21.
84 Convention on the Prevention and Punishment of the Crime of Genocide art. I, Dec. 9, 1948, 78 U.N.T.S. 277.
85 Crowe, at 30.
86 Priemel, at 410.
87 Bazyler, *In the Footsteps of Raphael Lemkin*, at 51.

Selected Bibliography

Bazyler, Michael, *Holocaust, Genocide and the Law* (2016).
Lemkin, Raphael, *Axis Rule in Occupied Europe: Laws of Occupation, Analysis of Government, Proposals for Redress* (1944).
Marrus, Michael R., *The Nuremberg War Crimes Trial, 1945–46: A Documentary History* (1997).
Priemel, Kim Christian, *The Betrayal: The Nuremberg Trials and German Divergence* (2016).
Taylor, Telford, *The Anatomy of the Nuremberg Trials: A Personal Memoir* (2013).

Part 2

The Nuremberg Principles

Trial of the Doctors and Judges: Reflections on Medical Ethics and the Rule of Law, 1946–1947

6

Thanatology and the Nuremberg Doctors' Trial

Conceptualizing the "Science of Killing"[1]

Ulf Schmidt

On November 27, 1946, a few days before the Nazi doctors' trial commenced, the Austrian-Jewish émigré-physician and medical expert for the US prosecution, Leo Alexander, who, in the weeks after the end of hostilities, had produced a series of Combined Intelligence Operative Sub-Committee (CIOS) reports on Nazi human experiments and the "euthanasia" program, wrote to his wife "Fifi" to give her a first impression about Nuremberg:

> I have been here about a week, and what an interesting week it was. The mass of material that has been unearthed since the days of my reports is tremendous. I have delved into that mass of material, and have finally grasped its meaning and have come out with an appraisal that makes sense. It is thanatology pure and simple, and it is the technique of genocide. Thanatology is a word I have coined: thanathos in Greek, means death. Genocide is the "murder of people", a word coined by our old friend Lemkin. I shall send you the carbon of an appraisal of the whole problem which I have been writing for General Taylor, the chief prosecutor.[2]

In March 2023, following investigations into war crimes, crimes against humanity, and genocide in the Russo-Ukrainian war, the International Criminal Court (ICC) issued an arrest warrant for Vladimir Putin and Maria Lvova-Belova, the Russian Commissioner for Children's Rights, for their involvement in the unlawful deportation of children. The arrest warrant against the president of the Russian Federation, coupled with compelling evidence of war crimes and crimes against humanity in one of the most brutal and expansionist wars Europe has witnessed since the end of the Second World War, has propelled the subject of the Nuremberg trials to the forefront of scholarly and political debates.[3] Experts recognize that the legal challenges and (geo) political and public relations implications of an international trial at the ICC, where Putin would probably be tried in absentia, are formidable. It has also highlighted the need for a deeper understanding of the historical, ethical, and legal underpinnings of the Nuremberg trials, which has become more important than ever.

Of particular concern for scholars has been the impact of the Holocaust on the international reputation of the medical profession, the practice of medicine, and the field of medical and research ethics. How was it possible that men and women sworn to the Hippocratic medical tradition of *primum non nocere* (first do no harm) could ignore principles of beneficence, non-maleficence, and consent, and commit medical crimes of previously unseen proportions on vulnerable communities? What were their motives? Were the doctors aware—as Primo Levi asked in *The Drowned and the Saved*—that they were committing a crime?[4] How did they legitimize their actions toward fellow human beings to themselves and society? How did post-war doctors explain and justify the fact that their profession had been heavily implicated in Nazi medical atrocities and genocide? While most of these questions were outside the scope of the trial, in preparing for the US prosecution, legal and medical experts made a first, albeit in retrospect too simplistic, attempt to construct a framework using the concept of thanatology, the "science of killing," to address these issues.

Bioethicists have previously questioned why the US prosecution in the Doctors' Trial, instead of concentrating on genocide and mass murder, focused the main thrust of their case against the Nazi doctors on human experiments where "at most, only a few thousand people" perished.[5] The answer to this question apparently lay in the weakness of their case concerning the charge of genocide and crimes against humanity, whereas evidence of criminal medical experiments was irrefutable and could be proven in open court at what was "no mere murder trial."[6] Viewed from a historical perspective, however, this line of argument reveals a certain misconception of how the prosecution's case was constructed and evolved during the Doctors' Trial.

Established by the US Military authorities on the basis of Control Council Law No. 10, the Nuremberg Doctors' Trial was the first of twelve war crimes trials that followed the International Military Tribunal (IMT) in 1945–6 to prosecute the major war criminals. Its official title was United States of America versus Karl Brandt et al. (Case I). Twenty doctors, including Hitler's personal escort physician Karl Brandt and three administrators, were charged with a common design or conspiracy, war crimes, crimes against humanity, and membership of an organization declared criminal by the IMT.[7] The Doctors' Trial resulted in the formulation of the Nuremberg Code, one of the landmark documents in the history of biomedical research ethics. It should not be confused with the Nuremberg Principles, which the United Nations adopted as the legal principles underpinning the Nuremberg trials.[8] To this day, the Nuremberg Code continues to be of global relevance in ongoing debates about human experimentation and voluntary consent.[9]

In the weeks preceding the opening of the Doctors' trial, discussions about the nature of German medical science and the principles of permissible and non-permissible experiments on humans emerged as a result of concerted efforts among the US prosecution to construct a legally viable prosecution case. The pressure on the medical and legal experts on the ground at Nuremberg was immense. Even as relations with the Soviet Union were deteriorating, support for war crimes trials was rapidly disappearing in Washington once the IMT had been completed. These factors contributed to a sense of urgency and the need for improvisation.

This chapter aims to demonstrate that, rather than having been conceived months in advance, the concept of thanatology used by medical experts such as Alexander and his colleagues from the US prosecution, led by General Telford Taylor, was, in fact, only developed in the days before the trial against the Nazi physicians commenced, and was expanded upon throughout the prosecution. By building on the legal precedent set by the IMT, and by borrowing from, and also interpreting, Raphael Lemkin's genocide concept, thanatology was understood to refer to the systematic development of scientific, inconspicuous, and effective methods to commit murder.[10] Whereas few international law and human rights experts have recognized or engaged with the concepts of thanatology and ktenology, which were used interchangeably, they played an important role not only in framing the prosecution case, but also in distinguishing more clearly between permissible and non-permissible human experiments, which served as the basis for the judges to construct the ten principles of the Nuremberg Code.

The Nuremberg Prosecution

Highly motivated and fascinated by one of the "most tremendous" things he had ever been involved with, Alexander felt like a "hunter who suddenly finds himself in a swarm of the most amazing birds with only one gun in his hand and a limited number of bullets to bring those trophies home."[11] At the same time, he realized that he and the US prosecution were part of the "maelstrom of the biggest, most hectically working legal machine ever assembled with inevitable improvisations."[12] Apart from the logistical problems, experts arriving at Nuremberg were shocked to see the city in such a state of destruction. Allied bombing had reduced the place in which Hitler had held his Party rallies to a "heap of rubble,"[13] Alexander observed on his journeys from the hotel to the courthouse. Those who had hoped to do some sightseeing were quickly disappointed. In the aftermath of the war, walking unarmed or without an escort police around the inner-city walls had become inadvisable since the ruins had apparently become "hangouts for thugs of all kinds."[14] Consequently, most focused on the work at hand in what turned into a relatively self-contained cosmos of Allied military personnel, lawyers, secretaries, and support staff.

The organizational setup of the prosecution team was unusual, to say the least, as many of the US legal experts employed their spouses in the prosecution and interrogation teams to justify their presence at Nuremberg. The chief prosecutor, General Telford Taylor, aged thirty-eight, was a Harvard-trained lawyer; his wife, described by Alexander as "highly intelligent and charming," worked in the interrogation section (albeit not as an interrogator). Their children had been sent to a boarding school in Washington, D.C., to avoid unnecessary distraction. The wife of Taylor's assistant, Mr. Erwin, was in charge of the location bureau to track down missing war criminals. While the office worked reasonably well, "it sports an air of amateurishness and erudition which would make a Boston cop's hair stand on end," Alexander observed. James M. McHaney, "a smooth Southern lawyer from Arkansas," had been put in charge of the prosecution in the Doctors' Trial.[15] The Sudeten-German émigré Arnost Horlik-Hochwald (originally called Ernst Hochwald), who had worked for the prosecution in the IMT, served as an assistant prosecutor.[16]

On October 25, 1946, the Chief of Counsel for War Crimes filed the indictment against the defendants in the Doctors' Trial. On November 5, the indictment was served, with the defendants given thirty days to prepare their defense. In the Doctors' Trial, the legal concept of a "common design" was adopted instead of the concept of a "common plan" after it had become apparent that the latter was difficult to prove in open court during the IMT, and was largely abandoned in the subsequent Nuremberg proceedings.[17] All twenty-three defendants pleaded not guilty.

By talking to the defendants prior to and during the trial, Alexander documented some of their deeply rooted cultural and racial prejudices. As it turned out, the defendant Wilhelm Beiglböck had been one of Alexander's former classmates in Austria. Charged with conducting deadly seawater experiments, Beiglböck was convinced that Germans had "culturally achieved more than the Polynesians."[18] People of color, according to Beiglböck, were either porters in hotels or jazz musicians. Shocked about such explicit racism, Alexander told his wife: "He did not recognize me, but I vaguely remembered him. He always was a Nazi rough-neck, and I guess he still is."[19] Whereas some Allied interrogators, such as Robert Kempner, gained a reputation for their aggressive line of questioning defendants, Alexander took a more gentle and pragmatic approach. His aim was to elicit information from the defendants about their underlying psychological motives for having agreed to become involved in Nazi crimes. By talking to men such as Hans Wolfgang Romberg, one of Sigmund Rascher's collaborators in the notorious Dachau high-altitude experiments, he wanted to understand how expert scientists had managed to justify their participation in unethical research and human experimentation. In particular, he wanted to know "how these men had come into a situation of order and obedience . . . and why certain other people . . . had kept at a distance."[20] There was certainly a strong tendency among some of the Nuremberg defendants to subordinate themselves to higher authorities, or justify their actions through alleged military necessity. Indeed, the defendant Fritz Fischer, charged with conducting deadly sulphonamide and bone transplantation experiments at the Ravensbrück camp, argued that "obedience and the acceptance of the community" had the highest priority during the war. "This is where the great inner conflict between individualists and collectivists begins,"[21] he told Alexander. In addition to prioritizing collectivism, factors such as anti-Semitism, extreme forms of nationalism, idealism, scientific opportunism, and careerism also played an important role. What was shocking, and required explanation, was the extent to which the suffering of experimental subjects had not evoked the slightest sense of moral or individual responsibility among the defendants.

Crimes against Humanity versus Genocide

The concept of crimes against humanity, three words describing the murder of "four million Jews and Poles on the territory of Poland," had been proposed in July 1945 by the Jewish émigré lawyer Hersch Lauterpacht in the build-up to the Nuremberg trials to strengthen the protection of individuals rather than groups, and subsequently been introduced into the Nuremberg statute. His book *An International Bill of the Rights of Man*, published in the same year, became one of the seminal texts in international human rights law.[22] The concept of genocide, on the other hand, an extension of related terms such as infanticide and homicide, had been developed during the Second World War by the lawyer Raphael Lemkin and publicized in the 1944 book *Axis Rule in Occupied Europe* in order to prevent—and by implication prosecute—the deliberate attempt to destroy national, ethnic, racial, or religious groups.[23] Genocide has been called the "crime of all crimes."[24]

Unlike crimes against humanity, genocide was not introduced as a separate charge in the Nuremberg indictment from October 1945, but it found expression in Count 3 on war crimes, which included the mass murder and ill-treatment of civilians in the occupied territories.[25] Between 1945 and 1946, Lemkin served as an expert advisor to the IMT's chief prosecutor, Robert Jackson, and was thus able to influence some of the discussions within the US prosecution team. Lauterpacht and Lemkin took different views with regard to the development of international law and the prosecution of Nazi war crimes, and although they both lived and studied in Lviv in the early twentieth century are not known to have met in person during their lifetime. Nonetheless, they shared a common desire to not only hold German mass murderers to account for exterminating entire Jewish and other minority communities, including Lauterpacht's immediate Jewish family, but also to establish new international legal concepts that would improve the protection of individuals and groups in the future.[26] Their approaches differed, but backed up by international law and the creation of an international court, both men wanted to limit the executive power of states so that it would no longer be possible to discriminate against individuals and groups without due regard for human rights and the rule of law. The introduction of the concept of crimes against humanity as one of the central charges in the Nuremberg trials bolstered the belief among experts that a new post-war order, underpinned by international law and overseen by international bodies such as the United Nations, could protect the world from another potentially catastrophic military conflict.

During the war, Lemkin and Alexander had apparently known each other as colleagues working at Duke University in Durham, North Carolina, which is why Alexander referred to him as "his old friend" in his correspondence.[27] On November 12, after having been briefed by officials from the War Crimes Branch, Civil Affairs Division at the Pentagon, Washington D.C., he noted in his diary that Lemkin's "genocide policy" was to serve as the basis in the Doctors' Trial.[28] To prepare himself, he asked his assistant Marian Shelley to procure further "genocidal material" as background reading.[29] The US prosecution knew that it had to have strong arguments to succeed with the medical case if they wanted to hold further trials against Nazi lawyers, police officers, and civil servants. Although the IMT offered legal and procedural guidance, Taylor and his staff found themselves in unfamiliar territory in the weeks prior to the trial. Under pressure, any concept members of the prosecution could come up with to secure the defendants' conviction was considered. Due diligence was not always applied to test the legal applicability of some of these concepts, one of which was Alexander's concept of thanatology. Having been omitted from the IMT statute book, and replaced with the concept of crimes against humanity, it was Alexander's attempt to introduce, essentially through the back door in one of the subsequent Nuremberg trials, a distinct variation of Lemkin's concept of genocide.[30]

Thanatology

Although the *tu quoque* (you likewise) argument had been ruled inadmissible under the statutes of the London Charter, Allied legal experts expected that the main thrust of the German defense would be directed along similar lines. By arguing that US American medical research on human participants in research institutions, penitentiaries, and asylums had been similar or identical in character, the defense lawyers wanted to demonstrate that US researchers were equally guilty of unethical and potentially prosecutable medical conduct, and thus expose the US prosecution's moral and ethical hypocrisy in the eyes of the world. As early as November 13, Kempner had briefed Alexander about his assignment at Nuremberg. He was supposed to help the prosecution to win the case after it had become apparent that the indictment had been "sloppily drawn."[31] US legal experts were expecting the German defense to argue that similar experiments had been performed in the "US and other countries." For the case against the doctors, it was consequently critical to "stress [the] differences."[32] US prosecutors had to show that the type of research performed in the camps had been a crime according to German law. "Sight should not be lost of that it is part of the general framework of genocidal activity," he told Alexander.[33]

The conversation with Kempner prompted Alexander to immediately reach out to the Commissioner for Mental Health in the Commonwealth of Massachusetts to gain a better understanding of the "nature and procedural characteristics of the experimentation on human beings" in the United States. Such information would place the US prosecution in a better position to "effectively contrast ethical with non-ethical experimentation on human beings."[34] Alexander wanted to know not only what conditions had to be met for the approval of state-funded human trials from US health officials, but also how the voluntary nature of the experiments was to be ensured. In his official capacity as the expert for the prosecution, Alexander also approached universities, hospitals, and research institutions in the United States, including the Rockefeller Institute for Medical Research, to supply him with details about

> the general rules which govern such experimentation [on humans], any procedure for approval of particular experiments by a board of research scientists or officials of the hospital, and the requirements laid down as to the need for consent of next of kin or guardian as well as for the consent and cooperation of the part of the patient.[35]

At Nuremberg, the US prosecution used the concept of thanatology as shorthand for the scientific means to systematically kill other people in order to link the crimes committed by German medical scientists to the broader framework of genocide. On November 21, three days after his arrival at Nuremberg, once the indictment had been read out in court and he had apparently told General Taylor that the US prosecution had had given the defense "too much credit, and Himmler too little," Alexander mentioned the thanatology concept for the first time in his diary.[36] Several days later, on November 27, after having worked on the seawater case, he recorded in his diary that the evidence from the interrogations suggested that the majority of experiments "had revealed nothing new beyond universal experimentation."[37] It prompted him to consider whether this might be an angle that the prosecution could take to highlight the differences between Allied and German medical science. The study of German medical science seemed to suggest, in the eyes of Alexander, that the overarching objective had not been the procurement of new and useful knowledge, but the development of methods to kill large numbers of people by the "most scientific" and "least conspicuous" means possible.[38]

Officially, Alexander first referred to the concept in his memorandum "Thanatology as a Scientific Technique of Genocide," which he submitted to General Taylor on November 30, 1946.[39] While acknowledging the German military's attempt to discover effective medical treatments and solutions for aeronautical and air-sea rescue problems, the US prosecution recognized a marked discrepancy between the ostensible purpose of the human experiments and their outcomes. Anyone studying the experiments from the perspective of "usefulness," Alexander argued, had to realize that the majority of the experiments contributed little or no new knowledge to medical science. He concluded that the "experiments were amateurish and poorly coordinated, that they failed to give the scientific information which was claimed to be desired, and that a unified policy was completely absent, except for the barbaric manner of their execution."[40] A few days later, on December 3, Alexander recorded in his diary:

> Many of these so-called experiments are frankly and openly devoted to methods of destroying or preventing life, namely to "euthanasia" and extermination methods, and to methods of sterilization. But the preoccupation with methods of producing death runs also through many of the other investigations like a red thread, irrespective of the ostensible other purpose of the experiment. The frightful body of new methods of killing—the new lethal injections, the new gases, the poison bullets, constitute a formidable body of new and dangerous knowledge, useful to criminals everywhere, and to a criminal state if another one is permitted to establish itself again, so as to constitute a new branch, a destructive perversion of medicine worthy of a new name, for which thanatology had been suggested by our medical consultant. This thanatological knowledge supplied the technological methods for genocide, a policy of the German Third Reich, which could not have been carried out without the active participation of its medical scientists.[41]

Two days later, on December 5, four days before the Doctors' Trial commenced, and after Taylor had approached him to help with the drafting of the opening speech, Alexander submitted another briefing paper to Taylor about a possible discussion of the "Thanatology Genocide Angle."[42] On December 7, he corrected the "General's opening address" as it came off the typewriter. The day before the opening of the Doctors' Trial, he continued to work with Taylor on the speech before relaxing at the General's party at Villa Schickedanz in Dambach, a large estate located southwest of Fürth.[43] Proudly, he told his wife that he had performed a "complete analysis of all the experiments, have completed studies of motives, techniques and personalities of all the 23 accused men, have put the salient features of all this into clear and lucid writing, and have submitted it, as it came off the typewriter, in installments, to General Taylor for inclusion into his opening speech. He has used it well."[44]

On November 9, Taylor took the stand in a packed courtroom 600 to deliver his opening speech. He made it clear that the court, as the agent of the United States and the "voice of humanity," found the acts of the defendants and the ideas which engendered them to be "barbarous and criminal."[45] The defendants were not "ignorant men," he told the court. While some of them may have been sadists, the majority were trained doctors and distinguished scientists who "were fully able to comprehend the nature of their acts" and "form a moral judgement" about their involvement in "wholesale murder and unspeakable cruel torture."[46] Before discussing the types of experiments in turn—the high altitude, malaria, mustard gas, sulphanilamide, bone transplantation, seawater, epidemic jaundice, sterilization, typhus, poison bullet, incendiary bomb, and related experiments, as well as the Jewish skeleton collection—Taylor told the court about the applied thanatological framework in the medical case:

> Mankind had not theretofore felt the need of a word to denominate the science of how to kill prisoners most rapidly and subjugated people in large numbers. This case and these defendants have created this gruesome question for the lexicographer. For the moment we will christen this macabre science thanatology, the science of producing death. The thanatological knowledge, derived in part from these experiments, supplied the techniques for genocide, a policy of the Third Reich, exemplified in the "euthanasia" program and in the widespread slaughter of Jews, Gypsies, Poles, and Russians. This policy of mass extermination could not have been so effectively carried out without the active participation of German medical scientists.[47]

As far as the subject of medical ethics was concerned, there was apparently no disagreement within the literature that "it is a fundamental and inescapable obligation of every physician under any known system of law not to perform a dangerous experiment without the subject's consent."[48] From the outset, the US prosecution attached critical importance to the principle of voluntary consent, since it allowed them, so they hoped, to demonstrate the differences between "human" Allied science and "inhuman" German science. All of the defendants, according to Taylor, had departed from "every known standard of medical ethics."[49]

Although Taylor's powerful rhetorical display highlighted the deadly nature of the experiments, from a legal perspective, the application of the thanatology concept, a variation of the concept of genocide, posed numerous problems that resulted in the exclusion of certain victim groups. Conceptually, genocide focused on the murder of another people, mainly European Jewry, and excluded groups such as the victims of the "euthanasia" program, which some members of the US prosecution, such as Kempner, regarded as "merely a training center for killer personnel of the Holocaust." Demonstrating the murder of German asylum patients did not strengthen the case of the US prosecution, unless it was possible to show that the "euthanasia" program included non-German nationals. It explains why US officials asked Alexander to "play down euthanasia" in his assessment of German medical war crimes. On balance, the approach taken by the US prosecution, as I have argued elsewhere, "prevented, rather than facilitated, a full investigation of the first systematic mass murder of the Nazi regime."[50] Recognizing this glaring omission led the trial observer Alice von Platen-Hallermund to publish one of the first accounts of the "euthanasia" program, entitled *Die Tötung Geisteskranker in Deutschland*, in July 1948.[51] The tens of thousands of sterilization victims likewise fell outside the remit of the court since the trial was concerned with crimes committed after the outbreak of war. Linking otherwise isolated experimental programmes, which showed that German medical scientists had acted according to a "common design," was not without its merits, because it allowed the prosecution to demonstrate degrees of culpability among sections of German society. Yet, it equally glossed over differences in the motivations and origins of the experiments. Thanatology might well have convinced the international media of the criminal conduct of the Nazi regime, but it offered little explanatory potential to engage with the defendants' lack of individual moral responsibility. By projecting the broader genocide concept onto the conduct of the camp experiments, the US prosecution wanted to make sense of Nazi medical science and create the conditions which would allow the court to sentence the defendants for war crimes and crimes against humanity. However, by doing so, they inadvertently overlooked processes of cumulative radicalization, the relationship between medical science and the German military and industry, and broader structural, institutional, and ideological factors, as well as the organizational and communicational chaos that lay at the heart of much of the decision-making. Above all, the thanatology concept, by implication, credited the Nazi regime with a degree of long-term genocidal planning and effective organization, which was rarely the case in practise during the Holocaust.[52]

However, by distinguishing between Allied and German medical science, the thanatology concept helped to define and construct medical ethical principles that exceeded the sentencing of the defendants. Thanatology made it possible to distinguish more clearly between permissible and non-permissible experiments. On December 3, the same day that Alexander outlined the thanatology concept in his diary, he produced a first draft of a memorandum on "Ethical and Non-Ethical Experiments in Human Beings" to demonstrate that the majority of the experiments had been inadequately prepared, inaccurate, unnecessary, and misleading in their approach and execution.[53] The high altitude and seawater experiments served to illustrate that many of the trials had been "non-crucial experiments," since the findings could have been obtained without the use of human participants.[54] The final text of the memorandum was completed on December 7, forty-eight hours before the start of the trial. A few months later, in April 1947, after evidence from medical experts such as Werner Leibbrand had pushed the US prosecution onto the defensive, Alexander produced a second memorandum on the same subject, which detailed a series of principles to ensure that research on human participants would be ethical and legally permissible.[55] It became part of the material that influenced the ongoing discourse on research ethics. As the trial progressed, the debates among the US prosecution about the ethics of human experimentation shaped the formulation of the Nuremberg Code.

When examining the approach of the US prosecution, we need to distinguish between two interrelated developments at the end of 1946. Whereas the first was closely related to the application of Lemkin's genocide principle during the Doctors' Trial to explain German medical science and secure the conviction of the defendants, the second created the conditions for a discursive environment within which the judges included a set of ethical principles in the judgment to offer future researchers ethical guidance through the Nuremberg Code. Following the IMT, the genocide concept had received additional backing from the United Nations. Discussions among the legal committee of the United Nations Assembly in November 1946 had concluded that the genocide concept expressed not only the "specific criminal intent" to exterminate large numbers of victims, but, like Lauterpacht's concept of crimes against humanity, it also called for "greater condemnation because it implied mass criminality and very great losses to humanity and civilization."[56] A few weeks into the Doctors' Trial, Lemkin himself had stressed to the US War Department the need to "develop the genocide concept" in the case.[57] Rather than conducting deadly experiments on individuals, he argued, the overarching objective of the Nazi regime had been the systematic murder of ethnic and religious groups. The Nazis "did not know the names of the victims but handled them by numbers. They did not hate nor had any particular interest to kill Mr. X, Y, or Z, but their acts were motivated by the desire to eradicate the particular national or racial group to which Mr. X, Y, or Z happened to belong."[58] The aim of US prosecution was to apply the force and stigma of the genocide concept, as the "crime of all crimes," to prevent the defendants from claiming that their research had been scientific, and thus unrelated to the exterminatory policies of the Third Reich.[59]

The second development was related to the expected line of defense of the defendants. The US prosecution correctly assumed that the defense lawyers would claim that Allied medical scientists had conducted similar unethical experiments, and that any trials against German scientists would necessitate a similar prosecution of US researchers or else expose the moral hypocrisy of the United States.[60] The *tu quoque* argument, US prosecutors feared, was likely to create an impasse in which medical scientists in Germany and the United States had either both breached the code of conduct of the medical profession, or none at all. Stressing the differences between Allied and German medical science through the concept of thanatology thus assumed a disproportionate importance. At the same time, it focused minds and resources to develop guidelines that would allow the judges to distinguish between ethical and non-ethical human experiments. The discussions about the thanatology concept and the ethics of human experiments were closely interrelated and mutually influential. Indeed, on December 3, after completing most of the interrogations, Alexander formulated the key arguments about both thanatology and ethical experiments.[61] "This dual focus," as Katz has pointed out, "led the prosecution and its expert witnesses, in what otherwise might have been a murder trial, to defend ethical research practices in the non-Nazi world in ways that tried to deny any past ethical transgressions."[62]

Post-Nuremberg

As the world was moving on from the Nuremberg and Tokyo trials, and other post-war medical trials in eastern and western Europe, it became clear that international medical law, a particular branch of international law, was still in its infancy and that the international standing of medicine could no longer be taken for granted.[63] In 1950, General Jules Voncken from the International Committee of Military Medicine and Pharmacy (ICMMP) told a gathering of physicians and lawyers at the Palais de Monaco that there had been "very regrettable delays in the construction of an international treaty which would be a safeguard for the peoples and nations subject to the war."[64] The moral toll, *le bilan moral*, from Nazi human experimentation had been *désastreux*.[65] According to historian of science Robert Proctor, writing decades later, it constituted the "low water mark in twentieth century moral culture."[66] Neither the Nuremberg Code nor the WMA international code of ethics from 1949 offered sufficient safeguards. Only a new "international code," Voncken claimed, which would outline the duties and rights of doctors in time of war, would protect modern societies from the "imminent danger of the medical mind."[67] The fact that scientists had developed new methods of human destruction with biological, chemical, or radiological agents, and used innovative means of propaganda to "annihilate or disempower the human personality," was of particular concern to medical ethicists and legal experts such as Voncken. They feared that the combination of non-conventional weapons in conjunction with advances in the behavioral and psy-sciences might produce a particularly lethal cocktail in future armed conflicts, and potentially sideline the role of international humanitarian law. That is why the fundamental principles of medical ethics had to be impressed upon the "soul of every doctor," not by asking them to swear a non-binding oath to their physician colleagues, but by integrating a "course in international medical ethics," which would be run under the auspices of the International Court of Justice, into their medical training. "By involving the International Court of Justice," argued Voncken, "the importance of the oath could not be ignored by anyone, and any perjury could be prosecuted and punished."[68] Doctors, in other words, would have to swear an oath in an international court of law which would summarize international medical ethics in order to protect the rights of "the wounded, the sick, prisoners and even civilians," and thus empower those whose rights and dignity had been violated with the possibility to enforce these rights. He also called upon the community of criminal lawyers, who had come together in Brussels for the unification of penal law, to regard the International

Conventions of Geneva and The Hague, which had been ratified by most nations, as the "expression of universal conscience," and thus any breaches of said conventions as "crimes or offences against humanity."[69]

What is remarkable in this context is the extent to which Voncken's paper foreshadowed the debates about human rights in human experimentation half a century later, in which scholars such as Robert Drinan, George Annas, and Michael Grodin argued for the establishment of a "permanent Nuremberg" and an "international medical tribunal."[70] What is perhaps less surprising, though, is the extent to which attempts to develop universally applicable and legally enforceable medical principles ran counter to the post-war interests of the WMA and its national associations. However, rather than engaging in open confrontation, senior WMA officials, after having considered Voncken's paper in July 1949, invited him to join an internal "working group" to study the future role of medical law, and to make proposals for "defining the rules of medical ethics in time of war."[71] It signaled the start of the WMA's campaign to contain, as much as possible, the role of international medical law, while at the same time claiming to be the sole authority for the codification of international medical ethics principles. It was a complicated balancing act which by the late 1950s was no longer sustainable, and eventually resulted in the Declaration of Helsinki in 1964.[72] While post-war efforts by medical ethicists such as Voncken to develop more robust and legally enforceable ethics principles may, in retrospect, be viewed as unsuccessful, they nonetheless reflected a broader deontological landscape in Europe which, often against the odds, tried to establish a conceptual and legal framework for the "protection of the human person" in modern medicine, several decades before a bioethics movement was on the horizon.

Conclusion

When, in May 1999, I talked to Alexander's daughter Cecily Alexander-Gable[73] at their holiday cottage on Cape Cod, Massachusetts, about what had motivated her father to spend a year away from his family and his career as a neuropsychiatrist to prosecute Nazi doctors at Nuremberg, she replied:

> He told me that he had worked on the creation of the Nuremberg Code for human experimentation and that, while there were still discussion[s] to be brought up about how to implement these rules in the Code, but that these were the basis, and that there had to be a lot of development and that people needed to really pay attention to that, that these, these things should never ever ever [sic] happen again, that's why he was at Nuremberg to see to it.[74]

Her observation brings to light the continued importance of individuals and organizations dedicated to the development and enforcement of the rule of law. It is thanks to them and their unwavering efforts over the last eighty years that fundamental violations against international laws and customs such as war crimes,

crimes against humanity, and genocide are being documented "so that no one can ever doubt that they were fact and not fable," as Taylor pointed out. Earlier, Robert Jackson had stressed that the wrongs that the IMT wanted to address had been "so calculated, so malignant, and so devastating, that civilization cannot tolerate their being ignored because it cannot survive their being repeated."[75] As we are moving into the fourth year of the Russo-Ukrainian war, in which the Russian dictator and his regime have trampled on all existing rules and customs of war, and the United States no longer appears to be committed to the international rules-based order which it helped to establish after the war, we are a long way from ensuring that those who have initiated and committed these acts will be held accountable. Only recently has Putin's regime attempted to smother even the slightest form of discontent and public criticism by ensuring that his main political rival, Alexei Navalny, met an untimely death. The civil courage shown by those who attended his funeral despite a draconian police presence can only be described as heroic. The above reflections should not only give us pause for thought, and a better understanding of existing historical precedents, but also a renewed determination to work toward international justice and the rule of law, regardless of how difficult and futile it may seem at times.

Notes

1 Research for this paper, which is part of the project "Taming the European Leviathan: The Legacy of Post-War Medicine and the Common Good," has been supported by the European Research Council under the European Union's Horizon 2020 research and innovation program (grant agreement no. 854503).

2 For a study of Leo Alexander and a discussion about the origins of the Nazi Doctors' Trial and the Nuremberg Code, see Ulf Schmidt, *Justice at Nuremberg. Leo Alexander and the Nazi Doctor's' Trial* (Basingstoke and New York: Palgrave Macmillan, 2004). Also Alexander papers, Leo Alexander to Phyllis Alexander, November 27, 1946. For a critical edition of Leo Alexander's diary and correspondence, see Ulf Schmidt, Kate Docking, Andreas Frewer, and David Peace, eds., Leo Alexander at the Nuremberg Doctors' Trial. The Nuremberg Diary and Correspondence (Stuttgart: Franz Steiner, 2025).

3 International Criminal Court press release, March 17, 2023, https://www.icc-cpi.int/news/situation-ukraine-icc-judges-issue-arrest-warrants-against-vladimir-vladimirovich-putin-and (accessed March 27, 2024).

4 Primo Levi, *The Drowned and the Saved* (London: Abacus, 1996); see also Primo Levi, *If This Is a Man and The Truce* (London: Abacus, 2001).

5 Arthur L. Caplan, "The Doctors' Trial and Analogies to the Holocaust in Contemporary Bioethical Debates," in *The Nazi Doctors and the Nuremberg Code. Human Rights in Human Experimentation*, eds. George J. Annas and Michael A. Grodin (New York and Oxford: Oxford University Press, 1992), 259–75, here 265f.

6 See Opening Statement of the Prosecution, December 9, 1946; George J. Annas and Michael A. Grodin, eds., *The Nazi Doctors and the Nuremberg Code. Human Rights in Human Experimentation* (New York and Oxford: Oxford University Press, 1992), 67–93, here 68.

7 Since the 1990s, there has been a burgeoning literature on the Nuremberg Doctors' Trial and its impact on modern biomedical ethics. For some of the literature, see George J. Annas and Michael A. Grodin, eds., *The Nazi Doctors and the Nuremberg Code. Human Rights in Human Experimentation* (New York and Oxford: Oxford University Press, 1992); Michael A. Grodin, "Historical Origins of the Nuremberg Code," in *The Nazi Doctors and the Nuremberg Code. Human Rights in Human Experimentation*, eds. George J. Annas and Michael A. Grodin (New York and Oxford: Oxford University Press, 1992), 121–44; Jürgen Peter, *Der Nürnberger Ärzteprozeß im Spiegel seiner Aufarbeitung anhand der drei Dokumentensammlungen von Alexander Mitscherlich und Fred Mielke* (Münster: Lit-Verlag, 1994); George J. Annas and Michael A. Grodin, "Medicine and Human Rights: Reflections on the Fiftieth Anniversary of the Doctors' Trial," in *Health and Human Rights*, eds. Jonathan M. Mann et al. (New York: Routledge, 1999), 301–11; Klaus Dörner and Angelika Ebbinghaus, eds., *The Nuremberg Medical Trial 1946/47. Transcripts, Material of the Prosecution and Defense, Related Documents* (Munich: K.G. Saur, 1999) Microfiche (in the following referred as: NDT-Documents); Ulf Schmidt, *Justice at Nuremberg. Leo Alexander and the Nazi Doctors' Trial* (Basingstoke and New York: Palgrave Macmillan, 2004); Ulf Schmidt, "Medical Ethics and Nazism," in *The Cambridge World History of Medical Ethics*, eds. Laurence B. McCullough and Robert Baker (Cambridge and New York: Cambridge University Press, 2009), 595–608; Ulf Schmidt and Andreas Frewer, eds., *History and Theory of Human Experimentation. The Declaration of Helsinki and Modern Medical Ethics* (Stuttgart: Franz Steiner Verlag, 2007); Jonathan D. Moreno, Ulf Schmidt, and Steve Joffe, "The Nuremberg Code Seventy Years Later," *Journal of the American Medical Association* 318 (2017): 795–6; for recent work about the history and global role of the World Medical Association's Declaration of Helsinki see Susan E. Lederer, "Research Without Borders: The Origins of the Declaration of Helsinki," in *Twentieth Century Ethics of Human Subjects Research—Historical Perspectives on Values, Practices, and Regulations*, eds. Volker Roelcke and Giovanni Maio (Stuttgart: Franz Steiner Verlag, 2004), 199–217; Ulf Schmidt, "Reflections on the Origins of the Declaration of Helsinki," in *Jahrbuch Medizinethik*, eds. Hans-Joerg Ehni and Urban Wiesing (Köln: Deutscher Ärzteverlag, 2012), 1–17; Ulf Schmidt, Andreas Frewer, and Dominque Sprumont, eds., *Ethical Research: The Declaration of Helsinki—Past, Present and Future of Human Experimentation* (Oxford and New York: Oxford University Press, 2020).

8 See, for instance, Robert F. Drinan, "The Nuremberg Principles in International Law," in *The Nazi Doctors and the Nuremberg Code. Human Rights in Human Experimentation*, eds. George J. Annas and Michael A. Grodin (New York and Oxford: Oxford University Press, 1992), 174–82.

9 Jonathan D. Moreno, Ulf Schmidt, and Steve Joffe, "The Nuremberg Code Seventy Years Later," *Journal of the American Medical Association* 318 (2017): 795–6.

10 See also Hilary Earl, "Prosecution Genocide before the Genocide Convention: Raphael Lemkin and the Nuremberg Trials, 1945–1949," *Journal of Genocide Research* 15, no. 3 (2013): 317–37, for the role of the genocide concept in the *SS-Einsatzgruppen* trial of 1947–8 in which the US prosecution charged high-ranking SS officers with crimes against humanity.

11 Alexander papers, Leo Alexander to Phyllis Alexander, December 21, 1946.

12 Alexander papers, Leo Alexander to Phyllis Alexander, December 21, 1946.
13 Alexander papers, Leo Alexander to Phyllis Alexander, November 27, 1946.
14 Alexander papers, Leo Alexander to Phyllis Alexander, November 27, 1946.
15 Alexander papers, Leo Alexander to Phyllis Alexander, November 27, 1946.
16 Duke University Medical Centre, Durham, Alexander diary (1946/47), p. 19, November 23, 1946; also Paul Weindling, *Nazi Medicine and the Nuremberg Trials. From Medical War Crimes to Informed Consent* (Basingstoke: Palgrave Macmillan, 2004), 136.
17 In March 1946, the Deputy Judge Advocate General outlined the connection between "conspiracy" and "common plan": "The legal characteristics of common design are in all material respects the same as conspiracy, as the latter is recognized in U.S. municipal criminal law, except that a previously conceived plan is not an essential element."; see Kerstin von Lingen, *Allen Dulles, the OSS, and Nazi War Criminals* (Cambridge and New York: Cambridge University Press, 2013), p. 2 (note 2).
18 Staatsarchiv Nürnberg, KV-Anklage, Interrogations, B49, Wilhelm Beiglböck, February 28, 1947.
19 Alexander papers, Leo Alexander to Phyllis Alexander, November 27, 1946; also Ulf Schmidt, *Justice at Nuremberg. Leo Alexander and the Nazi Doctors' Trial* (Basingstoke and New York: Palgrave Macmillan, 2004), 156.
20 Staatsarchiv Nürnberg, KV-Anklage, Interrogations, R128, Hans Wolfgang Romberg, February 27, 1947.
21 Staatsarchiv Nürnberg, KV-Anklage, Interrogations, F36, Fritz Fischer, December 24, 1946. For the experiments conducted at Ravensbrück concentration camp see Ulf Schmidt, "The Scars of Ravensbrück: Medical Experiments and British War Crimes Policy, 1945–1950," *German History* 23, no. 1 (2005): 20–49; Kate Docking, "Gender, Recruitment and Medicine at Ravensbrück Concentration Camp, 1939–1942," *German History* 39, no. 3 (2021): 419–41.
22 Philippe Sands, *East West Street. On the Origins of Genocide and Crimes Against Humanity* (London: Orion Publishing Group, 2017), 57–114; for Lauterpacht's role at the Nuremberg trials see Churchill College Cambridge, Churchill Archive, GBR/0014/LAUT 1/File 59–File 62.
23 Raphaël Lemkin, *Axis Rule in Occupied Europe. Laws of Occupation, Analysis of Government, Proposals for Redress* (Washington, DC: Carnegie Endowment for International Peace, 1944).
24 For the notion of genocide as the "crime of all crimes" see Nicole Rafter, *The Crime of All Crimes: Towards a Criminology of Genocide* (New York: New University Press, 2016); see also Chloe R. Edmunds, "The Crime of all Crimes: Genocide's Primacy in International Criminal Law" (MA Thesis, Georgetown University, Washington, DC, 2016).
25 Philippe Sands, *East West Street. On the Origins of Genocide and Crimes Against Humanity* (London: Orion Publishing Group, 2017), 137–89.
26 Philippe Sands, *East West Street. On the Origins of Genocide and Crimes Against Humanity* (London: Orion Publishing Group, 2017), xxi–xxx, and 57–114.
27 Alexander papers, Leo Alexander to Phyllis Alexander, November 27, 1946.
28 Duke University Medical Centre, Durham, Alexander diary (1946/47), p. 1, November 13, 1946.

29 Duke University Medical Centre, Durham, Alexander diary (1946/47), p. 1, November 13, 1946.
30 Philippe Sands, *East West Street. On the Origins of Genocide and Crimes Against Humanity* (London: Orion Publishing Group, 2017), 57–114, and 137–189.
31 Duke University Medical Centre, Durham, Alexander diary (1946/47), p. 1, November 13, 1946.
32 Duke University Medical Centre, Durham, Alexander diary (1946/47), p. 1, November 13, 1946.
33 Duke University Medical Centre, Durham, Alexander diary (1946/47), p. 1, November 13, 1946.
34 National Archives and Records Administration (NARA), RG 153/86-3-1, book 2, box 10, Alexander to Perkins, November 13, 1946.
35 National Archives and Records Administration (NARA), RG 153/86-3-1, book 2, box 10, Alexander to Cramer, November 14, 1946; Alexander to Overholser, November 14, 1946; Alexander to Taliaferro, November 14, 1946; Alexander to Rappleye, November 14, 1946; Alexander to Chesney, November 14, 1946; Alexander to Chairman, Board of Scientific Directors, Rockefeller Institute of Medical Research, November 15, 1946.
36 Duke University Medical Centre, Durham, Alexander diary (1946/47), p. 11, November 21, 1946.
37 Duke University Medical Centre, Durham, Alexander diary (1946/47), p. 32, November 27, 1946.
38 Ulf Schmidt, *Justice at Nuremberg. Leo Alexander and the Nazi Doctors' Trial* (Basingstoke and New York: Palgrave Macmillan, 2004), 165f.
39 Alexander Paper 1: The Fundamental Purpose and Meaning of the Experiments of the Experiments in Human Beings of which the Accused (Military Tribunal No. 1, Case No. 1) have been Indicted: Thanatology as a Scientific Technique of Genocide, November 30, 1946.
40 Alexander Paper 1: Thanatology as a Scientific Technique of Genocide, November 30, 1946.
41 Ulf Schmidt, Kate Docking, Andreas Frewer, and David Peace, eds., Leo Alexander at the Nuremberg Doctors' Trial. The Nuremberg Diary and Correspondence (Stuttgart: Franz Steiner, 2025).
42 Alexander Paper 2: Suggestions for a Discussion of the Thanatology Genocide Angle, December 5, 1946; Ulf Schmidt, *Justice at Nuremberg. Leo Alexander and the Nazi Doctors' Trial* (Basingstoke and New York: Palgrave Macmillan, 2004), 166f.
43 Duke University Medical Centre, Durham, Alexander diary (1946/47), p. 105, December 7, 1946.
44 Alexander papers, Leo Alexander to Phyllis Alexander, December 7, 1946.
45 George J. Annas and Michael A. Grodin, eds., *The Nazi Doctors and the Nuremberg Code. Human Rights in Human Experimentation* (New York and Oxford: Oxford University Press, 1992), 67–104.
46 George J. Annas and Michael A. Grodin, eds., *The Nazi Doctors and the Nuremberg Code. Human Rights in Human Experimentation* (New York and Oxford: Oxford University Press, 1992), 68.
47 George J. Annas and Michael A. Grodin, eds., *The Nazi Doctors and the Nuremberg Code. Human Rights in Human Experimentation* (New York and Oxford: Oxford University Press, 1992), 70f.

48 George J. Annas and Michael A. Grodin, eds., *The Nazi Doctors and the Nuremberg Code. Human Rights in Human Experimentation* (New York and Oxford: Oxford University Press, 1992), 89.
49 George J. Annas and Michael A. Grodin, eds., *The Nazi Doctors and the Nuremberg Code. Human Rights in Human Experimentation* (New York and Oxford: Oxford University Press, 1992), 89.
50 Alice Platen-Hallermund, *Die Tötung Geisteskranker in Deutschland* (Frankfurt: Psychiatrie-Verlag, [1948] 1998). Reprint; Alexander Mitscherlich and Fred Mielke, eds., *Das Diktat der Menschenverachtung. Der Nürnberger Ärzteprozeß und seine Quellen* (Heidelberg: Lambert Schneider, 1947); Alexander Mitscherlich and Fred Mielke, eds., *Medizin ohne Menschlichkeit* (Frankfurt: Fischer Verlag, 1960).
51 Duke University Medical Centre, Durham, Alexander diary (1946/47), p. 79, December 3, 1946.
52 See also Saul Friedländer, *The Years of Extermination. Nazi Germany and the Jews, 1939–1945* (London: Weidenfeld & Nicolson, 2007).
53 Duke University Medical Centre, Durham, Alexander diary (1946/47), p. 79, December 3, 1946.
54 George J. Annas and Michael A. Grodin, eds., *The Nazi Doctors and the Nuremberg Code. Human Rights in Human Experimentation* (New York and Oxford: Oxford University Press, 1992), 92.
55 For Leibbrand's testimony see Ulf Schmidt, *Justice at Nuremberg. Leo Alexander and the Nazi Doctors' Trial* (Basingstoke and New York: Palgrave Macmillan, 2004), 205–8; also Andreas Frewer, ed., *Psychiatrie und „Euthanasie" in der HUPFLA. Debatten zu Werner Leibbrands Buch "Um die Menschrechte der Geisteskranken"* (Erlangen-Nürnberg: Verlag Ph.C.W. Schmidt, 2020); Andreas Frewer, *Werner Leibbrand: Leben—Weiterleben—Überleben* (Stuttgart: Franz Steiner, 2021).
56 NDT-Documents and Material, fiche 303, frames 1803.
57 NDT-Documents and Material, fiche 303, frames 1802–1804.
58 NDT-Documents and Material, fiche 303, frames 1802; see also Levi 1996, p.x.
59 NDT-Documents and Material, fiche 303, frames 1803.
60 Jon M. Harkness, "Nuremberg and the Issue of Wartime Experiments on US Prisoners. The Green Committee," *Journal of the American Medical Association* 276, no. 20 (1996): 1672–5; for human experiments conducted by the United States and the United Kingdom during the Cold War see Jonathan D. Moreno, *Undue Risk. Secret State Experiments on Humans* (New York: W.H. Freeman, 1999); Susan M. Reverby, "'Normal Exposure' and Inoculation Syphilis: A PHS 'Tuskegee' Doctor in Guatemala, 1946–1948," *The Journal of Policy History* 23, no. 1 (2011): 6–28; *Presidential Commission for the Study of Bioethical Issues, Ethically Impossible. STD Research in Guatemala from 1946 to 1948* (Washington, DC: Presidential Commission for the Study of Bioethical Issues, 2011), https://bioethicsarchive.georgetown.edu/pcsbi/node/654.html (accessed March 27, 2024); Ulf Schmidt, *Secret Science: A Century of Poison Warfare and Human Experiments* (Oxford and New York: Oxford University Press, 2015).
61 Duke University Medical Centre, Durham, Alexander diary (1946/47), p. 79, December 3, 1946.
62 Jay Katz, "The Nuremberg Code and the Nuremberg Trial: A Reappraisal," *Journal of the American Medical Association* 276, no. 20 (1996): 1662–6, here 1662; Jay

Katz, "The Consent Principle of the Nuremberg Code: Its Significance Then and Now," in *The Nazi Doctors and the Nuremberg Code. Human Rights in Human Experimentation*, eds. George J. Annas and Michael A. Grodin (New York and Oxford: Oxford University Press, 1992), 227–39.

63 For the history of Japanese human experiments and the Tokyo trial, see Peter Williams and David Wallace, *Unit 731: Japan's Secret Biological Warfare in World War II* (New York: Free Press, 1989); Till Bärnighausen, "Communicating 'Tainted Science': The Japanese Biological Warfare Experiments on Human Subjects in China," in *History and Theory of Human Experimentation. The Declaration of Helsinki and Modern Medical Ethics*, eds. Ulf Schmidt and Andreas Frewer (Stuttgart: Franz Steiner Verlag, 2007), 117–42. Jing-Bao Nie, Nanyan Guo, Mark Selden and Arthur Kleinman, eds., *Japan's Wartime Medical Atrocities: Comparative Inquiries in Science, History, and Ethics* (London and New York: Routledge, 2010); Mark Felton, *The Devil's Doctors. Japanese Human Experiments on Allied Prisoners of War* (Barnsley: Pen & Sword Military, 2012); Jeanne Guillemin, *Hidden Atrocities: Japanese Germ Warfare and American Obstruction of Justice at the Tokyo Trial* (New York: Columbia University Press, 2017); for the Khabarovsk trial, see Soviet Army Primorsky Military District, Military Court and Otozō Yamada [defendant] ("Khabarovsk War Crime Trials"), *Materials on the Trial of Former Servicemen of the Japanese Army charged with Manufacturing and Employing Bacteriological Weapons* (Moscow: Foreign Languages Publishing House, 1950); for the Ravensbrück trial, see Ulf Schmidt, "The Scars of Ravensbrück: Medical Experiments and British War Crimes Policy, 1945–1950," *German History* 23, no. 1 (2005): 20–49; for the Struthof Medical Trial, see Christian Bonah and Florian Schmaltz, "From Nuremberg to Helsinki: The Preparation of the Declaration of Helsinki in the Light of the Prosecution of Medical War Crimes at the Struthof Medical Trials, France, 1952–4," in *Ethical Research: The Declaration of Helsinki—Past, Present and Future of Human Experimentation*, eds. Ulf Schmidt, Andreas Frewer, and Dominique Sprumont (Oxford and New York: Oxford University Press, 2020), 69–100.

64 AICRC, B AG 045-001, General Correspondence, Axelroude 1959, p. 5; "Je ne veux pas dire que si nos travaux de 1934 avaient trouvé une consécration plus immédiate, il n'y aurait pas eu d'atrocités pendant la guerre 1939–45, mais on ne peut que constater que des retards bien regrettables ont été apportés à l'édification d'un traité international qui aurait quand même été une sauvegarde pour les peuples et les nations soumises aux horreurs de la guerre."

65 Jules Voncken, "Pour créer un Droit International Médical," *Bulletin International des Services de Santé des Armées de Terre, de Mer et de l'Air* 3, no. 4 (1949): 57–74, here 61.

66 Proctor, Nazi War on Cancer, p. 7.

67 Jules Voncken, "Pour créer un Droit International Médical," *Bulletin International des Services de Santé des Armées de Terre, de Mer et de l'Air* 3, no. 4 (1949): 57–74, here 61.

68 Jules Voncken, "Pour créer un Droit International Médical," *Bulletin International des Services de Santé des Armées de Terre, de Mer et de l'Air* 3, no. 4 (1949): 57–74, here 63.

69 Jules Voncken, "Pour créer un Droit International Médical," *Bulletin International des Services de Santé des Armées de Terre, de Mer et de l'Air* 3, no. 4 (1949): 57–74, here 65; see also Hilary Earl, "Prosecution Genocide before the Genocide Convention: Raphael Lemkin and the Nuremberg Trials, 1945–1949," *Journal of Genocide Research* 15, no. 3 (2013): 317–37.

70 Robert F. Drinan, "The Nuremberg Principles in International Law," in *The Nazi Doctors and the Nuremberg Code. Human Rights in Human Experimentation*, eds. George J. Annas and Michael A. Grodin (New York and Oxford: Oxford University Press, 1992), 174–82, here 176f; George J. Annas and Michael A. Grodin, eds., *The Nazi Doctors and the Nuremberg Code. Human Rights in Human Experimentation* (New York and Oxford: Oxford University Press, 1992), 307–14, here 312ff; George J. Annas, and Michael A. Grodin, "Medicine and Human Rights: Reflections on the Fiftieth Anniversary of the Doctors' Trial," in *Health and Human Rights*, eds. Jonathan M. Mann et al. (New York: Routledge, 1999), 301–11, here 307f.

71 Anonymous, "In Memory of Physician General Voncken," *International Review of the Red Cross* 176 (1975): 580–1.

72 Ulf Schmidt, Andreas Frewer and Dominque Sprumont, eds., *Ethical Research: The Declaration of Helsinki—Past, Present and Future of Human Experimentation* (Oxford and New York: Oxford University Press, 2020), 101–30, here 102ff; see also Christian Bonah and Florian Schmaltz, "From Nuremberg to Helsinki: The Preparation of the Declaration of Helsinki in the Light of the Prosecution of Medical War Crimes at the Struthof Medical Trials, France, 1952–4," in *Ethical Research: The Declaration of Helsinki—Past, Present and Future of Human Experimentation*, eds. Ulf Schmidt, Andreas Frewer, and Dominique Sprumont (Oxford and New York: Oxford University Press, 2020), 69–100.

73 Cecily Kate Alexander-Grable (November 23, 1938–January 7, 2024).

74 Interview by author with Cecily Alexander-Grable, May 1999. The interview was conducted as part of the authors' work on *Justice at Nuremberg. Leo Alexander and the Nazi Doctors' Trial* (2004).

75 George J. Annas and Michael A. Grodin, eds., *The Nazi Doctors and the Nuremberg Code. Human Rights in Human Experimentation* (New York and Oxford: Oxford University Press, 1992), 68.

Selected Bibliography

Grodin, Annas, and Michael A. Grodin (eds.)., *The Nazi Doctors and the Nuremberg Code. Human Rights in Human Experimentation* (New York and Oxford: Oxford University Press, 1992).

Moreno, Jonathan D., Ulf Schmidt, and Steve Joffe, "The Nuremberg Code Seventy Years Later," *Journal of the American Medical Association* 318 (2017): 795–6.

Schmidt, Ulf, *Justice at Nuremberg. Leo Alexander and the Nazi Doctors' Trial* (Basingstoke and New York: Palgrave Macmillan, 2004).

Schmidt, Ulf, and Karl Brandt, *The Nazi Doctor. Medicine and Power in the Third Reich* (London and New York: Hambledon Continuum, 2007).

Schmidt, Ulf, Kate Docking, Andreas Frewer, and David Peace (eds.), *Leo Alexander and the Nuremberg Doctors' Trial* (Stuttgart: Franz Steiner, 2024/2025, forthcoming).

Schmidt, Ulf, Kate Docking, Andreas Frewer, and David Peace eds., Leo Alexander at the Nuremberg Doctors' Trial. The Nuremberg Diary and Correspondence (Stuttgart: Franz Steiner, 2025).

7

The Judges' Trials

The Lawlessness of the Rule of Law

Christoph Safferling

The German judiciary had failed. Instead of putting the law against injustice, instead of protecting minorities against state arbitrariness, most lawyers acted as supporters of the Nazi regime. In the Reich Ministry of Justice (RMJ), laws were prepared to suppress entire sections of the population, draconian punishments were devised to protect the Führer and the party, the resolutions of the Wannsee Conference were implemented, judicial sentences that were deemed too lenient were "corrected" with the help of the Gestapo,[1] and opponents of the regime were subjected to "extermination through labor." The judiciary persecuted the victims and protected the perpetrators, supported the secret proceedings of the "Nacht und Nebel" (Night and Fog) decree, and exacerbated the hardships of the war years through judicial terror. It was an integral part of the system to pass traditional sentences against "normal people's comrades" for "normal criminality"; people who were not supposed to be part of the "people's community," on the other hand, were treated brutally. The judiciary thus proved to be one of the effective selection structures of the Nazi national community. This is not to deny that some lawyers in the traditional justice system tried to uphold the rule of law and pass just verdicts.[2]

However, it was precisely the young careerists, spurred on by the academic teachings of unscrupulous law professors, for example, from the Kiel School,[3] who preached Hitler's will and National Socialist ideology as the ultimate standard for interpreting the law, who brought about the implementation of judicial terror in critical positions in the Reich Ministry of Justice or the People's Court, the Reich Court Martial, special courts and more.[4]

The Legal Process

The temple of German justice had been disgracefully destroyed and had to be cleansed and reconsecrated, as the chief prosecutor of the USA, Telford Taylor, put it in his opening statement.[5] The Allies initially took on this task. In the main war crimes trial, which is known to be the first international criminal trial, the so-called Nuremberg Trial of 1945/46 before the International Military Tribunal (IMT), some lawyers, such as Ernst Kaltenbrunner, Rudolf Hess, and Hans Frank, founder and until 1942 president of the Academy of German Law, were also indicted, but not for legal activities, but as influential politicians in the Nazi regime, co-responsible for the war of aggression, criminal warfare, and massive human rights violations. [6]

On the basis of Control Council Law No. 10 of December 16, 1945, the US occupying power held a total of twelve so-called follow-up trials before American military tribunals in Nuremberg following the main war crimes trial. These trials were intended to focus on individual professional groups and Nazi government authorities in order to prove and prosecute the involvement of the entire German elite in aggression, war crimes, and crimes against humanity.

The third of these trials was the so-called Nuremberg Lawyers' Trial, "USA vs. Josef Altstötter et al.," as the trial was officially called.[7] The defendants were a total of thirteen Nazi lawyers[8] and one lay judge at the People's Court.[9] Eight of them were employees of the Reich Ministry of Justice, four judges, and two public prosecutors. It was, therefore, a trial against judicial lawyers and representatives of the ministerial bureaucracy. The most prominent defendant was Franz Schlegelberger, state secretary in the Reich Ministry of Justice under Franz Gürtner and, after his death on January 29, 1941, acting head of the Ministry until the appointment of the previous president of the People's Court, Otto Georg Thierack, as minister of justice on August 20, 1942. Schlegelberger's successor as state secretary and Thierack's right-hand man, Herbert Klemm, was also in the dock.[10]

On the basis of Control Council Law No. 10, the US chief prosecutor, Telford Taylor, charged the lawyers with war crimes and crimes against humanity. While under German law, judicial activity is privileged due to the independence of judges, and, according to the case law of the German Federal Court of Justice, judges can only be prosecuted for the offense of obstruction of justice (today Section 339 German Criminal Code),[11] the lawyers were held responsible here solely for the result of their actions: The mass killing of opponents of the regime, the destruction of supposedly unworthy lives of the mentally ill and physically disabled, as well as the persecution and sentencing of people solely on the basis of racial descent. The tribunal summarized the defendants' responsibility in the sentence: The dagger of the assassin was concealed beneath the jurist's robe.[12] Lawyers clothed serious crimes in the appearance of legality.

The Indictment

Brigadier General Telford Taylor (February 24, 1908–May 21, 1998) was the chief prosecutor for all Nuremberg Military Tribunals (NMT) proceedings. His deputy, Charles La Follette (February 27, 1898–June 27, 1974), prepared the indictment. According to Article II CCL 10, three crimes could be prosecuted: Crimes against peace, war crimes, and crimes against humanity.

Article II. 1 Each of the following offenses constitutes a crime:

a) Crimes against peace. The enterprise of invading other countries and waging aggressive war in violation of international law and international treaties, including but not limited to the following examples: planning, preparing, launching, or waging a war of aggression or war in violation of international treaties, agreements, or assurances; participating in a common plan or conspiracy for the purpose of executing any of the above crimes.
b) War Crimes. Acts of violence or offenses against life, limb or property committed in violation of the laws or customs of war, including but not limited to the following examples: Murder, ill-treatment of the civilian population of occupied territories or their deportation for forced labor or other purposes; murder or ill-treatment of prisoners of war or persons on the high seas; killing of hostages; plunder of public or private property; wanton destruction of town or country or devastation not justified by military necessity.
c) Crimes against humanity. Acts of violence and offenses, including but not limited to the following examples: Murder, extermination, enslavement; enforced disappearance, deprivation of liberty, torture, rape or other inhumane acts committed against a civilian population; persecution on political, racial or religious grounds, regardless of whether they violate the national law of the country in which the act was committed.
d) Membership of certain categories of criminal organizations or organizations whose criminal character has been established by the International Military Tribunal.

The prosecution endeavored to show that the defendants had participated in the conspiracy to commit war crimes and crimes against humanity (count I). However, the conspiracy charge was only applied to the war of aggression, in line with the verdict in the IMT trial, and was otherwise rejected by the NMT in case 3 as too vague and indeterminate.[13] However, in addition to the war of aggression, war crimes (count II) and crimes against humanity (count III) could be charged. Furthermore, seven of the defendants were accused of being members of the SS, which had been condemned as a criminal organization by the IMT (count IV).

The concept of war crimes was comparatively clear in legal terms. This was generally about crimes committed against the civilian population by the German occupying power in the occupied territory. Based on the Hague Land Warfare Convention (1907) and the Geneva Conventions (1929), the occupying power is responsible for public safety and order. However, he may not change the existing civil laws in the occupied territory. The implementation of racist terror laws by the National Socialists, therefore, already violated this principle of international law of war.[14]

The still-young model of crimes against humanity, which had only been applied by the IMT in connection with an armed conflict, emancipated itself from this war requirement in the subsequent trials. It was applied above all to facts that occurred before the start of the war on September 1, 1939, and to acts that were directed against the German population. Normally, international law may not interfere in domestic affairs. This is not the case with crimes against humanity. Telford Taylor clearly expressed this in the proceedings against Flick:

> This [meaning crimes against humanity, CS] constitutes an explicit recognition that acts committed by Germans against other Germans are punishable as crimes under Law No. 10.[15]

The legitimacy for this lies in the systematic nature and the mass of human rights violations, which shock the conscience of humanity as such and violate the "United Nations'" common "standard of civilization."[16] Since international law is involved in this respect, the defendants' reference to the fact that they merely applied German law cannot excuse them. This is not about German law. It is about international law that has been violated.[17]

General Legal Principles

In a general section, the Tribunal identified seven issues that were examined to determine whether they constituted crimes under international criminal law:

(1) cases against habitual criminals.
(2) cases of looting in the devastated areas of Germany; committed after air raids and under cover of black-out.
(3) crimes against the war economy-rationing, hoarding, and the like.
(4) crimes amounting to an undermining of the defensive strength of the nation, defeatist remarks, criticisms of Hitler, and the like.
(5) Crimes of treason and high treason.
(6) crimes of various types committed by Poles, Jews, and other foreigners.
(7) crimes committed under the Nacht und Nebel program, and similar procedures.[18]

Only points 5, 6, and 7 were declared criminal. This included the entire persecution legislation, that is, legislation that was implemented solely for reasons of racial discrimination. This also included the eleventh Ordinance to the Reich Citizenship Act, which legalized the expropriation of Jews by the Gestapo, the SD, the tax authorities, or even competitors of Jewish entrepreneurs.[19] The Ordinance on the Administration of Criminal Law against Poles and Jews in the Incorporated Eastern Territories of December 4, 1941, known as the Polish and Jewish Special Criminal Law Ordinance,[20] based on which 61,836 convictions were handed down in 1942 alone, according to the NMT, was also serious. The government program "Correction of Inadequate Judgments",[21] which had been agreed upon between Thierack, Himmler, Bormann, Rothenberger, and others on September 18, 1942, was also declared criminal.[22] According to this program, convicts were handed over to the Gestapo for further "treatment" after the RMJ had reviewed their sentences.[23] The defendants claimed that they had not known what would happen to these people at the hands of the Gestapo or in concentration camps.[24] This plea was answered by the tribunal in general terms:

> This Tribunal is not so gullible as to believe these defendants so stupid that they did not know what was going on. One man can keep a secret, two men may, but thousands, never.[25]

Incidentally, we will see later that the Federal German judiciary in the late 1960s judged precisely this point differently. For example, the proceedings against the former personal assistant to Franz Schlegelberger and Otto Thierack and later senior civil servant ("Ministerialrat") in the Federal Ministry of Justice, Heinrich Ebersberg, were dropped. He was responsible in the RMJ for preparing the decisions on "correction." Nevertheless, the public prosecutor's office did not believe in having had sufficient evidence to prove that he knew that the term "extermination through labor" referred to physical extermination. [26]

The NMT also dealt intensively with the Law for the Prevention of Offspring with Hereditary Diseases (Hereditary Health Law) and the system of forced sterilization and hereditary health courts based on it.[27]

Central to this, however, was the so-called Nacht- und Nebel-Erlass of December 7, 1941, which had already been declared criminal by the IMT.[28] Based on this so-called NN decree, alleged opponents of the regime were arrested in the occupied territories and deported to concentration camps in the German Reich, especially the SS-camp Hinzert (in Hunsrück) and the Esterwegen concentration camp (in Emsland), and tried in secret proceedings. The relatives were denied any information about the whereabouts of the victims; they remained missing.[29] The decree was enacted on December 7, 1941, as secret "Guidelines for the Prosecution of Crimes against the Reich or the Occupying Power in Occupied Territories" by the OKW (Oberkommando der Wehrmacht - Military High Command) under Wilhelm Keitel, who had been sentenced to death in the main war crimes trial.[30]

However, no crimes against humanity could be established in points 1–4, even though the judges condemned the draconian laws and punishments and expressed their disgust.[31] This includes, in particular, war-related legislation, such as the Special Criminal Law Ordinance of 1938[32] and the Ordinance against Social Parasites.[33] The 1934 Treachery Act[34] to punish any form of criticism of the Nazi regime was also included in this category. The NMT judges did find the measures against the decomposition of military power outrageous. Nevertheless, the measures to restrict freedom of expression, for example, were not classified as punishable.[35]

Similarly, no crime against humanity was seen in the 1933 Habitual Offender Act.[36] The judges reasoned that what was permitted in the USA in peacetime could not be described as criminal in Germany during wartime.[37] While the tribunal accepted harsh laws and excessive punishment, the American judges found these laws uneven and discriminatory application intolerable. Nevertheless, as a result, crimes against humanity were denied to the defendants:

> All of the laws to which we have referred could be and were applied in a discriminatory manner, and in the case of many, the Ministry of Justice and the courts enforced them by arbitrary and brutal means, shocking to the conscience of mankind and punishable here. We merely hold that under the particular facts of this case we cannot convict any defendant merely because of the fact, without more, that laws of the first four types were passed or enforced.[38]

For the other measures, however, which were obviously introduced solely for the purpose of discrimination, the criminal nature was clear to the judges; only the individual responsibility of each defendant had to be established:

> The pattern and plan of racial persecution has been made clear. General knowledge of the broad outlines thereof in all its immensity has been brought home to the defendants. The remaining question is whether or not the evidence proves beyond a reasonable doubt in the case of the individual defendants that they each consciously participated in the plan or took a consenting part therein.[39]

Justifying this attribution between the legislative measures on the one hand and the defendants on the other was more accessible for the lawyers at the RMJ than for the lawyers working as prosecutors and judges.

The Process

The trial against the fourteen defendants lasted from March 6 to October 13, 1947. One hundred eighty-three witnesses were heard, the prosecution presented 641 documents, and 1,452 by the defense. The verdict was announced on December 3 and 4, 1947: four life sentences, six suspended sentences, and four acquittals made for a comparatively lenient verdict. The lawyers did not receive the same severity as the doctors (case No. 1), the generals (case Nos. 2, 12), or the members of the Einsatzgruppen (case No. 10). Those who concealed the murderer's dagger under their robes were not punished "as murderers." The verdict was in line with the weakening interest of the US government in further criminal prosecution, which was also documented in the Ministries Trial (case No. 11) and in the trials against the industrialists (IG Farben, Krupp, Flick). The trials found little support among the American population. Recruiting personnel for the prosecution and the bench became increasingly difficult. Financial resources were reduced.

This structural weakness of the prosecution in the subsequent trials was exploited by an intellectually very capable team of German defense lawyers, whose experience in dealing with war crimes was also constantly growing. As a result, the Nuremberg trials laid the foundations for the German elite's narrative of exculpation. For the lawyers, this defense strategy can be summarized in four points: (1) They had remained "decent" despite the terror. (2) They had known nothing of the madness of systematic persecution and extermination. (3) They could also have given way, but then real perpetrators of conviction would have come to power, so they had "prevented worse things" by persevering. (4) After all, they had only applied the applicable laws and had no choice, for example, to demand the death penalty as prosecutors and impose it as judges. These strategies can be illustrated by the case of the most senior defendant in the lawyers with trial.

The Schlegelberger Case

Franz Schlegelberger, born on October 23, 1876, in Königsberg in Prussia, enjoyed a distinguished judicial career after studying law in Königsberg and Berlin. From 1914, he was promoted to the highest class of judges in Berlin and then moved to the Reichsjustizamt, the forerunner of the Reich Ministry of Justice, in 1918. In 1927, he became Ministerial Director in the Reich Ministry of Justice. From 1922, he also held an honorary professorship at the Faculty of Law in Berlin. On October 10, 1931, Schlegelberger became state secretary in the RMJ under Justice Minister Franz Gürtner. From 1934, Roland Freisler, later president of the People's Court, was his colleague as state secretary. Unlike Freisler, Schlegelberger was not initially a member of the NSDAP. It was not until 1938 that he was admitted to the party by Hitler's decree. After the death of Franz Gürtner, he temporarily headed the RMJ until the appointment of the former president of the People's Court, Otto Thierack, as the new minister of justice. Schlegelberger left the RMJ on August 24, 1942, and received a gift of 100,000 Reichsmark from Adolf Hitler.

When Otto Thierack and the new state secretary in the RMJ, Curt Rothenberger, took over the ministry, the judiciary's independence in Germany finally ended.[40] In this respect, Franz Schlegelberger was not so wrong, as the American military tribunal in Nuremberg also stated, when he pointed out that after his departure, real National Socialist criminals of conviction took over power in the Reich Ministry of Justice. In his defense, he argued that he had resisted the constant pressure on the judiciary from Himmler and other advocates of the police state.[41] Although the NMT described this defense argument as "plausible" in principle, on closer analysis, it is not at all consistent with the truth, logic, or circumstances. Schlegelberger had come to terms with the system and played along in the new political structures. As a member of the Academy of German Law, he naturally also represented the "new line" of jurisprudence. His support for the regime is particularly evident in his involvement in Action T 4, "Destruction of unworthy life," and the apparent legalization of euthanasia murders. He was also involved in the action to "correct judicial sentences," according to which the convicts were handed over to the Gestapo for execution, which resulted in certain deaths.[42]

The Nuremberg judges went on to say:

> . . . [t]hat Schlegelberger supported the pretension of Hitler in his assumption of power to deal with life and death in disregard of even the pretense of judicial process. By his exhortations and directives, Schlegelberger contributed to

> the destruction of judicial independence. It was his signature on the decree of February 7, 1942, which imposed upon the Ministry of Justice and the courts the burden of the prosecution, trial, and disposal of the victims of Hitler's Night and Fog. For this, he must be charged with primary responsibility. He was guilty of instituting and supporting procedures for the wholesale persecution of Jews and Poles. Concerning Jews, his ideas were less brutal than those of his associates, but they can scarcely be called humane.[43]

The fact that Schlegelberger wanted to give the "half-Jews" the choice of infertility or deportation shows an attempt to save them from deportation to the extermination camps in the East. However, this suggestion, mentioned in a letter to Lammers dated April 5, 1942,[44] only serves to illustrate Schlegelberger's involvement in the system in a macabre way.

Franz Schlegelberger may be regarded as a "tragic figure" by the highly sympathetic American judges. However, the trial for his creeping concessions to the Nazi regime also brought tremendous guilt upon him. The Nuremberg judges sentenced him to life imprisonment for war crimes and crimes against humanity. Schlegelberger was released from the Landsberg war crimes prison as early as 1951 due to incapacity. He received a state secretary's pension, which led to further lengthy legal proceedings.[45] He subsequently worked diligently as a commentator on the German Civil Code and the Code of Commercial Law.[46] He died on December 14, 1970, in Flensburg.

Franz Schlegelberger was not a radical National Socialist. On the day the Nazis seized power, he had already reached the top rung of the career ladder and came to terms with the new regime. In the almost ten years that followed until his retirement in 1942, he was drawn ever deeper into the maelstrom of Nazi politics. He had undoubtedly not "remained decent." The Poles and Jews Special Criminal Law Ordinance and the Night and Fog Decree alone contained massive discrimination and inhumane procedures that a lawyer could simply not support. The fact that things got even worse after his early retirement in no way exculpates Schlegelberger.

Reception in the Federal Republic of Germany

In the Federal Republic of Germany, the legal judgment tended to be ignored. Attempts by the occupying power to disseminate the German text of the judgment to the German population[47] were not particularly successful.[48] Reception of the judgment only began late. A new attempt to deal with the legal judgment was only made in 1996 with the publication of the text of the judgment by Lore Maria Peschel-Gutzeit.[49]

Prosecution in the Federal Republic of Germany was blind to the legal judgment. As an occupation law, Control Council Law No. 10 could only be applied by German courts in the British and French occupation zones.[50] Efforts were also quickly made in the Bonn Republic to finally repeal this law, which was frowned upon as a shameful occupation law.[51] The responsibility of lawyers for the murderer's dagger concealed under the robe was only prosecuted under the German Criminal Code and thus only on the basis of obstruction of justice. In addition, the German Federal Court of Justice developed an intensely subjective interpretation of obstruction of justice, according to which a judge can only be prosecuted if he also positively knows that he is violating the law. If, on the other hand, the judge believes that he is complying with the law, he could not be declared guilty. As a result, not a single judge was finally convicted for his activities during the Nazi era, and—as far as can be seen—only a single public prosecutor. This jurisdiction was particularly dramatic in the case of the People's Court judge Rehse and in the case of Thorbeck and Huppenkothen, who, as judges and prosecutors of the SS Standgericht trial, handed over Dietrich Bonhoeffer, Wilhelm Canaris, Hans von Dohnanyi, and others to be hanged in the Flossenbürg concentration camp on April 18, 1945, only days before the liberation of the camp. In the end, only Huppenkothen was sentenced due to a technicality. He should have had the death sentence confirmed by the court's master, which was the final accusation. In this intolerable German Federal Court of Justice ruling, the SS court was recognized as a legal procedure. It is no coincidence that the verdict remained unpublished for a long time, leading to a late public apology by the then president of the German Federal Court of Justice, Günter Hirsch, in 2004.[52]

Reception in the GDR

The situation was different in the GDR, where the verdict was reprinted and used for propaganda purposes. It was an interesting process because, after all, the lawyers' trial was a trial under the responsibility of the American enemy. However, the reprinting fitted in with the general attack on the German "blood lawyers" who were once again active in the Federal Republic's judiciary and the Bonn ministries after 1949.

In the introduction to the publication of the verdict in case 3 (lawyers' trial) from 1969, P.A. Steiniger also writes that the verdict was far too lenient.[53] It is also interesting to note the justification of the right of occupation as a "peace-bringing occupation," which was not based on the "imperialist international law overthrown by the peoples," but on the rights of the victims of aggression. However, it is then explained that the USA ultimately missed the moral opportunity of denazification. On the contrary, the emergence of an "imperialist separate state" was tolerated and promoted.

The commentator Steininger supports the extension of the forms of participation to include the model of "conspiracy." The IMT had only recognized this for aggressive war. This was a mistake. "By using the usual forms of participation, the criminal courts cannot do justice to the specific nature of this criminal phenomenon." Night and Fog Decree demonstrates this perfidious collaboration between the OKW, the Ministry of Justice, and the Gestapo.

The NMT was accused of lacking courage because the judges had refrained from criminalizing draconian punishments alone. The GDR commentator considers this judicial leniency to be unjustifiable.

The further development of the criminal prosecution of lawyers in West Germany was virtually ridiculed in the GDR. Only crimes against humanity could have led to a just verdict here. The efforts of the West Berlin judiciary against, for example, the former People's Court judge Hans-Joachim Rehse had been measured solely against the offense of obstruction of justice in a serious misjudgment of these international requirements and reduced to absurdity.[54] In retrospect, the German Federal Court of Justice in West Germany had thus also acquitted Freisler.

At the end of the 1960s, however, the commentator sees a development toward a new fascist state in the Federal Republic: the emergency constitution, the criminal law, the presumption of sole representation, and revanchist blackmail are nothing more than renewed preparations for aggression, which the legal verdict has clearly rejected. Indeed, these statements are based on the Cold War rhetoric from the Eastern Bloc's perspective. However, there is more than a grain of truth in the facts mentioned.

Conclusion

The lawyers' trial used the historic opportunity to measure the actions of the lawyers by the result itself and not just by the process in the context of the "bending of the law." Condemning systematic discrimination through laws and jurisprudence as a crime against humanity was the right response to international law. On the other hand, judicial terror, which manifested itself in an exuberant criminal law for the protection of the state, draconian punishments for recurrence, and the alleged protection of war aims, was precisely not regarded as criminal. This gave the lawyers arguments for their exculpation, which they gratefully accepted.[55] In fact, particularly in the area of political criminal law and the emergency constitution in the Federal Ministry of Justice, former Nazi lawyers resorted to similar means as before 1945.

Therefore, the lawyers' trial is perfectly suitable as an initial approach to evaluating legal activity under National Socialism, as it identifies criminal acts. However, one must not fall into the trap of concluding that acts below this standard can be regarded as justified or tolerable. Instead, the ruling is based on a high degree of collegial understanding on the part of the bench and is characterized by the fear of delegitimizing harsh punitive measures at home in the USA by condemning Nazi lawyers.

Notes

1 The program was called: "Correction of Inadequate Judgments," cf. order of discontinuation by the public prosecutor's office in Cologne of October 30, 1970—24 Js 88/68. Cf. also Gerhard Werle, *Justiz-Strafrecht und polizeiliche Verbrechensbekämpfung im Dritten Reich* (Berlin: De Gruyter, 1989), 599–602.

2 This is demonstrated by the work of Karl Scheib for the Ulm district court district, cf. Karl Scheib, *Justiz unterm Hakenkreuz: Strafjustiz im Nationalsozialismus bei der Staatsanwaltschaft Ulm und den Gerichten im Landesgerichtsbezirk Ulm* (Münster: Klemm + Oelschläger, 2012).

3 About the Kiel School: Christina Wiener, *Kieler Fakultät und "Kieler Schule": Die Rechtslehrer an der Rechts- und Staatswissenschaftlichen Fakultät zu Kiel in der Zeit des Nationalsozialismus und ihre Entnazifizierung* (Baden-Baden: Nomos, 2013). For a contemporary account cf. Friedrich Dahm (ed.), *Grundfragen der neuen Rechtswissenschaft* (Berlin: Junker & Dünnhaupt, 1935).
4 For a more detailed analysis in German, see: Manfred Görtemaker and Christoph Safferling, *Die Akte Rosenburg. Das Bundesjustizministerium und die NS-Zeit,* (Munich: C.H. Beck, 2016) 44–63 as well as Friedrich Kießling and Christoph Safferling, *Staatsschutz im kalten Krieg*, (Munich: dtv Verlagsgesellschaft, 2021), 82–100.
5 These were the introductory words of the chief prosecutor, Telford Taylor, in the opening statement of the jury trial. NMT III, 34.
6 Ernst Kaltenbrunner and Hans Frank were sentenced to death, Rudolf Hess to life imprisonment.
7 In this case, the naming in the US tradition follows the alphabetical order of surnames. Josef Altstötter was Ministerial Director and Head of the Department for Civil Law at the RMJ.
8 The original co-defendant Carl Westphal, formerly Ministerialrat in the RMJ, committed suicide while in custody in Nuremberg. The defendant Karl Engert, SS-Oberführer, who was vice president of the People's Court and subsequently transferred to the RMJ as head of the Secret Special Department XV, was declared unfit to stand trial due to illness. He died in 1951; cf. NMT III, 3.
9 The defendant Hans Petersen, who was, however, acquitted.
10 Thus, the statement by Schafheutle about Klemm in: Bundesministerium der Justiz, *Strafvollzug und gnadenerweise an als Kriegsverbrecher verurteilten Deutschen in Gefängnissen der Besatzungsmächte und des übrigen Auslandes: Einzelelsachen: Strafsache gegen Herbert Klemm* (Landsberg) Vol. 1, B141/27019, 9250/5E (5), 14.
11 On this so-called blocking effect, see Thomas Vormbaum, "Die strafrechtliche Aufarbeitung der nationalsozialistischen Justizverbrechen in der Nachkriegszeit," in *Die Rosenburg. Das Bundesministerium der Justiz und die NS-Vergangenheit—Eine Bestandsaufnahme,* eds. Manfred Görtemaker and Christoph Safferling (Göttingen: Vandenhoeck & Ruprecht, 2013), 142, 155, 157 et seq, 168; or, also in current commentaries: Detlev Schmedding, Section 339, in *Gesamtes Strafrecht. Handkommentar,* eds. Dieter Dölling et al., 2nd ed. (Baden-Baden: Nomos, 2011), para. 11.
12 NMT III, 985.
13 NMT III, 956; on the concept of conspiracy, see Christoph Safferling, "Die Strafbarkeit wegen 'Conspiracy' in Nürnberg und ihre Bedeutung für die Gegenwart," in: 93 *Kritische Vierteljahresschrift für Gesetzgebung und Rechtswissenschaft*, Vol. 93, cf. above (2010): 65–82.
14 Cf. NMT III, 1076 et seq.
15 Cf. NMT III, 973.
16 On this, Christiane Wilke, "Case 3: Jurists on Trial, Law on Trial and the Legacy of Civilianization," in *The Nuremberg Military Tribunals between History, Justice and the Creation of Law*, eds. Kim C. Priemel and Alexa Stiller; Hamburg: HIS, 2013, pp. 287–319, 288, 299 et seqq.
17 Clearly: "The argument that compliance with German law is a defense to the charge rests on a misconception of the basic theory which supports our entire proceedings," NMT III, 983.

18 NMT III, 1025.
19 NMT III, 1064.
20 RGBl. 1941 I 759 et seq.
21 Werle, *Justiz-Strafrecht und polizeiliche Verbrechensbekämpfung im Dritten Reich*, 599–602.
22 NMT III, 1065.
23 NMT III, 1066.
24 NMT III, 1078.
25 NMT III, 1081.
26 Order to discontinue proceedings, Cologne District Court, October 30, 1970—24 Js 88/68.
27 Law of July 14, 1933, RGBl. I, 529, entered into force on January 1, 1934.
28 IMT, Judgment, I, 232; see Whitney Harris, *Tyranny on Trial, The Trial of the Major German War Criminals at the End of the World War II at Nuremberg Germany 1945–1946* (Dallas, TX: Southern Methodist University Press, 1999), 213 et seq.
29 Modern international criminal law recognizes the crime of "enforced disappearance" as a crime against humanity, cf. for example Art. 7 para. 1 lit d) of the Rome Staute. Historically, however, this offense relates primarily to the practice of South American dictatorships.
30 Cf. Keitel's cross-examination by Sir David Maxwell-Fyfe, IMT X, 627 et seqq.
31 NMT III, 1025.
32 "Kriegssonderstrafrechtsverordnung" from August 17, 1938, entered into force on August 26, 1939.
33 "Verordnung gegen Volksschädlinge" from September 5, 1939, RGBl. I, 1679.
34 The Law against Insidious Attacks on the State and Party and for the Protection of Party Uniforms of December 20, 1934, RGBl. I, 1269. De facto, a tightening of the Insidious Attacks Act was enforced in 1938 by Section 5 KSSVO.
35 NMT III, 1025.
36 Law against dangerous habitual criminals and on measures of security and correction of November 24, 1933 (RGBl. I, 995).
37 NMT III, 1026.
38 NMT III, 1027.
39 NMT III, 1081.
40 On this: Sarah Schädler, *‚Justizkrise' und ‚Justizreform' im Nationalsozialismus. The RMJ under Reich Minister of Justice Thierack 1942–1945* (Tübingen: Mohr Siebeck, 2009).
41 NMT, III, 1086.
42 A particular example here is the case of Markus Luftgas, a Hamburg Jew, mentioned in the lawyers' trial, who was sentenced to two and a half years in prison by a special court in Katowice for stealing eggs and whom Schlegelberger had transferred to the Gestapo after Hitler's intervention, NMT III, p. 1048. An investigation initiated later by the Flensburg public prosecutor's office was terminated by the Flensburg Regional Court on April 14, 1959.
43 NMT III, p. 1083.
44 Cited in the judgment, NMT III, p. 1084.
45 Henning von Alten, *Recht oder Unrecht? Der Verwaltungsrechtsstreit des Staatssekretärs a.D. Prof. Dr. Dr. h.c. Franz Schlegelberger um seine beamtenrechtlichen Versorgungsbezüge* (Norderstedt: BoD 2009).

46 Franz Schlegelberger, *Gesetz über die Angelegenheiten der freiwilligen Gerichtsbarkeit*, 6th ed. (Berlin: Heymann, 1952) as well as later editions; Franz Schlegelberger, *Handelsgesetzbuch in der seit dem 1. Oktober 1937 geltenden Fassung (ohne Seerecht)*, vol. 1–2, 2nd ed. (Berlin: F. Vahlen, 1950/1953) as well as later editions.

47 Cf. Zentral-Justizblatt für die Britische Zone, *Das Nürnberger Juristenurteil* (Hamburg: Rechts- und Staatswissenschaftlicher Verlag GmbH, formerly Gesetz und Recht Verlag GmbH, 1948). However, only the so-called general part of the judgment was available in bookshops. Thomas Vormbaum, "Die 'strafrechtliche Aufarbeitung' der nationalsozialistischen Justizverbrechen in der Nachkriegszeit," in *Die Rosenburg. The Federal Ministry of Justice and the Nazi Past—A Review,* eds. Manfred Görtemaker and Christoph Safferling (Göttingen: Vandenhoeck & Ruprecht, 2013), 142, 145 fn. 10.

48 Heribert Ostendorf and Heino ter Veen, *Das 'Nürnberger Juristenurteil': Eine kommentierte Dokumentation*, (Frankfurt am Main: Campus, 1985), 40 et seq.; Klaus Kastner, *Der Dolch des Mörders war unter der Robe des Juristen verborgen. The Nuremberg Lawyers' Trial of 1947,* in Juristische Arbeitsblätter (1997); Hubert Rottleuthner, *Das Nürnberger Juristenurteil und seine Rezeption in Deutschland—Ost und West*, Neue Justiz (1997): 617.

49 Lore Maria Peschel-Gutzeit, *Das Nürnberger Juristen-Urteil von 1947. Historischer Zusammenhang und aktuelle Bezüge* (Baden-Baden: Nomos, 1996).

50 Authorization by Ordinance No. 47 of the British Military Government of August 30, 1946; British Military Government Gazette, 306; Order No. 154 of the French High Commissioner of June 1, 1950, AHK Gazette, 443. However, these authorizations were then revoked by Order No. 234 of August 31, 1951 (AHK Gazette, 1138) and by Order No. 171 of August 31, 1951 (AHK Gazette, 1137). See also Vormbaum, "Die 'strafrechtliche Aufarbeitung' der nationalsozialistischen Justizverbrechen in der Nachkriegszeit", 142, 150.

51 First Act on the Repeal of Occupation Law of May 30, 1956 (BGBl. I, 437). Cf. ORR Wohlfarth memo of May 11, 1955, for the Minister at the cabinet meeting of May 13, 1955, BA Koblenz B 141/21526, 132 ff., which speaks of the liberation of Germany from the shackles of occupation law.

52 Günter Hirsch at the 2nd Rosenburg Symposium in Nuremberg.

53 Peter Alfons Steiniger and Kazimierz Leszczynski, *Fall 3: Das Urteil im Juristenprozeß* (Berlin: VEB Deutscher Verlag der Wissenschaften, 1969).

54 See Christoph Safferling, "Durfte Volksgerichtshofrichter Hans-Joachim Rehse freigesprochen werden?," in *Strafrecht und Systemunrecht*, eds. Florian Jeßberger et al. (Tübingen: Mohr Siebeck, 2022), 635–48.

55 Letter from Dreher to State Secretary Ehmke of October 17, 1968, BEW 65 vol. 1, 214 et seq.

Selected Bibliography

Luber, Martin, *Strafverteidigung im Nürnberger Juristenprozess am Beispiel des Angeklagten Oswald Rothaug* (Berlin: Duncker & Humblot, 2018 2018).

Peschel-Gutzeit, Lore Maria, *Das Nürnberger Juristen-Urteil von 1947. Historischer Zusammenhang und aktuelle Bezüge* (Baden-Baden: Nomos, 1996).

Reicher, Harry, "The Jurists' Trial and Lessons for the Rule of Law," in: Reginbogin, Herbert and Christoph Safferling (eds.), *The Nuremberg Trials: International Law Since 1945* (Berlin: Saur, 2006 2006), 175.

Safferling, Christoph, and Martin Luber, "Der Tempel der deutschen Justiz muss wieder eingeweiht werden", in: 49 Juristische Arbeitsblätter (2017): 881-887.

Wilke, Christiane, "Case 3: Juristen vor Gericht, Recht auf dem Pruefstand und das Erbe der 'Zivilisation,'" in: Kim C. Priemel and Alexa Stiller (eds.), *NMT. The Nuremberg Military Tribunals between History, Justice and the Creation of Law* (Hamburg: HIS, 2013), 287–319.

Part 3

The Legacy of Nuremberg Principles

8

Locating Legitimacy Throughlines in the Structural Design of International and "Internationalized" Criminal Tribunals

Michael J. Kelly

While some might argue that the concept of justice is objective or even perfect as one of Plato's forms,[1] that proposition renders justice aspirational. Justice is subjective in nature—both for those who dispense it and those who receive it. In the modern era, courts dispense justice. Although the courts, the judges therein, and the laws thereunder can undoubtedly be manipulated in corrupt or authoritarian societies toward unjust ends, as was the case in Soviet Russia or Nazi Germany, liberal democracies and the international legal order attempt to deliver justice evenhandedly, dispassionately, and with an eye toward to the social good. Civil and criminal tribunals are the vehicle for delivering international justice. But if the victims and international society itself who receive this justice do not perceive it as satisfactory, the legitimacy of the tribunal as justice-giver comes into question. Mindful of these concepts, international tribunal designers, especially those concerned with designing criminal tribunals which must deliver justice against perpetrators of the worst atrocities, such as genocide, must try to build into the structures of their creations the foundations of legitimacy strong enough to convince both those who are dispensing justice and those who are receiving the justice that, albeit subjectively, the justice that is done comports with notions of fairness, moral integrity, and decisional rigor.

This chapter compares structural features across eleven international and "internationalized" criminal tribunals in search of legitimacy throughlines that, once identified, may prove helpful to future tribunal designers. A tribunal's structure is not wholly determinative of the twin traditional measures of its success: operations and outcomes. However, a tribunal's structure may inform its practice. While such linkages may also become evident over time, the influence of funding or politics cannot be underestimated.

Concerning funding, much frustration currently focuses on the International Criminal Court (ICC), which has become an emblem of slow-moving international criminal justice. Having detained only twenty-one people in the past two decades and yielded a paltry ten convictions and four acquittals. With a 2023 budget of €170 million,[2] many are left to wonder whether the tribunal's meager results justify its expense. Countering such legitimacy-undermining perceptions, Karim Kahn, the ICC's new prosecutor since 2021, demonstrated the tribunal's potential effectiveness and speed by converting the prior preliminary examination of the situation in Ukraine into a full-blown investigation complete with an arrest warrant for Russian President Vladimir Putin within a year of Russia's invasion.[3] The ICC's structure allowed for him to do so. With respect to politics, Khan's move to arrest Putin quickly placed him on the Russian Interior Ministry's "wanted" list.[4]

It is easier to assess the legitimacy of a tribunal's legitimacy once it has completed its mandate. For example, the IMT-Nuremberg, International Criminal Tribunal for the Former Yugoslavia (ICTY), and Special Court for Sierra Leone (SCSL) were widely perceived to be successes. However, those perceptions rested on different strengths. The IMT-Nuremberg was the first such tribunal, offered a fair trial process, established important precedents such as individual criminal liability, no sovereign immunity or superior orders defenses, and early definitions of substantive crimes. The ICTY was the first ad hoc court. It was a model of efficiency and output: sitting for 10,800 trial days where 4,650 witnesses were heard, producing 2.5 million pages of transcripts, indicting 161 individuals, of which ninety were sentenced, nineteen were acquitted, thirteen were referred to national courts, thirty-seven had their indictments withdrawn, and two were retried before the successor court, and zero fugitives remained at large as of the court's closing.[5] The SCSL was the first hybrid court where local counsel and judges could meaningfully participate in trials considered as fair to defendants at the end of the day—were spared the death penalty that they would have faced in the Sierra Leonean criminal justice system.[6]

Conversely, the Extraordinary Chambers of the Courts of Cambodia (ECCC), the Iraqi High Tribunal (IHT), and the Special Tribunal for Lebanon (STL) were widely regarded as failures. Like the successful tribunals, these perceptions derived from different points—albeit weaknesses. The ECCC was viewed as corrupt and captured by the national political elite. The IHT was staffed by unqualified trial judges implementing flawed procedures and executed its main defendant, Saddam Hussein, halfway through the second of his seven scheduled trials. The STL never secured any defendants to stand trial, spent large sums on "in absentia" proceedings, and ultimately closed under a chaotic cloud of inconclusiveness.

Today, the somewhat surprising and sudden surfeit of prosecutions for international crimes by states utilizing universal jurisdiction as we open the second decade of the twenty-first century may represent a preference for domestic over international criminal prosecution altogether. Yet, the legitimacy quotient remains a key part of the discussion. For example, as discussed in Section V below, with respect to the crime of Russian aggression against Ukraine, opinion is divided as to whether prosecution for this crime should proceed from a newly created international tribunal or from an "internationalized" court within the Ukrainian judicial system.[7] Ukraine backs the former precisely because they feel it would garner maximum legitimacy. The United States, Ukraine's largest financial, military, and political supporter in its war against Russia, prefers the latter, perhaps because of the very legitimacy it might garner—

thereby curtailing Washington's future options for acting in a manner that might come close to aggression, such as the illegal 2003 invasion of Iraq. Consequently, legitimacy is a critical component of discussions underlying both models.

Unfortunately, not much polling data exists to measure perceptions of legitimacy from the public, victims' groups, the international community in general, or the international criminal justice community in particular.[8] Anecdotal commentary, academic assessments, funding concerns, and annual reports from prosecutors to governing bodies such as the UN Security Council or the Assembly of States Parties form the broad basis for a legitimacy discussion—such as it is. What has been missing is a comprehensive comparative analysis that can better inform this discussion. While certainly not a replacement for robust polling data, the tabular data offered in Section III at least provides comparative points about structural choices that can better inform this conversation. Although, we begin, foundationally, at the beginning, with a brief consideration in Section II of the Nuremberg experience.

Jackson's Experience at Nuremberg

Justice Robert H. Jackson of the US Supreme Court was the first designer of the first international criminal tribunal. But to become such, he and his country had to successfully beat back global clamoring for summary justice without legal process—a not insignificant battle.[9] Jackson's thoughts on building the International Military Tribunal at Nuremberg (IMT-N) to deliver civilization's justice to captured Nazi leaders of the Third Reich are not cabined to post-war Germany. His experiences at Nuremberg also offers salient markers to today's tribunal designers, justifying this brief exposition before presenting the tabular data. Moreover, they raise important questions of legitimacy faced by every international criminal tribunal that came after. How those questions have been answered largely flows from the structural choices subsequent tribunal designers made. Those who design these institutions must strive for common values such as integrity, efficiency, fairness, and narrative relevance to maximize their creations' legitimacy.

Despite a laudatory institutional vision, international criminal tribunal designers rarely get everything they wish. By definition, such bodies are the result of negotiation. At Nuremberg, Jackson worked through all his design ideas with his British, Soviet, and French partners in crafting the London Agreement. Decisions about charging conspiracy (an alien concept to the French and Soviet counterparts), holding a joint trial for key Nazi leaders and subsequent subject-specific trials for the remainder, forgoing a jury, allowing broad discretion on choice of defense counsel, cabining aggression to only cover Germany and not the USSR,[10] and many others were trade-offs among allies in arriving at a mutually acceptable tribunal.

Thus, at the very start, before the Nuremberg IMT was impaneled, Jackson, as chief designer, was working with a compromise as he sought to open the first successful breach in the previously impenetrable wall of international legal impunity on the theoretically new basis of individual criminal responsibility[11] that would ultimately erode sovereign immunity and superior orders defenses.[12] Moreover, public sentiment overall showed frustration. "[T]he Germans generally were hostile to the trial of their former leaders."[13] Meanwhile, the American public was impatient. Even before he returned from London, the *New York Times* reported the length of the negotiation process, extending the start of the trial into the Fall of 1945, revealed "difficulties that have delayed the "master trial" to an extent that has become irritating to many Americans."[14] Over and above structural considerations, practical considerations such as compromise, delay, and cost may bedevil a tribunal's perceived legitimacy.

Doubtful or negative opinions of tribunal designers' peers can also delegitimize the effort from the beginning. Although such misgivings didn't dampen Jackson's efforts to create the first such tribunal at Nuremberg, they lurked about its creation. When US Supreme Court Chief Justice Harlan Stone was invited to swear in the American members of the tribunal, he declined, noting that he "did not wish to appear, in that remote way, to give my blessing or that of the Court on the proposed Nurnberg trials" which he characterized as a "high-grade lynching party."[15] Defendants, too, often target a court's jurisdictional legitimacy in order to undermine it, much as German defendants sought to argue against ex post facto application of law to them at Nuremberg.[16] Characterized as "the heavy artillery of the critics' attack," the argument "is, in essence, that the pre-war treaties, commentaries, and other sources of international law did not constitute a clear international agreement that individuals who launched an aggressive war were to be punished as criminals. This argument generally rests on the premise that, if the trials involved the application of a retroactive standard, they deserve condemnation."[17]

Decisions by the resulting tribunal also lay beyond the control of the designers. For example, although Jackson was able to get the conspiracy charge admitted as Count 1 at Nuremberg,

> The Tribunal had rejected the prosecution's argument that the conspiracy had begun with the creation of the Nazi Party in 1920. It had instead dated the conspiracy's start to the Hossbach Conference on November 5, 1937—when Hitler had revealed to his generals his plans to invade neighboring countries. Even more significantly, the Tribunal had limited the conspiracy charge to the planning and waging of aggressive war (crimes against peace). The judgment would only concern itself with the conspiracy insofar as it had led to the violent assault on the sovereignty of other states.[18]

Yet despite subjective opinions about a tribunal during its creation and early operation, which may affect perceptions of legitimacy, tribunal designers may be able to point to at least two more or less objective indicia as marks of legitimacy: fairness of process and outcomes. At Nuremberg, even "its critics and German citizens" found the trial to be "a model of forensic fairness."[19]

This perception was partly due to the extraordinary efforts made to ensure due process, present unimpeachable evidence, and render verdicts based upon this proof. The prosecution's case was based upon documents culled from Nazi files instead of rhetorical testimony that would have had greater public interest and made for a more dramatic case. It was thought that "witnesses, many of them persecuted and hostile to the Nazis, would always be chargeable with bias, faulty recollection, and even perjury. Prosecution documents were given to defense counsel in advance of presentation in court." These lawyers were chosen by the defendants and were paid, fed, and housed by the military government. A transcript of court proceedings was furnished daily (in German) to each counsel, access was provided to documents not used by the prosecution, and the defendants were granted the deposition or presence of any witness that had information relevant to their defense.

Finally, the Germans were afforded the common law right to testify on their behalf and the continental right to make an unsworn statement not subject to cross-examination after all proceedings. Because the defendants offered evidence for nearly five months, compared to the prosecution's three months, and the closing speeches of each side took twenty days and three days, respectively, Jackson was justified in saying that the "future will never have to ask, with misgiving: "What could the Nazis have said in their favor? History will know that whatever could be said, they were allowed to say.""[20]

As to outcomes, Jackson pointed squarely to the acquittals at Nuremberg as the best and most legitimizing rebuttal to allegations of victor's justice.

> The most convincing demonstration of impartiality came with the acquittal of three individual defendants—Schacht, Von Papan, and Fritsche. This result belied the early suspicion that "[t]he basic approach [at Nuremberg] is that these men should not have a chance to go free." Alternatively, it realized Jackson's hope that the Trial would be faithful to "[t]he ultimate principle . . . that you must put no man on Trial under the forms of judicial proceedings if you are not willing to see him freed if not proven guilty."[21]

The track record for such tribunals, post-Nuremberg, offers mixed results. While none have been perfect, some have sacrificed legitimacy for efficiency, some have achieved a tenuous balance, others have co-opted new design components to boost legitimacy, and some have outright failed. The International Military Tribunal for the Far East (IMTFE) encountered very different de-legitimizing strands from the forerunner dominated by Jackson in Germany, namely the absence of a US Supreme Court Justice at the helm of creation and prosecution, marked disinterest by the French, Soviets, and British in comparison to Nuremberg—leaving the Americans to "run the show," assigned US JAG attorneys to "work with" each Japanese defendant even though each defendant had their counsel, and vastly different outcomes: all guilty.[22] As a result, the reception of the IMTFE by the Japanese people was decidedly mixed.[23] The IMTFE's context was somewhat different as well. The Japanese people were recovering from two atomic blasts while watching their Emperor's divinity literally being stripped away[24] and were living under the uncontested dictatorship of General Douglas MacArthur.[25] Although military defeat was total, as with Germany, Japan was subjected to a kind of

Table 8.1 International Military Tribunals (IMT)

Design Elements	International Military Tribunal—Nuremberg (Major War Criminals)	International Military Tribunal for the Far East (IMTFE)
Geographic location. E.g., is it inside or outside the country where the atrocities occurred?	• Palace of Justice in Nuremberg, Germany.[28] • Also referred to as Courtroom 600.[29] • Former location of Nazi Party rallies.[30] • Purpose of the location: to symbolize the death of Nazi Germany.[31]	• Ichigaya, Tokyo.[32] • Former building of the Japanese Ministry of War, a center for Japanese war tactics and advancement of its military ideologies.[33]
Context. E.g., is it in an occupied area, or a free state?	• Free State of Bavaria[34]	• Became occupied by the Allied Powers following the end of WWII. • Today, it is largely a residential area.
Founding authority. Was it created by the UN, by a treaty, or by a statute?	• London Agreement of the International Military Tribunal [London Agreement] established the constitution, jurisdiction, and functions of the IMT.[35] • Signed in August 1945 by the Allies.[36] • § 2, Art. 6 of the Charter of the International Military Tribunal [IMT Charter] puts forth the jurisdiction and general principles that were to be applied in the trial and punishment of the major war criminals of the European Axis countries.	• Charter of the International Military Tribunal for the Far East.[37] [IMTFE Charter] • On January 19, 1946, General Douglas MacArthur (Supreme Commander of the Allied Powers) ordered the creation of the IMTFE and approved the Charter.[38] • 11 countries formed the International Military Tribunal for the Far East (IMTFE).[39]

Judicial arm. E.g., are the judges purely international, purely domestic, or mixed (if the latter, what ratio)? What is the appointment mechanism? How long to judges serve? Do judges have diplomatic immunity?	• Judges were a mix of the Allies—American, British, French, and Soviet.[40]
	• Judges were appointed to the Tribunal from the respective Ally States.[41]
	• The tribunal was created as an international military tribunal that would prosecute the Nazi Party leaders (also referred to as "Major War Criminals").[42]
	• IMT judicial term: length of Major Criminals Trial/London Agreement (1945–October 1946).[43] (Appointment term is not explicitly stated within the charter besides the agreement's effective dates.)
		• IMTFE Charter, Art. 2: "The Tribunal shall consist of not less than five nor more than nine Members, appointed by the Supreme Commander for the Allied Powers from the names submitted by the Signatories to the Instrument of Surrender."[44]
		• The judges were all international[45]:
		  • William Flood Webb—Australia
		  • Edward Stuart McDougall—Canada
		  • Ju-ao Mei—China
		  • Henri Bernard—France
		  • Radhabinod Pal—India
		  • Bernard Victor Aloysius Röling—the Netherlands
		  • Erima Harvey Northcroft—New Zealand
		  • Delfin Jaranilla—Philippines
		  • William Donald Patrick—United Kingdom
		  • Harlan F. Stone—United States
		  • Myron Cady Cramer—United States
		  • John Patrick Higgins—United States

Prosecutorial arm. E.g., is the prosecution purely international, purely domestic, or mixed?	• The chief prosecutors of the Nuremberg Trials came from international jurisdictions[46]: • Robert H. Jackson—United States • Sir Hartley Shawcross—United Kingdom • General Roman A. Rudenko—Soviet Union • François de Menthon/Auguste Champetier de Ribes—France	• Chief prosecutors were all from the United States[47]: • Ernest E. Danly—United States • Theodore Goulsby—United States • Carlisle Wallace Higgins—United States • Solis Horwitz—United States • Joseph Berry Keenan—United States • Luke Lea—United States • Edward P. Monaghan—United States • Roy L. Morgan—United States • Arthur A. Sandusky—United States
Defense arm. E.g., are defense counsel purely international, purely domestic, or mixed?	• The defense lawyers were either selected by the defendants themselves or appointed by the Tribunal at the defendant's request.[48] • The Allies arranged and paid for the defendants' attorneys.[49] • Counsel for the defense was largely German.[50]	• Defendants were represented by over 100 attorneys, 75 percent Japanese and 25 percent American.[51] • IMTFE Charter, Art. 9(d): "Each accused shall be represented by counsel of his own selection, subject to disapproval of such counsel at any time by the Tribunal. The accused shall file with the General Secretary of the Tribunal the name of his counsel, or of counsel whom he desires the Tribunal to Appoint. If an accused is not represented by counsel, the Tribunal shall designate counsel for him."[52]
Funding. E.g., is there adequate funding for all three components? What is the source of funding?	• IMT Charter, Art. 30: The expenses of the Tribunal and of the Trials, shall be charged by the Signatories against the funds allotted for maintenance of the Control Council of Germany.[53]	• The budget for war crimes trials in the third quarter of 1948 amounted to $740,000, but only $249,000 was available for continued activity in 1949.[54] • Funding ran out, and most of the suspects still at Sugamo were released without being tried.[55] • Where the actual funding came from is remains unclear in the sources found.

(*Continued*)

Table 8.1 (Continued)

Design Elements	International Military Tribunal—Nuremberg (Major War Criminals)	International Military Tribunal for the Far East (IMTFE)

Jurisdiction. E.g., what are the temporal and subject matter jurisdictional limitations?	• The Geneva and Hague Conventions had defined war crimes, laying the foundation for the Nuremberg Trials.[56]
	• Personal Jurisdiction:
	  • IMT Charter, Art. 6: Tribunal has the power to try and punish persons as individuals or as members of organizations.[57]
	• Subject Matter Jurisdiction[58]:
	  • Crimes Against Peace
	  • War Crimes
	  • Crimes Against Humanity
	• The crimes of waging of aggressive war (today, "aggression"), the violation of sovereignty, and the perpetration of crimes against humanity had not been defined under international law, which exposed the Allies to accusations of ex post facto prosecution.[59]
	• Tribunal served as the first time an international authority would hold political and military leaders accountable for atrocities committed in the name of a state.[60]
	• Concurrent jurisdiction
	  • IMT Charter, Art. 10: "Competent national authority of any Signatory shall have the right to bring individual to trial for membership before national, military or occupation courts."[61]
	  • IMT Charter, Art. 11: "Any person convicted by the Tribunal may be charged before a national, military or occupation court, referred to in Article 10 may impose upon him punishment independent of and additional to the punishment imposed by the Tribunal for participation in the criminal activities of such group or organization."[62]
		• The IMTFE was created to prosecute leaders of Japan for conspiracy to start and wage war.[63]
		• Only those whose crimes included the charge of crimes against peace could be prosecuted by the Tribunal.[64]
		• Personal Jurisdiction[65]:
		  • "The Tribunal shall have the power to try and punish Far Eastern war criminals who as individuals or as members of organizations."
		• Subject Matter Jurisdiction[66]:
		  • Crimes Against Peace
		  • War Crimes
		  • Crimes Against Humanity
		• Concurrent Jurisdiction[67]

Evidence. E.g., how are the rules of evidence adopted and who wrote them?	• IMT Charter, Art. 19: The Tribunal was not bound by the technical rules of evidence. Any evidence deemed to have probative value may be admitted.[68]	• IMTFE Charter, Art. 15(d): ◦ The prosecution and defense may offer evidence, with the admissibility determined by the Tribunal.[69] • IMTFE Charter, Art. 13: ◦ "The Tribunal shall not be bound by technical rules of evidence."[70] • IMTFE Charter, Art. 9(e) and (f): ◦ "An accused shall have the right through himself or through his counsel to present evidence at the trial in support of his defense, and to examine any witness called by the prosecution, subject to such reasonable restrictions as the Tribunal may determine."[71] ◦ "An accused may apply inwriting to the Tribunal for the production of witnesses or of documents. The application shall state where the witness or document is thought to be located. It shall also state the facts proposed to be proved by the witness or the document and the relevancy of such facts to the defense. If the Tribunal grants the application, the Tribunal shall be given such aid in obtaining production of the evidence as the circumstances require."[72]
Procedure. E.g., how are the rules of procedure adopted and who wrote them?	• The procedure was determined by the IMT Charter, § 5, Arts. 17–25.[73] • 24 Nazi leaders were indicted[74] ◦ However, only 22 stood trial, as Robert Ley committed suicide while in custody and Gustav Krupp was presumed dead.[75] • The trial ran from November 20, 1945—October 1946.[76]	• The Rules of Procedure are defined in IMTFE Charter, Art. 7: "The Tribunal may draft and amend rules of procedure consistent with the fundamental provisions of this Charter." • Testimony from 419 witnesses and 4,336 pieces of evidence were seen including depositions and affidavits from 779 individuals.[77]
Witness protection. E.g., how are witnesses protected?	• Due to the nature of the conflict and Nuremberg trial, documentary evidence was used more than eyewitness and oral testimony.[78]	• IMTFE Charter, Art. 11: Tribunal shall have the power (a) To summon witnesses to the trial, to require them to attend and testify, and to· question them.[79]
Coverage. E.g., are trial proceedings televised? Are they live or delayed? Are proceedings open or closed?	• Over 400 visitors attended the daily proceedings, with 325 correspondents representing 23 different countries.[80] • The press was allowed to attend the proceedings.[81] • The courtroom was equipped with a simultaneous translation system to translate the proceedings in English, French, German, and Russian.[82]	• IMTFE Charter, Art. 13(e): "The transcript of the proceedings, and exhibits and documents submitted to the Tribunal, will be filed with the General Secretary of the Tribunal and will constitute part of the Record."[83]

(Continued)

Table 8.1 (Continued)

Design Elements	International Military Tribunal—Nuremberg (Major War Criminals)	International Military Tribunal for the Far East (IMTFE)

Sentencing. E.g., what are the sentencing options?	• The Charter of the Nuremberg Tribunal, Art. 27: The Tribunal shall have the right to impose upon the Defendant, on conviction, death or such other punishment as shall be determined by it to be just."[84]
	• Nineteen of the twenty-two defendants were found guilty[85, 86]
	  • Three were sentenced to life in prison.
	  • Four were sentenced to prison terms of 10 to 20 years.
	  • Twelve were sentenced to death.
	• Three of the defendants were acquitted.[87]
		• IMTFE Charter, Art. 16: "The Tribunal shall have the power to impose upon an accused, on conviction, death, or such other punishment as shall be determined by it to be just."[88]
		• Seven defendants were sentenced to death by handing and sixteen defendants were sentenced to life imprisonment.[89]
		• Defendants sentenced to death were executed at Sugamo Prison on December 23, 1948.[90]

Incarceration. E.g., where are sentences served?	• Those sentenced to imprisonment remained in Nuremberg until July 18, 1947, when they were transported to the Allied War Criminals Prison in Berlin-Spandau for the remainder of their sentences.[91]	• Prison sentences were served in Sugamo Prison (located in Tokyo, Japan).[92]
Appeals. E.g., can judgments be appealed? If so, what is the standard of review? If so, what are the statistics for trial judgments being upheld, reversed, or sentences modified?	• The Charter of the Nuremberg Tribunal, Art. 26: "The judgement of the Tribunal as to the guilt or the innocence of any Defendant shall be final and not subject to review."[93]	• IMTFE, Art. 17: "Sentence will be carried out in accordance with the Order of the Supreme Commander for the Allied Powers, who may at any time reduce or otherwise alter the sentence, except to increase its severity."[94]
Activity. E.g., how many trials has the tribunal completed? Is it considered efficient and effective?	• After the Nuremberg Trial for Major War Criminals, subsequent trials conducted before US military tribunals were held between 1946 and 1949 in Nuremberg against 177 high-ranking physicians, judges, industrialists, SS commanders and police commanders, military personnel, civil servants, and diplomats.[95, 96] • Thirteen cases were tried by the Tribunal (one Major War Criminals Trial and twelve subsequent trials).[97]	• The IMTFE concluded in December 1948 and had tried twenty-eight Japanese war leaders.[98]

Polling data. E.g., is there any polling data available as to whether the tribunal is considered legitimate? By the international community, by the victims, or by the country at large where the atrocities took place?	• By October 1946, the month in which the sentences from the IMT were announced, more than 79 percent of Germans polled by American occupation authorities reported that they had heard about the tribunal's judgments and thought the trial was fair.[99] • Seventy-one percent of those surveyed confirmed they had learned something new from the trial.[100] • Some scholar and social commentators condemn the Nuremberg Trials and denazification was failures, but the procedures established for the IMT and Allies' efforts have established legal precedent and a record of evidence that serves as commemoration for the prosecution of war criminals.[101]	• "A majority of Japanese seem to support a key conclusion of the tribunal—that Japan waged a war of aggression."[102] • A poll conducted in 2000 showed that 51 percent of 1,468 respondents aged sixteen or older consider Japan the aggressor for the war it waged in the 1930s and 1940s, compared with 15 percent who feel otherwise. The same poll showed that an increasing number of young Japanese are questioning the validity of the tribunal.[103] • A poll conducted in 1982 found that out of 2,623 people, 10 percent of those aged sixteen to nineteen, and 11 percent of those in their 20s, replied that "they can't tell" whether Japan waged a war of aggression. Those ratios grew to 29 percent and 37 percent, respectively, in the 2000 poll.[104]

Use of the tribunal's location after conclusion of trial	• Used by the United States until 1949 to conduct twelve trials before US American military tribunals.[105]
	• The subsequent trials are referred to as:
	  • Doctors' Trial
	  • Milch Trial
	  • Judges' Trial
	  • Pohl Trial Flick Trial
	  • IG-Farben Trial
	  • Hostages Trial
	  • RuSHA Trial
	  • Einsatzgruppen Trial
	  • Krupp Trial
	  • Wilhelmstrasse Trial
	  • High Command Trial
	• In these subsequent trials, 177 defendants were tried, of which twenty-four were sentenced to death (thirteen were actually executed), twenty were sentenced to life in prison, and ninety-eight were sentenced to long prison sentences.[106] Twenty-five defendants were found not guilty.[107]
	• Courtroom 600 has been controlled by Bavarian justice authorities since June 30, 1961.[108]
	• March 1, 2020, marked the end of Courtroom 600's use for trials.[109]
	• Today, the building is used for a permanent exhibition of the Memorium Nuremberg Trials.[110]
		• Australia, China, France, the Netherlands Indies, the Philippines, the United Kingdom, and the United States convened separate trials convicting more than 5,500 more lower-ranking war criminals.[111]
		• The trials were held all over Asia and the Pacific, and the last one was in 1951. China held thirteen tribunals, resulting in 504 convictions and 149 executions.[112]
		• The total number of death sentences are as follows:
		  • United States—140
		  • The Netherlands—236
		  • United Kingdom—223
		  • Australia—153
		  • China—149
		  • France—26
		  • Philippines—17

Table 8.2 Ad Hoc Tribunals

Design Elements	International Criminal Tribunal for the Former Yugoslavia (ICTY)	International Criminal Tribunal for Rwanda (ICTR)
Geographic location. E.g., is it inside or outside the country where the atrocities occurred?	• The Hague, the Netherlands[113]	• The ICTR is in Arusha, Tanzania, and has offices in Kigali, Rwanda.[114] • The ICTR Appeals Chamber is in The Hague, the Netherlands.[115]
Context. E.g., is it in an occupied area, or a free state?	• Parliamentary democracy/free state[116]	• ICTR: Region of northern Tanzania/East Africa and considered a "partly free" state.[117] • ICTR Appeals Chamber: Parliamentary democracy/free state.[118]
Founding authority. E.g., is it created by the UN or by a treaty or by a statute?	• Established by Security Council Resolution 827 (1993).[119] • Subject to UN Resolution 1966 that established the Mechanism for International Criminal Tribunals and decided that "the Statutes of the Mechanism and of the ICTY and ICTR shall be subject to the transitional arrangements set out in Annex II [of the Resolution]."[120] • Ad hoc body established by the UN Security Council Resolution 1966 (2010) to continue the "jurisdiction, rights and obligations, and essential functions" of the ICTY, and to maintain the Tribunal's legacy.[121]	• Established by UN Security Council Resolution 995 (1994).[122] • Statute of the ICTR (January 31, 2010)[123] • Omits Grave Breaches of the Geneva Convention of 1949 and has a temporal jurisdiction.
Applicable law	• International humanitarian law[124] • ICTY Statute, Art. 1[125]	• International humanitarian law[126] • ICTR Statute, Art. 1[127]
Judicial arm. E.g., are the judges purely international, purely domestic, or mixed (if the latter, what ratio)? What is the appointment mechanism? How long to judges serve? Do judges have diplomatic immunity?	• The Chambers include the Trial and the Appeals Chambers.[128] • The judges consisted of a mix of international jurisdictions.[129] • Each Trial Chamber is composed of three permanent judges and a maximum of six ad litem judges. Ad litem judges are appointed by the UN Secretary-General at the request of the president of the Tribunal to sit on one or more specific trials, allowing for efficient use of resources in accordance with the court's changing caseload.[130] •	• The Chamber was originally composed of sixteen (16) judges and no two could been nationals of the same states.[134] • Judges were elected by the United Nations General Assembly for a term of four (4) years and were eligible for re-election.[135] • The Appeals Chamber consists of seven (7) permanent Judges, five (5) of whom are permanent judges of the ICTY and two (2) of whom are permanent judges of the International Criminal Tribunal for Rwanda (ICTR). Each appeal is heard and decided by a bench of five (5) judges of the Appeals Chamber.[136]

	• Three judges are assigned to hear each case, and at least one judge per case must be a permanent judge. Trial Chamber may be divided into sections of three (3) judges each, composed of both permanent and ad litem judges. Individual sections have the same powers and responsibilities as a Trial Chamber.[131]
	• The Appeals Chamber consists of seven permanent Judges, five (5) of whom are permanent judges of the ICTY and two (2) of whom are permanent judges of the International Criminal Tribunal for Rwanda (ICTR). These seven (7) judges also constitute the Appeals Chamber of the ICTR. Each appeal is heard and decided by a bench of five (5) judges of the Appeals Chamber.[132]
	• The ICTY Statute provides for the judges to enjoy the privileges and immunities, exemptions and facilities accorded to diplomatic envoys in accordance to the Convention on the Privileges and Immunities of the United Nations.[133]
		• ICTR Statute, Art. 29:
		  • "The Convention on the Privileges and Immunities of the United Nations shall apply to the ICTR and the judges."[137]
		  • "The judges shall enjoy the privileges and immunities, exemptions and facilities accorded to diplomatic envoys, in accordance with international law."[138]

Prosecutorial arm. E.g., is the prosecution purely international, purely domestic, or mixed?	• The Office of the Prosecutor (OTP) oversees the preparation and presentation of the prosecution's cases and appeals.[139]
	• The prosecutors were all from a variety of international jurisdictions, including[140]:
	  • Belgium
	  • Venezuela
	  • South Africa
	  • Canada
		• The Office of the Prosecutor (OTP) is responsible for investigating all crimes under which the ICTR has jurisdiction, prepares indictments, and prosecutes defendants.[141]
		• Hassan B. Jallow, Prosecutor of the ICTR to the United Nations Security Council (Gambia).[142]

Defense arm. E.g., are defense counsel purely international, purely domestic, or mixed?	• The Registry organ of the ICTY serves as the mechanism to oversee the Division of Judicial Support Services.[143] • Annex I to the Directive on the Assignment of Defense Counsel provides counsel rates for the ICTY.[144]	• Defense Counsel was made up of more than 200 lawyers from a mix of countries.[145]

Funding. E.g., is there adequate funding for all three components? What is the source of funding?	• Budget: $272 million USD[146]
	• The ICTY has been funded by foundations, institutions, and governments. Specifically,
	  • 32 Countries[147]
	  • Non-Governmental Organizations and Other Institutions[148]
	  • Charles Stewart Mott Foundation[149]
	  • ICTY Outreach Programme Trust Fund (a UN Trust Fund, i.e., funded with contributions from member states)[150]
		• Budget: $256 million USD[151]
		• Cost of between $10–15 million (6.4–9.5 million euros) per accused.[152]

(Continued)

Table 8.2 (Continued)

Design Elements	International Criminal Tribunal for the Former Yugoslavia (ICTY)	International Criminal Tribunal for Rwanda (ICTR)

Jurisdiction. E.g., what are the temporal and subject matter jurisdictional limitations?	• Temporal Jurisdiction: Since January 1, 1991 (ICTY Statute, Art. 8)[153]
	• Personal Jurisdiction: Natural persons (ICTY Statute, Art. 6)[154]
	• Territorial Jurisdiction: Territory of the former Yugoslavia. (ICTY Statute, Art. 8)[155]
	• Subject Matter Jurisdiction[156]:
	  ◦ Genocide
	  ◦ War Crimes—Grave Breaches, Violations of Laws and Customs of War
	  ◦ Crimes Against Humanity
	• Concurrent Jurisdiction, primacy of the ICTY (ICTY Statute, Art. 9)[157]
	
	Additional Jurisdiction Information:
	• The ICTY and national courts have concurrent jurisdiction over the violations of international humanitarian law, however, the ICTY has can claim primacy over national investigations and proceedings at any stage if in the interest of international justice.[158]
	• ICTY Statute, Art. 1 provides jurisdiction over individual persons (not organizations, political parties, army units, administrative units, or the legal subjects) who have committed serious violations of international humanitarian law in the territory of former Yugoslavia since 1991.[159]
	  ◦ An accused person who served in an official position whether as head of state or government, or as a responsible Government official is not protected from criminal liability nor will their position mitigate punishment.[160]
		• Temporal Jurisdiction: January 1, 1994—December 31, 1994 (ICTR Statute, Art. 7)[164]
		• Personal Jurisdiction: Natural persons (ICTR Statute, Art. 5)[165]
		• Territorial Jurisdiction: Territory of Rwanda (Rwandans, non-Rwandan citizens)/territory of neighboring countries (Rwandans) (ICTR Statute, Art. 7)[166]
		• Subject Matter Jurisdiction[167]:
		  ◦ Genocide
		  ◦ War Crimes—Violations of common Art. 3 Geneva Conventions I-IV and AP II
		  ◦ Crimes Against Humanity
		• Concurrent Jurisdiction, primacy of the ICTR (ICTR Statute, Art. 8)[168]

	• Arts. 2–5 of the ICTY Statute identify four categories of crimes which the Tribunal has jurisdiction.[161,162]
	  • Art. 2: Grave Breaches of the Geneva Conventions of 1949
	  • Art. 3: Violations of the Laws or Customs of War
	  • Art. 4: Genocide
	  • Art. 5: Crimes Against Humanity
	• ICTY Statute, Art. 7: "A person who planned, instigated, ordered, committed or otherwise aided and abetted in the planning, preparation or execution of a crime referred to in Arts. 2 to 5 shall be individually responsible for the crime."[163]	

Evidence. E.g., how are the rules of evidence adopted and who wrote them?	• Rules of Procedure and Evidence for the ICTY
	  • IT/32/Rev.50, July 8, 2015[169]
	  • Adopted pursuant to the ICTY Statute[170]
	• Amendments: IT/282, July 10, 2015[171]
		• Rules of Procedure and Evidence for the ICTR:
		  • ICTR Statute, Art. 12
		  • The judges of the International Tribunal for Rwanda shall adopt, for the purpose of proceedings before the International Tribunal for Rwanda, the rules of procedure and evidence for the conduct of the pre-trial phase of the proceedings, trials and appeals, the admission of evidence, the protection of victims and witnesses and other appropriate matters of the International Criminal Tribunal for the Former Yugoslavia with such changes as they deem necessary.[172]

Procedure. E.g., how are the rules of procedure adopted and who wrote them?	• Rules of Procedure and Evidence for the International Criminal Tribunal for the former Yugoslavia (IT/32/Rev.50, July 8, 2015)[173]
	• Practice Direction on Procedure for the Proposal, Consideration of, and Publication of Amendments to the Rules of Procedure and Evidence of the International Tribunal. (IT/143/Rev.2)[174]
	• Amendments: IT/282, July 10, 2015[175]
	• Procedure for the Variation of Protective Measures Pursuant to Rule 75 (h) of the Rules of Procedure and Evidence of the International Tribunal for Access to Confidential Tribunal Material, February 4, 2008[176]
	• Individuals awaiting sentencing were held in detention facilities, including:
	  • United Nations Detention Facility (UNDF) located in Arusha[177]
	  • United Nations Detention Unit (UNDU) located in The Hague.[178]
		• ICTR Rules of Procedure and Evidence (as amended May 13, 2015)[179]
		• Individuals awaiting sentencing were held in detention facilities, including:
		  • United Nations Detention Facility (UNDF) located in Arusha[180]
		  • United Nations Detention Unit (UNDU) located in The Hague.[181]

(*Continued*)

Table 8.2 (Continued)

Design Elements	International Criminal Tribunal for the Former Yugoslavia (ICTY)	International Criminal Tribunal for Rwanda (ICTR)
Witness protection. E.g., how are witnesses protected?	• Procedure for the Variation of Protective Measures Pursuant to Rule 75 (h) of the Rules of Procedure and Evidence of the International Tribunal for Access to Confidential Tribunal Material (February 4, 2008)[182] • Confidential information, such as a witness's name or pseudonym, testimony, or exhibit number is subject to an application under Rule 75 (h).[183]	• ICTR Statute, Art. 21: • The International Tribunal for Rwanda shall provide in its rules of procedure and evidence for the protection of victims and witnesses. Such protection measures shall include, but shall not be limited to, the conduct of in camera proceedings and the protection of the victim's identity.[184]
Coverage. E.g., are trial proceedings televised? Are they live or delayed? Are proceedings open or closed?	• Public • ICTY Statute, Art. 20(4): "The hearings shall be public unless the Trial Chamber decides to close the proceedings in accordance with its rules of procedure and evidence."[185] • The ICTY proceedings were recorded with audio-visual equipment to serve as a record of the proceedings for archiving and media purposes.[186] • Only recordings of public hearings were made available to the media and are available in ICTY archives.[187]	• Public • ICTR Statute, Art. 19(4): "The hearings shall be public unless the Trial Chamber decides to close the proceedings in accordance with its rules of procedure and evidence."[188]
Sentencing. E.g., what are the sentencing options?	• In accordance with Art. 40 of the Host State Agreements for both branches and Art. 25 of the Mechanism Statute, detainees subject to a final conviction are transferred to an Enforcement State to serve their sentences.[189] • The median sentence length at the ICTY was 18 years.[190] • ICTY Statute, Art. 24: The penalty imposed by the Trial Chamber shall be limited to imprisonment. In determining the terms of imprisonment, the Trial Chambers shall have recourse to the general practice regarding prison sentences in the courts of the former Yugoslavia.[191] • ICTY Statute, Art. 24 provides general instructions as to what factors the court should take into account, including gravity of the offense and the individual circumstances of the convicted person.[192]	• Practice Direction on the Procedure for Designation of the State in Which a Convicted Person is to Serve His/Her Sentence of Imprisonment (September 23, 2008)[193] • The median sentence length at the ICTR was 33.5 years.[194] • ICTR Statute, Art. 23: The penalty imposed by the Trial Chamber shall be limited to imprisonment. In determining the terms of imprisonment, the Trial Chambers shall have recourse to the general practice regarding prison sentences in the courts of Rwanda.[195] • ICTR Statute, Art. 23 provides general instructions as to what factors the court should take into account, including gravity of the offense and the individual circumstances of the convicted person.[196]

		• On July 1, 2012, the UN-MICT took over responsibility for the supervision of ICTR sentences.[197] • Sentences are enforced in accordance with international standards of detention and the applicable law of the enforcing state.[198] • The ICTR Judges have the responsibility of determining the guilt or innocence of those accused of committing genocide, war crimes, and/or crimes against humanity in Rwanda in 1994, and to sentence those whom they convicted to a period of imprisonment commensurate with their crimes. The maximum sentence that can be imposed by the Chambers on an accused is life imprisonment.[199]
Incarceration. E.g., where are sentences served?	• Procedure for the International Tribunal's Designation of the State in which a Convicted Person is to Serve his/her Sentence of Imprisonment, Rev.1, September 1, 2009.[200] • The median sentence at the ICTY is 15 years.[201] • As from July 1, 2013, the supervision of the enforcement of sentences for ICTY cases falls under the jurisdiction of the International Residual Mechanism for Criminal Tribunals (IRMCT).[202] • The IRMCT also has jurisdiction to designate enforcement states, including for persons thereafter convicted by the Tribunal.[203] • Sentences are enforced in accordance with international standards of detention and the applicable law of the enforcing state.[204] • As of September 1, 2016, the Host State Agreement between the Mechanism for International Criminal Tribunals and the Kingdom of the Netherlands applies mutatis mutandis to the ICTY.[205] • Full list of ICTY judgments from 1996 to 2017.[206]	• In accordance with Art. 40 of the Host State Agreements for both branches and Art. 25 of the Mechanism Statute, detainees subject to a final conviction are transferred to an Enforcement State to serve their sentences.[207] • As from July 1, 2012, the supervision of the enforcement of sentences for ICTR cases falls under the jurisdiction of the International Residual Mechanism for Criminal Tribunals (IRMCT).[208] The IRMCT also has jurisdiction to designate enforcement states, including for persons thereafter convicted by the Tribunal.[209]

(*Continued*)

Table 8.2 (Continued)

Design Elements	International Criminal Tribunal for the Former Yugoslavia (ICTY)	International Criminal Tribunal for Rwanda (ICTR)

Appeals. E.g., can judgments be appealed? If so, what is the standard of review? If so, what are the statistics for trial judgments being upheld, reversed, or sentences modified?	• Formal Requirements for Appeals from Judgement, March 7, 2002.[210]
	• Practice Direction on procedure for the filing of written submissions in appeal proceedings before the International Tribunal (IT/155/Rev.4).[211]
	• The Appeals Chamber hears appeals from either a person convicted by a Trial Chamber or from the Prosecutor.[212] Either party can appeal any element of the Trial Chamber's judgement—an alleged error on a question of law or an alleged error of fact.[213]
	• A party may submit additional evidence on appeal if the Appeals Chamber finds that the evidence was not available at trial, and is relevant, credible and could have been a decisive factor in reaching the decision at trial.[214]
	• The ability of the Appeals Chamber to receive additional evidence on appeal has been particularly important because many of the archives holding relevant material in the former Yugoslavia were not made available to the ICTY until some years into its proceedings.[215]
	• Upon examination of the submissions by the parties, the Appeals Chamber will render its judgement by majority.[216] The Appeals Chamber can affirm, reverse or revise the Trial Chamber's decision.[217] Under appropriate circumstances, the Appeals Chamber may also order a retrial.[218]
		• Practice Direction on Formal Requirements for Appeals from Judgment (June 15, 2007)[219]
		• Appeals can be made on the grounds of:
		  • Error on a question of law[220]
		  • Error of fact[221]

Activity. E.g., how many trials has the tribunal completed? Is it considered efficient and effective?	• The ICTY conducted 111 trials.[222] • 161 indicted defendants[223] • Ninety-three sentenced, eighteen acquitted, thirteen referred to national jurisdictions pursuant to Rule *11bis*,[224] and thirty-seven had indictments withdrawn or died.[225] • The maximum sentence that a Trial Chamber may impose is life imprisonment (ICTY Statute, Art. 24).[226]	• Ninety-three individuals indicted, sixty-two sentenced, fourteen acquitted, ten referred to national jurisdictions for trial, three fugitives referred to the Mechanism for International Criminal Tribunal (MICT), two deceased prior to judgment, and two indictments were withdrawn before trial.[229]

	• According to one legal scholar, when accounting for the complexity and efficiency of the ICTY, the Rules of Evidence and Procedure followed by the Tribunal appeared to provide fair and expeditious trials.[227] • Other scholars have noted that the actual procedures implemented to expedite the trials may not have actually done so without sacrificing some other aspect of the trials' fairness or procedures.[228]	• The ICTR is the first international tribunal to deliver verdicts in relation to genocide, to interpret the definition of genocide set forth in the 1948 Geneva Convention, and to define rape in international criminal law and to recognize rape as a means of perpetrating genocide.[230] • Completion strategy: • On August 28, 2003, the Security Council adopted resolution 1503 (2003), ordering the ICTR to "take all possible measure to complete investigations by the end of 2004, to complete all trial activities at first instance by the end of 2008, and to complete all work in 2010."[231]
Polling data. E.g., is there any polling data available as to whether the tribunal is considered legitimate? By the international community, by the victims, or by the country at large where the atrocities took place?	• According to the ICTY, the Tribunal laid the foundations for the now the accepted norms for international conflict resolution and post-conflict development, proved that efficient and transparent international justice is possible, and contributed to an indisputable historical record, combating denial and helping communities come to terms with their recent history.[232]	• The ICTR has been recognized for achievements in the prosecution of perpetrators, but also criticized in the court's efficiency and its procedures.[233]
Tribunal's use after conclusion of proceedings	• N/A	• Until the return of that judgment in 2015, the ICTR will continue its efforts to end impunity for those responsible for the Genocide through a combination of judicial, outreach, and capacity-building efforts.[234]
Reports and publications	• Annual Reports to General Assembly and Security Council.[235] • The Yearbook provides information about the work, members (with biographies), jurisdiction, organization, functioning and activities of the Tribunal in a given year.[236] • Includes a bibliography of publications relating to the Tribunal released during the reporting period.[237] • The Judicial Reports reprint all public indictments as well as the decisions and judgments.[238]	• Annual Reports to General Assembly and Security Council.[239] • Case information can be found on the UN Mechanism for International Criminal Tribunals website.[240]

Table 8.3 Hybrid Tribunals

Design Elements	Extraordinary Chambers for the Courts of Cambodia (ECCC)	Special Court for Sierra Leone (SCSL)
Geographic location. E.g., is it inside or outside the country where the atrocities occurred?	• Phnom Penh, Cambodia[241]	• Freetown, Sierra Leone[242]
Context. E.g., is it in an occupied area, or a free state?	• Not considered a free state, because its political system has been dominated by one political party.[243]	• Considered "partly free."[244]
Founding authority. E.g., is it created by the UN or by a treaty or by a statute?	• 2003 Law on the Establishment of the Extraordinary Chambers in the Courts of Cambodia (NS/RKM/0801/12), promulgated on Aug. 10, 2002, as amended on Oct. 27, 2004; agreement between the UN and the government of Cambodia, signed June 6, 2003[245]	• 2002 Agreement between the UN and the government of Sierra Leone, Jan. 16, 2002[246] • Mandated "to prosecute persons who bear the greatest responsibility for serious violations of international humanitarian law and Sierra Leonean law committed in the territory of Sierra Leone since November 30, 1996."[247]
Applicable law	• Cambodian penal law/humanitarian law and custom/international conventions recognized by Cambodia Public.[248]	• Humanitarian law/Sierra Leonean law.[249] • UN-Sierra Leone Agreement, Art. 1; SCSL Statute, Art. 1.[250]

Judicial arm. E.g., are the judges purely international, purely domestic, or mixed (if the latter, what ratio)? What is the appointment mechanism? How long to judges serve? Do judges have diplomatic immunity?	• Court Structure[251]
	  • Chambers (Supreme Court, Trial, Pre-Trial Chambers)
	  • Office of the Co-Investigating Judges
	  • Office of the Co-Prosecutors
	• International mix of judges[252]
	• The UN Secretary General nominates a list of international judges and Cambodia's Council of Magistracy makes the final appointments. Cambodia's Council of Magistracy appoints national judges.[253]
		• Court Structure[256]:
		  • Chambers (Trial and Appeals Chambers)
		  • Prosecutor
		  • Registry
		• Chambers shall be composed of not less than eight (8) or more than eleven (11) independent judges.[257]
		• Three judges serve in the Trial Chamber, one appointed by the Government of Sierra Leone, and two (2) appointed by the Secretary-General of the United Nations.[258]

	• Law on ECCC, Arts 41 and 42:
	  • The foreign judges, the foreign Co-Investigating Judge, together with their families forming part of their household, shall enjoy all of the privileges and immunities, exemptions and facilities accorded to diplomatic agents in accordance with the 1961 Vienna Convention on Diplomatic Relations.[254]
	  • Cambodian judges and the Co-Investigating Judge shall be accorded immunity from legal process in respect to words and acts performed in their official capacity. Such immunity shall continue to be accorded after termination of employment with the Extraordinary Chambers, the Pre-Trial Chamber and the Office of Administration.[255]
		• Five (5) judges serve in the Appeals Chamber, two (2) appointed by the Government of Sierra Leone, and three (3) judges appointed by the Secretary-General.[259]
		• Judges shall be appointed for three-year term and are eligible for re-appointment.[260]
		• SCSL Statute, Art. 12: "The judges, together with their families forming part of their household, shall enjoy the privileges and immunities, exemptions and facilities accorded to diplomatic agents in accordance with the 1961 Vienna Convention on Diplomatic Relations."[261]

Prosecutorial arm. E.g., is the prosecution purely international, purely domestic, or mixed?	• The Agreement between the United Nations and the Government of Cambodia (which established the ECCC) provides for a Cambodian prosecutor and an international prosecutor, serving as co-prosecutors.[262]
	• The national co-prosecutor is appointed by the Supreme Council of the Magistracy, and the international co-prosecutor is appointed by the Supreme Council of the Magistracy of Cambodia upon nomination by the United Nations Secretary-General.[263]
	• Office of the Co-Prosecutors:
	  • Ms. Chea Leang (National Co-Prosecutor—Cambodian)[264]
	  • Mr. Fergal Gaynor (Reserve International Co-Prosecutor—Ireland)[265]
	• The Supreme Council of the Magistracy appoints the Cambodian co-prosecutor and reserve prosecutors from among Cambodia's professional judges. The UN Secretary General nominates and the council appoints the international co-prosecutor.[266]
		• The UN Secretary General appointed the prosecutor Government of Sierra Leone appointed the deputy prosecutor.[267]
		• The UN Secretary General appointed two (2) judges to the trial chamber and three (3) judges to the appeals chamber. The Government of Sierra Leone appointed one (1) judge to the trial chamber and two (2) judges to the appeals chamber.[268]
		• Up to two alternate judges may be appointed after six months of the commencement of the Special Court.[269]

(*Continued*)

Table 8.3 (Continued)

Design Elements	Extraordinary Chambers for the Courts of Cambodia (ECCC)	Special Court for Sierra Leone (SCSL)
Defense arm. E.g., are defense counsel purely international, purely domestic, or mixed?	• Mix of Cambodian and foreign/international defense counsel.[270]	• Defense teams were made up of international and national counsel, although a Sierra Leonean held the position of principal defender near the end of the court's operations; before that, only internationals held the position. The registry allocated considerable human resources to the defense office, including a chief advisor, three defense associates, and financial and administrative support staff.[271]

Funding. E.g., is there adequate funding for all three components? What is the source of funding?	• Budget: $464.87 million USD (Official budget reports issued by ECCC from 2004 through 2018).[272]
	• Cost per trial of $36 million (23 million euros).[273]
	• Law on Establishment of the ECCC, Art. 44[274]:
	  • "The expenses and salaries of the Cambodian administrative officials, staff, judges, and prosecutors shall be borne by the Cambodian national budget."
	  • "The Extraordinary Chambers may receive additional assistance for their expenses from other voluntary funds contributed by foreign governments, international institutions, non-governmental organizations, and other persons wishing to assist the proceedings."
		• Budget: $292,363,461 million USD (2013)[275]
		• The Residual Special Court is funded by voluntary contributions from the international community.[276]

Jurisdiction. E.g., what are the temporal and subject matter jurisdictional limitations?	• Temporal Jurisdiction: April 17, 1975–January 6, 1979 (ECCC Establishment Law, Art. 2)[277] • Personal Jurisdiction: Senior leaders and those most responsible for crimes committed in Democratic Kampuchea (ECCC Establishment Law, Art. 2).[278] • Territorial Jurisdiction: Territory of Cambodia (senior leaders and those most responsible for crimes committed in Democratic Kampuchea) (ECCC Establishment Law, Art. 2)[279]	• Temporal Jurisdiction: Since November 30, 1996 (SCSL Statute, Art. 1)[282] • Personal Jurisdiction: Persons who bear the greatest responsibility for serious violations of international humanitarian law (SCSL Statute, Art. 1).[283]

	• Subject Matter Jurisdiction[280]:
	  • Genocide
	  • War Crimes—Grave breaches of the 1949 Geneva Conventions
	  • Crimes Against Humanity
	  • Other Crimes—Crimes defined by the Cambodian law (Establishment Law, Ch. II)
	• Exclusive Jurisdiction[281]
		• Territorial Jurisdiction: Territory of Sierra Leone (SCSL Statute, Art. 1)[284]
		• Subject Matter Jurisdiction[285]:
		  • War Crimes
		  • Crimes Against Humanity
		  • Other Crimes—Crimes under Sierra Leonean law (SCSL Statute, Art. 5)
		• Concurrent Jurisdiction (decisions of the SCSL take precedence)[286]
		• Parallel Truth and Reconciliation Commission, founded in 2002[287]

Evidence. E.g., how are the rules of evidence adopted and who wrote them?	• The Internal Rules of the Extraordinary Chambers in the Courts of Cambodia (ECCC) regulate what kind of evidence is admissible during trial. The main rule is that all evidence is admissible. Internal Rules (Rev. 10), Rule 87.[288] • Evidence presented at trial: 334 witnesses (as of September 27, 2017).[289]	• Evidence presented at trial: 552 witness testimonies (310 for the prosecution and 242 for the defense).[290] • Rules of Procedure and Evidence are governed by SCSL Statute, Art. 14.[291]
Procedure. E.g., how are the rules of procedure adopted and who wrote them?	• Procedure for the ECCC is governed by Section III (Rules 21–40).[292]	• Rules of Procedure and Evidence are governed by SCSL Statute, Art. 14.[293]

(*Continued*)

Table 8.3 (Continued)

Design Elements	Extraordinary Chambers for the Courts of Cambodia (ECCC)	Special Court for Sierra Leone (SCSL)
Witness protection. E.g., how are witnesses protected?	• The ECCC ensures "the protection of Victims who participate in the proceedings, whether as complainants, or Civil Parties, and witnesses, as provided in the supplementary agreement on security and safety and the relevant Practice Directions" (ECCC (2011b), Rule 29 "Protective Measures").[294] • Requests for protection measures or concerns about confidentiality or safety of a witness are referred to the Witness and Expert Support Unit (WESU), whom they can meet in person to develop a strategy for protection. Witnesses can request that judges order protective measures for them, which the judge can do after considering all aspects of the issue including witness' rights and rights of the accused to a fair trial.[295]	• The court provided assistance "for witnesses, victims who appear before the Court and others who are at risk on account of testimony given by such witnesses" (Statute of the Special Court of Sierra Leone, art. 16(4)).[296] • Witnesses included "potential witnesses and sources" (The Special Court for Sierra Leone (2003c), Rule 39: Conduct of Investigations).[297] • The Witnesses and Victims Section (WVS) makes determinations on requests for witness protection and support, in consultation with the offices of the prosecutor and the defense and based on the particular needs and circumstances (Special Court for Sierra Leone (2003c), Rules 34(A)).[298] Parties could also apply to the judge or the Trial Chamber, which could consult with the WVS to determine the form of protective measures for victims and witnesses.[299]
Coverage. E.g., are trial proceedings televised? Are they live or delayed? Are proceedings open or closed?	• Public • Establishment Law, Art. 34: "Trials shall be public unless in exceptional circumstances the Extraordinary Chambers decide to close the proceedings for good cause in accordance with existing procedures in force," Art. 12 of the Agreement "Any exclusion from such proceeding . . . shall only be to the extent strictly necessary in the opinion of the Chamber concerned and where publicity would prejudice the interests of justice."[300]	• Public • SCSL Statute, Art. 17(2): "The accused shall be entitled to a fair and public hearing, subject to measures ordered by the Special Court for the protection of victims and witnesses."[301]
Sentencing. E.g., what are the sentencing options?	• The maximum sentence the ECCC may issue for the crimes falling within its jurisdiction is life imprisonment.[302] • Number of convictions after trial: 3.[303]	• The maximum sentence that a Special Court may impose is life imprisonment (SCSL Statute, Art. 19).[304] • Convictions after trial: 9.[305]

Appeals. E.g., can judgments be appealed? If so, what is the standard of review? If so, what are the statistics for trial judgments being upheld, reversed, or sentences modified?	• Appellate proceedings are governed by ECCC Section III, Subsection F (Rules 104–114)[306] • "The Tribunal rejected an appeal by Khieu Samphan, the last surviving leader of the Khmer Rouge government, and reaffirmed the life sentence he received in 2018 for genocide, crimes against humanity, and war crimes."[307] • "Co-defendant Nuon Chea, the Khmer Rouge's No. 2 leader and chief ideologist, was convicted twice and received the same life sentence. Nuon Chea died in 2019 at age 93."[308] • "The tribunal's only other conviction was that of Kaing Guek Eav, also known as Duch, who was commandant of Tuol Sleng prison, was convicted in 2010 of crimes against humanity, murder, and torture and died in 2020 at age 77 while serving a life sentence."[309]	• Appellate proceedings are governed by SCSL Statute, Art. 20.[310] • "Many of the findings at the trial level were upheld by the Appeals Chamber. The few instances where the defense's arguments prevailed on appeal, or where the appeals judges reversed the findings at trial for certain errors, resulted in the revision of the global sentences to fifty-two, forty, and twenty-five years for Sesay, Kallon, and Gbao respectively."[311]
Incarceration. E.g., where are sentences served?	• Kandal Provincial Prison[312]	• Sentences are served in Sierra Leone.[313] • Convicts were transferred to Mpanga Prison in 2009.[314]

Activity. E.g., how many trials has the tribunal completed? Is it considered efficient and effective?	• The ECCC has heard four cases in the tribunal.[315]
	• Positive perception of the tribunal and its effectiveness is mostly positive.[316]
	  • See *Justice and Reconciliation for the Victims of the Khmer Rouge?* (Williams et al., 2018) for more statistics about the trust and effectiveness of the tribunal.
		• Charges were filed individually, with cases consolidated into four trials.[317]
		• Achievements:
		  • First-ever convictions for attacks against UN peacekeepers, convictions for forced marriage as a crime against humanity, and for the recruitment of children for combat.[318]
		• UN Secretary-General commented on Court's legacy and advancement of international criminal liability.[319]

(*Continued*)

Table 8.3 (Continued)

Design Elements	Extraordinary Chambers for the Courts of Cambodia (ECCC)	Special Court for Sierra Leone (SCSL)
Polling data. E.g., is there any polling data available as to whether the tribunal is considered legitimate? By the international community, by the victims, or by the country at large where the atrocities took place?	• Varying polling data from before and after the proceedings.[320] • Cambodian public opinion in 2008, one year after the commencement of the tribunal's work, did not show much difference from years prior to the ECCC's establishment.[321] • According to the results of the 2008 survey conducted by UCB, only 36 percent of Cambodians agreed that "they trusted Cambodian court system," and 37 percent agreed that they trusted Cambodian judges.[322] • Only 40 percent of the respondents agreed that "Cambodian judges treat everyone equally," and 44 percent responded that "justice in Cambodia is same for everyone."[323]	• The Special Court represents the first hybrid approach to international criminal justice and is a proven example that the hybrid model of national ownership complemented by international partnership is effective and efficient.[324] • SCSL was the first tribunal since Nuremberg to successfully bring to justice a former head of state (Charles Taylor).[325] • The SCSL was also the first to adjudicate crimes relating to enlistment, recruitment, conscription, or use of child soldiers; attacks on peacekeepers; forced marriage; sovereign immunity; effect of national amnesties on the jurisdiction of an international court and procedural relationships with a Truth and Reconciliation Commission.[326] • An independent survey conducted by "No Peace Without Justice" found that 91 percent of Sierra Leoneans and 78 percent of Liberians believe that the SCSL helped to bring peace to their countries.[327]
Use of the tribunal's location after conclusion of trial	• N/A	• Period of operation: 2002–13.[328] • Currently operating as a residual mechanism.[329] • The Residual Special Court for Sierra Leone was created by an agreement between the United Nations and the Government of Sierra Leone to oversee the continuing legal obligations of the Special Court for Sierra Leone after its closure in 2013.[330] These include ongoing functions such as the maintenance, preservation, and management of the SCSL archives, witness protection, sentence enforcement, and ad hoc functions such as reviewing convictions and acquittals and conducting contempt of court proceedings.[331]

Table 8.4 Internationalized Domestic Tribunals

Design Elements	Kosovo Specialist Chambers (KSC)	Iraq High Tribunal (IHT)
Geographic location. E.g., is it inside or outside the country where the atrocities occurred?	• The Hague, the Netherlands[332]	• Baghdad, Iraq[333]
Context. E.g., is it in an occupied area, or a free state?	• Parliamentary democracy/free state[334]	• Occupied by United States from 2003 to 2011.[335] • Not recognized as a free state.[336]
Founding authority. E.g., is it created by the UN or by a treaty or by a statute?	• Hybrid tribunal, blends aspects of international and domestical law and resources.[337] • Established pursuant to an international agreement ratified by the Kosovo Assembly, a Constitutional Amendment and the Law on Kosovo Specialist Chambers and Specialist Prosecutor's Office.[338]	• Statute of the Iraqi Special Tribunal (IST Statute), enacted by the Iraqi Governing Counsel on December 10, 2003.[339] The tribunal was known as the Iraqi Special Tribunal (IST) between December 2003 to October 2005 as on Order of the Coalition Provisional Authority.[340] In August 2005, the IST statute was revoked by Iraq's Transitional National Assembly and replaced by an amended statue that renamed the IST Statute as the Statute of the Iraqi High Tribunal (IHT Statute).[341] The IHT Statute established the Supreme Iraqi High Tribunal (IHT) when promulgated in the Official Gazette on October 18, 2005.[342]

(*Continued*)

Table 8.4 (Continued)

Design Elements	Kosovo Specialist Chambers (KSC)	Iraq High Tribunal (IHT)
Applicable law	• Law on ratification of the international agreement was ratified, ratified by the Kosovo Assembly on April 23, 2014.[343] • Law on Specialist Chambers and Specialist Prosecutor's Office was adopted by the Kosovo Assembly, August 3, 2015.[344] • Constitution and Amendment of the Constitution, Art. 162: The Specialist Chambers and the Specialist Prosecutor's Office—adopted by the Kosovo Assembly on August 3, 2015.[345] • Agreement between the Kingdom of the Netherlands and the Republic of Kosovo concerning the Hosting of the Kosovo Relocated Specialist Judicial Institution in the Netherlands (Host State Agreement) of February 2016.[346] • Parliamentary Assembly of the Council of Europe Report Inhuman treatment of people and illicit trafficking in human organs in Kosovo of January 2011[347] • Law on Ratification of International Agreement ("Exchange of Letters") adopted by the Kosovo Assembly in April 2014[348]	• International criminal law/humanitarian law/ Iraqi laws[349] • IST Statute, Arts. 11–14[350] • On December 10, 2003, the Iraqi Governing Council adopted the IST Statute, providing the legal foundation and laying out the jurisdiction and basic structure for the Tribunal that will be responsible for prosecuting acts of genocide, crimes against humanity, and war crimes committed in Iraq between 1968 and 2003.[351] • The IHT revised statute was October 2005.

Judicial arm. E.g., are the judges purely international, purely domestic, or mixed (if the latter, what ratio)? What is the appointment mechanism? How long to judges serve? Do judges have diplomatic immunity?	• Court Structure:[352]
	  • Chambers (Basic Court, Court of Appeals, Supreme Court, and Constitutional Court Chambers)
	  • Registry
	• The Judges were appointed to the Roster upon recommendation of an independent Selection Panel of International Judges on February 7, 2017, by the Appointing Authority. Six (6) new Judges were appointed on September 22, 2020.[353]
	• Judges are international (no Kosovo judges appointed as of March 2024).[354]
		• Court Structure:[355]
		  • One or more Trial Chambers
		  • Appeals Chamber
		  • Prosecutions Department
		  • Administrative Department
		• Judges are to be nominated and appointed by the Governing Council, after consultation with the Judicial Council, the permanent judges of each Trial Chamber shall elect a Presiding Judge, and both the permanent and reserve judges are appointed for five (5) years.[356]

Prosecutorial arm. E.g., is the prosecution purely international, purely domestic, or mixed?	• Prosecution is international (citizenship of either an EU member state or one of the five non-EU contributing countries: Canada, Norway, Switzerland, Turkey, and the United States).[357]	• Prosecutors must be Iraqi nationals and serve a three-year term (IST Statute, Art. 28).[358] However, the Chief Prosecutor is required to appoint non-Iraqi advisers to assist in prosecution and non-Iraqi observers to monitor prosecutorial performance (IST Statute, Art. 8(j)).[359]
Defense arm. E.g., are defense counsel purely international, purely domestic, or mixed?	• Mixed with both domestic and international defense counselors.[360]	• Mixed of with domestic and international defense counselors.[361]
Funding. E.g., is there adequate funding for all three components? What is the source of funding?	• The EU Member States and other contributing countries (Canada, Norway, Switzerland, Turkey, and the United States of America) have financially supported the work of the court.[362]	• Budget: provided by the regular budgets of Iraqi government[363]

Jurisdiction. E.g., what are the temporal and subject matter jurisdictional limitations?	• Jurisdiction over natural persons of Kosovo/Federal Republic of Yugoslavia (FRY) citizenship, or over persons accused of committing crimes against persons of Kosovo/FRY citizenship.[364]
	• Temporal Jurisdiction: crimes commenced or committed in Kosovo between January 1, 1998, and December 31, 2000, by or against citizens of Kosovo or the Federal Republic of Yugoslavia.[365]
	• Subject Matter Jurisdiction[366]:
	  • War Crimes
	  • Crimes Against Humanity
	  • Other Crimes under Kosovo Law
	• Concurrent jurisdiction (KSC with primacy)[367]
		• Temporal Jurisdiction: July 17, 1968–May 1, 2003 (IST Statute, Art. 1)[368]
		• Personal Jurisdiction: Any Iraqi national or resident of Iraq (IST Statute, Arts. 1 and 10)[369]
		• Territorial Jurisdiction: Territory of Iraq/"elsewhere," including crimes committed in connection with Iraq's wars against the Islamic Republic of Iran and the State of Kuwait (IST Statute, Art. 1)[370]
		• Subject Matter Jurisdiction[371]:
		  • Genocide
		  • War Crimes
		  • Crimes Against Humanity
		  • Other Crimes—Violations of Iraqi Laws (IST Statute, Art. 14)
		• Concurrent Jurisdiction, primacy of IST[372]
		• Parallel Truth and Reconciliation Commission, founded in 2002[373]

(*Continued*)

Table 8.4 (Continued)

Design Elements	Kosovo Specialist Chambers (KSC)	Iraq High Tribunal (IHT)
Evidence. E.g., how are the rules of evidence adopted and who wrote them?	• Rules of Procedure and Evidence of the Kosovo Specialist Chambers.[374] • Adopted pursuant to international agreement ratified by the Assembly of Kosovo.[375]	• The Rules of Procedure and Evidence are defined in the IST Statute, Art. 16.[376] • Iraqi Governing Council adopted the IST, which provided the legal foundation and basic structure for the Tribunal.[377]

Procedure. E.g., how are the rules of procedure adopted and who wrote them?	• The Rules of Procedure and Evidence were adopted on March 17, 2017 and revised on May 29, 2017 by the Specialist Chambers Judges. Following the Specialist Chamber of the Constitutional Court's (SCCC) determination that the Rules comply with Chapter II of the Kosovo Constitution, they entered into force on July 5, 2017, marking the date from which the Specialist Chambers became judicially operational. On May 26, 2020, the SCCC found that 30 amendments adopted by the Judges to the Rules comply with Chapter II of the Constitution. The amended Rules entered into force seven days thereafter.[378]	• Rules of Procedure and Evidence are defined in the IST Statute, Art. 16[379]:
		  • President of the Tribunal drafts the rules of procedure and evidence where the IST Statute "does not adequately provide for a specific situation."
		  • "President of the Tribunal shall be guided by Iraqi Criminal Procedure Law."
		• Investigation and Indictment Procedures are defined in the IST Statute, Art. 18.[380]
		• Trial Proceeding are defined in the IST Statute, § 8.[381]

Witness protection. E.g., how are witnesses protected?	• The Victims' Participation Office will treat all victims' applications and communications with potential victims and those who assist them as confidential.[382] • To qualify as a victim, the applicant must provide sufficient evidence of the harm suffered as a direct result of any crime in the indictment.[383]	• Witness Protection is defined in the IST Statute, Art. 22[384]: • "The Tribunal shall, in its rules of procedure and evidence, provide for the protection of victims and witnesses. Such protection measures shall take into account the rights of the accused and shall include, but shall not be limited to, the conduct of in camera proceedings and the protection of the identity of the victim or witness."

Coverage. E.g., are trial proceedings televised? Are they live or delayed? Are proceedings open or closed?	• Public • "Outreach Programme of the Kosovo Specialist Chambers (KSC), funded in part through a generous contribution from Switzerland, aims to promote understanding of the mandate and proceedings of the KSC and to foster dialogue about its work in Kosovo and the region."[385] • The KSC established a Court information Network (CIN) comprised of NGOs from Kosovo and Serbia.[386] • All public hearings are streamed in the three languages of the court and can be watched at: https://www.scp-ks.org/en/streaming.	• Public • IST Statute, Art. 21: ". . . unless the Trial Chamber decides to close the proceedings in accordance with its rules of procedure and evidence. The decision to close the proceedings shall be exercised on a very limited basis."[387]
Sentencing. E.g., what are the sentencing options?	• Determination of Punishment (i.e., sentencing) is governed by Section V, Rules 162–165 of the Rules of Procedure and Evidence Before the KSC[388] • Amendment of the Constitution of the Republic of Kosovo, Art. 162: "If found guilty and sentenced to imprisonment, any such persons may be transferred to serve their sentence in a third country, outside the territory of Kosovo." • It is unclear where those sentenced to imprisonment have been serving their sentences.	• The maximum sentence that a Trial Chamber may impose is life imprisonment (IST Statute, Art. 24).[389] • Penalties imposed by the Tribunal are those prescribed by Iraqi Law/Iraqi Criminal Code.[390]

Appeals. E.g., can judgments be appealed? If so, what is the standard of review? If so, what are the statistics for trial judgments being upheld, reversed, or sentences modified?	• Appeals proceedings are governed by Chapter 10 of the Rules of Procedure and Evidence Before the KSC.[391]
	• In 2023, appeals judges at the special Kosovo Tribunal confirmed the war crimes conviction of Salih Mustafa, a former Kosovo Liberation Army guerrilla commander, but reduced his sentence from 26 to 22 years in prison.[392]
		• Appellate and Review Proceedings are governed by the IST Statute, Section 9.[393]
		• Appeals may be heard on the ground of:
		  • Error on a question of law,
		  • Error of procedure, or
		  • Error of material fact.[394]
		• The Court upheld the convictions of the seven appellants and their sentences, with the exception of Taha Yassin Ramadan whose sentence was increased to the death penalty.[395]

Incarceration. E.g., where are sentences served?	• Rules of Procedure and Evidence Before the KSC, Rule 166: "The President shall decide in which State the Accused shall serve his or her sentence, from a list of States that have agreed to accept convicted persons."[396]	• Sentences shall be carried out by the legal system of Iraq in accordance with its laws.[397]

(*Continued*)

Table 8.4 (Continued)

Design Elements	Kosovo Specialist Chambers (KSC)	Iraq High Tribunal (IHT)
Activity. E.g., how many trials has the tribunal completed? Is it considered efficient and effective?	• In 2021, The first trial opened on Wednesday at a special court dealing with crimes during the 1998–9 Kosovo conflict.[398] • As of March 2023, 2 cases are still in the pre-trial phase, 2 have been to trial, 1 case is at the end of appeal phase, and 1 case is in the enforcement of sentence phase.[399] • More case information can be found at: https://www.scp-ks.org/en/cases.	• Five cases brought before the Tribunal.[400] • There is debate as to whether the Tribunal is fair and effective.[401]
Polling data. E.g., is there any polling data available as to whether the tribunal is considered legitimate? By the international community, by the victims, or by the country at large where the atrocities took place?	• Witness intimidation and political interference are cited as potential threats to the KSC's legitimacy.[402]	• In 2006, 56 percent of Iraqis believed that if Hussein is tried by an Iraqi court for the murder of Iraqi civilians, it would be conducted in a fair and impartial manner, 23 percent believe otherwise, and 21 percent were unsure.[403] • As of 2024, Iraqis' faith in their political and national institutions is at a record-high of 56 percent, and 57 percent have confidence in their judiciary (highest in over a decade).[404]

Table 8.5 Hybrid/Internationalized Domestic Tribunals

Design Elements	War Crimes Chamber of the Court of Bosnia and Herzegovina (BWCC or War Crimes Chamber)	Special Tribunal for Lebanon (STL)
Geographic location. E.g., is it inside or outside the country where the atrocities occurred?	• Sarajevo, Bosnia-Herzegovina[405]	• Leidschendam, the Netherlands (near The Hague) and Beirut, Lebanon[406]
Context. E.g., is it in an occupied area, or a free state?	• Considered "partly free."[407] • Local tribunal.[408]	• Netherlands: Parliamentary democracy/free state[409] • Lebanon: Considered "partly free."[410]
Founding authority. E.g., is it created by the UN or by a treaty or by a statute?	• Established on July 3, 2002, by Parliament by the Law on the Court of Bosnia and Herzegovina.[411] • Created as a joint initiative of the ICTY and the Office of the High Representative (OHR).[412]	• UN Security Council Resolution 1757 (2007)[413]
Applicable Law	• Bosnian and Herzegovina (BiH) penal code.[414, 415] • Law on Court of Bosnia and Herzegovina (BiH).[416]	• UN Security Council Resolution 1757 (2007).[417] • Attachment Statute of the Special Tribunal for Lebanon, UN Security Council Resolution 1757 (2007) [STL Statute].[418]

Judicial arm. E.g., are the judges purely international, purely domestic, or mixed (if the latter, what ratio)? What is the appointment mechanism? How long to judges serve? Do judges have diplomatic immunity?	• Court Structure[419]:
	  • Chambers (Criminal and Appellate Divisions)
	  • Prosecutor's Office
	  • The Registry
	• The High Representative for BiH initially appointed international judges. Later, the High Judicial and Prosecutorial Council (HJPC) appointed both international and national judges.[420]
	• Mix of both national and international judges.[421]
	• Judges appointed shall perform their duties until the age of seventy, except when appointed by the High Commissioner (where the maximum term is five years), there is a voluntary resignation, permanent inability to perform duties due to a medical condition, or removed from office by Parliament.[422]
		• Court Structure:[423]
		  • Chambers (Trial and Appeals Chambers)
		  • Prosecutor
		  • Registry
		  • Defense Office
		• The UN Secretary-General appointed international judges based on nominations forwarded by states (at the invitation of the UN Secretary General). The UN Secretary-General appointed Lebanese judges from a list of twelve persons presented by the Lebanese government and proposed by the Lebanese Supreme Council of the Judiciary.[424]
		• The judges shall be appointed by the Secretary-General for a three-year period and may be eligible for reappointment for a further period to be determined by the Secretary-General in consultation with the Government.[425]

(*Continued*)

Table 8.5 (Continued)

Design Elements	War Crimes Chamber of the Court of Bosnia and Herzegovina (BWCC or War Crimes Chamber)	Special Tribunal for Lebanon (STL)
Prosecutorial arm. E.g., is the prosecution purely international, purely domestic, or mixed?	• The High Representative for BiH initially appointed prosecutors. Later, the High Judicial and Prosecutorial Council (HJPC) conducted the appointment process.[426] • Until 2008 each of the five trial panels and the appellate panel included two international members and one national member.[427] • Currently national judges are in a majority; the panels now include two nationals and one international. Both the international and national judges may sit simultaneously in war crimes and organized crime chambers.[428]	• The UN Secretary-General, after consultation with the Lebanese government and upon the recommendation of a selection panel. The selection panel is composed of two judges, currently sitting on or retired from an international tribunal, and a representative of the UN Secretary-General. The government appoints a Lebanese deputy prosecutor, in consultation with the UN Secretary-General and the prosecutor.[429]
Defense arm. E.g., are defense counsel purely international, purely domestic, or mixed?	• As of December 31, 2012, 124 defense lawyers were certified to appear before the War Crimes Section. The quality of the section's work in providing counsel with both training and administrative support has been generally considered high. Counsel is offered training and must meet continuing professional training criteria in order to be certified to practice in the chambers. Defense lawyers receive advice and research assistance, including on international law and jurisprudence, from "five defense support teams."[430]	• Defense lawyer demographics include: six (6) Lebanese and twenty-four (24) international lawyers.[431]
Funding. E.g., is there adequate funding for all three components? What is the source of funding?	• Budget: $64,693,290 USD (from official annual reports of the BiH office of the prosecutor)[432] • Cost of $16 million (10 million euros) per year to run eight trial courts.[433] • Supported through voluntary contributions from international donors and the BiH state budget.[434]	• In 2020–21, the tribunal's budget was $67 million with Lebanon paying 49 percent and foreign donors and the UN members covering the other 51 percent.[435] • 1 billion spent (as of 2021) in 15 years of investigation and legal proceedings.[436]

Jurisdiction. E.g., what are the temporal and subject matter jurisdictional limitations?	• Temporal Jurisdiction: serious violations committed since 1991.[437]
	• The Court has jurisdiction over "criminal offences defined in the Penal Code of Bosnia and Herzegovina and other laws of Bosnia and Herzegovina."[438]
	• Subject Matter Jurisdiction[439]:
	  • Genocide
	  • War Crimes
	  • Crimes Against Humanity
	• Concurrent jurisdiction (BiH has primacy).[440]
	  • No person shall be tried before a court in the territory of BiH for which they have already been tried by the BWCC.[441]
		• Temporal Jurisdiction: over persons responsible for attacks between October 1, 2004, and December 12, 2005 if these attacks are connected to the Hariri attack.[442]
		• Subject matter jurisdiction: crimes defined under Lebanese Penal Code (LPC) including, terrorism, crimes and offenses against life and personal integrity, illicit associations, and failure to report crimes and offenses.[443]
		• Concurrent jurisdiction (STL has primacy).[444]

Evidence. E.g., how are the rules of evidence adopted and who wrote them?	• Evidence presented at trial: 6,427 witnesses (2005–12).[445]	• Evidence presented at trial: Over 260 individual witnesses and about 2,470 exhibits in documentary form at the conclusion of prosecution case in Ayyash et al.[446]

Procedure. E.g., how are the rules of procedure adopted and who wrote them?	• Procedure governed by the BiH penal code[447] and the Law on Court of BiH.[448]
	• Law on Court of BiH, art. 10:
	  • Rules of procedure of the Court regulate all divisions. Must follow minimum procedural guarantees (arts. 33–35).
	  • Rules of procedure is published in the Official Gazette of BiH.[449]
		• Rules of Procedure and Evidence are governed by UN Security Council Resolution 1757 (2007), Art. 28.[450]

(*Continued*)

Table 8.5 (Continued)

Design Elements	War Crimes Chamber of the Court of Bosnia and Herzegovina (BWCC or War Crimes Chamber)	Special Tribunal for Lebanon (STL)
Witness protection. E.g., how are witnesses protected?	• A "vulnerable witness" is one who has been "severely physically or mentally traumatized" by the offense or "otherwise suffers from a serious mental condition rendering him unusually sensitive, and a child and a juvenile." Under the law on the witness protection program in BiH, eligible persons are those "without whose testimony there would be no prospects in criminal proceedings of investigating the facts or of ascertaining the whereabouts of the suspect, or such would be made much more difficult" (Law on Witness Protection Program, Official Gazette of Bosnia and Herzegovina, art. 2(1)).[451] • The BiH courts and the judges determine both the form of support or protection and whether such measures are necessary (Law on Witness Protection Program, Official Gazette of Bosnia and Herzegovina, Art. 3).[452]	• Eligible persons are victims and witnesses and "others who are at risk on account of testimony given by such witnesses."[453] • The Victims and Witnesses Unit (VWU) within the registry makes determinations on requests for witness protection and support.[454]
Coverage. E.g., are trial proceedings televised? Are they live or delayed? Are proceedings open or closed?	• Public[455]	• Public[456]
Sentencing. E.g., what are the sentencing options?	• Convictions after trial: over 188 (as of November 2017).[457]	• The Trial Chamber shall impose upon a convicted person, other than a juvenile offender, imprisonment for a specified number of years.[458] • Convictions after trial: 0 (primary cases), 2 (on contempt charges), and other trials are still ongoing.[459]
Appeals. E.g., can judgments be appealed? If so, what is the standard of review? If so, what are the statistics for trial judgments being upheld, reversed, or sentences modified?	• Appellate proceedings are governed by Law on the Court of Bosnia and Herzegovina, Arts. 9 and 22.[460] • Appellate division may confirm, reverse, or revise decisions.[461]	• Appellate proceedings are governed by UN Security Council Resolution 1757 (2007), Art. 26.[462]

Incarceration. E.g., where are sentences served?	• Sentences are served in a Special Detention Facility located on the grounds of the Court of BiH.[463]	• UN Security Council Resolution 1757 (2007), Art. 29: "Imprisonment shall be served in a State designated by the President of the Special Tribunal from a list of States that have indicated their willingness to accept persons convicted by the Tribunal."[464]
Activity. E.g., how many trials has the tribunal completed? Is it considered efficient and effective?	• In the period 2004–08, a total of eighty-nine war crimes cases were finalized, concerning 136 defendants, an average of eighteen cases per year.[465] • In the following decade (2009–19), 555 cases (involving 842 defendants) were completed across the country—an average of around fifty-five cases per year. There are currently 245 ongoing cases before the courts of BIH.[466] • In 2018, 780 cases involving 5,390 individuals remained pending before the different prosecutors' offices.[467]	• Nine indictments and case outcomes[468]: • Salim Ayyash—fugitive, trial began on January 16, 2014 • Mustafa Badreddine—died on May 13, 2016, proceedings terminated on July 12, 2016 • Hussein Oneissi—fugitive, trial began on January 16, 2014 • Assad Sabra—fugitive, trial began on January 16, 2014 • Hassan Mehri—fugitive, trial began on June 18, 2014 • Akhbar Beirut S.A.L—sentenced to a 6000 Euro fine • Ibrahim al-Amin—sentenced to a 20,000 Euro fine • Al Jadeed S.A.L / New TV S.A.L—acquitted on September 18, 2015 • Karma Khayat—acquitted on March 6, 2016
Polling data. E.g., is there any polling data available as to whether the tribunal is considered legitimate? By the international community, by the victims, or by the country at large where the atrocities took place?	• There was a small increase in the public's perception of judicial effectiveness in 2020 relative to 2019.[469] • See full 2020 report for more data/statistics	• There appears to be a disproval of what the STL was able to accomplish and the "selective justice" it appeared to carry out.[470]
Use of the Tribunal's Location After Conclusion of Trial	• 2005–12 with international judges. The War Crimes Chamber continues to operate.[471]	• No existing mechanisms.[472]

Table 8.6 Permanent Court

Design Elements	International Criminal Court (ICC)
Geographic location. E.g., is it inside or outside the country where the atrocities occurred?	The Hague, the Netherlands[473] • "The Rome Statute provides that the Court may sit elsewhere whenever the judges consider it desirable. The Court has also set up offices in the areas where it is conducting investigations."[474]
Context. E.g., is it in an occupied area, or a free state?	Parliamentary democracy/free state[475]
Founding authority. E.g., is it created by the UN or by a treaty or by a statute?	• Rome Statute of the International Criminal Court (July 17, 1998), adopted by the United Nations Diplomatic Conference of Plenipotentiaries on the Establishment of an International Criminal Court (A/CONF.183/9). [476] • Entered into force on July 1, 2002[477]
Applicable law	• ICC Statute/international law, including humanitarian law/general principles of law[478] • ICC Statute, Art. 21[479]

Judicial arm. E.g., are the judges purely international, purely domestic, or mixed (if the latter, what ratio)? What is the appointment mechanism? How long to judges serve? Do judges have diplomatic immunity?	• Court Structure[480]:
	  • Chambers: (Pre-Trial, Trial, and Appeals Chambers)[481]
	  • Office of the Prosecutor (OTP)[482]
	  • Registry[483]
	  • Presidency[484]
	• "The ICC's 18 judges are elected by the Assembly of States Parties for their qualifications, impartiality and integrity, and serve 9-year, non-renewable terms."[485]
	• Judges are from a mix of international states.[486]
	• Judges per case[487]:
	  • Pre-Trial: 3
	  • Trial: 3
	  • Appeals: 5

Prosecutorial arm. E.g., is the prosecution purely international, purely domestic, or mixed?	• The Office of the Prosecutor (OTP) is an independent organ of the Court[488] • Elected by the Assembly of States Parties (the Assembly) for a non-renewable mandate of nine (9) years.[489] • The OTP is a mix of international attorneys. • Currently (as of March 2024) is comprised of attorneys from the United Kingdom, Senegal, and Fiji.[490]

Defense arm. E.g., are defense counsel purely international, purely domestic, or mixed?	• Independent and not ICC staff.[491] • Suspects and accused persons have the right to freely choose counsel.[492] • Defense counsel must be admitted to the List of Counsel to represent a defendant.[493] • There are currently (March 2024) 400 lawyers from various international states on the List of Counsel.[494]
Funding. E.g., is there adequate funding for all three components? What is the source of funding?	• "The Court is funded by contributions from the States Parties and by voluntary contributions from governments, international organizations, individuals, corporations and other entities."[495] • Budget: €169,649,200 in 2023.[496]

Jurisdiction. E.g., what are the temporal and subject matter jurisdictional limitations?	• Temporal Jurisdiction: Since July 2002 (ICC Statute, Art. 11(1))[497]
	  ◦ "Crimes were committed by a State Party national, or in the territory of a State Party, or in a state that has accepted the jurisdiction of the Court; or
	  ◦ the crimes were referred to the ICC Prosecutor by the United Nations Security Council (UNSC) pursuant to a resolution adopted under chapter VII of the UN charter."[498]
	  ◦ "As of 17 July 2018, a situation in which an act of aggression would appear to have occurred could be referred to the Court by the Security Council, acting under Chapter VII of the United Nations Charter, irrespective as to whether it involves States Parties or non-States Parties. In the absence of a UNSC referral of an act of aggression, the Prosecutor may initiate an investigation on her own initiative or upon request from a State Party."[499]
	  ◦ "If a State becomes a party to the Statute after its entry into force, the Court may exercise its jurisdiction only with respect to crimes committed after the entry into force of the Statute for that State, unless that State has made a declaration accepting the jurisdiction of the ICC retroactively. The the Court cannot exercise jurisdiction with respect to events which occurred before 1 July 2002."[500]

(Continued)

Table 8.6 (Continued)

Design Elements	International Criminal Court (ICC)

	• Personal Jurisdiction: Natural persons (ICC Statute, Art. 25)[501]
	  ◦ The Court does not have jurisdiction to prosecute any person who was under the age of eighteen (18) when the crimes were committed.[502]
	• Territorial Jurisdiction: Territory of states party/territory of non-party states when crimes committed by states party's nationals/territory of non-party states that accepted the jurisdiction of the court. (ICC Statute, Art. 12)[503]
	• Subject Matter Jurisdiction[504]:
	  ◦ Genocide
	  ◦ War Crimes
	  ◦ Crimes Against Humanity
	  ◦ Other Crimes—Aggression (ICC Statute, Art. 5)
	• Complementarity (ICC Statute, Art. 1)[505]
	  ◦ "The ICC is intended to complement, not to replace, national criminal systems; it prosecutes cases only when States do not are unwilling or unable to do so genuinely."[506]

Evidence. E.g., how are the rules of evidence adopted and who wrote them?	• Governed by ICC Rules of Procedure and Evidence[507] • "The Statute of the International Criminal Court (ICC) was adopted as the result of an international diplomatic conference organized under the aegis of the United Nations (UN)."[508] • "When investigating, the Prosecutor must collect and disclose both incriminating and exonerating evidence."[509]
Procedure. E.g., how are the rules of procedure adopted and who wrote them?	• Governed by ICC Rules of Procedure and Evidence[510] • "The Statute of the International Criminal Court (ICC) was adopted as the result of an international diplomatic conference organized under the aegis of the United Nations (UN)."[511]
Witness protection. E.g., how are witnesses protected?	• "ICC Registry staff offer various means of practical support to witnesses, from obtaining visas so they can travel to the seat of the Court in The Hague, the Netherlands, assistance during their travel and stay at the place of testimony, to setting up video link services so witnesses can testify closer to their place of residence when granted by the Chamber."[512] • "The Court has a number of protective measures that can be granted to witnesses, victims who appear before the Court and other persons at risk on account of testimony given by a witness. The Court's protection system is based on best practices which are aimed at concealing the witness's interaction with the Court from their community and from the public in general."[513]

	• These include Familiarization with the Courtroom, Allowances, Protection, and mitigating Trauma and Vulnerability.[514]
	• Familiarization with the Courtroom:
	  • Showing witnesses the Courtroom before the hearing starts and explaining the Courtroom's procedures.[515]
	• Allowances:
	  • Witnesses may receive two types of allowances for personal expenses or wages, earnings, and time lost to compensate for the financial burden of testifying.[516]
	• Protection:
	  • Witness Relocation: "Protective measures where witnesses reside aim to limit the witness's exposure to threats or provide an appropriate response to an identified threat. Measures must be proportional to the risk."[517]
	  • Identity: "The Chamber can order certain protective measures that apply while the witness testifies in order to protect the witness's identity and whereabouts. Such measures may consist of face/voice distortion while the witness is giving evidence and/or the use of a pseudonym. Judges can also conduct parts of hearings in private or closed sessions when necessary to protect the witness's identity or the identity of other persons at risk on account of testimony."[518]
	• Trauma and Vulnerability:
	  • "The Registry is equipped with staff members with expertise in trauma, including trauma related to crimes of sexual violence. The Registry is mandated to advise the Chambers on measures to be taken to facilitate their testimony and to prevent psychological harm resulting from appearing before the Court."[519]

Coverage. E.g., are trial proceedings televised? Are they live or delayed? Are proceedings open or closed?	• Public • ICC Statute, Art. 67(7): "The Trial Chamber may, however, determine that special circumstances require that certain proceedings be in closed session for the purposes set forth in Art. 68, or to protect confidential or sensitive information to be given in evidence."[520]
Sentencing. E.g., what are the sentencing options?	• The maximum sentence that a Trial Chamber may impose is life imprisonment (ICC Statute, Art. 77).[521]

(*Continued*)

Table 8.6 (Continued)

Design Elements	International Criminal Court (ICC)
Appeals. E.g., can judgments be appealed? If so, what is the standard of review? If so, what are the statistics for trial judgments being upheld, reversed, or sentences modified?	• "Both the Prosecutor and the Defense have the right to appeal a Trial Chamber's decision on the verdict (decision on guilt or innocence of the accused) and the sentence."[522] • "The victims and the convicted person may appeal an order for reparations."[523] • "An appeal is decided by five judges of the Appeals Chamber, who are never the same judges as those who gave the original verdict." • "The Appeals Chamber decides whether to uphold the appealed decision, amend it, or reverse it."[524] • Unless the Appeal Chamber orders a re-trial before the Trial Chamber, the Appeals Chamber's decision is a final judgment.[525]
Incarceration. E.g., where are sentences served?	• "Sentences are served in countries that have agreed to enforce ICC sentences. If a verdict of guilt is not upheld, the person may be released."[526]

Activity. E.g., how many trials has the tribunal completed? Is it considered efficient and effective?	• As of March 2024:
	  • "31 cases before the Court, with some cases having more than one suspect. ICC judges have issued 42 arrest warrants.
	  • 21 people have been detained in the ICC detention center and have appeared before the Court. (17 people remain at large.)
	  • Charges have been dropped against 7 people due to their deaths.
	  • ICC judges have also issued 9 summonses to appear.
	  • The judges have issued 10 convictions and 4 acquittals."[527]

Polling data. E.g., is there any polling data available as to whether the tribunal is considered legitimate? By the international community, by the victims, or by the country at large where the atrocities took place?	• In April 2018, 63% of Americans believe that the United States should dedicate resources, including financial, military and intelligence resources, to international organizations that support human rights and that hold individuals accountable for mass atrocities (an increase from 47% in 2014).[528] • "Just under half of Americans (45%) are aware of the Court, up from 40% when this tracking began in 2014. Almost four out of ten Americans incorrectly believe that United States is a member of the ICC. Awareness of the ICC is the strongest among millennials (age 18–34) at 57% and among men of all ages at 27%."[529] • "Survey research suggests that registered victims are on average pleased with their direct interactions with the ICC, but they often hold 'insufficient knowledge to make informed decisions about their participation in ICC cases' because Court actors have not been able to maintain long-lasting relationships or regularly update locals, especially in rural areas."[530] • "In countries where the ICC has intervened, interest in human rights spiked, and sustained."[531]

societal humiliation that Germany was not. Indeed, Japan still lives today under the post-war constitution largely drafted by the US military during the occupation.[26]

"If public perceptions of international courts are tainted by accusations of victor's justice, western domination, or disregard for local interests, the legitimacy of international justice will be undermined."[27] While the post-Cold War tribunal models do not suffer from the stigma of victor's justice, as the post-World War II models may have. Nevertheless, post-conflict ethnic tensions may still infuse such tribunals in delegitimizing ways, such as Shi'a Arabs and Sunni Kurds being seen to prosecute and judge Sunni Arabs in the post-Saddam regime Iraqi High Tribunal (IHT), which was carried out under the US military occupation of Iraq or perceptions of the ICTY's and BWCC's efficacy split mainly along ethnic lines.

The legitimacy throughlines located by the tables in the next section highlight such elements comparatively.

I. Comparative Structural Elements

International criminal tribunals are arrayed across the following tables by tribunal typology. All of the tables except the final one contain two examples of tribunal design within each category. Structural design choices are highlighted within each category, but the reader is encouraged to broaden the scope of their understanding by comparing design choices across categories as well. With this view, legitimacy throughlines emerge, which may better inform future choices of future tribunal designers, such as those working to build a new international criminal tribunal for the crime of Russian aggression, discussed in Section V.

Legitimacy Throughlines

The degree to which a tribunal is accepted (1) by the public in the state where the atrocities occurred, (2) by the international community, (3) by the victims, and (4) by defendants, goes to the heart of whether that tribunal is deemed legitimate. Polling data, albeit limited, can measure the first, legal opinions and funding levels can measure the second, participation can measure the third, and acceptance of verdicts and judgments can measure the fourth. Absent sufficient acceptance by these groups, the goal of transitional or restorative justice may prove elusive, leaving tribunal designers to be satisfied only with retributive justice.

Defendants rarely accept the legitimacy of the court prosecuting them. They often attack the court with structure-based arguments such as constitutional integrity, equality of arms between prosecution and defense, and impartiality—the legitimacy argument is a key legal and rhetorical weapon. Legally, it was deployed against the first international criminal tribunal, the IMT-Nuremberg, by German counsel, making much about *ex post facto* application of the law, but these arguments were to little avail.[532] The second tribunal, convened half a century later, faced similar doubts. ICTY defendants mounted legal challenges against the court's legitimacy, causing it too to defend its existence in its first judgment. Dusko Tadic, the ICTY's first defendant in its first case, argued against the legality of the tribunal on multiple fronts:

> It is said that, to be duly established by law, the International Tribunal should have been created either by treaty, the consensual act of nations, or by amendment of the Charter of the United Nations, not by resolution of the Security Council. Called in aid of this general proposition are a number of considerations: that before the creation of the International Tribunal in 1993 it was never envisaged that such an ad hoc criminal tribunal might be set up; that the General Assembly, whose participation would at least have guaranteed full representation of the international community, was not involved in its creation; that it was never intended by the Charter that the Security Council should, under Chapter VII, establish a judicial body, let alone a criminal tribunal; that the Security Council had been inconsistent in creating this Tribunal while not taking a similar step in the case of other areas of conflict in which violations of international humanitarian law may have occurred; that the establishment of the International Tribunal had neither promoted, nor was capable of promoting, international peace, as the current situation in the former Yugoslavia demonstrates; that the Security Council could not, in any event, create criminal liability on the part of individuals and that this is what its creation of the International Tribunal did; that there existed and exists no such international emergency as would justify the action of the Security Council; that no political organ such as the Security Council is capable of establishing an independent and impartial tribunal; that there is an inherent defect in the creation, after the event, of ad hoc tribunals to try particular types of offences and, finally, that to give the International Tribunal primacy over national courts is, in any event and in itself, inherently wrong.[533]

First, the trial court, then the appellate court, knocked down such arguments in ways similarly employed by the IMT-Nuremberg—by citing the binding power of the UN Security Council's resolutions acting under its Chapter XII authority granted by all nations in the UN Charter, together with other interpretive provisions of the Charter, and force of logic to conclude that the ICTY was indeed property constituted, could exercise judicial power, had the jurisdiction granted it by the UNSC, was itself an appropriate measure to deal with the conflict during the Balkan civil wars, and enjoyed jurisdictional primacy over domestic national courts.[534]

Rhetorically, Slobodan Milosevic continued to challenge the ICTY's legitimacy years later, noting in his opening statement, "I consider this tribunal a false tribunal and indictments are false indictments. It is illegal, not being appointed by the U.N. General Assembly."[535] The designers of both the ICTY and ICTR had sought initially to imbue both tribunals with greater independence, better security, and more impartiality by locating them in The Hague, away from Serbia, and in Arusha, away from Rwanda, and staffing them with purely international judges, attorneys, and registrars. This structural choice, however, had the unintended consequence of psychologically distancing both tribunals from Serbs and Rwandans.

Buffeted by allegations of remoteness and irrelevance, the ICTY and ICTR sought to "get back" to Serbia and Rwanda. Both tribunals engaged in this organic practice of trying to recapture lost legitimacy in an effort to compensate for the structural design choice to physically remove the tribunals from the country that was producing most of their defendants—a departure from the IMT-Nuremberg and IMTFE models, which situated the tribunals in Germany and Japan. Once the court is up and operating, it may, on its own initiative, attempt to boost public perceptions of its legitimacy. While such moves are outside the control of the initial tribunal designers, they are perhaps legacies of what those designers built. Both ad hoc tribunals made such attempts.

By the time Milosevic was launching his legitimacy-challenging rhetorical broadsides at the tribunal, the ICTY had begun broadcasting proceedings back to Serbia for the public to view; however, this only emboldened Milosevic to speak over the heads of the judges and directly to the Serbian people, opining with contempt, "[T]his show which is supposed to take place under the guise of a trial is actually a crime against a sovereign state, against the Serb people, against me."[536] Thus, ironically, the extra step of televising trial proceedings to legitimize the court with people in Serbia actually worked to further undermine it. Indeed, Milosevic retrieved enough of his own legitimacy, at the cost of the tribunal's legitimacy, that he was elected *in absentia* to the Serb parliament while still incarcerated, standing trial in The Hague.[537] As Figure 8.1 shows, Serbs remained largely convinced the ICTY was biased against them, even though it also prosecuted Croatians and Bosnians, such that, by the tribunal's completion, 81 percent of Serbs felt so.[538]

Not surprisingly, the second largest group of perpetrators behind Serbs, Croatians, also viewed the ICTY somewhat negatively, while Bosniaks and Kosovar Albanians, mostly victim groups, viewed the work of the tribunal positively.[539]

Meanwhile, the ICTR, overwhelmed by the sheer number of defendants it was faced with prosecuting, decided to turn this problem into an opportunity to co-opt

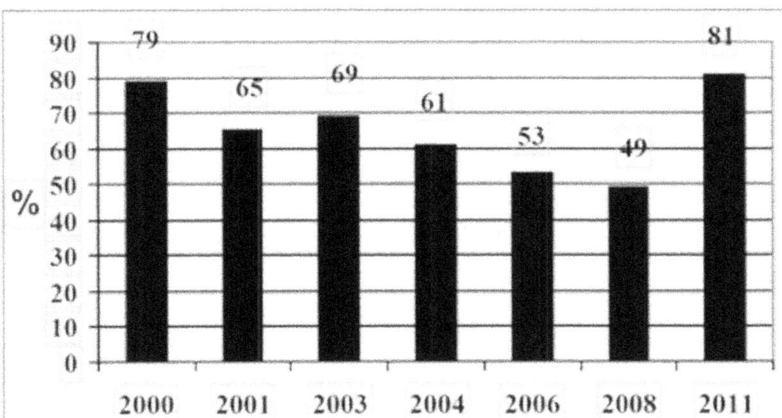

Figure 8.1 Percent of Serbs who feel ICTY is biased against them. Figure provided by author.

Rwanda's traditional tribal system of justice as a way to boost its own legitimacy among Rwandans who "view[ed] the tribunal as being distant from them both by proximity—as it [was] located in Arusha, Tanzania—and by the Western justice that it promot[ed] rather than the reconciliation that Rwandans desire[d]."[540] Partnering with tribal elders, the ICTR held onto the "big fish" in Arusha, but released the "small fish" back to their respective tribes in Rwanda to face the gacaca courts. Staffed by tribal elders elected by the community, these traditional courts eschewed strict evidentiary rules, emphasizing instead "reconciliation and the restoration of balance back in the community—including the reintegration of the perpetrator into community life."[541]

While achieving more acceptance than the ICTR, the looseness of the gacaca process left open the possibility of those seeking revenge to hijack the process through baseless accusations (convictions were based on witness testimony only—no physical evidence), lack of legal counsel for the accused, co-opting the accused to confess to lesser crimes for lighter sentences, and the traumatization and societal stigmatization of women witness who testified to traumatic events with no assistance of counsel or psychological support:[542]

> [I]nterviews revealed that each woman began to be harassed and threatened after giving testimony at a Gacaca trial. One woman described how not only her physical safety was threatened but also her livelihood. Her harassers brought their cows onto her land to graze and subsequently destroyed her crops. During the trials, many of the witnesses are harassed verbally by the shouts and contributions of those in attendance. One woman revealed that she no longer attends Gacaca because her sister was killed after testifying at a trial. The women also revealed the psychological side effects associated with testifying through their interviews. Many described the horror of reliving their experiences as they testified in court. Many of the women suffered physical trauma such as uncontrollable shaking, crying, and fainting while on the witness stand. The women are left vulnerable due to their testifying, and many confess to feeling lonely and isolated from the rest of their community. Sadly, these women who should feel comforted and relieved as their testimonies help to enact justice in the community instead are left feeling lonely, isolated, and fearful.[543]

Subsequent tribunal designers often take note of such structural arguments and attempt to adjust for perceived weaknesses. The structural evolution from the ad hoc models, represented by the ICTY and ICTR, to the hybrid models, represented by the SCSL and ECCC, amounted to an acknowledgment that such tribunals needed to re-anchor themselves among the people both physically and with respect to staffing. Consequently, the hybrid tribunals not only located themselves within Sierra Leone and Cambodia, but they also were staffed with local judges, attorneys, and registrars to sit alongside and work with international staff.[544]

In the case of the SCSL, this stratagem largely worked.[545] The only case that was held remotely was the case of former Liberian dictator Charles Taylor—which was moved to a special sitting of the SCSL in The Hauge under an agreement with The Netherlands because of security concerns about keeping him in Sierra Leone and running the trial there. As for the ECCC, this stratagem largely failed. One of the risks of incorporating the local population into the hybrid staffing model with the tribunal located in the country where the atrocities occurred, and which is producing the majority of the defendants is that local corruption and political interference may be incorporated as well. UN Secretary-General Kofi Annan was skeptical of the ECCC's structure, which placed too much emphasis on national rather than international components.[546] His worries proved to be true. The risks stemming from a shaky rule of law system, "incompetent" Cambodian judges emerging from a nascent legal system still not recovered from the Khmer Rouge wiping out the legal profession, endemic corruption, and lack of judicial independence from the government,[547] proved too much to save the ECCC from the context in which it was set.

In the end, only two cases were tried, and the tribunal was shuttered at the urging of Cambodia's prime minister, acting through the Cambodian national judges on the court against the wishes of the international judges:

> National judges' reluctance to try other members of the Khmer Rouge, despite the enormous legal and factual evidence to the contrary and the herculean effort of the international component of the ECCC, reflects Hun Sen's—Cambodia's longest-serving prime minister (since 1985) and a former defector of the Khmer Rouge—position that the ECCC will not be allowed "to expand its prosecutions beyond the two cases already underway." The political unwillingness coupled with "the continued . . . interference by the executive with the independence of the judiciary" (as noted by the General Assembly already in 2003 [Res. 57/225]), "little respect on the part of Cambodian courts for the most elementary features of the right to a fair trial" [Hans Corell's 2003 Report, p. 8], and the majority of national—Cambodian—judges at the ECCC, inevitably (and unfortunately for the international justice) lead to the crippling of the ECCC."[548]

The "takeaway" for designers from the hybrid model experience might be that location does not matter as much as an honest assessment of conditions on the ground of the host country, which could undermine the tribunal's legitimacy from a different direction.

> The legitimacy challenge for criminal prosecutions of former leaders and warlords lies in the ascription of forward-looking goals to an institutional mechanism—the criminal trial—that is, in its nature, mostly backward-looking. But, it is only through solving this challenge that transitional justice mechanisms can be legitimate, and the challenge is not easily solved by simply locating a court in the affected country.[549]

Similarly, the following two categories, internationalized domestic tribunals and hybrid/internationalized domestic tribunals, offer mixed results. Of the internationalized domestic tribunals, the Iraqi High Tribunal (IHT) was established under Iraqi law in

Baghdad to prosecute Saddam Hussein and his Ba'athist cronies, but during the US-led occupation of Iraq, failed on all counts—structure, process, and outcomes.[550] It was, perhaps, bedeviled from the outset. The American-led coalition invasion of Iraq in 2003 was illegal under international law.[551] Thus, the legitimacy of anything stemming from action, such as the IHT, was likely tainted from inception.

Moreover, the coalition's aggressive de-Ba'athification of Iraq wiped out the high-level judiciary, leaving behind only low-level judges to attempt to deal with the crimes of Iraq's former leaders—a task for which they were ill-equipped. International advisors sought to assist the judges and prosecution, and international defense counsel was introduced, but these devices did little to save the tribunal. Evaluations of its judgment and appeal in the first case were negative.[552] The chaotic courtroom environment, with defendants shouting out and trying to represent themselves, combined with the poor structural choice to proceed against the key defendant, Saddam Hussein, in seven sequential cases instead of building those into multiple charges under one case. The proceedings under Iraqi criminal law, which mandates the execution of death sentences within thirty days of the final appeal, guaranteed that millions of victims of Saddam's brutal dictatorship, such as survivors of the Kurdish genocide, would not receive justice.[553] He was, indeed, executed halfway through his second trial.

More successful is the relatively new Kosovo Specialist Chambers (KSC). Based in The Hague, the KSC operates under Kosovo's constitution, which was amended in 2015 to accommodate the court as a unique arm of the Kosovar judiciary, set up to prosecute crimes against humanity, war crimes, and other crimes under Kosovo law committed in Kosovo from 1998 to 2000. Unlike the IHT, this domestic tribunal's "internationalizing" aspect manifests as international staff, including judges, prosecutors, and the registrar's office. Security, however, is Kosovar. The European Union, as opposed to the United Nations for the hybrid models or the US-led coalition for the IHT, is the international partner with Kosovo in this arrangement and underwrites its funding. Also, unlike the IHT, the KSC is seen as a good working model.[554] Even though it is only now beginning its trial processes, it is already holding unruly defendants in contempt, thereby ensuring procedural accountability.[555] Despite public skepticism at its inception, this was driven largely by the identification of Kosovo Liberation Army staff as heroes who realized the new country's independence from Serbia, coupled with pushback from some academics that its structure is too internationalized.[556]

Several recent developments can be seen as legitimizing in nature. (1) with respect to charging, Kosovo's former prime minister is incarcerated and standing trial on six counts of crimes against humanity and four counts of war crimes committed via a joint criminal enterprise;[557] (2) concerning the high quality of its staff who have been selected for higher posts (always a mark of external validation), the French KSC judge, Nicolas Guillou, was elected in 2023 to the bench of the ICC and its chief prosecutor, Jack Smith, was selected to lead special prosecutions against former US president Trump with respect to the January 6th insurrection at the US Capitol and mishandling classified documents after leaving office.

Of the hybrid/internationalized domestic tribunals, the War Crimes Chamber in the Court of Bosnia and Herzegovina (BWCC) is much more successful[558] than the failed Special Tribunal for Lebanon (STL). Based in Sarajevo and staffed with a blend of international and local judges, the BWCC was initially designed to handle lower-level defendants accused of committing atrocities during the Bosnian phase of the Balkan civil wars, as was requested of all affected Yugoslavia successor states;[559] however, it was the BWCC rather than the Croatian or Serbian iteration that garnered the most respect, did the most work, and is now considered a model for domestic-based hybrid internationalized criminal justice.[560] The BWCC is very much the on-site successor to the ICTY;[561] the Hague-based MICT handling mostly post-conviction relief and archival duties.

In a 2023 assessment, the European Union noted: "[o]ut of 237 cases by the end of 2022 (including 103 in main trial phase), 91 proceedings (against 99 individuals) are pending as the indicted persons are not available."[562] This is due mainly to Serbia not handing over suspects.[563] Moreover, "The backlog in war crime cases continues to diminish . . .. From an estimated 1 210 cases in July 2013, unresolved war crime cases have been reduced to 395 (−67.5%) by the end of 2022."[564] Indeed, Bosnia-Herzegovina's handling of war crimes cases was noted as a point of progress in the European Commission's 2024 recommendation that the state be elevated to candidate status to join the EU with accession negotiations to begin forthwith.[565]

Despite these successes, Bosnian Serbs, not surprisingly, remain skeptical of possible BWCC bias against them, mostly because the largest number of defendants have been Bosnian Serb instead of Bosnian Croat or Bosnian Muslim[566]—which correlates directly to the Bosnian Serbs having committed the most atrocities during the war. "While the state court does not keep a record of the ethnicity of persons indicted for war crimes, the RS Centre for Investigating War Crimes, CIWC, claims that 70 percent of all indictees have been Serbs, around 16.5 percent Bosniaks (Bosnian Muslims), and 12.5 percent Croats."[567]

The STL was designed to investigate and prosecute those responsible for the 2005 assassination of the Lebanese prime minister Rafik Hariri. As such, it was not given the usual mandate of bringing those who commit war crimes, genocide, or crimes against humanity to justice. Rather, it was presented the opportunity to define international terrorism, which until then was not sufficiently defined. In seizing this opportunity, the STL's appeals chamber found that under customary international law, terrorism consisted of:

> The following three key elements: (i) the perpetration of a criminal act (such as murder, kidnapping, hostage-taking, arson, and so on), or threatening such an act; (ii) the intent to spread fear among the population (which would generally entail the creation of public danger) or directly or indirectly coerce a national or international authority to take some action, or to refrain from taking it; (iii) when the act involves a transnational element.[568]

Moreover, it found that joint criminal enterprise could be considered a viable mode of liability for the commission of international terrorism.[569] Despite this important contribution to international criminal jurisprudence, the STL is widely regarded as a failed institution.[570] Based in The Hague due to security risks in Lebanon, staffed with a combination of international and Lebanese judges, applying Lebanese law concerning international law, existing under Lebanese law as a component of that state's judiciary yet funded 51 percent internationally and 49 percent by Lebanon, the STL only convicted one person in absentia, acquitting three others, between 2009 and 2021 at the cost of nearly $1 billion.[571] When it was closed due to lack of funding, epithets such as "an expensive vanity project" and "no gleaming success" quickly surfaced.[572]

All of these international criminal justice projects were decidedly temporary in nature. The International Criminal Court (ICC) is not. Consequently, while the ICC's designers could certainly take comparative note of all the pros and cons offered by previous tribunals—chiefly the IMTs, ad hoc, and hybrids—those components could only be carried so far into an institution designed to persist, adapt, and evolve instead of one designed to wind up business as soon as its mandate was met. Moreover, since the Rome Statute creating the court was a large multilateral treaty, the ICC's designers faced the nearly impossible task of dealing with literally hundreds of states jockeying for structural and design aspects of the court that they individually wanted to see built into it. Some states, such as Saudi Arabia, participated in these negotiations only to water down provisions they found objectionable, with no intent whatsoever of actually signing the treaty. This atmosphere produced a court that was imbued with the power to investigate and prosecute major atrocities, but one which, under the principle of complementarity, could only do so if local states concerned were found to be unwilling or unable to investigate and prosecute. In other words, the permanent court that emerged is a back-up court.

Yet it is one that carries far more legitimacy than prior tribunals precisely because it is the product of so many states voluntarily ceding their sovereignty to it as opposed to being a product of militarily victorious states or an international body. Currently, 124 states have accepted the court's jurisdiction, although some point out that until major powers such as China, Russia, India, and the United States join, the Court's effectiveness is cripplingly undermined.[573] Moreover, the ICC was not designed as a tailored response to a specific conflict, as were all the others. The ICC's judges are well-regarded jurists, defense counsel has all the modern conveniences for fair representation and trial processes, and a special victims and reparation unit is a welcome addition to the international legal firmament. Still, the office of the prosecutor (OTP) isgenuinely the animating force behind the ICC.

Imbued with the power to open examinations and investigations, determine the willingness of states to begin proceedings or find those in progress to be unsatisfactory, and deploy an impressive evidence-gathering apparatus, the OTP is a walking accountability shop—ready and able to call out dictators such as Sudan's Omar al Bashir for committing genocide and Russia's Vladimir Putin for kidnapping children with arrest warrants supported by fact-based allegations. While the likelihood of apprehension for such leaders depends on several factors such as their overthrow, their surviving the overthrow, and the successor government deciding to give them up to The Hague in exchange for other international boons (often lifting of sanctions), the fact of an arrest warrant's issuance not only paints such leaders as war criminals or genocidaires but also may place them on a form of house arrest—sometimes unable to travel to states parties to the Rome Statute for fear of those states executing the warrant as they are legally obliged to do. That said, in the case of Libya's Muammar Gaddafi, although the ICC had issued an arrest warrant, he did not survive his overthrow to be extradited to The Hague, and in the case of Bashir, several ICC states parties such as Kenya and South Africa refused to arrest him during his visits.

Under its first three prosecutors, the OTP has also taken prosecutorial discretion in interesting directions to expand the purview of its structural capabilities. For example, Louis Moreno Ocampo wished to see corporations punished for participating in atrocity crimes, but this was not possible due to limitations of the Rome Statute, which was not amended to allow for such jurisdiction.[574] Fatou Bensouda opened the first case based on the destruction of cultural heritage following the leveling of kay sections of ancient UNESCO-protected Timbuktu in Mali.[575] Karim A. A. Khan is now developing the OTP's ability to investigate and prosecute environmental crime.[576] The Assembly of States Parties has also demonstrated that it can embrace structural innovations, such as adding the long-awaited crime of aggression to the Court's jurisdiction. This move wasn't possible during the Rome Statute's negotiations due to the participation of spoiler states such as the United States, which refused to agree to it but then refused to agree to it but never ratified the treaty.

Like the IMTs and the ad hocs, the ICC's staffing is purely international. Another legitimacy component may be that the Court benefits substantially from being able to draw upon international criminal justice "pros" who have served for decades in The Hague at previous tribunals and, therefore, understand how to undertake investigations, prosecutions, defense, write effective judgments, deal with victims and witnesses, handle evidence, and engage in public diplomacy. Still, key critiques of the Court focus on (1) its slowness, viewed as a byproduct of too much internal bureaucracy; (2) its cost, viewed as exorbitant (2023's budget was $185 million), and (3) its meager output (only fifty-four people have been indicted during the court's twenty-two-year history).

Locationally, the ICC has never left The Hague, although the Rome Statute permits it to do so. Like the International Court of Justice, which also can leave The Hague to sit elsewhere but never has, the ICC can export a trial chamber to a particular region to hold in situ proceedings or even trials, and it has been repeatedly requested to do so in Africa and Asia; however, the court has consistently denied these petitions.[577] Activating this feature may provide the court with yet another legitimacy component, especially as it would avoid importing local staff to its key operations and thereby avoiding the fate of the ECCC, because the local public would be able to attend such proceedings. But to do so, it would be advisable for the ICC's victims and reparations unit, working in conjunction with the OTP, to prepare the ground beforehand to make sure witnesses and victims are not coerced or harassed by local thugs associated with defendants who may have more opportunity to engage in such intimidation on site rather than in The Hague.

Building a Special Tribunal for Russian Aggression

As with defining terrorism, where one state's terrorist is another state's freedom fighter, taking the politics out of the definition of aggression is a fraught exercise. For example, while negotiating the IMT-Nuremberg at the London conference, the United States wanted the crime defined, but Moscow wanted the definition of aggression to solely concern Germany so as not to include the Soviet Union's aggression against Poland and Finland. While the Americans refused to define the crime that way, they agreed to limit the IMT-Nuremberg's jurisdiction over aggression to only include Germany, thereby bypassing Soviet resistance so the trial could proceed.[578] 1946 coverage of the London Conference noted Soviet consistency on this point at the San Francisco Conference as well:

> [T]he Russians have persisted in their refusal to permit the four-power agreement on the trials to contain a general definition of "aggression," holding that should any such definition be included, it be specifically limited to application only as to the conduct of the Germans in the war just ended. In other words, they have resisted a definition of "aggression" that could have general application. No official would hazard a guess as to what the Russian motivation might have been, but unofficially it was speculated that they might not want a set of rules devised for the trial of the Germans to be applicable to any acts of the Soviet Union, as in the Finnish case. The position on "aggression" is doubly interesting because the Soviet delegation at the San Francisco conference also strongly opposed efforts . . . to get such a definition into the United Nations Charter.[579]

By the Cold War, however, these positions had changed. The reference to aggression had made it into the UN Charter, but the term had been undefined. The Soviets petitioned the United Nations to define aggression in 1959, but this effort was opposed by the United States.[580] Ultimately, by 2017, two-thirds of the world's states, not including either Russia or the United States, agreed on a legal definition of aggression in amending the Rome State. However, the parameters of how the crime was defined limit its application to state parties only. Thus, while the ICC could charge Russia with crimes against humanity, war crimes, and genocide for atrocities committed during its invasion of Ukraine, Russia could not be charged with aggression.[581]

Nevertheless, both Ukraine and the international community are pushing to see Russia brought to account for its illegal invasion. Ukraine and much of the international community want a new international ad hoc tribunal established to deal with Russian aggression.[582] Such a tribunal, however, would be blocked by the Russian veto in the UN Security Council. Thus, to be a UN body, it would have to be constructed under the complex and untested legal rubric of "uniting for peace" by the General Assembly, as was debated with respect to creating a tribunal for accountability in Syria when Russia would have vetoed a similar proposal in the Security Council.[583] However, doing so would rob the tribunal of the ability to operate under Chapter VII authority, which is what provided the ad hoc tribunals for Yugoslavia and Rwanda the ability to override state opposition to their mandate or judicial order. Alternatively, such a tribunal could be set up by a group of states akin to the model for the ICC or perhaps as an extension of another international body such as the EU, although that would most certainly face jurisdictional issues.

The United States opposes an international tribunal, preferring instead Russia's aggression to be prosecuted by a special court with the Ukrainian judicial system as an "internationalized" Ukrainian court[584] along the lines of the IHT, which would require amending the Ukrainian constitution—a procedure not allowed while in a state of martial law, which Ukraine is now in.[585] America's position on this point ironically reflects Russia's position in 1946, the United States having arguably engaged in aggression against Iraq in 2003. Cabining aggression prosecutions either to courts the United States is not a party to, such as the ICC, or to domestic courts, which wouldn't have jurisdiction over it, thus suits Washington's worry about eventual legal blowback for past or future actions it may take. Ukraine opposes this domestic "internationalized" model because Kyiv feels an international court would command much more legitimacy. Moreover, under the international model, Vladimir Putin would enjoy no sovereign immunity defense, as he would under a domestic prosecution.[586] Figure 8.2 highlights a brief, non-exhaustive, side-by-side comparison of pros and cons of both models:

Thus, ironically, through its own actions, and nearly eighty after its opposition at Nuremberg, Russia may get exactly what it feared most—prosecution for the crime of aggression. Either model establishing a tribunal to prosecute Russian aggression is plausible. However, Kyiv is in a tricky position on this question. If it pushes too hard for an international tribunal, it risks alienating its biggest backer in the war against Russia. Not only would it run into opposition from the White House, which could likely be diplomatically overcome, it would very likely alienate key Republican allies in the US Senate—which Ukraine has assiduously cultivated and which it needs to secure further funding and military support, but who are simultaneously quite jealous of American sovereignty and what they consider to be threats to that sovereignty.

International Tribunal	**Internationalized Ukrainian Tribunal**
Maximum Legitimacy	Still Legitimate on National basis
U.N. Process (Not UNSC)	Adjustments to Ukrainian Law required
Hybrid or Ad Hoc Model	Ukrainian judges; International advisors
Potential Competition with ICC	Not in Competition with the ICC
No Sovereign Immunity	Immunity for Russia's Top Leaders
Supported by Ukraine	Models: IHT, KSC, STL
Opposed by the United States	Supported by the United States

Figure 8.2 International v. Internationalized Aggression Tribunals. Figure provided by author.

Conclusion

Notions of justice permeate humanity. Rooted in morality and religion and firmly implanted in our collective subconscious, justice is about righting wrongs. International criminal law is founded upon agreement among states and the international institutions they created about what is wrong. International criminal tribunals and internationalized hybrid tribunals are the institutions designed to address such wrongs by delivering justice. When that justice is too slow, biased, too expensive, or applied in a manner that creates more wrongs, it is rightly criticized. Those tasked with creating such tribunals must sail a safe path between Scylla and Charybdis lest their creations be dashed upon the rocks of illegitimacy.

Hopefully, the throughlines of legitimacy discussed here offer several markers for future tribunal designers, such as those working on the new tribunal for Russian aggression, to navigate this path. If such a tribunal emerges, it will need to do so in a way that the population in a post-Putin Russia understands to be just but also in a way that the population of Ukraine understands to be sufficiently retributive to deter future aggression. Seizing Russian assets to rebuild Ukraine will be part of this discussion,[587] but so will be providing a pathway for Russia to both demonstrate ownership of its crimes, as postwar Germany so dramatically did after the Holocaust, and rehabilitate itself through democratic and rule of law reforms that will enable to shed its pariah status and constructively reengage with the international community.

Notes

1 Charles A. Kahn, "The Meaning of 'Justice' and the Theory of Forms," *Journal of Philosophy* 69, no. 18 (October 1972): 568, http://www.jstor.org/stable/2025374.

2 "What is the International Criminal Court?," *Reuters*, March 17, 2023, https://www.reuters.com/world/europe/what-is-international-criminal-court-2023-03-17/.

3 Mike Corder and Raf Casert, "International Court Issues War Crimes Warrant for Putin," *Associated Press News*, March 17, 2023, https://apnews.com/article/icc-putin-war-crimes-ukraine-9857eb68d827340394960eccf0589253.

4 "Russia Places ICC Prosecutor Khan on the Wanted List," *Moscow Times*, May 19, 2023, https://www.themoscowtimes.com/2023/05/19/russia-places-icc-prosecutor-khan-on-wanted-list-a81210.

5 "Infographic: ICTY Facts & Figures," United Nations International Criminal Tribunal for the Former Yugoslavia, accessed May 16, 2024, https://www.icty.org/en/content/infographic-icty-facts-figures.

6 Charles C. Jalloh, "Special Court for Sierra Leone: Achieving Justice?," *Michigan Journal of International Law*, 32, no. 3 (2011): 456–8, https://repository.law.umich.edu/cgi/viewcontent.cgi?article=1047&context=mjil.

7 "Draft Law for a Ukrainian High War Crimes Court," *Public International Law & Policy Group*, July 22, 2022, https://www.publicinternationallawandpolicygroup.org/draft-law-ukrainian-high-war-crimes-court.

8 James Meernik, "Explaining Public Opinion on International Criminal Justice," *European Political Science Review* 7, no. 4 (December 10, 2014): 568, https://doi:10.1017/S1755773914000332.
9 Herbert Wechsler, "The Issues of the Nuremberg Trial," *Political Science Quarterly* 62, no. 1 (March 1947): 15–6.
10 Wechsler, "The Issues of the Nuremberg Trial," 26; John H. Crider, "Americans Doubt Trials by Sept. 1," *New York Times,* August 5, 1945, 12.
11 Gordon Dean, "Mr. Justice Jackson: His Contribution at Nuremberg," *American Bar Association Journal* 41, no. 10 (October 1955): 913.
12 Herman Phleger, "Nuremberg—A Fair Trial?," *Atlantic Monthly* 177, no. 4 (April 1946): 62, 64, https://cdn.theatlantic.com/media/archives/1946/04/177-4/132381393.pdf.
13 Dean, "Mr. Justice Jackson: His Contribution at Nuremberg," 13.
14 Crider, "Americans Doubt Trials by Sept. 1."
15 Jeffrey D. Hockett, "Justice Robert H. Jackson, the Supreme Court, and the Nuremberg Trial," *Supreme Court Review* 8 (1990): 258.
16 "Jackson Declares War Charge Legal," *New York Times*, October 21, 1945, 13.
17 Bernard D. Meltzer, "A Note on Some Aspects of the Nuremberg Debate," *University of Chicago Law Review* 14, no. 3 (1947): 456.
18 Francine Hirsch, "The Nuremberg Judgment," *Origins: Current Events in Historical Perspective*, September 2021, https://origins.osu.edu/milestones/nuremberg-judgment?language_content_entity=en.
19 Hockett, "Justice Robert H. Jackson, the Supreme Court, and the Nuremberg Trial," 263.
20 Hockett, "Justice Robert H. Jackson, the Supreme Court, and the Nuremberg Trial," 263–4.
21 Hockett, "Justice Robert H. Jackson, the Supreme Court, and the Nuremberg Trial," 264.
22 A. S. Comyns-Carr, "The Tokyo War Crimes Trial," *Far Eastern Survey* 18, no. 10 (May 18, 1949): 109, https://doi.org/10.2307/3024579.
23 Hiro Saito, "The History Problem: The Politics of War and Commemoration in East Asia" *The Asia-Pacific Journal* 15, no. 4 (August 1, 2017): 130–1, https://apjjf.org/2017/15/Saito.
24 Hal Brands, "Who Saved the Emperor? The MacArthur Myth and U.S. Policy Toward Hirohito and the Japanese Imperial Institution, 1942–1946," *Pacific Historical Review* 75, no. 2 (May 2006): 271, https://doi.org/10.1525/phr.2006.75.2.271.
25 William Manchester, *American Caesar: Douglas MacArthur 1880–1964* (Boston, MA: Little, Brown and Company, 1978).
26 Axel Berkofsky, "Japan's Post-War Constitution. Origins, Protagonists and Controversies," *Il Politico* 75, no. 2 (May–August 2010): 16.
27 Meernik, "Explaining Public Opinion on International Criminal Justice," 568.
28 "The Nuremberg Trials," The National WWII Museum | New Orleans, accessed February 2024, https://www.nationalww2museum.org/war/topics/nuremberg-trials.
29 "Use After 1945," Courtroom 600, Memorium Nuremberg Trials, accessed February 2024, https://museums.nuernberg.de/memorium-nuremberg-trials/permanent-exhibition/courtroom-600/use-after-1945.

30 "The International Military Tribunal," The Nuremberg Trials, PBS-American Experience, accessed February 2024, https://www.pbs.org/wgbh/americanexperience/features/nuremberg-military-tribunal/.
31 The National WWII Museum | New Orleans, "The International Military Tribunal."
32 "Tokyo War Crimes Trial," *The National WWII Museum | New Orleans*, accessed February 2024, https://www.nationalww2museum.org/war/topics/tokyo-war-crimes-trial.
33 The National WWII Museum | New Orleans, "Tokyo War Crimes Trial."
The National WWII Museum | New Orleans, "Tokyo War Crimes Trial."
34 "Nürnberg," United Nations Educational, Scientific, and Cultural Organization (UNESCO), European Coalition of Cities Against Racism (ECCAR), accessed February 2024, https://www.eccar.info/en/nurnberg.
35 United Kingdom of Great Britain and Northern Ireland, United States of America, France, and Union of Soviet Socialist Republics, "Agreement for the Prosecution and Punishment of the Major War Criminals of the European Axis ("London Agreement")," *United Nations Treaty Series* 82, no. 251 (August 8, 1945), https://www.refworld.org/legal/agreements/un/1945/en/56517 [hereinafter London Agreement]; United Kingdom of Great Britain and Northern Ireland, United States of America, France and Union of Soviet Socialist Republics, "Charter of the International Military Tribunal—Annex to the Agreement for the prosecution and punishment of the major war criminals of the European Axis ("London Agreement")," *United Nations Treaty Series* 82, no. 251 (August 8, 1945), https://www.refworld.org/legal/constinstr/un/1945/en/21123 [hereinafter IMT Charter].
36 PBS-American Experience, "The International Military Tribunal."
37 "Charter of the International Military Tribunal for the Far East (as amended on April 26, 1946)," January 19, 1946, *Treaties and Other International Acts Series no. 1589*, https://www.un.org/en/genocideprevention/documents/atrocity-crimes/Doc.3_1946%20Tokyo%20Charter.pdf [hereinafter IMTFE Charter].
38 The National WWII Museum | New Orleans, "Tokyo War Crimes Trial."
39 The National WWII Museum | New Orleans, "Tokyo War Crimes Trial."
40 The National WWII Museum | New Orleans, "The International Military Tribunal."
41 The National WWII Museum | New Orleans, "The International Military Tribunal."
42 "The Subsequent Nuremberg Trials," Memorium Nuremberg Trials, accessed February 2024, https://museums.nuernberg.de/memorium-nuremberg-trials/the-nuremberg-trials/the-subsequent-nuremberg-trials.
43 "Nuremberg Trials," Holocaust Encyclopedia, United States Holocaust Memorial Museum, January 5, 2018, https://encyclopedia.ushmm.org/content/en/article/the-nuremberg-trials.
44 IMTFE Charter, § 1, art. 2.
45 The National WWII Museum | New Orleans, "Tokyo War Crimes Trial."
46 "The Prosecution," The Nuremberg Trials, PBS-American Experience, accessed February 2024, https://www.pbs.org/wgbh/americanexperience/features/nuremberg-prosecution/.
47 The National WWII Museum | New Orleans, "Tokyo War Crimes Trial."
48 "The Defendants," The International Military Tribunal, Memorium Nuremberg Trials, accessed February 2024, https://museums.nuernberg.de/memorium

-nuremberg-trials/the-nuremberg-trials/the-international-military-tribunal/the-defendants.

49 PBS-American Experience, "The International Military Tribunal."

50 PBS-American Experience, "The International Military Tribunal."

51 The National WWII Museum | New Orleans, "Tokyo War Crimes Trial."

52 IMTFE Charter, § 3, art. 9(d).

53 IMT Charter, § 7, art. 30.

54 Mikaela Ediger, "Prosecuting the Crime of Aggression at the International Criminal Court: Lessons Learned from the Tokyo Tribunal," *NYU Journal of International Law and Politics* 51 (2018): 194 (*citing* Tim Maga, "Judgement at Tokyo: The Japanese War Crimes Trials" (2001): 128).

55 Ediger, "Prosecuting the Crime of Aggression at the International Criminal Court: Lessons Learned from the Tokyo Tribunal," 194.

56 PBS-American Experience, "The International Military Tribunal."

57 IMT Charter, § 2, art. 6.

58 IMT Charter, § 2, art. 6.

59 PBS-American Experience, "The International Military Tribunal."

60 PBS-American Experience, "The International Military Tribunal."

61 IMT Charter, § 2, art. 10.

62 IMT Charter, § 2, art. 11.

63 The National WWII Museum | New Orleans, "Tokyo War Crimes Trial."

64 The National WWII Museum | New Orleans, "Tokyo War Crimes Trial."

65 IMTFE Charter, § 2, art. 5.

66 IMTFE Charter, § 2, art. 5.

67 IMTFE Charter, § 1, art. 3.

68 IMT Charter, § 5, art. 19.

69 IMTFE Charter, § 4, art. 15(d).

70 IMTFE Charter, § 4, art. 13.

71 IMTFE Charter, § 3, art. 9(e).

72 IMTFE Charter, § 3, art. 9(f).

73 IMT Charter, § 5, arts. 17–25; The National WWII Museum | New Orleans, "The International Military Tribunal."

74 PBS-American Experience, "The International Military Tribunal."

75 PBS-American Experience, "The International Military Tribunal."

76 PBS-American Experience, "The International Military Tribunal."

77 The National WWII Museum | New Orleans, "Tokyo War Crimes Trial."

78 Michaela Halpern, "Trends in Admissibility of Hearsay Evidence in War Crime Trials," *Duke Journal of Comparative and International Law* 29, no. 1 (November 29, 2018): 109, https://scholarship.law.duke.edu/djcil/vol29/iss1/3.

79 IMTFE Charter, § 4, art. 11(a).

80 PBS-American Experience, "The International Military Tribunal."

81 PBS-American Experience, "The International Military Tribunal."

82 PBS-American Experience, "The International Military Tribunal."

83 IMTFE Charter, § 4, art. 13(e).
PBS-American Experience, "The International Military Tribunal."

84 IMT Charter, § 6, art. 27; The National WWII Museum | New Orleans, "The International Military Tribunal."

85 PBS-American Experience, "The International Military Tribunal."
86 Memorium Nuremberg Trials, "The Defendants."
87 PBS-American Experience, "The International Military Tribunal."
88 IMTFE Charter, § 5, art. 16.
89 The National WWII Museum | New Orleans, "Tokyo War Crimes Trial."
90 The National WWII Museum | New Orleans, "Tokyo War Crimes Trial."
91 "Verdicts," The International Military Tribunal, Memorium Nuremberg Trials, accessed February 2024, https://museums.nuernberg.de/memorium-nuremberg-trials/the-nuremberg-trials/the-international-military-tribunal/verdicts.
92 "Sugamo Prison and the Tokyo Trials," The National WWII Museum | New Orleans, last modified May 21, 2021, https://www.nationalww2museum.org/war/articles/sugamo-prison-and-tokyo-trials.
93 IMT Charter, § 6, art. 26; The National WWII Museum | New Orleans, "The International Military Tribunal."
94 IMTFE Charter, § 5, art. 16.
95 Memorium Nuremberg Trials, "The Subsequent Nuremberg Trials."
96 Memorium Nuremberg Trials, "Use After 1945."
97 "The Nuremberg Trial and Its Legacy," The National WWII Museum | New Orleans, last modified November 17, 2020, https://www.nationalww2museum.org/war/articles/the-nuremberg-trial-and-its-legacy.
98 Christopher W. A. Szplilman & Hantano Sumio, "History and the State in Postwar Japan," *The Asia-Pacific Journal: Japan Focus* 16, no. 9 (May 1, 2018): 4, https://apjjf.org/2018/09/Hatano.
99 The National WWII Museum | New Orleans, "The Nuremberg Trial and Its Legacy."
100 The National WWII Museum | New Orleans, "The Nuremberg Trial and Its Legacy."
101 The National WWII Museum | New Orleans, "The Nuremberg Trial and Its Legacy."
102 Yoshida Reiji, "60 Years on Japanese Debate the Tokyo Tribunal's Legitimacy," *The Asia-Pacific Journal: Japan Focus* 3, no. 10 (October 12, 2005): 2, https://apjjf.org/yoshida-reiji/1845/article.
103 Reiji, "60 Years on Japanese Debate the Tokyo Tribunal's Legitimacy," 2.
104 Reiji, "60 Years on Japanese Debate the Tokyo Tribunal's Legitimacy," 2.
105 Memorium Nuremberg Trials, "Use After 1945."
106 Memorium Nuremberg Trials, "The Subsequent Nuremberg Trials."
107 Memorium Nuremberg Trials, "The Subsequent Nuremberg Trials."
108 Memorium Nuremberg Trials, "Use After 1945."
109 Memorium Nuremberg Trials, "Use After 1945."
110 Memorium Nuremberg Trials, "Use After 1945."
111 The National WWII Museum | New Orleans, "Tokyo War Crimes Trial."
112 The National WWII Museum | New Orleans, "Tokyo War Crimes Trial."
113 "Courts & Tribunals," UN International Law Documentation Research Guides, United Nations Dag Hammarskjöld Library, accessed February 2024, https://research.un.org/en/docs/law/courts.
114 "The ICTR in Brief," About the ICTR, United Nations International Residual Mechanism for Criminal Tribunals, accessed February 2024, https://unictr.irmct.org/en/tribunal.
115 United Nations International Residual Mechanism for Criminal Tribunals, "The ICTR in Brief."

116 "Netherlands," Freedom in the World 2024, Freedom House, accessed February 2024, https://freedomhouse.org/country/netherlands/freedom-world/2024.
117 "Tanzania," Freedom in the World 2024, Freedom House, accessed February 2024, https://freedomhouse.org/country/tanzania/freedom-world/2024.
118 Freedom House, "Netherlands."
119 United Nations Security Council, *Updated Statute of the International Criminal Tribunal for the Former Yugoslavia (as Amended on July 7, 2009)*, S/RES/827, adopted May 25, 1993, https://www.icty.org/x/file/Legal%20Library/Statute/statute_sept09_en.pdf [hereinafter ICTY Statute]. See also United Nations Security Council, *Statute of the International Residual Mechanism for Criminal Tribunals (IRMCT)*, S/RES/1966, December 22, 2010, https://www.irmct.org/sites/default/files/documents/101222_sc_res1966_statute_en_0.pdf [hereinafter IRMCT Statute].
120 "Statute of the Tribunal," Documents, United Nations International Criminal Tribunal for the Former Yugoslavia, accessed February 2024, https://www.icty.org/en/documents/statute-tribunal.
121 "The Tribunal: Completion Strategy," About the ICTY, United Nations International Criminal Tribunal for the Former Yugoslavia, accessed February 2024, https://www.icty.org/en/about/tribunal/completion-strategy.
122 United Nations Security Council, *Statute of the International Criminal Tribunal for Rwanda (as Amended on October 13, 2006)*, S/RES/955, adopted November 8, 1994, https://www.refworld.org/legal/constinstr/unsc/1994/en/15174 [hereinafter ICTR Statute]. See also IRMCT Statute.
123 ICTR Statute.
124 ICTR Statute, art. 1; Robin Geiß and Noëmie Bulinckx, "International and Internationalized Criminal Tribunals: A Synopsis," *International Review of the Red Cross* 88, no. 861 (March 31, 2006): 54, 60, https://international-review.icrc.org/sites/default/files/irrc_861_3.pdf.
125 Geiß and Bulinckx, "International and Internationalized Criminal Tribunals: A Synopsis," 60.
126 Geiß and Bulinckx, "International and Internationalized Criminal Tribunals: A Synopsis," 54, 60.
127 Geiß and Bulinckx, "International and Internationalized Criminal Tribunals: A Synopsis," 60.
128 "The Tribunal: Organisational Chart," About the ICTY, United Nations International Criminal Tribunal for the Former Yugoslavia, accessed February 2024, https://www.icty.org/en/about/tribunal/organisational-chart.
129 "The Judges," About the ICTY, United Nations International Criminal Tribunal for the Former Yugoslavia, accessed February 2024, https://www.icty.org/en/about/organization/chambers/judges.
130 "Chambers," About the ICTY, United Nations International Criminal Tribunal for the Former Yugoslavia, accessed February 2024, https://www.icty.org/en/about/chambers.
131 United Nations International Criminal Tribunal for the Former Yugoslavia, "Chambers."
132 United Nations International Criminal Tribunal for the Former Yugoslavia, "Chambers."

133 "Chambers: Status of Judges," About the ICTY, United Nations International Criminal Tribunal for the Former Yugoslavia, accessed February 2024, https://www.icty.org/en/about/chambers/status-of-judges.
134 "The ICTR in Brief: Chambers," About the ICTR, United Nations International Residual Mechanism for Criminal Tribunals, accessed February 2024, https://unictr.irmct.org/en/tribunal/chambers.
135 United Nations International Residual Mechanism for Criminal Tribunals, "The ICTR in Brief: Chambers."
136 United Nations International Criminal Tribunal for the Former Yugoslavia, "Chambers."
137 ICTR Statute, art. 29.
138 ICTR Statute, art. 29.
139 United Nations International Criminal Tribunal for the Former Yugoslavia, "The Tribunal: Organisational Chart."
140 "Office of the Prosecutor," About the ICTY, United Nations International Criminal Tribunal for the Former Yugoslavia, accessed February 2024, https://www.icty.org/en/about/office-of-the-prosecutor.
141 Michael P. Scharf, "Statute of the International Criminal Tribunal for Rwanda," Historical Archives, Audiovisual Library of International Law, 2008, https://legal.un.org/avl/ha/ictr/ictr.html.
142 Scharf, "Statute of the International Criminal Tribunal for Rwanda."
143 United Nations International Criminal Tribunal for the Former Yugoslavia, "The Tribunal: Organisational Chart."
144 United Nations International Criminal Tribunal for the Former Yugoslavia, "Directive on the Assignment of Defence Counsel (Directive No.1/94) (as Amended June 29, 2006)," IT/73/Rev.11, Annex 1, September 1, 2009, https://www.icty.org/x/file/Legal%20Library/Defence/Assignment_of_counsel_july2006.pdf.
145 "The ICTR in Brief: Defence and Detention," About the ICTR, United Nations International Residual Mechanism for Criminal Tribunals, accessed February 2024, https://unictr.irmct.org/en/tribunal/defence.
146 Geiß and Bulinckx, "International and Internationalized Criminal Tribunals: A Synopsis," 59.
147 "Support and Donations," United Nations International Criminal Tribunal for the Former Yugoslavia, accessed February 2024, https://www.icty.org/en/content/support-and-donations.
148 United Nations International Criminal Tribunal for the Former Yugoslavia, "Support and Donations."
149 United Nations International Criminal Tribunal for the Former Yugoslavia, "Support and Donations."
150 United Nations International Criminal Tribunal for the Former Yugoslavia, "Support and Donations."
151 Geiß and Bulinckx, "International and Internationalized Criminal Tribunals: A Synopsis," 59.
152 Rupert Skillbeck, "Finding Justice: The Price of War Crimes Trials," *Human Rights Brief* 15, no. 6 (2008): 6, https://digitalcommons.wcl.american.edu/cgi/viewcontent.cgi?article=1028&context=hrbrief.

153 Geiß and Bulinckx, "International and Internationalized Criminal Tribunals: A Synopsis," 56, 60.
154 Geiß and Bulinckx, "International and Internationalized Criminal Tribunals: A Synopsis," 56, 62.
155 Geiß and Bulinckx, "International and Internationalized Criminal Tribunals: A Synopsis," 56, 62.
156 Geiß and Bulinckx, "International and Internationalized Criminal Tribunals: A Synopsis," 56.
157 Geiß and Bulinckx, "International and Internationalized Criminal Tribunals: A Synopsis," 56.
158 "The Tribunal: Mandate and Crimes Under ICTY Jurisdiction," About the ICTY, United Nations International Criminal Tribunal for the Former Yugoslavia, accessed February 2024, https://www.icty.org/en/about/tribunal/mandate-and-crimes-under-icty-jurisdiction.
159 United Nations International Criminal Tribunal for the Former Yugoslavia, "The Tribunal: Mandate and Crimes Under ICTY Jurisdiction."
160 United Nations International Criminal Tribunal for the Former Yugoslavia, "The Tribunal: Mandate and Crimes Under ICTY Jurisdiction."
161 United Nations International Criminal Tribunal for the Former Yugoslavia, "The Tribunal: Mandate and Crimes Under ICTY Jurisdiction."
162 ICTY Statute.
163 United Nations International Criminal Tribunal for the Former Yugoslavia, "The Tribunal: Mandate and Crimes Under ICTY Jurisdiction."
164 Geiß and Bulinckx, "International and Internationalized Criminal Tribunals: A Synopsis," 56, 62.
165 Geiß and Bulinckx, "International and Internationalized Criminal Tribunals: A Synopsis," 56, 62.
166 Geiß and Bulinckx, "International and Internationalized Criminal Tribunals: A Synopsis," 56, 62.
167 Geiß and Bulinckx, "International and Internationalized Criminal Tribunals: A Synopsis," 56.
168 Geiß and Bulinckx, "International and Internationalized Criminal Tribunals: A Synopsis," 56.
169 United Nations International Criminal Tribunal for the Former Yugoslavia, "Rules of Procedure and Evidence," IT/32/Rev.50, July 8, 2015, https://www.icty.org/x/file/Legal%20Library/Rules_procedure_evidence/IT032Rev50_en.pdf [hereinafter ICTY Rules of Procedure and Evidence].
170 ICTY Rules of Procedure and Evidence, Rule 1.
171 United Nations International Criminal Tribunal for the Former Yugoslavia, "Amendments to the ICTY Rules of Procedure and Evidence," IT/282, July 10, 2015, https://www.icty.org/x/file/Legal%20Library/Rules_procedure_evidence/150710-it-282-en.pdf.
172 ICTR Statute, art. 12.
173 ICTY Rules of Procedure and Evidence.
174 United Nations International Criminal Tribunal for the Former Yugoslavia, "Practice Direction on Procedure for the Proposal, Consideration of, and Publication of Amendments to the Rules of Procedure and Evidence of the

Tribunal," IT/143/Rev.2, January 24, 2002, https://www.icty.org/x/file/Legal%20Library/Rules_procedure_evidence/150710-it-282-en.pdf.

175 United Nations International Criminal Tribunal for the Former Yugoslavia, "Amendments to the ICTY Rules of Procedure and Evidence."

176 "Practice Directions," Documents, United Nations International Criminal Tribunal for the Former Yugoslavia accessed February 2024, https://www.icty.org/en/documents/practice-directions.

177 "United Nations Detention Facility (UNDF)," Detention at the IRMCT, United Nations International Residual Mechanism for Criminal Tribunals, accessed February 2024, https://www.irmct.org/en/about/functions/detention-irmct/united-nations-detention-facility-undf.

178 United Nations International Residual Mechanism for Criminal Tribunals, "United Nations Detention Facility (UNDF)."

179 United Nations International Residual Mechanism for Criminal Tribunals, "International Criminal Tribunal for Rwanda Rules of Procedure and Evidence (as amended on May 13, 2015)," ITR/3/Rev.19, June 29, 1995, https://unictr.irmct.org/sites/unictr.org/files/legal-library/150513-rpe-en-fr.pdf [hereinafter ICTR Rules of Procedure and Evidence].

180 United Nations International Residual Mechanism for Criminal Tribunals, "United Nations Detention Facility (UNDF)."

181 "United Nations Detention Unit (UNDU)," Detention at the IRMCT, United Nations International Residual Mechanism for Criminal Tribunals, accessed February 2024, https://www.irmct.org/en/about/functions/detention-irmct/united-nations-detention-unit-undu.

182 United Nations International Criminal Tribunal for the Former Yugoslavia, "Practice Directions."

183 United Nations International Criminal Tribunal for the Former Yugoslavia, "Practice Direction on Procedure for the Variation of Protective Measures Pursuant to Rule 75(H) of the Rules of Procedure and Evidence of the International Tribunal for Access to Confidential Tribunal Material," IT/254, February 4, 2008, https://www.icty.org/x/file/Legal%20Library/Practice_Directions/IT_254_e.pdf.

184 ICTR Statute, art. 21.

185 Geiß and Bulinckx, "International and Internationalized Criminal Tribunals: A Synopsis," 54, 60.

186 "A Report on the Audiovisual Coverage of the ICTY's Proceedings Finds That Cameras Contribute to a Proper Administration of Justice," Press Release, United Nations International Residual Mechanism for Criminal Tribunals, April 19, 2000, http://www.icty.org/sid/7869.

187 United Nations International Residual Mechanism for Criminal Tribunals, "A Report on the Audiovisual Coverage of the ICTY's Proceedings Finds That Cameras Contribute to a Proper Administration of Justice."

188 Geiß and Bulinckx, "International and Internationalized Criminal Tribunals: A Synopsis," 54, 60.

189 "Detention at the IRMCT," Functions of the Mechanism, United Nations International Residual Mechanism for Criminal Tribunals, accessed February 2024, https://www.irmct.org/en/about/functions/detention-irmct.

190 Barbora Holá, Alette Smeulers, and Catrien Bijleveld, "International Sentencing Facts and Figures: Sentencing Practice at the ICTY and ICTR," *Journal of International Criminal Justice* 9, no. 2 (May 2011): 420, https://doi.org/10.1093/jicj/mqr014.
191 ICTY Statute.
192 ICTY Statute.
193 United Nations International Criminal Tribunal for Rwanda, "Practice Direction on Procedure for Designation of the State in Which a Convicted Person is to Serve His/Her Sentence of Imprisonment," IT/137/Rev.1, September 23, 2008, https://unictr.irmct.org/sites/unictr.org/files/legal-library/pd-designation_state%20%281%29.pdf.
194 Holá, Smeulers, and Bijleveld, "International Sentencing Facts and Figures: Sentencing Practice at the ICTY and ICTR."
195 ICTR Statute.
196 ICTR Statute.
197 "The ICTR in Brief," About the ICTR, United Nations International Residual Mechanism for Criminal Tribunals, accessed February 2024, https://unictr.irmct.org/en/tribunal.
198 "Enforcement of Sentences: Enforcement Map," Functions of the Mechanism, United Nations International Residual Mechanism for Criminal Tribunals, accessed February 2024, https://www.irmct.org/en/about/functions/enforcement-of-sentences.
199 United Nations International Residual Mechanism for Criminal Tribunals, "The ICTR in Brief: Chambers."
200 United Nations International Criminal Tribunal for the Former Yugoslavia, "Practice Direction on Procedure for the International Tribunal's Designation of the State in Which a Convicted Person is to Serve His/Her Sentence of Imprisonment"; United Nations International Criminal Tribunal for the Former Yugoslavia, "Practice Directions."
201 Holá, Smeulers, and Bijleveld, "International Sentencing Facts and Figures: Sentencing Practice at the ICTY and ICTR."
202 "Enforcement of Sentences," Cases, United Nations International Residual Mechanism for the Former Yugoslavia, accessed February 2024, https://www.icty.org/en/cases/enforcement-of-sentences.
203 United Nations International Residual Mechanism for the Former Yugoslavia, "Enforcement of Sentences."
204 United Nations International Residual Mechanism for Criminal Tribunals, "Enforcement of Sentences: Enforcement Map."
205 "Member States Cooperation," Documents, United Nations International Residual Mechanism for the Former Yugoslavia, accessed February 2024, https://www.icty.org/sid/137.
206 "Judgement List," Cases, United Nations International Residual Mechanism for the Former Yugoslavia, accessed February 2024, https://www.icty.org/en/cases/judgement-list.
207 United Nations International Residual Mechanism for Criminal Tribunals, "Detention at the IRMCT."

208 "Bilateral Agreements," Documents, United Nations International Residual Mechanism for Criminal Tribunals, accessed February 2024, https://unictr.irmct.org/en/documents/bilateral-agreements.
209 United Nations International Residual Mechanism for Criminal Tribunals, "Bilateral Agreements."
210 United Nations International Criminal Tribunal for the Former Yugoslavia, "Practice Direction on Formal Requirements for Appeals from Judgement" IT/201, March 7, 2002, https://www.icty.org/x/file/Legal%20Library/Practice_Directions/it201_judgementappeals_procedure_en.pdf; United Nations International Criminal Tribunal for the Former Yugoslavia, "Practice Directions."
211 United Nations International Criminal Tribunal for the Former Yugoslavia, "Practice Direction on Procedure for the Filing of Written Submissions in Appeal Proceedings Before the International Tribunal," IT/155/Rev.4, April 4, 2012, https://www.icty.org/x/file/Legal%20Library/Practice_Directions/IT155_Rev4e.pdf; United Nations International Criminal Tribunal for the Former Yugoslavia, "Practice Directions."
212 "Chambers: Judgement and Sentencing," About the ICTY, United Nations International Criminal Tribunal for the Former Yugoslavia, accessed February 2024, https://www.icty.org/en/about/chambers/judgements-and-sentencing.
213 United Nations International Criminal Tribunal for the Former Yugoslavia, "Chambers: Judgement and Sentencing."
214 United Nations International Criminal Tribunal for the Former Yugoslavia, "Chambers: Judgement and Sentencing."
215 United Nations International Criminal Tribunal for the Former Yugoslavia, "Chambers: Judgement and Sentencing."
216 United Nations International Criminal Tribunal for the Former Yugoslavia, "Chambers: Judgement and Sentencing."
217 United Nations International Criminal Tribunal for the Former Yugoslavia, "Chambers: Judgement and Sentencing."
218 United Nations International Criminal Tribunal for the Former Yugoslavia, "Chambers: Judgement and Sentencing."
219 United Nations International Criminal Tribunal for the Former Yugoslavia, "Practice Direction on Formal Requirements for Appeals from Judgement."
220 ICTR Statute, art. 24(1)(a).
221 ICTR Statute, art. 24(1)(b).
222 "Public International Law Research: Ad Hoc International Criminal Tribunals," UNC School of Law | Katherine R. Everett Law Library, October 19, 2023, https://guides.lib.unc.edu/internationallaw/tribunals.
223 "Key Figures of the Cases," Cases, United Nations International Criminal Tribunal for the Former Yugoslavia, last modified September 2023, https://www.icty.org/en/cases/key-figures-cases.
224 "Transfer of Cases," Cases, United Nations International Criminal Tribunal for the Former Yugoslavia, accessed February 2024, https://www.icty.org/sid/103.
225 United Nations International Criminal Tribunal for the Former Yugoslavia, "Key Figures of the Cases."
226 Geiß and Bulinckx, "International and Internationalized Criminal Tribunals: A Synopsis," 54, 61.

227 Stuart Ford, "Complexity and Efficiency at International Criminal Courts," *Emory International Law Review* 29, no. 1 (2014), https://scholarlycommons.law.emory.edu/eilr/vol29/iss1/2.

228 Heidi L. Hansberry, "Too Much of a Good Thing in Lubanga and Haradinaj: The Danger of Expediency in International Criminal Trials," *Northwestern Law Journal of Human Rights* 9, no. 3 (Summer 2011): 357, https://scholarlycommons.law.northwestern.edu/njihr/vol9/iss3/4 (arguing that "judges tend to consider any reason for delay as unjustified and to be avoided at all costs in order to promote trial expediency" and that this has undermined the protection of witnesses at the ICTY and ICC); Michele Caianiello, "Law of Evidence at the International Criminal Court: Blending Accusatorial and Inquisitorial Models," *North Carolina Journal of International Law* 36, no. 2 (Winter 2011): 316–7, https://scholarship.law.unc.edu/ncilj/vol36/iss2/3 (expressing concern that the evidentiary rules at the ICTY were amended solely for purposes of expediency and not because of any legal deficiency in the previous rules); Charles Chernor Jalloh, "Does Living by the Sword Mean Dying by the Sword?," *Penn State Law Review* 117, no. 3 (2013): 751–2, https://ideas.dickinsonlaw.psu.edu/dlra/vol117/iss3/3 (arguing that over its lifetime the ICTY's decision-making with respect to assignment of defense counsel shifted from an emphasis on the rights of defendants to an emphasis on expediency); Anna Petrig and Fausto Pocar, "Case Referral to National Jurisdictions: A Key Component of the ICTY Completion Strategy," *Criminal Law Bulletin* 45 (2009): 1, 12 (worrying that referral decisions were driven largely by concerns of expediency in ways that undermined the legitimacy of those decisions); Daniel Tillay, "The Non-Rules of Evidence in the Ad Hoc Tribunals," International Lawyer 45, no. 2 (Summer 2011): 715–6, https://scholar.smu.edu/til/vol45/iss2/6 (worrying that rules about the presentation of evidence were changed largely for reasons of expediency without due regard for their effect on fairness); Maximo Langer and Joseph W. Doherty, "Managerial Judging Goes International, but Its Promise Remains Unfulfilled: An Empirical Assessment of the ICTY Reforms," *Yale Journal of International Law* 36 (2011): 245–51, https://hdl.handle.net/20.500.13051/6626 (concluding that the procedural changes made at the ICTY failed to meaningfully effect the length of the trials).

229 United Nations International Residual Mechanism for Criminal Tribunals, "The ICTR in Brief."

230 United Nations International Residual Mechanism for Criminal Tribunals, "The ICTR in Brief."

231 Scharf, "Statute of the International Criminal Tribunal for Rwanda."

232 "About the ICTY," United Nations International Criminal Tribunal for the Former Yugoslavia, accessed February 2024, https://www.icty.org/en/about.

233 "International Criminal Tribunal for Rwanda: Trials and Tribulations," Research, Amnesty International, April 20, 1998, https://www.amnesty.org/en/documents/ior40/003/1998/en/.

234 United Nations International Residual Mechanism for Criminal Tribunals, "The ICTR in Brief."

235 United Nations Dag Hammarskjöld Library, "Courts & Tribunals."

236 United Nations Dag Hammarskjöld Library, "Courts & Tribunals."

237 United Nations Dag Hammarskjöld Library, "Courts & Tribunals."

238 United Nations Dag Hammarskjöld Library, "Courts & Tribunals."

239 "Annual Reports," Documents, United Nations International Residual Mechanism for Criminal Tribunals, accessed February 2024, https://unictr.irmct.org/en/documents/annual-reports.
240 "The Cases," United Nations International Residual Mechanism for Criminal Tribunals, accessed February 2024, https://unictr.irmct.org/en/cases.
241 Geiß and Bulinckx, "International and Internationalized Criminal Tribunals: A Synopsis," 53.
242 Geiß and Bulinckx, "International and Internationalized Criminal Tribunals: A Synopsis," 53.
243 "Cambodia," Freedom in the World 2024, Freedom House, accessed February 2024, https://freedomhouse.org/country/cambodia/freedom-world/2024.
244 "Sierra Leone," Freedom in the World 2024, Freedom House, accessed February 2024, https://freedomhouse.org/country/sierra-leone/freedom-world/2024.
245 Government of Cambodia, *Law on the Establishment of the Extraordinary Chambers in the Courts of Cambodia for the Prosecution of Crimes Committed During the Period of Democratic Kampuchea, with Inclusion of Amendments as Promulgated on October 27, 2004 (NS/RKM/1004/006),* https://www.eccc.gov.kh/sites/default/files/legal-documents/KR_Law_as_amended_27_Oct_2004_Eng.pdf [hereinafter ECCC Law]; Geiß and Bulinckx, "International and Internationalized Criminal Tribunals: A Synopsis," 53.
246 Geiß and Bulinckx, "International and Internationalized Criminal Tribunals: A Synopsis," 53, 60.
247 "Residual Special Court for Sierra Leone—Fact Sheet," Residual Special Court for Sierra Leone (RSCSL), last modified March 8, 2023, https://rscsl.org/download/rscsl-fact-sheet-2022/.
248 Geiß and Bulinckx, "International and Internationalized Criminal Tribunals: A Synopsis," 55, 60.
249 Geiß and Bulinckx, "International and Internationalized Criminal Tribunals: A Synopsis," 55, 60.
250 Geiß and Bulinckx, "International and Internationalized Criminal Tribunals: A Synopsis," 60.
251 "Introduction to the ECCC," About ECCC, Extraordinary Chambers in the Courts of Cambodia, accessed February 2024, https://www.eccc.gov.kh/en/introduction-eccc.
252 "Judicial Chambers," Organs of ECCC, Extraordinary Chambers in the Courts of Cambodia, accessed February 2024, https://www.eccc.gov.kh/en/organs/judicial-chambers; Former Judicial Officers and Legal Representatives, Extraordinary Chambers in the Courts of Cambodia, accessed February 2024, https://www.eccc.gov.kh/en/person/formers.
253 Elena Naughton, *Committing to Justice for Serious Human Rights Violations: Lessons from Hybrid Tribunals* (New York: ICTJ, 2018), 63, https://www.ictj.org/sites/default/files/ICTJ_Report_Hybrid_Tribunals.pdf.
254 ECCC Law, art. 41.
255 ECCC Law, art. 42.
256 "Statute of the Special Court for Sierra Leone," conclusion date: January 16, 2002, *United Nations Treaty Series,* 2178, no. 38342, art. 2, https://treaties.un.org/doc/Publication/UNTS/Volume%202178/v2178.pdf [hereinafter SCSL Statute]. Annexed

to the Agreement between the United Nations and the Government of Sierra Leone on the Establishment of a Special Court for Sierra Leone.

257 SCSL Statute, art. 2.

258 SCSL Statute, art. 2.

259 SCSL Statute, art. 2.

260 SCSL Statute, art. 2.

261 SCSL Statute, art. 12.

262 "Office of the Co-Prosecutors," Organs of ECCC, Extraordinary Chambers in the Courts of Cambodia, accessed February 2024, https://www.eccc.gov.kh/en/organs/office-co-prosecutors.

263 Extraordinary Chambers in the Courts of Cambodia, "Office of the Co-Prosecutors."

264 Extraordinary Chambers in the Courts of Cambodia, "Office of the Co-Prosecutors"; "Office of the Co-Prosecutors—Ms. Chea Leang," Organs of ECCC, Extraordinary Chambers in the Courts of Cambodia, accessed February 2024, https://www.eccc.gov.kh/en/person/ms-chea-leang.

265 Extraordinary Chambers in the Courts of Cambodia, "Office of the Co-Prosecutors"; "Office of the Co-Prosecutors—Mr. Fergal Gaynor," Organs of ECCC, Extraordinary Chambers in the Courts of Cambodia, accessed February 2024, https://www.eccc.gov.kh/en/person/mr-fergal-gaynor-ireland.

266 Naughton, *Committing to Justice for Serious Human Rights Violations: Lessons from Hybrid Tribunals*, 69.

267 Naughton, *Committing to Justice for Serious Human Rights Violations: Lessons from Hybrid Tribunals*, 69.

268 Naughton, *Committing to Justice for Serious Human Rights Violations: Lessons from Hybrid Tribunals*, 63.

269 SCSL Statute, art. 2.

270 "Defence Teams," Organs of ECCC: Defense Support, Extraordinary Chambers in the Courts of Cambodia, accessed February 2024, https://www.eccc.gov.kh/en/organs/defence.

271 Naughton, *Committing to Justice for Serious Human Rights Violations: Lessons from Hybrid Tribunals*, 72.

272 Naughton, *Committing to Justice for Serious Human Rights Violations: Lessons from Hybrid Tribunals*, 99.

273 Skillbeck, "Finding Justice: The Price of War Crimes Trials, 7.

274 ECCC Law, art. 44.

275 Naughton, *Committing to Justice for Serious Human Rights Violations: Lessons from Hybrid Tribunals*, 97–8.

276 Residual Special Court for Sierra Leone (RSCSL), "Residual Special Court for Sierra Leone—Fact Sheet."

277 Geiß and Bulinckx, "International and Internationalized Criminal Tribunals: A Synopsis," 57, 62.

278 Geiß and Bulinckx, "International and Internationalized Criminal Tribunals: A Synopsis," 57, 62.

279 Geiß and Bulinckx, "International and Internationalized Criminal Tribunals: A Synopsis," 57, 62.

280 Geiß and Bulinckx, "International and Internationalized Criminal Tribunals: A Synopsis," 57.
281 Geiß and Bulinckx, "International and Internationalized Criminal Tribunals: A Synopsis," 57.
282 Geiß and Bulinckx, "International and Internationalized Criminal Tribunals: A Synopsis," 57, 62.
283 Geiß and Bulinckx, "International and Internationalized Criminal Tribunals: A Synopsis," 57, 62.
284 Geiß and Bulinckx, "International and Internationalized Criminal Tribunals: A Synopsis," 57, 62.
285 Geiß and Bulinckx, "International and Internationalized Criminal Tribunals: A Synopsis," 57.
286 Geiß and Bulinckx, "International and Internationalized Criminal Tribunals: A Synopsis," 57.
287 Geiß and Bulinckx, "International and Internationalized Criminal Tribunals: A Synopsis," 57; see "Witness to Truth: Final Report of the TRC," Sierra Leone Truth and Reconciliation Commission, accessed February 2024, https://www.sierraleonetrc.org/index.php/view-the-final-report/download-table-of-contents.
288 "Internal Rules (Concerning the Organization and Procedure of the Extraordinary Chambers) (Rev.10)," Extraordinary Chambers in the Courts of Cambodia, October 27, 2022, 67–68, https://www.eccc.gov.kh/sites/default/files/legal-documents/Internal%20Rules%20-%20EN.pdf [hereinafter Internal Rules (Rev.10)].
289 Naughton, *Committing to Justice for Serious Human Rights Violations: Lessons from Hybrid Tribunals*, 51.
290 Naughton, *Committing to Justice for Serious Human Rights Violations: Lessons from Hybrid Tribunals*, 32.
291 SCSL Statute, art. 14; "Special Court for Sierra Leone Rules of Procedure and Evidence (as amended May 14, 2005)," Residual Special Court for Sierra Leone, https://www.rscsl.org/Documents/RSCSL-Rules.pdf [hereinafter SCSL Rules of Procedure and Evidence].
292 Extraordinary Chambers in the Courts of Cambodia, "Internal Rules (Rev.10)," 21–80.
293 SCSL Statute, art. 14; SCSL Rules of Procedure and Evidence.
294 Naughton, *Committing to Justice for Serious Human Rights Violations: Lessons from Hybrid Tribunals*, 83.
295 Naughton, *Committing to Justice for Serious Human Rights Violations: Lessons from Hybrid Tribunals*, 86.
296 Naughton, *Committing to Justice for Serious Human Rights Violations: Lessons from Hybrid Tribunals*, 83.
297 Naughton, *Committing to Justice for Serious Human Rights Violations: Lessons from Hybrid Tribunals*, 83.
298 Naughton, *Committing to Justice for Serious Human Rights Violations: Lessons from Hybrid Tribunals*, 86.
299 Naughton, *Committing to Justice for Serious Human Rights Violations: Lessons from Hybrid Tribunals*, 86.
300 Geiß and Bulinckx, "International and Internationalized Criminal Tribunals: A Synopsis," 55, 60.

301 Geiß and Bulinckx, "International and Internationalized Criminal Tribunals: A Synopsis," 55, 60.
302 Cambodia and United Nations, "Agreement Between the United Nations and the Royal Government of Cambodia Concerning the Prosecution Under Cambodian Law of Crimes Committed During the Period of Democratic Kampuchea," conclusion date: June 6, 2003, *United Nations Treaty Series* 2329, no. 41723, art. 10, https://treaties.un.org/doc/Publication/UNTS/Volume%202329/Part/volume-2329-I-41723.pdf.
303 Naughton, *Committing to Justice for Serious Human Rights Violations: Lessons from Hybrid Tribunals*, 51.
304 Geiß and Bulinckx, "International and Internationalized Criminal Tribunals: A Synopsis," 55, 61; United Nations International Residual Mechanism for Criminal Tribunals, "Chambers: Judgement and Sentencing."
305 Naughton, *Committing to Justice for Serious Human Rights Violations: Lessons from Hybrid Tribunals*, 32.
306 Extraordinary Chambers in the Courts of Cambodia, "Internal Rules (Rev.10)," 67–80.
307 "After 16 Years and 3 Convictions, an International Tribunal Closes Down in Cambodia," Associated Press, September 22, 2022, https://apnews.com/article/crime-war-crimes-cambodia-khieu-samphan-government-and-politics-84728829003ab97b6ebe40c8d171bd45.
308 Associated Press, "After 16 Years and 3 Convictions, an International Tribunal Closes Down in Cambodia."
309 Associated Press, "After 16 Years and 3 Convictions, an International Tribunal Closes Down in Cambodia."
310 SCSL Statute, art. 20.
311 Jalloh, "Special Court for Sierra Leone: Achieving Justice?," 406.
312 "Statement by the Co-Prosecutors on the Transfer of Khieu Samphan to Kandal Province Prison," Extraordinary Chambers in the Courts of Cambodia, accessed February 2024, https://www.eccc.gov.kh/en/articles/statement-co-prosecutors-transfer-khieu-samphan-kandal-province-prision.
313 SCSL Statute, art. 22.
314 "Special Court Prisoners Transferred to Rwanda to Serve Their Sentences," Press Release, Outreach and Public Affairs Office, Special Court for Sierra Leone, October 31, 2009, https://www.rscsl.org/Documents/Press/2009/pressrelease-103109.pdf; "Amended Agreement Between the Special Court for Sierra Leone and the Government of the Republic of Rwanda on the Enforcement of Sentences of the Special Court for Sierra Leone," Special Court for Sierra Leone-Rwanda, March 18, 2009, https://www.rscsl.org/Documents/En-Rwanda-eng.pdf.
315 "Case Load," Cases, Extraordinary Chambers in the Courts of Cambodia, accessed February 2024, https://www.eccc.gov.kh/en/case-load.
316 Timothy Williams, Julie Bernath, Boravin Tann, and Somaly Kum, "Justice and Reconciliation for Victims of the Khmer Rouge? Victim Participation in Cambodia's Transitional Justice Process," Swiss Peace, November 2018, 62, https://www.swisspeace.ch/assets/publications/downloads/Reports/af32f3c3a1/Justice-and-Reconciliation-for-the-Victims-of-the-Khmer-Rouge-Report-2018-.pdf.

317 Residual Special Court for Sierra Leone (RSCSL), "Residual Special Court for Sierra Leone—Fact Sheet."
318 Lansana Gberie, "The Special Court for Sierra Leon Rests—For Good," United Nations Africa Renewal, April 2014, https://www.un.org/africarenewal/magazine/april-2014/special-court-sierra-leone-rests-%E2%80%93-good.
319 Gberie, "The Special Court for Sierra Leon Rests—For Good."
320 Jung Min Shin, "Inspiring Public Trust in the Domestic Legal System: The Impact of the Extraordinary Chambers in the Courts of Cambodia (ECCC)," *Independent Study Project (ISP) Collection* 2110 (Spring 2015): 34, https://digitalcollections.sit.edu/isp_collection/2110.
321 Center for Social Development (CSD), "Report on Corruption Perception Barometer (CPB): Voice of People 2005," Phnom Penh, November 2005, https://www.anti-corruption.org/wp-content/uploads/2016/11/Cambodia-Corruption-Barometer-CSD-2005.pdf.
322 Center for Social Development (CSD), "Report on Corruption Perception Barometer (CPB): Voice of People 2005."
323 Center for Social Development (CSD), "Report on Corruption Perception Barometer (CPB): Voice of People 2005."
324 Residual Special Court for Sierra Leone (RSCSL), "Residual Special Court for Sierra Leone—Fact Sheet."
325 Residual Special Court for Sierra Leone (RSCSL), "Residual Special Court for Sierra Leone—Fact Sheet"; *Prosecutor v. Charles Ghankay Taylor*, SCSL-03- 01-T, Special Court for Sierra Leone, May 18, 2012.
326 Residual Special Court for Sierra Leone (RSCSL), "Residual Special Court for Sierra Leone—Fact Sheet."
327 Residual Special Court for Sierra Leone (RSCSL), "Residual Special Court for Sierra Leone—Fact Sheet."
328 Naughton, *Committing to Justice for Serious Human Rights Violations: Lessons from Hybrid Tribunals*, 32.
329 Naughton, *Committing to Justice for Serious Human Rights Violations: Lessons from Hybrid Tribunals*, 32.
330 "The RSCSL," Residual Special Court for Sierra Leone (RSCSL), accessed February 2024, https://rscsl.org/the-rscsl/.
331 "The RSCSL: Mandate of the Residual Special Court for Sierra Leone," Residual Special Court for Sierra Leone (RSCSL), accessed February 2024, https://rscsl.org/the-rscsl/mandate-of-the-residual-special-court-for-sierra-leone/.
332 "Specialist Chambers: Background," Kosovo Specialist Chambers and Special Prosecutor's Office, accessed February 2024, https://www.scp-ks.org/en/background.
333 Geiß and Bulinckx, "International and Internationalized Criminal Tribunals: A Synopsis," 53.
334 Freedom House, "Netherlands."
335 "Iraq War: Occupation and Continued Warfare," Britannica, accessed February 2024, https://www.britannica.com/event/Iraq-War/Occupation-and-continued-warfare.
336 "Iraq," Freedom in the World 2024, Freedom House, accessed February 2024, https://freedomhouse.org/country/iraq/freedom-world/2024.

337 Sara L. Ochs and Kirbi Walters, "Forced Justice: The Kosovo Specialist Chambers," *Duke Journal of Comparative and International Law* 32 (May 8, 2022), https://scholarship.law.duke.edu/cgi/viewcontent.cgi?article=1586&context=djcil.
338 Kosovo Specialist Chambers and Special Prosecutor's Office, "Specialist Chambers: Background."
339 Geiß and Bulinckx, "International and Internationalized Criminal Tribunals: A Synopsis," 53; "Statute of the Iraqi Special Tribunal," December 10, 2003, https://www.legal-tools.org/doc/70f869/pdf/ [hereinafter IST Statute].
340 "Judging Dujail: The First Trial Before the Iraqi High Tribunal," Human Rights Watch, November 19, 2006, https://www.hrw.org/report/2006/11/19/judging-dujail/first-trial-iraqi-high-tribunal.
341 Human Rights Watch, "Judging Dujail: The First Trial Before the Iraqi High Tribunal."
342 "The Law of the Iraqi Criminal Tribunal Establishing the Supreme Iraqi High Tribunal (IHT) Law No. 10 of 2005," *Official Gazette of the Republic of Iraq*, no. 4006, October 18, 2005, https://menarights.org/sites/default/files/2016-11/IRQ_Supreme%20Criminal%20Court%20Act_2005_EN.pdf [hereinafter IHT Statute].
343 Kosovo Specialist Chambers and Special Prosecutor's Office, "KSC at a Glance," Fact Sheet, accessed February 2024, https://www.scp-ks.org/en/ksc-glance.
344 Kosovo Specialist Chambers and Special Prosecutor's Office, "KSC at a Glance."
345 Kosovo Specialist Chambers and Special Prosecutor's Office, "KSC at a Glance."
346 "SPO at a Glance," Fact Sheet, Kosovo Specialist Chambers and Special Prosecutor's Office, accessed February 2024, https://www.scp-ks.org/en/spo-glance.
347 Kosovo Specialist Chambers and Special Prosecutor's Office, "SPO at a Glance."
348 Kosovo Specialist Chambers and Special Prosecutor's Office, "SPO at a Glance."
349 Geiß and Bulinckx, "International and Internationalized Criminal Tribunals: A Synopsis," 55, 60.
350 Geiß and Bulinckx, "International and Internationalized Criminal Tribunals: A Synopsis," 60.
351 Laurel Miller, "Building the Iraqi Special Tribunal: Lessons from Experiences in International Criminal Justice," *United States Institute of Peace*, Special Report, June 13, 2004, 1, https://www.usip.org/sites/default/files/sr122.pdf.
352 Kosovo Specialist Chambers and Special Prosecutor's Office, "KSC at a Glance."
353 "Principals and Judges," Fact Sheet, Kosovo Specialist Chambers and Special Prosecutor's Office, accessed February 2024, https://www.scp-ks.org/en/principals-and-judges.
354 Kosovo Specialist Chambers and Special Prosecutor's Office, "Principals and Judges."
355 IST Statute, art. 3; IHT Statute, art. 3.
356 IST Statute, art. 5; IHT Statute, art. 4(3) (Under the revised statute, the judges and prosecutors are appointed by the Higher Judicial Council).
357 Kosovo Specialist Chambers and Special Prosecutor's Office, "KSC at a Glance"; Kosovo Specialist Chambers and Special Prosecutor's Office, "SPO at a Glance."
358 IST Statute, arts. 8(j), 28; IHT Statute, arts. 9, 28.
359 IST Statute, arts. 8(j), 28; IHT Statute, arts. 9, 28.

360 Kosovo Specialist Chambers and Special Prosecutor's Office, "Lists of Counsel," Counsel, accessed February 2024, https://www.scp-ks.org/en/counsel/lists-counsel.
361 IST Statute, art. 33; IHT Statute, art. 33; Human Rights Watch, "Judging Dujail: The First Trial Before the Iraqi High Tribunal."
362 Kosovo Specialist Chambers and Special Prosecutor's Office, "Specialist Chambers: Background."
363 IST Statute, art. 35; IHT Statute, art. 24; Geiß and Bulinckx, "International and Internationalized Criminal Tribunals: A Synopsis," 59.
364 Kosovo Specialist Chambers and Special Prosecutor's Office, "KSC at a Glance."
365 Kosovo Specialist Chambers and Special Prosecutor's Office, "Specialist Chambers: Background."
366 Kosovo Specialist Chambers and Special Prosecutor's Office, "Specialist Chambers: Background."
367 Kosovo Specialist Chambers and Special Prosecutor's Office, "SPO at a Glance."
368 Geiß and Bulinckx, "International and Internationalized Criminal Tribunals: A Synopsis," 57, 62.
369 Geiß and Bulinckx, "International and Internationalized Criminal Tribunals: A Synopsis," 57, 62.
370 Geiß and Bulinckx, "International and Internationalized Criminal Tribunals: A Synopsis," 57, 62.
371 Geiß and Bulinckx, "International and Internationalized Criminal Tribunals: A Synopsis," 57.
372 Geiß and Bulinckx, "International and Internationalized Criminal Tribunals: A Synopsis," 57.
373 Geiß and Bulinckx, "International and Internationalized Criminal Tribunals: A Synopsis," 57; Sierra Leone Truth and Reconciliation Commission, "Witness to Truth: Final Report of the TRC."
374 Kosovo Specialist Chambers and Special Prosecutor's Office, "Specialist Chambers: Background"; "Rules of Procedure and Evidence Before the Kosovo Specialist Chambers Including Rules of Procedure for the Specialist Chamber of the Constitutional Court," Kosovo Specialist Chambers and Special Prosecutor's Office, June 2, 2020, https://www.scp-ks.org/en/documents/rules-procedure-and-evidence-kosovo-specialist-chambers-including-rules-procedure-0.
375 "The Kosovo Specialist Chambers in a Nutshell," Fact Sheet, Kosovo Specialist Chambers and Special Prosecutor's Office, accessed February 2024, https://www.scp-ks.org/en/ksc-nutshell.
376 IST Statute, art. 16; IHT Statute, art. 16.
377 Laurel Miller, "Building the Iraqi Special Tribunal: Lessons from Experiences in International Criminal Justice."
378 Kosovo Specialist Chambers and Special Prosecutor's Office, "Rules of Procedure and Evidence Before the Kosovo Specialist Chambers Including Rules of Procedure for the Specialist Chamber of the Constitutional Court."
379 IST Statute, art. 16; "Rules of Procedure and Evidence of the Iraqi High Tribunal (IHT Rules of Procedure and Evidence)," *Official Gazette of the Republic of Iraq*, no. 4006, October 18, 2005, https://www.legal-tools.org/doc/bc23ac/pdf/.
380 IST Statute, art. 18; IHT Statute, art. 18.
381 IST Statute, arts. 21–4; IHT Statute, arts. 20–4.

382 "Victims' Participation at the KSC," Fact Sheet, Kosovo Specialist Chambers and Special Prosecutor's Office, accessed February 2024, https://www.scp-ks.org/en/victims-participation-ksc-0.
383 Kosovo Specialist Chambers and Special Prosecutor's Office, "Victims' Participation at the KSC."
384 IST Statute, art. 22; IHT Statute, art. 21.
385 "Outreach at the KSC," Fact Sheet, Kosovo Specialist Chambers and Special Prosecutor's Office, accessed February 2024, https://www.scp-ks.org/en/outreach-ksc.
386 Kosovo Specialist Chambers and Special Prosecutor's Office, "Outreach at the KSC."
387 Geiß and Bulinckx, "International and Internationalized Criminal Tribunals: A Synopsis," 55, 60.
388 Kosovo Specialist Chambers and Special Prosecutor's Office, "Rules of Procedure and Evidence Before the Kosovo Specialist Chambers Including Rules of Procedure for the Specialist Chamber of the Constitutional Court," § 5, Rules 162–5; United Nations International Residual Mechanism for Criminal Tribunals, "Chambers: Judgement and Sentencing."
389 Geiß and Bulinckx, "International and Internationalized Criminal Tribunals: A Synopsis," 55, 61; IST Statute, art. 24; IHT Statute, art. 24.
390 IST Statute, art. 24; IHT Statute, art. 24.
391 Kosovo Specialist Chambers and Special Prosecutor's Office, "Rules of Procedure and Evidence Before the Kosovo Specialist Chambers Including Rules of Procedure for the Specialist Chamber of the Constitutional Court," Chapter 10.
392 Stephanie van den Berg, "Kosovo Tribunal Confirms War Crimes Conviction of Ex-KLA Commander," *Reuters*, last modified December 14, 2023, https://www.reuters.com/world/europe/kosovo-tribunal-confirms-war-crimes-conviction-ex-kla-commander-2023-12-14/.
393 IST Statute, arts. 25–6; IHT Statute, arts. 25–6.
394 IST Statute, art. 25; IHT Statute, arts. 25–6.
395 *The Public Prosecutor in the High Iraqi Court et al. v. Saddam Hussein Al Majeed et al. (Al Dujail),* Case No. 29/C/2006 Iraqi High Tribunal (Appeals Commission), December 26, 2006, https://www.asser.nl/upload/documents/DomCLIC/Docs/NLP/Iraq/dujail_appellate_chamber_opinion_26-12-2006.pdf.
396 Kosovo Specialist Chambers and Special Prosecutor's Office, "Rules of Procedure and Evidence Before the Kosovo Specialist Chambers Including Rules of Procedure for the Specialist Chamber of the Constitutional Court," Rule 166.
397 IST Statute, art. 27; IHT Statute, art. 27.
398 Stephanie van den Berg and Anthony Deutsch, "Kosovo Tribunal: The Suspects, Allegations and History," *Reuters*, September 15, 2021, https://www.reuters.com/world/europe/kosovo-tribunal-suspects-allegations-history-2021-09-15/.
399 "Cases," Kosovo Specialist Chambers and Special Prosecutor's Office, accessed February 2024, https://www.scp-ks.org/en/cases.
400 "The Iraqi Tribunal: The Post-Saddam Cases," Chatham House, December 4, 2008, https://www.chathamhouse.org/sites/default/files/public/Research/International%20Law/il041208.pdf.

401 "Iraq: Iraqi Special Tribunal—Fair Trials Not Guaranteed," Amnesty International, Index no. MDE 14/007/2005, May 12, 2021, https://www.amnesty.org/en/documents/mde14/007/2005/en/.
402 Ochs and Walters, "Forced Justice: The Kosovo Specialist Chambers."
403 Richard Burkholder, "Gallup Poll of Iraq: Iraqis to Judge Saddam Hussein—But When?," *Gallup*, May 11, 2004, https://news.gallup.com/poll/11647/gallup-poll-iraq-iraqis-judge-saddam-hussein-when.aspx.
404 Benedict Vigers and Mohamed Youins, "Iraq: Signs of Stability in a Volatile Region," *Gallup*, February 16, 2024, https://news.gallup.com/poll/610355/iraq-signs-stability-volatile-region.aspx.
405 "Looking for Justice: The War Crimes Chamber in Bosnia and Herzegovina," Human Rights Watch, February 7, 2006, https://www.hrw.org/report/2006/02/07/looking-justice/war-crimes-chamber-bosnia-and-herzegovina.
406 Naughton, *Committing to Justice for Serious Human Rights Violations: Lessons from Hybrid Tribunals*, 10.
407 "Bosnia and Herzegovina," Freedom in the World 2024, Freedom House, accessed February 2024, https://freedomhouse.org/country/bosnia-and-herzegovina/freedom-world/2024.
408 Bogdan Ivanišević, "The War Crimes Chamber in Bosnia and Herzegovina: From Hybrid to Domestic Court," *International Center for Transitional Justice*, June 10, 2008, 7, https://www.ictj.org/sites/default/files/ICTJ-FormerYugoslavia-Domestic-Court-2008-English.pdf.
409 Freedom House, "Netherlands."
410 "Lebanon," Freedom in the World 2024, Freedom House, accessed February 2024, https://freedomhouse.org/country/lebanon/freedom-world/2024.
411 "The War Crimes Chamber in Bosnia and Herzegovina," Hybrid Justice, accessed February 2024, https://hybridjustice.com/the-war-crimes-chamber-in-bosnia-and-herzegovina/.
412 Human Rights Watch, "Looking for Justice: The War Crimes Chamber in Bosnia and Herzegovina"; United Nations Security Council, *Security Council Briefed on Establishment of War Crimes Chamber within State Court of Bosnia and Herzegovina*, S/RES/7888, October 8, 2003, https://press.un.org/en/2003/sc7888.doc.htm; Office of the High Representative, "War Crimes Chamber Project: Project Implementation Plan—Registry Progress Report," October 20, 2004, 4, http://www.ohr.int/ohr-dept/rule-of-law-pillar/pdf/wcc-project-plan-201004-eng.pdf.
413 Naughton, *Committing to Justice for Serious Human Rights Violations: Lessons from Hybrid Tribunals*, 10.
414 Ivanišević, The War Crimes Chamber in Bosnia and Herzegovina: From Hybrid to Domestic Court," 7.
415 "Criminal Code of Bosnia and Herzegovina," *Official Gazette of Bosnia and Herzegovina*, nos. 3/03, 32/03, 37/03, 54/04, 61/04, 30/05, 53/06, 55/06, 32/07, 8/10, and 47/14, arts. 11, 12https://www.tuzilastvobih.gov.ba/files/docs/zakoni/Criminal_Code_of_BH_-_Consolidated_text_47_14.pdf; "Criminal Procedure Code of Bosnia and Herzegovina," *Official Gazette of Bosnia and Herzegovina*, nos. 3/03, 32/03, 36/03, 26/04, 63/04, 13/05, 48/05, 46/06, 76/06, 29/07, 32/07, 53/07, 76/07,

15/08, 12/09, 16/09, 93/09, and 72/13, https://www.tuzilastvobih.gov.ba/files/docs/zakoni/Criminal_Procedure_Code_of_BH_-_Consolidated_text_72_13.pdf.

416 "Law on Court of Bosnia and Herzegovina—Consolidated Version," *Official Gazette of Bosnia and Herzegovina*, no. 49/09, December 4, 2008, https://www.un.org/en/genocideprevention/documents/atrocity-crimes/Doc.48_Law_on_Court_BiH_-_Consolidated_text_-_49_09.pdf.

417 Naughton, *Committing to Justice for Serious Human Rights Violations: Lessons from Hybrid Tribunals*, 10.

418 United Nations Security Council, *Attachment Statute of the Special Tribunal for Lebanon*, S/RES/1757, May 30, 2007, https://www.onlinelibrary.iihl.org/wp-content/uploads/2021/04/Statute-ICTL-EN.pdf [hereinafter Attachment Statute of STL].

419 Hybrid Justice, "The War Crimes Chamber in Bosnia and Herzegovina."

420 Naughton, *Committing to Justice for Serious Human Rights Violations: Lessons from Hybrid Tribunals*, 63.

421 Naughton, *Committing to Justice for Serious Human Rights Violations: Lessons from Hybrid Tribunals*, 51.

422 "Law on Court of Bosnia and Herzegovina—Consolidated Version," arts. 6, 7.

423 "Attachment Statute of STL," art. 7.

424 Naughton, *Committing to Justice for Serious Human Rights Violations: Lessons from Hybrid Tribunals*, 63.

425 "Attachment Statute of STL," art. 7.

426 Naughton, *Committing to Justice for Serious Human Rights Violations: Lessons from Hybrid Tribunals*, 69.

427 Ivanišević, "The War Crimes Chamber in Bosnia and Herzegovina: From Hybrid to Domestic Court," 7.

428 Ivanišević, "The War Crimes Chamber in Bosnia and Herzegovina: From Hybrid to Domestic Court," 7.

429 Naughton, *Committing to Justice for Serious Human Rights Violations: Lessons from Hybrid Tribunals*, 69.

430 Naughton, *Committing to Justice for Serious Human Rights Violations: Lessons from Hybrid Tribunals*, 73.

431 "STL Defense Office Publishes Names on Defense Counsel List," Naharnet Newsdesk, accessed February 2024, https://m.naharnet.com/stories/en/14518-stl-defense-office-publishes-names-on-defense-counsel-list.

432 Naughton, *Committing to Justice for Serious Human Rights Violations: Lessons from Hybrid Tribunals*, 103.

433 Skillbeck, "Finding Justice: The Price of War Crimes Trials, 10.

434 Naughton, *Committing to Justice for Serious Human Rights Violations: Lessons from Hybrid Tribunals*, 40.

435 Nicholas Blanford, David Daoud, Gissou Nia, and Reem Salahi, "The Special Tribunal for Lebanon: What does its closure mean for Lebanon?," *Atlantic Council*, July 13, 2021, https://www.atlanticcouncil.org/blogs/menasource/the-special-tribunal-for-lebanon-what-does-its-closure-mean-for-lebanon/.

436 Blanford, Daoud, Nia, and Salahi, "The Special Tribunal for Lebanon: What Does its Closure Mean for Lebanon?"

437 Hybrid Justice, "The War Crimes Chamber in Bosnia and Herzegovina."

438 Ivanišević, "The War Crimes Chamber in Bosnia and Herzegovina: From Hybrid to Domestic Court," 7.
439 Ivanišević, "The War Crimes Chamber in Bosnia and Herzegovina: From Hybrid to Domestic Court," 7 (*citing* "Law on the Court of Bosnia and Herzegovina," *Official Gazette of Bosnia and Herzegovina*, nos. 29/00, 15/02, 16/02, 24/02, 3/03, 37/03, 61/04, and 32/07, art. 13(1)).
440 "Law on Court of Bosnia and Herzegovina—Consolidated Version," arts. 22, 43.
441 "Law on Court of Bosnia and Herzegovina—Consolidated Version," art. 35.
442 Joseph Rikhof, "Analysis: The Special Tribunal for Lebanon: A Unique Institution," *Global Justice Journal, Queens Law*, July 30, 2018, https://globaljustice.queenslaw.ca/n.
443 Nidal Nabil Jurdi, "The Subject-Matter Jurisdiction of the Special Tribunal for Lebanon," *Journal of International Criminal Justice* 5, no. 5 (November 1, 2007): 2, https://doi.org/10.1093/jicj/mqm071.
444 "Special Tribunal for Lebanon," Hybrid Justice, accessed February 2024, https://hybridjustice.com/special-tribunal-for-lebanon/#:~:text=The%20STL%20and%20the%20National,matters%20outlined%20in%20the%20statute.
445 Naughton, *Committing to Justice for Serious Human Rights Violations: Lessons from Hybrid Tribunals*, 40.
446 Naughton, *Committing to Justice for Serious Human Rights Violations: Lessons from Hybrid Tribunals*, 50.
447 Ivanišević, "The War Crimes Chamber in Bosnia and Herzegovina: From Hybrid to Domestic Court," 7; "Penal Code of Bosnia and Herzegovina," *Official Gazette of Bosnia and Herzegovina*, nos. 37/03, 54/04, 61/04, 30/05, 53/06, 55/06, and 32/07, arts. 11, 12.
448 "Law on Court of Bosnia and Herzegovina—Consolidated Version," art. 10.
449 "Law on Court of Bosnia and Herzegovina—Consolidated Version," art. 10.
450 "Attachment Statute of STL," art. 28.
451 Naughton, *Committing to Justice for Serious Human Rights Violations: Lessons from Hybrid Tribunals*, 83.
452 Naughton, *Committing to Justice for Serious Human Rights Violations: Lessons from Hybrid Tribunals*, 86.
453 Naughton, *Committing to Justice for Serious Human Rights Violations: Lessons from Hybrid Tribunals*, 83.
454 Naughton, *Committing to Justice for Serious Human Rights Violations: Lessons from Hybrid Tribunals*, 86.
455 Robert Spano, "Transparency and the Importance of Increasing Trust in the Judicial System," Speech, European Court of Human Rights - Online Judicial Forum for Bosnia and Herzegovina, May 25, 2021, https://www.echr.coe.int/documents/d/echr/Speech_20210525_Spano_Judicial_Forum_BiH_ENG.
456 Martin Wählisch, "The Special Tribunal for Lebanon: An Introduction and Research Guide," *GlobaLex (NYU)* September 2012, https://www.nyulawglobal.org/globalex/Special_Tribunal_Lebanon.html.
457 Naughton, *Committing to Justice for Serious Human Rights Violations: Lessons from Hybrid Tribunals*, 40.
458 "Attachment Statute of STL," art. 18.
459 Naughton, *Committing to Justice for Serious Human Rights Violations: Lessons from Hybrid Tribunals*, 50.

460 "Law on Court of Bosnia and Herzegovina—Consolidated Version," arts. 9, 22.
461 "Law on Court of Bosnia and Herzegovina—Consolidated Version," art. 38.
462 "Attachment Statute of STL," art. 20.
463 Office of the High Representative, "War Crimes Chamber Project: Project Implementation Plan—Registry Progress Report."
464 "Attachment Statute of STL," art. 29.
465 Massimo Moratti, "Time is Running Out for War Crimes Prosecution in Bosnia," *JUSTICEINFO.NET*, November 14, 2022, https://www.justiceinfo.net/en/108796-time-running-out-war-crimes-prosecution-bosnia.html.
466 Moratti, "Time is Running Out for War Crimes Prosecution in Bosnia."
467 Moratti, "Time is Running Out for War Crimes Prosecution in Bosnia."
468 Hybrid Justice, "Special Tribunal for Lebanon."
469 Judicial Effectiveness Index of Bosnia and Herzegovina, "2020 Report: Monitoring and Evaluation Support Activity II (Measure II)," US Agency for International Development (USAID), 22, http://measurebih.com/uimages/JEI-BiH-2020-Report-Final-508.pdf.
470 "The Special Tribunal for Lebannon: Selective Justice?," Amnesty International, Index no: MDE 18/001/2009, February 25, 2009, https://www.amnesty.org/en/wp-content/uploads/2021/07/mde180012009en.pdf..
471 Naughton, *Committing to Justice for Serious Human Rights Violations: Lessons from Hybrid Tribunals*, 40.
472 Naughton, *Committing to Justice for Serious Human Rights Violations: Lessons from Hybrid Tribunals*, 50.
473 United Nations Dag Hammarskjöld Library, "Courts & Tribunals."
474 "Understanding the International Criminal Court," Fact Sheet, International Criminal Court, 2023, https://www.icc-cpi.int/sites/default/files/2023-03/understanding-the-icc.pdf.
"Defence Teams," Organs of ECCC: Defense Support, Extraordinary Chambers in the Courts of Cambodia, accessed February 2024, https://www.eccc.gov.kh/en/organs/defence.
475 Freedom House, "Netherlands."
476 *Rome Statute of the International Criminal Court*, adopted July 17, 1998 by A/CONF,183/9, https://www.icc-cpi.int/resource-library/Documents/RS-Eng.pdf.; Geiß and Bulinckx, "International and Internationalized Criminal Tribunals: A Synopsis," 52.
477 United Nations Dag Hammarskjöld Library, "Courts & Tribunals."
478 Geiß and Bulinckx, "International and Internationalized Criminal Tribunals: A Synopsis," 54, 60.
479 Geiß and Bulinckx, "International and Internationalized Criminal Tribunals: A Synopsis," 60.
480 "In the Courtroom," About the Court, International Criminal Court, accessed February 2024, https://www.icc-cpi.int/about/in-the-courtroom.
481 "Judicial Divisions," About the Court, International Criminal Court, accessed February 2024, https://www.icc-cpi.int/about/judicial-divisions.
482 "Office of the Prosecutor," About the Court, International Criminal Court, accessed February 2024, https://www.icc-cpi.int/about/otp.

483 "Registry," About the Court, International Criminal Court, accessed February 2024, https://www.icc-cpi.int/about/registry/default.
484 "The Presidency," About the Court, International Criminal Court, accessed February 2024, https://www.icc-cpi.int/about/presidency.
485 International Criminal Court, "Judicial Divisions."
486 "Current Judges—Who's Who," Judicial Divisions, International Criminal Court, accessed February 2024, https://www.icc-cpi.int/judges/judges-who-s-who.
487 International Criminal Court, "Judicial Divisions."
488 International Criminal Court, "Office of the Prosecutor."
489 International Criminal Court, "Office of the Prosecutor."
490 "Office of the Prosecutor—Who's Who," About the Court, International Criminal Court, accessed February 2024, https://www.icc-cpi.int/about/otp/who-s-who.
491 "Defence," About the Court, International Criminal Court, accessed February 2024, https://www.icc-cpi.int/about/defence.
492 "The Defence," Fact Sheet, International Criminal Court, accessed February 2024, https://www.icc-cpi.int/sites/default/files/DefenceEng.pdf.
493 International Criminal Court, "The Defence."
494 "List of Counsel Before the ICC," International Criminal Court, February 26, 2024, https://www.icc-cpi.int/sites/default/files/2024-02/list-of-counsel-eng.pdf.
495 International Criminal Court, "Understanding the International Criminal Court."
496 Janet Sankale, "Larger Budget Reflects Increased ICC Workload in 2023," Journalists for Justice, December 15, 2022, https://jfjustice.net/larger-budget-reflects-increased-icc-workload-in-2023/#:~:text=%E2%80%9CTo%20deal%20with%20this%20workload,current%20year%2C%E2%80%9D%20he%20said.
497 Geiß and Bulinckx, "International and Internationalized Criminal Tribunals: A Synopsis," 56, 62.
498 "How the Court Works," About the Court, International Criminal Court, accessed February 2024, https://www.icc-cpi.int/about/how-the-court-works.
499 International Criminal Court, "How the Court Works."
500 International Criminal Court, "Understanding the International Criminal Court."
501 Geiß and Bulinckx, "International and Internationalized Criminal Tribunals: A Synopsis," 56, 62.
502 International Criminal Court, "Understanding the International Criminal Court."
503 Geiß and Bulinckx, "International and Internationalized Criminal Tribunals: A Synopsis," 56, 62.
504 Geiß and Bulinckx, "International and Internationalized Criminal Tribunals: A Synopsis," 56.
505 Geiß and Bulinckx, "International and Internationalized Criminal Tribunals: A Synopsis," 56.
506 International Criminal Court, "How the Court Works."
507 *Rules of Procedure and Evidence*, International Criminal Court, adopted September 9, 2002, https://www.icc-cpi.int/sites/default/files/RulesProcedureEvidenceEng.pdf [hereinafter ICC Rules of Procedure and Evidence].
508 "The Practical Guide to International Humanitarian Law," Medecins Sans Frontieres, accessed February 2024, https://guide-humanitarian-law.org/content/article/3/international-criminal-court-icc/.
509 International Criminal Court, "How the Court Works."

510 *ICC Rules of Procedure and Evidence.*
511 Medecins Sans Frontieres, "The Practical Guide to International Humanitarian Law."
512 "Witnesses," About the Court, International Criminal Court, accessed February 2024, https://www.icc-cpi.int/about/witnesses.
513 International Criminal Court, "Witnesses."
514 International Criminal Court, "Witnesses."
515 International Criminal Court, "Witnesses."
516 International Criminal Court, "Witnesses."
517 International Criminal Court, "Witnesses."
518 International Criminal Court, "Witnesses."
519 International Criminal Court, "Witnesses."
520 Geiß and Bulinckx, "International and Internationalized Criminal Tribunals: A Synopsis," 54, 60.
521 Geiß and Bulinckx, "International and Internationalized Criminal Tribunals: A Synopsis," 54, 61; United Nations International Residual Mechanism for Criminal Tribunals, "Chambers: Judgement and Sentencing."
522 International Criminal Court, "How the Court Works."
523 International Criminal Court, "How the Court Works."
524 International Criminal Court, "How the Court Works."
525 International Criminal Court, "How the Court Works."
526 International Criminal Court, "How the Court Works."
527 "About the Court," International Criminal Court, accessed February 2024, https://www.icc-cpi.int/about/the-court.
528 "April 2018 Ipsos Poll Results," International Criminal Justice Today, accessed February 2024, https://www.international-criminal-justice-today.org/polling-data/2018/06/12/april-2018-ipsos-polling-results/.
529 International Criminal Justice Today, "April 2018 Ipsos Poll Results."
530 Geoffrey Thomas Dancy, "The Hidden Impacts of the ICC: An Innovative Assessment Using Google Data," *Leiden Journal of International Law* 34, no. 3 (May 14, 2021): 746, https://doi.org/10.1017/S0922156521000194 (*citing* Alexa Koenig, Mychelle Baltharzard, Eric Stover, and Stephen S. Cody, "The Victims" Court? A Study of 622 Victim Participants at the International Criminal Court," UC Berkley Human Rights Center, November 1, 2015, https://www.law.berkeley.edu/wp-content/uploads/2015/04/VP_report_2015_final_full2.pdf.
531 Dancy, "The Hidden Impacts of the ICC: An Innovative Assessment Using Google Data," 746.
532 Christian Tomuschat, "The Legacy of Nuremberg," *Journal of International Criminal Justice* 4, no. 4 (2006): 834–837, https://doi.org/10.1093/jicj/mql051.
533 *Prosecutor v. Dusko Tadic*, Decision on the Defence Motion for Interlocutory Appeal on Jurisdiction, ICTY Appellate Chamber, October 2, 1995, ¶27, https://www.icty.org/x/cases/tadic/acdec/en/51002.htm.
534 *Prosecutor v. Dusko Tadic*, ¶¶28–64.
535 "Transcript: Milosevic in Court," *Cable News Network (CNN)*, July 3, 2001, https://edition.cnn.com/2001/WORLD/europe/07/03/milosevic.hearing/.

536 Maya Steinitz, "The Milošević Trial—Live!: An Iconical Analysis of International Law's Claim of Legitimate Authority," *Journal of International Criminal Justice* 3, no. 1 (March 1, 2005): 109, https://doi.org/10.1093/jicj/3.1.103.
537 "Milosevic Due Seat in Serb Parliament," *Los Angeles Times*, December 30, 2003, https://www.latimes.com/archives/la-xpm-2003-dec-30-fg-serb30-story.html.
538 Mikloš Biro, "Public Opinion in Serbia on ICTY: A Chicken or an Egg?," *Primenjena Psihologjia* 10, no. 4 (December 29, 2017): 467, https://doi.org/10.19090/pp.2017.4.463–475.
539 Biro, "Public Opinion in Serbia on ICTY: A Chicken or an Egg?," 580–4.
540 Laruen Haberstock, "An Analysis of the Effectiveness of the Gacaca Court System in Post-Genocide Rwanda," *Global Tides* 8, no. 1 (2014): 6, https://digitalcommons.pepperdine.edu/globaltides/vol8/iss1/4.
541 Haberstock, "An Analysis of the Effectiveness of the Gacaca Court System in Post-Genocide Rwanda," 7–8.
542 Haberstock, "An Analysis of the Effectiveness of the Gacaca Court System in Post-Genocide Rwanda," 10–2.
543 Haberstock, "An Analysis of the Effectiveness of the Gacaca Court System in Post-Genocide Rwanda," 12.
544 Ellen Emilie Stensrud, "New Dilemmas in Transitional Justice: Lessons from the Mixed Courts in Sierra Leone and Cambodia," *Journal of Peace Research* 46, no. 1 (2009), https://doi.org/10.1177/0022343308096152.
545 Jalloh, "Special Court for Sierra Leone: Achieving Justice?."
546 Stensrud, "New Dilemmas in Transitional Justice: Lessons from the Mixed Courts in Sierra Leone and Cambodia," 10.
547 Stensrud, "New Dilemmas in Transitional Justice: Lessons from the Mixed Courts in Sierra Leone and Cambodia," 8–13.
548 Marija Đordeska, "The ECCC Begins Winding Down: In Cambodia, a Hybrid Tribunal's Hybrid Legacy," Just Security, October 3, 2022, https://www.justsecurity.org/83316/eccc-winding-down-in-cambodia-hybrid-tribunals-hybrid-legacy/.
549 Stensrud, "New Dilemmas in Transitional Justice: Lessons from the Mixed Courts in Sierra Leone and Cambodia," 13.
550 William H. Wiley, "Societal Reconciliation, the Rule of Law and the Iraqi High Tribunal," FICHL Policy Brief Series No. 35 (2015), https://www.toaep.org/pbs-pdf/35-wiley.
551 Nsama Jonathan Simuziya, "The (Il)legality of the Iraq War of 2003: An Analytical Review of the Causes and Justifications for the US-Led Invasion," *Cogent Social Sciences* 9, no. 1 (January 11, 2023), https://doi.org/10.1080/23311886.2022.2163066.
552 Nehal Bhuta, "Fatal Errors: The Trial and Appeal Judgments in the Dujail Case," *Journal of International Criminal Justice* 6, no. 1 (March 1, 2008), https://doi.org/10.1093/jicj/mqm081.
553 Michael J. Kelly, *Ghosts of Halabja: Saddam Hussein and the Kurdish Genocide* (Westport, CT: Praeger Security International, 2008).
554 Meris Mušanovic and Arolda Elbasani, "The Specialist Chambers" Hybrid Nature as a Promising Solution for Transitional Justice in Kosovo," *Osservatorio Balcani & Caucaso Transeuropa*, March 18, 2020, https://www.balcanicaucaso.org/eng/Areas/Kosovo/The-Specialist-Chambers-hybrid-nature-as-a-promising-solution-for-transitional-justice-in-Kosovo-200038.

555 Rogier Bartels, "Kosovo Specialist Chambers and the Unappreciated Necessity of Contempt Proceedings in International Criminal Accountability," Just Security, November 21, 2023, https://www.justsecurity.org/90213/kosovo-specialist-chambers-and-the-unappreciated-necessity-of-contempt-proceedings-in-international-criminal-accountability/.
556 Ochs and Walters, "Forced Justice: The Kosovo Specialist Chambers," 272.
557 "Kosovo: War Crimes Trial to Begin in The Hague," *Human Rights Watch*, March 31, 2023, https://www.hrw.org/news/2023/03/31/kosovo-war-crimes-trial-begin-hague.
558 Ivanišević, "The War Crimes Chamber in Bosnia and Herzegovina: From Hybrid to Domestic Court," 1.
559 Ivanišević, "The War Crimes Chamber in Bosnia and Herzegovina: From Hybrid to Domestic Court," 6–7, 43.
560 Param-Preet Sing, "Justice for Atrocity Crimes: Lessons of International Support for Trials before the State Court of Bosnia and Herzegovina," *Human Rights Watch*, March 12, 2012, https://www.hrw.org/report/2012/03/12/justice-atrocity-crimes/lessons-international-support-trials-state-court-bosnia.
561 Yaël Ronen, "The Impact of the ICTY on Atrocity-Related Prosecutions in the Courts of Bosnia and Herzegovina," *Penn State Journal of Law & International Affairs* 3, no. 1 (April 2014): 158.
562 European Commission, "Commission Staff Working Document, Bosnia and Herzegovina 2023 Report," SWD(2023) 691, November 8, 2023, 30, https://neighbourhood-enlargement.ec.europa.eu/system/files/2023-11/SWD_2023_691%20Bosnia%20and%20Herzegovina%20report.pdf.
563 European Commission, "Commission Staff Working Document, Bosnia and Herzegovina 2023 Report," 30.
564 European Commission, "Commission Staff Working Document, Bosnia and Herzegovina 2023 Report," 31.
565 European Commission, "Communication from the Commission to the Council and the European Parliament, Report on Progress in Bosnia and Hersegovina—March 2024," COM(2024) 129, March 12, 2024, 5, https://neighbourhood-enlargement.ec.europa.eu/document/download/fa9da504-4ecb-4317-b583-c9fff0b833b2_en.
566 Merdijana Sadović, "The Trials of Bosnia's War Crimes Court," *Institute for War & Peace Reporting*, April 1, 2011, https://iwpr.net/global-voices/trials-bosnias-war-crimes-court.
567 Sadović, "The Trials of Bosnia's War Crimes Court."
568 Michael P. Scharf, "Special Tribunal for Lebanon Issues Landmark Ruling on Definition of Terrorism and Modes of Participation," *American Society of International Law Insights* 15, no. 6 (March 4, 2011), https://www.asil.org/insights/volume/15/issue/6/special-tribunal-lebanon-issues-landmark-ruling-definition-terrorism-and.
569 Scharf, "Special Tribunal for Lebanon Issues Landmark Ruling on Definition of Terrorism and Modes of Participation." But see, Nidal Nabil Jurdi, "The Crime of Terrorism in Lebanese and International Law," in Amal Alamuddin, Nidal Nabil Jurdi, and David Tolbert (eds.), *The Special Tribunal for Lebanon: Law and Practice* (Oxford University Press, 2014), 73–87, https://doi.org/10.1093/acprof:oso/9780199687459.003.0005.

570 Anthony Dworkin, "Protected, Neglected, and Ineffective: Lessons from the Lebanon Tribunal," European Council on Foreign Relations, September 4, 2020, https://ecfr.eu/article/commentary_protracted_neglected_and_ineffective_lessons_from_the_lebanon_tr/.
571 Dworkin, "Protected, Neglected, and Ineffective: Lessons from the Lebanon Tribunal."
572 Mia Swart, "'No Gleaming Success': Special Tribunal for Lebanon to Close Because of Funding Shortage," *Al Jazeera Centre for Public Liberties & Human Rights*, June 13, 2021.
573 Matthew Gordin, "Can the International Criminal Court be Effective Without Support from the Major Powers?," *Western University Leadership and Democracy Lab*, accessed May 2024, https://www.democracylab.uwo.ca/research/opeds/can_the_international_criminal_court_be_effective_without_support_from_the_major_powers.html.
574 Michael J. Kelly, *Prosecuting Corporations for Genocide* (Oxford: Oxford University Press, 2016).
575 *Prosecutor v. Ahmad Al Faqi Al Mahdi*, Judgment and Sentence, ICC-01/12-01/15–171, September 27, 2016.
576 "The Office of the Prosecutor Launches Public Consultation on a New Policy Initiative to Advance Accountability for Environmental Crimes under the Rome Statute," Press Release, International Criminal Court, February 16, 2024, https://www.icc-cpi.int/news/office-prosecutor-launches-public-consultation-new-policy-initiative-advance-accountability-0.
577 Avinesh Bharadwaj, "One Size Does Not Fit All: A Quasi-Federal Solution to the Euro-Centric Structural Shortcomings of the ICC," *Cardozo International & Comparative Law Review* 7, no. 2 (2024), https://www.cardozociclr.com/_files/ugd/bc0e09_5847e9249ed545a5b52e44a6f0e413f2.pdf.
578 "Jackson Discusses Nuremberg Trials," *New York Times*, August 26, 1948, 4, https://www.nytimes.com/1948/08/26/archives/jackson-discusses-nuremberg-trials-says-russia-wished-to-define.html.
579 Crider, "Americans Doubt Trials by Sept. 1."
580 "Soviet Bids the U.N. Define Aggression," *New York Times*, April 15, 1959, 3, https://www.nytimes.com/1959/04/15/archives/soviet-bids-the-un-define-aggression.html.
581 "Statement of ICC Prosecutor, Karim A.A. Khan, on the Situation in Ukraine," Press Release, International Criminal Court, February 25, 2022, https://www.icc-cpi.int/news/statement-icc-prosecutor-karim-aa-khan-qc-situation-ukraine-i-have-been-closely-following.
582 "We Must Create a Special Tribunal on the Crime of Aggression Against Ukraine," Press Release, The Presidential Office of Ukraine, October 5, 2022, https://www.president.gov.ua/en/news/mayemo-stvoriti-specialnij-tribunal-shodo-zlochinu-agresiyi-78285; "Dmytro Kuleba: Coalition for the Establishment of a Special Tribunal for the Crime of Aggression of the Russian Federation Against Ukraine Will Continue to Grow," Press Release, Ministry of Foreign Affairs of Ukraine, February 27, 2023, https://www.kmu.gov.ua/en/news/dmytro-kuleba-koalitsiia-zi-stvorennia-spetstrybunalu-shchodo-zlochynu-ahresii-rf-proty-ukrainy-prodovzhyt-zrostaty.
583 Beth Van Schaack, "Options for Accountability in Syria," Just Security, May 22, 2014, https://www.justsecurity.org/10736/options-accountability-syria/.

584 Jennifer Trahan, "Don't Be Fooled by U.S. Smoke and Mirrors on the Crime of Aggression," Just Security, April 14, 2023, https://www.justsecurity.org/85986/dont-be-fooled-by-u-s-smoke-and-mirrors-on-the-crime-of-aggression/.
585 Alexander Komarov and Oona A. Hathaway, "Ukraine's Constitutional Constraints: How to Achieve Accountability for the Crime of Aggression," Just Security, April 5, 2022, https://www.justsecurity.org/80958/ukraines-constitutional-constraints-how-to-achieve-accountability-for-the-crime-of-aggression/.
586 Trahan, "Don't Be Fooled by U.S. Smoke and Mirrors on the Crime of Aggression."
587 See Public International Law & Policy Group, "Repurposing Frozen Russian Assets: Analysis under International Law," PILPG White Paper, March 2023, https://static1.squarespace.com/static/5900b58e1b631bffa367167e/t/6414b192b2d62a3f64fe2adb/1679077778313/2023-03+PILPG+-+Repurposing+Frozen+Russian+Assets+-+Analysis+Under+International+Law.pdf; Michael J. Kelly, Federica D'Alessandra, Dmytro Koval, Milena Sterio, and Lydia Korostelova, "Prosecution of Russian Corporations for War Crimes in Ukraine as a Precursor to Seizure of Frozen Corporate Assets in Foreign Jurisdictions," PILPG White Paper, January 25, 2024, https://static1.squarespace.com/static/5900b58e1b631bffa367167e/t/65b1707247caba2e860fc06d/1706127475750/PILPG+Foreign+Awards+What+Paper+Jan+24+2024.pdf.

Selected Bibliography

Fatic, Klaus Bachmann, *The UN International Criminal Tribunals, Transition without Justice?* (2017), https://www.amazon.com/International-Criminal-Tribunals-Transition-Routledge/dp/0815377800.

International Nuremberg Principles Academy, *A Practical Guide for Evaluating the Deterrent Effect of International and National Judicial Proceedings on Atrocity Crimes* (2020), available at https://www.nurembergacademy.org/fileadmin/media/images/projects/Practical_Guide_Deterrent_Effect.pdf.

Knoops, Geert-Jan, *An Introduction to the Law of International Criminal Tribunals* (2014), https://brill.com/display/title/16641?language=en&srsltid=AfmBOopHpEV9xFBc7jAiXH68sJ-hQd6p4jx7LKbggAN3z7EQH0uqXC7v.

Labuda, Patryk I., *International Criminal Tribunals and Domestic Accountability* (2023), available at https://global.oup.com/academic/product/international-criminal-tribunals-and-domestic-accountability-9780198868842?cc=us&lang=en&.

Schense, Jennifer and Linda Carter, *Two Steps Forward, One Step Back: The Deterrent Effect of International Criminal Tribunals* (2017), available at https://www.nurembergacademy.org/fileadmin/media/pdf/publications/2017_Two_Steps_Forward_One_Step_Back.pdf.

Schiff, Benjamin N., *Building the International Criminal Court* (Cambridge: Cambridge University Press, 2008), available at https://brill.com/display/title/16641?language=en.

9

The International Criminal Tribunal for Rwanda and Its Controversial Legacy

Gerd Hankel

Everything began on a discordant note. When Resolution 955 was adopted by the United Nations (UN) Security Council on November 8, 1994, Rwanda was the only country to speak out against the establishment of a tribunal to punish crimes committed during the genocide in Rwanda. Manzi Bakuramutsa, Rwanda's representative on the UN Security Council, demanded at the time that the tribunal's mandate should cover not only the year 1994 but the entire duration of the war from October 1, 1990, to July 1994, citing massacres that had been perpetrated against the Tutsi population from the beginning of the war. Eight thousand Tutsis had been arbitrarily imprisoned at the beginning of October 1990, and hundreds of them were killed. In the ensuing period, mass murder of Tutsis occurred repeatedly, in some cases claiming three hundred victims and once more than four hundred. The "Rwandan-style final solution" had not remained hidden from the international community; many diplomats and international organizations had been in the country. A court, Bakuramutsa argued, that would ignore the history of the genocide and not recognize the previous "experiments" in the form of a whole series of massacres would be of absolutely no use to Rwanda. It would not end the culture of impunity and in no way contribute to reconciliation.[1]

The Rwandan delegate added that the conception of the court as a mere appendage to the International Criminal Tribunal for the former Yugoslavia was indicative of the same disinterest. Only two criminal chambers with three judges each were planned. The five-member appeals chamber had to be shared with the Yugoslavia tribunal, as did the head of the prosecution authority, whose area of responsibility would simply be extended to include Rwanda.[2] Finally, apart from the fact that the court was not to be based in Rwanda, the country where the crimes were committed, and was not to include Rwandan judges familiar with Rwanda's history and culture, Bakuramutsa assailed the fact that the court would not be permitted to impose the death penalty, terming this an affront to the victims. According to Rwandan criminal law, as he pointed out, murder was punishable by death, but the maximum sentence that the international court could set was life imprisonment. The planners and organizers of the genocide would, therefore, receive lesser sentences than minor perpetrators who would have to answer to the Rwandan courts—a disparity that ran counter to the fundamental idea of reconciliation in Rwanda.[3]

Difficult Beginnings

The Rwandan delegate's criticism had no effect. Consequently, Rwanda voted against the court. The court's mandate covered only the year of the genocide, from January 1, 1994, to December 31, 1994; its seat was outside Rwanda, in Arusha, Tanzania; no Rwandan judges were appointed; and the court was not allowed to impose the death penalty. Regarding this last issue, New Zealand's delegate to the UN Security Council noted: "For over three decades, the United Nations has been trying progressively to eliminate the death penalty. It would be entirely unacceptable—and a dreadful step backwards—to introduce it here."[4] The only concession the UN made to Rwanda was to accept the creation of a prosecuting authority with a mandate to investigate the Rwandan genocide. However, this did not happen until nine years later, in September 2003. Until then, there was only the Office of the Prosecutor, which was responsible for both investigations conducted for the International Tribunal for the former Yugoslavia (established in May 1993 following a decision by the UN Security Council) and the investigation of the Rwandan genocide. That an Office of the Prosecutor was finally established in September 2003, rendering the Arusha Court complete, occurred, as I will show, under circumstances that highlighted the intertwining of law and politics. Until then, there was only an international court that took up the Rwandan case with great empathy for the country. Many Rwandans observed it with extreme suspicion.

Corruption, nepotism, incompetence, and mismanagement were the accusations that were regularly heard on the Rwandan side when the Arusha tribunal was discussed. These charges were by no means completely unfounded, as UN reports were forced to admit.[5] When the court hearings began in 1997, accusations were made that the judges lacked sensitivity and sufficient interest in resolving cases, especially when it came to charges of rape.[6]

The court's first verdict, which was also the verdict on genocide ever passed down by an international court, was received with almost grim satisfaction in Rwanda.[7] The court had finally established, on September 2, 1998, what everyone in Rwanda knew: that there had been a genocide, that the crime of rape was among the many atrocities that had made it possible, and that there had also been high-ranking perpetrators such as Jean-Paul Akayesu, the former mayor of Taba, a community about fifty kilometers southwest of Kigali.[8] The tortuous dogmatic considerations that the court made and applied for the first time to a concrete, real-life context—are the Tutsi, who share a culture with the Hutu, a national, ethnic, or racial group; how is the subjective characteristic of intent to destroy to be understood and proven?[9]—was acknowledged in Rwanda with pronounced indifference, as if to say "we know exactly who killed whom and why," a sentiment frequently heard in Rwanda. For many Rwandans, what was of decisive importance was merely the fact that Akayesu was sentenced to life imprisonment for genocidal crimes.

Two days later, on September 4, 1998, the second verdict followed. Jean Kambanda, Rwanda's prime minister at the time of the genocide, had pleaded guilty to all charges.[10] Thus, within a short period of time, the very highest "competent" authority had again confirmed before the world public that a genocide had taken place in Rwanda and that the genocide was intended to be as thorough as possible.

From the outset, it was apparent to all those involved that the court would be unable to do its job without a minimum willingness of Rwandan authorities to cooperate. Evidence had to be provided and witnesses had to be allowed to travel to Arusha and treated with respect and consideration there. From the Rwandan point of view, the court was always worthy of support when it was active, that is, when it handed down verdicts that demonstrated to the whole world the horror of the genocide and the suffering of the victims. On several occasions, Rwanda had already threatened to terminate all cooperation with the tribunal in Arusha due to sluggish court work or what was perceived as cynical questioning of witnesses by the defense that the court did not criticize. This was the case at the end of 1999 when the Appeals Chamber decided to dismiss the charges against Jean-Bosco Barayagwiza and order his immediate release. Barayagwiza had been in custody for over three hundred days without being told the reason for his arrest, which, in the opinion of the Chamber, was a blatant violation of the procedural guarantees resulting from the habeas corpus principle in favor of the accused.[11] However, the decision was overturned by the chamber a few months later because, it argued, new facts had emerged, making the violation of the habeas corpus principle appear far less serious and providing legal grounds to counter any release.

Rwanda, which was convinced of Barayagwiza's guilt,[12] had obviously prevailed. Although the chamber, in its corrective decision, had promised the defendant a reduced sentence in the event of his conviction,[13] the impression is that the court wanted to avoid severe strain on its relationship with Rwanda at all costs. This aim is understandable when one considers the increasing shift in focus of the Office of the Prosecutor at the time, a shift associated with its new head, the Swiss judge Carla Del Ponte. Up until September 1999, her predecessors, the South African Richard Goldstone and the Canadian Louise Arbour, had understood their mandate as applicable exclusively to crimes committed by extremist Hutus against Tutsis and oppositional Hutus. Del Ponte interpreted her mandate as calling for investigations in all directions. This included crimes committed by the RPF, which was now the ruling political power in Rwanda. The RPF and its army had allegedly committed crimes as it took power in the country in 1994; estimates range between 25,000 and 45,000 deaths caused by the RPF forces, with some witness testimony citing significantly higher figures.[14] "For me, a victim is a victim," Del Ponte commented. "Every crime that falls within my jurisdiction is a crime, regardless of the identity, ethnicity, or political views of the perpetrators. Justice does not obey political opportunism."[15]

Rwanda's Discontent and Its Victory

Del Ponte's statement, made quite matter-of-factly in 2002, sounded like a threat to Rwandan government representatives—an interpretation that meshed perfectly with their outrage over recent questioning of victims and witnesses that had been conducted in a degrading manner.[16] "Any crimes committed by individuals within the RPA [= Rwandan Patriotic Army, the military arm of the Rwandan Patriotic Front/RPF, G.H.] were investigated and punished," declared Rwanda's President Paul Kagame. Furthermore, he addressed the international community and the Rwanda tribunal, adding,

> They know that very well. We were not operating like forces that carried out the Genocide. On the side of the Government of that time, nobody was punishing those who were committing crimes, on the contrary, it was as if they were being rewarded for their crimes. How then does the ICTR attempt to place the RPA, who actually put an end to the Genocide, at the same level as the Genocidaire [*sic*], the very perpetrators of the Genocide? We do not agree with this kind of thinking.

Moreover, referring directly to the tribunal, he repeated an old accusation: "One only needs to compare the resources allocated to the tribunal with the results. Tens of millions of US Dollars are spent, yet trials take such a long time, and some cases have been pending for such a long time."[17]

In some cases, the outrage of the survivors was quite understandable. Following years of proceedings with numerous witnesses who had traveled from Rwanda, some of whom had to endure rugged, complex, and psychologically challenging questioning in court, many cases ended with verdicts that acquitted the accused due to lack of sufficient evidence, in keeping with the principle *in dubio pro reo* or to blatant procedural errors by lower courts.[18] For victims and witnesses, this was no doubt a sobering, shocking, and indeed humiliating experience. On the other hand, the nature of the crimes on trial required great sensitivity on the part of the court so as not to jeopardize the principles of a fair trial. The appearance of witnesses, if their appearance in person is significant for the proceedings, is an elementary component of a trial that respects the rule of law; at the same time, the accused must be presumed innocent until proven otherwise. These principles contrasted with the official views of Rwandan authorities, who claimed to "know exactly what had happened" and wanted this knowledge to be recognized by the court. In this perspective, the higher a person's position in the state apparatus, the more deeply they were involved in the genocide. In other words, there could not have been an officer, mayor, prefect, or minister who was not "somehow" involved in the genocide.

In this view, conversely, it was simply an incontrovertible truth that the RPF and its supporters were not guilty of any crime. If crimes were committed in the course of their gaining power over Rwanda between April and July 1994, then they were acts of revenge out of bitterness at the horrors and their aftermath revealed to advancing RPA soldiers. These were individual acts, nothing more. Regrettable but ultimately unavoidable. Anyone who claimed that these crimes were committed systematically and under orders was pronounced to be spreading lies and mocking the struggle to end the genocide.[19]

Carla Del Ponte did not heed this warning—which brings us to another aspect that evokes uneasiness with respect to Rwanda's role in influencing the tribunal. Just over a year after taking office, Del Ponte had already gathered sufficient evidence that RPA soldiers had committed crimes against the civilian population on a large scale in 1994. Kigali had even repeatedly declared its willingness to cooperate, without which, as everyone involved was aware, there would be no continuation of the proceedings (Kagame in April 2001 to Carla Del Ponte: "I decide and I have decided that we will cooperate in this investigation.").[20] However, the offer of cooperation was, in effect, merely a poorly veiled stalling tactic. A few months later, President Kagame made it clear to Chief Prosecutor Del Ponte in rather undiplomatic terms that there would be no transfer of RPA officers to the court. Kagame had already demonstrated that he meant business, as Rwanda hampered witnesses' travel to Arusha to testify and forced the Court to suspend its work temporarily.[21] But Carla Del Ponte did not let up and, driven by the fear that the court could fall into the trap of so-called victor's justice, insisted on investigations in all directions, including against RPA or RPF officials.[22]

The atmosphere between the prosecution in Arusha and Rwandan leadership continued to deteriorate. Rwanda sought to close ranks with Great Britain and the USA to exert more pressure on Del Ponte. The UK did not really need to be convinced, as London had been following the policies of the new Rwanda with some sympathy since 1994 and had no interest in destabilizing the regime by bringing charges against some of its representatives. The USA followed the British argument, especially in response to the fact that Rwanda had concluded, as a kind of advance payment, an agreement with Washington directed against the recently established permanent International Criminal Court in March 2003 (no accession by Rwanda to the Rome Statute, which established the International Criminal Court; no extradition of US citizens by Rwanda to the Court). UN Secretary-General Kofi Annan also supported a deal, which Rwanda hoped would mean that Carla Del Ponte would soon be relieved of her post as chief prosecutor for the Rwanda tribunal. According to this plan, the duties of the chief prosecutor, which had so far included the Rwandan and Yugoslavian ad hoc tribunals, were to be split between two people. Ideally, in the eyes of Rwandan authorities, Carla Del Ponte would lose responsibility for the Rwanda tribunal but remain prosecutor for the former Yugoslavia. Hassan Bubacar Jallow from Gambia would be named prosecutor for Rwanda. In return, Rwanda would agree to conduct its own proceedings against accused RPA officers.[23]

The plan was implemented according to Rwanda's expectations. Kofi Annan rejected Carla Del Ponte's last offer, made with quite subversive intentions, to voluntarily relinquish responsibility for the Yugoslavia tribunal in exchange for retaining responsibility for the Rwanda tribunal. In September 2003, the UN Security Council decided to divide up the powers of the Prosecutor for the ad hoc tribunals, which meant that Carla Del Ponte was no longer responsible for the Rwanda tribunal. Rwanda had previously agreed to a draft treaty that stated: "The [Office of the Prosecutor] will not seek an indictment or otherwise bring a case before the [tribunal] unless it is determined that the [government of Rwanda] investigation or prosecution was not genuine."[24] Carla Del Ponte had been elegantly silenced, and

Rwanda had prevailed and regained sovereignty over the prosecution of its own crimes—a questionable, sobering decision not only for the former chief prosecutor of the Rwanda tribunal.[25]

Questionable Prosecution in Rwanda

The time had finally come in 2008, fourteen years after the crimes. The expectation of the court in Arusha that Rwanda would prosecute members of the RPA forces accused of crimes had become too pressing, and four RPA soldiers had to stand trial before a Rwandan military court. The two officers in command were acquitted in the first trial ("they could not have foreseen the killings perpetrated by their subordinates"). In contrast, two accused sergeants were sentenced to eight years imprisonment each, with recognition by the court of mitigating circumstances ("especially agitated due to the massacres of Tutsis witnessed earlier"). The appeals court confirmed the acquittals and reduced the prison sentences to five years.[26]

In Rwanda's view, that was the end of the matter; after all, a high court had investigated the facts once again and made a final assessment. The sentences that it imposed in the last instance corresponded approximately to the sentences that had been imposed in previous proceedings before Rwandan courts against RPA soldiers. By the end of 1998, military courts had sentenced thirty-two soldiers to prison terms averaging between two and four years for twenty-one crimes with a total of ninety-two victims; all of these had been for manslaughter and not for war crimes or crimes against humanity.[27]

The prosecution in Arusha was satisfied with the verdicts. Carla Del Ponte's successor, Hassan Bubacar Jallow, declared, "[W]e gave the Rwandan prosecuting authorities the opportunity to proceed with that case against four senior military officers for the killings of those clergy and other civilians. . . . The report of my monitors indicates that the standards of fair trial were observed." A short time later, he added that "the trial had been open, public, free, and fair."[28]

The assessment of the non-governmental organization Human Rights Watch, which also monitored the proceedings in Arusha, differed fundamentally.

> The trial proved to be a political whitewash and a miscarriage of justice. . . . Both the prosecution and the defense presented the killings as spontaneous reactions by soldiers overcome with grief for their fellow RPF officers who had lost relatives in the genocide. The court heard testimony only from witnesses supporting this version of events, despite evidence you [prosecutor Jallow, G.H.] transmitted to Rwanda's prosecution service indicating that the killings were part of a planned military operation involving more senior officials.[29]

Carla Del Ponte came to a similar conclusion. The fact that the superior officers had been acquitted was confirmation "that shows that Rwanda did not want to do these cases. For me, it's the proof . . . that they are not able and they are not willing. I heard that myself directly from President Kagame. He told me at that time that they would not do them. This confirms that."[30]

In mid-2009, the prosecution in Arusha concluded that it would definitely not press charges for possible RPA crimes, arguing that there was a lack of reliable evidence, that the focus had to be placed on the time-consuming investigations into the genocide against the Tutsi, and that conducting proceedings in Rwanda was more conducive to furthering reconciliation.[31] In plain language, this meant that the deeds of the RPF would no longer be documented in court for the international public and world history. Only the Rwandan courts could conduct criminal proceedings to promote national reconciliation. Hopes that there would be a comprehensive reappraisal of the crimes committed by all sides—or even just the investigation of a few examples of crimes against humanity or war crimes perpetrated by RPF soldiers that would indicate that such cases could not be equated with genocide—were thus dashed. Not only were the crimes played down by the Rwandan judiciary (e.g., the officer indicted in the case of several thousand Rwandan refugees murdered in the Kibeho refugee camp in 1995 was merely charged with "failure to render assistance"). If the courts imposed any sentences at all, they were quite light and only partially served under comfortable circumstances and compensated for by subsequent accelerated promotion within the military. Under these conditions, it is simply inconceivable how reconciliation—or at least merely serious preparations for such a process—could be achieved. This was supposed to be the kind of reconciliation that the UN Security Council had in mind when it set up the international court and emphasized its conviction in the preamble to the Statute "that in the particular circumstances of Rwanda, the prosecution of persons responsible for serious violations of international humanitarian law would enable this aim to be achieved and would contribute to the process of *national reconciliation* and to the restoration and maintenance of peace."[32] Chief Prosecutor Jallow was familiar with this idea and was even aware of his own role in the process, which was revealed in a statement he made in 2005. "National reconciliation is anticipated to be an important outcome of the prosecution process," he said. "Hence, the extent to which the exercise of prosecutorial discretion impacts on this objective—positively or adversely—is a relevant consideration," he concluded.[33]

Obviously, it was Rwanda alone that determined what was meant by reconciliation and how it was to be brought about. Moreover, Rwanda alone obtained the necessary support to implement its ideas about reconciliation. At this point, the uneasiness about Rwanda's influence on the court in Arusha gives way to the sobering realization that the application of the law on international crimes not only follows legal standards but is also subject to political decisions. When seemingly overriding political rationales determine that no crimes were committed that can be brought to trial, there were indeed no crimes, even if the experience of the people concerned or the evidence gathered firmly suggests otherwise.

Law Was Applied, But Politics Proved to Be Stronger

Let us contrast this finding with the following statement:

> In appraising international trials, one should predicate such assessment on the notion that these tribunals have been established only to fill in for national courts, which tend to refrain from prosecuting and trying persons suspected of those widespread, large-scale and organized atrocities that are international crimes. Without the (relative) inertia or the reluctance of national courts, there would be no need for international criminal tribunals.[34]

The statement was made by Antonio Cassese, the first president of an international criminal court after the Second World War and an important voice in international criminal law. If we assume his assessment to be correct—and, strictly speaking, no other reasons can justify curtailing national sovereignty by an international criminal court—how is it compatible with the proceedings of the Rwanda tribunal?

One could argue simply that the court in Arusha only considered acts by perpetrators of the genocide, who were all Hutu, and acts that accompanied the genocide against the so-called "moderate Hutu" (primarily crimes against humanity). Then, one could also assert with satisfaction: "The ICTR cases, in particular, have shown that the international community is moving ever closer to the postulate that all human beings are equal before the law."[35] The crimes of the RPF would be ignored because they were not part of the genocide itself. Only perpetrators of genocidal acts would be condemned, right up to the highest-ranking officials.

This view would also be simplistic because it might be based on a widespread and, therefore, well-known perception of genocide as a "crime of crimes." Today, despite the decades of silence following the adoption of the Genocide Convention in December 1948, a crime that was outside the triad of "crimes against peace, war crimes, and crimes against humanity" formulated at the Nuremberg war crimes trial in 1945/1946 has become a crime that is regarded as the epitome of injustice worldwide. The crime of genocide, especially when it is associated with the Holocaust, evokes the association of massacres that come upon people like a disaster and are motivated solely by the will to exterminate.

Subsequent events and their international perception have confirmed agreement with the court's approach. "[W]idespread, large-scale and organized atrocities," which is how Antonio Cassese defined crimes of genocide, are obviously also what the crimes of genocide in Rwanda were. There is, thus, at least on the surface, much to be said in favor of the approach adopted by the court in Arusha, which was to concentrate solely on the investigation and prosecution of crimes perpetrated by Hutu against the Tutsi.

However, the acts that RPF members were accused of committing were also crimes under international law. The violent deaths of tens or even hundreds of thousands of people within just a few months are clearly evidence of a "widespread or systematic attack" against a civilian population and thus fulfill the definition in Article 3 of the statute of the Rwanda tribunal for crimes against humanity. If we perceive an independent and impartial judiciary as an essential prerequisite for achieving justice,[36] then the decision not to prosecute RPF crimes, which was presented as a pragmatic solution, was not in the interests of justice. One crime under international law cannot supersede another. This would only be acceptable if the crimes in question were less grave than violent crimes that breached international law, that is, if it were a crime that the Rwandan government was prepared to admit to and which the prosecuting authority in Arusha was willing to believe were merely acts of violence resulting from individual despair. The findings of UN envoy Robert Gersony, who had traveled through several regions of Rwanda in August and September 1994 to investigate whether the 2 million refugees who had fled the country since April 1994 could return home, had already cast considerable doubt on this version. He and his two colleagues had discovered, more or less by chance, that the RPA was involved in "clearly systematic murders and persecution of the Hutu population in certain parts of the country."[37] Gersony reported his findings to the UN High Commissioner for Refugees, who then informed UN headquarters. However, a report was never published, and in fact, the UN even denied the very existence of a report out of consideration for the new rulers in Kigali and in exchange for their promise to investigate the allegations themselves, as later became known. Thus, in November 1994, when the UN Security Council passed Resolution 955, in which the establishment of the International Tribunal for Rwanda was referred to as a contribution to national reconciliation, the council presumably adhered to the same understanding of the tribunal's aims. Only crimes of genocide and associated acts by the same group of perpetrators were to be put on trial. This was seen as meeting the most important prerequisite for reconciliation among Rwandans. Everything else was to be left up to the country's new leadership.

In the ensuing years, this understanding shaped by political expediencies became firmly entrenched, mainly at the instigation of Great Britain and the USA, soon becoming a fundamental principle—a principle that was at the root of Carla Del Ponte's failure. "Justice is always political, law is political," another judge who worked at an international criminal court asserted, adding as a warning that "everyday legal work must not be dependent on political influences, as I would like to emphasize."[38] But that was precisely what the court in Arusha allowed to happen. It conducted its work based on a political preconception without demonstrating any recognizable hesitance. And despite subsequent findings revealing that the RPA had killed about one hundred thousand people in 1994 alone[39] and regardless of the Rwandan-led wars in Congo, which further widened the rift between Hutu and Tutsi, the court maintained its stance. Even Rwanda's blatant lack of interest in investigating these crimes did not change its position.

As a result, I will summarize my assessment of the work of the Rwanda tribunal in the following paragraphs.

On the one hand, the court convicted dozens of high-ranking and influential people of genocide. Moreover, it dealt with essential substantive and dogmatic legal issues that include the following:

- Sexual violence and rape can be a form of genocidal violence.[40]
- A specific ethnic group protected under the Genocide Convention, like all other groups protected by it, should be defined not only based on objective criteria (language, religion, or cultural identity); processes of social attribution must also be taken into account (self-perception or perception of others, especially the perpetrators).[41]
- Expressions of opinions disseminated in the media that are intended to or are likely to promote hatred of a protected group—for example, hate speech disseminated in radio broadcasts—constitute an incitement to commit genocide and are thus genocidal crimes.[42]
- The responsibility of superiors and the fact that they are subject to prosecution for genocidal crimes if they did not take action to prevent their subordinates from perpetrating such crimes whenever they had (or should have had) prior knowledge of them must apply not only to the military sector but also to civilian authorities.[43]

Moreover, the court has also established important findings of fact. These include the following:

- There is no proof that plans were made to perpetrate the genocide before April 6, 1994. In the words of the court, "Accordingly, the Chamber is not satisfied that the Prosecution has proven beyond reasonable doubt that the four Accused conspired among themselves or with others to commit genocide before it unfolded on 7 April 1994."[44] According to the court elsewhere in the judgment, ethnic polarization had undoubtedly occurred since the end of 1990.[45] A civilian defense had also been organized and trained by the military, and death lists and death squads had been compiled and established.[46] However, whether and to what extent these findings suffice as evidence of an objective intention to exterminate the "Tutsi as such" could not be established with the necessary clarity, as much of the information was based on rumors or could not be confirmed beyond any doubt.[47]
- Nevertheless, the crisis unit and the interim government it set up on April 8, 1994, emphatically called for and facilitated the killing of political opponents and all Tutsi, regardless of age or gender. After April 18, 1994, when the last prefects, sub-prefects, and mayors in the southwest of the country who had opposed these plans had been murdered, expelled, or intimidated, there was no longer open resistance to the genocide.[48]
- Military units of the Rwandan army (Forces Armées Rwandaises), presidential guards, and paramilitary forces—above all, the Interahamwe—committed the murders and the accompanying acts of violence. Murdering Tutsis was perceived as a commendable act in the interests of the country's future, and the greatest possible participation of the Hutu population was aimed for.[49]
- Even representatives of churches and religious communities joined in the murders. Churches were not places of refuge but became the sites of massacres organized by Catholic priests.[50]

If we consider all this when assessing the work of the Arusha tribunal, we must conclude that its work was incomplete. The court disregarded the central reason for international criminal jurisdiction, which was also emphasized by Antonio Cassese—the investigation of crimes under international law because national courts tend to be biased. If it is true that it takes a generation before it is possible to address what really happened—in Germany, for example, where the majority of perpetrators and victims did not live in the same country, it was not until the 1960s that any significant reappraisal of Nazi injustice began—then it is all the more urgent that the facts be established as comprehensively as possible (as was the case in Germany with the Nuremberg Trials), before this process begins. Stopping investigations prematurely, suppressing investigation results, or making such results available to other law enforcement agencies that are likely to deal with them in a dilatory manner destroys the basis that is essential for a society to come to terms with its past and work for reconciliation. Although reconciliation may have been realized to a certain extent in some places in Rwanda, due to the partial success of the tribunal's work in Arusha, there is great danger that reconciliation will be eroded. Too many people failed to find recognition of their suffering in the genocide through the Arusha court.

Ultimately, this has led to a strange outcome. The people of Rwanda, at least the vast majority of them, reject the Arusha tribunal. Its decisions neither concern them nor interest them. The Rwandan authorities also rejected the court. Even though the court made numerous concessions to Rwanda, in the eyes of Rwandan officials, it acted too hesitantly and often enough in the wrong way. It has kept the memory of the genocide alive but has maintained a great distance to the victims and their lives. It would seem that the only ones who are satisfied with the outcome are Hassan Bubacar Jallow, who succeeded Carla del Ponte as the Rwanda tribunal's chief prosecutor, as well as the judges of the Arusha court, and—if appearances at memorial ceremonies commemorating the genocide are any indication—the representatives of the states that provided the money to finance it.

Notes

1 See UN document S/PV.3453, November 8, 1994, 15; https://documents.un.org/doc/undoc/pro/n94/869/74/pdf/n9486974.pdf?token=yw2xNPE3BBfenONA1T&fe=true; accessed February 29, 2024.

2 In 1994, the chief prosecutor of the United Nations International Criminal Tribunals for the former Yugoslavia and Rwanda was Richard Goldstone, a South African judge.

3 See UN document S/PV.3453, November 8, 1994, 16; https://documents.un.org/doc/undoc/pro/n94/869/74/pdf/n9486974.pdf?token=yw2xNPE3BBfenONA1T&fe=true; accessed February 29, 2024.

4 Ibid., 5.

5 See for example International Criminal Tribunal for Rwanda, Annual Report November 13, 1997, A/52/582, S/1997/868; https://unictr.irmct.org/sites/unictr.org/files/legal-library/971113-annual-report-en.pdf; accessed February 29, 2024.

6 See Binaifer Nowrojee, "'Your Justice is Too Slow.' Will the ICTR Fail Rwanda's Rape Victims?" United Nations Research Institute for Social Development, November 2005, 17 and 24; http://hdl.handle.net/10419/148772; accessed February 29, 2024.
7 This reaction is understandable, considering how long Europe, the USA, and the UN had hesitated in recognizing the genocide after it began on April 6, 1994. Indicative of this hesitant stance is a short dialog that took place on June 10, 1994 between Christine Shelly, speaker of the US Department of State, and a Reuters journalist, Alan Elsner, about the use of the g-word (g = genocide). See Samantha Power, *A Problem from Hell: America and the Age of Genocide* (New York: Basic Books, 2002), 363f.
8 Mayors were appointed directly by the Rwandan president and represented the president and his policies on the local level. They headed the local police forces.
9 See The Prosecutor vs. Jean-Paul Akayesu (Case ICTR-96-4-T), Judgment of September 2, 1998, para. 112–129, 492–548, 698–734.
10 See The Prosecutor vs. Jean Kambanda (Case ICTR-97-23-S), Judgment and Sentence, September 4, 1998, para. 3, 40.
11 See Jean-Bosco Barayagwiza vs. The Prosecutor (Case ICTR-97-19-AR72), Verdict of November 3, 1999, para. 113. Barayagwiza was accused of calling for genocide as a co-founder of the extremist *Coalition pour la Défense de la République* and of *Radio-Télévision Libre des Mille Collines*.
12 See Jean-Bosco Barayagwiza vs. The Prosecutor (Case ICTR-97-19-AR72), Verdict of March 31, 2000, para. 34.
13 Ibid., para. 75.
14 Gérard Prunier, *From Genocide to Continental War: The "Congolese" Conflict and the Crisis of Contemporary Africa* (London: Hurst, 2009), 15f.
15 My translation, quotation in French original: "Le procureur du TPIR accuse a nouveau le Rwanda de ne pas cooperer," *Hirondelle News*, November 29, 2004; https://www.justiceinfo.net/fr/7738-le-procureur-du-tpir-accuse-a-nouveau-le-rwanda-de-ne-pas-cooperer4528.html; accessed February 29, 2024.
16 See Filip Reyntjens, "Chronique politique du Rwanda et du Burundi, 2001–2002," in *L'Afrique des Grands Lacs: Annuaire 2001-2002*, eds. Filip Reyntjens, Stefaan Marysse (Paris: L'Harmattan, 2002), 60.
17 "ICTR being used—Kagame," *The New Times*, August 15–18, 2002, 1, 2.
18 See for example the court's decision from November 16, 2009 to acquit Protais Zigiranyirazo, brother-in-law of the former president Habyarimana, in which the Appeals Chamber noted "In reversing Zigiranyirazo's convictions for genocide and extermination as a crime against humanity, the Appeals Chamber again underscores the seriousness of the Trial Chamber's errors. The crimes Zigiranyirazo was accused of were very grave, meriting the most careful of analyses. Instead, the Trial Judgement misstated the principles of law governing the distribution of the burden of proof with regards to alibi and seriously erred in its handling of the evidence. Zigiranyirazo's resulting convictions relating to Kesho Hill and the Kiyovu Roadblock violated the most basic and fundamental principles of justice. In these circumstances, the Appeals Chamber had no choice but to reverse Zigiranyirazo's convictions." Zigiranyirazo vs. The Prosecutor (Case ICTR-01-73-A), Judgment of November 16, 2009, para. 75.
19 Frequently, RPF fighters had killed themselves after a killing spree, due to feelings of guilt or despair; see Stephen Kinzer, *A Thousand Hills: Rwanda's Rebirth and the Man Who Dreamed It* (Hoboken, NJ: John Wiley & Sons 2008), 190f.

20 See Carla Del Ponte (with Chuck Sudetic), *Madame Prosecutor: Confrontations with Humanity's Worst Criminals and the Culture of Impunity* (New York: Other Press, 2009), 183–6; quote 186.
21 See Del Ponte, *Madame Prosecutor*, 225–9.
22 Ibid., 296.
23 Ibid., 303; Thierry Cruvellier, *Le Tribunal des Vaincus: Un Nuremberg pour le Rwanda?* (Paris: Calmann-Lévy, 2006), 242f.
24 Quoted from Del Ponte, *Madame Prosecutor*, 233.
25 On criticism of the United Nations Security Council's decision, see Aryeh Neier, "Effort to Oust Prosecutor is Misguided, *International Herald Tribune*, August 7, 2003; https://www.opensocietyfoundations.org/voices/effort-oust-prosecutor-misguided; accessed February 29, 2024.
26 Lars Waldorf, "A Mere Pretense of Justice: Complementarity, Sham Trials, and Victor's Justice at the Rwanda Tribunal," *Fordham International Law Journal* 4 (2011): 1254.
27 Ibid., 1226f.
28 Both quotes ibid., 1255.
29 Quoted from ibid., 1257; see also Human Rights Watch Executive Director Kenneth Roth's letter to Hassan B. Jallow, the court's prosecutor, on May 26, 2009: http://www.hrw.org/node/83536; accessed February 29, 2024.
30 Quoted from Waldorf, "Mere Pretense," 1258.
31 See ibid., 1271f.
32 Emphasis G.H.
33 Quoted from Waldorf, "Mere Pretense," 1260.
34 Quoted from Antonio Cassese, *International Criminal Law*, 2nd ed. (Oxford: Oxford University Press 2008), 435.
35 Statement by Wolfgang Schomburg, former judge of the ICTTR Appeals Chamber in his article "Der Friedensbeitrag des UN-Tribunals für Ruanda: Strafgerichtsbarkeit kann auch transnational erfolgreich sein," *Vereinte Nationen*, no. 2 (2014): 64.
36 For details with respect to international criminal courts, see Cassese, *International Criminal Law*, 379f.
37 See https://www.hrw.org/legacy/reports/1999/rwanda/Geno15-8-03.htm; accessed February 29, 2024.
38 According to Christoph Flügge, judge at the International Criminal Tribunal for the former Yugoslavia in his text "Die juristische Aufarbeitung von Kriegsverbrechen am International Criminal Tribunal for the former Yugoslavia (ICTY) in Den Haag," in *Tribunale: Literarische Darstellung und juridische Aufarbeitung von Kriegsverbrechen im globalen Kontext*, eds. Werner Gephart, Jürgen Brokoff, and Jan Christoph Suntrup (Frankfurt am Main: Verlag Vittorio Klostermann, 2014), 63.
39 See Gérard Prunier, *The Rwanda Crisis: History of a Genocide* (New York: Columbia University Press, 1996), 359–63; Waldorf, "Mere Pretense," 1225.
40 See The Prosecutor vs. Jean-Paul Akayesu (Case ICTR-96-4), Judgment of September 2, 1998, para. 706, 731. "With regard, particularly, to the acts described in paragraphs 12(A) and 12(B) of the Indictment, that is, rape and sexual violence, the Chamber wishes to underscore the fact that in its opinion, they constitute genocide in the same way as any other act as long as they were committed with the specific

intent to destroy, in whole or in part, a particular group, targeted as such. Indeed, rape and sexual violence certainly constitute infliction of serious bodily and mental harm on the victims and are even, according to the Chamber, one of the worst ways of inflicting harm on the victim as he or she suffers both bodily and mental harm" (para. 731).

41 See The Prosecutor vs. Clément Kayishema et al. (Case ICTR-96-1), Judgment of May 21, 1999, para. 98.

42 See The Prosecutor vs. Georges Ruggiu, Judgment of June 1, 2000, 17; The Prosecutor vs. Ferdinand Nahimana et al., Judgment of December 3, 2003, para. 1091ff.

43 See The Prosecutor vs. Théoneste Bagosora et al. (Case ICTR-99-52-A), Judgment of December 18, 2008, para. 2158; The Prosecutor vs. Pauline Nyiramasuhuko, Judgment of June 24, 2011, para. 5610, 6088.

44 Quoted from The Prosecutor vs. Théoneste Bagosora et al. (Case ICTR-98-41), Judgment of December 18, 2008, para. 2113.

45 Ibid., para. 209.

46 Ibid., para. 446–53, 488–506, 521, 619.

47 Ibid., para. 222, 544–80.

48 See The Prosecutor vs. Jean Kambanda (Case ICTR-97-3-A), Judgment of October 4, 1998, para. 39; Cruvellier, *Le Tribunal des Vaincus*, 74–8.

49 See The Prosecutor vs. Georges Rutaganda (Case ICTR-96-3-A), Judgment of December 6, 1999, para. 2, 385–99; The Prosecutor vs. Tharcisse Renzaho (Case ICTR-97-31-A), Judgment of July 14, 2009, para. 779.

50 See The Prosecutor vs. Athanase Seromba (Case ICTR-01-66-A), Judgment of December 13, 2006, para. 322–38.

Selected Bibliography

Dallaire, Roméo, *Shake Hands with the Devil. The Failure of Humanity in Rwanda* (Toronto: Random House, 2003).

Fujii, Lee Ann, *Killing Neighbors. Webs of Violence in Rwanda* (Ithaca, NY and London: Cornell University Press, 2009).

Human Rights Watch, *Leave None to Tell the Story: Genocide in Rwanda* (New York: Human Rights Watch, 1999).

Kuperman, Alan J., *The Limits of Humanitarian Intervention. Genocide in Rwanda* (Washington, DC: Brookings Institution Press, 2001).

Prunier, Gérard, *The Rwanda Crisis. History of a Genocide* (London: C. Hurst & Co Publishers, 1995).

Wrong, Michela, *Do Not Disturb. The Story of a Political Murder and an African Regime Gone Bad* (New York: Public Affairs, 2021).

10

The Nuremberg Legacy in East Timor, Indonesia, and Cambodia

David Cohen

Telford Taylor, perhaps more than any other individual in the late 1940s, was in a position to assess the transformative nature of the historical trials in which he had played such a crucial role, first in the war crimes investigations that collected the evidence for the International Military Tribunal at Nuremberg (IMT). As the US deputy prosecutor, and finally as the chief prosecutor for the Nuremberg Subsequent Proceedings conducted under Control Council Law No. 10.[1] It was in particular at those subsequent proceedings before the National Military Tribunals at Nuremberg that the fundamental principles that guided the IMT were developed, interpreted, and elaborated into the more specific legal doctrines that would play such an important role when the enterprise of international criminal justice was reborn in 1993–4 with the establishment of the ICTY and the ICTR. Reflecting on his four years of leadership with the Nuremberg trials 1945–9, Taylor summarized the significance for the future of what he had experienced,

> International penal law—a mere embryo a few decades ago—has developed with phenomenal rapidity. Many concepts and doctrines previously embodied chiefly or solely in treaties, addresses, and textbooks have been expounded and applied in judicial proceedings. . . . Indeed, it is not too much to say that these trials, more than anything else in recent centuries, have brought international law out of the lecture hall and into the courtroom. Almost overnight, international penal law has become a living reality.[2]

It took another half century before that "living reality" actually came into being. Still, when it did, the ICTY and ICTR recognized the importance of Nuremberg and its legacy for the new era of international criminal justice.[3] Taylor reflected more deeply on the significance of Nuremberg in the Final Report he submitted to the US Army.[4] He began with the observation "Nuremberg is a historical and moral fact with which, from now on, every government must reckon in its internal and external policies alike." [5] From this starting point, he next took up the issue of what would be the legacy of the "Nuremberg principles" for governments and leaders in the future:

> It is undoubtedly a dim but growing awareness that we have deeply committed ourselves to the Nuremberg principles by undertaking *to judge men under them and punish men for their violation t*hat explains the comment one so often hears today that "Nuremberg has established a dangerous precedent." This remark reflects at least three quite distinct states of mind. Some people, unfamiliar with the Nuremberg record, continue to imagine that the German diplomats were punished for drafting notes, the generals for preparing military plans or leading armies in battle, and the businessmen for engaging in war production. The Nuremberg record itself will dispel these illusions. (my emphasis)[6]

Taylor's comment underscores the threat that the most fundamental of the Nuremberg principles represents to leaders contemplating conduct in violation of international criminal law: the principle of individual criminal responsibility for politicians, generals, officials, or those engaged in conflict-related economic activity.[7] There were extensive political and legal negotiations to try the German Kaiser after WWI, all of which failed. So it was Nuremberg's enduring contribution to have succeeded in establishing an enduring legal framework that could be used against the highest military and civilian leaders accused of having committed grave international crimes.[8]

Looking at the composition of the defendants at the IMT and the Subsequent Proceedings, one can understand the apprehension that viewed Nuremberg as a "dangerous precedent." The IMT did not select defendants, just those who might have been viewed as having the most blood on their hands. The defendants represented the German state and society as a whole, embracing the ruling political party, the military, the ministerial bureaucracies, the administration of occupied territories, the executive, and the German economic enterprises that fed the war machine.[9] The breadth and depth of that representation were expanded in the Subsequent Proceedings where not only the scope of governmental, economic, military, and Nazi party institutions and organizations significantly expanded but where the prosecution reached down into the secondary and tertiary leadership echelons, the domain of the professionals whose expertise made these institutions function as vital critical components of the Nazi program of conquest, occupation, exploitation, and extermination. With some prescience, Taylor also identified that newly born doctrine established in the Nuremberg Charter that, in his view, would play an increasingly important role in what today is called international criminal law: "The concept of 'crimes against humanity,' however, if it becomes an established part of international penal law-as it seems to be doing will be of the greatest practical importance in peacetime."[10] In this, as in many other things, Taylor has been proved correct, though the fulfillment of that prophetic statement took many decades.

While fully recognizing the magnitude of what these prosecutions and convictions *potentially* represented for the future, Taylor, well aware of the impact of the Cold War on the aspirations embodied in the UN Charter and other instruments, fully recognized the challenges that lay ahead and the overarching question that remained: "Now that the Nuremberg trials are concluded, probably most of the doubts concerning their wisdom are those conjured up by events in the world around us. In the last analysis, the 'Nuremberg question' is whether international law has intrinsic validity or practical efficacy in this day and age."[11]

That "Nuremberg question" so eloquently articulated by Taylor is still with us today. One need only turn on the BBC to see the challenge that contemporary events pose to Taylor's hope. "Nuremberg is a historical and moral fact with which, from now on, every government must reckon in its internal and external policies alike." Rather than concluding with the "Realists" that the state of the world provides ample evidence that international criminal law, if not all international law, provides only an empty promise, it is worth examining contexts where the international community did summon the political will to create tribunals within the legacy of Nuremberg. What answer, if any, have such tribunals provided to Taylor's "Nuremberg question"?

As noted above, the creation of the ICTY and ICTR marked a new beginning and was followed by a plethora of other tribunals of various kinds in the 1990s and early 2000s. While the formation of new international criminal tribunals has now seemingly come to a halt, the vision generated by Nuremberg for a permanent international criminal court has been fulfilled with the advent of the ICC. Whether the ICC can meet the demands of that vision and mandate, however, remains to be seen. From this perspective, there would appear to be value in determining how the "Nuremberg question" has been answered in some tribunals outside of the ICC.

One of the issues plaguing the ICC, of course, is the absence of the so-called "great powers" in the Assembly of State Parties: China, the USA, Russia, and India. With ICC membership seemingly stalled at the current 123, its potential for universal coverage remains in doubt. In no other region is the reluctance to accept the obligations that ICC membership imposes so apparent as in Asia, and particularly in Southeast Asia, where nine of the ten ASEAN member states have thus far refused to ratify the Rome Statute. For this reason, it may be instructive to examine the experience of the three Southeast Asian countries that conducted trials under international criminal law and explore what their varied experiences tell us about Taylor's question about the "intrinsic validity or practical efficacy in this day and age."

While much has been written about the successes and failures of the ICTY and the ICTR, less attention has been paid to attempts to promote individual criminal responsibility in the trials that were conducted in Southeast Asia from 2000 to 2022 in Timor Leste (East Timor), Indonesia, and Cambodia. These three cases allow us to compare three very different institutional settings that all aim to provide individual criminal responsibility for serious international and domestic crimes.[12] Although sharing some common goals, the extent to which they achieved their goals varied widely among the UN Special Panels for Serious Crimes in East Timor, the purely domestic Ad Hoc Human Rights Court in Jakarta, and the Extraordinary Chambers in the Courts of Cambodia. It is to the search for accountability through the application of the Nuremberg principles in these contexts that the remainder of this chapter now turns.

Seeking Justice in East Timor and Indonesia: The Special Panels for Serious Crimes and the Jakarta Ad Hoc Human Rights Court

The three experiences of international criminal justice in Southeast Asia may have incorporated similar legal frameworks drawn from contemporary international criminal law, but they could not have been more different in other ways. Because both the UN Special Panels for Serious Crimes (SPSC) in East Timor (now Timor Leste) and the Ad hoc Human Rights Court in Jakarta had similar mandates and jurisdictional features, both focusing solely on the 1999 violence in East Timor, it may be instructive to consider them together. The Jakarta trials amply illustrate the challenges of relying on domestic courts still enmeshed in a period of political transition. The UN's mission to East Timor, on the other hand, functioned as the de facto government for the two years before independence, facing the task of nation-building in a context characterized by massive physical destruction, displacement of at least one-third of the population, and the absence of an existing domestic judiciary or any other governmental institutions to build upon. As will be seen, neither setting produced satisfactory results.[13]

The Special Panels for Serious Crimes were thus solely a creation of the UN Mission that functioned as the government of the yet-to-be-independent country, the UN Transitional Authority for East Timor (UNTAET). UNTAET established the first "hybrid" tribunal within a nascent and notionally Timorese justice system that it alone created through a series of UN regulations. The UN regulations enacted by UNTAET encompassed both international crimes as well as domestic crimes within a domestic legal structure that it also invented. As will be seen, a concatenation of circumstances and constraints leads to serious questions as to whether the "Nuremberg principles" were implemented only in form rather than in substance.

The Indonesian initiative for accountability for the 1999 violence in East Timor arose in part from the aim of warding off the international tribunal that global and Indonesian human rights organizations were calling for. It was, however, also a product of the powerful movement for democratization, the rule of law, and reform that was unleashed by success in overthrowing the Suharto dictatorship that had been in place for more than three decades. Thus, in response to both international and domestic pressures at the beginning of Indonesia's transition to a fledgling democracy, Indonesia's Parliament adopted Law 26/2000, creating a specialized system of human rights courts. One of them, the Ad Hoc Jakarta Human Rights Court, was the first to function, and it conducted twelve trials involving eighteen accused persons, focusing on the 1999 violence in East Timor, a parallel mandate to the UN Special Panels for Serious Crimes operating simultaneously in Dili, East Timor.[14] Those human rights trials in Jakarta were a landmark in that they represented the first criminal prosecution of Indonesian military officers in a civilian court. The eighteen defendants included three generals, a colonel and the former Indonesian Governor and Chief of Police of East Timor. While the UN Serious Crimes Unit in Dili, in total, issued ninety-five indictments against 440 individuals, including both East Timorese and Indonesians, 339 of those accused were in Indonesia or elsewhere beyond the reach of the SCU's jurisdiction.[15] In the end, although the SPSC completed trials against eighty-seven accused persons, none of them were Indonesian, and all were low-level Timorese militia members.[16] Apart from quantitative considerations, Nuremberg's fair trial standards of procedural justice set a high standard that neither the UN nor the Jakarta trials met.[17]

The overlapping aims of these two judicial processes will permit us to consider how the Nuremberg legacy was carried over into, on the one hand, a hybrid international-Timorese justice process and, on the other hand, one operating solely within a domestic jurisdiction empowered to apply both international and domestic criminal law. As noted above, one of the most serious challenges facing UNTAET in East Timor was building a judicial process from "ground zero." In Jakarta, however, the search for accountability faced the opposite challenge. Indonesian judicial institutions, courts, and public prosecution service remained intact from the Suharto "New Order" era, in which they were reduced to tools supporting the military dictatorship. The outcome of the Jakarta Human Rights Court trials was significantly impacted by this legacy. While key reforms were initiated in the judiciary, most importantly by taking the judiciary out from under the executive branch and making it independent, the same never happened in the Attorney General's Office (AGO), under which the national public prosecution service operated. While judges were prepared to convict six of the eighteen defendants, including two generals, a colonel, and high-ranking officials, the prosecution in most cases did little to establish the culpability of the accused.[18] Ultimately, all those convicted were acquitted on appeal or judicial review. As Indonesian human rights organizations were quick to point out, the quest for accountability under the provisions of the Rome Statute incorporated into Indonesian Law 26/2000 had resulted in a reconfirmation of impunity.

The failure of the Jakarta trials on East Timor points up some fundamental differences with the context in which the IMT operated, providing insight into the structural challenges of prosecuting military officers and government officials in the immediate period of transition. While it is true that in postwar Germany, there was significant continuity in the judiciary, academia, and governmental bureaucracies from the Nazi era, this did not pose the kind of problems for the IMT that the judges in Jakarta faced.[19] As the Allies were in complete control of occupied Germany and could operate independently under their own authority, as Control Council Law No. 10 provided, the kinds of issues that plagued the Jakarta trials because of unreformed institutions did not occur. The IMT was solely a creation of the victorious allies who conquered, occupied, and governed postwar Germany following the unconditional surrender they demanded. These brute facts enabled investigation and prosecution backed by the uncontested coercive force and political control exercised by the Allied occupation regime. As is well known, in most cases of political transition, while the political appointees may change, the bureaucrats who populate the ministries remain. Thus, in Indonesia, the legacy of Suharto's policy of the "militarization of the public prosecution service" informed the Jakarta trials and still makes itself felt today. In East Timor, on the other hand, creating new institutions from the ground up also failed to provide a satisfactory application of the Nuremberg principles.

After the withdrawal of Indonesian forces and officials from East Timor in October 1999, the UN entered the power vacuum, assuming the uncontested role as the sole source of security, governance, reconstruction, and the creation of what would become Timorese state institutions after independence in May 2002. A prominent focal point of comparison here is what the UN accomplished in regard to accountability, given the very significant control it exerted over almost every aspect of seeking justice in East Timor. The situation of the UN in East Timor thus differs in important ways from the challenges it confronted in Cambodia, where, from the negotiation stage onward, the interests and goals of the UN and the government of Cambodia diverged. It also differs fundamentally from the situation in Jakarta, where the Indonesian government, newly embarked on its reform journey from the Suharto dictatorship, decided to create a tribunal for the 1999 violence in East Timor without any international assistance or participation.

As noted above, UNTAET created an internationalized tribunal within the nascent Timorese justice system that it was in the process of developing.[20] The Special Panel for Serious Crimes operated within the Dili District Court, also under UNTAET direction, until independence on May 20, 2002, when it nominally came under Timorese governmental authority. In thinking about the relation of the Nuremberg legacy to the tribunal in East Timor, one of the most important features was that the Special Panels were created, staffed, funded, and managed by the UN Mission. Thus, the impetus for accountability was grounded in the UN mandate, not, as became ever more apparent after independence, on the priorities of the Timorese government. The situation in which a national government and the UN share responsibility for the quest for accountability for international crimes bears within it the potential for conflicts born of divergent interests. Those divergences played a vital role in East Timor in ways that ultimately undermined accountability (and in Cambodia, as will be explored below). To put it bluntly, neither the UN nor the Timorese government demonstrated the political will necessary to achieve real accountability.[21] While the SPSC convicted eighty-four persons (a troubling 96.5 percent conviction rate), they were all low-level Timorese militia members. The indicted Timorese pro-Indonesian militia leaders and all of the Indonesian military and civilian personnel were in Indonesia. On the other hand, the Jakarta Ad Hoc Human Rights Court was able to prosecute those kinds of accused but, as noted above, ultimately failed in their mandate. The lack of political will to reform the Attorney General's Office and the military doubtless contributed to this result, as it had in East Timor. The Indonesian governmental institutions were divided in how they perceived their roles and their interests in the process of *Reformasi*. They remain so today.[22]

Apart from the failure to achieve accountability for the 1999 violence in East Timor, another dimension of the East Timor conflict remains even more unaddressed. For reasons related to the lack of political will, as well as other factors, both the SPSC and Jakarta trials focused only on the violence between January 1 and October 26, 1999. The 24 years of Indonesian occupation of East Timor and the massive violence that it produced were omitted from the mandates of both courts. The extent of the crimes committed, including those of both sides, was extensively documented in the voluminous report of the Timorese Truth Commission in its report Chega![23] The end result, however, of 10 years of multiple transitional justice mechanisms in East Timor and Indonesia is that there has never been judicial investigation or prosecution of crimes committed during the 1974–99 period, estimated to have claimed the lives of some 200,000 victims and encompassed virtually every other crime against humanity. While it requires little explanation to understand why the Indonesian prosecutions adopted the same temporal limitations employed in trials in East Timor, the failure of the UN to pursue accountability for the vastly more numerous and graver crimes committed during the preceding decades of occupation has never been fully explained. Among other factors, however, the politics of the UN Security Council doubtless played a role. Nuremberg, like all international criminal tribunals, was a political creation. The same is true for all three of the Southeast Asian tribunals as well.

The Extraordinary Chambers in the Courts of Cambodia and the Trial of the Khmer Rouge Leaders

While the Special Panels and the Indonesian Ad Hoc Human Rights Court in Jakarta were in full operation, the UN and the Cambodian government were engaged in protracted negotiations over the structure of what would become the Extraordinary Chambers in the Courts of Cambodia (ECCC). After eight years of often tense negotiations over the decision-making processes within each of the tribunal's divisions (chambers, prosecution, court administration), the ECCC came into being in 2006, the year after the trials in Timor Leste and Indonesia had ended. It soon became clear that the extended negotiations over control of the tribunal had not been fully resolved, as reflected in the compromise supermajority voting system and other institutional features that paved the way for some of the ongoing divisions that characterized the relations between the Cambodian government and the UN on the one hand, and on the other hand, within the court itself. It is also telling that the UN designated its operations as UNAKRT (United Nations Assistance to the Khmer Rouge Tribunal) instead of the clear Cambodian ownership of the tribunal expressed in the official Cambodian name, the Extraordinary Chambers *in the Courts of Cambodia* (my emphasis). Here again, we find an opportunity to assess how Nuremberg principles were applied in a hybrid judicial setting where there were both common goals and deep divisions over fundamental issues of accountability. The opportunity to compare these three cases with their different constellations of international and domestic engagement is important because it has been increasingly recognized, both through the ICC's principle of complementarity, as well as by the various challenges facing the ICC in fulfilling its ambitious mandate, that the involvement of domestic justice institutions is crucial to the future of efforts to fulfill the Nuremberg legacy.

When the ECCC was established in 2006, it had, as noted above, structural features that were later only partially remedied through various internal reforms aimed at addressing the problems left by the compromises that finally enabled the court to come into being. The underlying issue, of course, had been over who controlled the court and whether it would or could operate independently. Despite the changes, however, the issues that divided the Cambodian and international sides of the court were never fully dealt with (and perhaps could not have been). In the end, the controversies generated by the important differences in the respective ways in which the two sides attempted to meet their varying interpretations of their mandate resulted, perhaps inevitably, in a divergence within the court and among domestic and international observers as to whether accountability had in fact been achieved.

From the period before the court came into existence, the Cambodian government had repeatedly stated that only the six individuals in custody would be the "senior leaders" who would be tried. This, in the government's view, met the terms of the court's statute, which provided that it could exercise its jurisdiction only over "senior leaders of Democratic Kampuchea and those who were most responsible for the crimes and serious violations of Cambodian laws related to crimes, international humanitarian law and custom, and international conventions recognized by Cambodia, that were committed during the period from April 17 1975 to January 6 1979."[24]

One of the most serious disagreements over the mandate that arose was over how many and which individuals fell within the terms of that provision. A very significant amount of judicial effort went into resolving this dispute, as well as the disputes that arose about how to interpret the authority and limitations adhering to the principal organs of the court. For example, the statute of the court, as originally drafted, made no provision for how differences of opinion between the Cambodian and international co-prosecutors were to be resolved. The same issue arose over the functions of the Cambodian and international co-investigating judges. Since no majority was possible with only two co-prosecutors and two co-investigating judges, it was inevitable that deadlock would arise over sensitive issues, as they did over the crucial question of whether the court would move beyond the prosecution of the accused persons drawn from the six initially identified by the Cambodian government and handed over to the court for trial once the ECCC began to function.

The creation of a Pre-Trial Chamber, specifically to deal with such disputes, did little to resolve the issues because, like the other judicial chambers of the court, a supermajority of at least 4-1 was required for a decision (the Pre-Trial and Trial Chambers each had five judges, three Cambodian and two international). What should be the result of a non-decision because of a 3-2 split was also contested even though it had always been clear that on such issues the chambers would almost certainly split into national-international lines. Such disputes also impacted the work of the co-prosecutors, and such examples could be multiplied. In the end, in the opinion of many international observers, the ECCC failed in its mandate because only Cases 001 and 002, involving four of the original six indictees, were tried, and Cases 003 and 004 were dismissed.[25] In the view of the Cambodian government, however, the ECCC had fulfilled its mandate and brought to justice the Khmer Rouge leaders.[26] To some observers, however, the divisions within the ECCC and the shortcomings that ensued were entirely predictable, given the failure to address these issues in creating the court and the willingness of the UN to accede to such a structure because it was unwilling to have the process of creating the court fail.

The contestation over what the ECCC did or did not accomplish raises questions that arose at Nuremberg and remain unresolved in the arena of international criminal justice. The ECCC succeeded in holding accountable the most senior surviving Khmer Rouge leaders from Pol Pot's inner circle as well as the commander of the most notorious detention center, Tuol Sleng. As we have seen, the UN could make no such claim for the Special Panels for Serious Crimes. While the Cambodian government only made six such individuals available for trial, when the UN established the Special Court for Sierra Leone, its mandate was also limited to those who bore "the greatest responsibility."[27] Given the scale of the mass atrocity crime committed in Sierra Leone, many more individuals, beyond the thirteen indictees, could have been prosecuted by the court. How many more would depend on how one interpreted the vague formula of "greatest responsibility." This was perhaps even more the case in Cambodia, where approximately 20–25 percent of the Cambodian population perished under four years of the Khmer Rouge regime of terror. How many more "senior leaders" or those who were "most responsible" could have, or should have, been tried under those formulae? In its sixteen years of existence (2006–22), the ECCC succeeded in bringing four individuals to trial at a cost of some USD 300 million. Only one of those nonagenarians remains alive in 2024. Should more octogenarians have been brought before the court to, in all likelihood, die in custody over another ten years of trial at an estimated cost of an additional $200 million to just one or two of them? It is telling that neither the UN nor the Cambodian government has allowed the Cambodian people to answer this question.

I don't have the answer to such questions, nor did Nuremberg. As Telford Taylor's Final Report indicates, many more could have been tried at the IMT and several thousand more at the National Military Tribunals at Nuremberg. As Taylor noted, applying the same standard that informed the mandate of the ECCC, although there were several hundred thousand potential indictees in the American Occupation Zone alone,

> Yet it had never been my thought that more than a few hundred individuals could or should be tried before the Nuernberg tribunals. These few hundred, obviously, should be those highly placed individuals who *bore the greatest responsibility* for formulating and ordering the execution of the criminal policies which directly led to and instigated the aggressive wars and mass atrocities launched and committed under the authority of the Third Reich.[28] (my emphasis)

In the end, Taylor narrowed down the candidates for the Subsequent Proceedings to approximately 570 high-ranking individuals then in custody. Of these, 177 were eventually tried and either convicted or acquitted.[29] Of the many thousands of others in detention or under investigation by the US war crimes program, a substantial number, but by no means all, found themselves before a very different kind of US Army war crimes court at Dachau.

Ultimately, it was only the Cold War and the lack of political and public commitment to further war crimes trials that brought the USA and most other national war crimes programs in Europe and Asia to a close. The point is that international criminal justice is always selective and always serves a symbolic function in addition to its concrete task. Who and how many are tried, and for what crimes, is a product of prosecutorial discretion, availability of witnesses and accused persons, and, more fundamentally, political will and international and domestic politics. While the achievements of the ICTR are notable, it is a blemish on its record that the alleged crimes of the RPF were never investigated or prosecuted. This was due to the politics of the Kagame government and the acquiescence of the UN. The ICTY's ability to bring senior military and political leaders to trial was in no small part due to the political and economic pressures brought to bear by the EU, the UN, and the US. We have seen the way that political dynamics, as well as other factors, exerted their influence in East Timor, Indonesia, and Cambodia.

Reflecting on Nuremberg in this context, one is struck by the uniqueness of the circumstances that allowed it to succeed in its foundational role. It could do so because of the absolute control the Allies exercised over a defeated Germany placed under military occupation. It succeeded as well because of the decision of the four allied nations to cooperate despite their various differences over some matters pertaining to the trials. Those circumstances have never since been duplicated in a context enabling an international criminal tribunal to exert its legal authority. The challenges facing the ICC today, as well as the modest number of accused brought to trial in each ICC case, make this all too clear. For this reason, the answer to Taylor's "Nuremberg question" remains, at best, a work in progress.

Notes

1 Brigadier General Telford Taylor served as Chief of Counsel for War Crimes for the Control Council Law No. 10 trials conducted at Nuremberg. He of course later gained further renown as a scholar and law professor at Columbia University.

2 Taylor, "Forum Juridicum: An Outline of the Research and Publication Possibilities of the War Crimes Trials," *Louisiana Law Review* 9 (May 4, 1949), p. 498.

3 Although properly speaking, the IMTFE at Tokyo was an equal part of the Second World War foundational legacy, the jurisprudence of the 1990s drew more heavily on the IMT and the Subsequent proceedings. This is not surprising as the Tokyo Tribunal (IMTFE) has long been overshadowed by Nuremberg for a variety of reasons. There are exceptions, of course. See, for example, the discussion of the IMTFE's conviction of Hirota Koki, foreign minister during the Nanjing Massacre, in the Celebici Case (ICTY Prosecutor v Delalic et. al., IT-96-21-T, paras. 357–8 and 368–9.

4 Taylor, "Final Report to the Secretary of the Army on the Nuremberg War Crimes Trials Conducted under Control Council Law No. 10."

5 Talor, "Final Report," 234.

6 Ibid., p. 235. See also R. Hilberg's, *The Destruction of the European Jews* (1961). Hilberg's central thesis is that it was the German state and society as a whole, in

all of their organizational and institutional aspects, whose collective action and contributions were necessary to accomplish the Nazi extermination program. His thesis, as elaborated in the first, 1961 edition, relied heavily upon his groundbreaking research in the collection of IMT and Subsequent Proceedings records at the US National Archives,

7 As examples in Southeast Asia of this fear, we might recall Indonesia's efforts to avoid the creation of an international ad hoc tribunal for its role in East Timor 1975–99, discussed below, or, more recently, Philippine president Duterte's withdrawal from the Rome Statute of the ICC in an attempt to avoid prosecution for thousands of alleged extra-judicial killings in his so-called war on drugs.

8 See the definitive study by W. Schabas, *The Trial of the Kaiser* (2018).

9 The IMT prosecution mistakenly indicted Gustav Krupp, who was declared unfit to stand trial. The error was corrected with the indictment of Alfried Krupp in the Subsequent Proceedings.

10 Taylor, "Forum Juridicum," p. 510.

11 Final Report, p. 236.

12 All three of the tribunals established in these countries applied both national criminal law as well as international crimes such as crimes against humanity or genocide. This was perhaps most significant in East Timor where the UN Special Panels for Serious Crimes only dealt with thirteen crimes against humanity cases out of fifty-five cases brought to trial. The remainder applied only national criminal law for crimes such as homicide.

13 When Indonesia withdrew from East Timor in 1999, that territory was left, quite literally, with no judges, prosecutors, judicial administration, or legal framework for the administration of justice. It fell to the UN to create a national judiciary, relying upon international appointments and drawing on the few young Timorese who had recently graduated from Indonesian law faculties.

14 As will be briefly explained below, both the UN and the Indonesian trials ignored the 24 years of violence, 1975–99, during the Indonesian occupation of East Timor after Portugal precipitously abandoned its colony.

15 Cohen, "Accountability in the Balance: Trials Before the Special Panels for Serious Crimes in East Timor 1999–2005," *Law in Context Special Issue* (2010), pp. 108–9.

16 Ibid.

17 See, for example, Cohen, *Indifference and Accountability* (East-West Center, 2006).

18 See, for example, Cohen, *Intended to Fail: Trials before the Jakarta Ad Hoc Human Rights Court* (ICTJ, 2006).

19 On the continuity in postwar Germany see, for example, J. Friederich, *Die Kalte Amnestie* (1982).

20 UNTAET Regulation 2000/15.

21 Among many other examples, this was demonstrated most vividly when both the Timorese government and the UN in New York failed to support the SCU's indictment of Indonesian General Wiranto, who had been the commander in chief of Indonesia's armed forces during the 1999 violence. Indeed, Timorese president, Xanana Gusmao, flew to Bali immediately after the indictment was issued to hold a joint press event with Wiranto, assuring him of their mutual friendship. Likewise, the Timorese prosecutor general refused to request Interpol to issue a red card for Wiranto.

22 Even though the ICTY and the ICTR did not have a system of hybrid dual governances, the politics of relations with the states where the crimes occurred

produced, as is well known, myriad difficulties for those tribunals. Nuremberg, on the other hand, provides an example of the advantages that accrue when the search for accountability is unencumbered by such divisions. This is not to say that politics played no role at Nuremberg, but the issues arose more out of relations between the four Allies participating in the trials rather than interference by a national government.

23 Chega! Final Report of the Timor-Leste Commission for Reception, Truth, and Reconciliation (CAVR 2013).

24 Article 2, Law on the establishment of Extraordinary Chambers in the Courts of Cambodia for the prosecution of crimes committed during the period of Democratic Kampuchea, as amended October 27, 2004.

25 Ieng Thirith was declared unfit to stand trial, and Ta Mok died in custody before the court began trials.

26 All those brought to trial were convicted. All have died in detention apart from 93-year-old Khieu Samphan, who alone remains alive. Case 001 did not involve a "senior leader" because Kaing Guek Eav, aka Duch, was deemed to be one of those "most responsible."

27 Statute of the Special Court for Sierra Leone, Article 1.

28 Final Report, p. 54.

29 Final Report, p. 91.

Selected Bibliography

Chandler, David, *Voices from S-21* (UC Press).

Kiernan, Ben, *Genocide and Resistance in Southeast Asia* (Transaction Publishers).

Kiernan, Ben, *The Pol Pot Regime*, 2nd edition (Yale UP).

Lindsey, Tim (ed.), *Indonesia Law and Society*, 2nd edition (Federation Press).

Robinson, Geoffrey, *If You Leave Us Here, We Will Die: How Genocide was Stopped in East Timor* (Princeton UP).

Tomte, Aksel and Eko Riyadi, *International Human Rights and Local Courts* (Routledge).

Part 4

Nuremberg Law Principles and Contemporary Challenges

Continuity or Change?

11

The United States and International Criminal Law After Eighty Years

Continuity or Change from Victor's Justice to the Rule of Law

Herbert R. Reginbogin

The International Military Tribunal (IMT) trial of twenty-one major war criminals began on November 20, 1945, and concluded with its verdict on October 1, 1946. The American occupying authorities organized an additional twelve trials between 1946 and 1949. The official opening session occurred in Berlin, while the remaining sessions were held in Nuremberg, a city in ruins. Ironically, the courtroom mainly remained intact, having survived the Allied bombings. This location was historically significant, as it was where the infamous racist laws of 1935 were enacted and where the Nazi Party held its annual mass rallies. As a result, the name "Nuremberg" became synonymous with Nazi Germany.

On November 21, 1945, during the second day of the Trial of the Major War Criminals before the IMT at the Palace of Justice at Nuremberg, Germany, the chief US prosecutor and chief counsel, Justice Robert H. Jackson, delivered a meaningful address. He states, "While having the privilege to open the first trial in history for crimes against peace . . . imposes great responsibility,"[1] he acknowledged a pattern of cruelty, brutality, and legalized barbarism. He emphasized the importance of international criminal law condemning and punishing those who had committed such "calculated, so malignant, and so devastating [wrongs] that civilization cannot tolerate,"[2] as ignoring such acts threatens its survival because it cannot "survive being repeated."[3] In the words of Robert H. Jackson, "This inquest represents the practical effort of four of the most mighty of nations, with the support of 17 more, . . . flushed with victory and stung with injury, stay the hand of vengeance and voluntarily . . . utilize international law to meet the greatest menace of our times—aggressive war"[4]—among other war crimes including violations of the laws of war, crimes against humanity from extermination, deportation, and genocide and lastly conspiracy to have a joint plan to commit the crimes listed in the first three counts. They had decided to "submit their captive enemies to the judgment of the law is one of the most significant tributes that Power has ever paid to Reason."[5] Robert Jackson pointed out that this Tribunal is directed at "men who possess themselves of great power and make deliberate and concerted use of it to set in motion evils which leave no home in the world untouched."[6] He continued in his opening speech at Nuremberg to explain the role of international criminal law:

> But the ultimate step in avoiding periodic wars, which are inevitable in a system of international lawlessness, is to make statesmen responsible to law. And let me make clear [Justice Robert Jackson said] that while this law is first applied against German aggressors, the law includes, and if it is to serve a useful purpose, it must condemn aggression by any other nations, including those which sit here now in judgment. We are able to do away with domestic tyranny, violence, and aggression by those in power against the rights of their people only when we make all men answerable to the law. This trial represents mankind's desperate effort to apply the discipline of the law to statesmen who have used their powers of the state to attack the foundations of the world's peace and to commit aggressions against the rights of their neighbors[7]

and to hold "for the first time in history . . . central military, economic, and political leaders as Major Offenders of crimes against peace and humanity."[8]

In achieving these goals of justice and accountability, significant novel rulings were made in the first Nuremberg trial in 1945–6. These unique rulings formed the basis of the Nuremberg Principles, a document created by the International Law Commission of the United Nations to codify the legal principles underlying the Nuremberg Trials of Nazi party members following the Second World War. These principles include a set of guidelines for determining what constitutes a war crime.[9]

The rulings were further affirmed by the United Nations General Assembly in 1946 through Resolution 95(I), which directed the International Law Commission to formally codify them as the Nuremberg Principles in 1950. The Nuremberg Principles consist of seven foundational principles established by the International Law Commission of the United Nations to codify the legal principles underlying the Nuremberg Trials of Nazi party members following the Second World War. These principles provide a framework for determining what constitutes a war crime and form the basis of international criminal law.

The seven guidelines are:

1. Individual criminal accountability: Anyone who commits an international crime is responsible and liable for punishment.
2. No impunity: People are not exempt from responsibility for international crimes even if their internal law does not punish them or if they act on orders from a government or superior.
3. Equality before the law: No one is above the law, including heads of state.
4. Fair trial rights: The accused has the right to a fair trial on the facts and law.
5. Crimes against peace, war crimes, and crimes against humanity: These crimes are punishable under international law.

6. Complicity: Complicity in the commission of these crimes is also a crime under international law.
7. Genocide: This crime is also included in the principles.[10]

With the subsequent Nuremberg trials (1946–9), many rulings have been criticized and vehemently discussed as an exercise in Victor's Justice. The IMT was the first and most prominent international criminal trial to this day dubbed "the trial of the century," and for some, the birth of international criminal law, leading to the Genocide Convention, the Universal Declaration of Human Rights, and the Geneva Conventions. The trials displayed publicly through photos and films the devastation and hideous unparalleled atrocities committed by the planners and commanders of the Axis Powers that fully incarcerated the responsibility for the insanity of "war of all hells."

The Allied powers declared retribution for these crimes as one of their main war aims in 1941. By 1943, they had decided to establish a commission to collect evidence of Nazi crimes. In August 1945, the Four Powers (France, the Soviet Union, the United Kingdom, and the United States) signed the London Agreement, which paved the way to establish a tribunal to prosecute major Axis war criminals before the IMT. The Tribunal narrowly construed its jurisdiction to the German crimes committed exclusively by persons who acted in the interests of the European Axis. It did not address potential war crimes committed by the Allied forces, leading to criticism that Allied atrocities during the Second World War were not adequately investigated or punished, most notably mass killings of German civilians in Eastern Europe, the mistreatment of prisoners of war in Allied camps, the forced displacement of ethnic Germans, and the mass executions of nearly 22,000 Polish military officers and intelligentsia in the Katyń Forest, Poland by Soviet NKVD secret police. All are considered violations of international laws regarding the treatment of civilians and prisoners of war. These war crimes by the Allies were overlooked to give the appearance of standing together as victors over evil. The Court prohibited using the tu quoque defense—(a Latin phrase that translates to "you too") designed to discredit and make the court appear hypocritical for alleging the Allies had committed some of the same crimes. For example, they did not allow the defense to present evidence of Soviet responsibility for those crimes and conduct. The Soviet leader, President Mikhail Gorbachev, admitted in 1990 that, indeed, the Poles had been executed at Katyń by the Soviet Union.[11]

Same Law for All or Victor's Justice

On May 14, 1946, Lord Justice Geoffrey Lawrence, the primary British judge at the IMT, interrupted the German defense lawyer's efforts to demonstrate that the Allies had also committed similar war crimes. He stated, "We are not sitting here in court to decide whether other powers have committed breaches of international law, crimes against humanity, or war crimes. Here we are dealing with whether these [German] accused have committed such atrocities."[12] This highlighted the reality that only the defeated were charged with war crimes, while the victors defined the nature of those crimes. The court's role was to assess the guilt of the accused rather than vindicate the principles of law for all powers.

In contrast to the moral ambiguities presented earlier, which stand alongside the unimaginable injustices wrought by Nazi criminality, the Nuremberg trials played a crucial role in establishing accountability for these war crimes. They helped reintroduce a sense of moral principles that contributed to proving guilt for these atrocities. The trials aimed to restore some understanding of moral principles to human life, even as leaders navigate a world marked by double standards. Fairness and justice were fundamental principles that remained constant throughout the proceedings, accompanied by flexibility and adaptability alongside a conscious effort to prevent "victor's justice." This was exemplified by trials given to the German leaders of the Third Reich. International criminal law aimed to create a more just world, eliminate impunity, and replace violence with peace, striving for an ideal vision of society—"utopia."[13]

The legacy of the IMT and the subsequent twelve trials marked a significant turning point in the pursuit of justice, as they aimed to establish the guilt of those responsible for war crimes. Although the Soviet side made productive contributions to the history of international criminal law, its legal system continued to lack the rule of law. In one crucial respect, though, the Soviet trials of Axis soldiers were distinct from the Soviet prewar show trials. The difference lay in fabricated or imagined versus actual and visible acts, and in the extent to which almost everyone in occupied territory had suffered under the Germans. This, in turn, not only seems to have affected public perception of the trials, it also accounted for differences within illiberal justice. In contrast, Stalin envisioned an international trial court like the Soviet show trials of the 1930s.[14] These trials were primarily for propaganda purposes and to provide justifications to execute thousands of German Nazis.[15]

Initially, British Prime Minister Winston Churchill initially opposed the establishment of the Nuremberg war crimes tribunals at the end of the Second World War, favoring summary executions of Nazi leaders. However, his perspective changed after the 1943 Tehran Conference, where the Allied powers discussed the post-war order, including the prosecution of war criminals.[16]

Guy Liddell, the head of counter-espionage at MI5, kept a diary during the 1940s and 50s. As Allied leaders sought to determine the political structure of postwar Germany, some members of the British government and intelligence services supported the idea of eliminating Nazis rather than putting them on trial. In July 1946, Liddell traveled to Nuremberg with M15's deputy head, Oswald Harker, to observe the prosecution of twenty-one senior Nazis, including Hermann Göring and Albert Speer. Liddell noted,

> One cannot escape the feeling that most of the things the 21 are accused of having done over 14 years, the Russians have done over 28 years. This adds considerably to the somewhat phony atmosphere of the whole proceedings and leads me to the point which, in a way, worries me most, namely, that the court is one of the victors

> who have framed their charter, their procedure, and their own rules of evidence to deal with the vanquished.[17]

While the Nuremberg tribunals are now widely regarded as a pivotal moment in international justice, laying the groundwork for prosecuting war criminals, Liddell believed it was unwise to prosecute the Nazis for waging a war of aggression. He expressed concern that "a dangerous precedent is being created."[18]

Furthermore, there were significant contradictions in how the Nuremberg legacy was portrayed. Although it was depicted as a moral commitment rooted in international criminal law to pursue justice, the narratives often obscured the business and financial collaborations between American, British, and German industrialists in the 1930s. These collaborations aimed to monopolize global markets and ensured that business could continue as usual, even during war or in the aftermath of extensive destruction.[19]

International Criminal Law, Morality, and Justice

Over the past eighty years, the practice of international criminal law has significantly expanded, leading first to the establishment of several international ad hoc tribunals to address war crimes committed in the former Yugoslavia, Rwanda, and other regions. This evolution culminated in the formation of the permanent International Criminal Court (ICC). These international tribunals were built on the legal precedents set by the Nuremberg trials to uphold morality and justice by providing "something that broken societies cannot do for themselves: an honest account of past events and a clear demarcation of right and wrong, delivered by rule-respecting international models of good governance."[20] Additionally, these tribunals have aimed to avoid the criticism that the IMT faced for applying retroactive law to prosecute Nazi war criminals.

Some contemporary critics, including US Supreme Court Chief Justice Harlan F. Stone, described the Nuremberg efforts as fundamentally flawed. Stone remarked, "Jackson is away conducting his high-grade lynching party in Nuremberg. I don't mind what he does to the Nazis, but I hate to see the pretense that he is running a court and proceeding according to common law. This is a little too sanctimonious a fraud to meet my old-fashioned ideas."[21]

US Senator Robert Taft also criticized the Nuremberg trials, stating,

> I believe that most Americans view with discomfort the war trials which have just been concluded in Germany. . . . They violate the fundamental principle of American law that a man cannot be tried under an ex post facto statute. The trial of the vanquished by the victors cannot be impartial, no matter how it is hedged with the forms of justice. I question whether the hanging of those who, however despicable, were the leaders of the German people will ever discourage the making of aggressive war, for no one makes aggressive war unless he expects to win. There is the spirit of vengeance about this whole judgment, and vengeance is seldom

> justice. The hangings of the eleven men convicted will be a blot on the American record, which we shall long regret.[22]

As courts went, the IMT at Nuremberg was deeply flawed. Some say that ex-post facto laws were crafted to include only selected acts and enemies, which would fail to satisfy any Kantian notion of moral law or any established index of transparency.

Nevertheless, history has often overlooked the respected legal theorists who joined the German defendants in accusing the IMT of applying "Victor's Justice."[23] Today, the IMT symbolizes the triumph of the rule of law over vengeance and retribution, serving as "one of the most significant tributes that Power has ever paid to Reason."[24] Despite the criticism, the Nuremberg trials functioned to prove guilt for such atrocities of war crimes. Still, selective justice and the legality and thus legitimacy of the Nuremberg proceedings were substantive at the time and are today matters of ongoing scholarly debate. Where does the United States stand in the case of Justice for victims of international war crime abuses? The United States has actively supported the prosecution of war crimes in Bosnia and Rwanda and by the International Criminal Tribunal for the former Yugoslavia (ICTY) and the International Criminal Tribunal for Rwanda (ICTR)—these were Nuremberg-modelled ad hoc tribunals. Conversely, the United States, under President Donald Trump, imposed sanctions (withdrawn under President Joe Biden) on the International Criminal Court and its international civil servants charged with upholding human rights and humanitarian law in their investigation and potential prosecution of US personnel for possible war crimes in Afghanistan. This was reversed under President Joe Biden upon becoming President of the United States. In stark contrast the Justice for Victims of War Crimes Act became law at the start of 2023 expanding U.S. jurisdiction over war crimes, removing the statute of limitations to strengthen the efforts to ensure justice and accountability by enabling the Department of justice to prosecute alleged war crimes who are found in the United States, regardless of the location of the crime and nationality of the perpetrator or the victim. Today, President Donald Trump is serving a second term in office and has reversed the decision made by President Joe Biden, condemning the International Criminal Court and its judges again. Does the United States demonstrate a pattern of choosing alleged war crimes to prosecute over the last 80 years that are amenable to its political agenda, or will there be changes to serve justice at all costs?[25]

Law, Not War

This was Benjamin Ferencz's recurring message throughout his lifetime (1920–2023). He was an American prosecutor at Nuremberg, an advocate for Holocaust victims, and integral to the creation of the International Criminal Court, which reflected the ideas and spirit of the Nuremberg legacy. Notwithstanding legacy, the United States never demonstrated enough much-needed leadership by applying international criminal law to hold the heads of all states accountable for their actions.

The current conflict in Ukraine began on February 24, 2022 when Russian military forces entered the country from Belarus, Russia, and Crimea, blatantly violating its territorial integrity in a significant escalation of the Russo-Ukrainian conflict. Before the invasion, there had already been eight years of conflict in eastern Ukraine between Ukrainian Government forces and Russia-backed separatists.[26] The invasion, the most critical conflict in Europe since the Second World War, has caused thousands of Ukrainian military casualties and tens of thousands of civilian casualties. The General Assembly of the United Nations deplored in the strongest terms its aggression against Ukraine in violation of the Charter of the United Nations. The General Assembly of the United Nations condemned this aggression against Ukraine in the strongest terms, noting it as a violation of the Charter of the United Nations. The Assembly also demanded that the Russian Federation immediately and unconditionally reverse its February 21 decision related to the status of certain areas of the Donetsk and Luhansk regions of Ukraine.[27] The measure was adopted by a vote of 141 in favor, five against (Belarus, Democratic People's Republic of Korea, Eritrea, Russian Federation, and Syria) with thirty-five abstentions—a clear reaffirmation by the 193-member world body's commitment to Ukraine's sovereignty, independence, unity, and territorial integrity.[28] This decision reflected a long journey since the Cold War, including the Kampala Amendments of 2010 and their ratification in 2018, which aimed to address the crime of aggression—a crime considered among the most severe war crimes highlights the reluctance of the United States to accept international control over their sovereignty.

On March 27, 2023, Beth van Schaack, the Ambassador-at-Large for Global Criminal Justice, delivered a speech at the Catholic University of America in Washington, D.C. She called the United States' "leading role in prosecuting the crime of aggression at Nuremberg," and described it as "a critical moment in history" by emphasizing that "there are compelling arguments for why this crime must be prosecuted alongside the Rome Statute crimes."[29] As distinguished professor of international criminal law Claus Kress notes,

> With the U.S. appearance on the public scene, it had become abundantly clear that the new momentum concerning the crime of aggression impacted even the attitude of some of those governments that had for decades adopted a position of sovereigntist resistance. However, the critical question remains whether one is witnessing a genuine change by embracing Jackson's call for a consistent, non-selective application of the Nuremberg precedent on crimes against peace.[30]

Will the phenomenon of "Victor's Justice" continue to allow superpowers to selectively apply international criminal law to serve their interests, or will it hold Russia's leaders accountable for the atrocities committed in Ukraine through an international criminal response? Where does the United States stand on seeking justice for victims of international war crimes?

The United States has historically been involved in prosecuting war crimes in Bosnia and Rwanda. It has played a significant role in the International Criminal Tribunal for the former Yugoslavia and the International Criminal Tribunal for Rwanda. Since 2001, the United States has been involved in the war in Afghanistan, resulting in alleged war crimes involving US troops, Afghan forces, and the Taliban. Despite initial involvement, the United States later refused to ratify the ICC treaty. It even passed a law to discourage cooperation with the ICC. The ICC began investigating war crimes in Afghanistan, including those involving the US military and the CIA. In 2017, the ICC released a report suggesting that US armed forces and the CIA committed acts of torture and other crimes against detainees in Afghanistan. However, in September 2021, Prosecutor Karim Khan of the ICC announced that it would not pursue a war crimes investigation against the United States.[31] This decision to terminate the investigation by the ICC left many crimes undocumented and victims without justice. The standard federal statute of limitations also applied, which meant that the United States had control over the investigation and prosecution of war crimes and could only file charges within five years of the offense.[32]

Over the past 80 years, the United States has supported international criminal law inconsistently. These developments are historically significant for the legacy of the Nuremberg trials and the expansion of international criminal law within humanity's moral and legal framework. It is crucial to understand the challenges posed by criminal states today. Nations cannot engage in total warfare that violates international law and the laws of war without facing impunity, as these principles have been recognized as components of international law since the Middle Ages. Some argue that the Nuremberg Trials were an example of Victor's justice.

In contrast, others claim that they established the Nuremberg Principles, which state that individuals can be held accountable for crimes against international law. This was confirmed in a 1948 UN General Assembly resolution. The Nuremberg Trials also established that a global legal framework should protect all humanity and that even heads of state could be held criminally responsible for aggression and crimes against humanity.

The challenge faced by the Allied Powers at the end of the war was establishing laws to define future peace. Concerns arose regarding profound procedural shortcomings in the trial and the application of substantive norms, particularly the principle *opprobrium nulled crimen sine lege* (no crime without law), which prohibits retroactive criminalization of acts violating fundamental tenets of the rule of law systems and notions of justice.[33] This principle is essential for the rule of law (Rechtsstaat), as it maintains that "an act may be punished only if a law defined it as a criminal offense before the act was committed."[34] However, Professor Christoph Safferling, an expert in International Criminal Law at the University of Erlangen, Germany, points out that this principle had also been misused to excuse highly immoral acts on merely formal grounds. The High Court of Justice in West Germany, in the post-1950s period, found "those judges who energetically flexed and bent the law to bring Nazi ideology and politics to reality, who sentenced to death thousands of innocent victims in blatant breach of any known legal methodology, were acquitted because they had acted in accordance with their convictions and believed they were fulfilling the law."[35]

In contrast, today's judges employ an approach aimed at combating impunity and "meting out punishment to those who deserve it"[36] guided by the European Court of Human Rights, which recognizes the legitimacy of the Nuremberg trials. The crimes committed by Nazi leaders, which the Allies sought to prosecute, were not merely acts of lawlessness; but were carried out under the horrific laws of the Nazi regime. The written laws of the Nazi government sanctioned many atrocities committed before and during the war.

The prosecution at the IMT invoked John Locke's idea that people are inherently reasonable and moral. Their experiences and environment shape their behavior in contrast to the Hobbesian view that humans are naturally "nasty, brutish, and short."[37] This discussion addressed the tension between natural law principles of human rights and the positivist concern about making laws retroactively applicable.

Following the Russian invasion of Ukraine on February 24, 2022, a "critical moment in history" arose.[38] Russia's aggressive war against Ukraine has created a turning point in global governance. It is time for the United States and the other major powers of the Second World War to step up and address their reluctance to establish a moral jurisdictional regime for such crimes. This is necessary to avoid perpetuating a double standard in the existing international legal system.[39]

It is essential to avoid perpetuating a double standard within the existing international system. The balance of power shifted, and the belief that sovereign leaders had the unquestionable authority to justify their political actions through laws deemed abhorrent by universal principles of natural law is no longer absolute. This indicates that civil laws should be grounded in morality, ethics, and what is inherently right. The normative architecture developed in America's fight against National Socialism has advanced the notion of human rights in contrast to legal positivism, "which says that the sole criterion of a rule's legality"[40] is that the sovereign has enacted it according to his chosen procedures. This viewpoint holds that individuals in a foreign country have universal, objective human rights, irrespective of that country's laws.

At the time of the Nuremberg Trials, there were no international laws protecting fundamental human rights. International law did not prohibit the wholesale slaughter or elimination of groups of people on the grounds of religion or ethnicity, or political belief—as had happened in Nazi Germany, the Soviet Union, and many other places. Furthermore, there were no restraints on territorial domination or the creation of colonies. The notion that a group of people had a right to self-determination remained a distant dream. While piracy and slavery were outlawed, discrimination, racism, apartheid, and colonial domination and exploitation were not.[41]

After the Second World War, the tables would turn; sovereignty no longer had the absolute prerogative to absolve leaders' political conduct sanctioned by horrific laws that were judged wrong. America's struggle against fascism led to the drafting of a normative architecture anchored in the principles of the US Constitution, which protects individual human rights, and the Declaration of Independence, which asserts that the people's will is supreme and legitimizes the right of democratic self-determination.

Based on the foundations of international law, the paradigmatic implications of this normative architecture promoted the US perspective of human rights against legal positivism. This asserts that individuals in a foreign country have universal, objective human rights, regardless of the content of that foreign state's positive law. In the United States, the concept of human rights is constrained by the doctrine of legal realism. This perspective emerged in the early twentieth century.

European positivism in the nineteenth century maintained that scientific knowledge was the only way to understand the law, viewing social sciences as analogous to physical sciences. It cultivated "the vision of law's ultimate supersession [. . .] through the perfection of society, achieved [. . .] by a science-based manipulation, or by a natural evolutionary process."[42] This suggests that social science could identify the social good or facilitate its achievement through law. However, without an agreement on a common good between competing interests within a democratic process, there is a lack of integrity. In such a scenario, former UN General Secretary Kofi Annan underscores that the "winner-takes-all" mentality is counterproductive, with which many leaders approaching elections lead to abuses of power by the winner and encourage losers to reject democracy as a peaceful means of change.[43]

The Legacy of Nuremberg and Impact on International Criminal Law and the United States

The relativism of law as an instrument of legal barbarism became apparent during the Nuremberg trials. It was essential for the American legal culture to reaffirm that law was not merely a tool of politics but instead embodied principles and morality. As a result, American jurisprudence embraced the direction of natural law foundationalism. The decoupling of morality from the law by Nazi Germany's jurists was compellingly illustrated during the Nuremberg Trials. The legacy of the Nuremberg Trials firmly established the need for an ethical foundation in law.[44]

While the American legal system of the 1990s used or saw litigation involving constitutional and international law to redress past injustices, a new generation of legal scholars began challenging the previous generation's internationalist assumptions and outlook. Among America's international legal academia, a group of scholars writes from the perspective of what is known in the United States as foreign relations law rather than international law.[45] Their analysis is based on a perception that not only the outside world is dangerous and corrupt, but America's core values are threatened. Realist political thinkers like Hans Morgenthau,[46] John Mearsheimer,[47] and Stephen Walt[48] supported a liberal view to the extent that they argued that the domestic political order was overtly critical of the liberal international institutions. That line is being questioned by some conservative writers like John Yoo and Robert Bork to the extent that there is no difference between the domestic and international order. They argue for fewer constraints "on the executive branch to enable it to be effective in a world full of dangers that international law and institutions are inherently powerless to avert."[49] Other scholars like Bradley and Goldsmith advanced positions objecting to international law in the domestic legal system that are primarily grounded in American constitutionalism and, to an extent, in liberal constitutionalism in general, raising tension between the values of internationalism and those of American constitutionalism when international norms come into conflict with domestic laws, particularly regarding issues of individual rights and state power[50]

The events of 9/11 prompted President George W. Bush, Jr. to adopt a new approach to the rule of law in the fight against terrorism. This approach included the use of rendition and torture, which challenged international law but was based on the interpretation of the US Constitution by his advisors. While European liberal democracies committed to the Kantian vision of a cosmopolitan order, emphasizing civil liberties and a strong international law, the United States under President Bush. Jr. disavowed international law. In his book, *The Divided West*, Juergen Habermas pointed out a realist approach—relying on brute force—over the rule of law, or embraced hegemonic liberalism, which he describes as "the liberal ethos of a superpower as an alternative to law."[51]

Eli Rosenbaum, an American lawyer and the former Director of the US Department of Justice Office of Special Investigations (OSI), highlights a perceived double standard in the treatment of the ICC Office of the Prosecutor (OTP) treats the United States. During the Trump administration, sanctions were imposed on the OTP after US National Security Advisor John Bolton publicly criticized the office for investigation of the allegations of torture and other crimes committed by US military and intelligence personnel following the invasion of Afghanistan during the George W. Bush Administration. This investigation focused on US detention and interrogation sites in Afghanistan and CIA "black sites" at other locations.

However, in September 2021, Prosecutor Karim Khan, who succeeded Ms. Bensouda, announced that he would deprioritize the investigation into US actions related to Afghanistan due to limited resources. This decision came despite former president Bush's admission of authorizing the use of "waterboarding" during interrogations. Although the US government has taken steps to disclose post-9/11 abuses and prevent their recurrence, not a single senior official involved in approving or ordering waterboarding or alleged torture has been prosecuted, even two decades after the first "DOJ torture memos" were made public.[52]

Many argue that this inaction meets the ICC "complementarity" requirement, as the torture memos provide sufficient evidence of the alleged crime. Despite the ample evidence available to the ICC Prosecutor's Office, the Office of the Prosecutor continues to remain passive. Prosecutor Khan has effectively shut down the investigation, citing budget constraints as one reason for deprioritizing the inquiry into war crimes in Afghanistan by the US and Afghan national forces, 2021, which has been criticized for prioritizing the interests of powerful states over victims.[53]

Prominent American statesmen, scholars, and jurists, including former Ambassador of the United States to the United Nations, John Bolton, and Judge Robert Bork, who was nominated to the Supreme Court by President Ronald Reagan (but whose nomination was rejected by the Senate), have argued that the United States has been hampered by international law. Judge Bork contends that America's sovereignty and domestic laws are threatened by international law. Bolton has stated that "International law" today is very much about binding, restricting, and limiting the United States.

Alfred van Staden, a Professor of International Relations at Leiden University, critiques contemporary American foreign policy for its insufficient commitment to international law. The United States has rejected numerous treaties that have garnered widespread support from other countries, including the Statute of the International Criminal Court, the Landmines Treaty, the Comprehensive Nuclear Test Ban Treaty. Additionally, the United States has been criticized for withdrawing from the ABM Treaty and failing to comply with its obligations under the Non-Proliferation Treaty (NPT), which requires nations to pursue nuclear disarmament. The Bush administration's decision to use military force against the regime of Saddam Hussein in 2003 without explicit authorization from the UN Security Council was widely condemned as unjustified and detrimental to the effectiveness of the UN Charter. "The contention has been made that the prevailing American approach to international law is such that it defines this corpus of law basically in terms of private contractual relationships." Consequently, international law is not viewed as a tool for transforming the international system into a society of nations—much less a global society unified by common bonds. Instead, it is seen as a vehicle to serve national policy goals.

The powers, complexities, and limitations of an imperial force became evident during the US invasion of Iraq, as described by Alfred van Staden. This conflict highlighted both the extent of American power and its constraints. It also led to the silencing or moderation of dissenting voices, resulting in people being detained without charge or denied habeas corpus rights under the Patriot Act. Furthermore, images of the mistreatment of detainees at Abu Ghraib prison suggested that the United States disregarded the Geneva Conventions and international human rights laws. The use of waterboarding as a form of torture and the treatment of non-combatants at Guantanamo Bay contradicted America's obligations under international conventions. Such actions were widely viewed as violations of fundamental prohibitions against cruel, inhuman, or dangerous treatment, regardless of the individuals' combatant status.

Both the Geneva Conventions and the UN Convention Against Torture explicitly prohibit torture and inhumane treatment, making the practices used at Guantanamo Bay clear violations of international law concerning non-combatants. A significant point of contention is the categorization of detainees at Guantanamo Bay as "enemy combatants," which critics argue allowed the United States to circumvention legal protections afforded to prisoners of war under the Geneva Conventions. The use of "enhanced interrogation techniques" such as waterboarding, which many legal experts deem torture, further compounded the issue of violating international norms. Human rights organizations and legal scholars have consistently criticized the treatment of detainees at Guantanamo Bay, leading to numerous legal challenges against the practices.

In a recent *New Yorker* article titled "The War Crimes That the Military Buried," Parker Yesko reports that US soldiers returning to the United States from Iraq and Afghanistan would often "confess—to women, healthcare workers, and job interviewers—that they had murdered civilians or prisoners."[54] The most comprehensive investigations into possible war crimes in Iraq and Afghanistan since 9/11 have revealed 781 cases. Of these, 572 alleged perpetrators were linked to 151 criminal cases, yet only 130 were convicted, usually receiving short sentences. Commanders handled many cases by imposing light punishments, such as extra duty or demotion, by passing formal prosecution. Furthermore, fewer than one in five alleged perpetrators faced prison time, and at least 65 percent of allegations were dismissed as unsubstantiated. Detainees at Abu Ghraib prison reported abuse by their guards. Still, investigators did not find sufficient evidence to confirm it happened. In some cases, young men were found unresponsive at Camp Bucca prison, and their deaths were attributed to natural causes. According to Yesko's report, the military often lacks transparency and fails to deliver justice.[55]

Although the United States does not recognize the International Criminal Court's jurisdiction, it supported the Hague Tribunal in bringing Slobodan Milosevic to justice. American policies frequently prioritize national security over noble principles. However, the US Supreme Court's ruling in the Boumediene vs. Bush case affirmed the constitutional right to *habeas corpus* for Guantanamo detainees in 2008.[56] Some fifteen-plus years later, on July 1, 2024, the US Supreme Court ruled that former president Trump is at least presumptively immune from criminal liability for his official acts and is immune for some "core" of them—including his attempts to use the US Justice Department to obstruct the results of the election. In other words, the court granted functional absolute immunity to President Trump's improper use of the Justice Department.[57]

Concluding Remarks

The implications of international law for the United States are distinct and significant. Starting in 1919, after the collapse of the Austrian-Hungarian, German, Ottoman, and Russian Empires, the United States began propagating concepts that placed restrictions on sovereign rights. It acknowledged that individuals are not merely objects of international regulation. This recognition influenced international law profoundly in the mid-to-late twentieth century.

International law is not irrelevant, as some American legal scholars assert, nor can it be discarded because the United States has become a powerhouse with extensive reach across various areas of human rights. The influence is embedded in a normative framework that includes four key documents (the UN Charter, The Universal Declaration of Human Rights (UDHR), The Convention on the Rights of the Child, and the Statute of the International Court of Justice) designed to embrace international human rights law, international humanitarian law, refugee law, maritime law as well as parts of labor and migration law.

The global community relies on international treaties, customary international law, and non-consensual sources of law (i.e., ius cogens). Secondly, the Alien Claims Tort Act clause in the US Constitution refers to the "laws of nations" (international law), which paved the way to redress past injustices, although in a limited capacity.[58] Thirdly, the United States is deeply entangled in economic activities shaped by globalization, managing the global market through the implementation of international regulations (international public law) governing trade and financial flows (e.g., WTO, World Bank, IMF, Basel III) since the end of the Second World War. Fourthly, the global protection of life on earth against the boundless nature of environmental threats that the United States has historically used international law in the form of conventions dealing with climate change and wildlife conservation for more than a hundred years.

The norms of international law significantly influence America's constitution, foreign policy initiatives, and support of individual human rights, as well as its rise to power through globalization. The United States has primarily been a benevolent hegemon. However, it has been undermined by forces influenced by Karl Schmidt (1888–1985), a conservative German legal, constitutional, and political theorist often considered one of the most influential critics of liberalism, parliamentary democracy, and liberal cosmopolitanism. Schmidtian views prioritizing the US Constitution over International Law or sovereignty and emergency powers are often seen as the intellectual basis of contemporary calls for a strong executive power unhampered by constraints of legality. These views depict international law as "empty formalism, irresponsible utopianism, or a set of moralistic platitudes cynically invoked"[59] to justify the power maneuvers of a superpower or a few great powers against the weaker nations in a bid for control and legitimacy. A contempt for compromise. An expansive vision of executive power. Both owe much to Carl Schmitt.

From this perspective, actions such as humanitarian intervention, foreign aid, and the work of international criminal courts in pursuit of an enlightened universal morality legitimized by human rights, as well as efforts to address environmental issues such as the greenhouse effect (Kyoto Protocol), are seen as merely driven by political self-interest and superficial concerns. Proponents of this view argue that international customary law should be entirely discarded and not interpreted as domestic federal law.

The moral cosmopolitan perspective shares similarities in elements of power politics influenced by national interests and strategic calculations of raison d'état. However, human rights advocates diverge from realists by suggesting that we must go beyond the discussions surrounding state sovereignty and international law to prioritize the protection of human rights.

Since Russia invaded Ukraine on February 24, 2022, there has been a profound and alarming shift in global governance, reminiscent of Nazi Germany's invasion of the Soviet Union on June 22, 1941. This situation necessitates four fundamental principles—protecting populations from genocide, war crimes, crimes against humanity, and ethnic cleansing—taking precedence over sovereignty and formal international law, often called "legalism." To the moral cosmopolitan, the legalistic discourse of sovereignty and power-oriented international organizations must not be permitted to block rescue operations (R2P—The Responsibility to Protect), a significant global principle since the adoption of the UN World Summit Outcome Document in 2005.[60]

Russia's brutal invasion represents the most significant challenge to international humanitarian law, human rights law, and international criminal law since the Nuremberg Trials of 1945–9. The precarious situation facing Ukraine suggests that the legacy of Nuremberg is at risk. This raises the critical question of when international courts will effectively utilize their prosecutorial powers to hold heads of state accountable for war crimes, regardless of their identity.

Ultimately, contemporary international humanitarian law (IHL) is essential for protecting civilians and upholding the principles of a rules-based world. These include the basic human right to security, the fundamental right to protection, the principle of civilian inviolability, and the human right to popular sovereignty. These principles supersede the just war theory of the Middle Ages, which justified the use of force with the caveat of minimizing civilian casualties.

It was easier for the United States to adopt a moralistic stance and stress the importance of law before assuming its global responsibilities. The United States continues to advocate for the rule of law, provided it does not constrain their freedom of action. In many respects, the American dilemma regarding the role of law is not new. Despite numerous inconsistencies, neglect, and misuse of international law, the United States will not abandon its support for international law, its procedures, and its institutions. America has learned to navigate the system and often operates around its edges like many other nations.

While it is tempting to argue that the emergence of human rights as a dominant force in international law was made possible by the triumph of liberalism internationally since 1989, this alone was insufficient to create the established legal framework evident today. Instead, the normative architecture developed after the Second World War, enshrined in the legacy of the Nuremberg trials and the aims of the UN charter—Security, Peace, and Justice—served as the pillars of global security.

Philosophers and legal scholars have long attempted to justify a country's actions. History shows that human beings can be either peaceful or hostile. While humans may resort to violence, they simultaneously aspire to a quiet life. Grotius viewed war as a natural process aimed at achieving peace. The use of international law still operates on a Westphalian model and has not yet produced worldwide peace.

Power is needed at a supra-national level to effectively control and intervene at the level of a sovereign state. Moreover, there must also be protection at the level of popular sovereignty to ensure individual rights. Only when the norms of international customary law, as part of natural law, become mainstream—bringing to light issues such as the demise of heads of state immunity after the Second World War—will we be closer to achieving "perpetual peace." This would help end the imperial prerogatives and address undermining the legitimacy of international criminal law through selective justice. Instead, there should be justice for all, where everyone stands equally before the rule of law in the twenty-first century.

Notes

1 Robert H. Jackson Center, "Opening Statement before the International Military Tribunal," available at https://www.roberthjackson.org/speech-and-writing/opening-statement-before-the-international-military-tribunal.

2 Ibid.

3 Ibid.

4 Ibid.

5 Ibid.
6 Ibid.
7 Ibid.
8 Ibid.
9 International Law Commission, "The Charter and Judgment of the Nürnberg Tribunal—History and Analysis:
Memorandum submitted by the Secretary-General Formulation of the Nürnberg Principles," Document:A/CN.4/5, available at http://www.un.org/law/ilc/index.htm and https://legal.un.org/ilc/documentation/english/a_cn4_5.pdf.
10 United Nations, "Principles of International Law Recognized in the Charter of the Nürnberg Tribucnt of the Tribunal," available at https://legal.un.org/ilc/texts/instruments/english/draft_articles/7_1_1950.pdf.
PrincipleI
Any person who commits an act which constitutes a crime under international law is responsible therefor and liable to punishment.
Principle II
The fact that internal law does not impose a penalty for an act which constitutes a crime under international law does not relieve the person who committed the act from responsibility under international law.
Principle III
The fact that a person who committed an act which constitutes a crime under international law acted as Head of State or responsible Government official does not relieve him from responsibility under international law.
Principle IV
The fact that a person acted pursuant to order of his government or of a superior does not relieve him from responsibility under international law, provided a moral choice was in fact possible to him.
Principle V
Any person charged with a crime under international law has the right to a fair trial on the facts and law.
Principle VI
The crimes hereinafter set out are punishable as crimes under international law.
(a) Crimes against peace:
(i) Planning, preparation, initiation or waging of a war of aggression or a war in violation of international treaties, agreements or assurances.
(ii) Participation in a common plan or conspiracy for the accomplishment of any of the acts mentioned under (i).
(b) War crimes:
Violations of the laws or customs of war, which include, but are not limited to, murder, ill-treatment or deportation to slave labor or for any other purpose of the civilian population of or in occupied territory, murder or ill-treatment of prisoners of war, of persons on the seas, killing of hostages, plunder of public or private property, wanton destruction of cities, towns, or villages, or devastation not justified by military necessity.
(c) Crimes against humanity:
Murder, extermination, enslavement, deportation and other inhuman acts done against any civilian population, or persecutions on political, racial or religious

grounds, when such acts are done or such persecutions are carried on in execution of or in connection with any crime against peace or any war crime.

Principle VII

Complicity in the commission of a crime against peace, a war crime, or a crime against humanity as set forth in Principle VI is a crime under international law

11 History, "Soviets admit to Katyn Massacre of World War II," available at https://www.history.com/this-day-in-history/soviets-admit-to-katyn-massacre.

12 Reinhard Merkel, "The Law of the Nuremberg Trial: Valid, Dubious, Outdated," in Guenael Mettraux, ed., *The Perspectives of the Nuremberg Trial* (Oxford University Press, 2008), 570–1;

William A. Schabas, "Victor's Justice: Selecting 'Situations' at the International Criminal Court," *The John Marshall Law Review* 43 (2010): 535, 536. available at https://repository.law.uic.edu/cgi/viewcontent.cgi?article=1085&context=lawreviewbid.

13 Kerstin Bree Carlson, "International Criminal Law and Its Paradoxes Implications for Institutions and Practice," *Journal of Law and Courts* 5, no. 1 (Cambridge University Press, October 21, 2022), available at https://www.cambridge.org/core/journals/journal-of-law-and-courts/article/international-criminal-law-and-its-paradoxes/91724E14F76FD69E9017C5747C5D2643; See, Antonio Cassese, *Realizing Utopia: The Future of International Law* (Oxford: Oxford University Press, 2012).

14 Stephen Tonge, "4 Case Study: Stalin's Show Trials, 1936–1938," in *Case Studies: Dictatorship and Democracy 1920–1945* (The Educational Company of Ireland, 2022), available at https://issuu.com/edcoireland/docs/case_studies_dictatorship_and_democracy_1920.1945/s/15697820.

15 Carlos Augusto Canedo Goncalves da Silva and Amexia Alvim Machado Faria, "The Nuremberg Trial Court: Between Discourse and Negotiations in Post-War International Law," in Rainer Schroeder et al. (eds.), *Forum Historiae Iuris* (August 2017), 3, available at https://www.researchgate.net/publication/319069049_The_Nuremberg_Trial_Court_-_Between_discourse_and_negotiations_in_post-war_International_Law.

16 Ian Cobain, "Britain Favoured Execution over Nuremberg Trials for Nazi Leaders," October 26, 2011, available at https://www.theguardian.com/world/2012/oct/26/britain-execution-nuremberg-nazi-leaders.

17 Ibid.

18 Ibid.

19 G. Baars, "Capitalism Victor's Justice? The hidden story of the Prosecution of Industrialists post-WW II," in K. J. Heller and Simpson (eds.), *The Hidden Histories of War Crimes Trials* (Oxford, Oxford University Press, 2013), 165. See, Walther Hofer and Herbert R. Reginbogin, *Hitler, der Westen und die Schweiz 1936–1945* (Zurich: Neue Zurcher Zeitung Verlag, 2001).

Also, for an overview of theories of war responsibility between the importance of politics and the privacy of economics, see Norbert Frei and Tim Schanetzk (eds.), *Unternehmen im Nationalsozialismus: Zur historisierung einer Forschungskonjunktur* (Goettingen: Wallstein Verlag, 2010),

Some scholars follow an "agency theory" approach to argue that Hitler was a mirror puppet in the employment of German industrialists, but the better view is one of control by the German elites from all three sectors, which, particularly after the Nazification of industrial leadership and the assignation of military ranks to industrialists, became difficult to distinguish clearly and can be said to have formed a state capitalist trust.

20 Kestin Bree Carlson, "International Law and Its Paradoxes," *Journal of Law and Courts* 5, no. 1 (Spring 2017): 33.

21 Graeme A. Barry, "'The Gifted Judge': An Analysis of the Judicial Career of Robert H. Jackson," *Alberta Law Review* 38, no. 3 (2000): 880, 883, available at https://albertalawreview.com/index.php/ALR/article/view/1433/1422.

22 Mary Margaret Penrose, "Lest We Fail: The Importance of Enforcement in International Criminal Law," *American University International Law Review* 15, no. 2 (1999): 34, available at https://digitalcommons.wcl.american.edu/cgi/viewcontent.cgi?article=1265&context=auilr.

23 Ibid.

24 Robert H. Jackson Center, "Opening Statement before the International Military Tribunal," available at https://www.roberthjackson.org/speech-and-writing/opening-statement-before-the-international-military-tribuna.

25 Herbert Reginbogin, "The Nuremberg Principles: The Contemporary Challenges," Conference Presented by the Catholic University of America, Institute for Policy Research, March 27, 2023, available at https://www.gtlaw.com/en/events/2023/03/the-nuremberg-principles-the-contemporary-challenges.

26 Masahiko Asada, "The War in Ukraine Under International Law: Its Use of Force and Armed Conflict Aspects," in Masahiko Asada and Dai Tamada (eds.), *The War in Ukraine and International Law* (Singapore: Springer Publisher, 2024), 3–33.

27 United Nations General Assembly Eleventh Emergency Special Session, "General Assembly Overwhelmingly Adopts Resolution Demanding Russian Federation Immediately End Illegal Use of Force in Ukraine, Withdraw All Troops," GA/12407 March 2, 2022, available at https://press.un.org/en/2022/ga12407.doc.htm.

28 Ibid.

29 U.S. Department of State, "Ambassador Beth van Schaack's Remarks on the U.S. Proposal to Prosecute Russian Crimes of Aggression," March 27, 2023, available at https://www.state.gov/ambassador-van-schaacks-remarks.

30 Claus Kress, "Russia's War of Aggression Against Ukraine and the Crime of Aggression," in Masahiko Asada and Dai Tamada (eds) *The War in Ukraine and International Law* (Singapore: Springer Nature, 2024), 65.

31 Anthony Deutsch and Stephanie van den Berg, "War Crimes Prosecutor Would Not Focus on U.S. Forces in New Afghanistan Probe," *Reuters*, September 27, 2021, available at https://www.reuters.com/world/asia-pacific/icc-prosecutor-seeks-authorisation-resume-afghanistan-war-crimes-investigation-2021-09-27.

32 Adam R. Pearlman, "The Justice for Victims of War Crimes Act (U.S.)," *International Legal Materials* 62 (December 6, 2023): 1084–8, available at https://www.cambridge.org/core/journals/international-legal-materials/article/justice-for-victims-of-war-crimes-act-us/A942F71C8EE80401639F1BD21C445668.

33 William A. Schabas, "Victor's Justice: Selecting 'Situations' at the International Criminal Court," *John Marshall Law Review* 43 (2010): 535, available at https://repository.law.uic.edu/cgi/viewcontent.cgi?article=1085&context=lawreview.

34 Christoph J. M. Safferling, "German Participation in the Nuremberg Trials and Its Implications for Today," in *The Nuremberg War Crimes Trial and its Policy Consequences Today* (2020), 45, available at https://www.researchgate.net/publication/368136687.
35 Ibid., 47, Most dramatic in this regard was the acquittal of the former Judge at the Volksgerichtshof (The Peoples Court) Hans-Joachim Rehse, Bundesgerichtshof, 30 April 1968 – 5 StR 670/67, Neue Juristische Wochenschrift (1968), 1339.
36 Ibid.
37 Yale University Press London, "Thomas Hobbes: 'Solitary, Poor, Nasty, Brutish, and Short,'" April 5, 2013, available at https://yalebooksblog.co.uk/2013/04/05/thomas-hobbes-solitary-poor-nasty-brutish-and-short.
38 Ibid.
39 Claus Kress, "Russia's War of Aggression Against Ukraine and the Crime of Aggression," in Masahiko Asada and Dai Tamada (eds.) *The War in Ukraine and International Law* (Singapore: Springer Nature, 2024), 65.
40 David Luban, "The Legacies of Nuremberg," in Guenael Mettraux (ed.) *Perspectives of the Nuremberg Trial* (Oxford: Oxford University Press, 2008), 641.
41 Philippe Sands, *Lawless World: Making and Breaking Global Rules* (London: Penguin Books, 2005), 8.
42 Guglielmo Verdirame, "The Divided West: International Lawyers in Europe and America," *The European Journal of International Law* 18, no. 3 (2007): 557–8.
43 Kofi Annan Foundation, "The Electoral Integrity Initiative," May 2, 2016, available at https://www.kofiannanfoundation.org/news/electoral-integrity-initiative.
44 Roger D. Citron, "The Nuremberg Trials and American Jurisprudence," in Herbert Reginbogin and Christoph J. M. Safferling (eds.) *The Nuremberg Trials: International Criminal Law Since 1945* (Munich: Saur, 2006), 139–52.
45 Detlev Vagts, "American International Law: A Sonderweg?," in K. Dicke et al. (eds.) *Weltinnenrecht: Liber Amicorum Jost Delbrück* (2005), (Duncker Humblot, Berlin: Germany), 841.
46 Hans Joachim Morgenthau, *Politics Among Nations: The Struggle for Power and Peace* (New York: Alfred A. Knopf, 1962).
47 John J. Mearsheimer, *The Tragedy of Great Power Politics* (New York: Norton, 2001).
48 Stephen M. Walt, *Taming American Power: The Global Response to U.S. Primacy* (New York: Norton, 2005).
49 Guglielmo Verdirame, "The Divided West: International Lawyers in Europe and America," *The European Journal of International Law* 18, no. 3 (2007): 557–8.
50 Curtis A. Bradley and Jack L. Goldsmith III, "Current Illegitimacy of International Human Rights Litigation," *Fordham Law Review* 66, no. 2 (1997): 319.
51 Jürgen Habermas, *The Divided West*, trans. Ciaran Cronin (Cambridge: Polity, 2006), 161.
52 Eli M. Rosenbaum, "Amicus Curiae Observations Pursuant to Rule 103 Situation in the State of Palestine," International Criminal Court, No.: ICC-01/18, August 6, 2024, available at https://www.icc-cpi.int/sites/default/files/CourtRecords/0902ebd180922ed1.pdf.
53 Anthony Deutsch and Stephanie van den Berg, "War Crimes Prosecutor Would Not Focus on U.S. Forces in New Afghanistan Probe," *Reuters*, September 27, 2021, available at https://www.reuters.com/world/asia-pacific/icc-prosecutor-seeks-authorisation-resume-afghanistan-war-crimes-investigation-2021-09-27.

54 Parker Yesko, "The War Crimes That the Military Buried," *The New Yorker*, September 10, 2024, available at https://www.newyorker.com/podcast/in-the-dark/the-war-crimes-that-the-military-buried?utm_source=nl&utm_brand=tny&utm_mailing=TNY_Daily_Paid_091024&utm_campaign=aud-dev&utm_medium=email&utm_term=tny_daily_digest&bxid=079e5a6b25af9f3f05c348&cndid=646&hasha=260a136b6fc2a28b65f1e7a4bb4c12&hashb=a94f33dde16408caf8d286812a3c2b8ea97a365e&hashc=d9f7aa119411e8f93a34f1d2937e9cef81fc675465c7784e5bc41707b032616c&esrc=MARTECH_ORDERFORM&mbid=CRMNYR012019.

55 Ibid.

56 Boumediene vs. Bush (Nos. 06–1195 and 06–1196) 476 F. 3d 981.

57 Supreme Court of the United States Trump v. United States Certiorarito to the United States Court of Appeals for the District of the United States Court of Appeals for the District of Columbia Circuit, No. 23–939. Argued April 25, 2024—Decided July 1, 2024, available at https://www.supremecourt.gov/opinions/23pdf/23-939_e2pg.pdf See, ACLU of Washington, D.C., "Supreme Court Grants Trump Broad Immunity for Official Acts, Placing Presidents Above the Law. Case: Trump v. United States," July 1, 2024, available at https://www.aclu.org/press-releases/supreme-court-grants-trump-broad-immunity-for-official-acts-placing-presidents-above-the-law.

58 28 US Code § 1350—Alien's action for tort US Code—The Alien Tort Statute (ATS), also known as the Alien Tort Claims Act (ATCA), is a US law that allows non-US citizens to sue in US federal courts for violations of international law or US treaties (June 25, 1948, ch. 646, 62 Stat. 934.)

59 Jean L. Cohen, "Whose Sovereignty? Empire Versus International Law," *Ethics and International Affairs* 18, no. 3 (2004): 4, available at https://www.proquest.com/docview/200509023/fulltextPDF?_oafollow=false&accountid=9940&pq-origsite=primo&sourcetype=Scholarly%20Journals See, Carl Schmitt, *The Concept of the Political*, trans. George Schwab (Chicago, IL: The University of Chicago Press, 1996), 54

60 Global Centre for the Responsibility to Protect, available at https://www.globalr2p.org/.

Selected Bibliography

Cassese, Antonio. *Realizing Utopia: The Future of International Law* (Oxford: Oxford University Press, 2012).

Kreß, Claus. "The Ukraine War and the Prohibition of the Use of Force in International Law" (Brussels: Torkel Opsahl Academic EPublisher, 2022), available at https://www.toaep.org/ops-pdf/13-kress/.

Pearlman, Adam R. "The Justice for Victims of War Crimes Act (U.S.)," *International Legal Materials* 62 (December 6, 2023): 1084–8, available at https://www.cambridge.org/core/journals/international-legal-materials/article/justice-for-victims-of-war-crimes-act-us/A942F71C8EE80401639F1BD21C445668.

Reginbogin, Herbert and Christoph Suffering. *The Nuremberg Trials: International Criminal Law Since 1945* (Munich: K.G. Saur, 2006).

Safferling, Christoph and Eckhart Conze (eds.). *The Genocide Convention Sixty Years after its Adoption* (The Hague: T.M.C. Asser Press, 2010).

Schaack, Beth Van and Ronald C. Slye. *International Criminal Law and Its Enforcement: Cases and Materials*. 4th edition Thomson Reuters/Foundation Press (St. Paul, MN, 2020.

12

Nuremberg's Confused Construction of Crimes Against Peace[1]

Lawrence Douglas

Public international law long vouchsafed the prerogatives of sovereignty—the state's claim to unreviewable powers to police its own subjects and to wage war to advance its interests. The horrors of the Great War shocked this system but did not fundamentally alter it. Hitler's Germany changed all that. Nuremberg's International Military Tribunal (IMT) trial promised to radically recenter the fundamental commitments of international law. International law would liberate itself from its origins in sovereign practice. It would forthwith stand above and over the state, subjecting its exercise of power to an emerging regime of criminal law.

Nuremberg may have failed to deliver on its radical promise, but the radical promise was there, as the IMT Charter makes clear. The Charter—framed by legal teams from the United States, Britain, France, and the Soviet Union in London in the summer of 1945 and officially adhered to by an additional nineteen nations—established the constitution, jurisdiction, and functions of the IMT. In addition to the conspiracy charge, the Charter established the IMT's jurisdiction over three international crimes: "crimes against peace," "war crimes," and "crimes against humanity." Of these three, "war crimes" had the clearest pedigree in international law as outlined in the Hague Conventions of 1899 and 1907 and the Geneva Conventions of 1929, which had laid down principles for the treatment of Prisoners of War and sick and wounded combatants. The Leipzig trials staged after the Great War and at the Allies' behest established a precedent for prosecuting such offenses, albeit a weak and disappointing one.[2]

The legal status of "crimes against peace" and "crimes against humanity" was a very different matter. Consider the Charter's definition of "crimes against humanity." Jurists, journalists, and diplomats had used the term over the course of decades to great rhetorical effect, though without any clear meaning. Acts of piracy, the slave trade, Leopold's atrocities in the Congo, Turkish extermination of Armenians, and even aggressive war itself—all had been decried as "crimes against humanity."[3] So, while the term served as a powerful register of moral outrage, it lacked legal content and failed to name an independent crime in international law. (Piracy and the slave trade constituted their own crimes.[4])

By the terms of the Nuremberg Charter, "crimes against humanity" now gained recognition as an independent crime in international law. And while the definition of this crime appears to repeat many of the offenses that the Charter lists as "war crimes," it also divides "crimes against humanity" into two categories: "atrocity" crimes—that is, murder, extermination, enslavement, deportation, and other inhumane acts committed against any civilian population; and "persecution" crimes—that is, "persecutions on political, racial, or religious grounds." Concerning the first type of crime against humanity, the Charter declares that the enumerated acts of atrocity constitute international crimes whether "committed before or during the war," and it declares all crimes against humanity as justiciable "whether or not in violation of the domestic law of the country where perpetrated."[5] On its face, the language is astonishing, especially when read in tandem with Article 7 of the Charter, which announces that the "official position of the defendants, whether as Heads of State or responsible officials in Government Departments shall not free them from responsibility."[6] Not only does the Charter strip heads of state of immunity from international prosecution, it declares that acts *authorized by domestic law* directed against the state's own subjects can constitute international crimes. In point of fact, the IMT ended up framing a restrictive interpretation of crimes against humanity, limiting its jurisdiction over these crimes to those connected to the other two crimes within the Tribunal's jurisdiction—war crimes and "crimes against peace."

More radical still was Nuremberg's definition of "crimes against peace—Planning, preparation, initiation or waging a war of aggression, or a war in violation of international treaties, agreements or assurances."[7] Participants at the Paris Peace Conference convened after the Great War concluded that similar actions did not constitute crimes in international law, much less ones that could be charged against the former Kaiser. In a remarkable paradigm shift, Nuremberg promised to make "crimes against peace" the centerpiece of an emerging post-war system of international criminal law. The Charter itself makes this clear, as the "crime against peace" enjoys pride of place in the enumeration of the three international crimes over which the IMT was granted jurisdiction. Allied prosecutors followed the lead of the Charter, treating aggression as the paradigmatic offense of the defendants in the dock. And in its final judgment, the Tribunal famously declared that to "initiate a war of aggression . . . is not only an international crime; it is the supreme international crime differing only from other war crimes in that it contains within itself the accumulated evil of the whole."[8]

It was the American team that most aggressively pushed to make crimes against peace the gravamen of the prosecution's case.[9] The historian Francine Hirsch has shown how the US embrace of the "aggression paradigm" was powerfully influenced by the great Soviet jurist Aron Naumovich Trainin, who pioneered the term "crimes against peace" and offered a crucial pre-Nuremberg elaboration of the incrimination.[10] In 1944, Trainin published a short book called *Hitlerite Responsibility under Criminal Law*. In the same year, the book appeared in English translation and was closely studied by Murray Bernays, among others, in the US War Department.[11] Expanding on points he had made in articles published earlier in the war, Trainin argued that the primary offense of the "Hitlerites" was what he called "crimes against peace," his famous coinage adopted at Nuremberg. Trainin was hardly the first jurist to insist that aggression constituted an international crime. The effort to criminalize state aggression had emerged as a major preoccupation of jurists in the interwar period, with important work done by the likes of Vespasian Pella and Nikolaos Politis. Shortly before the publication of Trainin's book, Hersch Lauterpacht had addressed many of the same themes in an influential article called "The Law of Nations and the Punishment of War Crimes," published in the *British Yearbook of International Law*.[12] What is distinctive and original in *Hitlerite Responsibility under Criminal Law* is not Trainin's claim that "crimes against peace" constitute international crimes but his insistence that they constitute "the first species of international crime."[13] In a formulation that powerfully anticipates the position framed at Nuremberg, Trainin insists that "Aggression is therefore the most dangerous international crime." And in arguing that the perpetrators of "crimes against peace" must include "not only those guilty of carrying out aggression" but also "those who try to fan the flame of war, who prepare aggression," Trainin again powerfully influenced the framing of the London Charter, which likewise included planning as a key element of the incrimination.[14]

After sketching the contours of "crimes against peace" as an international crime, Trainin devoted two chapters to specifically enumerating the crimes of Nazi Germany. These two chapters again anticipate the structure of the prosecution at Nuremberg. The first, "Crimes of the Hitlerites against peace," described Nazi aggression, while the second, "Crimes of the Hitlerites connected with the War," enumerated what at Nuremberg would be disaggregated into "war crimes" and "crimes against humanity." But here we need to note that when Trainin applied his scheme to describing Nazi crimes, his priorities and distinctions lost their neat conceptual separation. His discussion of the "crimes of the Hitlerites against peace" barely takes up three and a half pages of his book, while his enumeration of the "crimes of Hitlerites connected with the war" runs a full twenty-four pages. This is not to say that Trainin was wrong to identify "crimes against peace" as the core international crime; instead, it is to claim that Trainin's understanding of the criminality of aggression was forged by the "monstrous" quality of Hitler's war in the east. Trainin could insist that aggression, and not, say, extermination, was the paradigmatic crime of the Nazi state for the simple reason that he understood the latter as a feature of the former. The core criminality of Nazi Germany lay in its *Ostkrieg*—that is, in its war of annihilatory aggression waged against the Soviet Union.

Trainin's understanding of Nazi aggression was, then, forged by the Soviet experience. From the outset, Hitler's *Ostkrieg* had been a war of annihilation and extermination—a war waged not to conquer territory but to eradicate a state, an ideology, and a people. While the Jews were undeniably the target of the Reich's most extreme race-hatred and its most systematic genocidal campaign, we also know the larger *Generalplan Ost*—General Plan for the East—contemplated further acts of mass extermination, ethnic cleansing, and mass death through slave labor that would transform much of Eastern Europe into a depopulated space for German expansion. For Trainin, Hitler's *Ostkrieg* split the difference between aggression and atrocity. Therein lay its "monstrous peculiarity." The mass atrocities that followed fast on the heels of the Wehrmacht's advance into Soviet territory were all part of a unified criminal plan.

Notwithstanding Trainin's decision to devote separate chapters to the Nazis' "crimes against peace" and their "crimes connected to war," Trainin ultimately treats Nazi aggression as indistinguishable from the mass atrocities visited on the Soviet nation. The wholesale destruction of cities and villages, the mass die-off of Soviet POWs, the targeting of Soviet commissars, and the extermination of Jewish civilians—all were features of Nazi aggression itself. This point is crucial, as I will argue that the extraordinary quality of Nazi criminality made for confusions in Nuremberg's concept of "crimes against peace"—confusions that continue to vex the body of international criminal law.

To appreciate this, let's consider the work of another leading jurist who insisted that state aggression constituted the primary international crime. Like Trainin, the Czech jurist Bohuslav Ečer had described aggression as the Nazis' "fundamental crime," noting "without war there would be no 'war crimes.'"[15] Ečer had been an early opponent of Nazism, and with the occupation of Czechoslovakia, he fled with his family to Paris and later to London. There he was named as the Czech government-in-exile's delegate to the newly formed UN War Crimes Commission (UNWCC). The UNWCC had been established in October 1943 with the participation of the United States, Britain, France, the Netherlands, and a clutch of other Allies—though not the Soviet Union—and charged with compiling evidence of Axis war crimes and lists of alleged war criminals to be used as possible future war crimes trials. In the first meeting of the legal committee in March 1944, Ečer insisted that the "launching and waging of the war" be treated as the "paramount crime of the Axis powers." In describing the criminality of Nazi aggression, Ečer, who had closely read Trainin's book and shared its conclusions with his fellow delegates, emphasized that the Axis powers had sought "to enslave foreign nations, to destroy the civilization of those nations, and physically to annihilate a considerable section of their populations on racial, political and religious grounds."[16] Insisting that Nazi aggression could not be distinguished from its acts of atrocity, Ečer proposed that Nazi aggression "be treated as crimes within the scope of the [UN War Crimes] Commission's work," whether or not "this was the case with any aggressive war in general."[17] Let us pause over these words, as here Ečer suggests not all aggressive wars necessarily constitute international crimes. Axis aggression, however, had earned this special status as it took the form of "criminal events without precedent."[18] And yet, a couple of years earlier, Ečer had argued that aggressive warfare "even if waged without 'atrocities' and in full compliance with conventions of The Hague and Geneva, is a crime."[19] Why Ečer came to retreat from this position remains unclear, although he certainly had sound strategic reasons for doing so. In March 1944, the UNWCC was debating whether to include aggression in its investigative remit; in arguing that Nazi aggression constituted an international crime even if other forms of state aggression might not, Ečer presumably was trying to craft an argument narrowly tailored to convince colleagues who remained doubtful that aggression in whatever form constituted an international crime.

As noted, American jurists assumed the decisive role in making "crimes against peace" the gravamen of the prosecution's case at Nuremberg and the primary focus of the international trial. And yet, in emphasizing the centrality of aggression, American jurists appeared to miss or overlook how Trainin and Ečer had framed the criminality of Nazi war-making. Indeed, the Americans embraced Ečer's earlier, more capacious understanding that insisted on the criminality of aggressive warfare "even if waged without 'atrocities' and in full compliance with conventions of The Hague and Geneva." By this understanding, aggression constitutes an international crime, even if waged in a manner fully respectful of *jus in bello.* As Robert Jackson, chief US prosecutor and on leave from his position as Associate Justice on the Supreme Court, put it in his opening address, "Any resort to war—to any kind of war—is a resort to means that are inherently criminal."[20] Invoking the classic figure of the pirate—the paradigmatic *hostis humani generis*—the American team insisted that acts of piracy remained criminal whether or not accompanied by acts of terror and killing. Like piracy, war itself was a crime.[21] In the span of less than a quarter-century, the United States had been dragged into two horrific European conflicts; demonstrating the criminality of war would offer powerful post-hoc justification for the nation's sacrifices. For Jackson, the focus on "crimes against peace" would also prove the lawfulness of both the US's Destroyers-for-Bases deal of 1940 (which "lent" Britain 50 destroyers in exchange for leases on British bases in Newfoundland and the Caribbean) and the US's Lend-Lease Act of 1941 (which provided food, oil and other critical material to Allies free of charge).[22] Jackson, at the time Roosevelt's Attorney General and relying on arguments developed by Hersch Lauterpacht, had argued in support of Lend-Lease, despite the fact that it represented a clear departure from principles of neutrality. Nuremberg now promised to deliver a more convincing vindication for the US program. Finally, fresh in the mind of US jurists was the fact that the nation had achieved victory over Japan by unleashing the unprecedented destructive power of nuclear weapons—a dramatic reminder of the horrors that may follow from even the justified uses of force to defeat aggression. Given how victory in the Pacific had been achieved, many shared the fear expressed by Justice Jackson in his opening address at Nuremberg that civilization itself could not survive another global conflict.

In making "crimes against peace" the centerpiece of the Nuremberg trial, Allied jurists were forced to confront the *nullum crimen* concern—the claim that "crimes against peace" was an invention of Nuremberg, and thus an application of retroactive law in violation of the basic principle of legality. To successfully rebut the retroactivity argument, voiced not only by lawyers for the defense but by skeptics in the legal community, Allied jurists would have to argue that sometime before the Wehrmacht crossed the Polish frontier on September 1, 1939, international law had come to recognize state aggression as an international crime, a fact that IMT's Charter formally recognized.

Although jurists could cite protocols and treaties such as the Pact of Paris of 1928—commonly called the Kellogg-Briand Peace Pact, after the American secretary of state and the French foreign minister who first proposed the agreement—which, by its lapidary terms, claimed to outlaw war, other jurists expressed doubts that the Pact had achieved anything of substance. Hans Kelsen spoke for many when, from his US exile, he branded the Pact's effort to deal with "cases of external aggression" a "complete failure."[23] But even if we believe that interwar instruments had outlawed aggression, the claim that the international community had agreed that aggression constituted an international *crime* for which individuals could be held accountable seems quite a stretch.

Unsurprisingly, then, the issue caused considerable controversy at the London Conference, where, in an oak-paneled room in Westminster's Church House, a group of world-class legal talent representing the four Allies gathered to draft the Charter for the IMT. The sharpest differences emerged between Jackson and André Gros, a French delegation member and a prominent human rights scholar. Gros had served on the UNWCC, where, to Ečer's chagrin, he had signed on to the Commission's majority position that "war was not a crime in positive international law."[24] Speaking for the French delegation at the London Conference, Professor Gross repeated this conclusion:

> We do not consider as a criminal violation the launching of a war of aggression. If we declared war a criminal act of individuals, we are going farther than the actual law . . . We do not want criticism in later years of punishing something that was not actually criminal.[25]

Gros cited the 1919 American Report of Lansing and Scott at the Paris Peace Conference, which emphatically concluded that there is "no legal basis to say that launching a war of aggression shows criminal responsibility of the people who launched the war." Gros argued that the case against the Nuremberg defendants should be organized around "something that is not in doubt—that the conduct of a war in violation of international law is a crime."[26]

We might have expected Professor Trainin, who served as a member of the Soviet delegation at the London Conference, to rebut Gros, but the most vehement pushback came from Justice Jackson. "I must say," Jackson declared with barely concealed irritation, "sentiment in the United States and the better world opinion have greatly changed since Mr. James Brown and Secretary Lansing announced their views."[27] The question that troubled Jackson was not whether aggression constituted an international crime but whether the Charter and the prosecution could adequately define the incrimination. Jackson argued that the problem of defining aggressive war was unavoidable. "We either define it now," he declared at the conference, "in which case it will end argument at trial, or define it at the trial, in which case it will be subject of an argument in which the Germans will participate."[28]

Rightfully concerned about handing the defense an opportunity to haggle about the prosecution's main charge was something Jackson wanted to avoid at all costs. Professor Gros argued that framing a definition in the Charter wouldn't solve the problem, as the judges or the defense could still question the adequacy of the definition. General Nikitchenko, head of the Soviet delegation, agreed with the French professor, noting that "however perfect our definition would be, . . . the defendants

. . . might question it."[29] Chief of the British delegation, Attorney General Sir David Maxwell Fyfe, suggested that the Charter simply rely on the definition in the Kellogg-Briand Pact and the declaration of the United Nations, seemingly unaware that the Pact and the statement of the fledgling body had utterly neglected to define aggression. General Nikitchenko then suggested that in the absence of a complete definition, the Charter should simply define aggression as a crime "carried out by the European Axis," a proposal that, given its most sympathetic gloss, could be heard as echoing Ečer's notion that the UNWCC should treat Nazi aggression as a crime whether or not "this was the case with any aggressive war in general." That, in any case, is not how Jackson, generally suspicious of the Soviets, heard Nikitchenko's proposal. Confronted with what he considered a Soviet-style attempt to shape the law of the Charter into a partisan tool of score-settling, he bluntly observed that to define aggression as acts carried out by Axis powers "deprives it of all standing and fairness as a juridical principle."[30] Better to scuttle the entire Allied trial, he testily remarked, than to sign on to such a manifest perversion of legal principle.

Ultimately convinced that any definition would invite challenge and unable to agree on one anyway, the conference chose not to supply a definition. And so the description of "aggressive war" in Article 6(a) of the IMT charter remained startlingly imprecise, a fact only highlighted by the relatively well-framed definitions of war crimes 6(b) and crimes against humanity 6(c). Still, the agreement not to define "crimes against peace" left Professor Gros's deeper concern unaddressed: that the very criminalization of aggression was "*ex post facto* legislation"—"a creation of by four people who are just four people."

The delegates' struggle to agree whether the Charter recognized law that had already been established or was creating new law out of whole cloth continued to play itself out in a debate over the Charter's language. Should, for example, as Professor Trainin suggested, the Charter "*declare* certain acts to be criminal"? Or should it adopt the wording of Sir David Maxwell Fyfe—"the following acts *shall be considered* criminal violations"—a formulation that also omitted the words "international crimes." The conference quickly tried and rejected various formulations:

- The following acts *shall be considered* criminal violations of International Law and shall come with the jurisdiction of the Tribunal.
- The following acts or designs or attempts at any of them *shall be deemed* crimes . . .
- The following acts, designs or attempts at any of them shall be deemed crimes and shall come within the jurisdiction of the Tribunal.
- The following acts *are deemed* criminal violations of International law and do come within . . .[31]

Finally, the delegates agreed on the lapidary formulation, "The following acts, or any of them, *are* crimes coming within the jurisdiction of the Tribunal . . .," wording which allowed the conferees to finish drafting the Charter without resolving the deeper jurisprudential question. Still, the *nullum crimen* problem hardly went away. At the trial, lawyers for the defense, as feared, raised it. Most trenchant were the arguments of

Hermann Jahreiß, a prominent professor of law at the University of Köln and counsel for Alfred Jodl, the former chief of staff of the *Oberkommando der Wehrmacht* (Military High Command). To the prosecution's annoyance, if not discomfort, Jahreiß quoted Oxford's authority on international law, J.R. Brierly, who had written that whatever Kellogg-Briand might have achieved, it had most certainly failed to criminalize aggression. Also quoting from the Kellogg-Briand ratification debates held in the US Senate, Jahreiß pointedly noted that US Senators had variously dismissed the Pact as "worthless . . . at best a feeble or friendly gesture" and at worst "a gigantic piece of hypocrisy" that sought to freeze the "unjust status quo of Versailles for France and Great Britain"—a claim that awkwardly appeared to anticipate arguments deployed by Hitler.[32]

Jahreiß might also have noted the *volte-face* of Sheldon Glueck, professor of law at Harvard and one of Jackson's leading legal advisors. In February 1946, as the trial was entering its fourth month, Glueck published an article in the *Harvard Law Review* called "The Nuremberg Trial and Aggressive War" (republished as a book by Knopf later that year bearing the same title) that supported the prosecution's insistence that aggression had clearly been criminalized before the beginning of the Second World War. Inconveniently, however, two years earlier, in 1944, Glueck had published another slender volume called *War Criminals: Their Prosecution and Punishment*, in which he insisted that trying Nazis for aggressive war "would only drag a red herring across the trial and confuse the much clearer principle of liability for atrocities committed during the conduct of war."[33]

In a sense, however, the *nullum crimen* problem was itself a red herring. As the tribunal noted in its judgment, *nullum crimen* is not a "limitation on sovereignty"—it is "a principle of justice" that can be weighed against countervailing interests in justice. Given the extreme nature of Nazi aggression, the Tribunal reasoned, "the attacker must know that he is doing wrong." In such a case, "it would be unjust if his wrong were allowed to go unpunished."[34] The cause of justice would be perverted by *failing* to treat aggression as an international crime, irrespective of whether the tribunal recognized a pre-existing incrimination or established a new one.

The more intractable question, however, was not when aggression had become a crime but the question that neither Trainin nor Ečer had precisely answered—what was being criminalized. This went beyond the problem of definition. Again, it was Professor Gros who framed the problem most clearly. "I don't quite see," the professor said at the conference, "how if Germany had launched a war of aggression but had not committed any acts in (b) and (c), we could actually set up a court to judge members of the German Government."[35] In the IMT Charter, (b) and (c) came to refer to "war crimes" and "crimes against humanity," respectively. The question that the Professor had implicitly raised went to the heart of the issue: Would a war of aggression, waged in the absence of war crimes and crimes against humanity, constitute an international crime? And if so, why? Unfortunately, in Jackson's escalating impatience, the French professor's concern was never satisfactorily answered. But it brought to light the central confusion at the heart of Nuremberg's attempt to make aggressive war the centerpiece of a postwar system of international criminal law.

As we've seen, both Trainin and Ečer had at least publicly altered their positions on precisely this issue—in earlier writings, both had suggested that aggression should be considered an international crime, regardless of how it was waged. In later writings, however, both focused on the "monstrous peculiarity" of Nazi aggression, which included the full range of Nazi atrocity. In these writings, the criminality of Nazi aggression was inextricably connected to Nazi war crimes and acts of mass atrocity.

Not only did Jackson and his team fail to answer Gros's concern satisfactorily, but they also offered no apparent response to a deeper question implicit in the French delegate's concern: Assuming an aggressing state acts in full compliance with *jus in bello*, what is it about state aggression that warrants its criminalization? Does the criminalization of aggression protect the "territorial integrity" or "political independence" of states? But why should the violation of the territorial integrity of a state be considered an international crime to which individual liability attaches? Does it matter if the aggressed-against state is a rogue state or one committing systematic abuses of its own population? If framed as a protection of territorial integrity and political independence, the incrimination looks a great deal like a conservative effort to enlist international criminal law to add another layer of protection to sovereign privilege. Or does the criminalization of aggression seek to defend human life? Yet this understanding is hard to square with the law of armed conflict framed in the Hague and Geneva conventions, which insists that war can be waged lawfully if not humanely. So even if we concede that aggressive war is an illegal act that warrants sanctioning the trespassing state, it is far from obvious why such a war, if waged in compliance with *jus in bello*, should render leaders of the offending state liable to criminal prosecution.[36]

In a sense, the IMT had the luxury of never properly answering these questions. Regardless of how one framed the criminality of aggression, Nazi Germany was going to more than fit the bill. As Hartley Shawcross emphasized in his opening address (largely drafted by Hersch Lauterpacht):

> The Tribunal will not allow itself to be deflected from its purpose by attempts to ventilate in the Court what is an academic and, in the circumstances, an utterly unreal controversy as to what is the nature of a law of aggression, for there is no definition of aggression, general or particular, which does not cover abundantly and irresistibly in every detail, the premeditated onslaught by Germany."[37]

Like the later Trainin and Ečer, Shawcross insisted that Nazi aggression was inextricably bound with acts that "plunged millions of people to their death, which . . . brought about the torture and extermination of countless thousands of innocent civilians, which devastated cities, which destroyed . . . the most rudimentary necessities of civilization" and "has brought the world to the brink of ruin."[38]

This understanding was also powerfully expressed by Francis Biddle, former US Attorney General who served as the principal US judge at Nuremberg. One month after the Tribunal delivered its judgment, Biddle urged President Truman to petition the fledgling UN to develop a body of international criminal law with Nuremberg's jurisprudence at its core. In emphasizing the centrality of crimes against peace to this project, Biddle wrote, "A war to conquer territory and subdue populations necessarily resulted in the kind of savagery in which the German leaders indulged, the torture rooms of the Gestapo and the concentration camps."[39] The words *necessarily resulted* jump out at us, as they underscore the understanding of crimes against peace framed at Nuremberg. Atrocity followed ineluctably from Nazi aggression. This was, of course, a fair and accurate understanding of Hitler's war. The problem was that the IMT treated an utterly extraordinary case as an exemplar of a category of criminality. What would happen when jurists confronted wars of aggression that did not feature the deformations of Nazi violence?

As we have noted, the IMT famously declared that to "initiate a war of aggression . . . is not only an international crime; it is the supreme international crime differing only from other war crimes in that it contains within itself the accumulated evil of the whole."[40] Now, however, we can appreciate the instabilities contained in Nuremberg's bold effort to erect an edifice of international law around the crime of aggressive war. For as we have seen, the spectacular nature of Nazi state-sponsored violence allowed the Tribunal to essentially overlook the unresolved conceptual differences percolating in the understanding of what Nuremberg framed as the core international crime. While this simplified matters for the IMT, it also meant that the fledgling jurisprudence of state aggression was based on a display without precedent in world history. In constructing its aggression paradigm in response to a form of state war-making that was unlikely to find repetition, the IMT left unanswered how the paradigm would apply to less egregious instances of aggression. To put the matter more pointedly, Nuremberg left unclear what exactly "crimes against peace" criminalized.

Notes

1 This chapter is adapted from my forthcoming book, *The Criminal State: War, Atrocity and the Cloak of the Sovereign,* to be published by Princeton.

2 Gerd Hankel, *The Leipzig Trials: German War Crimes and Their Legal Consequences after World War I*, trans. Belinda Cooper, Library of Human Rights (Dordrecht: Republic of Letters Publishing BV, 2014).

3 In 1890, George Washington Williams, a Black American veteran of the Civil War and journalist who had traveled around the Congo, described the atrocities he had witnessed as "crimes against humanity; in a statement issued on May 24, 1915, France, Russia and Great Britain condemned the mass killings of Armenians by Turks as a crime against humanity and civilization; and in 1917, Lloyd George had called Germany's deliberate "planning and plotting a great war" nothing less than a "great crime against humanity.

4 D. H. N. Johnson, "Piracy in Modern International Law," *Transactions of the Grotius Society* 43 (1957): 63–85; Jenny S. Martinez, *The Slave Trade and the Origins of International Human Rights Law*, Reprint edition (Oxford: Oxford University Press, 2014).

5 Charter of the International Military Tribunal, *Trial of the Major War Criminals Before the International Military Tribunal, Nuremberg, 14 November 1945–1 October 1946*, 1947, vol. 1, 11.
6 Charter of the International Military Tribunal, vol. 1, 12.
7 6(a) Charter of the International Military Tribunal, vol. 1, 12.
8 International Military Tribunal, vol. 1, 186.
9 The history of how this came to be has been told in detail, most attentively by Jonathan Bush, and we need not review the involved story of the intramural skirmishes among the likes of Professor Glueck, Colonel Chanler, Colonel Bernays, President Roosevelt, Secretary Stimson, Justice Jackson, and Baron Shawcross that resulted in the decision to frame the trial around the crime of aggressive war. Jonathan A. Bush, "'The Supreme . . . Crime' and Its Origins: The Lost Legislative History of the Crime of Aggressive War," *Columbia Law Review* 102, no. 8 (2002): 2324–424, https://doi.org/10.2307/1123729. See also, Bradley F. Smith, *The Road to Nuremberg* (New York: Basic Books, 1981). Also Telford Taylor, *The Nuremberg War Crimes Trials: War Crimes and International Law* (New York: Literary Licensing, 1949) and Robert Jackson, "The Significance of the Nuremberg Trials to the Armed Forces: Previously Unpublished Personal Observations by the Chief Counsel for the United States," *Military Affairs* 10, no. 4 (1946): 2–15.
10 Francine Hirsch, *Soviet Judgment at Nuremberg: A New History of the International Military Tribunal after World War II* (Oxford and New York: Oxford University Press, 2020).
11 Francine Hirsch, *Soviet Judgment at Nuremberg: A New History of the International Military Tribunal after World War II* (Oxford and New York: Oxford University Press, 2020).
12 H. Lauterpacht, "The Law of Nations and the Punishment of War Crimes," *British Year Book of International Law* 21 (1944): 58. Here we should note that Trainin himself had insisted on the criminality of state aggression in an earlier work called *The Defense of Peace and Criminal Law*, published in 1937. This earlier book bore the clear trademarks of Soviet jurisprudence, treating aggression as a predatory feature of fascist and capitalist states while casting the Soviet Union as the paragon of the peace-loving nation. See Rohini Sen and Rashmi Raman, "Aron Trainin," in *The Dawn of a Discipline: International Criminal Justice and Its Early Exponents*, ed. Frédéric Mégret and Immi Tallgren, (Cambridge: Cambridge University Press, 2020), 260–279.
13 Traĭnin, 37.
14 Traĭnin, 37.
15 Bohuslav Ečer, The Lessons of the Kharkov Trial (Russia Today Society, 1977), 9.
16 United Nations War Crimes Commission, *History of the United Nations War Crimes Commission and the Development of the Laws of War* (London: H.M. Stationery Office, 1948), 180.
17 Commission, 180–2, 182.
18 Commission, 182.
19 William Schabas, "Origins of the Criminalization of Aggression: How Crimes against Peace Became the "Supreme International Crime," in Mauro Politi and Giuseppe Nesi (eds.), *The International Criminal Court and the Crime of Aggression* (Abingdon and New York: Routledge/Taylor & Francis Group, 2017), 23.

20 International Military Tribunal, *Trial of the Major War Criminals Before the International Military Tribunal, Nuremberg, 14 November 1945–1 October 1946*, 1947, vol. 2, 146.
21 Quincy Wright, "The Law of the Nuremberg Trial," *The American Journal of International Law* 41, no. 1 (1947): 38–72, 64.
22 Robert H. Jackson, *Report of Robert H. Jackson: United States Representative to the International Conference on Military Trials, London, 1945*, Publication No. 3080 (Washington, DC: U.S. Department of State, U.S. Government Publishing Office, 1949), 363.
23 Hans Kelsen and John H. Herz, "Essential Conditions of International Justice," *Proceedings of the American Society of International Law at Its Annual Meeting (1921–1969)* 35 (1941): 70–98, 80.
24 Commission, *History of the United Nations War Crimes Commission and the Development of the Laws of War*, 182.
25 Robert H. Jackson, *Report of Robert H. Jackson, United States Representative to the International Conference on Military Trials, London, 1945,* Publication No. 3080 (Washington, DC: U.S. Department of State, U.S. Government Publishing Office, 1949), 295.
26 Jackson, 297, 296.
27 Jackson, 299.
28 Jackson, 302.
29 Jackson, 308.
30 Jackson, 330.
31 Jackson, 387.
32 International Military Tribunal, *Trial of the Major War Criminals Before the International Military Tribunal, Nuremberg, 14 November 1945–1 October 1946*, 1947, vol. 17, 470.
33 Sheldon Glueck, *War Criminals : Their Prosecution & Punishment* (New York: Alfred A. Knopf, 1944), 38.
34 International Military Tribunal, vol. 1, 219.
35 Jackson, *Report of Robert H. Jackson, United States Representative to the International Conference on Military Trials, London, 1945*, 379, 386.
36 This matter is dealt with in greater detail in my forthcoming book from which this chapter was adapted.
37 International Military Tribunal, vol. 3, 108.
38 International Military Tribunal, vol. 3, 104.
39 Biddle quoted in Hirsch, *Soviet Judgment at Nuremberg, 395.*
40 International Military Tribunal, vol. 1, 186.

Selected Bibliography

Dannenbaum, Tom. *The Crime of Aggression, Humanity, and the Soldier*. Cambridge: Cambridge University Press, 2018.

Douglas, Lawrence. The Criminal State: War, Atrocity and the Cloak of the Sovereign. Princeton, NJ: Princeton University Press, forthcoming, 2026.

Hirsch, Francine. *Soviet Judgment at Nuremberg: A New History of the International Military Tribunal after World War II*. Oxford and New York: Oxford University Press, 2020.

Jackson, Robert H. *Report of Robert H. Jackson: United States Representative to the International Conference on Military Trials, London, 1945*. Publication No. 3080. Washington, DC: U.S. Department of State, U.S. Government Publishing Office, 1949.

Sellars, Kirsten. *"Crimes against Peace" and International Law*. Reprint edition. Cambridge: Cambridge University Press, 2015.

Traĭnin, Aron Naumovich. *Hitlerite Responsibility Under Criminal Law*. London: Hutchinson & Company, 1945.

United Nations War Crimes Commission. *History of the United Nations War Crimes Commission and the Development of the Laws of War*. London: H.M. Stationery Office, 1948.

Part 5

Implementing the Nuremberg Principles in the Contemporary Context of the Criminalization of War Crimes and Current International Humanitarian Codes of War

13

The Nuremberg Principles and Constraints on Armed Conflict

Change and Continuity in the Effort to Limit Warfare in World History

Michael S. Bryant

Men who take up arms against one another in public war do not cease on this account to be moral beings, responsible to one another and to God.

Francis Lieber, Article 15, General Orders 100 (1863)

The laws of war do not recognize in belligerents an unlimited power in the adoption of means of injuring the enemy.

Brussels Declaration, Article 12 (1874)

The High Contracting Parties . . . [base] themselves on the principle of international law that the right of the parties to an armed conflict to choose methods or means of warfare is not unlimited, and on the principle that prohibits the employment in armed conflicts of weapons, projectiles and material and methods of warfare of a nature to cause superfluous injury or unnecessary suffering.

Preamble to the Convention on Prohibitions or Restrictions on the Use of Certain Conventional Weapons Which May Be Deemed to Be Excessively Injurious or to Have Indiscriminate Effects (1980)

The awful and interminable war in Ukraine has revived interest in the Nuremberg Principles and their continuing relevance to international criminal law. This subject aroused political leaders, judicial officials, and concerned citizens worldwide to explore how Russian perpetrators might be held legally responsible for their international crimes. In my chapter, I would like to contribute a deep historical perspective to our conversation. My hope is that my words might be a source of encouragement and solace during a dark time of Russian aggression, Ukrainian suffering, mass death in Israel and Gaza, and growing friction between the United States and China.

The words "encouragement" and "solace" may ring hollow in a time as bleak as the present moment. Yet, we may find hope in our species' historical efforts to limit warfare. Despite the many atrocities that stain the past, human beings have always limited the resort to and practice of war-making. Long before the terms "jus ad bellum" and "jus in bello" even existed, human beings had ensconced warfare within a network of cultural understandings that both structured and limited its occurrence. All human activity in the ancient past, including warfare, had a sacramental quality. By embedding their actions in a system of ritual performance, ancient peoples sought to recreate the cosmic world of the gods within their own societies. Nearly every purposive act had a place in this conjuring of the divine realm on earth. Thus, in the architecture of their houses and sacred buildings, ancient peoples likened the pillar or pole at the structure's center to the "axis of the world" (*axis mundi*) they believed supported the earth, heaven, and underworld. The sacred pole, moreover, was analogized to the "cosmic mountain" thought to be the world's midpoint, linking the earth with heaven. In Harappa, Mohenjo Daro, and Sumer, the ziggurat—a terraced edifice surmounted by a temple—was a homology of the cosmic mountain.[1]

Everywhere in antiquity, human cultures told stories about the origins of the world from the body of a slain dragon or primal monster. The dragon/monster represented darkness and disorder; its death was the victory of light and order over chaos. In ancient Egypt, the sun-God Re's procession across the sky each day routed the darkness and disorder of the night, represented by the serpent Apophis. As Re's living embodiment on earth, the Pharoah reproduced Re's victory through successful warfare. By defeating enemy armies, who represented in the Egyptian imagination the forces of dissolution and chaos that Re subdued daily, the Pharoah reenacted the victory over night. It preserved order (which the Egyptians called "ma'at") from world-destroying chaos. Like other ancient peoples, the Egyptians believed war should imitate celestial patterns observed in the heavens and, moreover, had to be ratified by the gods. Pharaohs visited cult centers like the Temple of Karnak before they embarked on military campaigns. The pharaohs sought divine approval for their impending wars at these sacred centers. Only through this ritual performance could Re's cosmic act be reenacted and ma'at sustained on earth.[2]

It is my contention that the Egyptian requirement of divine approval before a war could be fought was a type of *jus ad bellum* (right to go to war), which, while differing culturally from the subsequent *jus ad bellum* of the Roman world, was functionally quite similar to it. For all his seeming omnipotence as a living god, the Pharoah could not wage war without divine approval. The same principle existed in Mesopotamian warfare, where the Babylonians imposed the duty to secure the gods' approval on their kings before initiating armed conflict. In Babylon, war had to be both declared by the king and justified before it was legitimate. Thus, we read in a letter of the king of Yamhad, Yarim-Lim (reigned ca. 1780 BCE–ca. 1764 CE), to the king of Der, Yasub-Yahab, a declaration of war accompanied by a justification for waging it. "You are continually responding to me with lies and provocation," Yarim-Lim charged. He went on:

> I swear to you by Addu, my city's god, and by Sin, my own god: [may I be punished] should I ever go away before annihilating your land and you! Now therefore, I shall

> come at springtime and shall pitch camp at your city's gate. I shall have you witness the galling weapons of Addu and Yarim-Lim.[3]

Similar injunctions that prescribed divine approval before war could be waged occurred in the Zhou Dynasty in China (ca. 1046–256 BCE). Zhou armies embellished their military campaigns with elaborate ritualized ceremonies which, in the words of historian Mark Lewis, "linked actions in the field to the state cults and guaranteed the sacred character of the battle."[4] Zhou armies waged war only after consulting oracles and reciting a war prayer. The commander then issued a ceremonial command (called the *ming*). Reminiscent of Yarim-Lin's recitation of Yasub-Yahab's derelictions, the *ming* contained a summary of the enemy's crimes as well as an assertion that the declarant, in waging war, was fulfilling the will of Heaven. The *ming* sometimes included affirmations of personal responsibility by the commanding general for achieving victory. One such example is the affirmation of a commander fighting for the lord of Jin, Zhao Yang, who execrates himself should he lose the battle. "Should I be guilty [of defeat]," he avers, "then may I be punished by strangulation, may I only have a thin coffin with no outside layers, may it be drawn by an unornamented horse and wagon, and may I not be buried in the graveyard of my lineage."[5] Warfare has always been a serious business, but the general's vow of self-annihilation in the event of defeat is simply incomprehensible outside a religious worldview. These features of Zhou warfare evoke a *jus ad bellum* compounded of Chinese religious elements, especially ancestor worship and the notion of the will of Heaven. When these elements are set beside the honor of the state and the duty of each combatant to fulfill the demands of his ancestors, the general's all-or-nothing declaration becomes less enigmatic. Clearly, for the Zhou, warfare was not simply a matter of killing the enemy.

By the third century BCE, the Chinese had come to believe that the ruler's actions on earth, including his manner of warfare, must conform to natural processes in the heavens and on earth. The autumn and winter periods were set aside for waging war. To depart from this custom and wage war during spring and summer was regarded with horror—it signified a breach of the ruler's duties to imitate nature and its cycles. Commentators at the time, like Sima Qian, denounced those kings who violated the calendrical system and fought during the spring and summer periods as evil. Such kings put themselves at odds with the rhythms of the natural world. They were offenders against the cosmic Way prescribed by Heaven.[6]

Warfare in ancient India, too, was governed by a cosmo-religious model called dharma. According to the Vedas, dharma consisted of performing religious rituals believed to sustain the cosmic order. It was bound up with the idea of caste, and together, these two concepts held that every creature in the universe had a specific duty or ethic to fulfill. On the battlefield, dharma and caste prescribed that soldiers could make war only on their social equals. Hence, a king could only fight against another king, an officer with another officer, but never a foot soldier. Mounted cavalry could only engage other mounted warriors. Elephant riders were allowed to fight only against other elephant riders. These principles gave rise to a sharp distinction in Indian thinking about the law of war: the distinction between warfare fought in accordance with dharma (*dharmayudda*) and wars fought in violation of dharma (*kuttayudda*). These are the rough Indian counterparts of the Western *jus in bello* and *jus ad bellum*.[7] Their opposite, so-called "adharmic" warfare (war fought in violation of dharma), anticipates by two millennia the concept of war crimes.

The Greeks and the Romans imposed conditions on both the resort to warfare and the manner of its waging. In Greece a set of battlefield constraints had crystallized between 700 and 450 BCE, the "common customs of the Hellenes" (*koina nomina*), which demanded constraints on military actions, such as limiting the hot pursuit of a retreating enemy by the non-hoplite phalanxes (a limitation that served the social interests of elites among the hoplite formations). During the Roman Republic, a "fetial college" emerged, whose priests determined whether a just cause existed to support a declaration of war against another nation. The fetials also heard allegations of wrongdoing committed by a Roman citizen on a foreigner; if the claim was approved, then the offender was handed over to his accusers. Although the fetial system broke down during the imperial phase of Roman history, its *jus ad bellum* continued to resonate in the philosophy of Stoicism and the jurisprudence of Cicero and the jurisconsults. Their thought would go on to influence the just war theory of Medieval Europe, giving rise to some of the most consequential limitations on warfare in world history.[8]

A type of restraint on warfare derived, as in Egypt, Mesopotamia, China, India, Greece, and Rome, from religious belief also appears in the indigenous cultures of the Americas. Mayan kings of the Classic period (beginning in the second century CE) sought to reenact the victory over "Death" of their legendary heroes called the Twins. Recreation of the Twins' triumph involved the capture and ritualized sacrifice of high-born enemies, whose stylized deaths were believed to open the portal to the Otherworld. This practice became intertwined with the Mayan ballgame and its playing field, where noble captives were forced to play in front of spectators. The losers were beheaded and thrown down the temple steps. For the Maya, the game reenacted the Twins' victory over Death.[9]

Sacrificing war captives for cosmological reasons was also central to Aztec religion. So far as we can tell, Aztec warfare was driven less by material considerations like the acquisition of land and other resources than by the seizure of enemy soldiers for sacrifice to the Aztec god Huitzilopochtli. The sacrifices were intended to placate Huitzilopochtli and, like the Egyptian Pharaoh, to reproduce his victory over chaos and darkness.[10] Further north in modern-day New Mexico, the Pueblo Indians constructed a religious cult around war-making and scalp-taking. As anthropologist Adolf Bandelier has observed, the Pueblo attributed metaphysical properties to enemy scalps and believed that the powers of the slain warrior were transferred to the scalp-taker. Whether or not warfare among the Pueblo was ultimately motivated by the aim of harvesting scalps from the enemy dead, the scalps became a venerated object of the Pueblo religion, celebrated and honored in tribal ceremonies.[11]

Among the Santa Ana Pueblos, a law of war arose from the tribe's origins myth. American anthropologist Leslie White retells the myth:

> [Twin war gods] Masewi and Oyoyewi, full of zest, go about the country "killing people for nothing." This angers the gods and they decide to teach the twins a lesson. They cause a hideous corpsewoman . . . to pursue them to the four corners of the earth. At last the boys are spared. The gods now lay down the rules for killing and scalping people. They instruct Masewi and Oyoyewi in all that pertains to war: how the scalping is to be done, how to fast and observe continence, how to dance for the scalps and how to take care of them. Chastened, the war gods organize the Opi (Warriors) society and teach how to take scalps, how to fast and observe continence, how to take care of the scalps and how to dance for them. In this way Keresan war customs were established.[12]

Scalping and human sacrifice related to war-making are obnoxious to the modern conscience. The point, however, is that the Maya, Aztecs, and Pueblo, like many other civilizations of antiquity, invested warfare with their deepest cosmological concerns. For these people, war was serious not just because human lives and the survival of their communities frequently hung in the balance. War was serious because cosmic issues were at stake, so it had to be tamed and bent to conform with cosmological ideas and their associated practices. At the very genesis of human communities, the initiation and waging of war were subject to constraint.

The human tendency to impose restrictions on armed conflict was evident during the European High Middle Ages, which became fertile soil for the growth of limitations on battle. Church councils legislated into canon law earlier proclamations that forbade armed conflict during prescribed times, a practice called the "Truce of God." It prohibited fighting on Lent at Advent and during the week between Thursday and Sunday. On the other hand, the "Peace of God" declared that knights were responsible for protecting not just the Church but also women, merchants, and civilians. Neither the "Truce of God" nor the "Peace of God" successfully shielded civilians from military attack, yet each asserted the distinction between combatants and noncombatants, a principle of discrimination that would much later become a centerpiece of international humanitarian law.[13]

The Church's restrictions on warfare were extended to types of weaponry. The Second Lateran Council in 1139 banned the crossbow and ballista, the "weapons of mass destruction" of their day, because these armor-piercing devices were considered too violent. By the 1300s, a body of customary law regulated the behavior of knights in peace and wartime. Formal military courts of chivalry tried cases of alleged violations. It would be a misinterpretation to discern in these courts a forerunner of modern humanitarian tribunals; sovereign authorities of European states convened them, and most of the cases dealt with matters remote from the concerns of our own era, like "treason" charged against a knight for betraying his liege. Nonetheless, the courts of chivalry developed a body of law, the *jus militare*, or law of the knights, which formed a body of customs and practices applied to resolve real-world cases. These chivalric customs and practices imposed a grammar of proper behavior on both the resort to war and its conduct.[14]

During the High Middle Ages, moreover, kings issued national laws that imposed restrictions on warfare. The first was King John's Constitutions of 1214, which broadened the class of protected persons in wartime to include not only the church but peasants and their property. King Richard II's Ordinances of 1385 banned robbery, plunder, and killing or capturing unarmed women and clergymen during battle. They also forbade contact with the pyx (the container for the Eucharist), for which the punishment was the same as for rape, namely hanging. Richard's Ordinances would later serve as the model for Henry V's Ordinances of War, decreed at Mantes in July 1419. The specific provisions of Richard II's Ordinances incorporated into Henry's Ordinances were the prohibition of rape, killing/capturing unarmed women and clergymen, and sacking churches.[15]

Arguably, the most advanced and prescient of Medieval restrictions on warfare was the French King Charles VII's Ordinance to Prevent Pillage and Abuses by Soldiers, which was issued at Orléans in November 1439. It recited numerous prohibitions, including plunder, imprisonment or ransoming civilians, and removal of livestock, carts, and tools. The Ordinance forbade the destruction of food and storage bins containing it, as well as the common practice of soldiers to extort payments from peasants by ransoming their produce. Further, it set forth an extraordinarily modern principle of command responsibility, according to which a captain was responsible not only for his subordinates' crimes but also for his own failure to punish them. Soldiers who witnessed such crimes yet failed to report them could be charged as accomplices. They would, in the words of the Ordinance, "be held responsible for the offence as accessories to it and . . . be punished in the same manner as the offenders."[16]

Ecclesiastical and royal limitations prepared the way for the most extraordinary early modern effort to restrict warfare, the Scottish Articles of 1643. In addition to the familiar condemnations of rape, murder, and plunder, the Scottish Articles required armies to pay for food they seized from locals. Soldiers were required to give quarter to a surrendering enemy (i.e., spare his life). The Scottish Articles adumbrated the Martens Clause of the 1899 and 1907 Hague Convention in their affirmation that matters not addressed in the Articles could be decided by the customary law of war and the "law of nature."[17]

By the early modern period, the ancient world's concern to align warfare with cosmic and natural processes had long since given way in the West to national laws and royal decrees imposed on the waging of war. Through the nineteenth century, a new set of constraints gradually emerged. European jurists began to think of limitations on warfare as enforceable not just at the level of the nation-state but increasingly through international law and convention. For the first time, nations signed multilateral treaties explicitly aiming to reduce the suffering of war. The First Geneva Convention of 1864 and the creation of the Red Cross, the Hague Conventions of 1899 and 1907, the Geneva Conventions of 1929 and 1949, and the anti-chemical weaponry conventions of the 1920s were responses to catastrophic wars that revealed the need for an international regulation of armed conflict. By 1945, the Allied victors were ready to assert the criminal responsibility of political and military leaders for violating international norms. Through the Charter written in London in the summer of 1945, the Allies established the first international tribunal to prosecute crimes against peace, war crimes, and crimes against humanity. The Charter insisted on the criminal responsibility of heads of state (Art. 7) and declared the superior orders defense inadmissible to excuse humanitarian offenses (Art. 8). By December 1945, the Allies ventured yet farther with the promulgation of Control Council Law No. 10, which created the legal basis for the subsequent national trials of Nazi offenders. Specifically, Law No. 10's definition of crimes against humanity, in contrast with the London Charter, freed the charge from its dependence on wartime conditions, meaning that such crimes might be prosecuted with or without a linkage to war.[18] A new era of accountability, flawed though it may have been, was dawning. We are living in this era today.

When we compare the stylized warfare of the ancient world with the law-based approaches of modernity, we might be inclined to deny much of a resemblance. Waging war following the seasons or the position of the stars would seem to be a far cry from war crimes trials. What could these seemingly disparate social practices have in common? I would suggest they have a great deal in common. Both the cosmic-based restrictions on war followed by ancient cultures and the legalistic approach characteristic of modernity have to do with constraints placed on the conduct of war. The word "constraint" is important for clarifying this affinity. The roots of the word go back to the fourteenth century when it initially meant "binding together" or "drawing tight." The forces that have bound together or drawn tight the violence of war have changed depending on the variables of time and place. In one era, it was a religious ritual. In another, it was the recouping of damages for injury done. In still others, it reaffirmed social class, "good order and discipline," or fair play. Today, the constraint on warfare has taken a decidedly legal turn, and its motive is humanitarian—that is, the aim in our time is to reduce the awful, gratuitous suffering and cruelties of war. Because the dominant constraint on war in our time is humanitarian, we may be tempted to believe that all prior limitations on battle were simply forerunners of our own. This assumption is untrue.

Nonetheless, the persistence of constraints on warfare gives us reasonable grounds for optimism. The doomsday weapons forged in anxious thoughtlessness—technologies that today include the superproduction of greenhouse gasses—now torment their inventors with the prospect of extinction. Their existence must elicit the capacity of human beings to moderate their behavior. Countering nihilism with self-restraint should become the most urgent task of our species.

The greatness of Nuremberg consists in its recognition of limitations. We tend to think of Nuremberg as a true innovation, as breaking with a history burdened with unchecked command authority and licentious power. In fact, seeing Nuremberg as a recognition of limitations reveals it not as a break with the past but as being in continuity with what has gone before. Nuremberg is a fulfillment of the age-old notion that warfare, itself an extreme activity, is nonetheless conditioned by behavioral norms. Ethics, morality, and law govern the waging of war just as they do other human actions.

The concept of limitation may be the most crucial discovery of the human mind. In the observation and enforcement of limits reside the keys to human survival and, indeed, the survival of life on our planet. For humankind has become not just the master of the earth; it has become the lord of all life and death. In human hands rests the power to destroy life that has existed here for over 500 million years. A 2019 United Nations assessment of global biodiversity announced that 1 million plant and animal species were under threat of extinction due to human activities, especially anthropogenic climate change. In the last century, a cascade of human factors—poaching, farming, logging, fishing, mining, and the release of carbon dioxide into the atmosphere—caused a decline of 20 percent in plants and animals worldwide. Journalist Brad Plumer writes in the *New York Times*:

> [T]he report warms of a looming extinction crisis, with extinction rates currently tens to hundreds of times higher than they have been in the past 10 million years. . . . Unless nations step up their efforts to protect what natural habitats are left, they could witness the disappearance of 40 percent of amphibian species, one-third of marine mammals, and one-third of reef-forming corals. More than 500,000 land species, the report said, do not have enough natural habitat left to ensure their long-term survival.[19]

For moral philosopher John Gray, the crux of the problem lies not with "global capitalism, industrialization, 'Western civilization' or any flaw in human institutions. It is a consequence of the evolutionary success of an exceptionally rapacious primate."[20] Gray calls the boundless, self-aggrandizing creature that humans have become *homo rapiens*, or "rapacious man."[21] The actions of this creature pose the main threat to life on Earth.

If we have become *homo rapiens*, we are not fated by our biology to remain so. We can overcome this rapacious avatar of our natures. As Gray himself concedes, "the Inuit and the Bushmen stumbled into ways of life in which their footprint was light."[22] Our challenge is to rediscover the means of rendering our footprints light. The capacity for drawing and enforcing limits is one such means. Without boundary-setting, *Homo sapiens* will scud toward self-destruction and, like Captain Ahab, take everything—his cause, his ship, his crew, himself—down with it. Standing in the shadows of Birkenau and Hiroshima, the architects of Nuremberg understood this. They grasped that, as Robert H. Jackson said in his opening address before the IMT, civilization must not ignore the Nazis' crimes "because it cannot survive their being repeated."[23] This is the message and warning of Nuremberg: in constraint and accountability lies life abundant, and in the denial of limits lurks universal death.

The genius of our species may not be abstract reasoning, as is so often supposed. Our genius may be self-restraint informed by the awareness that action without limits tends toward the annihilation of all life and all reason, of the thinker and the thought. The boundless, the rampant, the unconstrained all sweep forward into the death pit. Their signposts are Babi Yar and Belzec, Nagasaki and My Lai, Rwanda and Srebrenica. More recently, we can trace their spoor in Darfur, Bucha, and Kibbutz Re'im. The creators of Nuremberg saw where the trail of human action divorced from restraint leads: into the killing fields, the mass grave, and the crematorium.

Recognizing constraints may be a critical part of becoming a complete human being. The great novelists understood this; Joseph Conrad certainly did. His character in *Heart of Darkness*, the colonial agent Mr. Kurtz, falls into madness and genocide because of his inability or refusal to discipline his "monstrous passions." Conrad's protagonist, Marlowe, talks with Kurtz in his final moments and comes to realize that he

> had to deal with a being to whom I could not appeal in the name of anything high or low, I had…to invoke him—himself—his own exalted and incredible degradation. There was nothing either above or below him, and I knew it. He had kicked himself loose of the earth. Confound the man! He had kicked the very earth to pieces.[24]

Leo Tolstoy appreciated this as well: War and Peace is a story of excess and the calamity it produces . Tolstoy's Napoleon thinks of himself, much like Kurtz, as kicking the earth to pieces. In his egotistical self-regard, he is the hero acclaimed by Hegel as the "world-soul on horseback," a dominator who has led history toward greater heights. In reality, like all men lacking restraint, Napoleon is a fattened lamb being led to the slaughter.[25] Tolstoy writes of Napoleon as an unwitting pawn of forces beyond his ken in section 2 of the first epilogue of *War and Peace*. Here, the author compares him to a ram whom his companions envy for his special "genius." Like Napoleon or Alexander, the ram is seen within the herd as a master of fortune, vaulting heedlessly over the limits that restrain everyone else. The reality is that the farmer is preparing him for his dinner table:

> To a herd of rams, the ram the herdsman drives each evening into a special enclosure to feed, and that becomes twice as fat as the others, must seem to be a genius. And it must appear an astonishing conjunction of genius with a whole series of extraordinary chances that this ram, who instead of getting into the general fold every evening goes into a special enclosure where there are oats—that this very ram, swelling with fat, is killed for meat.[26]

Cormac McCarthy understood this, too, as he shows us in his novel *The Road*. The world through which McCarthy's father and son wander has been sand-blasted and charred by a technology run amok—Technē gone badly, disastrously wrong. Every limit has been violated, and Technē, no longer a stone tool gripped in the hand of a hominid crouching beside a Pleistocene Sea, has instead become the human race's suicide weapon.[27]

Religion has been a fecund source of constraints on warfare. American Protestant theologian Reinhold Niebuhr placed religion's insistence on constraint at the very center of his theology. For Niebuhr, human beings stand at the crossroads of nature and spirit. A creature of evolutionary descent, the human being bears the total weight of its animal origins, yet the human ability to transcend its animality pricks it with anxiety. To overcome this anxiety, the human being transgresses every limitation disrupting "the harmony of creation." Niebuhr writes:

> Man is insecure and involved in natural contingency; he seeks to overcome his insecurity by a will-to-power which overreaches the limits of human creatureliness.

> . . . Man is ignorant and involved in the limitations of finite mind; but he pretends he is not limited. He assumes he can gradually transcend finite limitation until his mind becomes identical with universal mind. All of his intellectual and cultural pursuits, therefore, become infected with the sin of pride. Man's pride and will-to-power disturb the harmony of creation. . . . The ego which falsely makes itself the center of existence in its pride and will-to-power inevitably subordinates other life to its will and thus does injustice to other life.[28]

Niebuhr's voice joined an ancient prophetic tradition that exhorted humans to accept their creatureliness and the limitations associated with finitude. One need not be Christian, nor even religious, to perceive wisdom in his counsel.

In a remarkable exchange of letters in 1932, Albert Einstein and Sigmund Freud pondered the evils of war and the ways to avoid them.[29] Both men agreed that only an international solution to preventing war would be effective. Ruling cliques at the level of the nation-state would impede the peaceful settlement of conflict. This being the case, an international body vested with superior authority to avoid war had to be instituted. The two men found additional common ground on the source of evil: they located it within the human heart. Writing about the success of "the ruling class" in shaping the minds of the common people, Einstein asked, "How is it these devices succeed so well in rousing men to such wild enthusiasm, even to sacrifice their lives? Only one answer is possible. Because man has within him the lust for hatred and destruction."[30] Freud concurred with Einstein and attached a name to this "lust for hatred and destruction," the "death drive." He wrote that the death drive was one of two human instincts, the other being eros, which "represent[s] life." The death drive, when turned outward, sought the destruction of the external other; when directed inward, it caused psychopathology. The death drive was fundamental to human nature. It could only be restrained through coercive international legal bodies but never wholly eliminated.[31]

Einstein's and Freud's critiques notwithstanding, the nation-state has, until today, been the primary enforcer of domestic and international law. Whether enforced nationally or internationally, modern humanitarian law demands restrictions on when war may be resorted to and how it may be fought. It does not claim to eliminate war's ugliness, tragedy, and violence; all these properties are as natural to war as heat is to the face of the sun. Instead, with moorings in the Nuremberg principles, humanitarian law accomplishes the rarest of all actions: it rescinds our species' pact with mass death. In its bid to annul this contract, it opens to us the promise of a gentler and finer world.

Notes

1 Mircea Eliade, *The Sacred and the Profane: The Nature of Religion* (New York: Harcourt, Brace & World, 1959), 35 ff.

2 Mircea Eliade, *A History of Religious Ideas: From the Stone Age to the Eleusinian Mysteries*, vol. 1 (Chicago, IL: The University of Chicago Press, 1978), 91; Colin

Renfrew, *Prehistory: The Making of the Human Mind* (London: The Folio Society, 2013), 174; Jan Assman, *Ma'at: Gerechtigkeit und Unsterblichkeit im Alten Ägypten* (Munich: Verlag C. H. Beck, 2006), 9–10.

3 Quoted in Amnon Altman, "Tracing the Earliest Recorded Concepts of International Law. (3) The Ancient Near East in the Old Babylonian Period (2000–1595 BCE)," *Journal of the History of International Law* 19, no. 1 (2008): 7.

4 Mark Edward Lewis, *Sanctioned Violence in Early China* (Albany, NY: SUNY Press, 1990), 22–25.

5 Quoted in Lewis, *Sanctioned Violence*, 24.

6 Lewis, *Sanctioned Violence*, 138 ff.

7 On the Indian law of war, see Michael Bryant, *A World History of War Crimes: From Antiquity to the Present* (London: Bloomsbury, 2021), 37–43.

8 On the Greek *koina nomina*, see Adriaan Lanni, "The Laws of War in Ancient Greece," *Law and History Review* 26, no. 3 (Fall 2008), 469–89; Yvon Garland, *War in the Ancient World: A Social History* (New York: W. W. Norton, 1975); Josiah Ober, "Classical Greek Times," in *The Laws of War: Constraints on Warfare in the Western World*, ed. M. Howard, G. J. Andreopoulos, and M. R. Shulman (New Haven, CT: Yale University Press, 1994), 12–26. On the Roman *jus ad bellum*, see Garlan, *War in the Ancient World*; John Rich, "Roman Rituals of War," in *The Oxford Handbook of Warfare in the Classical World*, ed. Brian Campbell and Lawrence A. Tritle (Oxford and New York: Oxford University Press, 2013), 542–68; Alan Watson, *International Law in Archaic Rome* (Baltimore, MD and London: The Johns Hopkins University Press, 1993), 1–10.

9 Linda Schele and David Freidel, *A Forest of Kings: The Untold Story of the Ancient Maya* (New York: William Morrow and Co., 1990), 65.

10 Nigel Davies, *The Aztecs* (London: Folio Society, 2000), 103–4, 184.

11 Adolf Bandelier, *Final Report of Investigations among the Indians of the Southwestern United States*, Part 1 (Boston, MA: Papers of the Archaeological Institute of America, American Series, No. 3, 1890), 153.

12 Leslie A. White, *The Pueblo of Santa Ana, New Mexico. Memoirs of the American Anthropological Association*, No. 43 (Menasha, WI: American Anthropological Association, 1942), 304.

13 Bryant, *World History of War Crimes*, 94–5.

14 Bryant, *World History of War Crimes*, 95; James A. Brundage, *The Crusades, Holy War, and Canon Law* (Lawrence, KS: Variorum, 1991), 78–9.

15 Theodore Meron, "Medieval and Renaissance Ordinances of War: Codifying Discipline and Humanity," in *War Crimes Law Comes of Age: Essays* (Oxford: Oxford University Press, 1998), 2.

16 Meron, "Medieval and Renaissance Ordinances of War," 7.

17 Meron, "Medieval and Renaissance Ordinances of War," 10.

18 Copies of the London Charter and Control Council Law #10 are reproduced in Michael S. Bryant, *Nazi Crimes and their Punishment 1943–1950: A Short History with Documents* (Indianapolis, IN and Cambridge: Hackett Publishing Co., Inc., 2020), 98–107.

19 Brad Plumer, "Report Details Global Shrink in Diversity, *New York Times*, May 7, 2019, A10.

20 John Gray, *Straw Dogs: Thoughts on Humans and Other Animals* (New York: Farrar, Straus and Giroux, 2002), 7.

21 Gray, *Straw Dogs*, 7.
22 Gray, *Straw Dogs*, 7. Gray is doubtful that modern humans can follow the example of the Bushmen and Inuit; their sheer numbers preclude it.
23 Robert H. Jackson, "Opening Address for the United States, November 21, 1945," in *The Nuremberg War Crimes Trial, 1945–46: A Brief History with Documents*, ed. Michael R. Marrus (Boston, MA: Bedford Books; New York: St. Martin's Press, 2018), 124.
24 Joseph Conrad, *Heart of Darkness* (London: Penguin Books, 1983), 107.
25 See the discussion of *War and Peace* in Isaiah Berlin, "The Hedgehog and the Fox: An Essay on Tolstoy's View of History," in *The Proper Study of Mankind: An Anthology of Essays*, ed. Henry Hardy and Roger Hausheer (New York: Farrar Straus and Giroux, 1998), 457.
26 Leo Tolstoy, *War and Peace*, trans. Louise and Aylmer Maude (Norwalk, CT: Easton Press, 1981), 953.
27 Cormac McCarthy, *The Road* (New York and Toronto: Vintage International, 2006). A recurrent theme of McCarthy's *oeuvre* is the monstrous effects of human grandiosity. See, for example, *No Country for Old Men*; *Blood Meridian*; and his final two novels, *The Passenger* and *Stella Maris*.
28 Reinhold Niebuhr, *The Nature and Destiny of Man: A Christian Interpretation*, vol. 1 (New York: Charles Scribner's Sons, 1953), 178–9.
29 Albert Einstein and Sigmund Freud, "Why Are There Wars?," in *The Many Faces of Evil: Historical Perspectives,* ed. Amélie Oksenberg Rorty (New York and London: Routledge, 2001), 253–64.
30 Einstein and Freud, "Why Are There Wars?," 255.
31 Einstein and Freud, "Why Are There Wars?," 261.

Selected Bibliography

Altman, Amnon. "Tracing the Earliest Recorded Concepts of International Law. (3) The Ancient Near East in the Old Babylonian Period (2000–1595 BCE)." *Journal of the History of International Law* 19, no. 1 (2008): 1–33.

Bandelier, Adolf. *Final Report of Investigations among the Indians of the Southwestern United States, Part 1.* Boston: Papers of the Archaeological Institute of America, American Series, No. 3, 1890.

Brundage, James A. *The Crusades, Holy War, and Canon Law*. Lawrence, KS: Variorum, 1991.

Bryant, Michael S. *Nazi Crimes and their Punishment 1943–1950: A Short History with Documents*. Indianapolis, IN and Cambridge: Hackett Publishing Co., Inc., 2020.

Bryant, Michael S. *A World History of War Crimes: From Antiquity to the Present*. London: Bloomsbury, 2021.

Davies, Nigel. *The Aztecs*. London: Folio Society, 2000.

Eliade, Mircea. *A History of Religious Ideas: From the Stone Age to the Eleusinian Mysteries*, vol. 1. New York: Harcourt, Brace & World, 1959.

Einstein, Albert, and Sigmund Freud. "Why are there wars?" In *The Many Faces of Evil: Historical Perspectives*, edited by Amélie Oksenberg Rorty, 253–64. New York and London: Routledge, 2001.

Gray, John. *Straw Dogs: Thoughts on Humans and Other Animals*. New York: Farrar, Straus, and Giroux, 2002.

Lanni, Adriaan. "The Laws of War in Ancient Greece." *Law and History Review* 26, no. 3 (Fall 2008): 469–89.

Lewis, Mark Edward. *Sanctioned Violence in Early China*. Albany, NY: SUNY Press, 1990.

Meron, Theodore. "Medieval and Renaissance Ordinances of War: Codifying Discipline and Humanity." In *War Crimes Law Comes of Age: Essays*, edited by Theodore Meron, 1–10. Oxford: Oxford University Press, 1998.

Ober, Josiah. "Classical Greek Times." In *The Laws of War: Constraints on Warfare in the Western World*, edited by M. Howard, G. J. Andreopoulos, and M. R. Shulman, 12–26. New Haven, CT: Yale University Press, 1994.

Plumer, Brad. "Report Details Global Shrink in Diversity." *New York Times*, May 7, 2019. https://www.nytimes.com/2019/05/06/climate/humans-are-speeding-extinction-and-altering-the-natural-world-at-an-unprecedented-pace.html.

Rich, John. "Roman Rituals of War." In *The Oxford Handbook of Warfare in the Classical World*, edited by Brian Campbell and Lawrence A. Tritle, 542–68. Oxford and New York: Oxford University Press, 2013.

Schele, Linda, and David Freidel, *A Forest of Kings: The Untold Story of the Ancient Maya*. New York: William Morrow and Co., 1990.

Watson, Alan. *International Law in Archaic Rome*. Baltimore, MD and London: The Johns Hopkins University Press, 1993.

14

The Unlawful Transfer and Deportation of Children

Noëlle Quénivet

The conflict between Russia and Ukraine has not spared Ukrainian children. They have not only been direct victims of armed attacks, used as human shields by Russian forces and recruited in the armed forces of Russia, but also essential services (e.g., education and health care) for them have been destroyed. In areas occupied by Russian armed forces, some have been unlawfully confined in inhumane conditions or have suffered from sexual violence. These violations of international humanitarian law (IHL) are all too often prevalent in modern armed conflicts. One such violation that is less commonplace is the transfer and deportation of children from conflict zones and occupied territories. As Mark Kersten states, "The scale of efforts to abduct and transfer children from Ukraine to Russia is staggering."[1]

In April 2022, Ukraine's Commissioner for Human Rights claimed that children had been taken by force by Russia.[2] Two years on, the fact that children have been relocated to either Russian or Ukrainian territory under Russian occupation is not only well-established but also uncontested by both Ukraine and Russia.[3] Depending on sources, it is estimated that between 150,000 and 740,000 Ukrainian children are in Russia.[4] The practice of forcible transfer and deportation of children has been widely condemned by the United Nations Committee on the Rights of the Child,[5] the Parliamentary Assembly of the Council of Europe,[6] the OSCE,[7] the European Union,[8] the United States,[9] etc.

The transfer and deportation of children has been classed as a war crime, a crime against humanity, and an act of genocide. This chapter will demonstrate that such conduct[10] amounts to a violation of IHL. It starts by retracing the process whereby Ukrainian children were transferred onto Russian (occupied) territory, then presents the applicable legal framework, and then provides an in-depth analysis of the unlawful transfer and deportation of Ukrainian children.

The Transfer and Deportation of Children

From the early inception of the 2022 conflict, massive civilian deportations were taking place from the Ukrainian-occupied territories of Donbas and Luhansk toward Russia.[11] Among them were alleged orphans officially transferred to Russia on the basis that the breakaway republics had given their consent.[12] Ukraine's Commissioner for Human Rights alerted various official bodies, but this practice continued unabated without much success. It emerged that these children essentially came from two groups: children who had been separated from their parents and children from orphanages and other institutions. In both cases, no attempt was made by the Russian authorities to find the parents or guardians.

Later reports highlighted four categories of children who had been removed from Ukraine: (1) so-called "children of war," that is, children who lost (perhaps temporarily) their parents and were collected by Russian authorities, (2) children separated from their parents following the detention of and thus separation from them at filtration camps,[13] (3) children in institutions (e.g., orphanages, boarding schools, and hospitals) who were systematically displaced by the Russian authorities, and (4) children in occupied territories sent on vacation in Crimea or Russia but who, after the agreed recreation period, were not returned to their legal guardians.[14] Most of these children have close relatives or other legal guardians in Ukraine.[15] A lack of information compounds the complexity of the situation on the ground, the shame that some parents carry for having allowed their children to be sent to Russia or for having placed them in institutions, and so on.

The breadth and depth of the issue are revealed by the wide range of officials involved in the "operational as well as political implementation of Russia's child deportation [. . .] programme."[16] The transfers were coordinated by Russian officials and the local authorities[17] and "[t]he system of camps and adoptions [. . .] appears to be authorized and coordinated at the highest levels of Russia's federal government."[18] Moreover, the organized and systematic nature of the conduct and the fact that operations were conducted similarly over time and across different regions tend to show that these acts were "neither random nor unplanned."[19]

To support its actions, the Russian Federation passed several laws and regulations facilitating the transfer and assimilation of such children in Russia,[20] including an amendment to presidential decrees simplifying the procedure for Ukrainian children without parental care to obtain Russian nationality[21] and, in 2023, a law enabling the withdrawal of Ukrainian citizenship from children under the age of 14 years.[22] Two reasons for loosening the rules regulating Russian nationality were that the conferral of Russian nationality allowed for temporary custody to become permanent[23] and ensured access to social guarantees[24] in the form of medical insurance, health care, etc., thereby encouraging potential adoptive and foster parents to take these children. Financial incentives were also used to boost the number of adoptive families.[25]

All this indicates that should the conduct be found in violation of IHL, Russia can be held responsible.

Applicable Legal Framework

Since (at least) February 24, 2022, Ukraine and Russia have been involved in an international armed conflict under Common Article 2 GCs[26] thus triggering the applicability of the Geneva Conventions and Additional Protocol I.[27] The territorial, personal, and temporal scopes of their application need careful consideration.

Concerning the territorial scope of application of IHL, it applies to the entire territory of both parties to the conflict to the extent that such activities relate to the armed conflict. As the OSCE report stresses, "Ukrainian children brought to Russia in relation to the armed conflict are protected by IHL in the entire territory of the Russian Federation."[28] Specific rules also apply to occupied territories. Under IHL, a "territory is considered occupied when it is actually placed under the authority of the hostile army. The occupation extends only to the territory where such authority has been established and can be exercised."[29] Accordingly, Crimea is a territory occupied by Russia since 2014. At least since the incorporation of the territories of Donetsk and Luhansk into Russia, they are occupied territories. Moreover, as soon as the Russian armed forces can exercise authority over a territory, it is deemed occupied.[30] At this point, it should be noted under IHL the occupying party does not acquire sovereignty over the territory. The fact that the occupying power, that is, Russia, unilaterally annexes all or part of an occupied territory or make changes "into the institutions or government of the said territory"[31] does not deprive the protected persons of the benefits of the Geneva Convention IV.[32]

The personal scope of application of IHL covers all persons affected by the armed conflict on the territory of the parties to the conflict. Once civilians, including children, fall within the hands of the enemy, they are considered "protected persons" under GCIV.[33] Although this seems limited to occupied territories, there is no requirement to prove that the occupying power has actual authority as long as the individuals have fallen into the hands of the Occupying Power.[34] Resultantly, Ukrainian but not Russian children[35] are covered. API states that "children shall be the object of special respect [. . .] Parties to the conflict shall provide them with the care and aid they require."[36] Further, under Article 8 GCIV, individuals are not allowed to renounce their rights, and thus, a change of nationality does not mean that Ukrainian children have lost the benefit of the protection under IHL.[37] Accordingly, even though the hostilities might have ceased, those with a protective status under IHL will keep such status and "benefit from the relevant provisions of the Conventions and Protocols until their final release, repatriation or reestablishment."[38] This means that Ukrainian children transferred to Russia or Russian-occupied territories are still under the protection of IHL until returned or repatriated. Likewise, IHL applies to those separated from their parents until reunified with their families.[39]

As for the temporal scope of application of IHL, its application starts from the moment the conflict starts, though it also extends to some activities before the conflict, provided they are concerned with military operations.[40] This accordingly offers protection to Ukrainian children evacuated from zones that were under impending military offensive.[41]

The Prohibition of Transfer and Deportation and Specific Rules for Children

During the war, the civilian population is ineluctably displaced, willingly or unwillingly. While IHL recognizes this, it has also set boundaries to avoid the forceful (i.e., intended)[42] relocation or transfer of the civilian population. Some of these rules apply in occupied territories, others in any territory that belongs to the parties to the conflict. Moreover, while some apply to the civilian population generally, others address the specific situation of children.

Article 49 GCIV bans the deportation and forcible transfer of protected persons from occupied territory to the territory of the Occupying Power or another country. This provision aims at preventing the kind of deportations seen in the Second World War,[43] which led to the displacement and eventual destruction of entire communities. More generally, "[t]he prohibition against forcible displacements aims at safeguarding the right and aspiration of individuals to live in their communities and homes without outside interference."[44] Conventionally, while deportation denotes displacement across a border, forcible transfer takes place within national boundaries.[45] This prohibition is of a customary nature.[46] The case law has expanded the applicability of such prohibition to deportation from any territory, thus delinking it from the exigency of the violation starting in an occupied territory.[47] All kinds of transfers or deportations are banned "regardless of their motive."[48] Except for the provisions found in the GCs and API, nothing might justify the forcible transfer or deportation of protected persons in occupied territory.[49] The destination of the transfer or deportation is irrelevant, too.[50]

Owing to their inherent vulnerability, children benefit from specific protection in armed conflict.[51] "The purpose of these rules is to protect children from the scourges and scars of war, to shield their families from the scare and grief of loss, and to guard each belligerent party to the armed conflict and their populations against the unbearable prospect of losing their future generations, either to the war itself or to the enemy belligerent."[52] While the GCs are dotted with provisions offering such protection, API states in clear terms that "children shall be the object of special respect [. . .] Parties to the conflict shall provide them with the care and aid they require, whether because of their age or for any other reason."

Consensual Transfer and Relocation

Falling outside the scope of Article 49 GCIV is consensual transfer or relocation since the act is not *forcible*. As the Commentary points out, some protected persons "might [. . .] wish to leave the country."[53] Undoubtedly, the question is what qualifies as "forcible." The case law of the ICTY specifies that the test is whether the civilians had a "genuine choice"[54] in light of the relevant factual circumstances.[55] An additional issue is that while adults can express their consent to be relocated, this is not so concerning children whose parents or legal guardians must consent on their behalf.

Concerning the situation in Ukraine, two issues, that of "consent" and "genuineness" must be raised. First, it is the parent or the legal guardian who must consent to the transfer. The 2022 OSCE report notes that children were transferred from orphanages and institutions, and no attempt was made to find their parents, relatives, or legal guardians,[56] despite the fact that very few of these children lacked legal guardianship.[57] In other instances, consent was obtained from the directors of such facilities, although they were not authorized to do so.[58] In contrast, most children in recreation camps were sent with the consent of their parents.[59] Yet, consent was only obtained for an agreed period of stay, so the prolonged stay, without further consent, amounts to forcible transfer or deportation.[60]

Second, the "genuineness" of such transfers ought to be assessed. The ICTY explained that genuine choice means no threatening or intimidating acts are aimed at depriving the civilian population of exercising its free will.[61] Accordingly, taking advantage of a coercive environment will turn the transfer into a forcible one.[62] Thus, the transfer of a population going through a filtration camp set up by the Russian authorities is not consensual.[63] The broader issue of an atmosphere of assimilation and propaganda, especially in occupied territories, to which Ukrainian nationals have been subjected, must be emphasized as well. It is clear, "Russia's intense national and international propaganda campaigns, its multivariate war [. . .] against Ukraine, its terroristic occupation as well as the bombardment of Ukrainian territories, and its child as well as adult education programmes are designed to generate expressions of consent."[64] How genuine the opinions expressed by Ukrainians under occupation or those already transferred to Russia are is difficult to determine. Regarding the children sent to recreation camps more specifically, it seems that the Russian authorities used "the vulnerable position of the parents, their desire to protect the children from shelling and the difficulties of life in the occupied territory, misleading them about the nature and duration of the so-called 'vacation.'"[65] Consent in such cases might not be meaningful and genuine.

Overall, it is unlikely that the acts fall outside the purview of the ban on *forcible* transfer or deportation.

Evacuation

Article 49 para 2 GCIV contains the only exception to the absolute prohibition of forcible transfer and deportation, that of an area's total or partial evacuation. Yet, such evacuations are strictly regulated: they must be justified and temporary, there is a strong presumption against evacuations outside of the occupied territory, consent of the parents or legal guardians must be sought, and specific rules apply to children who have been evacuated or transferred. To put it bluntly, most of these rules have been violated by Russia.[66]

Article 49 para 2 GCIV specifies the conditions under which transfers or deportations are allowed: first, the justifications are limited to "the security of the population or imperative military reasons so demand."[67] Second, transfers must take place within the occupied territory unless "material reasons make it impossible to avoid"[68] transfers outside of that territory, and third, there is an obligation to allow the population to return "as soon as hostilities in the area in question have ceased."[69] Rule 129 of the ICRC Study on CIHL and the Guiding Principles on Internal Displacement[70] reiterate the former by specifying "unless the security of the civilians involved or imperative military reasons so demand."[71]

The classic example of lawful displacement is to clear a combat zone[72] which is connected to the IHL principle of precautions.[73] Shortly before Russia attacked Ukraine in 2022, a large number of the civilian population of the occupied territories of Donetsk and Luhansk moved to Russian territory. Russia specifically indicated that it was evacuating the population "from dangerous regions," that is, for security reasons,[74] an argument it also used concerning civilians in temporarily occupied territories who were moved to Crimea or Russia.[75] The evacuation of children from institutions in the initial phase of the invasion, as well as those in active combat theatre, can, to some extent, be justified on this ground.[76]

Article 78(1) API allows for the non-consensual temporary evacuation of children[77] for three additional reasons: health, medical treatment, and safety,[78] the last one not being applicable in the situation of children in occupied territories.[79] The three reasons are exhaustive because, as the Commentary explains,

> evacuations have been carried out for other reasons, for example, to educate children according to certain political or religious views, or to prepare them to serve in the armed forces of a State. Sometimes, they have been carried out in conditions such as to result in the children losing their identity or being raised in a manner foreign to that of their family or their country.[80]

Sadly, this rings true of the situation of Ukrainian children transferred to Russia.[81]

Besides being justified under IHL, the evacuation must be temporary to remain lawful.[82] The 2023 OSCE report exemplifies a breach of this rule in the case of medical evacuations, which, while initially lawful, became unlawful as the children moved to the territory of the Occupying Power were kept there "for reasons unrelated to the medical treatment."[83] Likewise, Ukrainian children from institutions who were evacuated because of impending hostilities were further moved from occupied Crimea to Russia without justification.[84] Also, children were "moved among various camps, without the consent of (and the information being sent to) their parents or legal guardians."[85] This tends to show that such evacuations were relied on for ulterior motives.

Both Articles 49 GCIV and 78 API also contain a strong presumption against evacuations outside of the occupied territory. The OSCE has documented several instances whereby children were moved not only outside of the occupied territory to another occupied territory but also to the territory of the Occupying Power.[86] In case of evacuation, the Occupying Power must "to the greatest practicable extent" ensure "that members of the same family are not separated."[87] As Vité explains, "international humanitarian law seeks first to prevent family separation."[88] Likewise, the Commentary to Article 78 API emphasizes that "everything possible should be done to avoid separating children (especially young children) from their natural protectors."[89]

While Article 49 GCIV does not indicate the procedure to be followed in case families cannot be evacuated together, Article 78 API specifies that "[w]here the parents or legal guardians can be found, their written consent to such evacuation is required. If these persons cannot be found, the written consent to such evacuation of the persons who by law or custom are primarily responsible for the care of the children is required."[90] The wording includes a broader set of individuals whose consent should be sought,[91] and thus, directors of institutions could fall within the scope of relevant persons, an interpretation supported by the Commentary, which avows that a child "may be left to reception centres."[92] This means that evacuations with the consent of such individuals are lawful. Yet, again, the consent would need to be genuine, a question already raised earlier as being somewhat problematic.

Particular attention is paid to children's needs as Article 78(2) API specifies that in cases of evacuations, "each child's education, including his religious and moral education as his parents desire, shall be provided while he is away with the greatest possible continuity."[93] Such responsibility seems to lie both in the state carrying out the evacuation, that is, Russia, and in the receiving country, that is, Russia and Belarus. The Commentary expressly states that "indoctrination must be prohibited."[94] Several reports indicate that Ukrainian children were not given the opportunity to be educated in the Ukrainian language or follow the Ukrainian school curriculum. On the contrary, it does not appear that Russia complied with the "all possible measures should be taken" wording of the Commentary.[95] The practice of "Russification" is widespread and systematic: children undergo indoctrination courses that advance nationalist messaging on the politics, military accomplishments, culture, and history of Russia[96] and denigrate the Ukrainian language, culture, and history.[97] Some reports also claim that Ukrainian children are undergoing military training to be recruited into the Russian armed forces.[98]

More generally, the displacement must be carried out so as to facilitate reunification with families,[99] and so it is imperative that children, should they be separated from their parents or legal guardians, are properly identified. For transfers and deportations under Article 49 GCIV, a duty to identify them is enshrined in Article 24 para 3 GCIV. As for evacuations under Article 78 API, the third paragraph mandates the parties arranging for the evacuation and the receiving country to "establish for each child a card [with specific information] with photographs, which they shall send to the Central Tracing Agency of the International Committee of the Red Cross." Unfortunately, "[t]o date, there is no available evidence to indicate that these identification cards have been issued to Ukrainian children or that the ICRC has been informed."[100]

Return and Reunification

In addition to the unlawful transfer and deportation of children, Russia has been widely condemned for failing to return these children and re-establish contact with their families.[101] Two specific issues warrant attention: first, the delay in returning children to their homes, and second, family reunification being prevented by an array of unlawful measures, all reinforcing the claim of the unlawful forcible displacement of Ukrainian children.

Article 49 para 2 GCIV mandates the return of displaced civilians in the context of evacuations in situations of occupation "as soon as hostilities in the area in question have ceased."[102] Since this legal provision includes the possibility of forcible transfer outside the occupied territory, the right of return is also applicable to such a situation and, *a fortiori*, to unlawful displacement.[103] Rule 132 of the ICRC Study on CIHL summarizes this obligation well: "Displaced persons have a right to voluntary return in safety to their homes or places of habitual residence as soon as the reasons for their displacement cease to exist."[104] Article 49 para 2 GCIV states that civilians must "be transferred back to their homes."[105]

Concerning the evacuation of children under Article 78 API, the Commentary spells out that once the justifications (health, medical treatment, and safety) for the evacuation have disappeared, children should be returned.[106] The Guidelines for the Alternative Care of Children specify that when children are evacuated, "a clear return plan should be established."[107] Denying the possibility to return as soon as possible is viewed as an indication of the unlawfulness of the displacement,[108] and a displacement that becomes permanent is considered an IHL violation. In many instances, the delays in the repatriation of children are unjustified.[109] As explained earlier, Russia has, instead of returning children to their homes, transferred them to further places[110] when it should have returned them to their homes or, if not possible, because of active hostilities, other parts of Ukraine or at least a neutral country. In fact, Article 133 GCIV encourages parties to the conflict to conclude agreements for the return, repatriation, or accommodation in a neutral party, of transferred children. Interestingly, it is in this provision that a solution to the current issue might be found: children transferred to Russia could be handed over to a neutral state that would take care of them.

Furthermore, Article 74 API requires all parties involved in the conflict to facilitate the reunion of families separated because of the armed conflict. As Bisset recalls, "the need to maintain and reinstate family unity is a central theme in Geneva Convention IV."[111] This includes a positive, that is, the parties should enable communication between the members of the family,[112] and a negative, that is, the parties should ensure that reunification is made possible by notably avoiding prolonged separation and refraining from assimilation in a different culture, duty.

In addition to Article 78(3) API, which obliges a detailed identification card for each transferred child to be completed and sent to the ICRC, Article 50 para 2 GC IV obliges the Occupying Power "to facilitate the identification of children and the registration of their parentage." This is all carried out with the view to facilitating family reunification.[113] This has not been carried out and thus made reunification extremely difficult. Several reports pinpoint that Russia has failed to set up a mechanism to trace Ukrainian children, communicate their location to Ukraine, and assist in their family reunification.[114] Russia has also actively prevented family reunions: children have been spread across the Russian territory,[115] do not know where they are or how to contact their families, or are falsely informed that their parents have died,[116] all of this leading to prolonged family separations.[117] Families have also faced unfounded logistical hurdles at variance with the obligation to facilitate reunification.[118]

A more worrying point is that Russia has actively prevented the reunification of families by changing the nationality of Ukrainian children, indoctrinating them, placing them in foster homes, and putting them up for adoption, thereby rendering family reunification nearly impossible: "the Russian Federation often forces Russian citizenship on them, which also leads to violation of the children's right to identity and promotes illegal adoptions of Ukrainian children by Russian families."[119] It should be remembered that under IHL, occupation is, per se, a situation of a temporary nature. According to Article 50 para 2 GCIV, the Occupying Power cannot in any circumstances change the personal status of children, including their nationality. Bearing in mind that genuine evacuation is also temporary, any alteration of personal status that has long-term effects violates IHL. A combination of elements, including the simplified procedure for the adoption of Russian citizenship, the "russification" of the occupied territories,[120] and the benefits gained by having Russian nationality, has led to Ukrainian children acquiring, often without being consulted, Russian nationality. In some instances, the children's names have been changed,[121] thus further increasing the difficulty of tracing them and so reuniting them with their families. The "re-education" of children, especially those in so-called recreation centers, and the assimilation with Russian culture, accompanied by a denigration of Ukrainian culture, further impedes family reunification. There is no doubt that "[t]he passage of time will inevitably weaken those children's links with their families and complicate their eventual reunification."[122]

Under Russian Law, there are, in addition to children placed under supervision in organizations, three types of family placement: adoption, the foster family, and custody, and guardianship.[123] While the Guidelines for the Alternative Care of Children recommend that children be cared for as a priority in family-based settings rather than in residential care, which is considered as a temporary measure, it also stresses that the state should "make cooperation with family tracing and reintegration efforts mandatory."[124] Adoption should only be envisaged when family reintegration proves impossible or is deemed contrary to the best interests of the child.[125] In the case of Ukrainian children, Russia has actively prevented family reunification, and it would be in the children's best interests to be reunited with their parents. The problem of adoption is compounded by the fact that "it may entail the change of the name, surname and the date and place of birth of the child [and] [. . .] is guided by the principle of secrecy, due to which there is not, and there cannot be, any database of adopted children."[126] The permanent integration of Ukrainian children into Russian families or institutions is not only a violation of IHL but also a confirmation that the Ukrainian children were victims of deportation under Article 49 GCIV.[127]

In sum, altering the nationality of Ukrainian children and facilitating their placement in foster homes or adoption families is in contravention of IHL.

Conclusion

The transfer and deportation of Ukrainian children, the rushed housing and adoption of children, and the prolonged custody of children without permitting contact with families are all violations or signs that confirm the violations of IHL by Russia. Parental consent was not sought, and when it was, it was eventually circumvented. The political indoctrination of such children and their being granted Russian nationality further support the view that such transfers and deportations were not conducted according to IHL, even more so as they have made family reunification extremely difficult, if not impossible, and are thus in contravention of IHL. The scale and systematicity of the conduct reveal a much darker objective behind the "evacuation" of the Ukrainian children.

It is thus not surprising that the first two arrest warrants issued by the International Criminal Court were against Vladimir Putin, president of the Russian Federation and Maria Lvova-Belova, commissioner for Children's Rights in the Office of the President of the Russian Federation for the war crimes of "unlawful deportation of population (children) and [. . .] unlawful transfer of population (children) from occupied areas of Ukraine to the Russian Federation (under articles 8(2)(a)(vii) and 8(2)(b)(viii) of the Rome Statute)."[128]

Notes

1 Mark Kersten, "Why Did the International Criminal Court Focus on the Transfer and Deportation of Children from Ukraine to Russia?", *Justice in Conflict*, March 21, 2023, https://www.proquest.com/docview/2788604956/citation/604AE260219846A3PQ/1.
2 Yulia Ioffe and Andreas Umland, "Forcible Transfer and Deportation of Ukrainian Children: Responses and Accountability Measures," January 2024, 34.
3 OSCE, "Report on Violations and Abuses of International Humanitarian and Human Rights Law, War Crimes and Crimes Against Humanity, Related to the Forcible Transfer and/or Deportation of Ukrainian Children to the Russian Federation," May 4, 2023, 12.
4 OSCE, 12. See also Ioffe and Umland, "Forcible Transfer and Deportation," 53. Parliamentary Assembly of the Council of Europe, "Deportations and Forcible Transfers of Ukrainian Children and Other Civilians to the Russian Federation or to Temporarily Occupied Ukrainian Territories: Create Conditions for Their Safe Return, Stop These Crimes and Punish the Perpetrators," Resolution 2495 (2023), para. 5.
5 Committee on the Rights of the Child, "Concluding Observations on the Combined Sixth and Seventh Periodic Reports of the Russian Federation," March 1, 2024, paras. 45–6.
6 Parliamentary Assembly of the Council of Europe, "Deportations and Forcible Transfers," para. 2.
7 OSCE, "Forcible Transfer and/or Deportation," 45–6.

8 European Parliament of the European Union, "Human Rights Violations in the Context of Forced Deportation of Ukrainian Civilians to and Forced Adoption of Ukrainian Children in Russia," P9_TA(2002)0320, September 15, 2022, https://eur-lex.europa.eu/legal-content/EN/TXT/PDF/?uri=CELEX:52022IP0320.

9 Resolution Condemning the Illegal Abduction of Children from Ukraine to the Russian Federation, H. RES. 149, *Congressional Record,* Vol. 170, No. 48, March 19, 2024.

10 This paper only covers events around and after February 24, 2022, until April 2024.

11 OSCE, "Forcible Transfer and/or Deportation," 19.

12 Ioffe and Umland, "Forcible Transfer and Deportation," 32. See also OSCE, "Forcible Transfer and/or Deportation," 19; Kaveh Khoshnood, Nathaniel Raymond, and Caitlin Howarth, "Russia's Systematic Program for the Re-Education and Adoption of Ukraine's Children" (New Haven, CT: Humanitarian Research Lab at Yale School of Public Health, February 14, 2023), 11.

13 Ukrainians leaving combat zones are often unable to flee into Ukrainian-held territory. To enter Russia or Russian-occupied territories, they have to undergo filtration which is a process whereby the Russian authorities interrogate them to establish whether they are involved in combat activities and/or are a threat to the security of the Russian state.

14 See also Ioffe and Umland, "Forcible Transfer and Deportation," 30; Council of Europe Commissioner for Human Rights, "Urgent Action Needed to Reunite Ukrainian Children Transferred to Russia and Russian-Occupied Territories with Their Families," Press Release, March 6, 2023.

15 Ioffe and Umland, "Forcible Transfer and Deportation," 28.

16 Ioffe and Umland, 33; Parliamentary Assembly of the Council of Europe, "Deportations and Forcible Transfers," para. 4.

17 Khoshnood, Raymond, and Howarth, "Russia's Systematic Program," 6.

18 Khoshnood, Raymond, and Howarth, 17.

19 Parliamentary Assembly of the Council of Europe, "Deportations and Forcible Transfers," para. 8.

20 Ioffe and Umland, "Forcible Transfer and Deportation," 32.

21 OSCE, "Forcible Transfer and/or Deportation," 19.

22 OSCE, 20. See also Committee on the Rights of the Child, "Concluding Observations," para. 45(c) and (d) and 46(e).

23 See OSCE, "Forcible Transfer and/or Deportation," 20.

24 Ioffe and Umland, "Forcible Transfer and Deportation," 33.

25 OSCE, "Forcible Transfer and/or Deportation," 20.

26 Convention for the Amelioration of the Condition of the Wounded and Sick in Armed Forces in the Field 1949, 75 UNTS 31 (GCI); Convention for the Amelioration of the Condition of the Wounded, Sick and Shipwrecked Members of the Armed Forces at Sea 1949, 75 UNTS 85 (GCII); Geneva Convention Relative to the Treatment of Prisoners of War, 75 UNTS 135 (GCIII); Geneva Convention Relative to the Protection of Civilian Persons in Time of War 1949, 75 UNTS 287 (GCIV).

27 Protocol Additional to the Geneva Conventions of 12 August 1949, and Relating to the Protection of Victims of International Armed Conflicts, 1125 UNTS 3 (API).

28 OSCE, "Forcible Transfer and/or Deportation," 24.

29 Hague Convention (IV) of 1907, Respecting the Laws and Customs of War on Land and its Annex: Regulations Concerning the Laws and Customs of War on Land, art. 42
30 OSCE, "Forcible Transfer and/or Deportation," 25.
31 Art. 47 GCIV.
32 Art. 47 GCIV.
33 GCIV, arts. 4(1) and (2). Alison Bisset, "Russia's Forcible Transfer of Children," *Lieber Institute West Point*, October 5, 2022, https://lieber.westpoint.edu/russias-forcible-transfer-children/.
34 ICTY, Prosecutor v. Naletilić and Martinović, IT-98-34-T, Judgment, Trial Chamber, March 31, 2003, para. 221.
35 Art. 49 GCIV.
36 Art. 77(1) API.
37 Art. 8 GCIV.
38 Art. 6(4) GCIV and art. 3(b) API.
39 OSCE, "Forcible Transfer and/or Deportation," 24.
40 Art. 57(4) and 58(a) API and art. 17 GCIV.
41 OSCE, "Forcible Transfer and/or Deportation," 24.
42 ICTY, Prosecutor v Gotovina and Markač, IT-06-90-A, Judgment, November 16, 2012, paras. 96 and 114.
43 Jean Pictet, ed., *Commentary on the Geneva Conventions of 12 August 1949: IV Geneva Convention Relative to the Protection of Civilian Persons in Time of War* (Geneva: International Committee of the Red Cross, 1958), 278.
44 ICTY, Prosecutor v. Krnojelac, IT-97-25-A, Appeal Judgement, September 17, 2003, para. 218.
45 Jean-Marie Henckaerts, "Deportation and Transfer of Civilians in Time of W Er of Civilians in Time of War," *Vanderbilt Journal of Transnational Law* 26, no. 3 (1993): 472. See also ICTY, Prosecutor v Naletilić and Martinović, para. 670.
46 Nuremberg Military Tribunals, Case of the United States of America v Erhard Milch, April 17, 1947, p. 789, and Rule 129 of the ICRC Study on Customary International Humanitarian Law.
47 ICTY, Prosecutor v Gotovina, Čermak and Markač, IT-06-90-PT, Decision on Several Motions Challenging Jurisdiction, March 19, 2007, para. 55. See also Ken Roberts and James G. Stewart, "Delimiting Deportation, Unlawful Transfer, Forcible Transfer and Forcible Displacement in International Criminal Law: A Jurisprudential History," *African Journal of International Criminal Justice* 5, no. 1 (2019): 68.
48 Art. 45 GCIV.
49 Pictet, *Commentary on the Geneva Conventions*, 279.
50 Vincent Chetail, "Is There Any Blood on My Hands? Deportation as a Crime of International Law," *Leiden Journal of International Law* 29, no. 3 (2016): 921.
51 Sylvain Vité, "Protecting Children during Armed Conflict: International Humanitarian Law," *Human Rights & International Legal Discourse* 5, no. 1 (2011): 19.
52 OSCE, "Forcible Transfer and/or Deportation," 22.
53 Pictet, *Commentary on the Geneva Conventions*, 279.
54 ICTY, Prosecutor v. Naletilić and Martinović, para. 519.

55 ICTY, Prosecutor v. Krnojelac, para. 229.
56 OSCE, "Report on Violations of International Humanitarian and Human Rights Law, War Crimes and Crimes Against Humanity Committed in Ukraine (April 1–June 25, 2022)," July 14, 2022, 95.
57 Ioffe and Umland, "Forcible Transfer and Deportation," 30. See also Khoshnood, Raymond, and Howarth, "Russia's Systematic Program," 11.
58 OSCE, "Forcible Transfer and/or Deportation", 33.
59 OSCE, 34.
60 See OSCE, 34.
61 ICTY, Prosecutor v. Simić, Tadić and Zarić, IT-95-9-T, Judgment, October 17, 2003, para. 126.
62 ICTY, Prosecutor v. Karadžić, IT-95-5/18-T, Judgment, March 24, 2016, paras. 488–90.
63 OSCE, "Forcible Transfer and/or Deportation," 35–6.
64 Ioffe and Umland, "Forcible Transfer and Deportation," 29.
65 OSCE, "Forcible Transfer and/or Deportation," 34. See also Khoshnood, Raymond, and Howarth, "Russia's Systematic Program," 11 and 13–14.
66 Parliamentary Assembly of the Council of Europe, "Humanitarian Consequences and Internal and External Displacement in Connection with the Aggression of the Russian Federation against Ukraine," Resolution 2448 (2022), para. 2; Parliamentary Assembly of the Council of Europe, "Legal and Human Rights Aspects of the Russian Federation's Aggression against Ukraine," Resolution 2482 (2023), para. 20.5; United Nations Human Rights Council, "Conference Room Paper of the Independent International Commission of Inquiry on Ukraine," August 29, 2023, para. 721.
67 Art. 49 para 2 GCIV.
68 Art. 49 para 2 GCIV.
69 Art. 49 para 2 GCIV.
70 United Nations Commission on Human Rights, "Guiding Principles of Internal Displacement," E/CN.4/1998/53/Add.2 (1998), art. 6(2)(b).
71 Rule 129 of the ICRC Study on CIHL and Guiding Principles of Internal Displacement, art. 6(2)(b).
72 See explanation in Rule 129 of the ICRC Study on CIHL.
73 Art. 58(a) and (c) API. It should be noted that Article 58(a) API expressly states that such action should not be in violation of Article 49 GCIV.
74 OSCE, "Forcible Transfer and/or Deportation," 15.
75 OSCE, 15.
76 OSCE, 37–9.
77 Yves Sandoz, Christophe Swinarski, and Bruno Zimmermann, eds., *Commentary on the Additional Protocols to the Geneva Conventions* (Geneva: International Committee of the Red Cross, 1987), para. 3237.
78 See also United Nations General Assembly, "Guidelines for the Alternative Care of Children," A/RES/64/142 (2010), para. 160.
79 Sandoz, Swinarski, and Zimmermann, *Commentary on the Additional Protocols*, para. 3227. It should thus be noted that Ukrainian children in occupied territories benefit from the concurrent protection afforded by the GCIV and API.
80 Sandoz, Swinarski, and Zimmermann, para. 3211.

81 Parliamentary Assembly of the Council of Europe, "Deportations and Forcible Transfers," para. 8.
82 OSCE, "Forcible Transfer and/or Deportation," 38.
83 OSCE, 40.
84 OSCE, 39.
85 OSCE, 17.
86 OSCE, 39.
87 Art. 49 para 3 GCIV. See also Sandoz, Swinarski, and Zimmermann, *Commentary on the Additional Protocols*, para. 3223.
88 Vité, "Protecting Children during Armed Conflict: International Humanitarian Law," 20.
89 Sandoz, Swinarski, and Zimmermann, *Commentary on the Additional Protocols*, para. 3213.
90 Art. 78(1) API.
91 Sandoz, Swinarski, and Zimmermann, *Commentary on the Additional Protocols*, para. 3233.
92 Sandoz, Swinarski, and Zimmermann, para. 3213.
93 Art. 78(2) API.
94 Sandoz, Swinarski, and Zimmermann, *Commentary on the Additional Protocols*, para. 3238.
95 Sandoz, Swinarski, and Zimmermann, para. 3239.
96 Ioffe and Umland, "Forcible Transfer and Deportation," 55; OSCE, "Forcible Transfer and/or Deportation," 42; Khoshnood, Raymond, and Howarth, "Russia's Systematic Program," 14–15.
97 Parliamentary Assembly of the Council of Europe, "Deportations and Forcible Transfers," para. 7.4; Council of Europe Commissioner for Human Rights, "Urgent Action Needed."
98 Ioffe and Umland, "Forcible Transfer and Deportation," 55; Khoshnood, Raymond, and Howarth, "Russia's Systematic Program," 6.
99 OSCE, "Forcible Transfer and/or Deportation," 41.
100 Ioffe and Umland, "Forcible Transfer and Deportation," 55; OSCE, "Forcible Transfer and/or Deportation," 41.
101 OSCE, "Forcible Transfer and/or Deportation," 42. Parliamentary Assembly of the Council of Europe, "Legal and Human Rights Aspects," para. 20.5.
102 Art. 49 para 2 GCIV.
103 E.-C. Gillard, "The Role of International Humanitarian Law in the Protection of Internally Displaced Persons," *Refugee Survey Quarterly* 24, no. 3 (2005): 41–2.
104 Rule 132 of the ICRC Study on CIHL.
105 Art. 49 para 2 GCIV.
106 Sandoz, Swinarski, and Zimmermann, *Commentary on the Additional Protocols*, para. 3218.
107 United Nations General Assembly, "Guidelines for the Alternative Care of Children," para. 160.
108 ICTY, "Prosecutor v. Naletilić and Martinović," para. 526.
109 Parliamentary Assembly of the Council of Europe, "Deportations and Forcible Transfers," para. 6.
110 See Ioffe and Umland, "Forcible Transfer and Deportation," 12.

111 Bisset, "Russia's Forcible Transfer of Children"; OSCE, "Forcible Transfer and/or Deportation," 43.
112 See in particular Article 25 GCIV. See discussion in Vité, "Protecting Children during Armed Conflict: International Humanitarian Law," 33–4.
113 See also United Nations General Assembly, "Guidelines for the Alternative Care of Children," para. 167.
114 OSCE, "Forcible Transfer and/or Deportation," 44.
115 Ioffe and Umland, "Forcible Transfer and Deportation," 55–6; Khoshnood, Raymond, and Howarth, "Russia's Systematic Program," 9.
116 Parliamentary Assembly of the Council of Europe, "Deportations and Forcible Transfers," para. 7.4.
117 Ioffe and Umland, 'Forcible Transfer and Deportation," 55–6.
118 OSCE, "Forcible Transfer and/or Deportation," 44; Council of Europe Commissioner for Human Rights, "Urgent Action Needed."
119 Parliamentary Assembly of the Council of Europe, "Deportations and Forcible Transfers," para. 2.
120 See OSCE, "Forcible Transfer and/or Deportation," 28; Committee on the Rights of the Child, "Concluding Observations," para. 45(h).
121 Ioffe and Umland, "Forcible Transfer and Deportation," 55–6.
122 Council of Europe Commissioner for Human Rights, "Urgent Action Needed."
123 OSCE, "Forcible Transfer and/or Deportation," 18.
124 United Nations General Assembly, Guidelines for the Alternative Care of Children, para. 154.
125 United Nations General Assembly, para. 161.
126 OSCE, "Forcible Transfer and/or Deportation," 18.
127 OSCE, 43.
128 International Criminal Court, "Situation in Ukraine: ICC Judges Issue Arrest Warrants against Vladimir Vladimirovich Putin and Maria Alekseyevna Lvova-Belova," Press Release, March 17, 2023, available at https://www.icc-cpi.int/news/situation-ukraine-icc-judges-issue-arrest-warrants-against-vladimir-vladimirovich-putin-and.

Selected Bibliography

Amann, Diane Marie, "Child-Taking," *Michigan Journal of International Law* 45 (2024), https://papers.ssrn.com/sol3/papers.cfm?abstract_id=4610553.

Bisset, Alison, "The UN Committee on the Rights of the Child and Russia's Deportation of Children from Ukraine," Opinio Juris, April 12, 2024, https://opiniojuris.org/2024/04/12/the-un-committee-on-the-rights-of-the-child-and-russias-deportation-of-children-from-ukraine.

Ioffe, Yulia, "Forcibly Transferring Ukrainian Children to the Russian Federation: A Genocide?," *Journal of Genocide Research* 25 (2023): 315–51.

Ioffe, Yulia and Andreas Umland, "Forcible Transfer and Deportation of Ukrainian Children: Responses and Accountability Measures," January 2024, PE 754.442, https://www.europarl.europa.eu/RegData/etudes/STUD/2024/754442/EXPO_STU(2024)754442_EN.pdf.

15

A Special Tribunal for the Crime of Aggression Against Ukraine

Beyond the Nuremberg Principles?

Vaios Koutroulis

This chapter[1] aims to examine the extent to which the Nuremberg precedent and principles remain relevant today, not in a general and abstract way but by looking into the discussions relating to establishing a special tribunal for the crime of aggression against Ukraine. Indeed, the war of aggression against Ukraine and the multiple views expressed in favor of the establishment of a special tribunal make this precedent ideal to evaluate whether what has been called the "Nuremberg legacy" has concretely been invoked and the influence it has had so far (June 2024) on the discussions on the special tribunal.

The open military invasion of Ukraine by Russia on February 24, 2022, and the ensuing military operations, including the annexation by Russia of the regions of Donetsk, Luhansk, Kherson, and Zaporizhzhia in Eastern Ukraine, have met with widespread condemnation by the United Nations General Assembly (UNGA),[2] by international organizations (e.g., the Organization of American States (OAS),[3] the African Union,[4] the European Union,[5] and the Council of Europe[6]), by states, as well as by an overwhelming number of international law scholars.[7]

The blatant character of Russia's violation of the prohibition to use force enshrined in article 2 (4) of the UN Charter—which was qualified as an act of aggression by the UNGA already since March 2, 2022[8]—triggered calls for accountability since the very beginning of the military intervention, insisting particularly on the criminal responsibility associated with the violation of Article 2(4) of the UN Charter. The most prominent proposal related to the creation of a special tribunal vested with the competence to judge those responsible for the aggression committed against Ukraine.

By virtue of a declaration lodged by Ukraine on September 8, 2015, in conformity with article 12 (3) of the International Criminal Court (ICC) Statute, the ICC has jurisdiction for the crimes committed in Ukrainian territory since February 20, 2014, "for an indefinite duration."[9] In this context, as of June 2024, four warrants of arrest have been issued by the ICC. The first two were issued on March 17, 2023, for Vladimir Putin, president of the Russian Federation, and Maria Alekseyevna Lvova-Belova, commissioner for Children's Rights in the Office of the President of the Russian

Federation, for war crimes in relation to the unlawful deportation and transfer of children from occupied Ukrainian territories to Russia.[10] The other two were issued on March 5, 2024, for Sergei Ivanovich Kobylash, lieutenant general in the Russian Army, and Viktor Nikolayevich Sokolov, admiral in the Russian Navy, for the war crimes of directing attacks against civilian objects and causing excessive incidental harm to civilians or damage to civilian objects, and for the crime against humanity of inhumane acts.[11]

Importantly, this declaration cannot cover the crime of aggression. Indeed, according to article 15*bis* of the ICC Statute, the Court cannot exercise its jurisdiction over the crime of aggression if either the state in whose territory the crime has been committed or the state whose nationals have committed the crime are not parties to the Statute.[12] Thus, the implementation of individual criminal responsibility for the crime of aggression committed against Ukraine became one of the thorniest issues in the discussions relating to accountability for the war in Ukraine.

On February 28, 2022, Professor Philippe Sands first launched the idea of a special tribunal,[13] followed very closely by several high-level politicians and international lawyers who, on March 4, 2022, published a statement in favor of creating such a tribunal.[14] The idea of this special judicial body for the crime of aggression committed against Ukraine (hereafter: special tribunal for Ukraine or special tribunal) gained much traction and was supported by Ukraine,[15] by other states like, for example, Estonia, Latvia and Lithuania,[16] France,[17] Switzerland,[18] Germany,[19] by the Council of Europe,[20] the Organization of Security and Co-operation in Europe (OSCE) Parliamentary Assembly,[21] the North Atlantic Treaty Organization (NATO) Parliamentary Assembly,[22] as well as by the European Union, namely the European Parliament[23] and the European Commission.[24]

Since January 2023, a group of states—the "Core Group"—has been actively examining the different models and legal basis for the establishment of the tribunal.[25] The need not to leave the crime of aggression committed against Ukraine unpunished is highlighted in the positions taken by the members of the group, as is illustrated by the following excerpt from a joint statement published on May 9, 2023, after a meeting of Core Group representatives:

> We (. . .) reaffirm that those responsible for committing the crime of aggression against Ukraine must not go unpunished, and call on the international community to consider appropriate actions, including through the establishment of an appropriate justice mechanism to ensure effective accountability for the crime of aggression, which is of concern to the international community as a whole.
>
> We therefore support exploring the creation of a tribunal to ensure effective accountability for the crime of aggression against Ukraine.'[26]

The first step in the direction of ensuring accountability for the crime of aggression against Ukraine was made with the creation of an International Centre for the Prosecution of the Crime of Aggression Against Ukraine, which was announced on February 2, 2023, by the president of the European Commission, Ursula von der

Leyen.[27] The Center's task is to "support the preparation of crime of aggression cases by securing crucial evidence and facilitating the process of case building at an early stage."[28] The Center is hosted in the European Union Agency for Criminal Justice Cooperation (Eurojust) and began its operations in July 2023.[29]

On April 2, 2024, a Ministerial Conference was held at The Hague with the participation of forty-four states.[30] At the political declaration issued at the end of the conference, the participating states reaffirmed their commitment to work toward the establishment of a special tribunal:

> We remain committed, in the context of the Core Group in which many of our Governments participate, to work towards the establishment of a special tribunal for the investigation and prosecution of the crime of aggression against Ukraine, that would contribute to accountability of the highest levels of military and political leadership; we welcome significant progress made in this regard, and we encourage interested States and international organisations to strengthen their efforts to secure a sound legal basis and broad international support for the completion of this process; we welcome the conditional offer of the Netherlands to host a special tribunal.[31]

This proposal has spawned numerous reactions from both legal scholars and institutions, some being favorable to the idea and others pointing out the legal problems that the creation of such a special tribunal entails.[32]

The discussion on the legal issues linked to establishing and functioning a special tribunal for Ukraine is ongoing at the time of writing (June 2024). A number of proposals have been on the table, and almost every possible scenario for the creation of the tribunal has been suggested at some point or another A first option would be to create the tribunal by an agreement between the UN and Ukraine. In this respect, the Special Court for Sierra Leone,[33] the Special Tribunal for Lebanon,[34] and the Extraordinary Chambers in the Courts of Cambodia[35] have been cited as relevant precedents. A second option would be to establish the tribunal by virtue of an agreement between a regional international organization—such as the Council of Europe or the European Union—and Ukraine. The Extraordinary African Chambers, created by an agreement between the African Union and Senegal in order to judge the former president of Chad, Hissène Habré, for international crimes, are sometimes mentioned as a useful precedent in this respect. However, substantial differences exist between the two situations: the Chambers tried a former, not an acting, head of state, whose immunity had been waived by the government of the state concerned (Chad), and, contrary to Russia, Chad was a member of the regional organization participating in the agreement.[36] Finally, the tribunal could be set up outside any existing institutional framework, under an agreement between Ukraine and other, "like-minded" states. Unsurprisingly, Nuremberg is the leading precedent invoked in connection to this last scenario.[37]

The object of this chapter is not to offer a detailed analysis of the several legal questions raised by the creation of a special tribunal for Ukraine, as interesting as these legal questions may be. Such analysis has already been done elsewhere, and the main arguments are known and remain fundamentally unchanged.[38] Instead, in accordance with the general line followed in this book, the chapter will focus on the International Military Tribunal for Nuremberg (IMTN or Nuremberg Tribunal) and the principles of international law recognized in both the Charter of the Nuremberg Tribunal and the tribunal's judgment, as they were set down by the UN International law Commission (ILC) in 1950 (Nuremberg Principles).[39] Since the precedent of the establishment of the IMTN and the Nuremberg Principles are very intimately connected, they will sometimes be referred to as the "Nuremberg precedent and principles." As has already been mentioned, not only does the Nuremberg tribunal come up quite often in the discourse relating to the establishment of a special tribunal for the crime of aggression against Ukraine, but the whole idea of the establishment of such a tribunal was borne out of a comparison with Nuremberg. Therefore, the views and discussions relating to the establishment of the tribunal for Ukraine offer an excellent opportunity to measure the influence that the Nuremberg precedent and principles have exerted on the question of criminal responsibility for the crime of aggression against Ukraine and its implementation. By looking more closely at the discourse of states, international organizations, and scholars relating to the creation of the special tribunal for Ukraine, this chapter will try to identify the place attributed to the Nuremberg precedent and principles to appreciate the impact that these principles have on the debate about this intricate question of international criminal law. We will first focus on the aspects on of the creation of a special tribunal for Ukraine which the Nuremberg precedent and principles do seem to have exercised considerable influence before looking into the questions that appear to have resisted such an influence.

The Continuing Relevance of the International Military Tribunal for Nuremberg and the Nuremberg Principles

As has already been mentioned, the IMTN and the Nuremberg Principles have been at the origin of the idea of creating a special tribunal for the crime of aggression against Ukraine. The steps leading to this creation are relatively simple: (i) Russia has committed an act of aggression; (ii) aggression is not only a violation of international law but also an international crime; (iii) individuals, especially high-ranking officials, bear criminal responsibility for this crime and must be brought to justice; (iv) the best forum before which the persons responsible for this crime of aggression can be judged is an international tribunal; (v) since the ICC does not have jurisdiction over this crime, the best alternative is an *ad hoc* tribunal. In this respect, referring to the Nuremberg experience has proven remarkably influential. This is manifest, firstly, in reaffirming the existence of individual criminal responsibility for the commission of aggression. Secondly, when envisaging the possible ways of implementing this criminal responsibility, Nuremberg is used as a key precedent in calls for general support for the creation of a special tribunal.

Nuremberg as the foundation of individual criminal responsibility for State aggression

In an address to the participants of a public debate held on October 9, 2022, in Paris, the president of Ukraine, Volodymyr Zelenskyy, made a forceful plea in favor of establishing a special tribunal for the crime of aggression against Ukraine. The excerpt includes a direct quote from the judgment of the International Military Tribunal of Nuremberg and deserves to be reproduced in extenso:

> And I will now add one more quote: "Crimes against International Law are committed by men, not by abstract entities, and only by punishing individuals who commit such crimes can the provisions of International Law be enforced." End of quote.
>
> Probably, you have read or heard these and other words that I have just given—they are from the verdict of the Nuremberg trials. The trials established by an international treaty. The trials punished the perpetrators of the previous full-scale war in Europe and proved that justice exists in the world.
>
> All of us who have studied jurisprudence have seen and analyzed this fundamental document—the Nuremberg verdict. And I am sure that there will be times when students who study law in the same way will be able to compare the text of the Nuremberg verdict with the text of the verdict that will be passed by the Special Tribunal regarding the crime of Russia's aggression against Ukraine.
>
> I invite all of you to participate in the establishment of appropriate legal institutions. Anyone who joins in restoring justice now will join in guaranteeing long-term peace for all of us in Europe and the world.[40]

Along similar lines, the statement signed by politicians and experts in public international law and published on March 4, 2022, referred implicitly to the Nuremberg precedent in connection with individual criminal responsibility for the crime of aggression: "international law has, at least since the end of the Second World War, provided for individual criminal responsibility for those who plan, prepare, initiate or execute wars of aggression."[41]

These statements reflect the first Nuremberg Principle according to which: "[a]ny person who commits an act which constitutes a crime under international law is responsible therefor and liable to punishment," as well as Principle VI, which reproduces the definition of the crime of aggression ("crime against peace" in the terminology used at the time) found in the Charter of the Nuremberg Tribunal:

> The crimes hereinafter set out are punishable as crimes under international law:
> a. Crimes against peace
> (i) Planning, preparation, initiation, or waging of a war of aggression or a war in violation of international treaties, agreements, or assurances.
> (ii) Participation in a common plan or conspiracy for the accomplishment of any of the acts mentioned under (i).[42]

An explicit reference to the Nuremberg Principles is included in the declaration made by the representatives of states and international organizations that participated in a summit on Russia's accountability for the crimes in Ukraine held in Bucha on March 31, 2023:

> *Recalling* the UN General Assembly resolution A/RES/95 (1946), entitled Resolution on the Affirmation of the Principles of International Law Recognized by the Charter of the Nuremberg Tribunal, which affirmed the principles of international law recognized by the Nuremberg Charter and Judgment, and recalling further again that aggression is criminalized in many national criminal codes, including that of Ukraine,
>
> (...)
>
> *Affirm* that those responsible for planning, masterminding, and committing the crime of aggression against Ukraine must not go unpunished, and call on the international community to consider appropriate actions, including through the establishment of an appropriate justice mechanism to ensure effective accountability for the crime of aggression, which is of concern to the international community as a whole.[43]

The phrase from the Nuremberg judgment, according to which international crimes "are committed by men, not by abstract entities, and only by punishing individuals who commit such crimes can the provisions of international law be enforced,"[44] is one of the most-cited parts of the judgment and indeed underpins the principle of individual criminal responsibility for crimes committed by states.[45]

Similarly, the ruling of the Nuremberg Tribunal that aggression is "the supreme international crime"[46] has been invoked a lot,[47] including to underlie the gravity of Russia's aggression against Ukraine. One of the preambular paragraphs of the resolution adopted on January 19, 2023, by the European parliament explicitly mentions this phrase of the Nuremberg judgment: "whereas the International Military Tribunal at Nuremberg, which focused on the crime of aggression, ruled in 1946 that aggression was 'the supreme international crime.'"[48]

In the context of Ukraine, this has been used to highlight the need to move beyond the "regular" war crimes and crimes against humanity committed in the context of the military operations conducted by Russia against Ukraine and shift the attention to punishing those responsible for the war itself. This is evident in the declaration made by the Ministry of Foreign Affairs of Poland on March 7, 2023:

> As it was stated by the Nuremberg Tribunal, the crime of aggression is the supreme international crime. The act of Russia's aggression has led to an unimaginable scale of other international crimes. Leaving the perpetrators of this unprecedented crime unpunished while trying to hold to account the perpetrators of other crimes will lead to injustice and undermine the fundamental principles of international law.

> In this context, Ukraine's proposal to establish a Special Tribunal for the Crime of Aggression deserves full support.[49]

Along the same lines, the states supporting the creation of a special tribunal for Ukraine highlighted that

> The crime of aggression is at the origin of all the other crimes committed in Ukraine. Without the aggression against Ukraine, the other Rome Statute crimes would not have been and continue to be committed. Thus, the crime of aggression is the "supreme international crime" in this situation, and those who are most responsible—the persons in senior political and military leadership positions who decided to commit the aggression—must be held to account.[50]

As indicated above, several options have been proposed and are being explored for establishing a judicial body that could judge those responsible for the aggression against Ukraine. In this respect, the INTM's precedent comes into play in support of creating a special tribunal that would fill the accountability gap created by the conditions imposed by Article 15*bis* of the ICC Statute.

Nuremberg as the key precedent in favor of the creation of a special tribunal

Those favoring the creation of a special tribunal for the crime of aggression against Ukraine have been swift in invoking Nuremberg as a guiding precedent. In their March 4, 2023, statement, the politicians and international law experts affirmed that "[t]he Special tribunal for the Punishment of the Crime of Aggression against Ukraine can be set up quickly. During the Second World War, nations met in London in 1942 to draft a resolution on German war crimes, which led, at the end of the conflict, to the creation of an International Military Tribunal and the Nuremberg trials."[51]

Similar references to Nuremberg and its legacy are found in declarations made by states supporting the creation of a special tribunal. The Ambassador of Estonia to the UN explained that "the whole aim of the undertaking is universal—to ensure justice and delegitimize aggression as a tool of statecraft, as it was after WWII with the Nuremberg trials"[52] and highlighted the importance of political will: "[i]f States want to achieve a just and lasting peace in Ukraine, and delegitimize aggression again, we should shake off our fears and find the political will to collectively reinforce the legacy of Nuremberg through action by the General Assembly."[53] Along the same lines, the US ambassador-at-large for Global Criminal Justice asserted that

> we are participating in negotiations to develop a tribunal dedicated to prosecuting the crime of aggression against Ukraine. We remain actively engaged in the Core Group that has convened to develop a modality to prosecute this international crime. (. . .) "These five pathways (ie including the establishment of a special tribunal)" are

> the legacy of Nuremberg. Just as the Allies at the end of the Second World War advanced the imperative of justice and ushered in a new era of accountability for the worst imaginable crimes, it falls on all of us to ensure that the legacy of Nuremberg and the promise of the Nuremberg Principles are not merely history.[54]

In this respect, it is perhaps worth reminding that the IMTN is the only *ad hoc* tribunal whose jurisdiction includes the crime of aggression (or "crime against peace"). Indeed, aggression was not included among the list of crimes falling under the jurisdiction of the two international criminal tribunals established by the UN Security Council in 1993 and 1994 for ex-Yugoslavia and Rwanda, respectively, nor of any other specialized or hybrid criminal jurisdictions established afterward (e.g., the Special Court for Sierra Leone, the Extraordinary Chambers in the Courts of Cambodia, the Special Tribunal for Lebanon, or the Extraordinary African Chambers). It is thus unsurprising that Nuremberg—alongside its sister jurisdiction, the International Military Tribunal for the Far East—is invoked as a precedent for establishing a tribunal whose jurisdiction would be limited to the crime of aggression. As one author has put it

> [t]he establishment of the proposed tribunal to prosecute crimes of aggression committed against Ukraine has the potential to demonstrate that might will not be allowed to have an untrammeled path of triumph over right. Discussions of the proposal have frequently cited Nuremberg as a relevant precedent. This is accurate insofar as Nuremberg, together with Tokyo, represent the only international trials of the crime we now know as the crime of aggression.[55]

Similarly, the non-governmental organization International Crisis Group insisted on the singularity of the Nuremberg precedent in terms of prosecuting aggression:

> Precedents for prosecuting the crime of aggression are limited. The overwhelming majority of prior prosecutions are from the World War II era, following the defeat and occupation of Nazi Germany and imperial Japan. In Germany, as noted above, the allies created the International Military Tribunal at Nuremberg. The Tribunal was the primary forum where the Allies prosecuted German political, military and economic leaders in connection with "crimes against the peace"—i.e., the "planning, preparation, initiation and waging of wars of aggression". A similarly named successor body, the Nuremberg Military Tribunal, subsequently tried German officials in the Ministries case. On the Asian front, Japanese leaders faced prosecution for crimes against the peace at the International Military Tribunal for the Far East, which the victorious allies established in Tokyo.
>
> (. . .)
>
> The first option would be a tribunal based on a multilateral treaty among Ukraine and a "coalition of the willing" states, styled after the International Military Tribunal at Nuremberg.[56]

The references mentioned above seem to indicate that the Nuremberg precedent and principles were highly influential in advocating for the creation of a special tribunal for Ukraine. This is indeed the case at the general level described above. However, as the discussions go on and the legal aspects of the tribunal are analyzed in greater detail, the complexity of the relevant legal issues gain in visibility, and the limits of the usefulness of Nuremberg become apparent.

The Limits of the Nuremberg Influence

From the outset, it is useful to keep in mind that the Nuremberg Principles focus on key aspects of individual criminal responsibility for international crimes[57] but are silent on the tribunal that will be called upon to enforce this responsibility.[58] Thus, the principles themselves cannot influence the choice of the model to be followed for the establishment of the special tribunal. In any event, it is not the establishment *per se* of the tribunal which is problematic. Indeed, there does not seem to be any difficulty in accepting that, from a legal perspective, it is perfectly possible to set up a tribunal competent to judge individuals suspected of committing international crimes in the context of the war in Ukraine either by international treaty between states or by an agreement with the UN or with any other international organization. The legal difficulties relate to some key aspects of the exercise of jurisdiction of such a tribunal, particularly the question of immunities and the obligation of third states to cooperate with the tribunal by, for example, executing the arrest warrants issued by it.[59] Given their silence on the judicial body that will implement individual criminal responsibility, the Nuremberg Principles do not take a position on the question of cooperation. They are, however, relevant for the question of immunities and also, more generally, for the connected issue of the *ratione personae* scope of application of the crime of aggression—in other words, the question of which persons may be considered as bearing criminal responsibility with respect to the crime of aggression. As it will be apparent from the analysis below, although the Nuremberg Principles can be read as favoring a "relaxed" approach to both questions, allowing for a broad scope of persons to be susceptible to prosecution for the crime of aggression and advocating for the exclusion of immunities in case of international crimes, these views have not (yet) prevailed in the discussions relating to the special tribunal for Ukraine.

The problem of the *ratione personae* scope of criminal responsibility: Kampala rather than Nuremberg?

Principle VI of the Nuremberg Principles, which contains the list of international crimes, defines "crimes against peace" as the "planning, preparation, initiation or waging of a war of aggression or a war in violation of international treaties, agreements or assurances" but, as the commentary to this principle rightly points out, there is no definition of what constitutes a "war of aggression":

> The Charter of the Nürnberg Tribunal did not contain any definition of "war of aggression", nor was there any such definition in the judgment of the Tribunal. It was by reviewing the historical events before and during the war that it found that certain of the defendants planned and waged aggressive wars against twelve nations and were therefore guilty of a series of crimes.[60]

This difficulty was overcome by the UNGA's adoption of a definition of aggression in resolution 3314(XXIX).[61] The definition remained unchanged and was confirmed several decades later in Kampala when the states parties to the Rome Statute adopted the resolution on the crime of aggression.[62]

However, one issue that has triggered some discussion is who can be considered criminally responsible for the crime of aggression. The generally accepted view is that aggression is a "leadership crime," implying that only high-ranking officials bear criminal responsibility for their commission. In this respect, the definition of crimes against peace, which includes the "planning, preparation, initiation or waging of a war of aggression," is phrased in rather broad terms. In its comments on the Nuremberg Principles, Norway communicated to the Commission its apprehension on this point:

> [t]he Norwegian Government is of the opinion that the words "waging of a war", etc., (. . .) should be qualified by some additional words that would make it clear that the provision cannot be made to apply to military personnel who have taken part in warlike operations in a more subordinate capacity. Such a limitation would be in agreement with the legal principles embodied in the judgment of the Nurnberg Tribunal.[63]

Subordinates do not fall under the scope of the crime of aggression, as confirmed by the ILC commentary to Principle VI. Indeed, the Commission specified that

> [t]he terms "planning" and "preparation" of a war of aggression were considered by the Tribunal as comprising all the stages in the bringing about of a war of aggression from the planning to the actual initiation of the war. In view of that, the Tribunal did not make any clear distinction between planning and preparation. As stated in the judgment, "planning and preparation are essential to the making of the war".
>
> The meaning of the expression "waging of a war of aggression" was discussed in the Commission (. . .). Some members of the Commission feared that everyone in uniform who fought a war of aggression might be charged with the "waging" of such a war. The Commission understands the expression to refer only to high-ranking military personnel and high State officials, and believes that this was also the view of the Tribunal.[64]

The Commission gives no further details as to exactly which "high-ranking military personnel and high State officials" come under this provision, and there seems to be some ambiguity as to the precise interpretation of the leadership criterion in Nuremberg.[65] Be that as it may, the leadership criterion was confirmed in the negotiations in Kampala, and the text of article 8*bis* of the Rome Statute, as adopted in the relevant resolution, mentions it specifically:

> For the purpose of this Statute, "crime of aggression" means the planning, preparation, initiation or execution, *by a person in a position effectively to exercise control over or to direct the political or military action of a State*, of an act of aggression which, by its character, gravity and scale, constitutes a manifest violation of the Charter of the United Nations.[66]

This is further confirmed by the elements of the crime of article 8*bis* and by the text of article 25 (3)*bis*, also inserted in the Rome Statute as part of the Kampala amendment on the crime of aggression:

> 3 *bis*. In respect of the crime of aggression, the provisions of this article shall apply only to persons in a position effectively to exercise control over or to direct the political or military action of a State.[67]

As some scholars have highlighted, by limiting the personal scope of application of the crime of aggression in the Rome Statute to persons "in a position effectively to exercise control over or to direct the political or military action" of the state which committed the act of aggression, the states parties to the ICC seem to propose an interpretation of the leadership criterion which may be more restrictive than the one established in Nuremberg:

> The leadership criterion does not appear as such in the Charters of the Nuremberg and Tokyo Military Tribunals, despite the fact that the object of these tribunals, in a more general sense, was to try only major war criminals. The criterion applied by the national military tribunals that tried war criminals in the wake of the Nuremberg Tribunal on the basis of Control Council Law No. 10, namely the power to "shape or influence policy", was broader than that currently laid down in the Rome Statute ("control or direct"). It is therefore debatable whether the definition contained in the Rome Statute fully corresponds on this point with the definition that exists under customary international law.[68]

Similarly, Tom Dannenbaum has stressed that

> individual liability for waging aggressive war attaches only to those in leadership positions. This, however, does not mean that liability is restricted to the single individual at the apex of a state's command structure. As articulated in the *High Command* case at Nuremberg, the leadership element limits criminal responsibility to those "in a position to shape or influence the policy that brings about [the criminal war's] initiation or its continuance after initiation, either by

> furthering, or by hindering or preventing it." (p. 488). The ICC's jurisdiction is limited to those in a position "effectively to exercise control over or direct the political or military action of a state." (art. 8 bis(1)). It has been suggested that the latter standard is narrower than that elaborated at Nuremberg, although its precise scope has yet to be tested and one might question whether any narrowing reflects customary international law. It is notable in this respect that those advocating the creation of a special tribunal for the current war have invoked language reminiscent of Nuremberg, calling for the tribunal to hold accountable those "who have materially contributed to or shaped the commission" of aggression.[69]

It should be borne in mind that the restrictive view adopted in Kampala should not necessarily be seen as reflecting current customary international law on this matter. This is expressly stated in the Kampala understandings, which make clear that

> the amendments that address the definition of the act of aggression and the crime of aggression do so for the purpose of this Statute only. The amendments shall, in accordance with article 10 of the Rome Statute, not be interpreted as limiting or prejudicing in any way existing or developing rules of international law for purposes other than this Statute.[70]

In other words, as far as the Nuremberg precedent does point to a broader view on the interpretation of the leadership criterion (a point which is not uncontested) and as far as such a view can be considered as reflecting customary international law, it continues to be valid and exists in parallel to the narrow view which will be applied in the ICC context. The states and stakeholders involved in the discussions relating to creating a special tribunal will consequently have to choose between the two views. The public international law professors who compose the Dutch Advisory Committee on Public International Law seem to favor the Rome Statute interpretation:

> The [Advisory Committee] considers that the leadership criterion as laid down in the Rome Statute ('control or direct') should be taken as the starting point because this was the wording agreed upon following extensive negotiations between States. It follows that the group of persons who can be held criminally responsible for aggression is limited.[71]

Irrespective of what scholars may advise, the final decision on this issue will be decided by those involved in creating the tribunal. What is certain is that a choice of the broad interpretation borne out of the Nuremberg tribunals will be an additional testimony to Nuremberg's continuing influence.

Intimately linked to the question of the personal scope of application of the crime of aggression is the problem of immunities, to which we will now turn.

The problem of immunities: beyond or below the Nuremberg Principles?

Article 7 of the Charter of the International Military Tribunal at Nuremberg stipulated that "[t]he official position of defendants, whether as Heads of State or responsible officials in Government Departments, shall not be considered freeing them from responsibility or mitigating punishment."[72] This article was taken up almost word for word in Principle III of the Nuremberg Principles, which reads as follows:

> [t]he fact that a person who committed an act which constitutes a crime under international law acted as Head of State or responsible Government official does not relieve him from responsibility under international law.[73]

Although the text of Principle III does not mention immunities explicitly, the commentary makes it clear that the ILC members had immunities in mind when they adopted the principle. Indeed, the commentary reproduces the following excerpts from the Nuremberg judgment in support of the exclusion of immunity of state officials for the commission of international crimes:

> "The principle of international law which, under certain circumstances, protects the representatives of a State" said the Tribunal "cannot be applied to acts which are condemned as criminal by international law. The authors of these acts cannot shelter themselves behind their official position in order to be freed from punishment . . .". The same idea was also expressed in the following passage of the findings: "He who violates the laws of war cannot obtain immunity while acting in pursuance of the authority of the State if the State in authorizing action moves outside its competence under international law."[74]

As this excerpt makes clear, Principle III of the Nuremberg Principles adopts the view that the immunities of state officials cannot be invoked with respect to international crimes. This exception to immunities is broadly formulated, applying both to personal immunities (or immunities *ratione personae*)—which cover all acts (both public and private) of a limited number of state officials of the highest rank, such as heads of state, Heads of Government, or Ministers of Foreign Affairs—and to functional immunities (or immunities *ratione materiae*)—which cover only official acts committed during the time when the state official is in office (but not private acts) and apply to all state officials, irrespective of their rank. Moreover, since, as explained above, the Nuremberg Principles do not explicitly limit their application to international tribunals, nothing in the ILC text prevents the exception to immunities from being also invoked before national courts.

The exception to immunities in case of international crimes was confirmed by the ILC in its Draft Code of Crimes against the Peace and Security of Mankind of 1954.[75] It was reiterated in the Draft Code adopted in 1996, whose article 7 repeats Principle III of the Nuremberg Principles: "[t]he official position of an individual who commits a crime against the peace and security of mankind, even if he acted as Head of State or

Government, does not relieve him of criminal responsibility or mitigate punishment."[76] The commentary to draft article 7 deserves to be reproduced *in extenso* because it gives a clear indication of how influential the Nuremberg precedent and principles have been on the inclusion of this rule in the Draft Code:

> The official position of an individual, including a head of State, was excluded as a defence to a crime under international law or as a mitigating factor in determining the commensurate punishment for such a crime in the Charter of the Nurnberg Tribunal (. . .).
>
> In accordance with this provision, the Nurnberg Tribunal rejected the plea of act of State and that of immunity which were submitted by several defendants as a valid defence or ground for immunity (. . .).
>
> The official position of an individual has been consistently excluded as a possible defence to crimes under international law in the relevant instruments adopted since the Charter of the Nurnberg Tribunal, including the Charter of the Tokyo Tribunal (art. 6), Control Council Law No. 10 (art. 4) and, more recently, the statute of the International Tribunal for the Former Yugoslavia (art. 7) and the statute of the International Tribunal for Rwanda (art. 6). The absence of such a defence was also recognized by the Commission in the Nurnberg Principles (Principle III) and the 1954 draft Code (art. 3).
>
> (. . .)
>
> As recognized by the Nurnberg Tribunal in its Judgment, the principle of international law which protects State representatives in certain circumstances does not apply to acts which constitute crimes under international law. Thus, an individual cannot invoke his official position to avoid responsibility for such an act. As further recognized by the Nurnberg Tribunal in its Judgment, the author of a crime under international law cannot invoke his official position to escape punishment in appropriate proceedings. The absence of any procedural immunity with respect to prosecution or punishment in appropriate judicial proceedings is an essential corollary of the absence of any substantive immunity or defence. It would be paradoxical to prevent an individual from invoking his official position to avoid responsibility for a crime only to permit him to invoke this same consideration to avoid the consequences of this responsibility.[77]

In this respect, it is interesting to note that in its draft articles on the immunity of state officials from foreign criminal jurisdiction, which were adopted along with their commentaries on first reading in 2022, the ILC has included a reference to Principle III of the Nuremberg Principles only in the introductory part of the commentary.[78] There is no reference to Principle III in the commentary of draft article 7, which sets out the list of international crimes to which immunity *ratione materiae* does not apply.[79] Because the draft articles "apply to the immunity of State officials from the criminal jurisdiction of another State" and not of an international tribunal,[80] this omission of the ILC can be interpreted as undermining the relevance of the Nuremberg Principles for national criminal proceedings of international crimes.

In its judgment in the case of the *Arrest Warrant of 11 April 2000* opposing Belgium to the Democratic Republic of the Congo (DRC), the International Court of Justice (ICJ) seems to confirm this view. Having issued an arrest warrant against the incumbent DRC's Minister for Foreign Affairs for war crimes and crimes against humanity, Belgium argued that under customary international law there existed an exception to immunities in case the suspect was accused of severe international crimes like war crimes and crimes against humanity.[81] In support of its view, among other sources, Belgium referred extensively to the Nuremberg precedent, Principle III of the Nuremberg Principles, and all the relevant ILC practices mentioned above.[82] The DRC accepted the existence of a principle of international criminal law, deriving from the decisions of the Nuremberg and Tokyo international military tribunals, that the accused's official capacity at the time of the acts cannot, before any court, whether domestic or international, constitute a 'ground of exemption from his criminal responsibility or a ground for mitigation of sentence.' The DRC then stresse[d] that the fact that an immunity might bar prosecution before a specific court or over a specific period of time does not mean that the same prosecution cannot be brought, if appropriate, before another court which is not bound by that immunity, or at another time when the immunity need no longer be taken into account."[83] The ICJ sided with this approach. It asserted that, after having "examined the rules concerning the immunity or criminal responsibility of persons having an official capacity contained in the legal instruments creating international criminal tribunals, and which are specifically applicable to the latter (. . .)", it found that "these rules (. . .) do not enable it to conclude that any such an exception exists in customary international law in regard to national courts."[84] The Court did go on to declare that immunities "do not represent a bar to criminal prosecution in certain circumstances," among which the Court listed "criminal proceedings before certain international criminal courts, where they have jurisdiction," without, however, mentioning the Nuremberg and Tokyo international criminal tribunals among the relevant examples cited.[85]

The scope of this finding of the ICJ is subject to debate. In a judgment handed down in 2019 concerning the non-execution of an arrest warrant issued for Sudan's President Omar Al-Bashir, the ICC Appeals Chamber concluded that customary international law did not allow for immunities to be invoked before international tribunals in general.[86] According to the Appeals Chamber, this rule applies even to heads of states that have not ratified the ICC Statute and cannot, therefore, be considered as having accepted the provision that precludes the invocation of immunities before the Court.[87] As the following excerpt from the reasoning of the Appeals Chamber shows, the Nuremberg precedent and principles played a significant role in the establishment of this customary exclusion of immunities before international courts and tribunals:

> Article 27(2) of the Statute is a clear provision in conventional law; but it also reflects the status of customary international law. In this regard, the Appeals Chamber notes, first, article 7 of the Nuremberg Charter of the International Military Tribunal at Nuremberg (…).

> On 11 December 1946, the UN General Assembly expressly affirmed the "principles of international law recognized by the Charter of the Nürnberg Tribunal and the judgment of the Tribunal" and directed the newly established International Law Commission to "treat as a matter of primary importance plans for the formulation [. . .] of the principles recognized" therein. The International Law Commission subsequently formulated the Nuremberg Principles, Principle III of which reads as follows (. . .).
>
> The same principle was included in article 3 of the International Law Commission's draft Code of Offences against the Peace and Security of Mankind.[88]

In connection to creating a special tribunal for Ukraine, the discussion has focused on what type of tribunal can qualify as "international" to come within the ICJ's finding in the 2002 *Arrest Warrant* judgment. A joint statement on the accountability for the crime of aggression committed on the territory of Ukraine, adopted on April 17, 2023, by thirteen states, reflects the quest for the right mode of establishment of the special tribunal for it to come under the ICJ finding:

> We believe that an international tribunal, before which the immunities granted by international law to the most senior leadership of a state do not apply, is best placed to deliver the abovedescribed (*sic*) objectives. We therefore call on the international community to actively engage in discussions on the establishment of such a tribunal, in particular through decisions of the United Nations General Assembly.[89]

The precedent of the Nuremberg tribunal and the Nuremberg Principles have been invoked by the proponents of a broad view according to which there can be no immunity before any international court or tribunal. Under this view, this exception will apply to the special tribunal for Ukraine, provided that an international treaty creates it:

> there was legal precedence in numerous instances of international criminal tribunals, distinctly noting within their statutes that the official status of defendants would not serve as impediments to the court's personal jurisdiction over them. Examples include provisions in Article 7 of the IMT Charter also known as the Nuremberg Charter—a reformulation of which was incorporated by the International Law Commission in its report and accepted by the UN General Assembly (UNGA) as early as 12 December 1950 (. . .).
>
> (. . .)
>
> For the first time since the Nuremberg trials, the international community is looking to bring perpetrators of the crime of aggression to justice. Head of State immunity from jurisdiction in other States has for centuries been considered a core principle of sovereignty, recognized by the ICJ. The sitting Heads of State enjoy immunity *ratione personae*, personal or procedural immunity, which protects them from being adjudicated by the courts of another state. Immunity *ratione materiae*,

> substantive or functional immunity, instead shields the acts committed as a Head of State, and it extends also to former heads of state. Functional immunity, as explained below, has eroded in international criminal law since the Nuremberg trials. Contemporary international criminal law recognizes that the principle is not absolute.[90]

Other scholars are more skeptical about whether this broad view does indeed correspond to existing customary international law. Already back in 1951, in its comments on the Nuremberg Principles transmitted to the ILC, Denmark had insisted on the immunity of its head of state under the Danish constitution:

> With regard to principle III—the fact that a person who committed an act which constitutes a crime under international law acted as Head of State or responsible Government official does not relieve him from responsibility under international law—I beg to add that in accordance with article 12 of the Constitution of the Kingdom of Denmark the King cannot be made responsible for his acts.[91]

Most importantly, the establishment of the Nuremberg and Tokyo tribunals was grounded on the unconditional surrender of Germany and Japan and on the exercise of legislative power by the victors of the Second World War in the name of the two defeated states:

> The IMT, of course, adopted a model of pooled jurisdictional authority, holding that the states involved did "together what any one of them might have done singly". However, in that context, their individual (and thus collective) authority to do so was understood to be grounded not in universal jurisdiction, but in their "sovereign legislative power" in light of Germany's unconditional surrender and the ensuing right of the victors to "legislate for the occupied powers" (…).[92]

Indeed, as we have argued elsewhere,

> States that set up the NIMT assumed "supreme authority with respect to Germany" and exercised "all the powers possessed by the German government"; they could thus set aside the immunities attached to German State officials; a similar reasoning can be applied in the case of Japanese officials' immunity before the IMTFE since the authority of the Supreme Commander for the Allied Powers who set up the tribunal was superior even to that of the Emperor and Japanese Government; in any event, Japan had accepted that war criminals should be brought to justice.[93]

This debate on the scope of the exception to the immunities of state officials is reflected in the discussions and hesitation concerning the model that will be adopted to establish the special tribunal for Ukraine. This question is particularly salient because states cannot hide behind a *sui generis* reasoning: the solution that will be adopted in this case will set the standards for future similar cases, and whatever is applied to Putin in the context of this war of aggression will have to be equally valid for any other head of state with respect to any other war of aggression.

Here again, the final take on this issue will be decided by the states and other stakeholders involved in the negotiations on establishing the tribunal. The solution adopted will, in all probability, have a defining role in the interpretation of the exception to immunities before international courts. If the special tribunal is established based on an international treaty—either between Ukraine and the UNGA (an option which currently seems unlikely) or between Ukraine and a regional organization to which the Russian Federation is not a party, like the Council of Europe, or between Ukraine and other "like-minded" states—and it excludes the invocation of immunities, this will confirm the rule formulated in Principle III of the Nuremberg Principles thus consolidating the principles' influence on this question.

Concluding Remarks

As was shown above, Nuremberg has had an undeniable impact at the general level of the underlying premises of the discussion on the creation of a special tribunal for aggression against Ukraine: it has solidified the tenets that a war of aggression is an international crime, that high-ranking officials, including heads of state, bear international criminal responsibility for such crime, and that international tribunals can be established in order to judge those responsible for the crime of aggression, setting aside any immunities that would normally apply. However, when it comes to concrete legal issues such as the personal scope of the crime of aggression and the question of immunities, the influence of Nuremberg becomes less decisive: the precedent of the IMTN and the Nuremberg Principles are invoked by the proponents of broad interpretations of the relevant international rules, but they are counterbalanced by arguments pointing toward more restrictive interpretations as established international law. Indeed, in some cases, such as the question of immunities, the international practice seems to have moved toward stricter standards than the ones that could have been established based on the Nuremberg Principles.

Nevertheless, it should not be forgotten that, in acquiring their importance, the Nuremberg Principles had to overcome two significant obstacles: legal and political. The legal obstacle concerns the legal value of the principles themselves. The discussions within the ILC at the time of the elaboration of the principles reveal a fierce debate about the interpretation of the mandate given to the Commission by the UNGA. While some members of the ILC were of the view that in formulating these principles, the Commission also had to identify the underlying established rules of international law, the majority view, which prevailed, disagreed:

> [t]he conclusion of the Commission is that it is not asked to express any appreciation of the principles applied in the Charter and the Tribunal of Nüremberg as principles of international law. It is asked merely to give formulation to those principles without any indication of their authority.[94]

Thus, formally, the Nuremberg Principles were not, in their inception, intended to codify existing international law. This was obvious to states as the following comment by Denmark clearly indicates:

> Since the Commission in accordance with its terms of reference has formulated only such principles of international law as have been recognized in the Charter of the Nürnberg Tribunal and in the judgment of the Tribunal, the Danish Government finds no occasion to furnish any observations concerning the formulation submitted by the Commission.[95]

The second obstacle is political and has to do with the legitimacy of the Nuremberg tribunal. The association of the IMTN with what has been called "victor's justice" has led some scholars to treat with caution references to Nuremberg in the context of the establishment of the special tribunal for Ukraine: "The proposal (ie to establish a special tribunal) should be distinguished from Nuremberg in that the latter reflects the use of law by powerful states against defeated enemies."[96] Indeed, it has been convincingly argued that the establishment of the special tribunal for Ukraine under a multilateral treaty between "like-minded" states *à la* Nuremberg would not be the best way to enhance its legitimacy:

> The main problem is the legitimacy of such a Special Tribunal. This problem can only be overcome, if at all, by involving the UN, in particular the General Assembly ("GA"). In contrast, regional initiatives (e.g., at the level of the Council of Europe, "CoE") or a multilateral treaty between interested States and Ukraine (Nuremberg model) may only produce a limited (only European) legitimacy.[97]

Despite both obstacles, the Nuremberg precedent and principles managed to become one of the main arguments used to reinforce international criminal law and enhance accountability for international crimes. And although their impact and influence on some specific legal questions must be nuanced, their overall successful trajectory is undeniable. Not a minor achievement for a small number of principles that were not even supposed to be codifications of international law in the first place.

Notes

1 The Chapter was finalised on June 30, 2024. Developments which occured after that date have not been taken into account. All internet references were last accessed on June 30, 2024.

2 UNGA Res ES-11/1, March 18, 2022: the Assembly "[*d*]*eplore*[*d*] *in the strongest terms* the aggression by the Russian Federation against Ukraine in violation of Article 2(4) of the Charter" (para. 2); UNGA Res ES-11/4, October 13, 2022: the Assembly condemns the organization of the illegal referendums in regions belonging to Ukraine and the "attempted illegal annexation of Donetsk, Kherson, Luhansk and

Zaporizhzhia" and declares that these actions "have no validity under international law" (paras. 2 and 3); UNGA Res ES-11/5, November 15, 2022: the Assembly "Recognizes that the Russian Federation must be held to account for any violations of international law in or against Ukraine, including its aggression in violation of the Charter of the United Nations" (para 2).

3 OAS, Statement from the OAS General Secretariat on the Russian Attack on Ukraine, February 24, 2022, Doc E-008/22, https://www.oas.org/en/media_center/press_release.asp?sCodigo=E-008/22.

4 African Union, Statement from Chair of the African Union, H.E President Macky Sall and Chairperson of the AU Commission H.E Moussa Faki Mahamat, on the situation in Ukraine, February 24, 2022, https://au.int/sites/default/files/pressreleases/41529-pr-english.pdf.

5 EU, Russia's aggression against Ukraine: Press Statement by High Representative/Vice-President Josep Borrell, February 24, 2022, https://www.eeas.europa.eu/eeas/russias-aggression-against-ukraine-press-statement-high-representativevice-president-josep_en.

6 Council or Europe, Committee of Ministers, Decision "2.3 Situation in Ukraine," February 24, 2022, Doc CM/Del/Dec(2022)1426bis/2.3, https://search.coe.int/cm/Pages/result_details.aspx?ObjectID=0900001680a5a1f1.

7 For a full list of references to positions condemning Russia's resort to force against Ukraine, see, among many, Olivier Corten and Vaios Koutroulis, *Tribunal for the Crime of Aggression against Ukraine – A Legal Assessment*, in-depth analysis requested by for the Policy Department of the Directorate-General for External Policies, European Parliament, December 14, 2022, 3–4, https://www.europarl.europa.eu/RegData/etudes/IDAN/2022/702574/EXPO_IDA(2022)702574_EN.pdf.

8 UNGA Res ES-11/1 (18 March 2022) UN Doc A/RES/ES-11/1.

9 Declaration accepting the jurisdiction of the International Criminal Court for crimes committed in the territory of Ukraine since February 20, 2014, September 8, 2015, https://www.icc-cpi.int/sites/default/files/iccdocs/other/Ukraine_Art_12-3_declaration_08092015.pdf#search=ukraine.

10 Situation in Ukraine: ICC judges issue arrest warrants against Vladimir Vladimirovich Putin and Maria Alekseyevna Lvova-Belova, press release, March 17, 2023, https://www.icc-cpi.int/news/situation-ukraine-icc-judges-issue-arrest-warrants-against-vladimir-vladimirovich-putin-and.

11 Situation in Ukraine: ICC judges issue arrest warrants against Sergei Ivanovich Kobylash and Viktor Nikolayevich Sokolov, press release, March 5, 2024, https://www.icc-cpi.int/news/situation-ukraine-icc-judges-issue-arrest-warrants-against-sergei-ivanovich-kobylash-and.

12 ICC Statute, Article 15bis, Resolution RC/Res.6, The Crime of Aggression, adopted on June 11, 2010, Annex 1, para. 3, https://treaties.un.org/doc/source/docs/RC-Res.6-ENG.pdf.

13 Philippe Sands, "Putin's Use of Military Force is a Crime of Aggression," *Financial Times*, February 28, 2022, https://www.ft.com/content/cbbdd146-4e36-42fb-95e1-50128506652c.

14 Gordon Brown et al., "Statement calling for the Creation of a Special Tribunal for the Punishment of the Crime of Aggression against Ukraine," March 4, 2022, https://gordonandsarahbrown.com/wp-content/uploads/2022/03/Combined-Statement-and-Declaration.pdf.

15 Statement by the Minister of Foreign Affairs of Ukraine at the SC Meeting on Russia's Aggression against Ukraine, Ministry of Foreign Affairs of Ukraine, September 22, 2022, https://mfa.gov.ua/en/news/statement-minister-foreign-affairs-ukraine-dmytro-kuleba-united-nations-security-council-meeting-russias-aggression-against-ukraine; President of Ukraine Volodymyr Zelenskyy, We must create a Special Tribunal on the crime of aggression against Ukraine—address by president Volodymyr Zelenskyy to the participants of the public debate "War and Law" in Paris, October 5, 2022, https://www.president.gov.ua/en/news/mayemo-stvoriti-specialnij-tribunal-shodo-zlochinu-agresiyi-78285.

16 Ministry of Foreign Affairs of Lithuania, The Ministers of Estonia, "Latvia and Lithuania Call to Establish a Special Tribunal to Investigate the Crime of Russia's Aggression," Joint Statement, October 16, 2022, https://urm.lt/default/en/news/the-ministers-of-estonia-latvia-and-lithuania-call-to-establish-a-special-tribunal-to-investigate-the-crime-of-russias-aggression. See also, "Law Not War: A Special Tribunal for the Crime of Aggression," side event organized in the margins of the International Law Week at the UN exploring relevant aspects of the creation of a Special Tribunal on the Crime of Aggression on the recommendation of the UN General Assembly, October 25, 2022, https://media.un.org/en/asset/k1q/k1qyewjw26.

17 France, Ministère de l'Europe et des affaires étrangères, "Ukraine – Tribunal spécial pour les crimes d'agression de la Russie," November 30, 2022, https://www.diplomatie.gouv.fr/fr/dossiers-pays/ukraine/evenements/article/ukraine-tribunal-special-pour-les-crimes-d-agression-de-la-russie-30-11-22.

18 Switzerland, Federal Department of Foreign Affairs, "War in Ukraine: Switzerland Calls for Special Tribunal," press release, November 16, 2023, https://www.admin.ch/gov/en/start/documentation/media-releases.msg-id-98640.html.

19 Germany, Federal Foreign Office, "Strengthening International Law in Times of Crisis," Speech by Federal Foreign Minister Annalena Baerbock in The Hague, January 16, 2023, https://www.auswaertiges-amt.de/en/newsroom/news/strengthening-international-law-in-times-of-crisis/2573492.

20 Council of Europe, Committee of Ministers, 1442nd meeting, September 14–15, 2022, Consequences of the aggression of Russian Federation against Ukraine, CM/Del/Dec(2022)1442/2.3, https://search.coe.int/cm/pages/result_details.aspx?objectid=0900001680a8135 a Parliamentary Assembly, resolution 2436 (2022), The Russian Federation's aggression against Ukraine: Ensuring accountability for serious violations of international humanitarian law and other international crimes, April 28, 2022.

21 OSCE Parliamentary Assembly, Resolution on the Russian Federation's war of aggression against Ukraine and its People, and its threat to Security across the OSCE region, July 6, 2022, paras 35–6, https://www.oscepa.org/en/documents/annual-sessions/2022-birmingham/4409-birmingham-declaration-eng/file.

22 NATO Parliamentary Assembly, Declaration Standing with Ukraine, 111 SESP 22 E rev.1, May 30, 2022, urging member governments and parliaments of the Alliance to support the initiatives aiming at establishing an *ad hoc* tribunal to investigate and prosecute the crime of aggression (§18j)).

23 European Parliament resolution on the fight against impunity for war crimes in Ukraine, 2022/2655, May 19, 2022, https://www.europarl.europa.eu/doceo/document/B-9-2022-0285_EN.html; European Parliament resolution on the establishment of

a tribunal on the crime of aggression against Ukraine, 2022/3017(RSP), January 19, 2023, https://www.europarl.europa.eu/doceo/document/TA-9-2023-0015_EN.html.

24 EU European Commission, "Statement by President von der Leyen on Russian Accountability and the Use of Russian Frozen Assets," November 30, 2022, https://ec.europa.eu/commission/presscorner/detail/en/statement_22_7307; EU European Commission, "Ukraine: Commission Presents Options to Make Sure that Russia Pays for its Crimes," press release, November 30, 2022, https://ec.europa.eu/commission/presscorner/detail/en/ip_22_7311.

25 Ukraine, Ministry of Foreign Affairs, "Dmytro Kuleba: Coalition for the Establishment of a Special Tribunal for the Crime of Aggression of the Russian Federation against Ukraine Will Continue to Grow," February 27, 2023, https://www.kmu.gov.ua/en/news/dmytro-kuleba-koalitsiia-zi-stvorennia-spetstrybunalu-shchodo-zlochynu-ahresii-rf-proty-ukrainy-prodovzhyt-zrostaty.

26 Italy, Ministry of Foreign Affairs, "Joint Statement on Efforts to Establish a Tribunal on the Crime of Aggression against Ukraine," May 9, 2023, https://www.esteri.it/en/sala_stampa/archivionotizie/comunicati/2023/05/joint-statement-on-efforts-to-establish-a-tribunal-on-the-crime-of-aggression-against-ukraine/.

27 Statement by President von der Leyen at the joint press conference with Ukrainian President Zelenskyy, February 2, 2023, https://neighbourhood-enlargement.ec.europa.eu/news/statement-president-von-der-leyen-joint-press-conference-ukrainian-president-zelenskyy-2023-02-02_en.

28 European Union Agency for Criminal Justice Cooperation (EUROJUST), "History in the Making – The International Centre for the Prosecution of the Crime of Aggression Against Ukraine Starts Operations at Eurojust," press release, July 3, 2023, https://www.eurojust.europa.eu/news/history-making-international-centre-prosecution-crime-aggression-against-ukraine-starts-operations-at-eurojust.

29 European Union Agency for Criminal Justice Cooperation (EUROJUST), "History in the Making – The International Centre for the Prosecution of the Crime of Aggression Against Ukraine Starts Operations at Eurojust," press release, July 3, 2023, https://www.eurojust.europa.eu/news/history-making-international-centre-prosecution-crime-aggression-against-ukraine-starts-operations-at-eurojust.

30 Albania, Andorra, Australia, Austria, Belgium, Bosnia and Herzegovina, Bulgaria, Canada, Croatia, Cyprus, Czechia, Denmark, Estonia, Finland, France, Georgia, Germany, Greece, Iceland, Ireland, Italy, Japan, Latvia, Liechtenstein, Lithuania, Luxembourg, Malta, Moldova, Monaco, Montenegro, the Netherlands, New Zealand, North Macedonia, Norway, Poland, Portugal, Romania, San Marino, Slovenia, Spain, Sweden, Ukraine, the United Kingdom, and the United States.

31 Restoring Justice for Ukraine, Political Declaration, The Hague, April 2, 2024, 3, para. 15, https://www.government.nl/documents/diplomatic-statements/2024/04/02/political-declaration-of-the-ministerial-restoring-justice-for-ukraine-conference.

32 Corten and Koutroulis, *Tribunal for the Crime of Aggression against Ukraine*, 3–4; Global Accountability Network, *Considerations for the setting up of the Special Tribunal for Ukraine on the Crime of Aggression*, report, July 2022, https://www.globalaccountabilitynetwork.org/_files/ugd/a982f0_6c35a85b089746a18a6334d2801e9c5d.pdf; Patrick Butchard, *Conflict in Ukraine: A Special Tribunal on the Crime of Aggression*, Research Briefing, House of Commons Library, February 22, 2024, 23, https://commonslibrary.parliament.uk/research-briefings/cbp-9968/#:~

:text=Conflict%20in%20Ukraine%3A%20A%20Special%20Tribunal%20on%20the %20Crime%20of%20Aggression,-Research%20Briefing&text=Two%20years %20after%20Russia's%20full,to%20prosecuting%20aggression%20against%20 Ukraine.; Claus Kreß, "Russia's War of Aggression Against Ukraine and the Crime of Aggression," in *The War in Ukraine and International Law*, ed. Masahiko Asada and Dai Tamada (Singapore: Springer, 2024), 55–78; Tom Dannenbaum, "A Special Tribunal for the Crime of Aggression?," *Journal of International Criminal Justice* 20, no. 4 (September 2022): 859–73; Advisory Committee on Public International Law, *Challenges in Prosecuting the Crime of Aggression: Jurisdiction and Immunities*, Advisory Report No. 40, September 12, 2022, https://www.advisorycommitteeinternationallaw.nl/publications/advisory-reports/2022/09/12/challenges-in-prosecuting-the-crime-of-aggression-jurisdiction-and-immunities; Jennifer Trahan, "The Need for an International Tribunal on the Crime of Aggression Regarding the Situation in Ukraine," *Fordham International Law Journal* 46, no. 5 (2023): 671–90; Carrie McDougall, "The Imperative of Prosecuting Crimes of Aggression Committed against Ukraine," *Journal of Conflict and Security Law* 28, no. 2 (summer 2023): 203–30; Rosanne van Alebeek, Larissa van den Herik, and Cedric Ryngaert, "Prosecuting Russian Officials for the Crime of Aggression: What about Immunities?," *European Convention of Human Rights Law Review* 4, no. 2 (2023): 115–32; Larry D. Johnson, "United Nations Response Options to Russia's Aggression: Opportunities and Rabbit Holes", *Just Security*, March 1, 2022, https://www.justsecurity.org/80395/united-nations-response-options-to-russias-aggression-opportunities-and-rabbit-holes/; Chatham House, *A Criminal Tribunal for Aggression in Ukraine*, March 4, 2022, https://www.chathamhouse.org/events/all/research-event/criminal-tribunal-aggression-ukraine; Kevin Jon Heller, "Creating a Special Tribunal for Aggression Against Ukraine is a Bad Idea," *Opinio Juris*, March 7, 2022, https://opiniojuris.org/2022/03/07/creating-a-special-tribunal-for-aggression-against-ukraine-is-a-bad-idea/; Jennifer Trahan, "U.N. General Assembly Should Recommend Creation of Crime of Aggression Tribunal For Ukraine: Nuremberg Is Not The Model," *Just Security*, March 7, 2022, https://www.justsecurity.org/80545/u-n-general-assembly-should-recommend-creation-of-crime-of-aggression-tribunal-for-ukraine-nuremberg-is-not-the-model/; Tom Dannenbaum, "Mechanisms for Criminal Prosecution of Russia's Aggression Against Ukraine," *Just Security*, March 10, 2022, https://www.justsecurity.org/80626/mechanisms-for-criminal-prosecution-of-russias-aggression-against-ukraine/; Carrie McDougall, "Why Creating a Special Tribunal for Aggression Against Ukraine is the Best Available Option: A Reply to Kevin Jon Heller and Other Critics," *Opinio Juris*, March 15, 2022, http://opiniojuris.org/2022/03/15/why-creating-a-special-tribunal-for-aggression-against-ukraine-is-the-best-available-option-a-reply-to-kevin-jon-heller-and-other-critics/; Kevin Jon Heller, "The Best Option: An Extraordinary Ukrainian Chamber for Aggression," *Opinio Juris*, March 16, 2022, https://opiniojuris.org/2022/03/16/the-best-option-an-extraordinary-ukrainian-chamber-for-aggression/; Dapo Akande, "Use of Force Under International Law – The Case of Ukraine," 62nd Meeting of the Committee of Legal Advisers on Public International Law (CAHDI), March 25, 2022, Strasbourg, 6–7, para. 28, https://rm.coe.int/cahdi-62-akande-use-of-force-under-pil-the-case-of-ukraine-25-march-20/1680a67f82; Owiso Owiso, "An Aggression Chamber for Ukraine Supported by the Council of Europe," *Opinio Juris*, March 30, 2022, http://

opiniojuris.org/2022/03/30/an-aggression-chamber-for-ukraine-supported-by-the-council-of-europe/; Janet H. Anderson, "A Nuremberg for Russia's Crime of Aggression?," *JusticeInfo.net*, April 22, 2002, https://www.justiceinfo.net/en/91135-nuremberg-russia-crime-of-aggression.html; Letter dated August 12, 2022, from the representatives of Latvia, Liechtenstein and Ukraine to the United Nations addressed to the Secretary-General, Chair's summary of an event organized by the permanent missions of Latvia and Liechtenstein to the United Nations in June 2022, reported in UN General Assembly – UN Security Council, UN Doc. A/ES-11/7 – S/2022/616, August 17, 2022, 3, https://www.justsecurity.org/wp-content/uploads/2022/09/UNSC-Letter-12-August-2022.pdf; Oona Hathaway, "The Case for Creating an International Tribunal to Prosecute the Crime of Aggression Against Ukraine. Part I," *Just Security*, September 20, 2022, Astrid Reisinger Coracini, "The Case for Creating an International Tribunal to Prosecute the Crime of Aggression Against Ukraine. Part II: Jurisdiction and Composition", *Just Security*, September 23, 2022, Jennifer Traham, "The Case for Creating an International Tribunal to Prosecute the Crime of Aggression Against Ukraine. Part III: How Many to Prosecute, Immunity, Amnesty and More," *Just Security*, September 26, 2002, David Scheffer, "The Case for Creating a Special Tribunal to prosecute the Crime of Aggression Committed Against Ukraine. Part IV: Information Sharing, Victim participation, Outreach and More," *Just Security*, September 28, 2002, all available at https://www.justsecurity.org/tag/u-n-general-assembly-and-international-criminal-tribunal-for-russian-aggression-against-ukraine/.

33 Chair's summary of an event organized by Latvia and Liechtenstein, A/ES-11/7 – S/2022/616, comments by Yale Law School Professor Oona Hathaway.

34 Akande, "Use of Force Under International Law – The Case of Ukraine", 6–7, para. 28.

35 Chair's summary of an event organized by Latvia and Liechtenstein, A/ES-11/7 – S/2022/616, 3; Hathaway, "International Tribunal. Part I"; Scheffer, "International Tribunal. Part IV"; Johnson, "Opportunities and Rabbit Holes"; Trahan, "Nuremberg is Not the Model"; Dannenbaum, "Mechanisms."

36 Heller, "The Best Option"; Global Accountability Network, *Considerations for the Setting up of The Special Tribunal*, 7.

37 See, among many, Brown, Statement; Philippe Sands, "Why We Need a New Nuremberg Trial to Make Putin Pay," *Daily Mail*, March 4, 2022, https://www.dailymail.co.uk/news/ukraine/article-10579137/PHILIPPE-SANDS-need-new-Nuremberg-trial-make-Putin-pay.; see some of the scholars interviewed in Anderson, "A Nuremberg for Russia's Crime of Aggression?"; UN Security Council, Verbatim record, UN Doc. S/PV.9011, April 5, 2022, 9 (speech made by President of Ukraine Volodymyr Zelenskyy).

38 See, among many, Corten and Koutroulis, *Tribunal for the Crime of Aggression*, 3–4.

39 ILC, Principles of international law recognized in the Charter of the Nürnberg Tribunal and in the Judgment of the Tribunal, with commentaries, *Yearbook of the International Law Commission*, 1950, vol. II, 374.

40 Volodymyr Zelenskyy, President of Ukraine, "We Must Create a Special Tribunal on the Crime of Aggression against Ukraine," Address by President Volodymyr Zelenskyy to the participants of the public debate "War and Law" in Paris, October 9, 2022, https://www.president.gov.ua/en/news/mayemo-stvoriti-specialnij-tribunal-shodo-zlochinu-agresiyi-78285.

41 Brown, Statement.
42 ILC, Nuremberg principles with commentaries, 374–8.
43 President of Ukraine, Bucha Declaration on accountability for the most serious crimes under international law committed on the territory of Ukraine, March 31, 2023, https://www.president.gov.ua/en/news/buchanska-deklaraciya-shodo-vidpovidalnosti-za-najtyazhchi-z-82005> (emphasis in the original).
44 International Military Tribunal (Nuremberg), Judgment of October 1, 1046, *The Trial of German Major War Criminals: Proceedings of the International Military Tribunal sitting at Nuremberg, Germany*, Part 22 (London, 1950), 447.
45 See among many, ICTY, *Prosecutor v. Dusko Tadic*, Decision on the Defence Motion for Interlocutory Appeal on Jurisdiction, Appeals Chamber, Decision, October 2, 1995, para. 128; ICTY, *Prosecutor v. Anto Furundzija*, Judgment, Trial Chamber, December 10, 1998, para. 140; The London Conference on International Law: "Engaging with International Law," keynote Speech of Judge Abdulqawi A. Yusuf, President of the International Court of Justice, October 3, 2019, 5, para. 27, https://www.icj-cij.org/sites/default/files/press-releases/0/000-20191003-STA-01-00-EN.pdf; Statement of Minister of Foreign Affairs of Armenia Ararat Mirzoyan at the official welcoming ceremony for Armenia as a new State party to the ICC Statute, February 8, 2024, pronounced at the ceremony for the accession of Armenia to the ICC Statute, https://www.mfa.am/en/speeches/2024/02/08/Ararat_Mirzoyan_ICC/12478; Judge Philippe Kirsch, President of the International Criminal Court, "Applying the Principles of Nuremberg in the ICC," Keynote Address at the Conference "Judgment at Nuremberg" held on the 60th Anniversary of the Nuremberg Judgment, Washington University, September 30, 2006, 3, https://www.icc-cpi.int/sites/default/files/NR/rdonlyres/ED2F5177-9F9B-4D66-9386-5C5BF45D052C/146323/PK_20930_English.pdf; Chantal Meloni, "Individual Criminal Responsibility," *Oxford Bibliographies*, October 28, 2020, https://www.oxfordbibliographies.com/display/document/obo-9780199796953/obo-9780199796953-0215.xml; Andreas Zimmermann, "The Creation of a Permanent International Criminal Court," *Max Planck Yearbook of United Nations Law* 2 (1998): 169.
46 IMTN, *Judgment*, Part 22, 421.
47 ICJ, *Armed Activities on the Territory of the Congo (Democratic Republic of the Congo v. Uganda)*, judgment of December 19, 2005, Declaration of Judge Elaraby, *ICJ Reports 2005*, 329, para. 10; ICTY, *Prosecutor v. Anto Furundzija*, Appeals Chamber, Judgment, July 21, 2000, case no. IT-95-17/1-A, Declaration of Judge Lal Chand Vohrah, para. 3; Judge Hans-Peter Kaul, Second Vice-President of the International Criminal Court, "The Crime of Aggression after Kampala – Some Personal Thoughts on the Way Forward," Remarks at the international law symposium "Beyond Kampala: The ICC, the Crime of Aggression, and the Future of the Court," May 13, 2011, 9, https://www.icc-cpi.int/sites/default/files/NR/rdonlyres/2054CCC9-4FB7-4839-B847-292206BF6E16/283357/12052011_TheCrimeofAggressionafterKampala.pdf; Benjamin B. Ferencz, "Ending Impunity for the Crime of Aggression," *Case Western Reserve Journal for International Law* 41, no. 2 (2009): 281–90.
48 European parliament resolution of 19 January 2023 on the establishment of a tribunal on the crime of aggression against Ukraine (2022/3017(RSP)), P9 TA(2023)0015, paragraph M.
49 Poland, Ministry of Foreign Affairs, "Poland supports the creation of a Special Tribunal for Crimes of Aggression against Ukraine," March 7, 2023, https://www.gov

.pl/web/diplomacy/poland-supports-creation-of-a-special-tribunal-for-crimes-of-aggression-against-ukraine.

50 Albania, Belgium, Estonia, Guatemala, Latvia, Liechtenstein, Lithuania, Luxembourg, Marshall Islands, North Macedonia, Poland, and Ukraine, Frequently Asked Questions: A Special Tribunal for the Crime of Aggression against Ukraine, Permanent Mission of the Republic of Latvia to the United Nations, March 5, 2024. Footnote 4, to which the text refers, states that "In its judgment, the International Military Tribunal at Nuremberg declared, '*To initiate a war of aggression . . . is not only an international crime; it is the supreme international crime differing only from other war crimes in that it contains within itself the accumulated evil of the whole.*' IMT, judgment of 1 October 1946, in The Trial of German Major War Criminals," https://www2.mfa.gov.lv/en/newyork/news/69560-frequently-asked-questions-a-special-tribunal-for-the-crime-of-aggression-against-ukraine.

51 Brown, Statement.

52 Ambassador Rein Tammsaar (Estonia), "An International Special Tribunal is the Only Viable Path to a Just and Lasting Peace in Ukraine", *Just Security*, May 9, 2023, https://www.justsecurity.org/86516/an-international-special-tribunal-is-the-only-viable-path-to-a-just-and-lasting-peace-in-ukraine/.

53 Tammsaar, "Only Viable Path". The reference to the UN General Assembly points to the adoption of a resolution by the Assembly either actively participating in the creation of the special tribunal (similar to the precedent of the Extraordinary Chambers in the Courts of Cambodia) or at least endorsing it.

54 Beth Van Schaack, Ambassador-at-large for Global Criminal Justice, US Department of State, Remarks to the Helsinki Commission: "Holding Russia Accountable for War Crimes Against Ukraine: Lessons from Nuremberg," February 20, 2024, https://www.state.gov/remarks-to-the-helsinki-commission-holding-russia-accountable-for-war-crimes-against-ukraine-lessons-from-nuremberg/. See also Beth Van Schaack, "Ambassador Van Schaack's Remarks on the US Proposal to prosecute Russian Crimes of Aggression," Remarks at the Nuremberg Principles Meeting, Catholic University of America, March 27, 2023, https://www.state.gov/ambassador-van-schaacks-remarks/:

> there are compelling arguments for why this crime [ie the crime of aggression] must be prosecuted alongside the Rome Statute crimes. In my public remarks, I often emphasize that we are at an historic moment for international justice. Today's efforts reflect the tremendous legacy of the Nuremburg and Tokyo Tribunals established after World War II, the work of the *ad hoc* international tribunals dedicated to the conflicts in the former Yugoslavia and Rwanda, the establishment of a permanent International Criminal Court, and the plethora of international justice mechanisms that have followed since.
>
> These were times when the world came together to deliver a measure of justice in the face of atrocities. I am proud that at each of these moments, the United States supported the advancement of international criminal law and accountability. At Nuremburg, for example, the United States led the prosecution of the crime of aggression—deemed "crimes against the peace" in the lexicon of the era.
>
> Again now, at this critical moment in history, I am pleased to announce that the United States supports the development of an internationalized tribunal dedicated to prosecuting the crime of aggression against Ukraine.

55 McDougall, "The Imperative," 229.
56 International Crisis Group, *A New Court to prosecute Russia's Illegal War?*, March 29, 2023, https://www.crisisgroup.org/global-ukraine/new-court-prosecute-russias-illegal-war.
57 ILC, Nuremberg principles with commentaries, pp. 374–8: affirmation of individual criminal responsibility for crimes under international law (principle I); irrelevance of internal law (principle II); irrelevance of official position (principle III); irrelevance of superior orders (principle IV); right to a fait trial of persons charged with an international crime (principle V); definitions of international crimes (principle VI); responsibility for complicity(principle VII).
58 It is true that, in parallel to the formulation of the Nuremberg principles, the UN General Assembly also directed the ILC to "prepare a draft code of offences against the peace and security of mankind"; see A/RES/177(III) adopted November 21, 1947. One year later, when the Convention on the prevention and punishment of the crime of genocide was adopted, the General Assembly invited the Commission to "study the desirability and possibility of establishing an international judicial organ for the trial of persons, charged with genocide and other crimes over which jurisdiction will be conferred upon that organ by international conventions"; see A/RES/260(III)B, adopted on December 9, 1948. Nevertheless, despite the obvious connection to these topics, the Nuremberg principles do not refer explicitly to an international court or tribunal as the judicial body vested with the competence to judge individuals responsible for international crimes.
59 See among many, Corten and Koutroulis, *Tribunal for the Crime of Aggression*, 14–35.
60 ILC, Nuremberg principles with commentaries, 376, para. 113.
61 A/RES/3314(XXIX), adopted on December 14, 1974, Annex: Definition of Aggression, article 3.
62 ICC Statute, Article 8bis, Resolution RC/Res.6, The Crime of Aggression, adopted on June 11, 2010, https://treaties.un.org/doc/source/docs/RC-Res.6-ENG.pdf.
63 Note from the permanent Delegation of Norway, April 10, 1951, reproduced in *Yearbook of the International Law Commission*, 1951, vol. II, p. 105.
64 ILC, Nuremberg principles with commentaries, 376, paras. 116–7.
65 Kevin Jon Heller, "Retreat from Nuremberg: The Leadership Requirement in the Crime of Aggression," *European Journal of International Law* 18, no. 3 (June 2007): 477–97; Carrie McDougall, *The Crime of Aggression under the Rome Statute of the International Criminal Court* (2nd ed., Cambridge: Cambridge University Press, 2021), 214–32.
66 ICC Statute, Article 8*bis*, Resolution RC/Res.6, Annex I, para 2 (emphasis added).
67 ICC Statute, Article 25(3)*bis*, Resolution RC/Res.6, Annex I, para 5. For the elements of the crime of aggression see Annex II, Amendments to the elements of the crimes, element no. 2.
68 Advisory Committee on Public International Law, *Challenges in Prosecuting the Crime of Aggression*, 9.
69 Dannenbaum, "Mechanisms." See also Heller, "Retreat from Nuremberg", 477–97.
70 ICC Statute, Article 25(3)*bis*, Resolution RC/Res.6, Annex III, Understandings regarding the amendments to the Rome Statute of the International Criminal Court on the crime of aggression, para 4.

71 Advisory Committee on Public International Law, *Challenges in prosecuting the crime of aggression*, 10. See also McDougall, "A Reply to Kevin Jon Heller and Other Critics": "I agree that others in Russia and Belarus who meet the definition of a potential perpetrator found in Article 8bis(1) of the Rome Statute ('a person in a position effectively to exercise control over or to direct the political or military action of a State') should be investigated and, if warranted, prosecuted."
72 Charter of the International Military Tribunal, Annexed to the London Agreement, Article 7, https://www.legal-tools.org/doc/64ffdd/pdf.
73 ILC, Nuremberg principles with commentaries, 375.
74 ILC, Nuremberg principles with commentaries, 375, para. 103.
75 Draft Code of Offences against the Peace and Security of Mankind, *Yearbook of the International Law Commission*, 1954, vol. II, 137: "Article 3: The fact that a person acted as head of State or as responsible government official does not relieve him from responsibility for committing any of the offences defined in this Code." The Commentary reproduces article 7 of the Charter of the Nürnberg Tribunal and Principle III of the ILC Nuremberg Principles but without any substantive analysis.
76 Draft Code of Crimes against the Peace and Security of Mankind, *Yearbook of the International Law Commission*, 1996, vol. II, part two, 26.
77 Draft Code of Crimes against the Peace and Security of Mankind, 1996, 27, paras. 2–4 and 6.
78 Immunity of State officials from foreign criminal jurisdiction, *Report of the International Law Commission*, 73rd session (April 18–June 3 and July 4–August 5, 2022), A/77/10, 195, para. 2.
79 Immunity of State officials from foreign criminal jurisdiction, A/77/10, 230–42.
80 Immunity of State officials from foreign criminal jurisdiction, A/77/10, 189–90, draft article 1 (Scope of the present draft articles), paras. 1 and 3.
81 ICJ, *Arrest Warrant of 11 April 2000 (Democratic Republic of the Congo v. Belgium)*, judgment of 14 February 2002, *I.C.J. Reports 2002*, 23, para. 56; ICJ, *Arrest Warrant of 11 April 2000 (Democratic Republic of the Congo v. Belgium)*, Counter-Memorial of the Kingdom of Belgium, September 28, 2001, 131–85.
82 *Arrest Warrant of 11 April 2000*, Counter Memorial of the Kingdom of Belgium, 134–5, paras. 3.5.21–3.5.23; 137, para. 3.5.26; 143–4, paras. 3.5.46–3.5.49; 147–9, paras. 3.5.61–3.5.66; 164–8, paras. 3.5.105–3.5.114.
83 ICJ, *Arrest Warrant* judgment, 20, para. 48.
84 ICJ, *Arrest Warrant* judgment, 24, para. 58.
85 ICJ, *Arrest Warrant* judgment, 25–6, para. 61.
86 ICC, Appeals Chamber, *Judgment in the Jordan Referral re Al-Bashir Appeal*, May 6, 2019, ICC-02/05-01/09 OA2, 52–60, paras. 100–19, https://www.icc-cpi.int/sites/default/files/CourtRecords/CR2019_02856.PDF.
87 Rome Statute of the International Criminal Court, UNTS 2137, no 38544, 106, Article 27(2).
88 ICC, *Jordan Appeal* Judgment, 53–4, paras. 103–5.
89 Permanent Mission of Estonia to the UN, Joint statement by Albania, Belgium, Costa Rica, Czech Republic, Estonia, Guatemala, Latvia, Liechtenstein, Lithuania, Luxembourg, Marshall Islands, North-Macedonia, and Poland on the accountability for the crime of aggression committed on the territory of Ukraine, April 17, 2023, https://un.mfa.ee/joint-statement-on-the-accountability-for-the-crime-of-aggression-committed-on-the-territory-of-ukraine/.

90 Global Accountability Network, *Considerations for the Setting up of The Special Tribunal*, 4–5 and 21 (references omitted). See also Trahan, "The Need for an International Tribunal on the Crime of Aggression," 687–8 (discussing a tribunal based on a treaty between the UN and Ukraine on the basis of a UNGA recommendation).
91 Letter from the Permanent Delegation of Denmark, April 4, 1951, reproduced in *Yearbook of the International Law Commission*, 1951, vol. II, 104.
92 Dannenbaum, "Mechanisms"; see also, Advisory Committee on Public International Law, *Challenges in Prosecuting the Crime of Aggression*, 8.
93 Corten and Koutroulis, *Tribunal for the Crime of Aggression*, 30.
94 *Yearbook of the International Law Commission*, 1949, 133, para. 35 and 282, para. 27.
95 Letter from the Permanent Delegation of Denmark, April 4, 1951, reproduced in *Yearbook of the International Law Commission*, 1951, vol. II, 104.
96 McDougall, "The Imperative," 229.
97 Ambos, "A Ukraine Special Tribunal with Legitimacy Problems?"; see also Corten and Koutroulis, *Tribunal for the Crime of Aggression*, 40–3.

Selected Bibliography

Corten, Olivier, and Vaios Koutroulis, "Tribunal for the Crime of Aggression against Ukraine - A Legal Assessment, In-depth Analysis Requested by for the Policy Department of the Directorate-General for External Policies," European Parliament, December 14, 2022, https://www.europarl.europa.eu/RegData/etudes/IDAN/2022/702574/EXPO_IDA(2022)702574_EN.pdf.

Dannenbaum, Tom, "A Special Tribunal for the Crime of Aggression?," *Journal of International Criminal Justice* 20, no. 4 (September 2022): 859–73.

International Law Commission, "Principles of International Law Recognized in the Charter of the Nürnberg Tribunal and in the Judgment of the Tribunal, with Commentaries." New York: Yearbook of the International Law Commission, 1950, vol. II, 374–8.

Kreß, Claus, "Russia's War of Aggression Against Ukraine and the Crime of Aggression," in *The War in Ukraine and International Law*, eds. Masahiko Asada and Dai Tamada (Singapore: Springer, 2024), 55–78.

McDougall, Carrie, "The Imperative of Prosecuting Crimes of Aggression Committed against Ukraine," *Journal of Conflict and Security Law* 28, no. 2 (summer 2023): 203–30.

Trahan, Jennifer, "The Need for an International Tribunal on the Crime of Aggression Regarding the Situation in Ukraine," *Fordham International Law Journal* 46, no. 5 (2023): 671–90.

Part 6

The Nuremberg Principles

Theology–Philosophy–Reconciliation

16

Meditation on Truth, Memory, Justice, and Deterrence[1]

Marshall Breger

Now that the International Criminal Court has announced two indictments of Vladimir Putin for war crimes, the process of applying the international rule of law to Russia's invasion of Ukraine has begun.[2] In March 2024, the International Criminal Court issued arrest warrants for Russian General Sergei Kobylash, commander of the Russian long-range aviation force, and Admiral Viktor Sokolov, head of the Black Sea fleet, for their leadership roles in bombing Ukrainian civilian population centers and critical infrastructure.[3]

It may seem presumptuous to point this out before war crimes trials are even started, but it is a fact that most war crimes tribunals have an endpoint—they stop investigating before all the perpetrators have been found. The Nuremberg Military Tribunals themselves were wound down in 1948 (and the caseload handed over to the German authorities) in recognition of "pressure from a Washington administration whose enthusiasm for war crimes trials was rapidly ebbing away."[4]

The rule-of-law community instinctively supports the accountability provided by war crimes trials—after all, it's what we do. However, one must ask how much of this is virtue signaling? It is hard to imagine how political leaders like Putin or the Russian generals will be actually hauled into the dock. For one, who would hand them over for trial? Russia would have to be defeated and sued for peace, or Putin would have to be removed by an internal coup—and not just a coup by right-wing revanchists who thought Putin was not authoritarian enough, but by those who want to transform Russia into a democracy abiding by the rule of law.

There are probably thousands of low-level soldiers and bureaucrats who might be—surely should be—charged with crimes. Ukraine already has opened 47,000 war crime cases and at least 100,000 collaboration cases.[5] International or even domestic Ukrainian tribunals cannot deal with all of them. This does not mean that such institutions should not be created—there is a benefit in perpetrators knowing that they may end up before a tribunal if they travel to the wrong place. And there is a benefit in the international community facilitating a culture of accountability in war.

When we speak about the Nuremberg Principles and war crimes, we speak of justice for victims. The goals of war crimes trials are a mixture of accountability, memory, truth, and deterrence. But it is worth considering how alternative approaches to justice—beyond the Nuremberg-style tribunal—might help achieve these goals.

Accountability

By accountability, I mean that the perpetrators are identified and held accountable for their actions. In the rule-of-law community that means some form of justice—most usually retributive justice.

To be frank, war crimes trials are a way of structuring a legal process without the whiff of revenge (parenthetically, that is why many support international rather than domestic tribunals). The Nuremberg trials focused on retributive justice. At the 1943 Tehran Conference, the Russians wanted revenge, but the United States and Britain insisted on war crimes trials.[6] Thus, the Allies tried high-level Nazis for crimes against humanity, and those who were found guilty after a full trial were punished. For those concerned about the rule of law, this was a significant advance over revenge.

Retributive justice usually means that punishment is proportionate to the seriousness of the crime—that the perpetrator will receive just desserts. But "an eye for an eye" is impossible in most war crimes trials. The crimes are simply too gargantuan. Indeed, if the EU is involved, the most extreme penalty—death—is likely off the table. What is the proportional punishment for bombing a children's nursery and killing scores of infants?

Memory

One stated value of war crimes trials, besides justice, is memory. Memory has at least four functions in this area.

Hòmage

The first function of memory allows one to fulfill what the French call *devoir de mémoire*, the duty to remember.[7] It can be seen as a form of hòmage, a way of keeping individuals and their lives from falling into oblivion.

The minimum indicium of memory is one's name. That is why, on 9-11 each year, the names of those individuals murdered in that terror attack are read so that they may not be forgotten.[8] It is why the Vietnam War Memorial in Washington lists by name the over 58,000 soldiers killed in that conflict[9] and why the Hall of Names at Yad Vashem seeks to register the names of every individual murdered in the Shoah.[10] All this is a kind of "sacralization of names."[11] It is why churchyards all over the English countryside contain stone memorials to the fallen of the First World War. All to ensure, as Lawrence Binyon has written, "at the going down of the sun and in the morning/we will remember them."[12]

To whom do we owe this duty? Avishai Margalit, in his powerful book *The Ethics of Memory,* says that what he calls "thick" duties of memory exist for those who are in a "community of memory," including a "parent, friend, lover, fellow-countryman." Thus, it is to one's fellow citizens that one owes a duty of memory.[13]

Collective Memory

At the same time, collective memory can also increase collective trauma. A cult of memory can make reconciliation near impossible. The Jewish quarter of Hebron derives its identity from the massacre of Hebron Jews by Arabs in 1929. The "contemporary community of Hebron now resides in the houses of the former community—even in the same rooms where the killings took place."[14] Journalists covering the siege of Srebrenica in the Balkan War in 1992 recounted that when they asked Serbians why they were fighting, they simply answered "1453"—the year the Ottomans conquered Christian Constantinople.[15]

Forgetting is an element of human consciousness that is of great value. Without forgetting, we would have only the past but no present (and perhaps no future). We could never move forward with our lives.[16] Sadly, the truth may not always set us free. One must balance forgetting and remembering. Of course, it may well be the case that one has to actively remember before one actively forgets. As Martin Imbleau suggests, "Before turning the page on events, a population needs to know what it is turning that page on."[17]

Collective amnesia may allow not just a society but also its citizens to rebuild their lives. Some years ago, the Rwandan ambassador to the United States, speaking of the murder of 1 million, told me that Rwandans had no choice but to forget because, "we have to live with the fact that our neighbors committed these atrocities. We see them every day. They are still our neighbors. We have no choice—if our community is to survive, we must find a way to reconcile with them. We live next to each other cheek-by-jowl."[18]

Collective memory may also serve to foster group solidarity. Indeed, one must keep in mind that collective memory is a social construct—in the words of French sociologist Maurice Halbwachs—"a reconstruction of the past in light of the present."[19] Indeed, it can be seen as "the selective reconstruction and appropriation of aspects of the past that respond to the needs of the present."[20] The "March of the Living," which takes Israeli high school youth to the death camps in Poland, has become a mandatory milestone in shaping their collective identity as Israeli Jews, underscoring what would happen if Jews again became weak.[21]

Of course, victims may not want to reconcile. They may not want to forgive.[22] Indeed, there may be tension between individual and communal reconciliation. In the early 1950s, Israel reached a restitution agreement with Germany for financial reparations vital to the survival (or so it was thought) of the Jewish state.[23] Blood flowed in the streets as individual Holocaust survivors recoiled from what they considered state reconciliation with Germany.[24] The state was prepared for some degree of reconciliation for reasons of *realpolitik*, but many individuals were not.

Truth

A third function of memory is to ensure that the horrors are not forgotten or, even worse, that a false narrative is accepted. In the Warsaw Ghetto, Emanuel Ringelblum collected documentation of Nazi atrocities (code name *Oyneg Shabes*), knowing he and his community were doomed. The documentation, buried in milk cartons, was his group's answer to the question, "Who will write our history?"[25]

On that point, we must consider how best to secure the truth. The UN Human Rights Commission has suggested that there is, in some sense, a "right to know," a "right to be informed," or a "right to the truth."[26] This right may in some formulations be independent from the "right to justice."

This right to truth has been a developing concept in human rights discourse. Still, "its definition as a general right remains elusive."[27] Indeed, some suggest that its status leaves "it somewhere above a good argument and somewhere below a clear legal rule."[28] In many ways, a right to truth is predicated on a duty to investigate (so as to uncover the truth). The Inter-American Court of Justice has determined in *Velasquez Rodriguez* that there is a duty to investigate individual human rights violations and, in later cases, found that with serious violations, there is a duty to prosecute.[29] The European Court of Human Rights found there is a duty to investigate but not necessarily a duty to prosecute.[30]

A unique approach to uncovering truth was the Argentine creation of a judicial forum for enforcing "the right to truth."[31] The Court is charged with making a declarative judgment, not a punitive one. In this sense, they saw the "truth" not as a precondition for accountability or punishment but as an end in itself. This approach developed during the period of legal amnesty for the Argentine dictatorship.[32] With accountability seemingly stalled, using the courts in a truth-finding role at least would allow the right to truth to be adjudicated. Most cases of this kind are related to the time of the dictatorship. However, in one unusual proceeding, the Argentine judicial system in 2011 found that Turkey committed genocide against the Armenians during and after the First World War.[33]

Deterrence

A final purpose of focusing on memory is the belief that knowledge of such crimes will lead to deterrence. In this view, memory is a prophylactic that can avert future horrors. As George Santayana iconically stated, "Those who refuse to remember the past are condemned to relive it."[34] That is the gravamen of the clarion call "Never Again." But there is scant evidence that "never again" is more than a shibboleth. David Rieff wrote, "After Sarajevo, after Srebrenica, we now know what 'never again' means. Never again simply means never again will Germans kill Jews in Europe in the 1940s. That is all it means."[35]

Alternatives

If war crimes trials cannot do the entire job, is it too soon to broach alternatives? The reasons for doing so may be both pragmatic and moral—pragmatic as the accountability of war crimes trials for all perpetrators may be infeasible, and moral in that justice might be better pursued by other means. One increasingly popular option has been the Truth and Reconciliation Commission.

After the 1994 South African election, when non-whites were first able to vote, the question was how to deal with the crimes of apartheid and with those who committed those crimes. Many wanted revenge. Others called for justice. But what kind of justice? There is justice in ethics and justice in law, and there are different principles of legal justice, including distributional justice (aimed at equity) and procedural justice (aimed at fairness). Two other essential principles of justice that have long been discussed are retributive justice (letting the punishment fit the crime) and restorative justice (focusing on the victim and what "restoreth [his] soul").[36]

After his election, President Nelson Mandela set up a Truth and Reconciliation Commission (TRC). Archbishop Desmond Tutu was chosen as its chairman. Tutu understood that South African society would need more than retributive justice. Such justice can be harsh and may not lead to peace. Indeed, it can lead to resentment and even violence (whether warranted or not).

Thus, Tutu sought less retributive justice and more what he called a "higher form of justice"—restorative justice. Restorative justice is the "process of bringing together individuals who have been affected by an offense and having them agree on how to repair the harm caused by the crime."[37] Restorative justice concerns itself not only with the treatment of the offender but with the healing of the victims—focusing on values of dignity, of redemption, of self-worth, and the healing values of forgiveness. These values enhance the idea of justice, rather than substitute for it.

The Commission began work in 1996 and issued a final report in 1998.

The Report was five volumes and totaled more than 3000 pages.[38] It laid out in public view a gruesome litany of the crimes of apartheid.

In a sense, TRC was a Plan B. The report states, "Nuremberg-style tribunals were simply not a viable political option, given the balance of military and political forces that prevailed at the time."[39] This is often true whenever alternative justice approaches are tried. The "old regime" may still have some modicum of state power. Thus, after the death of the Generalissimo in 1975, all parties in Spain accepted the Pacto del Olvido (the path of forgetting) to allow Spain to move forward.[40]

Many interest groups in South Africa objected to the report's publication. Indeed, "the TRC was sued by nearly every major political party in South Africa."[41] The ANC opposition was particularly instructive. While the ANC supported the creation of the TRC (after all, Nelson Mandela was in favor), days before the publication of the Final Report, they sought to censor some of the report's criticism of ANC activities. The commission rejected the ANC's request by one vote (Desmond Tutu's). The ANC then went to the Supreme Court and lost. There is little doubt that the Commission's willingness to take on the ANC increased its legitimacy.[42]

Some early truth commissions did not publicly identify persons responsible for human rights violations. At least four truth commissions urged some level of lustration provision, but only one—El Salvador—followed through (albeit only partially).[43] The demand for a truthful narrative is seen in the lustration laws passed in Eastern European countries after the collapse of the Soviet Union, all designed to learn who among the population were informers.[44]

A cognate question is whether the victim's testimony should be confidential. "[D]ifferent societies have made different decisions regarding the publicity or privacy of the testimonies . . . provided under the veil of confidentiality."[45] In some countries, confidentiality was maintained to protect witnesses' safety, while in other cases, it was to defend their right to privacy or dignity.[46] In Chile, for example, victims' testimonies must remain secret until 2054.[47] In other countries, such as Sierra Leone, the Commission can decide to maintain confidentiality at its own discretion.[48] In El Salvador, the testimony must be made public "when there is reliable testimony available, especially when the persons identified occupy senior positions and perform official functions directly related to violations or the cover-up of violations."[49]

Truth Commission reports often differ from the transcripts of war crimes trials. They are less interested in adjudicating the guilt or innocence of specific persons than in developing a historical narrative. In that way, they differ radically from war crimes tribunals. That may be why in 1946, George Orwell, Arthur Koestler, and other intellectuals urged that the Nuremberg trials include a component that would explore "historical truths related to Stalin's claim that Leon Trotsky had collaborated with Hitler," not only the guilt or innocence of individuals.[50] And why, in a *Financial Times* article, Quentin Peel suggested that the Yugoslav war crimes tribunal "confused the need to bring one man to account with the need to produce a clear narrative of war crimes and direction for the history books."[51]

There is a natural tension between truth and reconciliation. It is not clear why truth will lead to reconciliation. Indeed, it has been argued that full knowledge can exacerbate, not heal, social tensions. The South African Report directly responds to this conclusion, comparing the harms caused by apartheid to "scars" that "often conceal festering wounds" and claiming that these wounds must be opened for healing to take place. At the same time, the Commission acknowledged that truth-telling, while necessary, was insufficient for reconciliation.[52]

Notably, in the South African Truth and Reconciliation framework, the victim did not have to forgive the oppressor. And to receive amnesty, the perpetrator did not have to show remorse. He or she only had to tell the truth,[53] the truth being "a good in and of itself."[54] As Martha Minow incisively put it, the Commission offered "the trade of amnesty for talking."[55]

To his credit, Tutu demanded consistency in the truth and reconciliation process. All parties to the conflict needed to confess their crimes. He "threatened to resign when the African National Congress said they didn't think they needed to apply for amnesty because they had been engaged in a just war. Essentially, they were granting themselves amnesty. This would have turned the commission process into a charade."[56]

The South Africa Truth and Reconciliation Commission has been a template for restorative justice efforts in countries all over the world, including but not limited to Chile, Ecuador, Ghana, Guatemala, Kenya, Liberia, Morocco, the Philippines, Sierra Leone, South Korea, and most unfortunately, in Rwanda after the horrendous genocide there.[57] The Transitional Justice Data Base project suggests that sixty truth commissions were established between 1970 and 2007.[58] Some efforts, such as Bosnia–Herzegovina, admittedly failed.[59] Interestingly, one commentator has urged the creation of a permanent truth commission to investigate state misconduct.[60]

Two of the most interesting truth commissions were those in Rwanda and Sierra Leone.

The challenge of securing justice in Rwanda was daunting. Around a million people were killed between April and July 1994 in internal strife, about 10 percent of the national population. The victims were mostly Tutsis, the perpetrators largely Hutus, the country's two largest ethnic groups.[61]

Three separate forums were used for accountability: the International Criminal Tribunal for Rwanda (ICTR), Rwanda's national criminal justice system, and an informal, traditional adjudication system—the *Gacaca* courts.[62] The justice and reconciliation process lasted from 1994 to 2014. The ICTR completed trials of eighty people. By 2006, the national courts tried approximately 10,000 suspects. Since 2005, the Gacaca courts have tried 1.2 million cases throughout the country.

In the Gacaca court system, communities at the local level elect judges to hear the trials of suspects accused of all crimes except planning genocide. The courts give lower sentences if the person is repentant and seeks reconciliation with the community. As an indigenous grassroots form of reconciliation, Gacaca soon became a much-lauded, non-conventional option.[63]

After the initial, perhaps "Panglossian" enthusiasm, the possibly inevitable revisionist view emerged.[64] It focused on the Gacaca courts' failures to track traditional notions of due process,[65] corruption among judges,[66] and violence against witnesses.[67] Some called it a "failed experiment,"[68] asserting that the Gacaca was an opportunity for "corruption, score-setting, vengeance, the search for profit, and power plays"[69] and was manipulated by the state to underpin an authoritarian regime.[70]

Sierra Leone was a "hybrid" situation where war crimes tribunals existed together with a truth and reconciliation commission. The question, of course, is how they coordinate—if at all. Indeed,

> in late 1998, when leaders of the three ethnic groups in Bosnia were discussing creating a joint truth commission to establish a common record of the past decade, they were told bluntly by ICTY's Chief Prosecutor, Louise Arbour, that such an effort would contaminate her evidence. Arbour also told aid donors not to support the Bosnian initiative, which set back its plans considerably.[71]

In Sierra Leone, "[t]he Truth Commission was . . . [originally] . . . presented as an alternative to prosecutions, not a complement to them."[72] However, a resurgence of the conflict led Sierra Leone to request that the UN establish an international criminal court. The interplay between the criminal court and the truth and reconciliation commission was remarkably vague.[73]

As has been made clear earlier, the purposes of the two are distinct. Still, in the UN Secretary General's words, they were considered as "mutually reinforcing instruments through which impunity will be brought to an end and long-term reconciliation may be achieved."[74] In its enabling act, the Sierra Leone TRC was charged with "creat[ing] an impartial historical record."[75]

Applicability to Ukraine[76]

As noted earlier, almost all the energy and thinking in the international community about post-war accountability has been on war crime tribunals—international and domestic. That is what one would expect in the middle of a conflict.

At this time, the Ukrainians themselves reject any sort of reconciliation. As Prime Minister Denys Shmyhal proclaimed as regards Russia: "Reconciliation and cooperation—no, not in the next hundred years."[77] As of 2023, a majority of Ukrainians agreed.[78]

At some point, however, the war will have to end, either by formal agreement or by petering out, and it is not likely to end with unconditional surrender by one side or the other. At that point, Ukraine may begin to consider alternatives, or at least supplements, to war crime trials.

As discussed earlier, Truth Commissions are often married to a reconciliation function. But the reality is that reconciliation may well be a bridge too far for Ukrainians today.[79] Further, the case of Ukraine differs considerably from those of societies that have previously made use of truth and reconciliation commissions. For one, those societies were coming out of a civil war or transitioning from a dictatorship to some semblance of a democracy.[80] Their "official" judicial systems are often compromised or under-resourced. The preconditions for the kind of reconciliation that was attempted in South Africa or Rwanda do not exist in Ukraine. Still, time has its own way of healing. Who would have imagined that France and Germany would ever reconcile after 1945? There may yet be a possibility of some form of reconciliation (if not forgiveness) if Ukraine is to move forward.[81]

In 2022, the UN created a Truth Commission to document the facts of the invasion.[82] The Commission was empowered "to investigate all alleged violations and abuses of human rights and violations of international humanitarian law and related crimes in the context of the aggression against Ukraine by the Russian Federation."[83] The annual reports since the Commission's inception have documented human rights abuses and mass usage of explosive weaponry in predominantly civilian areas, incidents of torture and horrific treatment of prisoners of war, removal of Ukrainian children to regions under Russian control, and some instances of human rights abuses by Ukrainian authorities against individuals suspected of cooperating with Russian forces.[84]

It is important that any truth commission be prepared to examine Ukrainian war practices as well. Bishop Tutu understood this in South Africa when he refused the ANC's demand for blanket amnesty as a liberation organization and, further, when the Commission repeatedly criticized various ANC practices. This is easier said than done. In 2022, when Amnesty International released a report criticizing the Ukrainian defense forces for endangering civilians by purposefully placing troops near schools, hospitals, and residential buildings, it was excoriated by civil officials, journalists, and even Amnesty International's own Ukraine office for shifting blame for the conflict from Russia to Ukraine.[85] This criticism prompted Amnesty International to provide an apologetic clarification three days later.[86] This said, if the Truth Commission is to gain legitimacy, it must be prepared to focus on all sides.

Amnesty

The need to move forward, if not "close the books" on the past, may lead to consideration of some form of amnesty. After defeating the Ukrainians at Ilovaisk in August 2014 and again in January 2015, Russia forced Ukraine to sign two agreements negotiated by Russia, Ukraine, and the Organization for Security and Co-operation in Europe (OSCE). The agreements, Minsk I and Minsk II, provided, in part, that Ukraine must "[e]nact a law prohibiting the prosecution and punishment of persons in connection with the events that took place in certain areas of the Donetsk and Luhansk regions of Ukraine."[87]

But Minsk was, to some extent, *force majeure*, and it is doubtful that Ukraine would consider an amnesty of any kind for Russians in the near term, at least after the depredations of the 2022 invasion.

One may hope that any suggestion of amnesty could be complemented with a requirement for confession and "truth-telling," as in the South African experience.

Reparations

As a practical matter, what Ukraine needs most is funding for reconstruction.[88] The likely source is reparations from Russia. In November 2022, the General Assembly resolved that Russia "must bear the legal consequences of all of its internationally wrongful acts, including making reparations."[89] Proposals have included the repurposing of seized Russian sovereign assets to Ukraine,[90] using such Russian assets as collateral for loans to Ukraine,[91] and using the interest on such assets to pay for Ukraine reparations.[92] In this volume, Eric Chang describes the use of state arbitration mechanisms to effectively secure reparations.[93] We also note a discussion of the merits of the international law doctrine of countermeasures—a doctrine that allows a harmed state "to take an action that would otherwise be unlawful—a 'countermeasure'—against a state that is responsible for an internationally wrongful act in order to induce that state to comply with its international obligation."[94]

The Ukrainian government has already begun formal efforts to secure reparations. In May 2023, the UN General Assembly created the Register of Damage for Ukraine.[95] It was opened for Claim Submissions on April 2, 2024.[96]

Less attention has been paid to reparations for individual victims. The Global Survivors Fund uses funds provided by donor governments to victims of sexual violence.[97] A similar limited program has been available for a one-time payment of circa 3,000€ to victims of Russian unlawful detention.[98] More comprehensive legislation was adopted in January 2022.[99] One significant concern is that the reparation legislation to date has focused on compensation for Russian crimes. It is not focused on harm to victims, and thus does not have a framework to address, for example, a Ukrainian child hit by a Ukrainian drone gone astray. And of course, we must understand that securing reparations money from Russia may present an obstacle to reaching a peace arrangement.

Religious Reconciliation

The one sector in Ukraine that might seek reconciliation, however gingerly, is the religious communities. However, the spiritual landscape in Ukraine is very complicated. The Orthodox churches are the dominant religious force in the country, with over 70 percent of Ukraine's population identifying as Orthodox. However, Orthodoxy in Ukraine is split into two churches, one connected to the Moscow patriarchate—the Ukrainian Orthodox Church-Moscow Patriarchate (UOC-MP) (25 percent)—and one connected to an autocephalic Ukrainian Orthodox church. The autocephalic Orthodox Church, known as the Orthodox Church of Ukraine (OCU), is the most prominent and largest sect (about 58 percent of the population).[100] The UOC-MP claimed to have broken its ties to Moscow, but the Ukrainian authorities consider them a "fifth column" and recently all but banned the UOC-MP.[101] Under these circumstances, it is hard to imagine religious reconciliation undergirding national reconciliation.

The Roman Church (1.7 percent of the population) is the one denomination focused on reconciliation. When the war began, Pope Francis broke all diplomatic protocol by visiting the Russian Embassy to the Holy See and sending a message to Putin that he "was willing to travel [to Moscow] on condition that [Putin] allowed him a tiny window to negotiate."[102] In March 2024, he argued that Ukrainians should have the courage of the "white flag" and negotiate an end to the war with Russians.[103] The Pope was quoted as saying, "The strongest one is the one who looks at the situation, thinks about the people and has the courage of the white flag, and negotiates."[104] Many Ukrainians strongly criticized these comments, pushing back against the connotation of the "white flag" of surrender.[105]

Conclusion

Accountability will undoubtedly be critical to any post-war scenario for the Ukrainians. However, war crime tribunals are only one form of accountability. At some point in time, there will be a need to think of ways other than war crimes tribunals to achieve some of the same goals—justice, deterrence, memory, truth, and dare one say, forgiveness and reconciliation.

I must admit that most truth commissions have developed in the aftermath of a civil war or a nation transitioning from dictatorship to democracy. The characteristics of such transitional justice are different from the situation in Ukraine. Still, one may wish to look seriously at the application of truth commissions and other alternative forms of accountability for the current crisis.

Notes

1 This chapter is drawn from a larger work in progress, co-authored by Jessica Blumberg, on Alternatives to War Crime Tribunals in Ukraine.

2 International Criminal Court, "Situation in Ukraine: ICC judges issue arrest warrants against Vladimir Vladimirovich Putin and Maria Alekseyevna Lvova-Belova," *International Criminal Court*, March 17, 2023, https://www.icc-cpi.int/news/situation-ukraine-icc-judges-issue-arrest-warrants-against-vladimir-vladimirovich-putin-and.

3 International Criminal Court, "Situation in Ukraine: ICC Judges Issue Arrest Warrants Against Sergei Kobylash and Admiral Viktor Sokolov," *International Criminal Court,* March 5, 2024. https://www.icc-cpi.int/news/situation-ukraine-icc-judges-issue-arrest-warrants-against-sergei-ivanovich-kobylash-and.

4 Kim Christian Priemel, *The Betrayal: The Nuremberg Trials and German Divergence* (Oxford: Oxford University Press, 2016), 406. The reason, of course, was the Cold War. As an IG Farben manager observed, "Now that they have Korea on their hands, the Americans are a lot more friendly" (ibid., 353).

5 Nette Nöstlinger, Oliver Elltrult, and Sepia Limmabrink, "Ukraine Probing Over 122,000 Suspected War Crimes, Says Prosecutor," *Reuters,* February 23, 2024, https://www.reuters.com/world/europe/ukraine-probing-over-122000-suspected-war-crimes-says-prosecutor-2024-02-23/.

6 Arieh Kochavi, "The Moscow Declaration, the Kharkov Trial, and the Question of a Policy on Major War Criminals in the Second World War," *History* 76, no. 248 (1991): 401–3. In negotiations during the Tehran Conference, Stalin advocated for the "liquidation" of the German general staff. Churchill disagreed, arguing that the British public would not tolerate mass retributive killings in that vein, and instead advocated for a short list to be created and approved by jurists of the top "50–100" criminals, offering immunity to anyone who killed someone on the list. In reply to Stalin's comment that 50,000 German officers ought to be executed and Churchill's response that that number was intolerable, Roosevelt quipped that a compromise of 49,000 would be amenable. For more detail on the disagreements within the Roosevelt administration prior to the end of the war, see Athan Theoharis,

"Roosevelt and Truman on Yalta: The Origins of the Cold War," *Political Science Quarterly* 87, no. 2 (1972): 211–4.

7 Miryam Bienenstock, "Is There A Duty Of Memory? Reflections On A French Debate," *Modern Judaism* 30, no. 3 (2010): 332–47; Olivier Lalieu, "L'invention du devoir de memoire," *Vingtième Siècle. Revue d'histoire*, no. 69 (2001): 83–94.

8 Dan Barry, "Vigilance and Memory: Ceremonies; A Day of Tributes, Tears, and the Litany of the Lost," *New York Times*, September 12, 2002, https://www.nytimes.com/2002/09/12/us/vigilance-memory-ceremonies-day-tributes-tears-litany-lost.html; Claire Fahy, "Somber 9/11 Ceremony Draws Mourners to Ground Zero," *New York Times*, September 11, 2023, https://www.nytimes.com/2023/09/11/nyregion/september-11-memorial-event.html.

9 Kristin Ann Hass, *Carried to the Wall: American History and the Vietnam Veterans Memorial* (Berkeley, CA: University of California Press, 1998), 14–15; "Vietnam Veterans Memorial," National Park Service, March 15, 2024, https://www.nps.gov/vive/index.htm.

10 Ran Puni, "People Are Astounded that Around a Million Names of Holocaust Victims Are Missing; 6 Million is Probably 5.8 Million," *Israel Hayom*, May 5, 2024, https://www.israelhayom.com/2024/05/05/people-are-astounded-that-around-a-million-names-of-holocaust-victims-are-missing-6-million-is-probably-5-8-million/.

11 Hass, *Carried to the Wall*, 39; For further discussion of memorialization by naming, see Thomas Laqueur, "Memory and Naming in the Great War," in *Commemorations; The Politics of National Identity*, ed. John R. Gillis (Princeton, NJ: Princeton University Press, 1994), 152–64.

12 Laurence Binyon, "For the Fallen," Poetry Foundation, https://www.poetryfoundation.org/poems/57322/for-the-fallen. Binyon's poem was initially published in *The Times of London* on September 21, 1914.

13 Avishai Margalit, *The Ethics of Memory* (Cambridge, MA: Harvard University Press, 2002), 7 and 36. There is a "thin" duty of memory for those to whom one's only connection is a shared humanity, while "thick" relations are grounded in a "shared memory."

14 Michael Feige, "Jewish Hebron Between Past and Present: A Case of Collective Memory," *Israel Studies Bulletin* 10, no. 2 (1995): 7. The birthday of every child murdered is commemorated, as is the place where every Jewish inhabitant was slaughtered.

15 David Rieff, "The Cult of Memory: When History Does More Harm than Good," *The Guardian*, March 2, 2016, https://www.theguardian.com/education/2016/mar/02/cult-of-memory-when-history-does-more-harm-than-good.

16 Nietzche goes further, stating, "It will be immediately obvious how there could be no happiness, no cheerfulness, no hope, no pride, no *present*, without forgetfulness." Friedrich Nietzsche, *On the Genealogy of Morals,* trans. Walter Kaufmann and R. J. Hollingdale (New York: Random House, 1989), 58.

17 Martin Imbleau, "Initial Truth Establishment by Transitional Bodies and the Fight Against Denial," in *Truth Commission and Courts: The Tension between Criminal Justice and the Search for Truth,* eds. William Schabas and Shane Darcy (Norwell, MA: Kluwer Academic, 2004), 161.

18 In a similar vein, Archbishop Tutu has opined: "While the Allies could pack up and go home after Nuremberg, we in South Africa had to live with one another." Desmond Tutu, *No Future Without Forgiveness* (New York: Doubleday, 1999), 21.

19 Maurice Halbwachs, *On Collective Memory*, ed./trans. Lewis A. Coser (Chicago, IL: The University of Chicago Press, 1992), 34.

20 Nancy Wood, *Vectors of Memory: Legacies of Trauma in Postwar Europe* (New York: Berg, 1999), 2.

21 Ariana Melamed, "It's Time to Abolish the March of the Living," *Haaretz*, April 13, 2008, https://www.haaretz.com/opinion/2018-04-13/ty-article-opinion/.premium/its-time-to-abolish-the-march-of-the-living/0000017f-e125-d38f-a57f-e777afd00000; Larry Derfner, "Rattling the Cage: Holocaust Denial and Jewish Liberals," *The Jerusalem Post*, December 13, 2006, https://www.jpost.com/opinion/columnists/rattling-the-cage-holocaust-denial-and-jewish-liberals.

22 The South African Final Report, for example, addresses the unwillingness of some to forgive if forgiveness requires forgetting the past. *Truth and Reconciliation Commission of South Africa Report* (1998), 1:116, https://www.justice.gov.za/trc/report/finalreport/volume%201.pdf.

23 Frederick Honig, "The Reparations Agreement between Israel and the Federal Republic of Germany," *American Journal of International Law* 48, no. 4 (1954): 564–65; Secretariat of the United Nations, *Treaties and International Agreements Registered or Filed with the Secretariat of the United Nations from 20 March 1953 to 31 March 1953*, vol. 162, no. 2137, 205–311, https://treaties.un.org/doc/Publication/UNTS/Volume%20162/v162.pdf.

24 Dave Adams Schmidt, "Israel Mob Riot over Bonn Talks," *New York Times*, June 8, 1952.

25 Samuel D. Kassow, *Who Will Write Our History?; Emanuel Ringelblum, The Warsaw Ghetto, and the Oyneg Shabes Archive* (Bloomington, IN: Indiana University Press, 2007), 225–283; See also Lucjan Dobroszycki, *The Chronicle of the Lodz Ghetto 1941–1944* (New Haven, CT: Yale University Press, 1984).

26 UN Human Rights Council, Resolution 9/11, Right to the Truth, A/HRC/RES/9/11 (2008), https://ap.ohchr.org/documents/E/HRC/resolutions/A_HRC_RES_9_11.pdf; UN Commission on Human Rights, Study on the Right to the Truth: Report of the Office of the United Nations High Commission for Human Rights, E/CN.4/2006/91, ¶ 4 (February 8, 2006), https://documents.un.org/doc/undoc/gen/g06/106/56/pdf/g0610656.pdf?token=NLawnQaFSDD5jlcrf4&fe=true.

27 Patricia Naftali, "Crafting a 'Right to Truth' in International Law: Converging Mobilizations, Diverging Agendas?," *Champ Pénal/Penal Field [En Ligne]* 13 (2016): 1, https://doi.org/10.4000/champpenal.9245.

28 Yasmin Naqvi, "The Right to the Truth in International Law: Fact or Fiction?," *International Review of the Red Cross* 88, no. 862 (2006): 273, https://doi.og/10.1017/S1816383106000518.

29 Velasquez Rodriquez v. Honduras, Judgment, Inter-Am.Ct.H.R. (ser C) No.4 (July 29, 1988), http://hrlibrary.umn.edu/iachr/b_11_12d.htm; for general information, see also Raquel Aldana-Pindell, "In Vindication of Justiciable Victims' Rights to Truth and Justice for State-Sponsored Crimes," *Vanderbilt Journal of Transnational Law* 35, no. 5 (2002): 1399–502.

30 McCann and others v. the United Kingdom, App. 18984/91, (Eur Ct H.R. 1995); Öneryildiz v. Turkey, App. 48939/99 (Eur. Ct H.R. 2004).
31 Sevane Garibian, "Ghosts Also Die: Resisting Disappearance through the Right to the Truth and the Jucios por la Verdad in Argentina," *Journal of International Criminal Justice* 12, no. 3 (2014): 518. *See also* Chiara Chisari, "The Judicial Implementation of the Right to the Truth: Some Thoughts on the Argentinian Experience of the Juicios Por La Verdad," *Union University Law School Review (Praai Zapisi)* 13, no. 3 (2022).
32 Chisari, "The Judicial Implementation of the Right to the Truth," 646–8.
33 "El Estado turco ha cometido el delito de genocidio contra el Pueblo Armenio en el period comprendido entre los anos 1915 y 1923." The full text of the decision rendered by the Buenos Aires Federal Court No. 5 for Criminal and Correctional Matters (case No 2.610/2001) may be found at http://www.genocidios.org (visited March 11, 2024).
34 George Santayana, *The Life of Reason* (New York: Open Road Integrated Media, Inc., 1981), vol. 1, *Reason in Common Sense*, ProQuest Ebook Central, 132.
35 David Rieff, *Slaughterhouse: Bosnia and the Failure of the West* (New York: Simon & Schuster, 1995), 27. Indeed, as an even greater cynic might suggest, "The lesson of Auschwitz is that you can get away with it." Isabel Wollaston, *A War Against Memory: The Future of Holocaust Remembrance* (London: Society for Promoting Christian Knowledge, 1996), 7.
36 Psalm 23:3 [KJV]
37 John Braithwaite, "A Future Where Punishment Is Marginalized: Realistic or Utopian?," *UCLA Law Review* 46, no. 6 (1999): 1743.
38 *Truth and Reconciliation Commission of South Africa Report* (1998), https://www.justice.gov.za/trc/report/finalreport/volume%201.pdf. For an account of the history of the Commission, see pp. 44–47 of the report.
39 Truth and Reconciliation Commission of South Africa Report, 1:118.
40 Spain may now be choosing to remember. The 2007 Historical Memory Law *Boletín Oficial del Estado,* BOE-A-2007-22296, no. 310, December 27, 2007 and the 2022 Democratic Memory Law *Boletín Oficial del Estado,* BOE-A-2022-17099, no. 252, October 20, 2022 begin to overcome that memory loss.
41 James L. Gibson, "On Legitimacy and the Effectiveness of Truth Commissions," *Law and Contemporary Problems* 72, no. 2 (2009): 138. The TRC treated "this as evidence of its own evenhandedness."
42 Stephen Ellis, "Review Essay: Truth and Reconciliation Commission of South Africa Report, Volumes 1–5. Pretoria: Government Printer, October 1998," *Transformation* 42 (2000): 57–8.
43 Onur Bakiner, *Truth Commissions: Memory, Power and Legitimacy* (Philadelphia, PA: University of Pennsylvania Press, 2016), 101; Joanna R. Quinn, "The Development of Transitional Justice," in *Research Handbook on Transnational Justice*, eds. Cheryl Lawther, Luke Moffett, and Dov Jacobs (Northampton: Edward Elgar Publishing, 2017), 24.
44 Cynthia M. Horne, "International Legal Rulings on Lustration Policies in Central and Eastern Europe: Rule of Law in Historical Context," *Law and Social Inquiry* 34, no. 3 (2009): 714; Hanna Suchocka, "Lustration: Experience of Poland," Venice Commission: European Commission for Democracy Through Law (2015), 5,

https://www.venice.coe.int/webforms/documents/default.aspx?pdffile=CDL-PI(2015)029-e; Czech Republic Act No 451/1991 Coll. and Act No 279/1992 Coll.; Pavel Žáček, "Lustration laws in the Czech Republic: The Application of Act No. 451/1991 Coll. and Act No 279/1992 Coll," https://www.ustrcr.cz/data/pdf/clanky/zacek-lustrace.pdf.

45 Juan Carlos Urquidi Herrera, "Victims' Testimonies in Truth Commissions: Who Owns the Memory?," *Oregon Review of International Law* 20, no. 1 (2018): 83. Herrera provides a good review of the different Commissions.

46 Herrera, "Victims' Testimonies in Truth Commissions," 92–3.

47 Ibid., 87.

48 Ibid., 95.

49 Margaret Popkin, "The Salvadoran Truth Commission and the Search for Justice," *Criminal Law Forum* 15, no. 1–2 (2004): 111.

50 George Orwell to the Editor of *Forward*, February 25, 1946, in *The Collected Essays, Journalism and Letters of George Orwell*, eds. Sonia Orwell and Ian Angus, vol. 4, *In Front of Your Nose, 1945–1950* (London: The Camelot Press, 1968), 115–6.

51 Quentin Peel, "Between the Lines: Lessons for Prosecutors of War Crimes Trials," *Financial Times*, March 13, 2006.

52 *Truth and Reconciliation Commission of South Africa Report*, 1:115. Interestingly, the Commission also described their role in the process of reconciliation as "an inclusive remembering of painful truths about the past," attempting to transcend partisan interpretations of history and to foster national unity (Ibid., 116).

53 In contrast, most other forms of restorative justice focus on the value of the oppressor seeking forgiveness and the psychological and spiritual value of the victim forgiving his oppressor.

54 Avishai Margalit, "Is Truth the Road to Reconciliation?," in *Experiments with the Truth*, eds. Okwui Enwezor, Carlos Basualdo, Ute Meta Bauer, Susanne Ghez, Sarat Maharaj, Mark Nash, and Octavio Zaya (Berlin: Hatje Cantz Verlag, 2002), 61–4, https://www.documenta-platform6.de/is-truth-the-road-to-reconciliation. Essay presented at a seminar on Truth and Reconciliation, organized by the Prince Claus Fund for Culture and Development, *The Hague*, July 6, 2000.

55 Martha Minow, *Between Vengeance and Forgiveness: Facing History after Genocide and Mass Violence* (Boston, MA: Beacon Press, 1998), 59.

56 Archbishop Desmond Tutu, "No Future Without Forgiveness," *New Perspectives Quarterly* 16, no. 5 (1999): 29.

57 Bonny Ibhawoh, "Do Truth and Reconciliation Commissions Heal Divided Nations?," *The Conversation*, January 23, 2019, https://theconversation.com/do-truth-and-reconciliation-commissions-heal-divided-nations-109925.

58 Tricia D. Olsen, Leigh A. Payne, and Andrew G. Reiter, *Transitional Justice in Balance: Comparing Processes, Weighing Efficiency* (Washington, DC: United States Institute for Peace, 2010). The most recent comprehensive list of truth commissions that we have found is at United States Institute of Peace, "Truth Commission Digital Collection," March 16, 2011, https://www.usip.org/publications/2011/03/truth-commission-digital-collection.

59 It failed because of opposition by the war crimes court as well as the unfortunate reality that "the most powerful political actors lack commitment to the values of a multiethnic society." Jacna Dragovic Soso, "History of a Failure: Attempts to Create

a National Truth and Reconciliation Commission in Bosnia and Herzegovina, 1997–2006," *Journal of Transitional Justice* 10 (2016): 309.

60 Michael P. Scharf, "The Case for a Permanent Truth Commission," *Duke Journal of Comparative & International Law* 7, no. 2 (1997): 375–410.

61 United States Institute of Peace, "Rwanda Accountability for War Crimes and Genocide," January 1, 1995, https://www.usip.org/publications/1995/01/rwanda-accountability-war-crimes-and-genocide.

62 Jeremy Sarkin, "The Tension Between Justice and Reconciliation in Rwanda: Politics, Human Rights, Due Process and the Role of the *Gacaca* Courts in Dealing with the Genocide," *Journal of African Law* 51, no. 2 (2001): 159–62.

63 An exhaustive study of the Gacaca courts can be found in Paul Christoph Bornkamm, *Rwanda's Gacaca Courts: Between Retribution and Reparation* (Oxford: Oxford University Press, 2012), 31–91.

64 Christopher J. Le Mon, "Rwanda's Troubled Gacaca Courts," *Human Rights Brief* 14, no. 2 (2007): 16.

65 In the words of Christopher Le Mon, "The Rwandan government has lowered its standards of justice in the name of expediting trials and convictions." Le Mon, "Rwanda's Troubled Gacaca Courts," 17. According to Human Rights Watch, "[T]he compromises made in adapting the customary community-based practice to try grave criminal offenses led to significant due process violations being built into the system." Human Rights Watch, *Justice Compromised: The Legacy of Rwanda's Community-Based Gacaca Courts* (New York: Human Rights Watch, 2011), 139, www.hrw.org/sites/default/files/reports/rwanda0511webwcover_0.pdf.

66 According to Bert Ingelaere, "It became common knowledge that one had to contribute to the *mutuelle de gacaca* by 'giving something' to the judges. That way, one would receive favorable treatment during the proceedings, and false testimony would more easily be accepted." Bert Ingelaere, *Inside Rwanda's Gacaca Courts: Seeking Justice after Genocide* (Madison, WI: University of Wisconsin Press, 2016), 125.

67 Le Mon, "Rwanda's Troubled Gacaca Courts," 17–8.

68 Sonali Chakravarti, "The Case of *Gacaca*—A Flawed Project and the Hope of Transitional Justice," *Theory and Event* 16, no. 3 (2013), https://muse.jhu.edu/article/520020.

69 Ingelaere, *Inside Rwanda's Gacaca Courts*, 12.

70 Timothy Longman, *Memory and Justice in Post-Genocide Rwanda* (New York: Cambridge University Press, 2017), 123–4. For a useful empirical study of how Gacaca helped consolidate the present authoritarian regime in Rwanda, see Anuradha Chakravarty, *Investing in Authoritarian Rule* (New York: Cambridge University Press, 2015).

71 Helena Cobban, "The Legacies of Collective Violence," *Boston Review*, April 2002.

72 William A. Schabas, "A Synergistic Relationship; The Sierra Leone Truth and Reconciliation Commission and the Special Court for Sierra Leone," in *Truth Commission and Courts: The Tension Between Criminal Justice and the Search for Truth*, eds. William A. Schabas and Shane Darcy (Darndacht: Kluwer Academic, 2004), 3.

73 Ibid., 29.

74 United Nations Security Council, "Eleventh Report of the Secretary-General on the United Nations Mission in Sierra Leone, S/2001/857," ¶ 66 (September 7, 2001),

https://documents.un.org/doc/undoc/gen/n01/529/63/pdf/n0152963.pdf?token=k0T2iVtdxIp4cxdo5S&fe=true.

75 The Government of Sierra Leone, The Truth and Reconciliation Commission Act 2000, Part III, ¶ 6(1); For commentary, see Michael Nesbitt, "Lessons from the Sam Hinga Norman Decision of the Special Court for Sierra Leone: How Trials and Truth Commissions Can Co-exist," *German Law Journal* 8, no. 10 (2007): 989–90.

76 The material on Ukraine has been informed and enhanced by the diligent work of my research assistant Emily Bushman.

77 Communication Department of the Secretariat of the CMU, "Reconciliation? Not Even in a Hundred Years: Prime Minister Denys Shmyhal in Interview with Focus Germany," February 26, 2023, https://www.kmu.gov.ua/en/news/prymyrennia-ne-bude-navit-cherez-sto-rokiv-interviu-premier-ministra-ukrainy-denysa-shmyhalia-nimetskomu-focus.

78 Halya Coynash, "Majority of Ukrainian Say Reconciliation with Russia is Impossible and Reject any Territorial Concessions," *Kharkiv Human Rights Protection Group*, May 7, 2023, https://khpg.org/en/1608812461.

79 Nonetheless, in mid-July 2024, perhaps because of the seeming stalemate in the military situation, Ukrainians began to shift their views. A media survey found that "about 44% of Ukrainian civilians favored starting official talks with Russia." Kim Barker, "As War Gets Bleaker, More Ukrainians Appear Open to a Peace Deal," *New York Times*, July 31, 2024.

80 One can define transitional justice as "forms of justice that seek to bring about social and political change following major episodes of societal trauma or crises including armed conflict, authoritarian repression, genocide, or other widespread human-rights violations." Mara Revkin, Ala Alrababah, and Rachel Myrick, "Evidence-Based Transitional Justice: Incorporating Public Opinion into the Field, with New Data from Iraq and Ukraine," *Yale Law Journal* 133, no. 5 (2024): 1593. For a different perspective, see Quinn, "The Development of Transitional Justice," 15.

81 Recently, the Templeton World Charity Foundation made a grant to an Israeli university to train religious leaders in the culture of forgiveness, exploring "the concept of unconditional forgiveness for the benefit of one's own psychological well-being." Judith Sudilovsky, "With a New $220,000 Grant, Israeli Researchers Look to Teach Rabbis the Latest Science of Forgiveness," *eJewish Philanthropy*, October 9, 2024. The grant does not specifically focus on October 7, but its resonance with Archbishop Tutu's view of truth commissions should be obvious—as should its relevance to Ukraine.

82 UN Human Rights Council, Resolution, Situation of Human Rights in Ukraine Stemming from the Russian Aggression, A/HRC/RES/49/1, (March 4, 2022), https://digitallibrary.un.org/record/3963815?ln=en&v=pdf.

83 Ibid., 11(a). The mandate of the Commission of Inquiry has been extended by the Council on a yearly basis. See "Independent International Commission of Inquiry on Ukraine," UN Human Rights Council, accessed July 27, 2024, https://www.ohchr.org/en/hr-bodies/hrc/iicihr-ukraine/index.

84 Human Rights Council, "Report of the Independent International Commission of Inquiry on Ukraine," U.N. Doc. A/HRC/55/66, (February 26–April 5, 2024).

85 Amnesty International, "Ukraine: Ukrainian Fighting Tactics Endanger Civilians," August 4, 2022, https://www.amnesty.org/en/latest/news/2022/08/ukraine-ukrainian

-fighting-tactics-endanger-civilians/. Regarding criticisms of Ukraine's report, see Julian Hayda, "Amnesty International's Report Criticizing Ukraine Is Dividing the Rights Group," *NPR*, August 5, 2022, https://www.npr.org/2022/08/05/1115767497/amnesty-international-ukraine-military-civilians-war-crimes; Uriel Epshtein, "Amnesty Got it Terribly Wrong," *Politico*, August 15, 2022, https://www.politico.eu/article/amnesty-ukraine-report-wrong/.

86 Amnesty International, "Statement on Publication of Press Release on Ukrainian Fighting Tactics," August 7, 2022, https://www.amnesty.org/en/latest/news/2022/08/statement-on-publication-of-press-release-on-ukrainian-fighting-tactics/.

87 United Nations Peacekeeper, *Protocol on the Results of Consultations of the Trilateral Contact Group (Minsk Agreement)*, February 24, 2015, https://peacemaker:un.org/sites/peacemaker:un,org/files/UA 140905 MinskCeasfire en.pdf. *See also* OSCE, *Protocol on the Results of Consultations of the Trilateral Contact Group*, September 5, 2014, https://www.osce.org/home/12357 (original Russian). The full text of the Minsk agreement can be found at *Financial Times*, February 12, 2015, https://www.ft.com/content/21b8f98e-b2a5-11e4-b234-00144feab7de. It states, in part, "Ensure pardon and amnesty by enacting the law prohibiting the prosecution and punishment of persons in connection with the events that took place in certain areas of the Donetsk and Luhansk regions of Ukraine."

88 In this regard, Ukraine's situation reminds one of Israel's need for German reparations (albeit, in that case, voluntary). See text at notes 23–4.

89 "General Assembly Adopts Resolution for Russian Reparations for Ukraine," *UN News*, November 14, 2022, https://news.un.org/en/story/2022/11/1130587.

90 This problem is discussed in Paul R. Williams and Alexandra Koch "Invoicing Russia for Ukraine's Recovery: The Complexities of Repurposing Frozen Russian Assets," *Opinion Juris*, December 5, 2023, https://opiniojuris.org/2023/05/12/invoicing-russia-for-ukraines-recovery-the-complexities-of-repurposing-frozen-russian-assets/.

91 Timothy Ash, "Who Can Pay for Putin's War? Step Forward Vladimir," *Center for European Policy Analysis*, March 7, 2023, https://cepa.org/article/who-can-pay-for-putins-war-step-forward-vladimir/.

92 Alan Rappeport and Jenny Gross, "G7 Finalizes $50 Billion Ukraine Loan Backed by Russian Assets," *New York Times*, October 23, 2024.

93 Eric Chang, chapter 21 of this volume.

94 Oona A. Hathaway, Maggie M. Mills, and Thomas M. Porton, "War Reparations: The Case for Countermeasures," *Stanford Law Review* 76, no. 5 (2024): 977. The article argues that "states may apply collective countermeasures by continuing to freeze Russian central bank assets in an effort to induce Russia to meet its reparations obligation (1049)."

95 Register of Damage for Ukraine, "First Preparatory Meeting on an International Instrument to Establish a Claims Commission for Ukraine," July 12, 2023, https://rd4u.coe.int/en/-/first-preparatory-meeting-on-an-international-instrument-to-establish-a-claims-commission-for-ukraine. In July 2024 the Council of Europe became a full "participant" in the Register. Register of Damage for Ukraine, "The Register of Damage for Ukraine Welcomes the European Union as a Fully Fledged Participant," July 24, 2024, https://rd4u.coe.int/en/-/the-register-of-damage-for-ukraine-welcomes-the-european-union-as-a-fully-fledged-participant.

96 Register of Damage for Ukraine, "Register of Damage for Ukraine to Open for Claims Submission on 2 April 2024," March 17, 2024, https://rd4u.coe.int/en/-/register-of-damage-for-ukraine-to-open-for-claims-submission-on-2-april-2024.

97 Weronika Strzyżyńska, "Reparations to be Paid to Survivors of Wartime Sexual Violence in Ukraine," *Guardian*, April 26, 2024, https://www.theguardian.com/global-development/2024/apr/26/reparations-survivors-wartime-sexual-violence-by-russian-soldiers-ukraine-war-olena-zelenska. As of June 2024, forty persons have received compensation. "40 Survivors of Wartime Sexual Violence Separation - Ukrainian Gender Policy Commissioner," *Ukraine Pravda English*, June 20, 2024.

98 Law on the social and legal protection of persons who have been deprived of personal liberty as a result of armed aggression against Ukraine, and their family members from January 26, 2022.

99 Law of Ukraine "On the Compensation for Damage or Destruction of Certain Categories of Immovable Property Resulting from Hostilities, Terrorist Acts, Sabotage Caused by Armed Aggression of the Russian Federation against Ukraine, and the State Register of Property Damaged and Destroyed as a Result of Hostilities, Terrorist Acts, Sabotage Acts Caused by the Armed Aggression of the Russian Federation against Ukraine," no. 2923-IX, February 23, 2023, https://zakon.rada.gov.ua/laws/show/2923-20#Text.

100 Denys Brylov, Tetiana Kalenychenko, and Andrii Kryshtal, "Mapping the Religious Landscape of Ukraine," *Peaceworks* 193 (2023): 8, https://www.usip.org/publications/2023/10/mapping-religious-landscape-ukraine.

101 Mykyta Vorobiov, "Ukraine Bans Russia's Orthodox Church," *CEPA*, August 20, 2024, https://cepa.org/article/ukraine-bans-russias-orthodox-church/.

102 Pope Francis, "Exclusive: Pope Francis Discusses Ukraine, U.S. Bishops and More," interview by Matt Malone et al., *America*, November 28, 2022, https://www.americamagazine.org/faith/2022/11/28/pope-francis-interview-america-244225.

103 Phillip Pullella, "Pope says Ukraine Should Have the 'Courage of the White Flag' of Negotiations," *Reuters*, March 9, 2024; Jonathan Luxmore, "Ukrainian's Top Catholic Bishop: Pope Calls for Negotiations with Russia are Hurtful," *America*, March 22, 2024.

104 "Ukraine Criticizes Pope's 'White Flag' Comment," *BBC*, March 10, 2024, https://www.bbc.com/news/world-europe-68528217.

105 Susie Blann, "Pope Francis' 'White Flag' Comment Is Met by Criticism from Ukraine and Its Allies," *CTV News*, March 10, 2024, https://www.ctvnews.ca/world/pope-francis-white-flag-comment-is-met-by-criticism-from-ukraine-and-its-allies-1.6801987; John L. Allen Jr., "This Time, a 'White Flag' Signals the Beginning of a Conflict, Not the End," *Angelus News*, March 14, 2024, https://angelusnews.com/voices/pope-white-flag-conflict/.

Selected Bibliography

Bass, Gary. *Judgment at Tokyo*. New York: Alfred Knopf, 2023.

Bass, Gary. *Stay the Hand of Vengeance: The Politics of War Trials*. Princeton, NJ: Princeton University Press, 2000.

Belgorodski, Erick. "Situating Reparations for Ukraine within a Broader Transitional Justice Process." *International Journal of Transitional Justice* (2024). https//doi.org/10.1093/ijtj/ijae028.

Kim Christian Priemel, *The Betrayal: The Nuremberg Trials and German Divergence* (Oxford: Oxford University Press, 2016), 406. The reason, of course, was the Cold War. As an IG Farben manager observed, "Now that they have Korea on their hands, the Americans are a lot more friendly" (ibid., 353).

Margalit, Avishai. *The Ethics of Memory*. Cambridge, MA: Harvard University Press, 2002.

Minow, Martha. *Between Vengeance and Forgiveness: Facing History after Genocide and Mass Violence*. Boston, MA: Beacon Press, 1999.

Teitel, Ruti G. *Transitional Justice*. New York: Oxford University Press, 2002.

17

A Theological Perspective of Law and Morality About the Just and the Unjust Russian-Ukrainian War

Father Mark Morozowich

Russia's war in Ukraine today provokes dismay and shock. In February 2022, Russia launched a full-scale invasion of Ukraine, starting the largest and most significant conflict in Europe since the Second World War. The war has resulted in a refugee crisis and tens of thousands of deaths and marks a historical milestone by ending a long-lasting period of peace in Europe. Global change and challenges to the concept of truth lie at the very heart of this war. Russia is attacking human freedom, freedom of conscience, freedom of speech, freedom of thought, and freedom of belief in Ukraine today. Ukraine's existence and its identity as a sovereign nation with a venerable culture are at risk from the brutal totalitarian regime of Russia's government.

This examination of the theological perspective of Russia's war in Ukraine begins with a thumbnail historical sketch from the beginning of the war in 2014 to the full-scale invasion on February 24, 2022. The surreptitious beginnings of this war back in 2014, with soldiers camouflaged as unidentified little green men,[1] demonstrated that secrecy, subterfuge, and suppression were the tools of the Russian military. This invasion began after months of peaceful protest in Kyiv following the 2013 decision by Yanukovich's Ukrainian government to turn its focus on Russia and away from the West. As the people protested, the Ukrainian armed forces waged a bloody attack on peaceful protestors, which began on February 20, 2014, killing 100 protestors. This fateful decision was met with outrage on the part of the people, and it marked the end of President Yanukovich's regime: he subsequently fled his country for Russia and was taken under Putin's protection.

This revolution of dignity, a revolution for the dignity of the human person, arose because Ukrainians remembered the lived reality under Russian domination. They remembered the atrocities of the 1932–33 Holodomor, and they remembered tales of deportation, life in the Gulag, and the type of controls limiting free speech. While younger generations, born since the collapse of the Soviet Union, never experienced these firsthand, they knew the stories of their parents and grandparents. Ukrainians mobilized in protest during the winter of 2014 because they were incredulous that their government would look to Russia rather than Europe. They demonstrated and voiced their desire for freedom. They did not want a life lived under the repressive restrictions and controls of the Russian state.

Putin's military and the decisions of the Russian government during and after the Revolution of Dignity validated their concerns. Angry at the botched handling of the protestors and the ability of Ukrainians to freely manifest their will by peaceful protest for civil liberties, Putin began a takeover on February 27, 2014. He sent little green men to seize control of government buildings in Crimea, as well as starting his war in the Donbas. This subterfuge blunted immediate reactions from governments throughout the world.

The world stood by as if stymied by Putin's tactics. This aggression and plausible deniability provided a bit of distance for the Kremlin. Russia, one of the signatories of the 1994 Budapest Memorandum of denuclearization of Ukraine, blatantly violated that agreement. In 1994, Russia joined the United States and the United Kingdom by agreeing to Ukraine's territorial integrity and political independence and not to use weapons against Ukraine. This denuclearization treaty guaranteed the protection of Ukraine. Russia stands in clear violation of this memorandum in 2014 by its war in Crimea, eastern Ukraine, and the 2022 full-scale invasion of Ukraine. The invasions of a peaceable neighbor violated moral and ethical standards. The violation of the treaty further compounds their culpability.

In the immediate aftermath of the full-scale 2022 invasion, the world quickly became surprised at the ability of Ukraine's armed forces to withstand the onslaught of a supposedly superior military force. This bravery shocked pundits who believed in the superiority of Russia's armed forces. Outnumbered and outgunned, Ukrainian soldiers defended their homeland and managed to force back the Russian invaders. The Russian soldiers thought this would be easy, and they had been told that they were to be accepted as liberators from the so-called Nazi regime. They believed that the people of Ukraine needed them. Much to the contrary, even old village women told Russian soldiers to leave their country.

All too often, modern political and military analysts fail to consider the complexities of what makes a nation. Often, they simply look at political or economic motivations without including a more profound knowledge of a nation's history and culture. This more complex understanding includes a broader historical, political, and religious context. If a person wants to truly understand Russia's war in Ukraine, they need to delve deeper to grasp the events' significance and impact.

There can be no doubt today that the initial subterfuge of the Russian 2014 invasion led to the 2022 full-scale invasion. These acts manifested a clear and apparent disregard for the norms of international law. Russia, the aggressor state, continues to violate international norms. These acts against human dignity are unsurprising: the Russian government does not respect the human dignity of its citizens. The lack of free speech in Russia continues today, as witnessed by the suppression of all dissent. The recent death of Alexei Anatolyevich Navalny and the massive arrests of protestors demonstrate the tactics of the Russian government.

The moral issues of Russia's war can best be understood by listening to Ukrainians in Ukraine. This study presents an overview of the various theological and moral issues of the war by focusing on a text published by the Ukrainian Greek Catholic bishops of Ukraine on March 5, 2024, entitled: "Rescue the victims from the hand of their oppressors (Jer. 22:3): The Letter of the Synod of Bishops of the Ukrainian Greek Catholic Church in Ukraine on War and Just Peace in the Context of New Ideologies."[2] This letter begins with a thumbnail sketch of the historical situation that helps to explain deeper motivations for this war. It then outlines and discusses theological issues regarding the morality of the war. An overview of this letter will deepen our understanding of these complex issues. The Ukrainian Bishop's letter consists of six principal parts: Introduction; (I) Causes and Origins of Russia's Contemporary War Against Ukraine; (II) From the *Russian World* (*Russkiy Mir)* to "ruscism": the Path of Degradation of the Aggressor State; (III) Non-violent Resistance; (IV) Defensive War and Legitimate Defense; (V) Neutrality in Time of War; (VI) The Goal of Legitimate Defense Is a Just Peace; and Conclusion. This comprehensive approach provides a framework for evaluating this war by addressing the moral issues involved.

The letter begins by acknowledging the real-life cost of war:

> The time of war is extremely painful and cruel: it causes countless traumas to every person and the whole of society. Every day, we receive tragic news about the death of Ukrainians; many have already lost family members and friends; we are witnessing the destruction of what is most precious to us—our Homeland, our families' well-being, our happiness, our dreams.[3]

This statement grounds the letter in the reality of the war, its human toll, and the travesty it exacts. This starting point keeps the focus on the plight of the people.

They then stipulate the moral and spiritual basis in paragraph 3: "Clear understanding of the moral and spiritual foundations that guide our actions during a time of war and upon which we will build our future after its end with the achievement of a just peace is absolutely necessary to ensure that our efforts are a purposeful movement toward the kind of victory we desire."[4] The bishops lay their foundation on Christian social and moral teaching, especially the theological and philosophical richness of the Catholic tradition. This elaboration on the principles of peace and war, as seen in the context of the war in Ukraine, provides a broader framework for analysis. They continue this introductory section in paragraph 4 by stressing that this letter is both for the residents of Ukraine and those in the international community.

The first section of this letter then goes on to treat the causes and analyze how this war originated. They identify the principle of human dignity as the fundamental cause of this war. This subjugation of the human person has a deep political past. In their analysis of the causes of Russia's war against Ukraine, they identify the evils of totalitarian regimes. In paragraph 5, they write:

> The twentieth century witnessed the emergence of totalitarian regimes in Europe, primarily in Germany and Russia, which caused terrible wars and committed

> numerous crimes against humanity. The main characteristic of totalitarianism is disregard for the freedom and dignity of the human person. In this sense, totalitarian regimes are forms of state structures that are called "tyranny" in the Christian intellectual tradition.[5]

This totalitarianism is evidenced in Russia today. In fact, the bishops believe that it was the lack of a "Nuremberg moment" in calling Russia to account for its crimes during the Communist period. This lack of public reckoning can be witnessed in multiple acts and statements by Russian leaders. As early as 2005, Putin stated that "the demise of the Soviet Union was the greatest geopolitical catastrophe of the century."[6] He continues this line of thinking today and strives to fashion this empire anew. The bishops forcefully accentuate this fact in paragraph 8:

> A significant error of the free world after the collapse of the communist bloc was that democratic countries did not demand post-Soviet Russia, which was recognized as the successor to the Soviet Union, condemn fully the crimes of the communist period and require the new Russian rulers to ensure decommunization, lustration, and purification of their state from the consequences of totalitarianism.[7]

The importance of Nuremberg in demonstrating the evils of totalitarianism brought about a catharsis in the general population and served to put Germany on a different path.

The evils of totalitarianism are the very enemy of human dignity. Then, the document develops a sense of hybrid totalitarianism that is being espoused in our contemporary context. The bishops posit a broad aim of this war by pointing to the historical evidence in a concise summation in paragraph 11:

> When it comes to Ukraine, all these features of hybrid totalitarianism are superimposed on another extremely important factor: the colonizing legacy of imperial, tsarist Russia. Most of the territory on which Ukrainians had lived was conquered and subjugated by Muscovy, a state entity that eventually adopted the name "Russian Empire" between the second half of the seventeenth and mid-eighteenth centuries. Since then, the Russian government has banned and suppressed Ukrainian culture, language, Churches, and identity; it has claimed that Ukrainians are only a more recent, smaller, lower-grade part of the Russian population. As indicated by numerous public texts and speeches of contemporary high-level Russian leaders and propagandists, today, this traditional Muscovite imperial ideology has acquired a radical militant character and calls for the complete destruction of the Ukrainian state and Ukrainian identity as such.[8]

This historical overview helps to remind the reader of the broader background and the mindset of a colonializing power. It clearly views Ukraine as a territory to be conquered and aims directly at its existence. The Bishops go on further to analyze the war:

> The war being waged by Russia against Ukraine has all the features of a neocolonial war on the European continent, with clear signs of genocide. The destruction of everything that is Ukrainian has become the political program of Russian leaders, their mania, which is supported by a significant portion of the citizens of the aggressor state, indicating the ailing state of Russian society. That is why calls for a compromise with Russia, which Ukraine occasionally hears from some representatives of the international community and even members of religious communities, have no real basis and demonstrate a lack of understanding of the situation in which Ukrainians find themselves. The problem lies not only in the fact that such calls lack solid moral foundations, in as much as they disregard the principles of respect for human dignity and just peace, but also in the fact that they are simply unrealistic: a compromise cannot be reached if one of the parties denies the very existence of the other. Russia leaves Ukraine no choice but to defend itself militarily. This war is a national struggle of liberation for the Ukrainian civil nation on behalf of the right to its own existence and future, as well as the independence, freedom, and dignity of our citizens.[9]

This argument stresses that not only does Moscow aim to subjugate the political apparatus of Ukraine but even the very idea of a Ukrainian identity. This approach denigrates the human dignity of the Ukrainian people, in fact, of all people, and it repeats past destructive actions of Russia. Perhaps the most jarring claim is the lack of recognition of the existence of the Ukrainians as a people and as a nation. The Ukrainians' response to this aggression is a just war from the theological point of view as they are trying to defend themselves from attack so that they can live as they choose.

The letter proceeds to its second section, which examines the political concept of the *Russian World* or Russian *Russkiy mir*. While the concept of the *Russian World* is supposedly a political ideal, it is clear that the Russian Orthodox Church espouses it. In paragraph 12, the letter posits that this is a logical outcome from the historical perspective:

> Therefore, it should not be surprising that the Patriarch of Moscow supported and blessed Russia's criminal war against the Ukrainian people. Such actions are in line with the Muscovite tradition of the Church's ideological service to the authorities and its servility to those in power. Unfortunately, now this long-standing imperial tradition combined with modern post-communist totalitarianism has led to a real crime committed by the leadership of the Moscow Patriarchate, namely to propagandizing the war. It was this church leadership that generated the new genocidal ideology now known as the "Russian World" and willingly offered its services to the criminal authorities and "sanctified" them.[10]

Some may find this conclusion to be jarring and even incredulous. However, the Russian Orthodox Church, long proponents of the *Russian World* concept, codified and ratified this ideology recently at a formal gathering on March 27, 2024, at the Cathedral of Christ the Savior in Moscow. The gathering of the World Russian People's

Council headed by Patriarch Kirill issued a document entitled: "The Present and Future of the Russian World."[11] While this formal declaration leaves no doubt about the intentions of the church and the Russian government, it is not a new stance. The Russian Orthodox Church utilized this so-called *Russian World* ideology from the very beginning as a justification for the war.

The *Russian World* ideology has drawn the scrutiny of many scholars. Already on March 13, 2022, Fordham's Orthodox Christian Studies Center, on their *Public Orthodoxy* webpage, posted an open letter inviting Orthodox theologians throughout the world to sign a joint declaration entitled: "A Declaration on the "Russian World" (Russkiy mir) Teaching."[12] This joint condemnation of this false ideology has over 1,500 signatures. Following the Mach 2024 endorsement, Dr. Paul Gavrilyuk analyzed the Moscow Orthodox Church statement. He published this short commentary on Fordham's *Public Orthodoxy* website entitled "When Theology Fuels the War: False Prophecy and State Policy in 'The Present and Future of the Russian World' Document." He critiques it:

> A manifesto of sorts, the document mixes apocalyptic rhetoric with mythology, moral exhortation, and policymaking. Using the euphemism "special military operation" for Russia's full-scale invasion of Ukraine in February 2022, the document introduces the war as "the new stage of the national liberation of the Russian people" and declares: "From the spiritual and moral point of view, the special military operation is a Holy War, in which Russia and its people, defending the unified spiritual space of the Holy Rus', fulfill the mission of the 'Restraining One' by protecting the world from the onslaught of globalism and the victory of the west that has fallen into Satanism." Apparently, by bombing Ukrainian cities, Russia is engaging in the holy war and is preventing the end of the world. With the stakes being so high, any destruction, no matter how horrific, is justified; any amount of violence is acceptable in the fight of the absolute good (i.e., Russia) against the satanic evil (i.e., the West).[13]

His analysis of the limitless war idea espoused by the Russian Orthodox Church is that it reaches a level of absurdity. No justification exists for the kind of destruction and terror that Russia continues to subject the people of Ukraine. The complete acceptance of this war and aggression on the part of the Russian Orthodox Church presents significant problems. There was no war of aggression against Russia. Simply put, this toxic stance of the Russian Orthodox Church is not morally flawed. Many of their own faithful, including priests and lay people, remain shocked by the blind acceptance of the Russian political ideals and the very war itself.

This stunning endorsement of violence displays a jarring reality. As we look more closely at moral principles violated by this *Russian World* ideology, we see more significant issues with even more disturbing elements. The Ukrainian Greek Catholic bishops outline these problems in paragraph 16: "Such a position to exclude or discriminate against others based on ethnicity or cultural affiliation, however, does not correspond to the foundations of the Christian faith as such. Inciting hatred and waging war based on the 'Russian World' ideology violates Christian principles and contradicts the spiritual norms that the Church is supposed to embody."[14] Once again, we see that the Russian authorities are violating fundamental moral principles of human dignity and the ability of the human person to be able to freely choose to act, believe, and speak without fear. The abhorrent policies of the Russian Orthodox Church and their complicity in this war demand justice.

The question of non-violent resistance marks the third section of the bishops' letter. They analyze the teaching of the Catholic Church and appeal to the Second Vatican Council's Gaudium et Spes as well as the Ukrainian Catholic Church's catechism, *Christ—Our Pascha*. They begin with a recognition of the call to seek peace among Christians, and in paragraph 23, they accentuate the pacifist tradition among the very first Kyivan Christian princes: "This very path was taken by the ancient Kyivan princes Borys and Hlib, who refused to engage in dynastic struggle and defend themselves by violent means (cf. Matt. 26:52). For this spiritual feat, the Kyivan Church proclaimed them among the first saints of the Kyivan lands."[15] The bishops develop this notion of non-violence in paragraph 26. They turn to St. Augustine to introduce the legitimacy of military service for Christians as they should strive for peace and justice. They see that the state has a duty to its citizens: "It does not eliminate the duty of the state to protect the life and freedom of its citizens."[16] They go on to commend society's proper ordering and remind us that while we are indeed called to forgive personal slights, we also have an obligation to protect those who have been wronged, especially through violence. Indeed, this type of protection remains at the foundation of a well-ordered community. In paragraph 30, we are reminded that true justice and genuine peace entail the naming of and accountability for the acts of aggression. They warn that if this does not occur, "the aggressor concludes that its violence becomes its legal right and tries by all means to achieve recognition of this 'right to crime' under the guise of the legitimacy of its geopolitical interests and their justification."[17]

The bishops posit that each person has a right and moral choice of discerning their activity in wartime. They respect the position of non-violence, but they also look to the need to defend the innocent. They ask in paragraph 32:

> Can the human community leave without condemnation and accountability the genocide of Ukrainians that the Russian army has organized in Bucha, Borodyanka, Irpin, Mariupol, and many other occupied territories of Ukraine? Who will stand up for the victims and their families? The current cry of Ukrainians to the international community for justice has the full support of the Church, as she has always made and continues to make a preferential option for the offended.[18]

They remind everyone that Ukraine's own signing of the Budapest memorandum was an affirmation of trust in the role of international law, of the vision of a just society that lives in accord with international law that seeks the common good and respects human dignity. They continue this analysis and ask: "How can we speak about international security today when a state that is a member of the UN Security Council and possesses one of the largest nuclear arsenals in the world itself poses a threat to this security and resorts to outright nuclear blackmail of the entire international community in order to achieve its aggressive goals?"[19] They continue this prophetic role and conclude this section in paragraph 32 by asking:

> The current cry of Ukrainians to the international community for justice has the full support of the Church, as she has always made and continues to make a preferential option for the offended. This choice is the essence of her mandate from our Lord Jesus Christ, and her warning against injustice does not come merely of itself: "Consider how one conceives iniquity; is pregnant with mischief, and gives birth to deception" (Ps. 7:15).[20]

As we continue to examine the various moral issues presented by Russia's war in Ukraine, the fourth part of the document discusses the notion of a defensive war and legitimate defense. Their explanation of a just war in terms of defense begins with an introductory appeal to St. Ambrose and St. Augustine. They continue their study by recounting Pope Pius XII and the Second World War with a treatment of the important measures the United Nations put forth. They recount the UN statements forbidding the use of "armed force against the territorial integrity or political independence of any state."[21] They acknowledge these ideals in the current situation. The bishops then turn their attention to understanding the concept of a just war. In paragraph 38, they further explicate the critical principles for understanding a just war:

> The Catholic Church teaches that legitimate armed defense against an unjust attacker, as well as war in general, is always the last means to which a party in danger can resort. This is emphasized by the Catechism of the UGCC *Christ — Our Pascha*: "The use of military force may be justified only in the event of extreme necessity as a means of legitimate self-defense, and the Christian soldier is always a defender of peace" [21]. The Catechism of the Catholic Church outlines the elements of a just defensive war: "The strict conditions for legitimate defense by military force require rigorous consideration. The gravity of such a decision makes it subject to rigorous conditions of moral legitimacy. At one and the same time: the damage inflicted by the aggressor on the nation or community of nations must be lasting, grave, and certain; all other means of putting an end to it must have been shown to be impractical or ineffective; there must be serious prospects of success; the use of arms must not produce evils and disorders graver than the evil to be eliminated," [22] that is, when negotiations, arbitration, compromise, and other means have failed. As a rational being, the human person is obliged to make decisions based on reasonable judgment and the law, rather than using force, whenever possible. For legitimate defense to be just, the safety of civilians must be kept in mind. This defense always has a clearly limited goal: a just peace, not the complete destruction of the enemy's people, economy, or political institutions. In order to achieve a just peace, limited and proportionate means must be used: armaments and force must be measured to what is absolutely necessary to repel aggression and deter future attacks.[22]

The bishops assist us in understanding how Ukraine's actions are indeed a just defense. This clear articulation of legitimate defense focuses on the protection of people. They clearly demonstrate that Ukraine's defensive war aims to find a just peace to enable the residents to live in peace and to have their inalienable right to human dignity.

This brief survey provides a useful point of departure for those unaware and unversed in this doctrine. I agree with the bishops' conclusion in paragraph 40 when they state: "In light of the teachings of the Catholic Church, the Security and Defense Forces of Ukraine are legitimately defending the state and the people."[23] They complete this presentation by looking at the core rationale for this war:

> The aggressor country rejects the very right to existence of the Ukrainian people and their state as a subject of international law, refusing to engage in dialogue and negotiations with a sovereign Ukraine. It is impossible to "engage in dialogue with someone who does not exist", as Russian propaganda constantly repeats. According to the already discussed modern Russian ideology of ruscism, the "Ukrainian issue" must be resolved once and for all through the complete destruction of everything Ukrainian.[24]

Russian propaganda sees the "Ukrainian issue" as something that needs to be resolved, thus continuing a policy and mode of action that began centuries ago. The systematic denigration of a people and an entire culture is a thorough assault on human dignity. Paragraph 44 states: "Russian aggression against Ukraine is not a struggle for disputed territory: it is an attack on international law and a crime against peace."[25] This movement to reestablish an empire, to undo the past wrongs in Putin's eyes, is being brought about by the subjugation of a freedom-loving nation. The bishops remind us, "The atrocities of the Russian army against civilians, which the whole world is watching almost live, are a brutal outrage on human dignity and a crime of genocide."[26] These conclusions follow directly from the stated objectives of the *Russian World* ideology and should be a source of moral outrage for all concerned citizens.

The following moral issue pertains to neutrality and is analyzed as the fifth point. The bishops recognize the importance of neutrality on behalf of countries and acknowledge this significant stance. However, they point out in paragraph 44 that all must join in condemning the atrocities of this war:

> Russian aggression against Ukraine is not a struggle for disputed territory: it is an attack on international law and a crime against peace. The current war in Europe is a zero-sum conflict of identities, as Ukrainians seek to preserve their independence as a state and the right simply to be Ukrainians, while Russians seek to deprive Ukrainians of their right to exist as such and revive their empire. The atrocities of the Russian army against civilians, which the whole world is watching almost live, are a brutal outrage on human dignity and a crime of genocide. Maintaining a performative neutrality in such a situation is a betrayal of the values of respect for international law, justice, and human dignity. This is a position based on interests, not principles.[27]

This challenge calls on all to adopt a posture of defending innocent victims. Neutrality can never forget the evils that are occurring. The bishops identify the neutrality of the Vatican as an example of a state that remains neutral, but clearly, the Vatican addresses the moral calamity of war. The document gives ample evidence of the Holy Father and the Vatican's diplomatic core's positive role in bringing decisive peace to conflictual situations.

The sixth and final moral theological consideration treats the relationship of legitimate defense in light of just peace. The bishops argue that a just peace is based on giving everyone their due, as seen in paragraph 50: "The ethics of just war, which determines the Christian understanding of war and peace, was formed in the Middle Ages when the Church used as the concept of justice the constant desire to give everyone his or her due."[28] This concept provides the basis for the idea that people and nations have the right to independence. Hopefully, the continued existence and ability of the Ukrainians to fight for self-determination will lead to a genuine peace. The bishops caution: "The end of war is not true peace, however, if it means the end of Ukraine."[29] This foreboding message motivates Ukrainians to fight even if they lack the means to complete their mission. They see the apparent aim of the *Russian World* propaganda and want to be sure that they will have a future. They want to ascertain peace based on human dignity and human liberty. The lack of free speech and freedom of the press in Russia reminds the world that Ukraine's issues have a broader impact. The bishops invite the reader in paragraph 61 to consider that this is not just a local conflict between two nations. They point out that the desire to restore the Russian empire and thwart free speech is a problem that we must confront. The bishops conclude: "Today, all the foundations of human civilization are under threat."[30] They continue this in their concluding paragraphs, especially in paragraph 63:

> By launching a hybrid war against Ukraine, Russia has, in fact, challenged the entire civilized world. Russia has disrupted it so much that many people have ceased to distinguish truth and deception, and thus, good and evil. Before our eyes, a terrible substitution takes place: what is evil is cloaked in the guise of good, and what is good is branded as if of hell. In such a distorted world, it will be impossible to avoid or stop wars. Blurred verbal declarations and vague political language will be powerless, and diplomatic neutrality without clear values and guidelines will gradually become moral relativism or weakness. This already prevents many politicians in the civilized world from recognizing Russian troops' atrocities in Ukraine as genocide because it would then demand their intervention. At present, many Christians who belong to the Western world's postmodern generation simply do not see the genocide of the Ukrainian people nor hear the victims' cries; yet, in order not to lose face, they continue to express their worry and deep concern.[31]

This haunting challenge from these bishops in a war-ravaged country provokes the reader to deepen their reflection and re-evaluate their understanding of Russia's war. This ultimatum of a "moral call to arms" forces the reader to question not only their response but also their response and the response of various countries and civilizations.

The insidious beginning in 2014 received only muted responses; Russia learned that the world would impose some sanctions, but there was no resolute reaction that would ultimately cause it to pause. The calculus regarding Russia's nuclear weapons and their continued threat, coupled with a veiled notion of self-defense, stymied governments from reacting more forcefully and empowered the Russian full-scale invasion.

Conclusion

The Nuremberg tribunals unveiled the evil atrocities of the German Nazi regime. When these cruel acts were exposed to the light of reason, it helped all to engage in a rejection of these Nazi principles and the underlying dispositions that gave rise to them. Today, totalitarianism still menaces the world in various different locales. As we have examined, the so-called *Russian World* concept seeks to eliminate Ukraine and its culture and heritage. Ukrainians have sought to identify this evil and have coined the phrase Ruscism (Рашизм)[32] to describe this phenomenon. The lack of accountability for the atrocities of the Soviet regime permitted Russia the ability to think that there was nothing wrong. Russia never condemned the barbaric acts committed by the Stalin and Lenin regimes that continued throughout the Soviet period. Putin boldly laments the dissolution of the Soviet Union and has created this false vision of a *Russian World*.

This brief investigation of the morality of Russia's war in Ukraine analyzes the various moral principles through the lens of Ukrainians. Of necessity, the complexities of the cultural, religious, and historical identities of these East Slavic people provide the context. We have seen how Russia continues to violate moral norms. Future generations will evaluate how the world responded to the horrors of Russia's twenty-first-century totalitarian regime. The examples and principles discussed in our Nuremberg conference can provide a model for resolving the underlying issues behind Russia's war on Ukraine. As Ben Ferencz stated at the conclusion of his opening argument at the Nuremberg trials: "The conscience of humanity is the foundation of all law. We seek here a judgment expressing that conscience and reaffirming the basic rights of man under law." I believe that by making the Russian government accountable for the suffering and horrors inflicted upon the Ukrainian people, making it responsible for trespassing on the fundamental human rights of the Ukrainian people, this accountability will help to irradicate these evil acts. The *Russian World* concept amounts to genocide. Its ultimate goal is the eradication of Ukrainian identity. The moral question is, what is our response? Will we stand up for human dignity? Will we stand up for the just?

Notes

1 John R. Haines, "How, Why, and When Russia Will Deploy Little Green Men – and Why the US Cannot," Foreign Policy Institute, March 9, 2016. https://www.fpri.org

/article/2016/03/how-why-and-when-russia-will-deploy-little-green-men-and-why-the-us-cannot/.

2 The Synod of Bishops of the Ukrainian Greek Catholic Church in Ukraine, Letter on War and Just Peace in the Context of New Ideologies "Rescue the victims from the hand of their oppressors" (Jer. 22:3). February 8, 2024 in Lviv, last update May 14, 2024. https://ugcc.ua/en/data/rescue-the-victims-from-the-hand-of-their-oppressors-jer-223-the-letter-of-the-synod-of-bishops-of-the-ugcc-in-ukraine-on-war-and-just-peace-in-the-context-of-new-ideologies-944/.

3 Ibid., 1.

4 Ibid., 3.

5 Ibid., 5.

6 Vladimir Putin, "Annual Address to the Federal Assembly of the Russian Federation," April 25, 2005. http://en.kremlin.ru/events/president/transcripts/22931.

7 Synod, "Letter on War," 8.

8 Ibid., 11.

9 Ibid., 11.

10 Ibid., 12.

11 "Наказ XXV Всемирного русского народного собора «Настоящее и будущее Русского мира»." http://www.patriarchia.ru/db/text/6116189.html.

12 "A Declaration on the 'Russian World' (Russkii mir) Teaching." March 13, 2022. https://publicorthodoxy.org/2022/03/13/a-declaration-on-the-russian-world-russkii-mir-teaching/

13 Paul Gavriluk, "When Theology Fuels the War: False Prophecy and State Policy in "The Present and Future of the Russian World" Document," April 8, 2024. https://publicorthodoxy.org/2024/04/08/when-theology-fuels-the-war/.

14 Synod, "Letter on War," 16.

15 Ibid., 23.

16 Ibid., 26.

17 Ibid., 30.

18 Ibid., 32.

19 Ibid., 31.

20 Ibid., 32.

21 Ibid., 35.

22 Ibid., 38.

23 Ibid., 40.

24 Ibid., 40.

25 Ibid., 44.

26 Ibid., 44.

27 Ibid., 44.

28 Ibid., 55.

29 Ibid., 55.

30 Ibid., 61.

31 Ibid., 63.

32 Timothy Snyder, "The War in Ukraine Has Unleashed a New Word." *New York Times*, 2022. https://www.nytimes.com/2022/04/22/magazine/ruscism-ukraine-russia-war.html?smid=url-share.

Selected Bibliography

Avvakumov, Yury, Oleh Turiy, Anatoliĭ Babyns'kyĭ, and Andrij M. Hlabse. *The Churches and the War: Religion, Religious Diplomacy, and Russia's Aggression Against Ukraine.* Lviv: Ukrainian Catholic University Press, 2024.

Denysenko, Nicholas E. *The Church's Unholy War: Russia's Invasion of Ukraine and Orthodoxy.* First edition. Eugene, OR: Cascade Books, 2023.

Hryts͡ak, I͡Aroslav. *Ukraine: The Forging of a Nation.* Translated by Dominique Hoffman. First US edition. New York: PublicAffairs, 2024.

Plokhy, Serhii. *The Gates of Europe: A History of Ukraine.* New York: Basic Books, 2015.

Snyder, Timothy. *Bloodlands: Europe Between Hitler and Stalin.* 1st ed. New York: Basic Books, 2010.

18

Legitimizing a New Ethics and Theology of "Holy War"

The Russian Orthodox Church's Path Justifying Russia's War Against Ukraine

Yuri Stoyanov

The expansion and aggravation of Russia's political and military interventionism in Ukraine, from the annexation of Crimea in 2014 and the subsequent unfolding of active hostilities in the Ukrainian eastern Donbas region to the full-scale invasion of Ukraine in February 2022, have rekindled interest in and debates on the role of religion in world politics and geopolitical confrontation, the proliferation of religiously motivated state-sponsored political violence, specifically but not only in conflicts displaying post-secular characteristics at various levels of intensity. The keen participation of high-ranking Russian Orthodox clerics of the Moscow Patriarchate in the theological and ideological justification of Russia's military aggression against Ukraine has invited criticism, condemnation, and investigation, as well as diverse arguments that the Russian-Ukrainian conflict could represent the first religious war of the twenty-first century,[1] that it was triggered by a Russian Orthodox version of Christian nationalism[2] or alternatively, religion was used mainly as a rhetorical tool for justifying the invasion and sacralizing the "Russian imperial project."[3] These war-legitimization stances and policies of the Moscow Patriarchate have significant repercussions for the current discussions on and reconceptions of religiously framed and secular just war traditions, historical and novel uses of the religious rationale for warfare, including articulations of revamped "holy war" paradigms.

The Russian Orthodox Church's close involvement in the justification of war and the formulation and dissemination of just war (and, more recently, holy war) narratives inevitably has strongly impacted Eastern Orthodox cultures and ecclesiastical bodies, triggering divisions and theological and geopolitical antagonisms and frontlines among them. These tensions and faultlines have highlighted the increasing challenges of finding a balance between the traditional legacy of Eastern Orthodox clerical pacific stances/precepts and the political-military strategies of Eastern Orthodox-majority state secular elites. The modern relevance and echoes of historical and more recent

Christian theological stances on war and peace have consequently reverberated intensely across the broader Eastern Orthodox world since the outbreak of full-scale war in Ukraine in February 2022.

Historically, the origins, development, and modern manifestations of Eastern Orthodox theological and socio-cultural stances on the ethics of war and peace display similarities with and divergences from the respective Western Christian attitudes, and this remains a much-underexplored field. Still, in the last three decades or so, the subject of Eastern Orthodox clerical and cultural approaches to the legitimization and conduct of just, justifiable, and "holy" war (or to pacifism and non-violence) has attracted some intense disputes among clerics, theologians, historians of the medieval and modern periods, and political scientists.[4]

The formative phases of East Roman Christian/Byzantine ideologies of war and peace display a synthesis of varied notions, normative rules, and rhetoric based on the late Roman just war tradition remolded through the lens of Christian ethics and the political theology of *imperium romanum christianum*. Unlike Western Christianity, no evidence of systematic efforts to formulate a just war theory within the Byzantine church has been unearthed as yet. Apart from a few exceptions, the mainstream Eastern Orthodox ecclesiastical elites successfully resisted the acceptance of notions such as Christian military martyrdom for fallen soldiers, notwithstanding periodic pressure from the Byzantine imperial court's keen intent on fostering forms of lay military piety among its warrior classes[5] with its focus on the notion of Byzantine Christian warriors receiving spiritual recompense for their fighting on behalf of Orthodoxy, blessings of standards and weapons, military religious services (including services for fallen soldiers), thanksgiving ceremonies to commemorate victory, and the progressively popular cult of military saints. Beyond the ecclesiastical sphere, the roots and norms of the maturing Byzantine imperial just war theory were followed and applied by the imperial court and government based on standard notions such as self-defense, recovery of lost territory, and so on.

This conglomerate Byzantine synthesis of pre-Christian and Christian concepts and precepts, ethics, and piety was adapted to the cultures of the Orthodox monarchies and principalities in the medieval "Byzantine Commonwealth" in South-Eastern Europe, Ukraine, and Russia. In the medieval East Slavonic Orthodox states and principalities (Kievan/Kyivan Rus', Grand Duchy of Moscow/Muscovy, etc.), the traditions of lay pacifism and secular and religiously colored just war came to be formulated and employed early in their political and religious history. Adopted and gradually developed after the Ottoman conquest of Constantinople in 1453, the Muscovite religio-political ideology of "Moscow the Third Rome" contributed to the Russian Empire's strategy of diplomatic and military interventionism in the late Ottoman Empire in fulfillment of its self-declared mandate as a protector of Eastern Orthodox polities and communities under Ottoman dominion. The last decades of the late Russian imperial era, from the Crimean War (1853–6) to the First World War, the Russian Civil War, and the inauguration of the USSR in 1922, witnessed heated debates in Russian Slavophile, Pan-Slav, ecclesiastical and intellectual circles on pacifism, Tolstoyism, and the justifiability and sanctification of warfare, which intensified in Russian émigré circles in the 1920s and 1930s. After several cycles of anti-church measures and persecution in the Soviet Union, the Russian Orthodox Church was reinstated during the Second World War with the explicit intention of mobilizing support for the "Great Patriotic War" against Nazi Germany, during which eminent Russian hierarchs blessed and praised the war endeavors as a "Holy War of Liberation" with a global ethical mission and importance.[6]

During the Cold War, along with the other Eastern Orthodox patriarchates and national churches, the restored Moscow patriarchate engaged in a series of international peace initiatives, forums, and declarations. These long-term engagements of the Moscow Patriarchate and the churches of the Eastern Bloc states proceeded under the tight surveillance of the respective Communist governments, which regularly attempted to use them as an extension of their foreign policy through international, transnational Orthodox ecclesiastic networks and inter-church organizations such as the World Council of Churches, as well as similar international bodies and campaigns, such as the World Peace Council, the Christian Peace Conference, the Peace and Disarmament Campaign of the 1980s, and so on. Throughout this period, the topics of Christian participation in warfare and the pertinence and applicability of just war theories in Eastern Orthodoxy remained a persistent focus of attention in the successive intra-Orthodox and ecumenical dialogues, statements, and exchanges.

Post-Cold War geopolitical crises and major armed conflicts such as the Wars of Yugoslav Succession in the 1990s brought to the fore warfare ethics and conduct issues and were accompanied by the growing politicization of varied trends in world religions, the somewhat unexpected deprivatization of religion and its resurgence in the political and public space. It was against the background of these shifts on the international scene that the Ecumenical Patriarch of Constantinople, Bartholomew I, reiterated the traditional Eastern Orthodox patristic and ecclesiastic pacific stances in a series of statements in the 1990s and 2000s in which he also grappled with crucial problems arising from the expansion, transmutations, and consequences of modern warfare: inter-religious violence, ethnic cleansing, militaristic religious nationalism, humanitarian intervention, the destructive impact of recent and contemporary armed conflicts on the environment, and so on.[7]

Committed to the complex processes of reenvisaging and reinventing new modes of coexistence and collaboration with post-Soviet Russian political and military institutions, the Russian Orthodox Church followed a somewhat contrasting path in its stances on war- and peace-making which found manifestation in its statement of faith, *The Basis of the Social Concept of the Russian Church*, issued by the Jubilee Council of Russian Bishops in 2000.[8] The statement includes a section on "War and Peace" which, on the one hand, reasserts the historical Eastern Orthodox precepts on warfare as categorically evil and the church's responsibility to promote international peacemaking while also stipulating that in some cases, war, though unwished-for, could be necessary. The document illustrates the growing involvement of the Russian Orthodox Church in the military institutions and procedures of the post-Soviet Russian federal state by emphasizing its significant role in the Christian education of the military and the respective responsibilities of the military chaplains. Symptomatically, the statement ventures to forge an Orthodox reevaluation of and counterpart to the Western just war tradition, adopting, reappraising, and referring to some of its principal *jus ad bellum* and *jus in bello* norms, acknowledging their roots in St Augustine's influential systematization in the patristic period. Characteristically, the document chooses to resort to somewhat ambiguous language when describing the "difficulty" of differentiating an aggressive war from a defensive war and the recognition of instances in which war might be necessary: national defense, defense of neighbors, and "restoration of trampled justice." Such vague criteria can be applied and mobilized in broader legitimization frameworks, opening vast possibilities for justifying potentially offensive military action.[9]

With the advance of the negotiation and search for viable post-Soviet models of church-state relations in the Russian Federation, the politicization of the Russian Orthodox Church started to gain momentum in the 1990s, and as an institution, it assumed a growing role in state-building and confessional identity formation processes, foreign policy approaches and strategies, as well as the expansion of religious diplomacy.[10] While not homogeneous in the ideological sphere, the principal trends in the Russian Orthodox Church (which can be roughly described as traditional, fundamentalist, and liberal, with their various sub-currents) interreacted with varied earlier and revived, as well as neoteric religious, philosophical, and geopolitical trends. The cross-fertilization between the traditionalist and fundamentalist Russian Church factions with rejuvenated and popular Neo-Slavophile and Neo-Eurasianist streams are patterns of sustained mutual enhancement. Consequently, various amalgams of chauvinistic, anti-Occidental, and neo-conservative narratives, notions, and rhetoric came to exploit Orthodox vocabulary and references to update and upgrade the historical conceptions and appeal of Russian exceptionalism and messianism (which were otherwise critically challenged in the 1990s).[11] Furthermore, pre-Soviet and Soviet-era underground apocalyptically leaning trends of Russian religious messianism[12] were brought to the surface to gain credibility, broader impact, and widespread acceptance, occasionally assuming the utopian and militant traits of an actual "apocalyptic imperialism."[13]

The interaction between these post-Soviet ideological currents and Russian Orthodoxy was also linked to the process of the securitization of Russian religious policies, whose initial phases can be traced to the early 2000s.[14] A series of legal "National Security" documents (published first in 2000, then re-issued and updated in 2009, 2015, and 2021), as well as the amended Russian Constitution of 2020, brought to the fore the newly conceptualized "inseparable" link between national security and traditional "spiritual-moral values."[15] In a related process, the concept of "spiritual security" was introduced into official Russian political, clerical, and public discourse,[16] frequently in connection with the "Russian World" ("Russkiy Mir") ideology, as formally adopted and publicized by the Russian political and clerical establishments since 2006–7 (forcefully endorsed by Patriarch Kirill, elected as a Patriarch of Moscow and All Rus in 2009).[17] The accentuated religious and ecclesiastic aspects of the "Russian World" ideology bolstered the status of the Russian Orthodox Church as an increasingly influential social, cultural, and political actor on the domestic and international scene, especially in the spheres of cultural and religious diplomacy.[18] In a series of official and public pronouncements, various high-ranking clerics of the Moscow Patriarchate increasingly dwelled on and praised traditional patriotic and Christian values, and hence, as a self-appointed agent of moral and national renewal, in the 2010s the Russian Orthodox Church attained a virtually hegemonistic and advantaged position in the Russian socio-religious and cultural spheres, while also acquiring a significant place in the transnational neo-Conservative Christian arena and the various global culture wars waged on its behalf.[19]

The post-Soviet renewal of closer and gradually expanding links between the Russian Orthodox Church and the military establishment was initially effected by the Moscow Patriarchate's reinstatement of the correlation and symbiosis between inherited patriotic values and religious faith.[20] The deepening ecclesiastical-military collaborations and partnerships included the reintroduction of military chaplains, church-building in military bases, the resumption of the controversial clerical practice of the blessing of weaponry, increasing clerical penetration of military structures, and the formation of a Synodal Department for Cooperation with the Armed Forces and Security Organs by the Moscow Patriarchate. The remarkably close cooperation between the church and the nuclear weapons corps has acquired the nature of the striking phenomenon of "Russian Nuclear Orthodoxy," arguably inaugurating a far-reaching process of "military theocratization."[21]

The outbreak of the initial post-Soviet armed conflicts, from the First and Second Chechen Wars (resp. 1994–6 and 1999–2000) to the Russian-Georgian war of 2008, demonstrated the currency of contrasting views within the Russian Orthodox Church regarding the nexus between military and religious values, some of which could be critical of disproportionate or extreme militarism.[22] However, in the wake of the so-called "conservative turn" of the Kremlin establishment in 2011/2012, various trends and wings of the Russian Orthodox Church started energetically to advance and popularize intensely militaristic narratives and notions, which contributed to the formation of a bellicose military-religious ideology[23] (as manifested, for instance, by emblematic projects like the opening of the monumental Main Cathedral of the Russian Armed Forces in Moscow in 2020).[24]

The proliferation of such Russian Orthodox military-religious ideologies in the 2010s was a clear indicator that the Russian Orthodox Church could provide appropriate legitimization narratives and frameworks for Russian military campaigns while also mobilizing some of the emotive and prevailing notions of post-Soviet chauvinist, messianic, neo-Slavophile and neo-Eurasianist discourses. The nebulous and protean concepts of "spiritual security" and the "Russian World" could be effectively employed for a religious justification of military planning and action across the so-called extended Russian Orthodox Church "canonical territory" (beyond Russia into Belarus, Ukraine, Moldova, etc.), hence bringing into convergence the declared and undeclared strategic aims of Russian political, military, and ecclesiastic establishments.[25]

Such harmonization and unification of strategic goals appear explicit in the Russian military intervention in Syria in 2015. As the intervention got underway, Patriarch Kirill stated that the campaign possessed a defensive and just character and aimed at the protection of genocide-threatened Syrian Christians and civilians, clearly reiterating the traditional Russian-imperial era self-understanding as a military defender of Christian communities and polities in the Balkans and the Middle East.[26] In a statement announcing the campaign, Patriarch Kirill had also declared that the war against terrorism in the Middle East is a "holy war"[27] but felt compelled to clarify and partially retract his statement once the campaign had started, claiming that his statement was misunderstood. He was referring to the global war on terrorism and not to the specific Russian intervention in Syria.[28] The Patriarch's qualified holy war disclaimer was clearly provoked by the highly adverse reactions of Middle Eastern Christian and Islamic clerics[29] to the assertion of the then chairman of the Synodal Department for the Cooperation of Church and Society of the Moscow Patriarchate, Vsevolod Chaplin that the battle against terrorism (of *Daesh*) is "a moral and holy fight."[30] Chaplin's public pronouncement was made at the very start of the Russian Syrian campaign. While echoing the same theme of Russia's historic mission of protection of the Middle Eastern Christians (and other oppressed communities), the widespread critique and controversies it incited contributed to his being released from his duties at the department soon afterward. The episode indicated that at that time, the Moscow Patriarchate was still cautious about employing a "holy fight" rhetoric coming from within its ranks of hierarchs; given the perils of framing a military engagement in the Middle East in religious terms, opting for a simple version of a traditional Christian just war legitimization seemed the preferable option.

However, a conscious religiofication of the military conflict in Donbas is discernible in the Moscow Patriarchate's statements after its outbreak, which strove to depict the hostilities as a war on Orthodoxy, its churches, and Orthodox Christians in the region.[31] These claims were strongly refuted as war propaganda by the Ukrainian Orthodox Church-Kyiv Patriarchate.[32] In the actual Donbas war zones, these statements provided a breeding ground for a holy war mentality reportedly emerging among the Russian-state-aligned regional "people's militias" and volunteers.[33] The unfolding conflict gravely affected Ukraine's tortuous and volatile post-Soviet ecclesial situation.[34]

These deepening ecclesial divisions and antagonisms intensified in the build-up to and the first stages of the Russian invasion of Ukraine in February 2022. On the eve of the invasion, Patriarch Kirill addressed the Russian military with a routine just war rhetoric on the significance of the military vocation in defending the Russian people and the "sacred borders" of the realm[35] and on the day of the incursion called for prayers for the swift restoration of peace.[36] However, as Russia's war of aggression entered its third week, Patriarch Kirill articulated its strategic and military aims in a more extensive, explicitly religious, and "metaphysical" context.[37] Exploiting standard attack lines from the global culture wars, he declared the Russian campaign a "struggle" waged in defense of traditional Christian norms, which has not a physical but a metaphysical significance, transcends international relations and politics, and bears on human salvation.

Patriarch Kirill's "metaphysical war" declaration was in stark contrast with the reactions and statements of the Ukrainian Orthodox ecclesiastical leaderships, whether issued by the Ukrainian Orthodox Church-Moscow Patriarchate or the newly autocephalous Orthodox Church of Ukraine.[38] One of Patriarch Kirill's preferred explanations of the conflict was that it was provoked by "diabolical attacks and provocations" as well as evil, dark, and hostile external forces and enemies who have always sought to destroy the unity of Rus' (described as including "Russia and Ukraine and Belarus and other tribes and peoples").[39] Denunciation of and opposition to the invasion in its immediate aftermath was manifested in varying degrees of magnitude in the Russian Orthodox Church's domestic and international dioceses. In early March 2022, nearly 300 Russian Orthodox priests and deacons from around the world signed an open letter calling for an immediate halt of the fratricidal war and the military coercion of Ukraine as a precondition for reconciliation.[40] In April 2022, hundreds of clergymen of the Ukrainian Orthodox Church-Moscow Patriarchate supported an appeal and petition accusing patriarch Kirill of being guilty of war crimes by blessing Russia's invasion of Ukraine in breach of Christian moral norms and the own regulatory documents of the Russian Orthodox Church.[41] The document also appealed for the establishment of an International Ecclesiastical Tribunal to condemn Russia's war of aggression against Ukraine, to theologically evaluate Patriarch Kirill's war-related public statements, and in the light of such assessment, to potentially bring Patriarch Kirill to justice and "deprive him of the right to hold the patriarchal throne." The appeal emphasized the necessity of pan-Orthodox doctrinal scrutiny of the "Russian World" ideology, which in March 2022 had already been execrated as non-Orthodox (in an international declaration backed by more than 1500 Orthodox clerics and theologians) and a "form of Orthodox ethnic-phyletic religious fundamentalism, totalitarian in character," providing the foundation for the backing of the war against Ukraine among a large part of the Moscow Patriarchate's ranks.[42]

In May 2022, the Ukrainian Orthodox Church-Moscow Patriarchate held a council that announced its independence and autonomy from the Moscow Patriarchate as an act of protest against the Russian invasion of Ukraine and expressly in response to Patriarch Kirill's public support for the military aggression.[43] The reliability and validity of this declaration of autonomy from Moscow, however, were mistrusted by most sectors of Ukrainian society, and the persisting ambiguity of the allegiance and ties of the self-announced autonomous church continues to trigger Ukrainian government security proceedings and legislative measures targeting its ecclesiastical body.

As the Moscow Patriarchate's explicit pro-war stances and pronouncements were starting to incite disapprovals, protests, and ecclesial divisions across the Russian Orthodox "canonical territory," within Russia itself, clergymen who openly inveighed against the invasion with anti-war statements and sermons began to face ecclesiastical and political pressure, prosecution and defrocking.[44] Throughout the Moscow Patriarchate-aligned dioceses outside Russia, opposition and protests against the Moscow Patriarchate's war-justification standpoint manifested in open letters and critical statements (or actual moves to seek independence from Moscow) initiated by the clerical leadership of the Archdiocese Orthodox Churches of Russian Tradition in Western Europe, the German Diocese of the Russian Orthodox Church Outside Russia, the Russian Orthodox parish in Amsterdam, the Lithuanian Orthodox Church, and so on, while in the broader Orthodox sphere, similar repudiations were issued by the Orthodox Churches of Cyprus and Finland, among others.[45] The Ecumenical Patriarch of Constantinople, Bartholomew, repeatedly condemned the invasion as a "blatant violation of any notion of international law and legality,"[46] in which the Russian state and church "cooperated in the crime of aggression and shared the responsibility for the resulting crimes" and that the Moscow Patriarchate had theologically "legitimized criminal behavior."[47] Patriarch Bartholomew defined the "Russian World" ideology as a crucial "instrument of legitimization of Russian expansionism" in which the church has entered into an alliance with the state to make faith "the backbone of the ideology" of the Kremlin's regime.[48]

The Moscow Patriarchate's multi-layered justification of the Russian war on Ukraine also became the target of attention, critique, and sanctions in the spheres of the ecumenical movement, international relations, and diplomacy. After appealing unsuccessfully to Patriarch Kirill to intervene to halt the war in Ukraine,[49] in June 2022, the Central Committee of the World Council of Churches (WCC) deplored in a formal statement "the illegal and unjustifiable war inflicted on the people and sovereign state of Ukraine," renounced "any misuse of religious language and authority to justify armed aggression," and urged "dialogue and negotiations to secure a sustainable peace."[50] At a meeting with a WCC delegation in October 2022, Patriarch Kirill ostensibly agreed with the delegates that war could not be holy, declared that his war-legitimizations statements had been quoted unfairly and out of context, and professed his trust in the peace-making and dialogue-seeking role of the church in conflict resolution. However, the actual evidence of his pre-war and war-time sermons and statements betray the vital elements of a new religion-military ideology that continues to be embellished and expanded in the latest dramatic conditions of Russia's war on Ukraine.

In the incubation period of this ideology preceding the invasion of Ukraine, Patriarch Kirill made use of the Gospel text of John 15:13 (periodically employed in earlier Orthodox theological efforts to envisage Orthodox versions of just war and military martyrdom)[51] to conceive a distinct Russian Orthodox military piety focused on the "holy feat" of self-sacrifice on the battlefield which would bring the Orthodox soldier to God, "God's Kingdom and eternal life."[52] In a later war-time sermon, the patriarch went much further and reinforced this military ideology with a remission of sins promise, stating that soldiers who are pursuing their vocation and duty and sacrifice themselves for others will have attained an act equivalent to sacrifice which "washes away all the sins" they may have previously perpetrated.[53]

These attempts to conceive a new Eastern Orthodox ideology of warfare have far-reaching implications—they display some general continuities but also some extreme ruptures from earlier comparable endeavors in Eastern Orthodox cultures. Patriarch Kirill's statements coalesce the concept of military battlefield martyrdom (which was by and large opposed by the medieval Byzantine Orthodox Church) and remission of sins granted in return for military service, a notion and practice not accepted or documented in Eastern Orthodox cultures.[54] Furthermore, aligning the Moscow Patriarchate with fundamentalist, radical apocalyptic trends in post-Soviet Russian Orthodoxy, Patriarch Kirill expanded the notion of Russia's war on Ukraine being a "metaphysical war," transforming it into an apocalyptic struggle for the future of mankind against "global evil" and the "movement of the Antichrist."[55]

The Moscow Patriarchate's progression toward the outright adoption and declaration of the "holy war" gained further momentum with the "ratification" and publication (on the patriarchate's official website) of the decree (or edict) of the XXV World Russian People's Council held in late March 2024 under the presidency of Patriarch Kirill (serving as the council's head). Dedicated to the Russian "special military operation" in Ukraine, the decree's first section presents it as "a new stage in the national liberation struggle of the Russian people" against the criminal Kyiv regime, a struggle which, from a spiritual and moral point of view assumes the nature of a "Holy War," "defending the single spiritual space of Holy Russia," so that it can "fulfill the mission" of the apocalyptic "Restraining Force," protecting the world from the "globalism's onslaught" and the "victory of the West, which has fallen into Satanism."[56] Whereas not a normative church document, the decree reflects the the Second World War Russian ecclesiastical and secular holy war statements and indicates that the Russian Orthodox Church has begun to play an increasingly central role in furnishing a more coherent, ideologically and theologically charged sacral legitimization of the war on Ukraine (with the accompanying narratives and rhetoric), indeed a possible blueprint for further Russian military and ecclesiastically sanctified expansionism.

The Ukrainian Orthodox Church promptly condemned the decree in an official statement that its "holy war" declaration contradicts the "basic principles of Christian morality" and advances an "apologia for violence" and a "justification of a military aggression" in contravention with the Gospel teaching.[57] The Hierarchical Council of the Orthodox Church of Ukraine condemned the new "theology of war/ holy war" promulgated in the decree intended to sacralize Kremlin's regime state power and its "neo-imperial geopolitics."[58] The Ukrainian Council of Churches and Religious Organizations (UCCRO) similarly strongly repudiated the decree's "holy war" proclamation as amounting to a "spiritual crime,"[59] which was followed by a condemnation of the document in a joint statement of the Conference of European Churches and UCCRO.[60] The WCC has requested an urgent meeting with the Moscow Patriarchate and a clarification if the "holy war" statement reflects the Russian Orthodox Church's position and how such ideology can be reconciled with it being a member church of the WCC.[61] In the secular realm, the Parliamentary Assembly of the Council of Europe has also reacted with the adoption of a resolution that also castigates the "holy war" promulgation as an "abuse of religion" and "distortion of the Christian Orthodox tradition" which makes the Russian Orthodox Church "complicit in war crimes and crimes against humanity, conducted in the name of the Russian Federation and the Russkiy Mir ideology."[62] In another recent resolution, the Parliamentary Assembly of the Council of Europe has recommended that the member states need to "recognize the role of the Russian Orthodox Church as a tool of Russian State propaganda, and evaluate and address the involvement of religious institutions that are used for spreading the Kremlin's propaganda in their countries."[63]

These latest resolutions of the Parliamentary Assembly of the Council of Europe indicate that the important and manifold role of the Moscow Patriarchate and Patriarch Kirill in providing the theological and ideological justification for Russia's war on Ukraine and its expansion and conduct will and need to continue to be under investigation.[64] The United Kingdom (followed by other countries) has already sanctioned Patriarch Kirill on account of his public support for the invasion of Ukraine,[65] and the growing list of individual Russian clergymen and representatives of church institutions sanctioned by a number of countries is already unprecedented.[66] New appeals continue to call for a comprehensive church document scrutinizing and denouncing the war in Ukraine and the Russian Orthodox Church's empowering and the bestowal of "divine approval upon violence, war, and aggression."[67] Such ecclesiastical documents and tribunals, as well as further legal moves and scrutinies of the militarism advocated by the Russian Orthodox Church, certainly would seem necessary before Eastern Orthodox churches and clerics could become involved in earnest in conflict resolution, peace negotiations, peace-building, and reconciliation in Ukraine.

Notes

1 Lucian N. Leustean, "Russia's Invasion of Ukraine is the First Religious War in the 21st Century," March 3, 2022, *London School of Economics*, https://blogs.lse.ac.uk/religionglobalsociety/2022/03/russias-invasion-of-ukraine-the-first-religious-war-in-the-21st-century/; Lucian N. Leustean, "Is Russia's Invasion of Ukraine still a Religious War?," *London School of Economics*, February 8, 2023, https://blogs.lse.ac.uk/religionglobalsociety/2023/02/is-russias-invasion-of-ukraine-still-a-religious-war/.

2 Jason Stanley, "The Antisemitism Animating Putin's Claim to "Denazify" Ukraine," *The Guardian*, February 26, 2022, https://www.theguardian.com/world/2022/feb/25/vladimir-putin-ukraine-attack-antisemitism-denazify; Ishaan Tharoor, "The Christian Nationalism behind Putin's War," April 19, 2022, https://www.washingtonpost.com/world/2022/04/19/patriarch-kirill-orthodox-church-russia-ukraine/.

3 Dmytro Voyk, "Religious Arguments and Political Goals Behind the Russian-Ukrainian War," *Canopy Forum*, June 23, 2022, https://canopyforum.org/2022/06/23/religious-arguments-and-political-goals-behind-the-russian-ukranian-war/

4 The whole recent issue of *St Vladimir's Theological Quarterly* (47:1, 2003) was devoted to these disputes.

5 Primary source texts and commentaries in Yuri Stoyanov, "Eastern Orthodoxy and the Ethics of War," in *Religion, War and Ethics: A Sourcebook*, eds. Greg M. Reichberg and Henryk Syse (Cambridge and New York: Cambridge University Press, 2014), 164–235, at 178–80, 183–7.

6 A selection of Russian Orthodox clerical sermons and statements made during the Second World War were assembled in *The Truth about Religion in Russia* (London: Hutchinson, 1944).

7 Statements collected and published in Bartholomew I, *Cosmic Grace – Humble Prayer: The Ecological Vision of the Green Patriarch Bartholomew*, ed. John Chryssavgis (Grand Rapids, MI: W. B. Eerdmans, 2003).

8 Russian Orthodox Church, *The Orthodox Church and Society: The Bases of the Social Concept of the Russian Orthodox Church* (Belleville, MI: St. Innocent, Firebird Publishers, 2000).

9 Yuri Stoyanov, "Norms of War in Eastern Orthodox Christianity," in *World Religions and Norms of War*, eds. Vesselin Popovski, Gregory Reichberg, and Nicholas Turner (Tokyo; New York; Paris: United Nations University Press, 2009), 166–219, at 206–7; Viorel Coman, "Critical Analysis of the Moscow Patriarchate Vision on the Russian–Ukrainian Military Conflict: *Russkiy Mir* and Just War," *Scottish Journal of Theology* 76 (2023): 332–44, at 334–6.

10 Zoe Knox, *Russian Society and the Orthodox Church: Religion in Russia after Communism* (London: Routledge, 2005); Zoe Knox and Anastasia Mitrofanova, "The Russian Orthodox Church," in *Eastern Christianity and Politics in the Twenty-First Century*, ed. Lucian Leustean (London: Routledge, 2014), 38–66; Katarzyna Chawryło, *The Altar and Throne Alliance. The Russian Orthodox Church vs. the Government in Russia* (Warsaw: Centre for Eastern Studies, 2015); Kristina Stoeckl, "Three Models of Church-State Relations in Contemporary Russia", in *Constitutions and Religion, Research Handbooks in Comparative Constitutional Law Series*, ed. Susanna Mancini (Cheltenham: Edward Elgar Publishing Ltd, 2020), 237–51.

11 For a recent analysis of the principal approaches to and reconstructions of the origins and historical development of the phenomenon of Russian messianism, see Alicja Curanović, "Conventional Wisdom and Contemporary Russian Messianism. A Critical Verification," *Vestnik MGIMO-Universiteta* 64, no. 1 (2019): 28–44. On its latest manifestations in Russian foreign policy, cf. Maria Engström, "Contemporary Russian Messianism and New Russian Foreign Policy," *Contemporary Security Policy* 35, no. 3 (2014): 356–79; Charlie Lewis, "Contemporary Russian Messianism under Putin and Russian Foreign Policy in Ukraine and Syria," *Slavonic and East European Review* 98, no. 3 (2020): 531–59; Alicja Curanović, "The Phantomic Nature of Missionary Nationalism in a Former Empire: The Case of Russia," in *Nationalism in a Transnational Age Irrational Fears and the Strategic Abuse of Nationalist Pride*, eds. Frank Jacob and Carsten Schapkow (Berlin: De Gruyter, 2022), 69–91; Alicja Curanović, "Mission Narrative in Russian Foreign Policy. The Comparative Perspective," in *Exploring Russia's Exceptionalism in International Politics*, ed. Raymond Taras (Abingdon; New York: Routledge, 2024), 33–53; Mikhail Suslov, "Messianic Discourses and the Ideology of Putinism," in Taras, *Exploring Russia's Exceptionalism*, (Abingdon; New York: Routledge, 2024), 82–99.

12 Peter J. S. Duncan, *Russian Messianism: Third Rome, Revolution, Communism and After* (London: Routledge, 2000), 87–8.

13 Victor Shnirelman, "Russian Neoconservatism and Apocalyptic Imperialism," in *Contemporary Russian Conservatism: Problems, Paradoxes and Dangers*, eds. Mikhail Suslov and Dmitry Uzlaner (Leiden: Brill, 2019), 347–78. Cf. Jardar Østbø, *The New Third Rome: Readings of a Russian Nationalist Myth* (Stuttgart: Ibidem, 2016), 181–223; Engström, "Contemporary Russian Messianism," 363–70 (exploration of post-Soviet Russian "katechonic" ideology and messianism); Suslov, "Messianic Discourses," 90–6.

14 Edwin Bacon, "Church and State in Contemporary Russia: Conflicting Discourses," in *Russia After Communism*, eds. Rick Fawn and Stephen White (London: Frank Cass, 2002), 97–116; Beth Admiraal, "A Religion for the Nation or a Nation for the Religion? Putin's Third Way for Russia," in *Russian Nationalism and the National Reassertion of Russia*, ed. Marlene Laruelle (London: Routledge, 2009), 203–18, at 204–6.

15 "O Kontseptsii natsional'noi bezopasnosti Rossiyskoi Federatsii," https://www.prlib.ru/item/352298; "Deklaratsiya Tsennostey Soyuznogo Gosudarstva Rossii i Belarusi," January 25, 2018, https://rosbelclub.ru/archives/3981; "Konstitutsiya Rossiyskoj Federatsii," *The State Duma. The Federal Assembly of The Russian Federation*, July 1, 2020, http://duma.gov.ru/legislative/documents/constitution/; "Executive Order Approving Fundamentals of State Policy for Preservation and Strengthening of Traditional Russian Spiritual and Moral Values," *President of Russia*, November 9, 2022, http://en.kremlin.ru/acts/news/69810 (the Moscow Patriarchate was involved directly in the formulation of the section on "spiritual-moral values" in the last document).

16 Kristina Stoeckl, "Russia's Spiritual Security Doctrine as a Challenge to European Comprehensive Security Approaches," *The Review of Faith & International Affairs* 20, no. 4 (2022): 37–44.

17 According to Patriarch Kirill's statements the "Russian World" represents a unique common civilizational and multi-national community and sphere (its nucleus being the "historical space of Russia": Russia, Belarus, and Ukraine), with a shared historical memory stemming from the Orthodox heritage of the cradle of medieval the East Slavonic Christian civilization of Kievan/Kyivan Rus. As the religious and spiritual pillar of the "Russian World," the Russian Orthodox Church and its canonical territory transcend current state borders; consequently it can play a vital role in the integration processes across this broader transnational sphere: Patriarch Kirill, "Vystuplenie Svyateishego Patriarkha Kirilla na torsheztvennom otkrytii III Assemblei Russkogo mira," *Official Site of the Moscow Patriarchate*, November 3, 2009, http://www.patriarchia.ru/db/print/928446.html.

18 Robert C. Blitt, "Russia's 'Orthodox' Foreign Policy: The Growing Influence of the Russian Orthodox Church in Shaping Russia's Policies Abroad," *University of Pennsylvania Journal of International Law* 33, no. 2 (2011): 363–460; Nicolai Petro, "Russia's Orthodox Soft Power," *Carnegie Council for International Affairs*, March 2015, http://www.carnegiecouncil.org/publications/articles_papers_reports/727; Daniel P. Payne, "Spiritual Security, the Russkiy Mir, and the Russian Orthodox Church: The Influence of the Russian Orthodox Church on Russia's Foreign Policy Regarding Ukraine, Moldova, Georgia and Armenia," in *Traditional Religion and Political Power: Examining the Role of the Church in Georgia, Armenia, Ukraine and Moldova*, ed. Adam Hug (London: The Foreign Policy Centre), 65–71; Cyril Hovorun, "Russian Church and Ukrainian War," *The Expository Times* 134, no. 1 (2022): 1–10, at 5–7.

19 Kristina Stoeckl, "The Russian Orthodox Church's Conservative Crusade," *Current History* 116, no. 792 (2017): 271–6; Alicja Curanović, *The Guardians of Traditional Values: Russia and the Russian Orthodox Church in the Quest for Status* (Washington, DC: Transatlantic Academy, 2015); Dimitry Uzlaner and Kristina Stoeckl, *The Moralist International: Russia in the Global Culture War* (New York: Fordham University Press, 2022); Kristina Stoeckl, *Russian Orthodoxy and Secularism* (Leiden: Brill, 2020), 47–59.

20 John Garrard and Carol Garrard, *Russian Orthodoxy Resurgent: Faith and Power in the New Russia* (Princeton, NJ: Princeton University Press, 2008), 207–42.

21 Dmitry Adamsky, *Russian Nuclear Orthodoxy: Religion, Politics, and Strategy* (Stanford, CA: Stanford University Press, 2019), 6, 234–5.

22 Knox, *Russian Society*, 124–5.

23 Symptomatic aspects of this ideology are discussed in Boris Knorre, "The Culture of War and Militarization within Political Orthodoxy in the Post-Soviet Region," *Transcultural Studies* 12 (2016): 15–38; Boris Knorre and Aleksei Zygmont, "'Militant Piety' in 21st-Century Orthodox Christianity: Return to Classical Traditions or Formation of a New Theology of War?," *Religions* 11 (2020): 2; Pär Gustafsson Kurki, *Apostles of Violence: The Russian Orthodox Church's Role in Russian Militarism* (Stockholm: Swedish Defence Research Agency, 2024).

24 Bojidar Kolov, "Main Cathedral of Mutual Legitimation: The Church of the Russian Armed Forces as a Site of Making Power Meaningful," *Religions* 12 (2021): 925.

25 Stoeckl, "Russia's Spiritual Security Doctrine," 39–40.

26 "Patriarkh Kirill: Voennoe uchastie Rossii v Sirii dolzhno prinesti dolgozhdannyy mir," *Komsomol'skaya Pravda*, September 30, 2015, https://www.kp.ru/daily/26439/3310649/; "Patriarkh Kirill podderzhal voennuyu operatsiyu Rossii v Sirii," *Interfaks*, January 7, 2016, https://www.interfax.ru/russia/488620. Generally, on the role of the Russian Orthodox Church in the Syrian campaign, see Dmitry Adamsky, "Christ-loving Diplomats: Russian Ecclesiastical Diplomacy in Syria," *Survival* 61, no. 6 (2019): 49–68; Dmitry Adamsky, "Christ-Loving Warriors: Ecclesiastical Dimension of the Russian Military Campaign in Syria," *Problems of Post-Communism* 67, no. 6 (2020): 433–45.

27 "Patriarkh Kirill: voina s terrorizmom - svyashchennaya voina," TASS, May 6, 2015, https://tass.ru/obschestvo/3263372.

28 "Patriarkh Kirill nazval voinu s terrorizmom svyashchennoi," TASS, October 18, 2015, https://tass.ru/obschestvo/3714937.

29 "Khristiane v Sirii razgnevany slovami RPTs o "svyashchennoi bor'be," *BBC Russian Service*, October 6, 2015, https://www.bbc.com/russian/news/2015/10/151006_syria_christians_holy_war; "Saudi Opposition Clerics Make Sectarian Call to Jihad in Syria," *Reuters*, October 5, 2915, https://www.reuters.com/article/us-mideast-crisis-saudi-clerics-idUSKCN0RZ1IW20151005/; Milo Comeford, "Defender of the Faith? Russia's 'Holy War' in Syria," *Tony Blair Institute for Global Change*, October 14, 2015, https://institute.global/insights/geopolitics-and-security/defender-faith-russias-holy-war-syria; "Met Elias Audi: Our Church Does Not Bless Wars," October 18, 2015, https://araborthodoxy.blogspot.com/2015/10/met-elias-audi-our-church-does-not.html.

30 "Vsevolod Chaplin ob operatsii VVS RF v Sirii: Bor'ba s terrorizmom – svyashchenna," *Ren. TV*, September 30, 2015, https://ren.tv/news/v-mire/50886-vsevolod-chaplin-ob-operatsii-vvs-rf-v-sirii-borba-s-terrorizmom-sviashchenna.

31 "Vsevolod Chaplin ob operatsii VVS RF v Sirii: Bor'ba s terrorizmom – svyashchenna," *Ren. TV*, September 30, 2015, https://ren.tv/news/v-mire/50886-vsevolod-chaplin-ob-operatsii-vvs-rf-v-sirii-borba-s-terrorizmom-sviashchenna gust18, 2014, https://mospat.ru/en/news/51174/; "Russkaya pravoslavnaya tserkov'prizvala vlasti Ukrainy ostanovit' goneniya na veruyushchikh," *Informatsionniy portal fonda "Russkiy mir,"* https://russkiymir.ru/news/253084/.

32 "Patriarch Filaret to Patriarch Bartholomew: Moscow Cynically Lies about the Events in Eastern Ukraine," *Religious Information Service of Ukraine*, September 1, 2014, https://risu.ua/en/patriarch-filaret-to-patriarch-bartholomew-moscow-cynically-lies-about-the-events-in-eastern-ukraine_n70497.

33 Tim Whewell, "The Russians Fighting a 'Holy War' in Ukraine," *BBC News Magazine*, December 18, 2014, https://www.bbc.co.uk/news/magazine-30518054; Knorre, "The Culture of War," 15–38.

34 The post-Soviet Ukrainian ecclesial configuration in Ukraine comprises the Ukrainian Orthodox Church-Kyiv Patriarchate, the Ukrainian Autocephalous Orthodox Church, and the Ukrainian Orthodox Church-Moscow Patriarchate (alongside smaller Orthodox churches and the Ukrainian Greek Catholic Church). The establishment of an autocephalous Orthodox Church of Ukraine in 2018–19 (largely based on the unification of the first two churches) under the jurisdiction of the Ecumenical Patriarchate of Constantinople provoked a schism between the Moscow and Constantinople Patriarchates, as the ecclesial confrontations intensified also on the political level.

35 "V Den' zashchitnika Otechestva Svyateishiy Patriarkh Kirill vozlozhil venok k mogile Neizvestnogo soldata u Kremlevskoi steny," *Official Site of the Moscow Patriarchate*, February 23, 2022, http://www.patriarchia.ru/db/text/5903402.html.

36 "Obrashchenie Svyateishego Patriarkha Kirilla k arkhipastyryam, pastyryam, monashestvuyushchim i vsem vernym chadam Russkoi Pravoslavnoi Tserkvi," *Official Site of the Moscow Patriarchate*, February 24, 2022,http://www.patriarchia.ru/db/text/5903795.htm.

37 "Patriarshaya propoved' v Nedelyu syropustnuyu posle Liturgii v Khrame Khrista Spasitelya," *Official Site of the Moscow Patriarchate*, March 6, 2022, http://www.patriarchia.ru/db/text/5906442.html.

38 Analysis of and references to these reactions/statements in Yuri Stoyanov, "Eastern Orthodox War Justification and Ecclesial Dilemmas Arising from the War in Ukraine," *Studies in World Christianity* 30, no. 2 (2024): 230–48, at 235–7.

39 "His Holiness Patriarch Kirill Calls on the Faithful to Pray for Peace and Unity of the Church," *Official Site of the Moscow Patriarchate*, February 27, 2022, http://www.patriarchia.ru/en/db/text/5904398.html.

40 "Obrashchenie svyashchennosluzhitelei russkoi pravoslavnoi tserkvi s prizyvom k primireniiyu i prekrashcheniyu voiny," https://docs.google.com/forms/d/1yOGuXjdFQ1A3BQaEEQr744cwDzmSQ1qePaaBi4z6q3w/viewform?edit_requested=true.

41 Appeal reproduced in https://risu.ua/en/international-ecclesiastical-tribunal-for-cyril---almost-200-priests-of-the-uoc-mp-demand_n128244; https://hrwf.eu/ukraine-russia-hundreds-of-priests-of-the-moscow-patriarchate-in-ukraine-condemn-the-role-of-russian-patriarch-kirill-in-the-war/.

42 Co-published by the Orthodox Christian Studies Centre at Fordham University and the Volos Academy for Theological Studies: *Public Orthodoxy*, March 13, 2022, https://publicorthodoxy.org/2022/03/13/a-declaration-on-the-russian-world-russkii-mir-teaching/.

43 "Resolutions of the Council of the Ukrainian Orthodox Church of May 27, 2022," *Ukrainian Orthodox Church*, https://news.church.ua/2022/05/28/resolutions-council-ukrainian-orthodox-church-may-27-2022/?lang=en#2024-02-04.

44 Jack Jenkins, "Russian Priest Speaks out Against War in Ukraine Despite Threats," *Washington Post*, April 8, 2022, https://www.washingtonpost.com/religion/2022/04/08/russia-ukraine-war-priest-police/; Maria Katamadze, "Anti-war Russian Clergy Face Punishment," *Deutsche Welle*, October 15, 2023, https://www.dw.com/en/like-partisans-anti-war-russian-clergy-face-punishment/a-67103511.

45 Summary of these statements and moves in Stoyanov, "Eastern Orthodox War Justification," 237–8.
46 "The Ecumenical Patriarch Condemns the Unprovoked Russian Invasion of Ukraine and Expresses His Solidarity to the Suffering Ukrainian People," *Ecumenical Patriarchate*, February 24, 2022, https://ec-patr.org/the-ecumenical-patriarch-condemns-the-unprovoked-russian-invasion-of-ukraine-and-expresses-his-solidarity-to-the-suffering-ukrainian-people.
47 "Ecumenical Patriarch: Russian Church Shares Blame for 'Crimes' in Ukraine," *Reuters*, March 22, 2022, https://www.reuters.com/world/europe/ecumenical-patriarch-russian-church-shares-blame-crimes-ukraine-2023-03-22.
48 "Speech by Ecumenical Patriarch Bartholomew in Abu Dhabi," *RISU. Religious Information Service of Ukraine*, December 22, 2022, https://risu.ua/en/speech-by-ecumenical-patriarch-bartholomew-in-abu-dhabi_n134828.
49 "WCC Acting General Secretary to Patriarch Kirill of Moscow: "Raise up Your Voice so That the War Can be Stopped," *World Council of Churches*, March 2, 2022, https://www.oikoumene.org/news/wcc-acting-general-secretary-to-patriarch-kirill-of-moscow-raise-up-your-voice-so-that-the-war-can-be-stopped.
50 "WCC Central Committee Statement on the War in Ukraine," *World Council of Churches*, June 18, 2022, https://www.oikoumene.org/resources/documents/wcc-central-committee-statement-on-the-war-in-ukraine.
51 Texts and commentaries in Stoyanov, "Eastern Orthodoxy and the Ethics of War," 186–7, 214, 221.
52 "Patriarshee slovo posle Liturgii po sluchayu pervoi godovshchiny osvyashcheniya glavnogo khrama Vooruzhennykh sil RF," June 13, 2021.
53 "Patriarshaya propoved' v Nedelyu 15-iu po Pyatidesiatnitse posle Liturgii v Aleksandro-Nevskom skitu," *Official Site of the Moscow Patriarchate*, September 25, 2022, http://www.patriarchia.ru/db/text/5962628.html.
54 Texts and commentaries in Stoyanov, "Eastern Orthodoxy and the Ethics of War," 178–80, 183–7.
55 References and analysis in Maureen Perrie, "Apocalypse Delayed: Patriarch Kirill on Restraining the Antichrist in Ukraine," *Public Orthodoxy*, January 23, 2023, https://publicorthodoxy.org/2023/01/23/apocalypse-delayed-restraining-antichrist/; Stoyanov, "Eastern Orthodox Just War and Ecclesial Dilemmas," 240.
56 "Nakaz XXV Vsemirnogo russkogo narodnogo sobora 'Nastoiashchee i budushchee Russkogo mira,'" *Official Site of the Moscow Patriarchate*, March 27, 2024,http://www.patriarchia.ru/db/text/6116189.html.
57 "Calls for the Destruction of Ukraine and the Justification of a Military Aggression Are Inconsistent with the Gospel Teaching — Statement from the UOC Department for External Church Relations," *Ukrainian Orthodox Church*, March 28, 2024, https://news.church.ua/2024/03/28/calls-for-the-destruction-of-ukraine-and-the-justification-of-a-military-aggression-are-inconsistent-with-the-gospel-teaching-statement-from-the-uoc-department-for-external-church-relations/?lang=en#2024-05-24.
58 "Letter of the Council of Bishops of the UOC (OCU) to Ecumenical Patriarch Bartholomew," *Orthodox Church of Ukraine*, May 11, 2024, https://www.pomisna.info/uk/document-post/lyst-arhiyerejskogo-soboru-upts-ptsu-vselenskomu-patriarhu-varfolomiyu/.

59 "Statement of the UCCRO on the Condemnation of the Documents of the 'World Russian People's Council' Containing Justification of Russian Aggression against Ukraine," *UCCRO*, March 29, 2024, https://vrciro.org.ua/en/news/statement-of-the-ukrainian-council-of-churches-and-religious-organizations.

60 "CEC-UCCRO Joint Statement Calls for Just and Lasting Peace in Ukraine," *Conference of European Churches*, April 15, 2024, https://ceceurope.org/cec-uccro-joint-statement-calls-just-and-lasting-peace-ukraine.

61 "WCC Statement on Decree of XXV World Russian People's Council," *World Council of Churches*, April 12, 2024, https://www.oikoumene.org/resources/documents/wcc-statement-on-decree-of-xxv-world-russian-peoples-council.

62 "Alexei Navalny's Death and the Need to Counter Vladimir Putin's Totalitarian Regime and its War on Democracy," *Parliamentary Assembly of the Council of Europe*, April 17, 2024, https://pace.coe.int/en/files/33511/html.

63 "Neutralising Harmful Propaganda while Preserving the Right to Freedom of Expression," *Parliamentary Assembly of the Council of Europe*, October 1. 2024, https://pace.coe.int/en/news/9610/neutralising-harmful-propaganda-while-preserving-the-right-to-freedom-of-expression.

64 Jonathan Luxmoore, "Prosecutors Set Out Case against Kirill," *Church Times*, November 10, 2023, https://www.churchtimes.co.uk/articles/2023/10-november/news/world/prosecutors-set-out-case-against-kirill.

65 "Consolidated List of Financial Sanctions Targets in the UK," *Office of Financial Sanctions Implementation HM Treasury*, June 16, 2022, https://assets.publishing.service.gov.uk/media/65c2535612d5f1000d375136/Russia.pdf.

66 Iuliia Korniichuk, "'This Did Not Happen Even during the Cold War': Religion and International Sanctions in the Russo-Ukrainian War," *Stosunki Międzynarodowe – International Relations* (2024): n. pag.

67 "Open Letter: War in Ukraine and the Russian Church," *The Orthodox Christian Studies Center of Fordham University, Public Orthodoxy*, February 20, 2024, https://publicorthodoxy.org/good-reads/open-letter-ukraine-war/.

Selected Bibliography

Adamsky, Dmitry, *Russian Nuclear Orthodoxy: Religion, Politics, and Strategy* (Stanford, CA: Stanford University Press, 2019).

Chawryło, Katarzyna, The Altar, and Throne Alliance, *The Russian Orthodox Church vs. the Government in Russia* (Warsaw: Centre for Eastern Studies, 2015).

Knox, Zoe, *Russian Society and the Orthodox Church: Religion in Russia after Communism* (London: Routledge, 2005).

Stoeckl, Kristina and Dimitry Uzlaner, *The Moralist International: Russia in the Global Culture War* (New York: Fordham University Press, 2022).

Stoyanov, Yuri, "Norms of War in Eastern Orthodox Christianity," in *World Religions and Norms of War*, Vesselin Popovski, Gregory Reichberg, and Nicholas Turner (eds.) (Tokyo; New York; Paris: United Nations University Press, 2009), 166–219.

Taras, Raymond (ed.), *Exploring Russia's Exceptionalism in International Politics* (Abingdon; New York: Routledge, 2024).

Part 7

Ukraine's Nuremberg

War Crime Issues

19

The Genocide Convention and the Russia-Ukraine War

Kristina Hook

This chapter focuses on Russian atrocities targeting the Ukrainian people, specifically the application of the United Nations Convention on the Prevention and Punishment of the Crime of Genocide (hereafter, Genocide Convention) in the Russia-Ukraine war. Russia first sparked armed conflict with Ukraine in 2014 through its annexation of Crimea and proxy forces in eastern Ukraine. However, due to space constraints, this chapter will focus on events following Russia's escalation and full-scale invasion of Ukraine on February 24, 2022.

This chapter proceeds as follows. First, distinctive areas of the Genocide Convention's definitional criteria are discussed, including establishing genocidal intent. Next, the acts prohibited by the Genocide Convention (Article II) are outlined, along with associated evidence of Russian violations. Finally, the acts punishable under the Genocide Convention (Article III) are discussed, particularly (1) the genocidal commission and (2) direct and public incitement to genocide, given their salience to this case. Critically, the central duty of the Genocide Convention remains prevention—not yet achieved in the Russia-Ukraine war. Russia's continuing atrocities, therefore, pose severe risks to the Ukrainian people, other atrocity crime victims, and international law more broadly.

The Application of the Genocide Convention in the Russia-Ukraine War

Genocide has been referred to by pioneering experts like Raphael Lemkin as the "crime of crimes" as perpetrators willfully target a group's most fundamental right: to exist.[1] When contrasted to other atrocity crimes like war crimes or crimes against humanity, two distinctive elements stand out. First, genocide requires not simply establishing that criminal violations of prohibited acts have occurred. It also requires establishing the motivation (i.e., intent) by which these prohibited acts were conducted. In addition, while genocide and crimes against humanity can share overlapping features, such as their large-scale, systematic, or coordinated nature, the prohibited acts associated with genocide are more tightly defined. In this section, these prohibited acts, and evidence of the intent by which they were committed will be explored, followed by a discussion of the punishable acts defined in the Genocide Convention.

Genocidal Intent

In international law, the crime of genocide was codified in the Genocide Convention, which, notably, the Soviet Union (and its legal inheritor, the Russian Federation) ratified in 1954.[2] The legal obligations to the Genocide Convention are *erga omnes*, meaning owed to the international community as a collective whole.[3] As defined under Article II of the Genocide Convention, three necessary parts of any claim of genocide (i.e., constituent elements) must be established: (1) any of the delineated genocidal acts in Article II, (2) as committed against a listed protected group, (3) with the "intent to destroy the group in whole or in part."[4]

Regarding protected groups, the Genocide Convention explicitly identifies "national, ethnical, racial or religious groups."[5] While this limited number of explicitly protected groups is an oft-critiqued feature of the Genocide Convention,[6] these limitations are circumvented in this case on the grounds that Russia is targeting Ukrainians along the lines of their national group membership. Requiring additional scrutiny is Russian *intent*—the most contested feature of genocide definitions in both jurisprudence and genocide scholarship.[7] Here, it is important to delineate that intent can be attributable to individual criminal liability or to determining state responsibility for breaches of international law, that is, "in the case of genocide, wrongful conduct of exceptional gravity that is attributable to the State."[8] With atrocity crimes by Russia or Russia-aligned actors continuing daily against Ukrainians at the time of this writing, engaging questions of individual criminal liability is presently less productive (as these crimes will continue to mount) than the question of whether the Russian Federation bears state responsibility for breaches of the Genocide Convention in Ukraine. This chapter takes this latter approach.

When assessing intentionality, international courts have indicated that intent can be attributed to a state through "evidence of a general plan (derived from official statements, documents, or policy) or can be inferred from a systematic pattern of atrocities targeting the protected group."[9] The five prohibited acts defined as genocide in the Convention (discussed next) can also provide supporting indications of intent when viewed in their totality and alongside other evidence. In the context of the Russia-Ukraine war, determining a "general plan" to destroy the Ukrainian national group in part is supported by language inciting genocide by key actors, by salient patterns of atrocities consistent across the areas controlled by Russian state actors since 2022, and by conspicuous and systematic methods of atrocities underlying military and occupational policy that implement expressed intent.[10]

With the Genocide Convention denoting the intent to destroy a protected group may be attempted "in whole or in part," jurisprudence has often stressed a threshold of a substantial, influential, and/or prominent component of the group.[11] More specifically, the International Court of Justice has evaluated three factors to interpret genocidal intent to destroy a group "in part," namely, whether (1) the targeted component of the group is "significant enough to have an impact on the group as a whole," (2) whether an indication of genocide can be drawn from the geographical area controlled by the perpetrators, should they be unable to access an entire group, and (3) if the targeted group segment is of such prominence to the group that the targeted part is essential to the broader group's survival.[12] Each of these criteria has been applied to the Russia-Ukraine context, with previous genocide assessments arguing that these criteria directly relate to Russia's intentional targeting of influential, prominent Ukrainians through coordinated, premeditated policies and through a systematic pattern of atrocities against Ukrainians that have been repeated in every area that the Russian military has controlled or accessed.[13] Together, these dynamics indicate an overlap of genocidal motive and means.[14] The extreme motivations of genocide perpetrators and the dynamics that arise from its corresponding logistical requirements also mark genocide as a process characterized by specific characteristics well-documented by scholars.[15]

Indeed, when assessing the scale of atrocities inflicted on Ukrainians by Russian actors relative to their area of access or control, a distinctive pattern of concentrated destruction and willfully inflicted atrocities has emerged. These range from large-scale destruction of cities, towns, and essential infrastructure to mass torture, close-range executions, rape, and other sexual violence.[16] Notably, the selective targeting of Ukrainian activists and community leaders—including those with no military affiliation, such as teachers—for violence, killing, and enforced disappearances can constitute evidence of Russian targeting of Ukrainian national group members vital to the group's survival and reproduction.[17] Further, such assessments are based upon available evidence, such as when the Ukrainian Armed Forces have liberated areas; when Ukrainian state, international, or civil society representatives have returned forcibly transferred citizens and children; and when the Russian military has rapidly retreated, most notably in the Kyiv and Kharkiv regions with little time to cover evidence of their criminal activities. This latter point is essential, as it suggests the presence of additional evidence not yet available to investigators in Ukrainian territories presently controlled by Russia.

Prohibited Acts (Article II)

As defined by the Genocide Convention, five specific acts committed with the intent to destroy a protected group in whole or in part denote the commission of genocide:

"(a) Killing members of the group;
(b) Causing serious bodily or mental harm to members of the group;
(c) Deliberately inflicting on the group conditions of life calculated to bring about its physical destruction in whole or in part;

(d) Imposing measures intended to prevent births within the group;
(e) Forcibly transferring children of the group to another group."[18]

In the case of the Russia-Ukraine war, the presence of substantial evidence of atrocities committed by Russian actors against Ukrainians corresponding to each of these five categories is both rare and striking. This chapter will examine evidence of Russian violations of each prohibited act, with the caveat that space constraints prohibit a full review of Russian atrocities corresponding to each category. These prohibited acts often overlap, as they together comprise the complex sociopolitical behavior of genocide. Of particular concern, more detailed assessments of Russian breaches of the Genocide Convention in Ukraine argue that Russian perpetrators have escalated their willful and systematic violations in these areas over the course of their full-scale invasion of Ukraine.[19]

While genocide is not exclusively determined by the number of fatalities or attempted fatalities,[20] such fatalities often occur during violence intended to destroy. In Ukraine, Russian forces have embarked upon extensive examples of lethal violence against Ukrainian men, women, and children, with executions of Ukrainian civilians recorded in all areas of their control.[21] These willful fatalities have been documented across Ukraine, including in areas of geographic, cultural, linguistic, religious, and other features of diversity.[22] Killings have occurred through summary executions, shelling, torture-induced fatalities, missile strikes, and willful targeting of evacuation caravans. Also pertinent for jurisprudence in this area,[23] Russian perpetrators have killed by omission in diverse ways, such as the deaths of Ukrainians held captive in squalid basements and starvation conditions.[24] Adding to evidence of state-sanctioned lethal actions, Russian military units have actively participated in the mass killing of civilians, including infamous examples in Bucha, where perpetrators later received national awards from Russian President Vladimir Putin himself.[25] Russian state and state-aligned media platforms have also regularly released celebratory communiques in the immediate aftermath of the targeting and killing of Ukrainian civilians.[26]

Next, when evaluating severe and willful bodily or mental harm by Russian actors against Ukrainians, a pattern of escalating, systematic, and diverse tactics has been employed against the Ukrainian national group.[27] As with fatalities, "consistent patterns of grievous physical and psychological harm inflicted by Russian forces and authorities against Ukrainian men, women, and children have been documented in geographically diverse areas of Ukraine and Russia."[28] The United Nations and other international human rights experts have documented extensive, systematic torture, rape, and other forms of conflict-related sexual violence with "extreme brutality and acts of torture" across age and gender divides and in all Ukrainian territories that Russia has controlled.[29] For example, documented cases of gender-based and sexual violence have been recorded involving children, women, and men from ages four to eighty-two years old across nine regions of Russian-occupied Ukraine as well as in Russian territory where Ukrainians have been transported.[30] Human rights experts have documented torture, violence, and rape occurring to "punish" Ukrainians for their national identity, as well as against large swaths of the civilian population, with "the primary targets Ukrainian civil servants, including teachers and community leaders, former and retired Ukrainian soldiers or policemen, and ordinary civilians, including children, known for patriotic sentiments."[31] Russia's willful campaign to induce severe psychological harm to Ukrainians nationwide has included numerous direct and indirect threats of a nuclear strike targeting the same population that survived the "world's worst-ever civil nuclear incident" in the Chornobyl disaster, exacerbated by Moscow itself in the 1980s.[32] Of special relevance to inquiries of genocide in the Russia-Ukraine war, multiple fact-finding reports have documented lethal or near-lethal torture aimed at a widening segment of the protected Ukrainian national group since the beginning of Russia's full-scale invasion.[33]

Such atrocities are linked to Russian state actors' additional documented prohibited acts explicated in Article II(c) of the Genocide Convention. These perpetrators have deliberately inflicted on Ukrainians conditions of life aimed at bringing about their destruction in part through a systematic, premeditated, and coordinated campaign that escalated through targeting an ever-widening group of Ukrainians. In particular, Russian perpetrators have engaged in unrelenting attacks on Ukrainian population centers in willful campaigns that have leveled numerous Ukrainian towns and cities (including but not limited to Mariupol, Bakhmut, Marinka, Volonvakha, Lyman, Rubizhne, Popasna, Sievierodonetsk, Bilohorivka, Hirske, Zolote, Kreminna, and Lysychansk).[34] These attacks have targeted Ukrainian cities' vital civilian infrastructure, including water, electricity, natural gas, and communication lines, in successive and close-time attacks across Ukraine's extensive territory and involving population centers far away from the war's frontline.[35] Notably, a Russian campaign during the 2022–3 winter season was "timed for Ukraine's harsh winter—the most vulnerable season for the physical survival of Ukrainians."[36] It was interpreted at the time by humanitarian specialists as posing serious risks to the survival, health, and well-being of millions of Ukrainians. Publicized reactions to these attacks by Russian state actors demonstrated awareness and intention for these attacks' destructive purposes, including from Russian parliamentarians who celebrated the coordinated missile attacks as making it "impossible to survive."[37] In March 2024, the International Criminal Court issued arrest warrants for Russian General Lieutenant Sergei Kobylash and Admiral Viktor Sokolov, commander of the Russian long-range aviation force and head of the Black Sea fleet, respectively, for their leadership roles in bombing Ukrainian civilian population centers and critical infrastructure.[38] While the range of evidence in this category is more expansive than space constraints in this short chapter allow, as one indicator, human rights experts have documented a doubling of premature births due to the war's impact in the eastern regions of Ukraine.[39] This harsh reality has corresponded with more than 1,000 attacks on Ukrainian hospitals, healthcare workers, and medical infrastructure from February 2022 to May 2023 alone.[40]

In the fourth category of acts defined by the Genocide Convention,[41] other analyses and jurisprudence, including in the Kosovo war and for ISIS crimes against the Yazidi people, have provided relevant guidance.[42] Such assessments have highlighted rape and conflict-related sexual violence as meeting the criteria of imposing measures intended to prevent births within the group. The deployment of sexual, gender-based violence and other forms of conflict-related sexual violence by the Russian military and authorities has been extensively documented in all Ukrainian areas under Russian control, with the United Nations concluding Russia's deployment of rape as a "military strategy" by October 2022.[43] A core similarity across multiple testimonies has involved sexual violence used to target Ukrainian identity, with testimonies from victims that Russian soldiers stated they would "beat the Ukrainian out of you"[44] or "rape them to the point where they wouldn't want sexual contact with any man, to prevent them from having Ukrainian children."[45] This type of violence has been described in other legal analyses of genocide as reducing women and girls' desires to procreate, marry, build families, or engage in future relationships.[46] In addition, rape, castration, and other conflict-related sexual violence have also been directed at Ukrainian males as well as females, including widespread reports in detention centers, with journalistic and other current reporting suggesting this practice is systematic and widespread.[47] No public response by the Russian government to United Nations reporting or other widely publicized accounts of systematic sexual violence has been recorded.

Finally, the fifth act delineated by the Genocide Convention prohibits the "forcible transfer of children from one group to another group." Coupled with the requisite genocidal intent, this category has proven rare in recent cases prosecuted and analyzed in the modern era for genocidal crimes, tragically setting the Russia-Ukraine war apart. Although Russian transfer of Ukrainian children existed in the areas of their conflict activities before its full-scale invasion, a notable escalation of policies, directives, and domestic legislation aimed at the coordinated, systematic, and large-scale transfer of Ukrainian children to Russia-controlled or Russian territory has escalated since this time.[48] Ukrainian authorities have verified the identities of 19,393 Ukrainian children taken by Russian state actors as of July 2023,[49] although Russian state actors, including key official Maria Lvova-Belova, have claimed that Russia has taken 700,000 Ukrainian children.[50] Her role in this forcible deportation program led to an International Criminal Court arrest warrant, along with Russian President Vladimir Putin, in March 2023.[51] For questions of genocide and genocidal intent, the level of extensive Russian state involvement, management, and coordination is particularly salient, with reporting and documentation recording Ukrainian children being taken from their guardians and communities against their expressed will.[52] Also of note, Russian legislation was rapidly adopted to "legalize" these compulsory transfers of children without the child or guardian's permission.[53] Russian authorities have made concerted efforts to hide these children or work against their return to Ukrainian guardians.[54] A growing body of evidence demonstrates that the Russian state has enacted procedures—including indoctrination camps—aimed at "re-educating" Ukrainian children and destroying their connection to their identity, language, citizenship, and national belonging.[55]

Punishable Acts (Article III)

As stated above, the evidence that Russian actors have engaged in at least one of these five genocidal acts must be accompanied by proof of intent to destroy the Ukrainian national group in part. Together, the consistent patterns across systematic atrocities allow for credible inferences of Russian genocidal intent, indicating Russian state breaches of the Genocide Convention, namely, the commission of genocide itself under Article III(a). As Article III of the Genocide Convention states, however, the commission of genocide is only one of five punishable acts, along with "(b) Conspiracy to commit genocide; (c) Direct and public incitement to commit genocide; (d) Attempt to commit genocide; (e) Complicity in genocide."[56]

Of such punishable acts, direct and public incitement to genocide by Russian actors has drawn significant international attention, with the United Nations Independent International Inquiry confirming their ongoing investigation in March 2024.[57] Such inciting statements also add to the portrait of Russian actors' expressed motivations for their unprovoked military aggression and atrocity crimes in Ukraine. Russian state actors have engaged in "eliminationist" rhetoric against Ukrainians before February 24, 2022, with this rhetoric sharply escalating as a core feature of Moscow's campaign against Ukraine.[58] Since 2022, experts have documented how high-level Russian officials have "repeatedly and publicly den[ied] the existence of a distinct Ukrainian identity, implying that those who self-identify as Ukrainian threaten the unity of Russia or are Nazis, and therefore deserving of punishment."[59] Specific indicators highlighted by the United Nations, including denials of identity and "accusation in a mirror" (where perpetrators accuse their victims of implementing or planning the crimes they themselves intend), have been regular features of Russia's inciting campaign against Ukrainians, such as claims by Russian president Vladimir Putin and other officials that Ukrainian identity does not exist or that Ukraine is committing genocide against itself.[60] As Ukrainians have increasingly been framed as posing an existential threat to Russia, regular dehumanizing tropes that Ukrainians must be "de-Nazified" or "de-Satanized" are regularly broadcast on Russian state media and uttered by influential Russian state actors, ranging from Russian President Putin down through Russian occupation officials with direct physical control over Ukrainians.[61] Calls for violence have been extended that target the killing of millions of Ukrainians by high-level Russian officials, with this direct and public incitement to genocide has been intended and has conditioned their audiences for violence against Ukrainians.[62] Documented instances of incitement by Russian state actors have adhered to scholarly frameworks in this area, such as Richter et al.'s five "D's" of incitement (demonization, delegitimization, dehumanization, denial, and disinformation).[63]

Conclusion: The Purpose of the Genocide Convention

Applying the Genocide Convention to the ongoing Russia-Ukraine war is a daunting but critical task. For actors working to prosecute Russian atrocity crimes in Ukraine, time-staking efforts to document, record witness statements, preserve the chain of custody for evidentiary processes, and more will continue for many years and decades to come. These investigations and the political will necessary to see the accused in courtrooms are critical steps for Ukrainians, for other global victims of atrocities, and for the essential deterrent effect that genocide prosecutions are intended to have on other would-be perpetrators.

Nevertheless, the central duty and primary purpose of the Genocide Convention remains the *prevention* of genocide—hence its inclusion as the operative and first term in the Convention on the Prevention and Punishment of the Crime of Genocide. As Article I of the Genocide Convention stresses, "genocide, whether committed in time of peace or in time of war, is a crime under international law which they [the Contracting Parties] undertake to prevent and punish."[64] In *Bosnia v. Serbia*, the International Court of Justice clarified when the signatories' duty to prevent is triggered: "A State's obligation to prevent, and the corresponding duty to act, arise at the instant that the State learns of, or should normally have learned of, the existence of a serious risk that genocide will be committed."[65]

As evident in this language—and in the Genocide Convention's name itself—the duty of state signatories to the Convention to prevent genocide is triggered prior to the onset of genocide and certainly prior to the conclusive proof required by future courtrooms to adjudicate claims. When applying a "fully convincing" or "conclusive" standard, experts have concluded that the duty to prevent genocide in Ukraine was triggered at least by May 2022.[66] The slow pace of international institutions and national government leaders explicitly addressing their moral and legal obligations in this area will bear historical scrutiny.

Of critical importance, the Genocide Convention's preamble—central to its interpretation today—references its mandating United Nations General Assembly Resolution, which states, "A denial of the *right of existence* of entire human groups . . . results in great losses to humanity in the form of cultural and other contributions represented by these human groups and is contrary to moral law and the spirit and aims of the United Nations."[67] While this short chapter has not referenced the tremendous cultural heritage destruction that Russia's unprovoked aggression on Ukraine has caused, this legacy of the Russia-Ukraine war echoes this 1946 language by the United Nations General Assembly. With genocide recognized as targeting a protected group—in this rare case, an entire national group consisting of millions of potential Ukrainian victims—the failure to prevent Russian genocidal aims would usher in nearly unimaginable human suffering and constitute a severe blow to international law and international human rights.

As this chapter has summarized, the available evidence indicates strong scholarly and legal arguments to consider the Russian Federation as in breach of the Genocide Convention through the willful commission of genocide and through direct and public incitement to genocide, among other crimes that are still under investigation. Despite expected academic and legal debates on these matters in the decades ahead, Russia's combined military aggression, nationwide assault on Ukraine, and clear evidence of atrocity crimes targeting Ukrainian civilians were evident from the earliest weeks of Russia's full-scale invasion. Thus, this case—and its outcome for the people of Ukraine—poses one of the most serious test cases of international commitments to the duty to prevent genocide as outlined in the Genocide Convention that the modern era has faced since Nuremberg.

Notes

1 See, William A. Schabas, "Convention for the Prevention and Punishment of the Crime of Genocide," *United Nations Audiovisual Library of International Law*, 2008, https://legal.un.org/avl/pdf/ha/cppcg/cppcg_e.pdf.
2 United Nations, *Convention on the Prevention and Punishment of the Crime of Genocide (Genocide Convention)*, December 9, 1948, (UN Doc. A/RES/260(III)).
3 International Court of Justice (ICJ), *Application of the Convention on the Prevention and Punishment of the Crime of Genocide (Bosnia and Herzegovina v. Serbia and Montenegro) - Preliminary Objections*, June 26, 1995: 595, para. 31, https://www.icj-cij.org/case/91/preliminary-objections.
4 United Nations, "General Assembly," Art. II.
5 Ibid.
6 See, Kristina Hook, "Pinpointing Patterns of Violence: A Comparative Genocide Studies Approach to Violence Escalation in the Ukrainian Holodomor," *Genocide Studies and Prevention* 15, no. 2 (October 2021): 10–36; Adam Jones, *Genocide: A Comprehensive Introduction*, 3rd ed. (London; New York: Routledge, Taylor & Francis Group, 2017).
7 Devrim Aydin, "The Interpretation of Genocidal Intent Under the Genocide Convention and the Jurisprudence of International Courts," *The Journal of Criminal Law* 78, no. 5 (October 2014): 423–41, https://doi.org/10.1350/jcla.2014.78.5.943; Ernesto Verdeja, "The Political Science of Genocide: Outlines of an Emerging Research Agenda," *Perspectives on Politics* 10, no. 2 (June 2012): 307–21, https://doi.org/10.1017/S1537592712000680; Maureen S. Hiebert, "Theorizing Destruction: Reflections on the State of Comparative Genocide Theory," *Genocide Studies and Prevention* 3, no. 3 (December 2008): 309–39, https://doi.org/10.3138/gsp.3.3.309.
8 Diamond et al., "Independent Inquiry."
9 Ibid., 2. See also, *Application of the Convention on the Prevention and Punishment of the Crime of Genocide (Bosnia and Herzegovina v. Serbia and Montenegro)*, Judgment, I.C.J. Reports 2007, para. 373.
10 See, Diamond et al., "Independent Inquiry"; Kristina Hook, "Why Russia's War in Ukraine Is a Genocide," *Foreign Affairs*, July 28, 2022, https://www.foreignaffairs.com/ukraine/why-russias-war-ukraine-genocide; Yulia Ioffe, "Forcibly Transferring Ukrainian Children to the Russian Federation: A Genocide?," *Journal of Genocide Research* 25, no. 3–4 (October 2, 2023): 315–51; Kristina Hook, John Packer, Erin Farrell Rosenberg, et al., "The Russian Federation's Escalating Commission of Genocide in Ukraine: A Legal Analysis," *New Lines Institute*, July 2023, https://newlinesinstitute.org/wp-content/uploads/20230726-Genocide-Ukraine-Report-NISLAP_.pdf; Denys Azarov et al., "Understanding Russia's Actions in Ukraine as the Crime of Genocide," *Journal of International Criminal Justice* 21, no. 2 (September 15, 2023): 233–64.
11 United Nations, "General Assembly," Art. II.
12 International Court of Justice (ICJ), *Application of the Convention on the Prevention and Punishment and Punishment of the Crime of Genocide (Bosnia and Herzegovina v. Serbia and Montenegro)*, February 26, 2007, para. 198–200 (ICJ Doc. 091-20070226-JUD-01-00-EN).
13 See, Hook et al., "Russian Federation's Escalating."

14 Scott Straus, "'Destroy Them to Save Us': Theories of Genocide and the Logics of Political Violence," *Terrorism and Political Violence* 24, no. 4 (September 2012): 544–60; U.S. Department of State, *Atrocity Assessment Framework: Supplemental Guidance to State/USAID Conflict Assessment Frameworks*, July 27, 2015, https://2009-2017.state.gov/j/cso/archive/ap/241116.htm.
15 Straus, "Destroy Them"; Hook, "Pinpointing Patterns"; Hook et al., "Russian Federation's Escalating."
16 Hook et al., "Russian Federation's Escalating."
17 Jason Beaubien, "Screams from Russia's Alleged Torture Basements Still HauntUkraine's Kherson," *NPR*, November 18, 2022, https://www.npr.org/2022/11/18/1137473863/ukraine-kherson-alleged-torture-russia; Advait Malviya, "New Torture Chamber Evidence Uncovered from Liberated Kherson," *Global Rights Compliance*, March 2, 2023, https://globalrightscompliance.com/2023/03/02/new-torture-chamber-evidence-uncovered-from-liberated-kherson/.
18 United Nations, "General Assembly," Art. II.
19 See, Hook et al., Russian Federation's Escalating."
20 See, Daniel Chirot and Clark R. McCauley, *Why Not Kill Them All? The Logic and Prevention of Mass Political Murder* (Princeton, NJ: Princeton University Press, 2010).
21 Erika Kinetz, Oleksandr Stashevskyi, Vasilisa Stepanenko, "How Russian Soldiers Ran a "Cleansing" Operation in Bucha," *PBS*, November 3, 2022, https://www.pbs.org/wgbh/frontline/article/russian-soldiers-cleansing-operation-bucha-ukraine/; "Russian Soldiers Emerge from Forest After Couple Makes Wrong Turn on Their Drive," *CNN*, March 21, 2023, https://edition.cnn.com/videos/world/2023/03/21/izium-ukraine-war-crimes-investigation-russia-watson-ac360-vpx.cnn; David Botti, Malachy Browne, Evan Hill, et al., "New Evidence Shows How Russian Soldiers Executed Men in Bucha," *New York Times*, May 19, 2022, https://www.nytimes.com/2022/05/19/world/europe/russia-bucha-ukraine-executions.html; "Ukraine: Apparent War Crimes in Russia-Controlled Areas," *Human Rights Watch*, April 3, 2022, https://www.hrw.org/news/2022/04/03/ukraine-apparent-war-crimes-russia-controlled-areas; "UN Report Details Summary Executions of Civilians by Russian Troops in Northern Ukraine," *OHCHR*, December 7, 2022, https://www.ohchr.org/en/press-releases/2022/12/un-report-details-summary-executions-civilians-russian-troops-northern; see also, "Detentions of Civilians in the Context of the Armed Attack by the Russian Federation Against Ukraine," *OHCHR*, June 27, 2023, https://www.ohchr.org/en/statements-and-speeches/2023/06/detentions-civilians-context-armed-attack-russian-federation.
22 Hook et al., "Russian Federation's Escalating."
23 International Criminal Tribunal for Rwanda (ICTR), *The Prosecutor v. Jean-Paul Akayesu (Trial Judgement)*, September 2, 1998, para. 589 (Case No. ICTR-96-4-T).
24 Oleksandr Stashevskyi, "Forced into a Basement in Ukraine, Residents Began to Die," *AP News*, April 13, 2022, https://apnews.com/article/russia-ukraine-kyiv-europe-8fc19b96f035bd21fe14a0ec71982aa9; "Agriculture Weaponized: The Illegal Seizure and Extraction of Ukrainian Grain by Russia," Global Rights Compliance, November 2023, https://globalrightscompliance.com/wp-content/uploads/2023/11/20231115-Grain-Report-External.pdf.
25 "64th Detached Motor Rifle Brigade Receives Honorary Guards Title," President of Russia, April 18, 2022, http://www.en.kremlin.ru/catalog/keywords/91/events/68235.

26 "Telegram," *Ministry of Defense Russia*, April 28, 2023, https://t.me/mod_russia/26000; "Putin Hails a 'Positive Dynamic' for His Troops in Ukraine," *AFP*, January 15, 2023, https://www.themoscowtimes.com/2023/01/15/putin-hails-a-positive-dynamic-for-his-troops-in-ukraine-a79950.
27 Hook, "Why Russia's War"; Diamond et al., "Independent Inquiry."
28 Hook et al., "Russian Federation's Escalating," 7.
29 "Independent International Commission of Inquiry on Ukraine," *OHCHR*, March 4, 2022, https://www.ohchr.org/en/hr-bodies/hrc/iicihr-ukraine/index; Human Rights Council, *Report of the Independent International Commission of Inquiry on Ukraine*, March 15, 2023 (A/HRC/52/62); Malviya, "New Torture."
30 Hook et al., "Russian Federation's Escalating."
31 Vadym Chovgan, Mykhailo Romanov, and Vasyl Melnychuk, "'Nine Circles of Hell:' Places of Detention in Ukraine Under the Russian Occupation," *Dignity Publication Series on Torture and Organized Violence Report*, December 2022, 7, https://www.dignity.dk/wp-content/uploads/42-Nine-circles-of-hell.pdf.
32 "World Health Organization Report Explains the Health Impacts of the World's Worst-ever Civil Nuclear Accident," *WHO*, April 26, 2006, https://web.archive.org/web/20110404181327/http:/www.who.int/mediacentre/news/releases/2006/pr20/en/index.html; see also, Vasilisa Stepanenko, "Ukrainians Mark Chernobyl Disaster Amid Nuclear Threats," *AP NEWS*, April 26, 2023, https://apnews.com/article/ukraine-chernobyl-disaster-anniversary-nuclear-9ea533917643d80a891d85a8552e2701.
33 See, Hook et al., "Russian Federation's Escalating," 34–40; Independent International Commission, 2023; Chovgan et al., "Nine Circles."
34 Hook et al., "Russian Federation's Escalating," 44.
35 Stanislav Pohorilov, "Russian Attack on Dnipro: Death Toll Rises to 46 People," *Ukrainska Pravda*, January 19, 2023, https://www.pravda.com.ua/eng/news/2023/01/19/7385596/; "Kyiv Falling into Darkness," *Ukraine Conflict Observatory*, December 13, 2022, https://hub.conflictobservatory.org/portal/apps/sites/#/home/pages/nightlights.
36 Hook et al., "Russian Federation's Escalating," 8. See also, "What Ukrainians Need to Survive Winter," *International Rescue Committee*, November 6, 2023, https://www.rescue.org/article/what-ukrainians-need-survive-winter-0.
37 Hook et al., "Russian Federation's Escalating," 43–4.
38 "Situation in Ukraine: ICC Judges Issue Arrest Warrants Against Sergei Ivanovich Kobylash and Viktor Nikolayevich Sokolov," *International Criminal Court*, March 5, 2024, https://www.icc-cpi.int/news/situation-ukraine-icc-judges-issue-arrest-warrants-against-sergei-ivanovich-kobylash-and.
39 Inna Varenytsia, "On Ukraine's Front Line, a Fight to Save Premature Babies," *AP News*, August 22, 2022, https://apnews.com/article/russia-ukraine-health-world-news-donetsk-50ae42150e64960eda574dd7769e0212.
40 "WHO Records Over 1,000 Attacks on Ukraine Healthcare During War," *Reuters*, May 30, 2023, https://www.reuters.com/world/europe/who-records-over-1000-attacks-ukraine-healthcare-during-war-2023-05-30/. See also, Elisabeth Mahase, "Ukraine: Over 700 Recorded Attacks on Health Facilities and Workers in Year Since Russia Invasion," *BMJ*, February 23, 2023, p. 451, https://doi.org/10.1136/bmj.p451.
41 United Nations, "General Assembly."

42 Human Rights Council, "'They Came to Destroy': ISIS Crimes Against the Yazidis," June 15, 2016 (A/HRC/32/CRP.2) para. 145; "Kosovo: Rape as a Weapon of "Ethnic Cleansing," *Human Rights Watch*, March 1, 2000, https://www.hrw.org/report/2000/03/01/kosovo-rape-weapon-ethnic-cleansing.
43 Philip Wang, Tim Lister, Josh Pennington, and Heather Chen, "Russia Using Rape as 'Military Strategy' in Ukraine: UN Envoy," *CNN*, October 15, 2022, https://www.cnn.com/2022/10/15/europe/russia-ukraine-rape-sexual-violence-military-intl-hnk/index.html. See also, Violetta Orlova, "Occupants at Checkpoints Demand the Most Expensive Dumplings and Condoms from Drivers," *UNIAN*, June 7, 2022, https://www.unian.ua/war/viyna-v-ukrajini-okupanti-na-blokpostah-vimagayut-naydorozhchih-pelmeniv-ta-prezervativiv-novini-vtorgnennya-rosiji-v-ukrajinu-11856963.html; Kateryna Busol, "Russia's Weaponizing of Sexual Violence, and Ukraine's Response, Reveals a Grim War of Values," *The Guardian*, March 25, 2024, https://www.theguardian.com/commentisfree/2024/mar/25/russia-weaponising-sexual-violence-ukraine-values.
44 Siobhán O'Grady, Anastacia Galouchka, and Whitney Shefte, "In Russian-Occupied Izyum, She Was Raped and Tortured," *The Washington Post*, October 9, 2022, https://www.washingtonpost.com/world/2022/10/09/izyum-rape-torture-occupation-russia/.
45 Yogita Limaye, "Ukraine Conflict: 'Russian Soldiers Raped me and Killed My Husband,'" *BBC News*, April 11, 2022, https://www.bbc.com/news/world-europe-61071243.
46 Human Rights Council, "*They Came*," para. 145.
47 Harriet Barber, "Castration, Gang-Rape, Forced Nudity: How Russia's Soldiers Terrorise Ukraine with Sexual Violence," *The Telegraph*, November 28, 2022, https://www.telegraph.co.uk/global-health/terror-and-security/how-russian-soldiers-terrorise-ukraine-sexual-violence/; Christina Lamb, "She Thought She was Unshockable, Then Two Castrated Ukrainian Soldiers Arrived, *The Sunday Times*, June 17, 2023, https://www.thetimes.co.uk/article/ukraine-soldiers-castrated-russia-war-0hflzhzlv.
48 "Evacuation from the DPR Began with Orphans from a Boarding School in Donetsk," *Interfax.ru*, February 18, 2022, https://www.interfax.ru/world/822971; Ioffe, "Forcibly Transferring."
49 Hook et al., "Russian Federation's Escalating."
50 "During the Year, 5.3 Million Refugees Arrived from Ukraine and Donbass [sic] to the Territory of the Russian Federation," *TASS*, February 20, 2023, https://tass.ru/obschestvo/17091725.
51 International Criminal Court, "Situation in Ukraine."
52 Khoshnood, Kaveh, Nathaniel Raymond, Caitlin Howarth, et al., "Russia's Systematic Program for the Re-education & Adoption of Ukraine's Children," *Conflict Observatory*, February 14, 2023, https://hub.conflictobservatory.org/portal/sharing/rest/content/items/97f919ccfe524d31a241b53ca44076b8/data; Human Rights Council, *Report*; "Deportation of Ukrainian Citizens from the Territory of Active Military Operations or from the Temporarily Occupied Territory of Ukraine to the Territory of the Russian Federation and the Republic of Belarus," *Zamina*, January, 2023, https://zmina.ua/en/publication-en/deportation-of-ukrainian-citizens-from-the-territory-of-active-military-operations-or-from-the-temporarily-occupied

-territory-of-ukraine-to-the-territory-of-the-russian-federation-and-the-republic-of/.

53 "Moscow Mechanism: Report on Violations and Abuses of International Humanitarian and Human Rights Law, War Crimes and Crimes Against Humanity, Related to the Forcible Transfer and/or Deportation of Ukrainian Children to the Russian Federation," *Organization for Security and Co-operation in Europe (OSCE)*, May 4, 2023, https://www.osce.org/odihr/542751.

54 Khoshnood et al., "Russia's Systematic Program."

55 Khoshnood et al., "Russia's Systematic Program"; Hook et al., "Russian Federation's Escalating."

56 United Nations, "General Assembly."

57 "Ukraine: UN Commission Concerned by Continuing Patterns of Violations of Human Rights and International Humanitarian Law," *United Nations Ukraine*, March 15, 2024, https://ukraine.un.org/en/263422-ukraine-un-commission-concerned-continuing-patterns-violations-human-rights-and.

58 Clara Apt, "Russia's Eliminationist Rhetoric Against Ukraine: A Collection," *Just Security*, January 11, 2024, https://www.justsecurity.org/81789/russias-eliminationist-rhetoric-against-ukraine-a-collection/.

59 Diamond et al., "Independent Inquiry," 1.

60 See, United Nations Office on Genocide Prevention and the Responsibility to Protect, *Analyzing Atrocities Crimes*, February 16, 2016 (UN Doc. A/70/741–S/2016/71); Ian Garner, "'We've Got to Kill Them:' Responses to Bucha on Russian Social Media Groups," *Journal of Genocide Research* 25, no. 3–4 (October 2, 2023): 418–25; Diamond, "Independent Inquiry."

61 Hook et al., "Russian Federation's Escalating."

62 Apt, "Russia's Eliminationist"; Hook et al., "Russian Federation's Escalating"; Martin Shaw, "Russia's Genocidal War in Ukraine: Radicalization and Social Destruction," *Journal of Genocide Research* 25, no. 3–4 (October 2, 2023): 352–70.

63 Elihu D. Richter, Dror Kris Markus, and Casey Tait, "Incitement, Genocide, Genocidal Terror, and the Upstream Role of Indoctrination: Can Epidemiologic Models Predict and Prevent?," *Public Health Reviews* 39, no. 30 (December 2018): 1–22.

64 United Nations, "General Assembly."

65 International Court of Justice, *Application*, para. 431.

66 See, Diamond et al., "Independent Inquiry."

67 United Nations General Assembly, "Crime of Genocide," *UN General Assembly*, December 11, 1946, A/RES/96, https://www.refworld.org/legal/resolution/unga/1946/en/27712.

Selected Bibliography

Azarov, Denys et al. *Journal of International Criminal Justice* 21, no. 2 (September 15, 2023): 233–64.

Diamond, Yonah, John Packer, Erin Farrell Rosenberg, Susan Benesch, Rayhan Asat, Adejoké Babington Ashaye, Christopher Atwood, et al. "An Independent Legal Analysis of the Russian Federation's Breaches of the Genocide Convention in

Ukraine and the Duty to Prevent." *New Lines Institute*, January 19, 2023. https://newlinesinstitute.org/an-independent-legal-analysis-of-the-russian-federations-breaches-of-the-genocide-convention-in-ukraine-and-the-duty-to-prevent.

Finkel, Eugene. *Intent to Destroy: Russia's Two-Hundred-Year Quest to Dominate Ukraine*. New York: Basic Books, 2024.

Hook, Kristina. "Why Russia's War in Ukraine Is a Genocide." *Foreign Affairs*, July 28, 2022. https://www.foreignaffairs.com/ukraine/why-russias-war-ukraine-genocide.

Hook, Kristina, John Packer, Erin Farrell Rosenberg, et al. "The Russian Federation's Escalating Commission of Genocide in Ukraine: A Legal Analysis." *New Lines Institute*, July 2023. https://newlinesinstitute.org/wp-content/uploads/20230726-Genocide-Ukraine-Report-NISLAP_.pdf.

Ioffe, Yulia. "Forcibly Transferring Ukrainian Children to the Russian Federation: A Genocide?" *Journal of Genocide Research* 25, no. 3–4 (October 2, 2023): 315–51.

20

Seeking Accountability for International Crimes Committed in Russia's War of Aggression against Ukraine

Domestically, Before the ICC and in Third States

Isabelle Hassfurther[1]

Since Russia started to invade and occupy Ukrainian state territory in 2014, Ukraine and its civil society have attempted to seek accountability through legal means. After the beginning of the full-scale invasion on February 24, 2022, a large alliance of states has pledged to support Ukraine in this quest. In the search for legal avenues to stop and account for breaches of international law by Russia, both the state of Ukraine itself and survivors of international crimes and grave human rights violations individually have turned to a variety of international and national legal fora.[2]

One field that has received great attention and is forming the focus of this contribution is international criminal law. The full-scale invasion was followed by the condemnation of the Russian acts as aggression by 141 states in the UN General Assembly.[3] The calls by third states for legal consequences and the assurances of efforts toward ensuring them have been manifold.[4] Investigations have been opened internationally by the International Criminal Court [ICC] and domestically by Ukrainian and third-state prosecutorial authorities. Against the background of this vocal commitment to accountability, the chapter explores what has been achieved so far [II.] and what obstacles have manifested [III.]. Indeed, despite the notable momentum, a resumé of the results over two years after the full-scale invasion began is rather sobering. What is called for are sustainable reforms of the international justice system at many levels and meaningful cooperation by all actors involved to close accountability gaps.

Efforts under Criminal Law to Hold Perpetrators of International Crimes Committed in Russia's War of Aggression against Ukraine Accountable

Ever since the ICC's Rome Statute entered into force in 2002, at least three judicial levels (ideally) complement each other in investigating and prosecuting cases of violations of international criminal law to prevent accountability gaps: First and foremost, the state, in which the international crime has been committed, is competent to investigate and prosecute under its territorial jurisdiction. Secondly, the ICC can step in where the territorial state is "unwilling or unable genuinely to carry out the investigation or prosecution", Art. 17(1)(a) Rome Statute,[5] if the case falls within the jurisdiction of the court,[6] is of sufficient gravity, and certain other admissibility criteria are met.[7] Finally, third states can open investigations based on their own jurisdiction, which may, on the one hand, result from the fact that their nationals have either committed the crime (the so-called active personality principle) or have been subjected to an international crime on foreign territory (the so-called passive personality principle).[8] On the other hand, they can prosecute international crimes based on universal jurisdiction. Even without a direct link to the territory or nationals of a state, it is customarily recognized that all states are empowered to prosecute international crimes due to the common aim to protect the underlying fundamental interests of the international community if "no state that is 'closer' to the crime is willing and able to prosecute the crimes."[9]

Concerning international crimes committed in the war of aggression against Ukraine, there has been an unprecedented readiness to take measures on all three of these levels to ensure comprehensive accountability. The following section aims to sketch out the specific steps taken to back up these commitments.

Investigative and Prosecutorial Steps in Ukraine

Ukrainian prosecutorial authorities had already been investigating and prosecuting crimes by Russian and Russian-affiliated suspects before February 2022,[10] given that the occupation of Crimea, Donetsk, and Luhansk, and the armed conflict in the Donbas had been ongoing for years. After the full-scale invasion, however, the number of potential international crimes registered reached a whole new level. In February 2024, Ukrainian Prosecutor General Andriy Kostin already spoke of more than 122,000 suspected cases of war crimes into which investigations had been launched within the past two years.[11] By this point in time, according to the Ukrainian authorities, 511 perpetrators had been identified, and 80 trials had been held in Ukrainian courts.[12] By April 2024, at least 101 people had already been convicted for "violations of the laws and customs of war" according to Art. 438 of the Ukrainian Criminal Code, the majority of them in trials in absentia.[13]

Besides the Ukrainian authorities, many civil society organizations on the ground have been going to great lengths to document the implications of the war of aggression, preserve evidence for future prosecutions, file cases, and support survivors in their efforts to seek justice through legal means. Among many others, two coalitions of Ukrainian organizations—the Ukraine 5 AM Coalition[14] and the Tribunal For Putin Initiative[15]—are making crucial contributions to the work toward accountability. As will be shown in more detail in due course, the Ukrainian authorities are, moreover, being supported on the ground by third states and investigative missions of international organizations.[16]

Investigations and Arrest Warrants by the ICC

The ICC is also investigating international crimes committed in Ukraine. While neither Russia nor Ukraine have ratified the Rome Statute, Ukraine has lodged two ad hoc declarations under Art. 12(3) Rome Statute in 2014 and 2015, accepting the court's jurisdiction.[17] Given that the crimes are being committed on Ukraine's territory, the ICC thus has jurisdiction to prosecute war crimes, crimes against humanity, and genocide, Art. 12(2)(a), 13(a), (c) Rome Statute.[18] As early as 2020, upon completion of a preliminary examination of the situation in Ukraine, former ICC Chief Prosecutor Fatou Bensouda concluded that there was a reasonable basis that war crimes and crimes against humanity had been committed in Eastern Ukraine and Crimea; she did not request the opening of investigations due to capacity constraints of the court.[19]

Immediately after the beginning of the full-scale invasion, however, the present ICC Chief Prosecutor, Karim Khan, declared his intention to move forward.[20] The announcement was followed by the referral of the situation to the ICC by as many as 43 ICC states parties.[21] Formal investigations were opened on March 2, 2022.[22]

The political momentum—the massive support by Ukraine itself and by third states—sped up the workings of the court: On March 17, 2023, ICC Pre-Trial Chamber II issued two arrest warrants against Vladimir Putin and his so-called "Commissioner for Children's Rights" Maria Lvova-Belova for the war crimes of unlawful deportation and transfer of population, namely Ukrainian children from Ukraine to the Russian Federation.[23] In the same month, the ICC opened an office in Ukraine to strengthen cooperation further.[24] On March 5, 2024, ICC Pre-Trial Chamber II issued two more arrest warrants for high-ranking members of the Russian military: Sergei Kobylash, a lieutenant general and commander of the Long-Range Aviation of the Aerospace Force, and Viktor Sokolov, an admiral in the Russian Navy and former commander of the Black Sea Fleet, based on suspicion of their responsibility for war crimes of direct attacks on and excessive incidental harm to civilians and civilian objects as well as crimes against humanity of inhumane acts through commanding a campaign of airstrikes on electric infrastructure in winter 2022/2023.[25] On June 24, 2024, Pre-Trial Chamber II then adopted two further arrest warrants against former Minister of Defense Sergei Kuzhugetovich Shoigu as well as Valery Vasilyevich Gerasimov, Chief of the General Staff of the Armed Forces of the Russian Federation and First Deputy Minister of Defense, on similar charges.[26] The issuance of these six arrest warrants was exceptionally made public in the hope that they would deter similar ongoing conduct. It is, thus, very well possible that further arrest warrants have been issued in secret and remain sealed.

Preservation of Evidence and Accountability Efforts by Third States and International Organizations

In addition to the ICC, numerous third states have opened investigations—by April 2024, 17 states had publicly stated to be looking into crimes committed in the war of aggression against Ukraine.[27] In an interview given in July 2023, the head of the War Crimes Department at the Office of the Prosecutor General of Ukraine even spoke of 24 states investigating.[28] While some domestic authorities focus on war crimes,[29] others are also looking into crimes against humanity[30] and the crime of aggression.[31]

As early as March 25, 2022, Ukraine, Poland, and Lithuania established a Joint Investigation Team [JIT] under the umbrella of the European Union Agency for Criminal Justice Cooperation [Eurojust][32] as a means to make cross-border investigations more efficient by enabling states to "directly exchange information and evidence, cooperate in real-time and jointly carry out operations."[33] Estonia, Latvia, Slovakia, and Romania joined the JIT soon after.[34] The ICC similarly announced its participation—this being a first in history.[35] A Memorandum of Understanding has since also been signed with the United States.[36]

In June 2022, the EU, United States, and United Kingdom moreover set up the Atrocity Crimes Advisory Group, whose purpose it is to provide strategic advice and operational assistance to the Ukrainian Office of the Prosecutor General, including through Mobile Justice Teams of international and Ukrainian experts to increase capacity to conduct field investigations on the ground.[37]

Besides the provision of on-site support, high hopes lie in the exercise of extraterritorial jurisdiction by domestic prosecutorial authorities as a means to support Ukrainian efforts and close accountability gaps. So far, reports on the advance of structural investigations to person-specific investigations—the first serving to collect evidence on the situation generally, the second targeting specific suspects—predominantly concern cases of third-state nationals who have been affected by international crimes: In Lithuania, three soldiers of the so-called Donetsk Peoples Republic have been charged with the unlawful arrest, deprivation of liberty, and killing of Lithuanian filmmaker Mantas Kvedaravičius[38]; Germany is investigating reportedly indiscriminate shootings at civilians, including a German national, in Hostomel[39]; in France, the case of a French journalist has advanced to an investigating magistrate[40]; in the United States, four Russia-affiliated soldiers have been charged with war crimes, including torture, inhuman treatment, and unlawful confinement, and conspiracy to commit war crimes to the detriment of a US citizen.[41]

Moreover, the international efforts to secure evidence for future cases are notable. In 2023, Eurojust set up a Core International Crimes Evidence Database to "preserve, store and analyse evidence of core international crimes in a secure mode."[42] To specifically collect evidence with regard to the crime of aggression, the International Center for the Prosecution of the Crime of Aggression against Ukraine has been founded under the umbrella of Eurojust.[43] Additionally, several international mechanisms have been activated to document grave human rights violations, violations of international humanitarian law, and possible international crimes committed in the Russian war of aggression. In March 2022, an Independent International Commission of Inquiry of the UN Human Rights Council was set up, which has published five consecutive reports pointing to the possible commission of war crimes and crimes against humanity.[44] Similarly, under the OSCE's Moscow Mechanism, various expert reports have been compiled.[45]

Critical Reflections on the Limitations of These Efforts to Seek Justice through Criminal Accountability

Despite these necessary steps to hold perpetrators of international crimes to account, stocktaking is impossible without critically pointing out the gaps that have become apparent. It currently seems like both legal lacunae and political considerations could ultimately affect comprehensive accountability.

Limitations of Accountability Efforts of the ICC

Concerning the ICC, it should initially be emphasized that its arrest warrants serve as an important legal and political labeling of international crimes. Therefore, the decisive steps taken are welcomed (and will hopefully also serve as a blueprint for other situations in the future). However, reactions to the ICC's swift action, particularly against Putin, have been ambiguous. While explicit endorsement came from most NATO- and EU-members and close allies, the overwhelming majority of states from the Global South remained silent[46]—despite the broad condemnation of the invasion as aggression. It thus remains to be seen whether ICC states parties will indeed abide by their obligation to arrest and extradite Putin upon entering their territory. South Africa even explicitly left open whether it would enforce the arrest warrant should Putin enter the state[47]—a scenario which was not unlikely at the time because of an upcoming BRICS summit. Its International Relations Minister, Naledi Pandor, criticized the ICC's issuance of the arrest warrant, stating that South Africa had hoped that other forms of warrants would be issued "because there are many countries and leaders who have practiced grave abuses in situations of conflict, but they remain unscathed in terms of the ICC."[48] Naturally, the argument that action can only be taken against international crimes committed by the Russian state leadership if the same is also done absolutely seamlessly against other suspects simultaneously is not convincing. Prosecuting criminal offenses is necessarily selective for factual reasons alone, and there is no such thing as "equality in injustice." Every perpetrator of international crimes should be held accountable, regardless of whether all others can also be apprehended. At the same time, the statement hints at a larger problem which the Minister reiterated later[49] that indeed threatens the legitimacy of international criminal justice and has already left visible traces: that of perceived double standards in its application, including upon either indifference or political pressure of powerful (Western) states.[50] The "deprioritization" of investigations into international crimes of

US forces in Afghanistan is but one example in point.[51] The lack of resources provided to the ICC concerning the situation in Ukraine before the full-scale invasion equally illustrates how political preferences can influence the court's workings. It remains to be seen if the situation of Palestine will serve as an example to prove the opposite.[52]

The situation of Ukraine demonstrates that to ensure the legitimacy of the court and the resulting willingness of member states to cooperate, it remains crucial to apply international criminal law indiscriminately in all situations and not just where it is politically convenient.

Moreover, and tying in with these considerations, the ICC's lack of jurisdiction over the crime of aggression concerning Russia and Ukraine due to the restrictions in its statute, entirely ruling out the prosecution of non-member state nationals,[53] and the resulting discussion about a Special Tribunal for this specific case[54] have similarly led to division in the international community.[55] Without a doubt, crimes of aggression must be accounted for—also right now, under the flawed framework we are confronted with. It is, therefore, more than understandable—and necessary—that solutions are being considered. However, establishing an *international* Special Tribunal alongside the ICC as an existing international court without at the same time moving toward a reform of the latter's jurisdictional regime raises the question of why a tribunal is set up in particular cases when the underlying problem is not solved on a more principled basis. By contrast, a hybrid tribunal embedded in the Ukrainian legal system would appear less like such an exception.

Moreover, a hybrid tribunal—ideally equipped with jurisdiction over all core crimes—could be an important support to the Ukrainian judiciary in dealing with the sheer mass of crimes.[56] However, as opposed to an international court[57] or arguably an *international* Special Tribunal, particularly if based on a broadly endorsed UN General Assembly Resolution,[58] this more domestic form of a tribunal would likely[59] be confronted with personal immunities of the head of state, head of government, and foreign minister while in office.[60] Given that the crime of aggression constitutes a leadership crime, holding those "in a position effectively to exercise control over or direct the political or military action of a state" to account, Art. 8*bis* Rome Statute, these highest ranks of state leadership are usually the principal suspects of crimes of aggression. Against this background, it is absolutely crucial for ICC member states to agree to reform the ICC's jurisdiction for the crime of aggression to ensure that both in the situation of Ukraine and other comparable situations, all four core crimes can be prosecuted by the ICC, even if the attack on an ICC member originates from the nationals of a non-member state.[61]

Need for Clear Political Commitment and Reform of Legal Obstacles to the Efforts by Ukraine

With regard to the Ukrainian legal framework, there is similarly a need to close lacunae, both to ensure that international crimes committed can be fully accounted for and to safeguard the legitimacy of the steps taken.

One crucial aspect in this regard is the ratification of the Rome Statute. Though civil society organizations have called for Ukraine's accession to the ICC,[62] it has so far only issued ad hoc declarations of acceptance of the court's jurisdiction—allegedly due to opposition from the Ukrainian military, though this claim remains unsubstantiated.[63] Independently of the fact that prosecution of both Russian and Ukrainian suspects is already legally possible through ad hoc declarations, becoming an ICC member would be an important step to show full acceptance of the indiscriminate application of international law.

Moreover, gaps in the domestic legal framework concerning international crimes remain. Two discrepancies that lead to particularly tangible consequences are that crimes against humanity are not criminalized under Ukrainian law and that the principle of command responsibility has not been incorporated.[64] Command or superior responsibility acknowledges that military or civilian superiors can be held criminally liable for crimes of subordinates under their effective control if they knew or should have known that the crimes would be committed but failed to take all necessary and reasonable measures within their power to prevent them or submit them for investigation afterward.[65] By contrast, under the Ukrainian criminal code, as it currently stands, only participation in the crimes or an order to commit them is punishable, concerning commanders who are not part of the Ukrainian armed forces.[66] It is, hence, considerably more difficult to hold higher-ranking perpetrators to account, given that it will be a lot more challenging to evidence orders or active involvement of persons who were not on-site compared to the failure to prevent crimes despite their foreseeability. This gap is particularly problematic in the context of an armed conflict in which a climate of impunity created by commanders in military structures can crucially contribute to the commission of crimes and in which said commanders wield particular power.[67] Similarly, the lack of a provision to prosecute crimes against humanity leads to the effect that a significant part of such macro criminality cannot be accounted for, namely the widespread and systematic character of the crimes committed against the civilian population.

Both shortcomings could have already been remedied in 2021 when Draft Law 2689, "On amendments to certain legislative acts on the Enforcement of International Criminal and Humanitarian Law,"[68] was adopted by the Verkhovna Rada, the Ukrainian parliament.[69] The Draft Law foresaw an alignment of the domestic legislation with international standards and would have closed the described gaps. President Zelenskyy has, however, refrained from signing and promulgating it.[70] In 2022, Draft Law 7290 was registered with the Verkhovna Rada, also addressing "amendments to the Criminal Code of Ukraine and the Criminal Procedure Code of Ukraine."[71] The draft foresees the introduction of crimes against humanity and provisions on war crimes in line with the Rome Statute. However, it stops short of fully implementing command responsibility, with the foreseen provision covering only *intentional* failure but leaving out the neglectful omission.[72] The Draft Law is, moreover, still under deliberation two years later. For the reasons above, it is hoped that both the Ukrainian parliament and the government will take decisive steps toward aligning the legislation to make the prosecution of the crimes according to international standards of material law and modes of liability possible.

Another obstacle to accountability is the criticism of a lack of adherence to fair trial standards voiced by both civil society and third states. In December 2023, Finland's Supreme Court blocked the extradition of a Russian suspect to Ukraine, pointing to potentially inhuman prison conditions.[73] A French court refused to extradite a Ukrainian suspect of embezzlement, holding that "the petitioning state (Ukraine) [was] not able to guarantee that [the accused] will be tried by a court that can ensure fundamental procedural guarantees and protection of the defence rights."[74] To ensure the legality and legitimacy of judgments rendered by Ukraine in the context of the war of aggression, which may pose an especially high challenge to judges' neutrality toward Russian perpetrators, it is, however, crucial to grant fair trials.[75]

This holds particularly true in the context of trials in absentia, the mode currently applied in most proceedings against Russian suspects. Such trials have been said to be "seen as problematic in many jurisdictions, given the difficulties they present in allowing the defendant their full rights."[76] While a trial in absentia need not automatically be unfair, according to the jurisprudence of the European Court of Human Rights [ECtHR], under the right to a fair trial, Art. 6 European Convention on Human Rights [ECHR],[77] the legality of a judgment rendered without the presence of the accused particularly necessitates that they have had actual knowledge of the trial taking place but still chose—explicitly or implicitly—not to attend the proceedings and that they have a defense.[78] The fact that a defendant waived their right to appear "must, if it is to be effective for Convention purposes, be established in an unequivocal manner."[79] That they cannot be traced does not automatically justify the conclusion that they fled and waived their right.[80] Furthermore, "[all] efforts that could reasonably be expected should be made to secure an accused's participation in the proceedings. The domestic authorities must act diligently in ensuring that an accused is duly and fully informed about the charges and the hearing at which s/he is to be tried."[81] At the same time, the ECtHR has acknowledged in a case concerning the prosecution of war crimes that moving forward with a trial despite lack of knowledge of the defendant may not contravene Art. 6 ECHR if it was impossible to notify them, due to the great interest of the public and survivors to "see the justice been done."[82] In this case, however, there must be a compelling opportunity for a retrial,[83] referring to a new trial in which "all the evidence should be examined in adversarial proceedings in the presence of an accused."[84] To benefit from this right, the person convicted in absentia may not be required to surrender to the authorities.[85]

Against the background of these requirements, Ukrainian lawyers and civil society organizations have particularly criticized the practice of publishing suspicions and summonses online on the Ukrainian Office of the Prosecutor General website and in Ukrainian print media.[86] According to the Ukrainian Code of Criminal Procedure, these two modes of publication are permissible, and summons shall moreover be sent to the last-known address. "The suspect shall [then] be deemed to have been properly informed about the summons content from the moment of its publishing in national mass media."[87] This assumption may, however, not meet the international standards just described since it is not a given that suspects based in Russia or the occupied territories of Ukraine have access to these sites, and no actual proof of their knowledge of the trial is explicitly required in the relevant provisions of the Ukrainian Criminal Procedure Code.[88] Therefore, to ensure the legality of judgments in absentia under international human rights law, it is necessary to either interpret the Ukrainian Criminal Procedure Code to require actual knowledge in light of general provisions protecting the rights of the accused in trials in absentia[89] or to reform the legislation to expressly reflect international standards.

Where it remains impossible to notify a suspect despite all reasonable efforts, it must be ensured that a definite and effective right to retrial is granted—an aspect which has similarly been questioned[90] and thus warrants scrutiny in future cases. The desire to move forward with procedures to give survivors of international crimes a sense of justice is more than understandable. To ensure the legitimacy of judgments, it is, however, crucial to pay close attention to fair trial standards.

Seeming Hesitance Concerning Complementary Efforts Based on Universal Jurisdiction

Regarding third states, investigations are ongoing, and it is hoped that the extensive evidence collected could form the basis of many cases in the following decades. However, so far, the announcements to close accountability gaps and support Ukraine's procedures in every way possible have not been met with corresponding prosecution efforts, at least from what is publicly known. As illustrated, there seems to be a tendency to merely advance from the collection of evidence to perpetrator-specific investigations in cases of crimes against third states' own nationals.[91] By contrast, states have stopped short of moving cases forward based on universal jurisdiction.

An example in point is a criminal complaint filed in Germany by the Ukrainian Legal Advisory Group [ULAG] and the European Center for Constitutional and Human Rights [ECCHR] in support of a Ukrainian survivor of sexual violence.[92] The complaint named two Russian soldiers and two of their superiors as suspects. Ukrainian authorities had already opened proceedings in absentia against one alleged direct perpetrator. However, given the gaps in the Ukrainian legal framework described above, investigations neither concerned the higher-ranking perpetrators' possible liability under command responsibility nor did they include the dimension of crimes against humanity. Nonetheless, the German Federal Prosecutor General decided not to open perpetrator-specific investigations, pointing to already ongoing investigations in Ukraine and arguing that there was no initial indicia for the responsibility of the superiors.[93] The Federal Prosecutor General did, furthermore, not consider the gap in Ukrainian law concerning crimes against humanity to call for further steps.

Given that Ukrainian authorities have opened so many investigations, third states will technically have the possibility to refrain from investigating based on arguments of subsidiarity in the vast majority of cases. However, with such a reluctant approach to step in and offer coordinated efforts to cover all possible crimes and perpetrators, the lacunae in the Ukrainian legal framework will not be closed. It is crucial to address the responsibility of higher-ranking, mid-level perpetrators, who are challenging to prosecute under the current Ukrainian framework and whom the ICC may not focus on at the same time. While the latter has already shown its readiness to prosecute perpetrators of the highest ranks, it seems unlikely to take on more than a dozen cases at best. Moreover, the sheer amount of proceedings underway in Ukraine calls for effective international cooperation and the initiative both of Ukraine to let other states take on cases and of third states to open proceedings based on their universal jurisdiction. They could also set varying foci in their investigations, thereby diversifying the types of crimes addressed. In this regard, it is crucial not to lose sight of crimes that are often awarded less priority. While Ukraine, for example, seems to have already started to look into attacks against the environment, attacks against cultural heritage, and conflict-related sexual violence,[94] third states could take on some of these complexes or prioritize other aspects.

Against this background, it would also be highly desirable for states with no legislation on universal jurisdiction or only restricted provisions—inter alia requiring the presence or even residence of the suspect—to enact reforms.[95] Similarly, strengthening the position of survivors in proceedings on international crimes should form a central goal of states. A reform process inter alia pursuing the latter aim has recently been concluded in Germany, introducing the entitlement to join proceedings as joint plaintiffs for most survivors of international crimes, entailing a right to legal representation and psycho-social support.[96] It would also be desirable for other third states to support initiatives in this direction.

Conclusions

To sum up, the war of aggression against Ukraine has provoked unprecedented and commendable efforts to ensure legal accountability for international crimes. However, upon closer examination, the steps taken so far seem less effective than expected, given the broad international condemnation of the Russian aggression. In particular, states from the Global South have remained a lot more hesitant in their reactions to the strong push for the prosecution of international crimes by the states of the Global North. In order not to deepen the divide and (further) endanger the legitimacy of international law and institutions, it is crucial to work toward applying international criminal law indiscriminately to all atrocities committed worldwide, independently of the political interests of powerful states. Therefore, it should be a priority to amend the ICC's jurisdiction over the crime of aggression and not stop short at setting up a Special Tribunal.

Moreover, Ukraine's commendable efforts on the international plane should be mirrored by the ratification and domestic implementation of the legal standards of the Rome Statute, as well as the strict adherence to fair trial requirements. Finally, it is somewhat sobering to see that after two years, besides the six arrest warrants against high-ranking perpetrators issued by the ICC, no arrest warrants are known to have been issued by third states in the exercise of universal jurisdiction. Given that Ukrainian warrants and prosecution are so far predominantly directed against low-level, direct perpetrators, a large group of suspects has thus been left out. To close accountability gaps, it is hoped that third states will eventually step up their efforts and open proceedings based on universal jurisdiction.

Notes

1 The author is a senior legal advisor at the Berlin-based European Center for Constitutional and Human Rights (ECCHR). Thanks for their valuable comments are owed to ECCHR-colleagues Andreas Schueller, Arne Bardelle, Kateryna Buriakovska, and Helena Krueger. (Note: This chapter is based on the status quo before June 2024)

2 For example through two proceedings before the International Court of Justice [ICJ] under the International Convention of Suppression of the Financing of Terrorism and of the International Convention on the Elimination of all Forms of Racial Discrimination since 2017 (ICJ, Application of the International Convention for the Suppression of the Financing of Terrorism and of the International Convention on the Elimination of All Forms of Racial Discrimination (Ukraine v. Russian Federation)) as well as under the Genocide Convention since 2022 immediately after the full-scale invasion started (ICJ, Allegations of Genocide under the Convention on the Prevention and Punishment of the Crime of Genocide (Ukraine v. Russian Federation)); through proceedings before the European Court of Human Rights [ECtHR] with four inter-state cases and over 7,400 individual applications pending; through arbitral proceedings before the Permanent Court of Arbitration [PCA] since 2019 (PCA, Dispute Concerning the Detention of Ukrainian Naval Vessels and Servicemen (Ukraine v. the Russian Federation), 2019–28); through proceedings before the International Tribunal of the Law of the Seas [ITLOS] in 2019 (ITLOS, Case concerning the detention of three Ukrainian naval vessels (Ukraine v. Russian Federation), Provisional Measures, No. 26).

3 UN General Assembly, Aggression against Ukraine, March 2, 2022, A/ES-11/L.1.

4 See, for example, G7, "Berlin Declaration," November 29, 2022, accessed June 28, 2024, https://www.bmj.de/SharedDocs/Downloads/DE/Themen/Nav_Themen/G7_Berliner_Erklaerung_en.pdf?__blob=publicationFile&v=3.

5 Rome Statute of the International Criminal Court, 2187 UNTS 90, entered into force on July 1, 2002.

6 See Arts. 11, 12, 13, 15*bis*, 15*ter* Rome Statute.

7 See Arts. 17, 53 Rome Statute.

8 See Gerhard Werle and Florian Jessberger, *Principles of International Criminal Law*, 4th ed. (Oxford: Oxford University Press, 2020), 95, para 258.

9 See Gerhard Werle and Florian Jessberger, *Principles of International Criminal Law*, 4th ed. (Oxford: Oxford University Press, 2020), 95 ff., esp. para. 260.

10 Diana Kolodiazhna, "How Ukraine Passes Judgment on Violations of the Laws and Customs of War?," *ZMINA*, April 24, 2024, accessed June 28, 2024, https://zmina.info/en/articles-en/how-ukraine-passes-judgment-on-violations-of-the-laws-and-customs-of-war/.

11 Nette Nöstlinger, Oliver Ellrodt and Sopia Linnebrink, "Ukraine Probing Over 122,000 Suspected War Crimes, Says Prosecutor," *Reuters*, February 23, 2024,

accessed June 28, 2024, https://www.reuters.com/world/europe/ukraine-probing-over-122000-suspected-war-crimes-says-prosecutor-2024-02-23/.

12 Ibid.

13 Diana Kolodianzha, "How Ukraine Passes Judgment on Violations of the Laws and Customs of War?," *ZMINA*, April 24, 2024, accessed June 28, 2024, https://zmina.info/en/articles-en/how-ukraine-passes-judgment-on-violations-of-the-laws-and-customs-of-war/.

14 "Ukraine 5 AM Coalition," accessed June 28, 2024, https://www.5am.in.ua/en.

15 "About the 'T4P'," T4P, accessed June 28, 2024, https://t4pua.org/en/1202.

16 See infra, 390.

17 "Ukraine," International Criminal Court, accessed June 28, 2024, https://www.icc-cpi.int/situations/ukraine.

18 On the restrictions of jurisdiction concerning the crime of aggression, see infra and Art. 15*bis* Rome Statute.

19 "Statement of the Prosecutor, Fatou Bensouda, on the Conclusion of the Preliminary Examination in the Situation in Ukraine," International Criminal Court, December 11, 2020, accessed June 28, 2024, https://www.icc-cpi.int/news/statement-prosecutor-fatou-bensouda-conclusion-preliminary-examination-situation-ukraine.

20 "Statement of ICC Prosecutor, Karim A.A. Khan QC, on the Situation in Ukraine: 'I Have Decided to Proceed with Opening an Investigation,'" International Criminal Court, February 28, 2022, accessed June 28, 2024, https://www.icc-cpi.int/news/statement-icc-prosecutor-karim-aa-khan-qc-situation-ukraine-i-have-decided-proceed-opening.

21 "Ukraine," International Criminal Court, accessed June 28, 2024, https://www.icc-cpi.int/situations/ukraine.

22 "Statement of ICC Prosecutor, Karim A.A. Khan QC, on the Situation in Ukraine: Receipt of Referrals from 39 States Parties and the Opening of an Investigation," International Criminal Court, March 2, 2022, accessed June 28, 2024, https://www.icc-cpi.int/news/statement-icc-prosecutor-karim-aa-khan-qc-situation-ukraine-receipt-referrals-39-states.

23 "Situation in Ukraine: ICC Judges Issue Arrest Warrants against Vladimir Vladimirovich Putin and Maria Alekseyevna Lvova-Belova," International Criminal Court, March 17, 2023, accessed June 28, 2024, https://www.icc-cpi.int/news/situation-ukraine-icc-judges-issue-arrest-warrants-against-vladimir-vladimirovich-putin-and.

24 "Ukraine and International Criminal Court Sign an Agreement on the Establishment of a Country Office," International Criminal Court, March 23, 2023, accessed June 28, 2024, https://www.icc-cpi.int/news/ukraine-and-international-criminal-court-sign-agreement-establishment-country-office.

25 "Situation in Ukraine: ICC Judges Issue Arrest Warrants against Sergei Ivanovich Kobylash and Viktor Nikolayevich Sokolov," International Criminal Court, March 5, 2024, accessed June 28, 2024, https://www.icc-cpi.int/news/situation-ukraine-icc-judges-issue-arrest-warrants-against-sergei-ivanovich-kobylash-and.

26 "Situation in Ukraine: ICC Judges Issue Arrest Warrants against Sergei Kuzhugetovich Shoigu and Valery Vasilyevich Gerasimov," International Criminal Court, June 24, 2024, accessed June 28, 2024, https://www.icc-cpi.int/news/situation-ukraine-icc-judges-issue-arrest-warrants-against-sergei-kuzhugetovich-shoigu-and.

27 "Ukraine: Commission Presents Options to Make Sure that Russia Pays for its Crimes," European Commission, November 30, 2022, accessed June 28, 2024, https://ec.europa.eu/commission/presscorner/detail/en/ip_22_731; Canada: "A Statement by the Partners of Canada's War Crimes Program on the Conflict in Ukraine," Royal Canadian Mounted Police, April 7, 2022, accessed June 28, 2024, https://www.rcmp-grc.gc.ca/en/news/2022/a-statement-the-partners-canadas-war-crimes-program-the-conflict-ukraine; Czech Republic: "Prověřování válečných zločinů," Policie Ceske Republiky, May 10, 2022, accessed June 28, 2024, https://www.policie.cz/clanek/proverovani-valecnych-zlocinu.aspx; Denmark (though apparently not through state institutions but supporting civil society): "Denmark Will Launch Project for International Crimes in Ukraine," Sayba Sagheer, September 23, 2022, accessed June 28, 2024, https://thediplomaticinsight.com/denmark-to-launch-project-for-international-crimes-in-ukraine/; Estonia: "Estonia's Internal Security Service also Investigating War Crimes Committed in Ukraine," *Baltic Times*, March 30, 2022, accessed June 28, 2024, https://www.baltictimes.com/estonia_s_internal_security_service_also_investigating_war_crimes_committed_in_ukraine/; France: "Crimes de guerre en Ukraine: la justice française "extrêmement décidée" à établir les responsabilités," *La Croix*, September 23, 2022, accessed June 28, 2024, https://www.la-croix.com/Crimes-guerre-Ukraine-justice-francaise-extremement-decidee-etablir-responsabilites-2022-09-23-1301234692; Germany: "Germany Probing Several Hundred Possible Ukraine War Crimes," *Justice Info*, June 18, 2022, accessed June 28, 2024, https://www.justiceinfo.net/en/102270-germany-probing-several-hundred-possible-ukraine-war-crimes.html; Latvia:, "Latvia Commences Criminal Procedure Over Crimes Committed by Russian Forces in Ukraine," *BNN*, March 17, 2022, accessed June 28, 2024, https://bnn-news.com/latvia-commences-criminal-procedure-over-crimes-committed-by-russian-forces-in-ukraine-233233; Lithuania: "Lithuania's Investigation Recognises 90 People as Victims of War Crimes in Ukraine," Ignas Jacauskas, LRT, March 30, 2023, accessed June 28, 2024, https://www.lrt.lt/en/news-in-english/19/1950516/lithuania-s-investigation-recognises-90-people-as-victims-of-war-crimes-in-ukraine; Norway: "The Norwegian Government is Tasking the National Criminal Investigation Service with Assisting in the Investigation of Possible War Crimes in Ukraine by the International Criminal Court," Norwegian Government, April 7, 2022, accessed June 28, 2024, https://www.regjeringen.no/en/aktuelt/the-norwegian-government-is-tasking-the-national-criminal-investigation-service-with-assisting-in-the-investigation-of-possible-war-crimes-in-ukraine-by-the-international-criminal-court/id2907846/; Poland: " Mazowiecki pion PZ PK wszczął śledztwo w sprawie napaści Rosji na Ukrainę," Prokuratura Krajowa, March 1, 2022, accessed June 28, 2024, https://www.gov.pl/web/prokuratura-krajowa/mazowiecki-pion-pz-pk-wszczal-sledztwo-w-sprawie-napasci-rosji-na-ukraine; Romania: "Romania Says Starting Probe Against Russia for Crimes in Ukraine," Andra Timu and Irina Vilcu, *Bloomberg*, July 11, 2022, accessed June 28, 2024, https://www.bloomberg.com/news/articles/2022-07-11/romania-says-starting-probe-against-russia-for-crimes-in-ukraine; Slovakia: "General Prosecutor Signs Memorandum about Cooperation with Ukraine Two Months after Signing it with Russia," *Slovak Spectator*, March 15, 2022, accessed June 28, 2024, https://spectator.sme.sk/c/22861200/general-prosecutor-signs-memorandum-about-cooperation-with-ukraine-two-months-after-signing-it-with

-russia.html; Spain: "La fiscalía espanola abre una investigación sobre la invasion rusa de Ucrania," Pablo Gabilondo, *El Confidencial*, March 8, 2022, accessed June 28, 2024, https://www.elconfidencial.com/espana/2022-03-08/fiscalia-investigacion-guerra-ucrania-rusia_3388023/; Sweden:, "Swedish Prosecutors Open Preliminary Investigation into War Crimes in Ukraine," *Reuters*, April 5, 2022, accessed June 28, 2024, https://www.reuters.com/world/europe/swedish-prosecutors-open-preliminary-investigation-into-war-crimes-ukraine-2022-04-05/; US: "US Attorney General and Ukrainian Prosecutor General Met to Strengthen Joint Efforts to Hold Accountable Perpetrators of War Crimes and Other Atrocities Committed in Ukraine," US Department of Justice, September 20, 2022, accessed June 28, 2024, https://www.justice.gov/opa/pr/us-attorney-general-and-ukrainian-prosecutor-general-met-strengthen-joint-efforts-hold.

28 "Yuriy Belousov, 'We Can't Lose Ukraine's Legal Battle'," Franck Petit, *Justice Info*, July 11, 2023, accessed June 28, 2024, https://www.justiceinfo.net/en/119268-yuriy-belousov-we-cant-lose-ukraine-legal-battle.html.

29 "Ukraine: enqueter sur les crimes de guerre," Quentin Lafay, *radiofrance*, March 18, 2023, accessed June 28, 2024, https://www.radiofrance.fr/franceculture/podcasts/et-maintenant-l-invite-e-des-matins-du-samedi/ukraine-enqueter-sur-les-crimes-de-guerre-2709170.

30 "Germany Opens Investigations Into Suspected Russian War Crimes in Ukraine," Bojan Pancevski, *The Wall Street Journal*, March 8, 2022, accessed June 28, 2024, https://www.wsj.com/livecoverage/russia-ukraine-latest-news-2022-03-08/card/germany-opens-investigation-into-suspected-russian-war-crimes-in-ukraine-bNCphaIWE30f2REH8BCi.

31 "Lithuania's Top Prosecutor, Eurojust Chief Discuss Probe on War Crimes in Ukraine," *The Baltic Times*, January 9, 2023, accessed June 28, 2024, https://www.baltictimes.com/lithuania_s_top_prosecutor__eurojust_chief_discuss_probe_on_war_crimes_in_ukraine/.

32 "Two Years on. A Timeline of Eurojust's Response to the War in Ukraine," European Union Agency for Criminal Justice Cooperation, February 29, 2024, accessed June 28, 2024, https://www.eurojust.europa.eu/publication/two-years-timeline-eurojusts-response-war-ukraine#.

33 "Joint Investigation Teams," European Union Agency for Criminal Justice Cooperation, accessed June 28, 2024, https://www.eurojust.europa.eu/judicial-cooperation/instruments/joint-investigation-teams.

34 "Joint Investigation Team into Alleged Crimes Committed in Ukraine," European Union Agency for Criminal Justice Cooperation, accessed June 28, 2024, https://www.eurojust.europa.eu/joint-investigation-team-alleged-crimes-committed-ukraine; "Two Years on: A Timeline of Eurojust's Response to the War in Ukraine," European Union Agency for Criminal Justice Cooperation, February 29, 2024, accessed June 28, 2024, https://www.eurojust.europa.eu/publication/two-years-timeline-eurojusts-response-war-ukraine.

35 "ICC Participates in Joint Investigation Team Supported by Eurojust on Alleged Core International Crimes in Ukraine," European Union Agency for Criminal Justice Cooperation, April 25, 2022, accessed June 28, 2024, https://www.eurojust.europa.eu/news/icc-participates-joint-investigation-team-supported-eurojust-alleged-core-international-crimes.

36 "National Authorities of the Ukraine Joint Investigation Team Sign Memorandum of Understanding With the United States Department of Justice," European Union Agency for Criminal Justice Cooperation, March 4, 2023, accessed June 28, 2024, https://www.eurojust.europa.eu/news/national-authorities-ukraine-joint-investigation-team-sign-memorandum-understanding-usa.

37 "Atrocity Crimes Advisory Group Press Release," Global Rights Compliance, June 21, 2022, accessed June 28, 2024, https://globalrightscompliance.com/2022/06/21/atrocity-crimes-advisory-group-press-release/.

38 "War Crimes in Mariupol: Justice for Lithuanian Filmmaker," European Center for Constitutional and Human Rights, accessed June 28, 2024, https://www.ecchr.eu/en/case/kriegsverbrechen-in-mariupol-gerechtigkeit-fuer-litauischen-filmemacher/.

39 "Germany Looks into War Crime Reports in Ukraine," Eugen Theise, *dw*, March 9, 2024, accessed June 28, 2024, https://www.dw.com/en/why-germany-is-investigating-war-crime-reports-in-ukraine/a-68469036.

40 "France Appoints Magistrates in Probe into Fox News Cameraman Death," *Justice Info*, April 17, 2024, accessed June 28, 2024, https://www.justiceinfo.net/en/131007-france-appoints-magistrates-in-probe-into-fox-news-cameraman-death.html.

41 "Four Russia-Affiliated Military Personnel Charged with War Crimes in Connection with Russia's Invasion of Ukraine," US Department of Justice, December 6, 2023, accessed June 28, 2024, https://www.justice.gov/opa/pr/four-russia-affiliated-military-personnel-charged-war-crimes-connection-russias-invasion.

42 "Start of Operations of Core International Crimes Evidence Database and New International Centre for Prosecution of the Crime of Aggression to be Based at Agency," European Union Agency for Criminal Justice Cooperation, February 23, 2023, accessed June 28, 2024, https://www.eurojust.europa.eu/news/start-operations-core-international-crimes-evidence-database-and-new-international-centre.

43 "International Centre for the Prosecution of the Crime of Aggression against Ukraine," European Union Agency for Criminal Justice Cooperation, accessed June 28, 2024, https://www.eurojust.europa.eu/international-centre-for-the-prosecution-of-the-crime-of-aggression-against-ukraine.

44 "Independent International Commission of Inquiry on Ukraine," United Nations Human Rights Council, accessed June 28, 2024, https://www.ohchr.org/en/hr-bodies/hrc/iicihr-ukraine/index.

45 "Report of the OSCE Moscow Mechanism's Mission of Experts Entitled 'Report On Violations Of International Humanitarian And Human Rights Law, War Crimes And Crimes Against Humanity Committed In Ukraine Since 24 February 2022'," Organization for Security and Co-Operation in Europe, April 13, 2022, accessed June 28, 2024, https://www.osce.org/odihr/515868; "Report of the OSCE Moscow Mechanism's Mission of Experts Entitled 'Report on Violations of International Humanitarian and Human Rights Law, War Crimes and Crimes Against Humanity Committed in Ukraine (1 April–25 June 2022)'," Organization for Security and Co-Operation in Europe, July 14, 2022, accessed June 28, 2024, https://www.osce.org/odihr/522616; "Moscow Mechanism: 'Report on Violations and Abuses of International Humanitarian and Human Rights Law, War Crimes and Crimes Against Humanity, Related to the Forcible Transfer and/or Deportation of Ukrainian Children to the Russian Federation'," Organization for Security and Co-Operation in Europe, May 4, 2023, accessed June 28, 2024, https://www.osce

.org/odihr/542751; "Moscow Mechanism: 'Report on Violations and Abuses of International Humanitarian and Human Rights Law, War Crimes and Crimes against Humanity, Related to the Arbitrary Deprivation of Liberty of Ukrainian Civilians by the Russian Federation,'" Organization for Security and Co-Operation in Europe, April 25, 2024, accessed June 28, 2024, https://www.osce.org/odihr/567367.

46 Alonso Gurmendi, "Tracking State Reactions to the ICC's Arrest Warrant against Vladimir Putin," *Opinio Juris*, March 29, 2023, accessed June 28, 2024, http://opiniojuris.org/2023/03/29/tracking-state-reactions-to-the-iccs-arrest-warrant-against-vladimir-putin/.

47 "Arrest Warrant for Putin: Presidency Won't 'Speculate' on Scenario if Russian President Arrives in SA," Jan Gerber, *news 24*, March 19, 2023, accessed June 28, 2024, https://www.news24.com/news24/politics/government/arrest-warrant-for-putin-presidency-wont-speculate-on-scenario-if-russian-president-arrives-in-sa-20230319.

48 "Cabinet to Meet to Discuss ICC Decision on Arrest Warrant for Vladimir Putin," Amanda Khoza, *Times Live,* March 23, 2023, accessed June 28, 2024, https://www.timeslive.co.za/politics/2023-03-23-cabinet-to-meet-to-discuss-icc-decision-on-arrest-warrant-for-russias-putin/?utm_medium=Social&utm_source=Twitter#Echobox=1679552973-2.

49 Amanda Khoza (@MandaKhoza), "Dirco Minister Naledi Pandor Reiterates Her Stance on the ICC's Warrant of Arrest against Russia's Vladimir Putin. Says Cabinet Must Discuss the Matter Asap Because There Are Obvious 'Double Standards'. @SundayTimesZA. Putin Has Been Invited to Attend BRICS Summit in SA," *X*, March 23, 2023, accessed June 28, 2024, https://twitter.com/MandaKhoza/status/1638827193236168706.

50 Similarly on this allegation with regard to Ukraine Chidi Anselm Odinkalu and Sharon Nakandha, "Putin Arrest Warrant: International Law and Perceptions of Double Standards," *Opinio Juris*, March 27, 2023, accessed June 28, 2024, http://opiniojuris.org/2023/03/27/putin-arrest-warrant-international-law-and-perceptions-of-double-standards/.

51 "Statement of the Prosecutor of the International Criminal Court, Karim A. A. Khan QC, Following the Application for an Expedited Order Under Article 18(2) Seeking Authorisation to Resume Investigations in the Situation in Afghanistan," International Criminal Court, September 27, 2021, accessed June 28, 2024, https://www.icc-cpi.int/news/statement-prosecutor-international-criminal-court-karim-khan-qc-following-application.

52 In May 2024, the Prosecutor applied to ICC Pre-Trial Chamber I for arrest warrants for Hamas leader Yahya Sinwar, head of Hamas's Political Bureau, Ismail Haniyeh, and the commander-in-chief of the military wing of Hamas, Mohammed Deif, as well as for Israeli Prime Minister Benjamin Netanyahu and Defence Minister Yoav Gallant ("Statement of ICC Prosecutor Karim A.A. Khan KC: Applications for Arrest Warrants in the Situation in the State of Palestine," International Criminal Court, May 20, 2024, accessed June 28, 2024, https://www.icc-cpi.int/news/statement-icc-prosecutor-karim-aa-khan-kc-applications-arrest-warrants-situation-state).

53 Art. *15bis*(5) Rome Statute. For a detailed account of the gaps, see Isabelle Hassfurther, "Accountability for the Crime of Aggression against Ukraine,"

Verfassungsblog, February 24, 2024, accessed June 28, 2024, https://verfassungsblog.de/aggression-ukraine/.

54 For an overview, see "Prosecuting the Crime of Aggression Against Ukraine (Series)," *Just Security*, accessed June 28, 2024, https://www.justsecurity.org/tag/prosecuting-the-crime-of-aggression-against-ukraine/.

55 Patryk Labuda, "Beyond Rhetoric: Interrogating the Eurocentric Critique of International Criminal Law's Selectivity in the Wake of the 2022 Ukraine Invasion," *Leiden Journal of International Criminal Law* 36, no. 4 (December 2023): 1096.

56 On this suggestion see "Needs Assessment of Ukraine's Justice System: Delivering Meaningful Justice to the Victims and Survivors of the Armed Conflict," Ukrainian Legal Advisory Group, June 2024, accessed June 28, 2024, https://ulag.org.ua/reports-and-materials/needs-assessment-ukraines-justice-system; Andreas Schüller, "What Can('t) International Criminal Justice Deliver for Ukraine?," *Verfassungsblog*, February 24, 2023, accessed June 28, 2024, https://verfassungsblog.de/justice-ukraine/.

57 International Criminal Court, The Prosecutor v. Omar Hassan Ahmad Al-Bashir, Judgment in the Jordan Referral re Al-Bashir Appeal, Appeals Chamber, ICC-02/05-01/09 OA2, May 6, 2019, particularly paras. 100–19.

58 Kevin Jon Heller, "The Jordan Appeal Supports a Hybrid Tribunal Denying Personal Immunity," *Opinio Juris*, February 6, 2023, accessed June 28, 2024, http://opiniojuris.org/2023/02/06/the-jordan-appeal-judgment-supports-a-hybrid-tribunal-denying-personal-immunity/. Kevin Jon Heller is also pointing out that it is questionable whether the same can be said about a hybrid tribunal established as part of the Ukrainian judicial system but with the support of the Council of Europe. In this regard, the Open Society Justice Initiative [OSJI] and the International Renaissance Foundation [IRF] came to the conclusion that a fully regional model of this kind may have some claim to the status of an international tribunal, given that it represents the interest of 46 states, see "Immunities and a Special Tribunal for the Crime of Aggression against Ukraine," February 2023, accessed June 28, 2024, https://www.justiceinitiative.org/publications/immunities-and-a-special-tribunal-for-the-crime-of-aggression-against-ukraine.

59 This refers to a tribunal embedded in the Ukrainian system with internationalized elements, such as international judges, but "without significant involvement of the international community" (OSJI and IRF, "Immunities and a Special Tribunal for the Crime of Aggression against Ukraine," February 20, 2023, accessed June 28, 2024, https://www.justiceinitiative.org/publications/immunities-and-a-special-tribunal-for-the-crime-of-aggression-against-ukraine). This form has been termed a hybrid or "internationalized" model (see e.g. James A. Goldstone and Anna Khalfaoui, "In Evaluating Immunities before a Special Tribunal for Aggression Against Ukraine, the Type of Tribunal Matters," *Just Security*, February 1, 2023, accessed June 28, 2024, https://www.justsecurity.org/84959/in-evaluating-immunities-before-a-special-tribunal-for-aggression-against-ukraine-the-type-of-tribunal-matters/.) Arguing that a hybrid tribunal could overcome personal immunities is Kevin Jon Heller. The evaluation, however, refers to a tribunal not in the sense used here but based on an agreement between UN/Ukraine and with UN General Assembly backing ("The Jordan Appeal Supports a Hybrid Tribunal Denying Personal Immunity." *Opinio*

Juris, February 6, 2023, accessed June 28, 2024, http://opiniojuris.org/2023/02/06/the-jordan-appeal-judgment-supports-a-hybrid-tribunal-denying-personal-immunity/).

60 Jennifer Trahan, "Why a 'Hybrid' Ukrainian Tribunal on the Crime of Aggression Is Not the Answer," *Just Security*, February 6, 2023, accessed June 28, 2024, https://www.justsecurity.org/85019/why-hybrid-ukrainian-tribunal-on-crime-of-aggression-is-not-the-answer/.

61 Isabelle Hassfurther, "Accountability for the Crime of Aggression against Ukraine." *Verfassungsblog*, February 24, 2024, accessed June 28, 2024, https://verfassungsblog.de/aggression-ukraine/.

62 "Ukrainian Civil Society Calls on Ukraine to Ratify the Rome Statute." Coalition for the ICC, May 5, 2023, accessed June 28, 2024, https://www.coalitionfortheicc.org/news/20230505/ukrainian-civil-society-calls-ukraine-ratify-rome-statute.

63 "Ratification Must Become a Clear Action Item, Rather than a Distant Goal | ULAG at the Embassies and International Organisations Briefing on RS Ratification," Ukrainian Legal Advisory Group, November 30, 2023, accessed June 28, 2024, https://ulag.org.ua/news/ratification-must-become-a-clear-action-item-rather-than-a-distant-goal-ulag-at-the-embassies-and-international-organisations-briefing-on-rs-ratification.

64 "Needs Assessment of Ukraine's Justice System: Delivering Meaningful Justice to the Victims and Survivors of the Armed Conflict," Ukrainian Legal Advisory Group, June 2024, accessed June 28, 2024, https://ulag.org.ua/reports-and-materials/needs-assessment-ukraines-justice-system, 37, 41 f.

65 See in detail Gerhard Werle and Florian Jessberger, *Principles of International Criminal Law*, 4th ed. (Oxford: Oxford University Press, 2020), 264 ff.

66 See Arts. 27, 28, 438 Criminal Code of the Republic of Ukraine, entered into force on September 1, 2001, last revision May 19, 2024, Document 2341-III, accessed June 28, 2024, https://zakon.rada.gov.ua/laws/show/en/2341-14#Text. Ukrainian military commanders (Art. 401(2)) can additionally be held accountable for neglect of duty in military service and for willful omission, Art. 425, 426 Ukrainian Criminal Code.

67 See Gerhard Werle and Florian Jessberger, *Principles of International Criminal Law*, 4th ed. (Oxford: Oxford University Press, 2020), 265.

68 "Проект Закону про внесення змін до деяких законодавчих актів України щодо імплементації норм міжнародного кримінального та гуманітарного права," May 15, 2024, accessed June 28, 2024, http://w1.c1.rada.gov.ua/pls/zweb2/webproc4_1?pf3511=67804. Comparing the Draft with the current legislation are Parliamentarians for Global Action, "Comparative Table to the Draft Law of Ukraine 'On Amendments to Certain Legislative Acts on the Enforcement of International Criminal and Humanitarian Law,'" accessed June 28, 2024, https://www.pgaction.org/pdf/2021/en-bill-2689-10-03-2021.pdf.

69 "Ukraine and the Rome Statute," Parliamentarians for Global Action, accessed June 28, 2024, https://www.pgaction.org/ilhr/rome-statute/ukraine.html.

70 Ibid.

71 "Файл 1271913," Verkhovna Rada, April 14, 2022, accessed June 28, 2024, https://itd.rada.gov.ua/billInfo/Bills/pubFile/1271913.

72 See Art. 442-2 Draft Law 7290. Critically for example "Appeal," Ukraine 5 AM Coalition, April 2022, accessed June 28, 2024, https://zmina.ua/wp-content/uploads/sites/2/2022/04/eng_7290_pozycziya-koaliczyi_suprovidnyj.pdf; "Новий

законопроект уряду р.н. 7290 штучно звужує можливості для притягнення до відповідальності військових командирів та цивільних начальників Російської Федерації за воєнні злочини," Ukrainian Helsinki Committee, April 21, 2022, accessed June 28, 2024, https://www.helsinki.org.ua/appeals/novyy-zakonoproekt-uriadu-r-n-7290-shtuchno-zvuzhuie-mozhlyvosti-dlia-prytiahnennia-do-vidpovidalnosti-viyskovykh-komandyriv-ta-tsyvilnykh-nachalnykiv-rosiyskoi-federatsii-za-voienni-zlochyny/.

73 "Finland's Supreme Court Blocks Extradition of Russian Terrorism Suspect to Ukraine," *Reuters,* December 8, 2023, accessed June 28, 2024, https://www.reuters.com/world/europe/finlands-supreme-court-blocks-extradition-russian-terrorism-suspect-ukraine-2023-12-08/.

74 "French Court Rejects Appeal to Extradite Ukrainian Billionaire Zhevago", *Reuters*, November 10, 2023, accessed June 28, https://www.reuters.com/world/europe/french-court-rejects-appeal-extradite-ukrainian-billionaire-zhevago-2023-11-10/.

75 For a critical assessment in this regard see Kai Ambos, "Ukrainian Prosecution of ICC Statute Crimes: Fair, Independent and Impartial?," *EJIL: Talk!*, June 10, 2022, accessed June 28, 2024, https://www.ejiltalk.org/ukrainian-prosecution-of-icc-statute-crimes-fair-independent-and-impartial/; for a more positive account see Gaiane Nurudzhanian, "Prosecuting War Crimes: Are Ukrainian Courts Fit to do it?," *EJIL: Talk!*, August 11, 2022, accessed June 28, 2024, https://www.ejiltalk.org/prosecuting-war-crimes-are-ukrainian-courts-fit-to-do-it/.

76 Victoria Matola, "Ukraine: Justice in Absentia," Institute for War and Peace Reporting, April 11, 2023, accessed June 28, 2024, https://iwpr.net/global-voices/ukraine-justice-absentia.

77 The provision foresees that "everyone is entitled to a fair and public hearing within a reasonable time by an independent and impartial tribunal established by law" and the minimum right "to be informed promptly, in a language which he understands and in detail, of the nature and cause of the accusation against him." See similarly Art. 14(3)(a)(d) International Covenant on Civil and Political Rights, entered into force on March 23, 1976, accessed June 28, 2024, https://www.ohchr.org/en/instruments-mechanisms/instruments/international-covenant-civil-and-political-right.

78 "Trials in Absentia," Global Rights Compliance, accessed June 28, 2024, https://www.asser.nl/media/795064/grc-trials-in-absentia-english.pdf; European Court of Human Rights [ECtHR], Case of Colozza v. Italy (Application no. 9024/80), Judgment, February 12, 1985, paras. 18, 19, 28; ECtHR, Case of Poitrimol v. France (Application no. 14032/88), Judgment, November 23, 1993, paras. 31 ff.; ECtHR, Case of Lala v. The Netherlands (Application no. 14861/89), Judgment, September 2, 1994, paras. 14, 33 f.; ECtHR, Case of Krombach v. France (Application no. 29731/96), Judgment, May 13, 2001, para. 85.

79 ECtHR, Case of Poitrimol v. France (Application no. 14032/88), Judgment, November 23, 1993, para. 31.

80 Nona Tsotsoria, "Information Note of the Council of Europe Expert Advisory Group to the Office of the Prosecutor General of Ukraine on the 'Trials *In Absentia* in War Crimes Proceedings: Compliance with Article 6 of ECHR'," Council of Europe, September 7, 2022, 4, w.f.r.

81 Ibid.

82 ECtHR, Case of Sanader v. Croatia (Application no. 66408/12), Judgment, April 7, 2015, paras. 68, 76 f.

83 ECtHR, Case of Sanader v. Croatia (Application no. 66408/12), Judgment, April 7, 2015, paras. 68, 78.

84 Council of Europe, Committee of Ministers, "On the Criteria Governing Proceedings Held in the Absence of the Accused," May 21, 1975, Resolution (75) 11, I.8. holds: "A person tried in his absence on whom a summons has not been served in due and proper form shall have a remedy enabling him to have the judgment annulled." Nona Tsotsoria, "Information note of the Council of Europe expert advisory group to the Office of the Prosecutor General of Ukraine on the 'Trials *In Absentia* in War Crimes Proceedings: Compliance with Article 6 of ECHR'", Council of Europe, September 7, 2022, 7, w.f.r.; ECtHR, Case of Sanader v. Croatia (Application no. 66408/12), Judgment, April 7, 2015, para. 78.

85 ECtHR, Case of Sanader v. Croatia (Application no. 66408/12), Judgment, April 7, 2015, paras. 70, 74, 84 ff.

86 Diana Kolodiazhna, "How Ukraine Passes Judgment on Violations of the Laws and Customs of War?," *ZMINA*, April 24, 2024, accessed June 28, 2024, https://zmina.info/en/articles-en/how-ukraine-passes-judgment-on-violations-of-the-laws-and-customs-of-war/; "Trials in Absentia," Global Rights Compliance, accessed June 28, 2024, https://www.asser.nl/media/795064/grc-trials-in-absentia-english.pdf, 11; "Needs Assessment of Ukraine's Justice System: Delivering Meaningful Justice to the Victims and Survivors of the Armed Conflict," Ukrainian Legal Advisory Group, June 2024, accessed June 28, 2024, https://ulag.org.ua/reports-and-materials/needs-assessment-ukraines-justice-system, 71.

87 See Art. 297-5 and Art. 323 Criminal Procedure Code of Ukraine, entered into force on November 20, 2012, revision on April 19, 2024, Document 4651-VI, accessed June 28, 2024. https://zakon.rada.gov.ua/laws/show/en/4651-17?find=1&lang=en&text=Absentia#w1_1; "Trials in Absentia," Global Rights Compliance, accessed June 28, 2024, https://www.asser.nl/media/795064/grc-trials-in-absentia-english.pdf, 11.

88 Diana Kolodiazhna, "How Ukraine Passes Judgment on Violations of the Laws and Customs of War?," *ZMINA*, April 24, 2024, accessed June 28, 2024, https://zmina.info/en/articles-en/how-ukraine-passes-judgment-on-violations-of-the-laws-and-customs-of-war/; Ukrainian Bar Association et al., "ЗВІТ, ЗА РЕЗУЛЬТАТАМИ ВПРОВАДЖЕННЯ ПРОЄКТУ «МОНІТОРИНГ СУДОВИХ ПРОВАДЖЕНЬ У СПРАВАХ ПРО ВОЄННІ ЗЛОЧИНИ," December 2023, accessed June 28, 2024, https://uba.ua/documents/1PR/PR%20%2620Communications%023/Monitoring%20report_UKR-1.pdf, 7, 15.

89 See "Trials in Absentia," Global Rights Compliance, accessed June 28, 2024, https://www.asser.nl/media/795064/grc-trials-in-absentia-english.pdf, 11 f., suggesting to interpret Art. 297-1(2), requiring that the suspect absconded "with a view of avoiding criminal liability" to require evidence of actual knowledge. Provisions which could be drawn on are Art. 7(2) and 374(5), explicitly enshrining fair trial rights of the defendant in absentia. Whether this could similarly be done with Art. 323(3), which includes the same wording, is more questionable since it considers proof sufficient, that the accused "was aware or *must have been aware* of the launch of criminal proceedings" [emphasis added].

90 Diana Kolodiazhna, "How Ukraine Passes Judgment on Violations of the Laws and Customs of War?," *ZMINA*, April 24, 2024, accessed June 28, 2024, https://zmina.info/en/articles-en/how-ukraine-passes-judgment-on-violations-of-the-laws-and-customs-of-war/; "Needs Assessment of Ukraine's Justice System: Delivering Meaningful Justice to the Victims and Survivors of the Armed Conflict," Ukrainian Legal Advisory Group, June 2024, accessed June 28, 2024, https://ulag.org.ua/reports-and-materials/needs-assessment-ukraines-justice-system, 71.

91 See supra, 390.

92 "Sexual Violence by Members of the Russian Armed Forces: Federal Public Prosecutor Must Investigate," European Center for Constitutional and Human Rights, accessed June 28, 2024, https://www.ecchr.eu/en/case/sexual-violence-by-members-of-the-russian-armed-forces-federal-public-prosecutor-must-investigate/.

93 "Sexual Violence by Members of the Russian Armed Forces: A Renewed Call to the German Authorities to Investigate," European Center for Constitutional and Human Rights, February 2024, accessed June 28, 2024, https://www.ecchr.eu/fileadmin/user_upload/QA_CRSV_Counterstatement.pdf.

94 "Environmental War Crimes Guide," Climate Counsel, accessed June 28, 2024, https://www.climatecounsel.org/warcrimes; "A Victim-Centred Approach to Prosecuting Sexual Violence," Olga Golovina, Institute for War & Peace Reporting, December 12, 2023, accessed June 28, 2024, https://iwpr.net/global-voices/victim-centred-approach-prosecuting-sexual-violence; "Preserving Ukraine's Identity: Law Enforcement Agencies Train on Crimes against Cultural Heritage," EUAM Ukraine, March 11, 2024, accessed June 28, 2024, https://www.euam-ukraine.eu/news/preserving-ukraine-s-identity-law-enforcement-agencies-train-on-crimes-against-cultural-heritage/.

95 Examples in point are among others France ("Universal Jurisdiction Law and Practice in France," OSJI, Briefing Paper, February 2019, accessed June 28, 2024, https://www.justiceinitiative.org/publications/universal-jurisdiction-law-and-practice-france) or Switzerland ("Universal Jurisdiction Law and Practice in Switzerland," OSJI, Briefing Paper, June 2019, accessed June 28, 2024, https://www.justiceinitiative.org/uploads/180eda19-de98-44f5-afc7-4dc25d42b1a0/universal-jurisdiction-law-and-practice-switzerland.pdf). For an overview of Universal Jurisdiction criteria in EU member states see "At a Glance: Universal Jurisdiction in EU Member States, European Union Agency for Criminal Justice Cooperation," May 23, 2023, accessed June 28, 2024, https://www.eurojust.europa.eu/publication/glance-universal-jurisdiction-eu-member-states.

96 For a critical overview of the reforms see Isabelle Hassfurther, "Reform of the International Criminal Law Framework in Germany – Successful Changes and Missed Opportunities: Part I and Part II," *Opinio Juris*, June 13 and 14, 2024, accessed June 28, 2024, http://opiniojuris.org/2024/06/13/reform-of-the-international-criminal-law-framework-in-germany-successful-changes-and-missed-opportunities-part-i/.

Selected Bibliography

European Center for Constitutional and Human Rights. "Pathways to Justice for Ukraine," Living Open Archive, accessed September 4, 2024, https://loa.ecchr.eu/de/dossiers/pathways-to-justice-for-ukraine.

Hassfurther, Isabelle. "Accountability for the Crime of Aggression against Ukraine," *Verfassungsblog*, February 24, 2024, accessed September 4, 2024, https://verfassungsblog.de/aggression-ukraine.

International Criminal Court. "Ukraine," accessed September 4, 2024, https://www.icc-cpi.int/situations/ukraine.

Schüller, Andreas. "What Can('t) International Criminal Justice Deliver for Ukraine?" *Verfassungsblog*, February 24, 2023, accessed September 4, 2024, https://verfassungsblog.de/justice-ukraine.

Ukrainian Legal Advisory Group. "Needs Assessment of Ukraine's Justice System: Delivering Meaningful Justice to the Victims and Survivors of the Armed Conflict," June 2024, accessed September 4, 2024, https://ulag.org.ua/reports-and-materials/needs-assessment-ukraines-justice-system.

United Nations Human Rights Council. "Independent International Commission of Inquiry on Ukraine," accessed September 4, 2024, https://www.ohchr.org/en/hr-bodies/hrc/iicihr-ukraine/index.

21

Designating Investment Arbitration as a Legal Mechanism under the REPO Act

Eric Chang

On April 24, 2024, President Joseph Biden signed into law a US$95.3 billion war aid package to assist Israel, Taiwan, and Ukraine.[1] Contained within this package is a law that authorizes the president to provide additional financial assistance to Ukraine using assets confiscated from the Central Bank of the Russian Federation, as well as other foreign assets of the Russian Federation.[2] Known as the "Rebuilding Economic Prosperity and Opportunity for Ukrainians Act," or the "REPO Act" for short, this law creates an extraordinary tool to seize frozen Russian state assets.

The REPO Act anticipates the creation of a future international compensation mechanism that may receive Russian assets seized via the Act. However, such a mechanism, assuming it is successful, will take time, and it will be years before Ukraine sees proper compensation flow in-country from positive awards. In the meantime, the cost of war to Ukraine has now reached over $411 billion,[3] and Russia is currently engaging in a renewed surge into Ukraine, seriously jeopardizing Ukraine's territorial integrity.[4] A much quicker interim solution would be to leverage the REPO Act to designate Ukraine-Russia-specific investor-state dispute settlement (ISDS) cases as an "international compensation mechanism," allowing Ukrainian investors to satisfy positive investment awards against Russia by receiving seized Russian state assets. Leveraging the ISDS system would provide an immediate solution with a high degree of legitimacy that would address a number of domestic and international law due process concerns. It would also amount to a remarkable example of "lawfare," or the use of legal means as a substitute to achieve a military objective.

Ukraine's Lawfare Efforts Leveraging International Investment Law

In the wake of Russia's 2014 invasion of Ukrainian Crimea, Ukraine undertook a concerted campaign of legal proceedings against Russia before various international fora. This strategy represents the most systematic deployment of lawfare in an ongoing international armed conflict today and perhaps at any time in history.[5] Lawfare describes the use of legal means to apply pressure against a military adversary, potentially forcing that adversary to defend itself in multiple arenas.[6] An updated definition views lawfare as:

> 1) the purposeful use of law taken toward a particular adversary with the goal of achieving a particular strategic, operational, or tactical objective, or 2) the purposeful use of law to bolster the legitimacy of one's own strategic, operational, or tactical objectives toward a particular adversary, or to weaken the legitimacy of a particular adversary's particular strategic, operational, or tactical objectives.[7]

Lawfare encompasses an astonishingly diverse array of legal activities. A now classic example is the United States use of targeted sanctions during the invasion of Iraq in 2003, which prevented the Iraqi Air Force from acquiring new aircraft and spare parts and which so debilitated Iraq's airpower that it was unable to launch a single aircraft against the Coalition air armada. This use of law, in the form of sanctions, was arguably as effective as any military engagement in aerial combat, if not more.[8]

In Ukraine's case, its Ministry of Justice has deployed a conspicuous "Lawfare Project" against Russia, going so far as publishing an informational website detailing this campaign:

> *[O]ne of the key areas of confrontation is the legal one. The legal front is inconspicuous, but extremely important. Its key feature is that there is no noticeable disproportion in weight with the enemy. It is not subject to force-sharing agreements. Where there are no weapons, there is international law, sanctions and a tribunal. In the West, "legal war" received a special term—lawfare. And on this front, Ukraine (state bodies and state-owned enterprises) is fighting quite well.*
>
> *We are moving from the sometimes chaotic hit-skip tactics to a well-thought-out, comprehensive and coordinated legal defense of our rights and interests, and for this purpose we have involved leading foreign legal advisers who help to develop a strategy for legal confrontation.*[9]

Following the invasion of Crimea, Ukraine launched a veritable legal blitzkrieg against Russia, including, for example, several inter-state proceedings before the European Court of Human Rights (ECtHR),[10] proceedings under the dispute settlement procedures of the UN Convention on the Law of the Sea (UNCLOS) and the International Tribunal for the Law of the Sea (ITLOS),[11] proceedings before the International Court of Justice,[12] and three consultations at the World Trade Organization.[13] Ukraine further lodged two declarations under Article 12(3) of the Rome Statute of the International Criminal Court (ICC), voluntarily accepting the jurisdiction[14] of the ICC in order to allege crimes committed in Crimea from November 21, 2013, to February 22, 2014, and from February 20, 2014, onward.[15] The Office of the Prosecutor of the ICC opened preliminary investigations in response to both declarations.[16] Beyond the Ukrainian government's direct involvement as a party in these proceedings, over 8,500 individual applications relating to the conflict in Crimea and eastern Ukraine have been submitted to the ECtHR.[17]

Ukraine has also leveraged investment treaty claims under the ISDS system, explicitly encouraging[18] Ukrainian investor claims against Russia filed pursuant to the bilateral investment treaty (BIT) between Russia and Ukraine, signed in 1998 (the Ukraine-Russia BIT).[19] These investors collectively seek billions USD in compensation for the seizure of their investments in Crimea, leveraging an innovative legal argument under the law of armed conflict (LOAC) that occupied Crimea forms part of Russian territory, thereby granting jurisdiction to investment tribunals to adjudicate the disputes under the BIT. (Without this jurisdictional hook under LOAC, Ukrainian investors would remain within Ukrainian territory and would not be considered foreign investors in Russia within the meaning of the BIT.[20]) These investment treaty claims have been largely successful and have resulted in significant monetary awards against Russia: Russia was held liable in the *Aeroport Belbek v. Russia* and *PrivatBank v. Russia* cases (PrivatBank sought over $1 billion in damages);[21] the *Everest Estate LLC v. Russia* tribunal awarded claimants $159 million in damages,[22] which was successfully enforced in Ukraine;[23] in *Ukrnafta v. Russia* and *Stabil LLC v. Russia*, the tribunal awarded claimants nearly $88 million, including legal fees and interest;[24] that same award survived Russia's challenge before the Swiss Federal Supreme Court (at the legal seat of the arbitration), with a four-to-one majority of the Swiss court ruling that Russia has assumed responsibility under the Ukraine-Russia BIT to protect Ukrainian investments in Crimea made prior to the Russian annexation of the territory in 2014;[25] the *Oschadbank v. Russia* tribunal awarded the claimant over $1.1 billion in damages;[26] finally, in the biggest award reported to date, a tribunal in *Naftogaz v. Russia* was awarded $4.2 billion plus compound interest (EURIBOR +2 percent compounded semi-annually until the date of full payment), $23.9 million in legal fees and costs plus interest.[27]

Russia risks continued and unlimited liability under such claims and awards for as long as its occupation of Crimea continues, and as long as existing awards remain unpaid. These awards will continue to accrue considerable legal interest until fully settled, leading to swiftly escalating interest sums that will far outstrip principal damages. Meanwhile, new claims may continue to be filed as the occupation persists. Thus, in a very real sense, Ukraine has utilized international investment law to make Russia pay for the damages of war.

The REPO Act and the Establishment of an International Compensation Mechanism

Parallel to Ukraine's lawfare efforts, the international community has stepped in to impose a series of sanctions against Russia. In particular, the G7 (the United States, France, Canada, Germany, Japan, Italy, the United Kingdom), Australia, and the European Union (EU) joined together to collectively freeze Russian state assets, including significant Russian Central Bank assets, located outside of Russia.[28] While the imposition of sanctions and asset freezing was not without debate, the widespread consensus was that the temporary freezing of Russian assets, in particular Russian Central Bank assets, was permissible as a matter of public international law.[29] Together, the United States, EU, G7, and other countries froze an estimated $300 billion in frozen sovereign assets.[30] An estimated 70 percent of the assets are held in Belgium at Euroclear, a clearinghouse that provides cross-border securities transactions and asset settlement and holding services; these funds, therefore, fall under the jurisdictional purview of the EU.[31] The United States holds a minor portion of the total, with a wide range of estimates reported to be anywhere from $5 billion to $40–60 billion.[32]

The legality under both domestic and international law to confiscate and repurpose those frozen Russian state assets has been less clear. The EU, which controls the lion's share of the frozen assets, has been exceptionally cautious about the legal ramifications of direct confiscation and disbursement of those frozen funds;[33] instead, it currently plans to sidestep these legal issues by only disbursing the €4.4 billion in generated interest from the estimated €191 billion in Russian Central Bank assets immobilized by Euroclear. The EU member states agreed to use 90 percent of that generated interest for lethal assistance to Ukraine, with the remaining 10 percent spent on non-lethal assistance, to appease a small group of member states unwilling or unable to fund weapons.[34]

By contrast, the US position has quickly evolved into a more assertive stance. Policymakers harbored initial doubts on the legality of sovereign asset forfeiture due to a lack of domestic legal authorities allowing Executive seizure (as opposed to mere freezing) of assets;[35] equally, under international law, the drastic measure of confiscating sovereign assets would require, at minimum, some elaboration, if not expansion, of certain international law concepts, such as the doctrine of countermeasures.[36]

Moreover, as a matter of policy, many experts were (and still are) concerned that a dilution of the legal protections the United States provides typically to sovereign assets could contribute to the trend of "de-dollarization" that might weaken the economy and undermine the effectiveness of future US sanctions.[37] As late as mid-2022, US secretary of the treasury Janet Yellen stated that the United States did not have legal authority (under US domestic law) to seize Russian Central Bank assets frozen by the United States.[38] Nevertheless, as the war ground on, opinion evolved in favor of seizure.[39] Congress and the Biden Administration eventually backed the idea, ultimately enacting the REPO Act to provide the required domestic legal authority.[40]

The REPO Act allows the US president to confiscate frozen Russian sovereign assets subject to the jurisdiction of the United States for the express purpose of supporting Ukraine. As a starting point, under Section 103(a) of the Act, the United States must continue to block or immobilize all Russian sovereign assets already frozen until hostilities between Russia and Ukraine have ended.[41] The central section of the Act, Section 104, states that "the President may seize, confiscate, transfer, or vest any Russian aggressor state sovereign assets, in whole or in part, and including any interests in such assets, subject the jurisdiction of the United States."[42] This explicitly includes Russian Central Bank assets.[43]

The REPO Act closely circumscribes Executive discretion by imposing specific conditions on the confiscation of Russian sovereign funds. First, the seizure, confiscation, or transfer of such funds must be for the benefit of Ukraine and in the national interest of the United States;[44] the president must also meaningfully coordinate with G7 leaders to take multilateral actions with regard to such actions.[45] The funds must be deposited into the Ukraine Support Fund.[46] This fund, created by the REPO Act, is available to the Secretary of State (in consultation with USAID) to assist Ukraine in addressing damage resulting from the Russian invasion.[47] The funds may further be merged with foreign assistance funds[48] or used for direct loans to Ukraine.[49]

In addition to these direct uses of Russian state funds, the United States may also disburse these funds "through contributions to an international body or mechanism charged with determining compensation and providing assistance to Ukraine."[50] Section 105 of the REPO Act directs the president to coordinate with the G7, the European Union, Australia, and other partners and allies of the United States regarding the establishment of the compensation mechanism and a possible register of damages and ensuring distribution of the assets or proceeds of the assets "based on determinations under that mechanism."[51] Notably, such a multilateral disbursement of funds is optional.

Parallel to the enactment of the REPO Act, there has been initial progress on the establishment of such an international compensation mechanism. By a Resolution passed in November 2022,[52] the United Nations General Assembly supported and created an impetus for the creation of an international compensation mechanism. Following this lead, the Council of Europe (COE) established in May 2023 the Enlarged Partial Agreement of the Register of Damage Caused by the Aggression of the Russian Federation Against Ukraine (the Register of Damages, or Register).[53] Thirty-seven COE members agreed on the Register, with representatives of the EU, Canada, Japan, and the United States present.[54] The broad mandate of the Register is to record and document evidence and claims information on damages caused by Russia's internationally wrongful acts in or against Ukraine.[55] Critically, the Register is only the first component of a future international compensation mechanism: the Register records information, but is not itself an adjudicatory body.[56] Therefore, the exact form and structure of the compensation mechanism are still to be negotiated and could include a claims commission and a compensation fund.[57]

Thus, both the United States and the Council of Europe (along with the remaining G7 partners) have much work ahead in coordinating, negotiating, and establishing a compensation mechanism, including possibly combining disparate sets of frozen funds and transferring these to a single unified compensation fund.

Designating the Investor-State Dispute Settlement System as a Parallel, Interim International Compensation Mechanism

Unfortunately, the time required for a fully operational compensation mechanism runs headlong against the current crisis in Ukraine, where its military is facing increasing critical losses of manpower, equipment, and territory against a surging Russia.[58] Indeed, a compensation mechanism is, in essence, more suited as post-conflict war reparations than a real-time effort to aid Ukraine's ongoing war efforts. Notwithstanding the time it will take to negotiate and establish such a mechanism, claims require intensive fact-gathering, preparation, and a long adversarial adjudication process before any positive awards are issued; it may well take years before Ukraine, its citizens, and corporations begin to see compensation funds flow in-country. In the meantime, Russia has surged across the border, outmanning and outgunning Ukraine.[59]

The existing Investor-State Dispute Settlement (ISDS) system can provide an immediate interim solution, providing a high degree of legitimacy while minimizing residual domestic and international law concerns, and help normalize the use of seized funds to assist Ukraine. This would amount to a novel use of US lawfare to further boost Ukraine's own lawfare efforts through its encouragement of investor-state disputes.

As a starting point, the REPO Act's reference to an international compensation mechanism is not limited to a future or even a single mechanism. Under the text of Sections 104 and 105, it is entirely within the president's powers, in coordination with the G7 and other partners, to designate that Russian sovereign funds frozen in the United States can be transferred into a separate, stand-alone fund created with the specific purpose of satisfying investment awards against Russia. By co-opting and leveraging the existing ISDS system—itself a specialized type of international compensation mechanism—the United States can achieve several important objectives. Indeed, strong legal and policy reasons favor the disbursement of Russian state assets through the ISDS system.

First, using the REPO Act to satisfy the investment awards will put that money into the hands of Ukrainian investors.[60] The largest of these, Naftogaz, is a state-owned entity, meaning that its $4.2 billion-plus award (likely much higher if accounting for compound interest on the principal) would effectively go back to Ukraine: as noted on Ukraine's Lawfare website, the Naftogaz group is the largest taxpayer in Ukraine, with 2018 revenues alone amounting to 137 billion hryvnias ($5.28 billion), or 15 percent of total state budget revenues.[61] Satisfaction of all awards, regardless of the investors' private or state-owned nature, would plow much-needed funds back into the Ukrainian economy—in the same way that a future international compensation mechanism will achieve. At the same time, this would permanently deny Russia use of these funds for its own war efforts.

Second, disbursing seized funds through investment awards would immediately funnel those funds into the Ukrainian economy. In contrast, a future compensation mechanism negotiated between the COE, the United States, and other partners will take years to result in any actual compensation to Ukraine or Ukrainian claimants. All of the current investment arbitration awards issued under the Ukraine-Russia Bilateral Investment Treaty arose from the 2014 Russian invasion of Crimea. The disputes have already wound their way through years-long proceedings. The resulting awards against Russia as Respondent are owed and due now, opening the way for immediate satisfaction through the use of Russian state assets seized in the United States (subject to any remaining enforcement challenges).

Third, transferring seized Russian assets (via the REPO Act) to satisfy investment treaty awards against Russia will enjoy a high degree of legitimacy and will respect due process principles. The investment awards were issued under the Ukraine-Russia Bilateral Investment Treaty. Pursuant to that Treaty, Russia explicitly agreed to ISDS for investor-claimants to bring claims before international arbitration tribunals in order to seek compensation for alleged losses or damages to their investments. In other words, by signing and ratifying the Ukraine-Russia BIT, Russia explicitly agreed to ISDS as a specialized international compensation mechanism—something that is not likely to happen for any future international compensation mechanism established by the COE. Given Russia's international agreement to arbitrate investment disputes, the legitimacy of ISDS as a designated compensation mechanism under the REPO Act is unimpeachable.

Furthermore, the arbitration proceedings themselves should satisfy any due process and/or taking claims concerns (under domestic laws and/or under international law) about the seizure of Russian state assets. In this sense, a full adversarial process under ISDS is superior to the scenario of the United States directly disbursing seized funds to Ukraine under the other available avenues under Section 104 of the REPO Act.[62] ISDS is a well-established dispute settlement system, and tribunals are composed of highly respected, independent, and impartial tribunal members. Russia received a full and fair opportunity to defend the Ukrainian investors' claims and cannot now complain about the use of seized funds to satisfy the awards against it. Further, using seized funds to satisfy investment awards against Russia will effectively act as a set-off against Russia's existing debts to Ukrainian investors under these awards, which would further help blunt any Russian objections regarding unlawful takings or lack of due process.[63]

Fourth, designating an interim ISDS compensation mechanism under the REPO Act can help further normalize the disbursement of seized Russian funds to satisfy awards under any future international compensation mechanism. Indeed, the ISDS system should look similar to any eventual compensation mechanism: current proposals look to the historic example of the Iran-United States Claims Tribunal established under the 1981 Algiers Accord to resolve the Iran hostage crisis.[64]

Fifth, as noted above, Russia's exposure to investment claims and awards will continue as long as its occupation of Crimea continues. Under the REPO Act, the United States can continue to satisfy such awards through seized funds while a more permanent international compensation mechanism is negotiated and established.

Finally, the enactment of the REPO Act is, in and of itself, a prime example of lawfare, broadly defined as the use of law or legal instruments as a substitute for traditional military means to achieve an operational or strategic objective in an ongoing armed conflict. Here, the United States is leveraging its legal-economic power to impose financial costs on Russia that will impose real-world constraints on its ability to prosecute its incursion against Ukraine.

The United States' designation of the ISDS system as a temporary and immediate compensation mechanism under the REPO Act would further dovetail effectively with Ukraine's own lawfare efforts, resulting in a synergistic, reciprocal leveraging of both lawfare campaigns. From this perspective, the REPO Act would be leveraged to the greatest effect if the funds were seized and immediately disbursed to Ukraine to aid its war efforts rather than waiting until an international compensation mechanism is established.

Conclusion

Designating the ISDS system as an "international compensation mechanism" will give teeth to the REPO Act by allowing immediate disbursement of seized Russian funds to Ukraine, at a time when it is most needed. Although the United States holds a fraction of the overall frozen funds, it can play an outsized role through the REPO Act and taking the lead in pushing for (and normalizing) immediate disbursement of Russian state funds. While the EU has so far taken a much more cautious approach to the same topic, it has nonetheless played an important role in developing a possible future international compensation mechanism. Designating an interim ISDS compensation mechanism will help bridge and leverage these strong points from each side of the Atlantic.

Notes

1 Zolan Kanno-Youngs, "Biden Says Aid Bill for Ukraine and Israel Will 'Make the World Safer,'" *New York Times*, April 24, 2024, available at <https://www.nytimes.com/2024/04/24/us/politics/biden-ukraine-israel-aid.html>.

2 S. 2003, 118th Cong. (2023–2024), available at <https://www.congress.gov/bill/118th-congress/senate-bill/2003/text>.

3 World Bank, "Updated Ukraine and Recovery and Reconstruction Needs Assessment," World Bank Press Release, March 23, 2023, available at <https://www.worldbank.org/en/news/press-release/2023/03/23/updated-ukraine-recovery-and-reconstruction-needs-assessment>.

4 Constant Méheut, Maria Varenikova, and Michael Schwirtz, "Facing Russian Advance, a Top Ukrainian General Paints a Bleak Picture," *New York Times*, May 13, 2024, available at <https://www.nytimes.com/article/russia-ukraine-kharkiv.html>.

5 Eric Chang, "Lawfare in Ukraine: Weaponizing International Investment Law and the Law of Armed Conflict Against Russia's Invasion," *Strategic Perspectives* no. 39 (August 9, 2022), available at <https://ndupress.ndu.edu/Media/News/News-Article-View/Article/3121131/lawfare-in-ukraine-weaponizing-international-investment-law-and-the-law-of-arme/>.

6 Gregory P. Noone, "Lawfare or Strategic Communications?" *Case Western Reserve Journal of International Law* 43, no. 1 (2010): 73–4. The modern definition of lawfare was advanced in large part by General Charles J. Dunlap, Jr., USAF (Ret.), who described it as "the strategy of using—or misusing—law as a substitute for traditional military means to achieve an operational objective." Charles J. Dunlap, Jr., "Lawfare Today: A Perspective," *Yale Journal of International Affairs* (Winter 2008): 146. *See*

also Orde F. Kittrie, *Lawfare: Law as a Weapon of War* (Oxford: Oxford University Press, 2016).

7 Jill I. Goldenziel, "Law as a Battlefield: The U.S., China, and the Global Escalation of Lawfare," *Cornell Law Review* 107 (2021): 1085, 1097.

8 Charles J. Dunlap, Jr., "Does Lawfare Need an Apologia?" *Case Western Reserve Journal of International Law* 43, no. 1 (2010): 121, 123–4. Another example is the US purchase, in 2001, of exclusive rights to selected commercial satellite imagery prior to operations in Afghanistan, which had the effect of denying the data to any hostile forces. *Ibid.* at 123.

9 "About Lawfare Project History," Law Confrontation with Russian Federation, last accessed May 15, 2024, available at <https://lawfare.gov.ua/about>.

10 Ukraine v. Russian Federation, App. Nos. 20958/14 and 38334/18 (re: Crimea) (re: allegations of systematic human rights violations committed by the Russian Federation in Crimea); Ukraine and the Netherlands v. Russian Federation, App. Nos. 8019/16, 43800/14, and 28525/20 (re: events in Eastern Ukraine, including the crash of Malaysian Airlines flight MH17); Ukraine v. Russian Federation (VIII), App. No. 55855/18 (re: naval incident in the Kerch Strait leading to the capture of three Ukrainian naval vessels and their crews); Ukraine v. Russian Federation, App. No. 10691/21 (re: allegations of Russian state-authorized assassination operations); Ukraine v. Russia (X), App. No. 11055/22 (re: "massive human rights violations committed by Russian troops in the course of the military aggression against the sovereign territory of Ukraine"); and Ukraine v. Russian Federation, App. No. 49537/14 (struck off list). *See also* "Full Court Venues List," Law Confrontation with Russian Federation, last accessed May 15, 2024, available at <https://lawfare.gov.ua/cases>.

11 Dispute Concerning Coastal State Rights in the Black Sea, Sea of Azov, and Kerch Strait (Ukraine v. the Russian Federation), Case No. 2017-06, Permanent Court of Arbitration, 2017; Detention of Three Ukrainian Naval Vessels (Ukraine v. Russia), Case No. 26, Permanent Court of Arbitration (2019); Immunity of Three Ukrainian Naval Vessels and the Twenty-Four Servicemen on Board (Ukraine v. Russia), Case no. 26, Request for Provisional Measures Submitted by Ukraine (2019).

12 Allegations of Genocide under the Convention on the Prevention and Punishment of the Crime of Genocide (Ukraine v. Russian Federation), Application, February 27, 2022, available at <https://www.icj-cij.org/case/182>; Application of the International Convention for the Suppression of the Financing of Terrorism and of the International Convention on the Elimination of All Forms of Racial Discrimination (Ukraine v. Russian Federation), January 16, 2017, available at <https://www.icj-cij.org/case/166>.

13 Request for Consultations by Ukraine, *Russia: Measures Concerning Traffic in Transit*, World Trade Organization (WTO) Doc. WT/DS512/1, September 14, 2016; Request for Consultations by Ukraine, *Russia: Measures Affecting the Importation of Railway Equipment and Parts Thereof*, WTO Doc. WT/DS499/11, October 21, 2015; Request for Consultations by Ukraine, *Anti-Dumping Measures on Ammonium Nitrate from Russia*, WTO Doc. WT/DS493/1, May 7, 2015.

14 Ukraine is not a party to the Rome Statute of the International Criminal Court.

15 Declaration of Ukraine, April 9, 2014, International Criminal Court, available at <https://www.icc-cpi.int/itemsDocuments/997/declarationRecognitionJuristiction09

-04-2014.pdf>; Declaration of Ukraine, September 8, 2015, International Criminal Court, available at <https://www.icc-cpi.int/iccdocs/other/Ukraine_Art_12-3_declaration_08015.pdf>.

16 On March 2, 2022, the Office opened formal investigations following referrals by 3939 ICC State Parties. *Statement of ICC Prosecutor, Karim A.A. Khan QC, on the Situation in Ukraine: Receipt of Referrals from State Parties and the Opening of an Investigation*, March 2, 2022, available at <https://www.icc-cpi.int/news/statement-icc-prosecutor-karim-aa-khan-qc-situation-ukraine-receipt-referrals-39-states#:~:text=Today%2C%20I%20can%20confirm%20that,Costa%20Rica%2C%20Republic%20of%20Croatia%2C>.

17 European Court of Human Rights Press Unit, "Factsheet: Armed Conflicts," April 20–23, 2022, available at <https://www.echr.coe.int/Documents/FS_Armed_conflicts_ENG.pdf>.

18 "Oschadbank Files Claim Worth UAH 15 Bln Against Russia for Losses Caused by Crimean Annexation—Yatseniuk," Interfax-Ukraine, August 7, 2015, available at <https://en.interfax.com.ua/news/economic/276618.html>. The former prime minister of Ukraine issued very public statements encouraging investor claims, amounting to an express call to action to wage a legal war against Russia's occupation of Crimea.

19 Agreement Between the Government of the Russian Federation and the Cabinet of Ministers of the Ukraine on the Encouragement and Mutual Protection of Investments, Russian Federation–Ukraine Bilateral Investment Treaty ("Ukraine-Russia BIT"), UN Conference on Trade and Development (UNCTAD) Investment Policy Hub, November 27, 1998, available at <https://investmentpolicy.unctad.org/international-investment-agreements/treaties/bilateral-investment-treaties/2859/russian-federation---ukraine-bit-1998->.

20 By definition, bilateral investment treaties only deal with *foreign* investments, that is, investments made by an investor from one contracting state in the territory of the other contracting state. Thus, Article 1 of the Ukraine-Russia BIT states that "'Investments' shall denote all kinds of property and intellectual values, which are put in by the investor of one Contracting Party on the territory of the other Contracting Party . . . ."

21 Aeroport Belbek LLC and Mr. Igor Valerievich Kolomoisky v. the Russian Federation, PCA Case No. 2015-07, PCA Case Repository, Interim Award, February 24, 2017; PJSC CB PrivatBank and Finance Company Finilon LLC v. The Russian Federation, PCA Case No. 2015-21, PCA Case Repository, Interim Award, February 24, 2017; Tom Jones, "Russia Held Liable Again over Crimean Assets," *Global Arbitration Review*, February 15, 2019, available at <https://globalarbitrationreview.com/russia-held-liable-again-over-crimean-assets>.

22 Everest Estate LLC and others v. the Russian Federation, PCA Case No. 2015-36, PCA Case Repository, Award, May 2, 2018; "Russia Held Liable for Crimea Real Estate Seizures," *Global Arbitration Review*, May 9, 2018, available at <https://globalarbitrationreview.com/russia-held-liable-crimea-real-estate-seizures>.

23 Sebastian Perry, "Enforcement of Crimea Award Upheld in Ukraine," *Global Arbitration Review*, February 7, 2019, available at <https://globalarbitrationreview.com/enforcement-of-crimea-award-upheld-in-ukraine>.

24 Stabil and others v. the Russian Federation, PCA Case No. 2015-35, PCA Case Repository, Award, April 12, 2019; PJSC Ukrnafta v. the Russian Federation, PCA

Case No. 2015-34, PCA Case Repository, Award, April 12, 2019; Tom Jones and Sebastian Perry, "Russia Ordered to Pay for Petrol Stations Seized in Crimea," *Global Arbitration Review*, April 16, 2019, available at <https://globalarbitrationreview.com/russia-ordered-pay-petrol-stations-seized-in-crimea>.

25 "Crimea Awards Upheld in Switzerland," *Global Arbitration Review*, October 16, 2018, available at <https://globalarbitrationreview.com/crimea-awards-upheld-in-switzerland>; Sebastian Perry, "Russia Fails to Overturn Crimea Awards," *Global Arbitration Review*, December 18, 2019, available at <https://globalarbitrationreview.com/russia-fails-overturn-crimea-awards>.

26 Oschadbank v. the Russian Federation, PCA Case No. 2016-14, PCA Case Repository, Award, November 26, 2018; Jones, "Russia Held Liable Again over Crimean Assets." However, Russia succeeded in annulling the *Oschadbank* award before the Paris Court of Appeal. See Cosmo Sanderson, "Russia Overturns Billion-Dollar Crimea Award," *Global Arbitration Review*, March 30, 2021, available at <https://globalarbitrationreview.com/russia-overturns-billion-dollar-crimea-award>. Despite this enforcement defeat, the *Oschadbank* claimants can appeal to France's supreme court, the *Cour de cassation*, and elsewhere, and can continue to enforce in other jurisdictions where Russian assets are discovered.

27 NJSC Naftogaz v. Russia, PCA Case no. 2017-16, Final Award dated June 16, 2023, available at < https://www.italaw.com/cases/4381>; Tom Jones, "Russia Liable for Seizure of Naftogaz Assets in Crimea," *Global Arbitration Review*, March 1, 2019, available at <https://globalarbitrationreview.com/russia-liable-seizure-of-naftogaz-assets-in-crimea>.

28 U.S. Dep't Treasury, "Russian Elites, Proxies, and Oligarchs Task Force Joint Statement," Press Release, June 29, 2022, available at <https://home.treasury.gov/news/press-releases/jy0839>.

29 *See, e.g.*, Anton Moiseienko, "Legal: The Freezing of the Russian Central Bank's Assets," *European Journal of International Law* 34, no. 4 (2023).

30 Ibid.; Fatima Hussein, "Yelen Urges World Leaders to 'Unlock' Frozen Russian Central Bank Assets and Send Them to Ukraine," *Associated Press*, February 27, 2024, available at <https://apnews.com/article/yellen-russia-ukraine-war-central-bank-finance-85e080fd78e9d37951e1e7dcd58fdc87>.

31 Henry Ridgwell, "Europe to Fund Ukraine Weapons with Profits from Frozen Russian Assets," *Voice of America*, May 9, 2024, available at <https://www.voanews.com/a/europe-to-fund-ukraine-weapons-with-profits-from-frozen-russian-assets/7604226.html>.

32 Fatima Hussein, "The US is Now Allowed to Seize Russian State Assets. How Would That Work?," *Associated Press*, May 10, 2024, available at <https://apnews.com/article/russia-ukraine-treasury-sanctions-assets-congress-0a3bc97a2d6d77ce365 0c767db6ea7ed>; Keithe Johnson and Amy Mackinnon, "The U.S. Is Considering Giving Russia's Frozen Assets to Ukraine," *Foreign Affairs*, January 30, 2024, available at <https://foreignpolicy.com/2024/01/30/biden-russia-ukraine-assets-banks-senate/>.

33 Julia Payne and Jan Strupczewski, "EU Unlikely to Confiscate Russian Central Bank Assets – Officials," *Reuters* January 23, 2024, available at <https://www.reuters.com/world/europe/eu-unlikely-confiscate-russian-central-bank-assets-officials-2024-01-23/>.

34 Jennifer Rankin, "EU Reaches Deal on Using Profits from Russia's Frozen Assets for Ukraine," *The Guardian*, May 8, 2024, available at <https://www.theguardian.com/world/article/2024/may/08/eu-reaches-deal-on-using-profits-from-russias-frozen-assets-for-ukraine>.

35 Scott R. Anderson and Chimène Keitner, "The Legal Challenges Presented by Seizing Frozen Russian Assets," *Lawfare*, May 26, 2022, available at <https://www.lawfaremedia.org/article/legal-challenges-presented-seizing-frozen-russian-assets>.

36 Under the doctrine of countermeasures, an injured State may take certain acts, including acts normally considered illegal under international law, against an offending State that is responsible for an internationally wrongful act, in order to induce that latter State to cease the internationally wrongful act or to make reparation for the internationally wrongful act. *See* Draft Articles on the Responsibility of States for Internationally Wrongful Acts, U.N. Doc. A/56/10 (October 24, 2001), Art. 49.

37 Ibid.

38 David Lawder, "Yellen: Not legal for U.S. to seize Russian official assets," *Reuters*, May 18, 2022, available at <https://www.reuters.com/world/yellen-not-legal-us-government-seize-russian-central-bank-assets-2022-05-18/>.

39 *See, e.g.*, "Confiscate Russian Assets? The West Should Resist," *The Washington Post*, July 18, 2023, available at <https://www.washingtonpost.com/business/2023/07/18/russian-assets-can-pay-for-ukraine-s-reconstruction-the-question-is-how/d5cfae0a-2564-11ee-9201-826e5bb78fa1_story.html>; Scott R. Anderson and Chimène Keitner, "The Legal Challenges Presented by Seizing Frozen Russian Assets," *Lawfare*, May 26, 2022, available at <https://www.lawfaremedia.org/article/legal-challenges-presented-seizing-frozen-russian-assets>; Laurence Tribe et al., "The Legal, Practical, and Moral Case for Transferring Russian Sovereign Assets to Ukraine," *Renew Democracy Initiative*, September 17, 2023, available at <https://rdi.org/articles/making-putin-pay/>; "Repurposing Frozen Russian Assets: Analysis Under International Law," *Public International Law & Policy Group*, March 2023, available at <https://www.publicinternationallawandpolicygroup.org/policy-planning-ukraine-sanctions-and-frozen-assets>.

40 Daniel Flatley, "White House Throws Support Behind Seizing Frozen Russian Assets," *Bloomberg*, January 10, 2024, available at <https://www.bloomberg.com/news/articles/2024-01-10/white-house-throws-support-behind-seizing-frozen-russian-assets>.

41 S. 2003 at s.104(b)(1).

42 S. 2003 at s.104(b)(1).

43 Ibid., at s. 2(3)(A). Section 104 also requires that all currently frozen Russian sovereign assets will remain frozen until Russia has ceased hostilities and withdrawn its forces (s. 103(a)(1)); and Russia has fully compensated Ukraine (s. 103(a)(2)), or is participating in an international mechanism that will do so (s. 103(a)(3)).

44 Ibid., at s. 104(c)(1).

45 Ibid., at s. 104(c)(3).

46 Ibid., at s. 104(b)(3)(A).

47 Ibid., at s. 104(e)(1).

48 Ibid., at s. 104(e)(2)(A).

49 Ibid., at s. 104(e)(2)(B).

50 Ibid., at s. 104(e)(1).
51 Ibid., at s. 105(a)(1)-(3).
52 United Nations (UN) General Assembly, "General Assembly Adopts Text Recommending Creation of Register to Document Damages Caused by Russian Federation Aggression against Ukraine, Resuming Emergency Special Session," UN Press Release GA/12470, November 14, 2022, available at <https://press.un.org/en/2022/ga12470.doc.htm>.
53 "About the Register," *Council of Europe RD4U*, last accessed May 14, 2024, available at <https://rd4u.coe.int/en/about-the-register>.
54 Chiara Giorgetti and Patrick Pearsall, "A Significant New Step in the Creation of an International Compensation Mechanism for Ukraine," *Just Security*, July 27, 2023, available at <https://www.justsecurity.org/87395/significant-step-in-creation-of-international-compensation-mechanism-for-ukraine/>.
55 "About the Register," *Council of Europe RD4U*, under "Mandate and Functions."
56 Ibid.
57 Chiara Giorgetti and Patrick Pearsall, "A Significant New Step in the Creation of an International Compensation Mechanism for Ukraine," *Just Security*, July 27, 2023, available at <https://www.justsecurity.org/87395/significant-step-in-creation-of-international-compensation-mechanism-for-ukraine/>. Some proposals have looked to the historic example of the Iran-United States Claims Tribunal established under the 1981 Algiers Accord to resolve the Iran hostage crisis. "Repurposing Frozen Russian Assets: Analysis Under International Law," *Public International Law & Policy Group*, March 2023, 45–47, available at <https://www.publicinternationallawandpolicygroup.org/policy-planning-ukraine-sanctions-and-frozen-assets>.
58 Dara Massicot, "Time is Running Out in Ukraine," *Foreign Affairs*, March 8, 2024, available at <https://www.foreignaffairs.com/ukraine/time-running-out-ukraine>; Victor Punchuk, "Time is Running Out to Help Ukraine and Defend the West," *Atlantic Council*, February 20, 2024, available at <https://www.atlanticcouncil.org/blogs/ukrainealert/time-is-running-out-to-help-ukraine-and-defend-the-west/>; Phil Steward and Idrees Ali, "US General Warns Time Running Out for Ukraine without US Aid," *Reuters*, April 10, 2024, available at <https://www.reuters.com/world/europe/us-general-warns-time-running-out-ukraine-without-us-aid-2024-04-10/>.
59 Constant Méheut, Maria Varenikova, and Michael Schwirtz, "Facing Russian Advance, a Top Ukrainian General Paints a Bleak Picture," *New York Times*, May 13, 2024, available at <https://www.nytimes.com/article/russia-ukraine-kharkiv.html>.
60 Because the REPO Act must be used specifically to assist Ukraine, these funds could not be used to satisfy investment treaty awards against Russia that are unrelated to Ukraine or Ukrainian investors.
61 "Naftogaz vs Russia," Law Confrontation with Russian Federation, last accessed May 15, 2024, available at <https://lawfare.gov.ua/cases/pca-case-no-2017-16>.
62 Of note, Section 104 of the REPO Act preserves Russia's right to seek compensation under the US Constitution's Takings Clause for injury arising out of the forfeiture of its assets. The use of seized state assets to satisfy the investment awards should help overcome such Takings Clause claims. This is especially so since the use of the funds would essentially amount to an enforcement of an arbitration award, and both Russia and the United States are signatories to the United National Convention on the

Recognition and Enforcement of Foreign Arbitral Awards (New York Convention) (1958).

63 An analogous idea was proposed to create syndicated loan facilities for Ukraine, with Ukraine's future compensation claims against Russia serving as collateral. The loan would be non-recourse, meaning Ukraine would not be liable to repay in the event of default, which would be very likely, if not expected. The creditors would then utilize the concept of set-off to seize the Russian state assets held in collateral. Ashley Deeks, Mity Gulati, Paul Stephan, "What Should the Biden Administration Do With REPO?," *Lawfare*, May 6, 2024, available at <https://www.lawfaremedia.org/article/what-should-the-biden-administration-do-with-repo>. *See also* Daniel Franchini and Astrid Iversen, "Frozen Russian Assets to Finance Ukraine: Collateralization Instead of Confiscation," *Lawfare*, March 15, 2024, available at <https://www.lawfaremedia.org/article/frozen-russian-assets-to-finance-ukraine-collateralization-instead-of-confiscation>.

64 "Repurposing Frozen Russian Assets: Analysis Under International Law," *Public International Law & Policy Group*, March 2023, 45–47, available at <https://www.publicinternationallawandpolicygroup.org/policy-planning-ukraine-sanctions-and-frozen-assets>.

Selected Bibliography

Anderson, Scott R., and Chimène Keitner, "The Legal Challenges Presented by Seizing Frozen Russian Assets," *Lawfare*, May 26, 2022.

Chang, Eric, "Lawfare in Ukraine: Weaponizing International Investment Law and the Law of Armed Conflict Against Russia's Invasion," *Strategic Perspectives* no. 39 (August 9, 2022) available at <https://ndupress.ndu.edu/Media/News/News-Article-View/Article/3121131/lawfare-in-ukraine-weaponizing-international-investment-law-and-the-law-of-arme/>..

Dunlap, Charles Jr, "Does Lawfare Need an Apologia?" *Case Western Reserve Journal of International Law* 43, no. 1 (2010).

Goldenziel, Jill I., "Law as a Battlefield: The U.S., China, and the Global Escalation of Lawfare," *Cornell Law Review* 106, 1085-1172 (2021).

Johnson, Keithe and Amy Mackinnon, "The U.S. Is Considering Giving Russia's Frozen Assets to Ukraine," *Foreign Affairs*, January 30, 2024.

Kittrie, Orde F., *Lawfare: Law as a Weapon of War* (Oxford: Oxford University Press, 2016).

Rankin, Jennifer, "EU Reaches Deal on Using Profits from Russia's Frozen Assets for Ukraine," *The Guardian*, May 8, 2024.

22

Destruction of Ukrainian Cultural Heritage

Anton Korynevych, Tymur Korotkyi, and Nataliia Hendel

Vandalism (barbarism) has taken different forms in different centuries, but it has always been a threat to civilization. Its victim has always been "culture" in the broadest sense. That is why Raphael Lemkin considered cultural genocide to be one of the forms of genocide.[1] Culture was one of the victims of the Nazis during the Second World War, a manifestation of barbarism and the desire to destroy entire peoples, to wipe them off the face of the Earth, their language, their religion, and their culture. In this way, 6 million Jews were exterminated, and Yiddish culture practically disappeared.[2] And it was Nuremberg that became a turning point in the reaction of civilized nations, including the destruction of cultural heritage, to the condemnation and prosecution of war crimes against cultural property.[3]

Now, in the twenty-first century, the "Russian world" has become the embodiment of barbarism, just as Nazism was in the twentieth century. The denial of the right to exist of the Ukrainian nation and culture by the apologists of the "Russian world" led to a colonial and genocidal war.[4] A war in which Russia's violations of international humanitarian law became part of its policy, a method of warfare in its legal context.[5] Russia's method of warfare in an ideological context is to rewrite the history of the Ukrainian people, erase their identity, and destroy their culture.[6]

These two contexts of Russian aggression against Ukraine were the impetus for writing this chapter. The destruction of Ukraine's cultural values and its national, moral, and cultural leaders has not only a legal dimension, which we will focus on but also a clear colonial and genocidal context that should be taken into account when assessing Russia's violations of international law against Ukraine's cultural heritage during its war of aggression. In a strictly legal sense, these violations began on February 19, 2014, with the occupation of Crimea,[7] but they have deep historical roots going back to Russia's colonial policies.

It was the occupation and attempted annexation of Crimea that underscored Russia's colonial policy toward Ukraine's cultural heritage. Russia's numerous violations of international law about cultural heritage in Crimea[8] epitomize Russia's true intentions to destroy the Ukrainian national identity, the identity of the Crimean Tatar people, clearly repeating the phases of genocide identified by Raphael Lemkin: the first is the destruction of the national characteristics of the oppressed group; the second is the imposition of the national characteristics of the oppressors.[9] Russia exacerbated all these cases during the full-scale invasion and were a reflection of Russia's colonial policy, starting with the traditional cultural appropriation of Ukrainian cultural heritage, the replacement of the identification of artists, attacks, abductions, torture, and murders of religious leaders and believers of various denominations in connection with the destruction of Ukraine's cultural heritage.[10]

Structure and Methodology

In what follows, we will present the facts in chronological order, starting with the occupation of Crimea in February 2014 and the full-scale invasion of 2022. We will assess (1) the Russian Federation's violations of international law norms relating to cultural property during the Russian Federation's aggression against Ukraine, (2) their possible international legal and criminal qualification, (3) the international community response to these violations, (4) the measures taken by Ukraine to protect cultural property during the international armed conflict provoked by the aggression of the Russian Federation against Ukraine and the implementation of the norms of international humanitarian law, and (5) specific issues of compensation and restitution of damage caused to the cultural heritage of Ukraine.

It is important to consider Russian encroachments on Ukraine's cultural heritage through a "colonial prism." The appropriation of Ukraine's cultural heritage by the Russian occupation authorities creates the basis for further crimes, such as unauthorized archaeological excavations or unlawful removal of artifacts.[11]

The participation of the parties to the armed conflict in international treaties for the protection of cultural property is a relevant circumstance for the international legal qualification of violations of international law applicable in an international armed conflict. Since Ukraine uses all possible international legal mechanisms for the protection of cultural heritage, we will not limit ourselves exclusively to the sources of international humanitarian law. Still, we will assess all special international treaties applicable to the protection of cultural property. First of all, these are the international treaties on international humanitarian law. Ukraine is a party to the Convention (IV) respecting the Laws and Customs of War on Land and its annex: Regulations concerning the Laws and Customs of War on Land (The Hague, October 18, 1907),[12] the Convention (IV) relative to the Protection of Civilian Persons in Time of War (Geneva, August 12, 1949),[13] the Convention for the Protection of Cultural Property in the Event of Armed Conflict (The Hague, May 14, 1954),[14] the Protocol for the Protection of Cultural Property in the Event of Armed Conflict (The Hague, May 14, 1954),[15] the Protocol Additional to the Geneva Conventions of August 12, 1949, and relating to the Protection of Victims of International Armed Conflicts (Protocol I), (Geneva, June 8, 1977),[16] the Second Protocol to the Hague Convention of 1954 for the Protection of Cultural Property in the Event of Armed Conflict (The Hague, March 26, 1999).[17] Naturally, the norms of customary international humanitarian law apply to belligerents.[18]

The Russian Federation is a party to all the treaties listed, with the exception of the Second Protocol to the Hague Convention of 1954 for the Protection of Cultural Property in the Event of Armed Conflict (The Hague, March 26, 1999).[19]

Cultural heritage treaties create a general protection regime. Ukraine participates in the Convention concerning the Protection of the World Cultural and Natural Heritage (Paris, November 16, 1972),[20] the Convention for the Safeguarding of the Intangible Cultural Heritage (Paris, October 17, 2003),[21] and the Convention on the Means of Prohibiting and Preventing the Illicit Import, Export, and Transfer of Ownership of Cultural Property (Paris, November 14, 1970).[22] The Russian Federation does not participate in the Convention for Safeguarding Intangible Cultural Heritage (Paris, October 17, 2003).[23]

About the Rome Statute of the International Criminal Court (July 17, 1998), Ukraine signed the Rome Statute in 2000 but has not yet ratified it. However, in two declarations in 2014 and 2015,[2425] Ukraine accepted the jurisdiction of the International Criminal Court under Article 12(3) of the Rome Statute, which applies from November 21, 2013, to all war crimes, crimes against humanity, and genocide committed on the territory of Ukraine.[26] Thus, the jurisdiction of the ICC extends to all war crimes against cultural property under Article 8 of the Rome Statute committed in the context of and in relation to an international armed conflict provoked by the aggression of the Russian Federation against Ukraine. In this way, a non-exhaustive description was given of the international regulatory framework applicable to the qualification of the actions of the Russian Federation and its representatives against the cultural heritage of Ukraine at the time of the aggression and to the application by Ukraine of the principle of the protection of cultural heritage in the event of an international armed confrontation. A new stage in Ukraine's relations with the ICC was the adoption by the Verkhovna Rada of Ukraine on August 21, 2024, of the Law of Ukraine on Ratification of the Rome Statute of the International Criminal Court and Amendments thereto, submitted by President of Ukraine Volodymyr Zelenskyy.[27] However, the Law of Ukraine on the Ratification of the Rome Statute of the International Criminal Court and Amendments thereto contains a provision for its entry into force simultaneously with the entry into force of the Law of Ukraine "On Amendments to the Criminal Code and the Criminal Procedure Code of Ukraine in connection with the ratification of the Rome Statute of the International Criminal Court and Amendments thereto," as a result of which several draft laws have been registered in the Verkhovna Rada of Ukraine, but none has been adopted as of September 27, 2024.

Violation by the Russian Federation of the Norms of International Law Concerning the Protection of the Cultural Heritage of Ukraine during the Aggression of the Russian Federation against Ukraine in Relation to the Occupation of Crimea

The occupation of Crimea resulted in an attempt to eradicate everything Ukrainian: language, religion, education, culture, persecution of its speakers, and direct violation of the norms of international humanitarian law regarding the protection of cultural property. These violations began immediately after the occupation of Crimea and are well documented. In particular, the information prepared by UNESCO is presented under 210 EX/Decision 5.I.C on the "Follow-up of the situation in the Autonomous Republic of Crimea (Ukraine)."[28]

Since 2014 and until today, the Russian occupation authorities have been erasing the Ukrainian and Crimean Tatar national identity, in particular by restricting education in the Crimean Tatar language and reducing the number of Ukrainian-language schools. The aggressor's restriction of the use of the Ukrainian language was legally assessed in the judgment of the International Court of Justice on January 31, 2024, as a violation of the International Convention on the Elimination of All Forms of Racial Discrimination of 1965,[29] political persecution, and repression.

Cultural monuments on the territory of occupied Crimea, including UNESCO World Heritage Sites, have suffered significant damage, destruction, and changes in the protection regime. In particular, the ancient city of Taurian Chersonese and its Chora World Heritage Site[30] and five other sites in Crimea inscribed by Ukraine on the Tentative List of World Heritage Sites, in particular the Bagçesaray Palace of the Crimean Khans, have been seriously damaged. Illegal appropriation and looting of cultural property and illegal archaeological excavations are taking place.[31] The Russian Federation changed its legal status and assigned the cultural values of Ukraine, which is located in Crimea, including more than 4,000 monuments of national and local importance.[32] Examples of such actions are (1) on August 8, 2014, the deputies of the so-called "State Council of the Republic of Crimea" adopted a "law" according to which cultural heritage sites in Crimea received the status of national heritage of the Russian Federation; (2) on February 13, 2015, Russian President Vladimir Putin signed a law simplifying the procedure for inclusion of these monuments in the Unified State Register of Cultural Heritage Sites of Russia; (3) on October 17, 2015, Russian Prime Minister Dmitry Medvedev signed a decree on the classification of more than 220 historical and cultural sites in Crimea as federal cultural heritage sites.[33]

Russia is using such appropriation to implement its comprehensive long-term strategy to consolidate its historical,[34] cultural, and religious dominance over Crimea's past, present, and future.[35]

Violation by the Russian Federation of the Rules of International Law Regarding the Cultural Heritage of Ukraine in the Temporarily Occupied Territories of the Donetsk and Luhansk Regions of Ukraine

Since the end of April 2014, these territories have been under the control of the Russian Federation and puppet entities, so-called "Donetsk" and "Luhansk" "people's republics," which were actually Russian occupation authorities created there.[36] The policy of these occupation authorities in the field of cultural heritage was aimed at the destruction of Ukrainian culture, language, and education[37] and was accompanied by illegal detentions, tortures, and murders of their carriers.[38] One of the reasons for the illegal detentions was the pro-Ukrainian position and authority among the population.[39] The infamous prison-torture "Isolation" (until 2014, it was an art object) became a symbol of the atrocities of Russian "proxies."[40]

During the ten years of temporary occupation of the regions of Eastern Ukraine, a purposeful campaign was carried out to eradicate from the collective memory everything Ukrainian: culture, literature, history, language, erasure of cultural identity, and destruction of Ukrainians as a nation. It manifested itself in the mystification of museum exhibits, the destruction of monuments related to Ukraine, the transformation of educational programs in schools and universities, the militarization of education,[41] the imposition of Russian historical and political imperatives, and the persecution of Ukrainian activists and bearers of Ukrainian identity.[42] The most false and illegal concept of the "people of Donbas," under the slogan of which the aggression of the Russian Federation against Ukraine in the East of Ukraine in 2014 was carried out,[43] became a tool for changing the Ukrainian identity during the entire temporary occupation of the eastern regions of Ukraine by the Russian Federation. The result was the destruction of the Ukrainian identity of the population of the temporarily Russian-occupied parts of the Donetsk and Luhansk regions of Ukraine and its replacement by the Russian one through the destruction of the cultural space.[44]

Dozens of Ukrainian museums, including the Mariupol Museum of Local Lore, the Art Museum named after Arkhyp Kuindzhi, the Donetsk Regional Museum of Local Lore, the Melitopol City Museum of Local Lore, the Picture Gallery named after Albi, Kherson Regional Art Museum named after O. O. Shovkunenko, suffered appropriation and looting of museum collections after the full-scale invasion. These are the most famous examples of destruction and looting of cultural property in Ukraine. At the same time, hundreds of other crimes against cultural heritage and thousands of cases of destruction and misappropriation of cultural values, including those in private ownership, remain unknown.[45]

Ukrainian organizations document these cases,[46] and they fall entirely under Rafal Lemkin's concept of "cultural genocide" and the concept of "cultural erasure," which the Committee on Culture of the Parliamentary Assembly of the Council of Europe recognized as an instrument of Russia's war against Ukraine and an element of the genocidal policy aimed at destroying the Ukrainian nation.[47] The Institute of Mass Information has prepared a report on the cultural genocide committed by the Russian Federation through the introduction of Russian education in the temporarily occupied territories of Ukraine.[48] The Russian Federation has implemented a policy of "denazification" by changing the educational programs for Ukrainian children.[49]

The cultural dimension, in a broad sense, was and remains one of the reasons for the aggression of the Russian Federation against Ukraine. The basis of the full-scale invasion is the idea of Russian neo-imperialism,[50] the denial of the right of the Ukrainian people to statehood, political and religious independence, and cultural identity.[51] Further, the erasure of Ukrainian identity and its replacement with Russian totalitarian culture is a tool for introducing the colonial narrative of the "Russian world" and the "united Russian people"[52] with the denial of the right to the existence of the Ukrainian people as the general goal of the full-scale invasion, which indicates the presence of genocidal intent to destroy the existence of the Ukrainian people as such. Cultural heritage as a manifestation of Ukrainian identity has become an object of extermination, physical—in relation to cultural property and cultural carriers,[53] and spiritual—the erasure of Ukrainian identity and its replacement by Russian identity in the territories of Ukraine occupied by the Russian Federation, as has been happening since 2014 in Crimea and the East of Ukraine. They continued with greater intensity and scale and with much more brutal, horrific methods.

Numerous objects of the cultural heritage of Ukraine have become everyday objects of attacks, looting, and destruction by the Russian Armed Forces. The intangible cultural heritage of Ukraine became a common victim as the main qualitative feature that allows identifying a group of people as a nation.[54]

Systematic attacks on civilian objects, including objects of cultural heritage,[55] destruction of everything Ukrainian in the occupied territories, distortion of history and appropriation of culture, distortion and promotion of neo-imperialism and militarism in the educational space in the occupied territories,[56] and illegal transfer and deportation of Ukrainian children[57] resulting in the deprivation of their national identity. All this indicates the desire to destroy Ukrainian culture and Ukrainian identity and the denial of the right to the existence of the Ukrainian nation.

The physical destruction of Ukraine's material cultural heritage became an integral part of Russia's full-scale invasion of Ukraine. Director of the USAID Mission in Ukraine, James Hope, at the opening of the "Postcards from Ukraine" project of the Ukrainian Institute, noted that "Russia's malicious, targeted destruction of Ukrainian cultural monuments is a huge loss for Ukraine, Europe, and the whole world. By trying to erase the culture and history of Ukraine, the Kremlin seeks to erase the very concept of the Ukrainian nation."[58]

According to the Ministry of Culture and Information Policy of Ukraine, from February 24, 2022, to April 25, 2024, the Russian Federation destroyed or damaged 1,062 cultural heritage objects.[59]

The list of cultural infrastructure objects that were destroyed or damaged due to Russian aggression is more exhaustive and includes 1,938 objects, including 113 museums and galleries, 154 art education institutions, and 689 libraries. The greatest losses and damage to the cultural infrastructure were experienced in the Donetsk, Kharkiv, Kherson, Kyiv, Mykolaiv, Luhansk, and Zaporizhia regions and Kyiv.[60] The attack of the Russian Armed Forces on the Kharkiv printing house "Faktor-druk," with the death of its employees, the destruction of printing facilities and 50,000 books[61] of "Vivat,"[62] "Ranok" ("Morning"),[63] and "Klub simeinoho dozvillia" ("Family Leisure Club")[64] on May 23, 2024, is not included in these figures but is definitely an attack on Ukrainian culture.

Religion is also a victim of Russian aggression, both freedom of religion[65] and religion as part of the spirituality and identity of the Ukrainian people.[66] The Russian occupation authorities restrict the activities of religious organizations in the controlled territories.[67] At least 580 religious buildings were damaged or completely destroyed after February 24, 2022, according to the Religion on Fire project as of the end of May 2024. Among them, at least thirteen objects have the status of monuments of regional importance and five have monuments of national importance.[68]

According to the experts of the KSE Institute project "Russia will pay," as of the beginning of 2024, direct losses caused to the spheres of culture, religion, and tourism amount to 2.4 billion dollars.[69] As of December 31, 2023, according to the Third Rapid Damage and Needs Assessment (RDNA3), the total damage caused to Ukrainian cultural heritage and objects is estimated at USD 2.85 billion.[70]

As of April 10, 2024, UNESCO has verified damage to 351 sites since February 24, 2022—129 religious sites, 157 buildings of historical and/or artistic interest, thirty-one museums, nineteen monuments, fourteen libraries, and one archive.[71] UNESCO has published a new assessment of the impact of the war on the country's culture and tourism sectors. The total cost of the damage to these sectors is estimated at nearly $3.5 billion, and almost $9 billion will be needed over the next ten years to enable them to recover.[72]

Architectural monuments and objects of monumental art, monuments, religious buildings, places of memory, etc. are subjected to direct, disproportionate, and indiscriminate attacks. Among them are the Holy Dormition Svyatogorsk Lavra, the Mariupol Drama Theater, the Kharkiv National Academic Theater of Opera and Ballet named after M. V. Lysenko, the building of the V. V. Tarnovsky Museum of Ukrainian Antiquities, and many others.

Special attention should be paid to alleged targeted attacks on museums and museum collections, which are a concentrated reflection of Ukrainian history and culture, the embodiment of the cultural heritage of Ukraine. As a result of a rocket attack, the National Literary and Memorial Museum of H. S. Skovoroda, a Ukrainian mystic philosopher and theologian of the eighteenth century, was utterly destroyed, as a result of artillery shelling by the Russian Armed Forces, the Ivankiv Historical and Local History Museum burned down, and the Arkhyp Kuindzhi Art Museum was destroyed as a result of aerial bombardment.[73]

Probable International Legal Qualification of Violations by the Russian Federation of the Norms of International Law Regarding Cultural Heritage during the Aggression against Ukraine

The Russian Federation has violated many mandatory norms of international law regarding Ukraine. These include those related to cultural heritage. Cultural identity is a constituent basis of the individual's rights, his/her rights to language, self-expression, freedom of opinion, and freedom of religion. As an aggressor state, the Russian

Federation bears full responsibility for all the damages caused to the cultural heritage of Ukraine.

The Russian Federation violated its obligations under the International Convention on the Elimination of All Forms of Racial Discrimination of 1965, recorded in the Judgment of the International Court of Justice dated January 31, 2024.[74] Para. 404 of the ICJ Judgment in Ukraine v. Russia (CERD and ICSFT) establishes that the ICJ "Finds that the Russian Federation, by how it has implemented its educational system in Crimea after 2014 with regard to school education in the Ukrainian language, has violated its obligations under Articles 2, paragraph 1 (a), and 5 (e) (v) of the International Convention on the Elimination of Racial Discrimination."[75]

The Russian Federation is also responsible for violations of the treaty and customary norms of international humanitarian law, particularly those that protect cultural property during an international armed conflict. Several serious violations of international humanitarian law regarding the cultural property of Ukraine committed by the Russian Federation during the international armed conflict provoked by the aggression of the Russian Federation can be singled out.

We will describe below four main groups of violations of international humanitarian law by the Russian Federation in relation to cultural property committed after the start of the full-scale invasion of Ukraine.

The first group includes damage to cultural property as a result of attacks on civilian objects or indiscriminate/disproportionate attacks.[76] This is the largest group of violations.[77] A dark symbol of a large-scale war crime and a crime against humanity by the Russian Armed Forces is the bombing of the Mariupol Drama Theatre with a significant number of civilians, which was also under the special protection of norms protecting cultural property.

These violations also include missile attacks by the Russian Armed Forces on Odesa, because of which civilian objects located in the central part of the city, including museums and historical monuments, were massively damaged. As a result of the attack of the Russian Armed Forces on Odesa on July 20, 2023, twenty-nine monuments of cultural heritage of national and local significance were damaged by the Oniks missile. Among them are objects included in the UNESCO World Heritage protection zone: the historical center of Odesa and its buffer zone.[78] The Odesa Literary Museum,[79] the Odesa Archaeological Museum,[80] the Odesa Museum of Western and Eastern Art,[81] the House of Scientists,[82] architectural landmarks, and the Holy Transfiguration Cathedral of the Ukrainian Orthodox Church (Moscow Patriarchate). This and previous attacks by the Armed Forces of the Russian Federation drew condemnation from UNESCO.[83]

Russia is causing damage due to direct attacks on cultural property as objects under special protection of international humanitarian law. Among such cases, the most "famous" are the destruction of the National Literary and Memorial Museum of H. S. Skovoroda and the Kupyan Museum of Local History as a result of direct missile attacks by the Russian Armed Forces, artillery shelling by the Russian Armed Forces and the subsequent fire of the Ivankiv Historical Museum with a unique collection of paintings by Maria Priymachenko, and the destruction of the Arkhyp Kuindzhi Art Museum as a result of aerial bombardment.[84]

The second group includes destruction or damage to cultural property in the territory of Ukraine temporarily occupied by the Russian Federation. There is no doubt that there is a significant number of such cases before and after the full-scale invasion. However, their identification is complicated due to the lack of access and availability of reliable information from the territories of Ukraine temporarily occupied by the Russian Federation. First of all, these are the actions of the Russian Federation in the temporarily occupied Crimea since 2014, a typical example of which is the Ancient City of Tauric Chersonese and its Chora, Bagçesaray Palace of the Crimean Khans, archaeological excavations that continue throughout the entire period of occupation.

The third group is related to the violations after the full-scale invasion of the Russian Federation into Ukraine. Such cases were often accompanied by the looting of museums, as happened in the Kherson Museum of Local History, the Museum of Weaving (Kyiv Region), and the Sniguriv Historical and Local History Museum. Acts of vandalism include the actions of persons who defaced the exhibition of the People's Museum of Marshal Rybalka.[85]

The fourth group includes damage to cultural objects due to the Kakhovka Hydro Power Plant dam explosion on June 6, 2023. These actions of the Russian Armed Forces, among other things, fell under the qualification of "large-scale destruction and appropriation of property not caused by military necessity and committed illegally and senselessly," which is a serious violation of international humanitarian law. As a result of the explosion and subsequent large-scale flooding, which caused an ecological and humanitarian disaster, five museums, ten libraries, a significant number of architectural monuments, and archaeological monuments were damaged or destroyed.[86]

Appropriation and Looting of Cultural Property in the Territory of Ukraine Temporarily Occupied by the Russian Federation

The number, scale, and severe violations of international humanitarian law testify, among other things, to the Russian Federation's neocolonial policy regarding Ukraine's cultural heritage. The status of about 85,000 cultural property objects in the territories of Ukraine occupied by the Russian Federation is unknown.[87]

In particular, with regard to museum collections, the actions of the perpetrators fell into two patterns: the seizure and appropriation of cultural property by individuals (Russian military or representatives of the occupation administration), who used the situation of occupation and the situation of coercion as favorable for committing any actions regarding cultural property, as well as conditions that contribute to their impunity; organized (planned) removal of cultural property from museums in the occupied territory and transfer of these values to other parts of the occupied territory of Ukraine or the Russian Federation, in particular to museum institutions under the jurisdiction of the Russian Federation.[88]

Among the most striking examples are the abduction and removal by the Russian occupation authorities of paintings and sculptures from the Arkhyp Kuindzhi Art Museum, artifacts from the Mariupol Museum of Local History,[89] the Melitopol City Museum of Local History, the Kherson Regional Museum of Local History, and almost the entire collection from the Kherson Regional Art Museum named after O. O. Shovkunenko.[90] In these and other cases, the Russian Federation violates its obligations under international humanitarian law to prohibit the export of cultural values from the territory occupied during the armed conflict. It carries out illegal export of cultural values, including to the Russian Federation.

The organized nature of the specified actions of the Russian occupation authorities may indicate not only the violation of the norms of international humanitarian law regarding the protection of cultural property and the commission of war crimes but also a broader context related to the extermination, distortion, and appropriation of the history and culture of Ukraine, the implementation of cultural genocide of Ukrainians according to R. Lemkin, which is consistent with the strategy of Russian aggression aimed at the destruction of the Ukrainian nation through the destruction and appropriation of objects of cultural heritage.

This is also confirmed by the fact that the analysis of satellite maps shows that Russia deliberately attacks educational and cultural facilities, including universities and museums. Thus, the legal qualification of the specified events related to the destruction or removal (theft) of cultural property may go beyond international humanitarian law violations.[91]

In the territories of Ukraine occupied by the Russian Federation, despite the norms of international law, the occupying power restricts and prohibits the use of the Ukrainian language and Ukrainian-language books, destroys such books,[92] introduces education in the Russian language and with a Russian ideological direction,[93] distorting the history of the Ukrainian people.[94] Such actions, together with the statements of the political and military leadership of the Russian Federation, testify to the existence of the official policy of the Russian state regarding the non-recognition of the Ukrainian people's right to self-identification, self-determination, the erasure of cultural identity, and the destruction of Ukrainians as a nation.

In particular, it may constitute a violation of the main provisions of international human rights law, the Convention (IV) respecting the Laws and Customs of War on Land and its annex: Regulations concerning the Laws and Customs of War on Land (The Hague, October 18, 1907), International Convention on the Elimination of All Forms of Racial Discrimination (1965). Also, these facts, with a high probability, indicate the presence of genocidal intent in the actions of the political and military leadership of the Russian Federation, which means Russia's violation of the Convention on the Prevention and Punishment of the Crime of Genocide (1948). This description of the actions of the Russian Federation is contained, in particular, in the Statement of the Verkhovna Rada of Ukraine, "On the Russian Federation's Commitment of Genocide in Ukraine."[95]

Alleged Criminal Offenses Committed against the Cultural Property of Ukraine, Committed in the Context of an International Armed Conflict, Are Duly Documented by Ukrainian Law Enforcement Agencies

Serious violations of international humanitarian law committed by any persons against protected persons and objects, in particular, Ukraine's cultural property, should be considered war crimes. Criminal accountability for war crimes is provided in Article 438, "Violation of laws and customs of war," of the Criminal Code of Ukraine.[96]

The total number of criminal proceedings regarding war crimes committed during the full-scale invasion of the Russian Federation in Ukraine is about 130,000. Among them, there are also proceedings related to the damage to cultural property as civilian objects, primarily during indiscriminate and disproportionate attacks and war crimes against persons committed on the grounds of denial of Ukrainian identity.

In particular, as part of the policy of erasing religious identity and Russification of the temporarily occupied territories, the Russian occupying power has systematically attacked religious groups in the regions of Ukraine occupied by the Russian Federation for almost ten years in Crimea and in occupied territories of Eastern Ukraine, creating such a practice in the territories of Ukraine occupied after 2022. Such actions of the Russian occupation authorities cover a wide range of crimes against humanity and war crimes.

On June 5, 2024, the Security Service of Ukraine served a notice of suspicion on Ivan Panchenko, commander of the 159th Fighter Aviation Regiment of the Western Military District of the Russian Armed Forces, who ordered an air strike on the Hryhorii Skovoroda National Museum in the Kharkiv region. As a result of the airstrike, the museum building was severely damaged, and one employee was seriously injured. On the basis of the evidence gathered, the investigators of the Security Service of Ukraine served Ivan Panchenko in absentia with a notice of suspicion under Article 28(2) and Article 438(1) of the Criminal Code of Ukraine (violation of the laws and customs of war, giving orders to commit such acts by prior conspiracy).[97]

The Prosecutor General's Office of Ukraine has established a specialized unit for procedural management of crimes against cultural heritage. Currently, about eighty episodes that are directly related to alleged war crimes against cultural property committed during the full-scale invasion of the Russian Federation into Ukraine will be investigated.

Law enforcement agencies of Ukraine are conducting pre-trial investigations in two dozen criminal proceedings on the facts of intentional destruction, destruction or damage to historical or cultural monuments, illegal conducting of search and archaeological works, removal of cultural values from the temporarily occupied territory of the Autonomous Republic of Crimea and the city of Sevastopol, which were committed from the moment of the occupation of Crimea since 2014. Procedural management of the pre-trial investigation of these criminal proceedings is carried out by the Prosecutor's Office of the Autonomous Republic of Crimea and the city of Sevastopol.

Within the International Board of Experts framework at the Prosecutor General's Office of Ukraine, a working group on combating crimes committed against objects of cultural heritage has been created. The group includes representatives of state bodies and institutions, representatives of civil society, and international and national experts.

Investigators, prosecutors, and security sector employees are trained on issues related to crimes against cultural heritage, particularly by the Consultative Mission of the European Union on reforming the civil security sector of Ukraine,[98] the Ukrainian expert environment.[99]

International cooperation in criminal cases regarding war crimes committed in the context of the Russian Federation's aggression against Ukraine is developing, including the fight against crimes committed by representatives of the Russian Federation against the cultural heritage of Ukraine. Law enforcement agencies of Ukraine and representatives of the Art Crime Team of the US Federal Bureau of Investigation plan to create a joint operational group, as well as training of the Ukrainian experts.[100]

Ukraine has recognized the jurisdiction of the International Criminal Court in accordance with Article 12(3) of the Rome Statute and actively cooperates with it. War crimes against the cultural property of Ukraine fall under the jurisdiction of the International Criminal Court.

In March 2024, the Prosecutor's Office of the Autonomous Republic of Crimea and the city of Sevastopol sent fourteen submissions from Ukraine to the International Criminal Court regarding alleged war crimes and crimes against humanity committed by the Russian occupation authorities of Crimea based on the facts of persecution of members of religious communities.[101]

Reaction of the International Community to Violations of International Law by the Russian Federation in Relation to Cultural Property during the Aggression against Ukraine

These violations are condemned at the international level, primarily by UNESCO. On March 18, 2022, the Committee for the Protection of Cultural Property in the Event of Armed Conflict at the 2nd Extraordinary Meeting adopted the Declaration on the protection of cultural heritage in Ukraine, where, in particular, it called on Russia to comply with its obligations under the Hague Convention on the Protection of Cultural Property in the Event of Armed Conflict (1954) and to ratify the Second Protocol to it. The Russian Federation was also called upon to stop any forms of robbery, misappropriation, and vandalism directed against Ukrainian cultural values and to refrain from requisitioning them.[102]

UNESCO is reacting to specific violations of the Russian Federation's obligations to protect cultural values during an armed conflict,[103] and it is conducting a preliminary damage assessment for cultural properties by cross-checking the reported incidents with multiple credible sources. UNESCO is also developing, with its partner organizations, a mechanism for independent, coordinated assessment of data in Ukraine, including satellite image analysis, in line with provisions of the Hague Convention for the Protection of Cultural Property in the Event of Armed Conflict (1954).[104]

On January 25, 2023, the World Heritage Committee decided to inscribe the Historic Centre of Odesa (Ukraine) on the World Heritage List. This decision recognizes the outstanding universal value of the site and the duty of all humanity to protect it. Given the threats to the city since the beginning of the full-scale invasion, the World Heritage Committee has used an emergency procedure provided in the Operational Guidelines of the World Heritage Convention. In parallel with the process of inscribing the Historic Centre of Odesa on the World Heritage List, UNESCO implemented emergency measures on the ground to help protect the site. Since the beginning of the full-scale invasion, UNESCO has notably ensured the repairs to damages inflicted on the Odesa Museum of Fine Arts and the Odesa Museum of Modern Art. The organization provided equipment for the digitization of nearly 1,000 works of art and the documentary collection of the Odesa State Archives. Equipment was also delivered to protect the buildings as well as the open-air works of art.[105]

On the Extended 45th Session of the World Heritage Committee held in Riyadh, Saudi Arabia, from 10 to September 25, 2023, relevant Additions to the List of World Heritage in Danger were made and now include: "Kyiv: Saint Sophia Cathedral and Related Monastic Buildings and Lavra of Kyiv-Pechersk" and "Lviv—the ensemble of the historical center (Ukraine)."[106]

UNESCO is also mobilized in Ukraine to protect heritage by preventing destruction and looting, assessing the damage to alert the international community, and fighting against the illicit trafficking of cultural property.[107]

On July 15, 2022, a meeting of the UN Security Council in the Arria format with the topic "Destruction of Cultural Heritage as a Result of Russian Aggression against Ukraine" was held. Lazar Assomo, Director of the UNESCO World Heritage Center, noted that war affects not only material heritage but the entire cultural sector of Ukraine. In particular, the mass displacement of the population threatens the protection of intangible heritage.[108] During the meeting, the Ukrainian side noted that the deliberate attacks on the cultural heritage of Ukraine are an attempt by Russia to erase Ukrainian identity, and the cultural heritage of the entire country, both tangible and intangible, is now under attack.[109]

In the Reports on violations of international humanitarian law and human rights law, war crimes, and crimes against humanity committed in Ukraine, prepared by the OSCE expert mission, the paragraphs "Cultural heritage and religious buildings" are included.[110] Regarding stolen cultural property, the Mission emphasizes "that the theft or illegal trade of artifacts and museum collections, if established, violates both IHL and IHRL." Neighboring states, as well as the international community, the OSCE emphasizes, "must remain vigilant" because "approximately 2,000 art objects were stolen. There are special squads that search for and remove antiquities, such as Scythian artifacts, from archaeological sites with the aim of transporting these objects to Russia."[111]

Measures Taken by Ukraine to Protect Cultural Property during the International Armed Conflict Provoked by the Aggression of the Russian Federation against Ukraine and the Implementation of Norms of International Humanitarian Law

Ukraine closely cooperates with UNESCO, is a member of the Committee for the Protection of Cultural Property in the Event of Armed Conflict, has actively participated in its work[112] since December 2021, and was elected to the World Heritage Committee in 2023.

To increase the level of protection of cultural objects, Ukraine activated the inclusion of the historical center of Odesa in the World Heritage List,[113] and on January 25, 2023, UNESCO decided favorably. Such inclusion will serve as a means of attracting additional global attention to its protection and a mechanism for using additional means of documenting and investigating actions against such objects and, notably, obtaining additional assistance for their protection and restoration.[114] These mechanisms were already used during attacks on the historic center of Odesa in the summer of 2023.

Ukraine provided enhanced protection of twenty objects central to its cultural values in accordance with the Second Protocol to the Hague Convention of 1954 for the Protection of Cultural Property in the Event of Armed Conflict (The Hague, March 26, 1999). At Ukraine's request, protection was granted at an extraordinary session of the Committee for the Protection of Cultural Property in the Event of Armed Conflict on 09/07/2023. The committee provisionally inscribed twenty cultural properties in Ukraine on the International List of Cultural Property under Enhanced Protection, including the Saint-Sophia Cathedral and Related Monastic Buildings (Kyiv), Kyiv-Pechersk Lavra, the Ensemble of the Historic Centre (L'viv), the Odesa National Academic Opera and Ballet Theater, and others.[115] Later, five more objects were included in the list.[116] This creates a higher threshold of negative informational, political, and legal consequences for the aggressor in the case of attempted attacks on cultural property objects under enhanced protection and will testify to Ukraine's conscientious fulfillment of its obligations under the Protocol (1999).

Issues of cultural heritage protection are included in the various bi-national agreements on security cooperation. Fifteen such Agreements have already been signed, and their number is growing. Provisions on the preservation, protection, and reconstruction of the cultural heritage of Ukraine are contained in the Agreement between Ukraine and the Republic of Latvia on long-term support and security obligations dated April 11, 2024.[117] The Agreement on Security Cooperation between Ukraine and Canada, dated February 24, 2024,[118] emphasizes that the participants recognize that Russia's war against Ukraine aims to destroy Ukrainian identity and silence the voices of Ukrainians. The participants will work together to expose the theft of landmarks and other works of art by Russia, as well as Russia's efforts to rewrite history and remove the Ukrainian language from school programs in the temporarily occupied territories of Ukraine. Recognizing that art, history, and language are critical aspects of culture, Canada will, in particular, work with Ukraine to gain access to audiences in the temporarily occupied territories of Ukraine, recognizing that Russia is deliberately targeting radio, television, and other broadcast infrastructure in Ukraine and redirects Internet traffic in temporarily occupied territories, and support and promote Ukrainian voices internationally, as well as support Ukrainian diplomatic presence as Ukraine expands its diplomatic presence in the world.

The Agreement on Security Cooperation between Ukraine and the Netherlands, dated March 1, 2024,[119] provides that

> Participants recognize that the armed conflict has caused damage to the cultural heritage of Ukraine through negligence, contempt or even targeted attacks on it, motivated by malice or malicious intent. In this context, we recall the UNESCO Hague Convention (and its protocols) on protecting cultural property in the event of armed conflict in 1954. Its observance is one of the main topics of the UNESCO conference, which will be held in The Hague on May 14–15, 2024, on the occasion of the 70th anniversary of the Convention. The Conference will seek to draw attention to the need for increased adherence to and adherence to the Convention and its Protocols, ultimately by all UNESCO Member States (para. 2, para. 1).

Recognizing the importance of cultural heritage in the context of the aggression of the Russian Federation against Ukraine, a draft law was prepared to supplement the list of fundamental national interests of Ukraine contained in the Law of Ukraine "On the National Security of Ukraine" with the provision of the following content: "the preservation of the cultural heritage of Ukraine and the national memory of the Ukrainian people as the main elements of the formation of its identity, consolidation, and development of the Ukrainian nation."[120]

On February 29, 2024, Ukraine held a High-Level Experts Conference, "United for Justice. United for Heritage." The event was devoted to numerous cases of destruction of cultural heritage due to Russian aggression. It brought together a wide range of political and legal experts. Its main goal was to consolidate the efforts of the international community to assess the damages caused by the war to Ukraine's cultural heritage.[121]

In compliance with the requirements of international humanitarian law, geospatial data of cultural heritage objects and other objects protected by international humanitarian law, which are taken into account when planning military operations, are entered into the situational awareness system "Delta"[122] used by the Ukrainian Defense Forces when conducting military operations. "Delta" is a national military situational awareness system used by Ukraine's Security and Defence Forces. The system is used for operational and combat planning. The system has been created, and the "Objects Protected by International Humanitarian Law" information layer has been updated. This electronic map contains information on more than 60,000 cultural heritage sites. In addition, the "Damages" layer has been created on the same platform, containing documented information on cultural heritage sites and cultural property destroyed or damaged during the armed conflict (almost 400 of them have been entered so far).[123]

Ukraine has launched the Information and Communication System for Accounting of Immovable Objects of the Cultural Heritage of Ukraine, "State Register of Immovable Monuments of Ukraine" ("ePamyatka").[124] The system will allow for the formation of a single array of data on all cultural heritage objects, including those located in temporarily occupied territories. ePamyatka will simultaneously function as a state management tool and an information base about monuments open to the public.[125]

To fully calculate the damage caused by the Russian Federation's aggression against Ukraine, a special state register of destroyed and damaged objects of cultural heritage "will be one of the tools for determining the amount of damage from Russia."[126]

The issues of restoring the cultural sector of Ukraine were considered at the International Conference "The Way to the Recovery of the Cultural Sector of Ukraine" on June 7, 2024, at which more than thirty countries supported the "Vilnius Call to Action for the Recovery of the Cultural Sector of Ukraine," prepared by the Ministries of Culture of Lithuania and Ukraine. They also emphasized the preparatory role of the Vilnius Conference for the Conference on the Recovery of Ukraine 2024, which was held on June 11–12, 2024, in Berlin. In particular, the countries emphasized the intention to promote the integration of culture in all relevant discussions on the restoration of Ukraine, including the Conference on the Recovery of Ukraine in Italy in 2025.[127]

Questions of Compensation for Damage and Restitution of Damage Caused to the Cultural Heritage of Ukraine

The Russian Federation must bear responsibility for the damages caused by its internationally wrongful acts in Ukraine and against Ukraine. Those damages include any damage caused as a result of aggression against Ukraine, including damage to Ukraine's cultural heritage. The Russian Federation must also compensate for the damage caused by violations of international humanitarian law.

Possibilities of applying to an international court or arbitration for compensation for damage to the cultural property of Ukraine caused by aggression against Ukraine are significantly limited due to the lack of jurisdiction of these bodies according to conventions dedicated to the protection of cultural heritage.[128] That means that compensation for the damage caused to Ukraine's cultural property due to international law violations by the Russian Federation will take place in accordance with the general norms of international law regarding the international responsibility of states. Therefore, it is important to carefully and qualitatively document the damage caused to the cultural heritage of Ukraine as a result of the aggression of the Russian Federation.

A separate area of recording the damage and losses caused to Ukraine as a result of the armed aggression of the Russian Federation is the loss of cultural heritage, which includes the loss of cultural heritage and cultural values.[129]

The restitution of cultural property may include all possible conventional and diplomatic mechanisms, including the application of sanctions within the framework of international organizations and individual states to force Russia to return the appropriated cultural values of Ukraine and to compensate for the value of destroyed property.

It is also possible to use the future International Compensation Mechanism for damage, loss, or destruction caused by Russian aggression, provided for by the UN General Assembly resolution of November 14, 2022,[130] to compensate victims for the cost of lost cultural values, if they belonged to individuals and legal entities. The Statute of the Register of Damages for Ukraine has already been approved,[131] and the Register of Damages has started its operations.

At the level of bilateral cooperation, a positive example of the application of administrative procedures is the return of cultural property of Ukraine illegally exported from the temporarily occupied territories of Ukraine, which were tried to be imported into the territory of the United States of America and seized by the US Customs and Border Protection. On September 2, 2022, US Customs and Border Protection officers at the International Mail Office at JFK International Airport seized cultural property that was being illegally smuggled into the United States. Among the stolen valuables were, in particular, Akinaki swords of the Scythian culture of the VI–V centuries BCE (the area of distribution is the forest-steppe, steppe part of Ukraine and the Crimea), a flint polished ax of the III millennium BCE, Polovtsian sabers from the times of the Old Russian state of the XI–XII centuries-, and many other artifacts. US Customs and Border Protection employees identified the items as cultural values of Ukraine. On March 10, 2023, the Embassy of Ukraine in the United States held an official handover ceremony for the return of cultural heritage items of Ukraine.[132] On October 20, 2023, representatives of the ICIP handed over returned archaeological values from the territories temporarily occupied by Russia to the National Reserve "Kyiv-Pechersk Lavra" for temporary storage.[133] Also, cooperation with Europol regarding the tracking and return of cultural values is actively being developed.

The case of "Scythian Gold" testifies to Ukraine's exclusive right to cultural heritage compared to the demands of representatives of the aggressor state and the importance of the consistent defense of national interests in the judicial institutions of third countries, as was the case in the Amsterdam District Court, the Amsterdam Court of Appeal and the Supreme Court of the Netherlands. The Judgement of the Court of Appeal of Amsterdam of October 26, 2021, states,

> Although the museum pieces come from Crimea and can also be regarded as Crimean heritage, they are part of the cultural heritage of Ukraine as the latter has existed as an independent state since 1991. In light of this, the cultural interest in

the preservation of the museum pieces must be considered as an overriding public interest of the State of Ukraine.[134]

Afterword

In conclusion, we will provide a quote that reflects the barbarism, cynicism, and inhumanity of the Russian government, which strives to destroy Ukrainian national identity, Ukrainian culture, and the Ukrainian people. And the strength of this people is contained in the words of the schoolboy M.,[135] despite the danger of persecution, he sent his essay from the territory of Ukraine occupied by Russia to the All-Ukrainian Contest of Student Works "Human rights and the rights of the child in conditions of war"[136]:

> Also, in the conditions of occupation, the right to a name and citizenship is also violated. Forced change of documents under the threat of reprisal (how my parents cope with it, I don't know . . .), constant propaganda from everywhere about the "great and mighty," the ban on getting an education (but despite everything, we fight). This is all so that we forget our roots, lose our Ukrainian identity, become like them. I don't want to, and I won't. My parents taught me to be worthy, I am a UKRAINIAN.[137]

Notes

1 Raphael Lemkin's, *Axis Rule in Occupied Europe: Laws of Occupation—Analysis of Government—Proposals for Redress* (Washington, DC: Carnegie Endowment for International Peace, 1944), pp. 79–95. http://www.preventgenocide.org/lemkin/AxisRule1944-1.htm.

2 Noelle Higgins, *The Protection of Cultural Heritage During Armed Conflict. The Changing Paradigms* (New York:Routledge, Taylor & Francis Group, 2020), p. 48.

3 Toman Jiri, *The Protection of Cultural Property in the Event of Armed Conflict* (Dartmouth Publishing Company: Legal Monographs and Treatises, 1996), pp. 10–11, 20–1.

4 Статья Владимира Путина "Об историческом единстве русских и украинцев" [Vladimir Putin's article "On the historical unity of Russians and Ukrainians"]. http://www.kremlin.ru/events/president/news/66181.

5 "Russia's disregard for basic principles of humanitarian law and its human rights obligations, the Independent International Commission of Inquiry on Ukraine said in its report published on Friday. The Commission found new evidence that Russian authorities have committed violations of international human rights and international humanitarian law, and corresponding war crimes, in areas that came under their control in Ukraine." See: Ukraine: UN Commission concerned by continuing patterns of violations of human rights and international humanitarian law. https://www.ohchr.org/en/press-releases/2024/03/ukraine-un-commission

-concerned-continuing-patterns-violations-human-rights; "In its previous reports, the Commission has found that Russian authorities have committed a wide range of violations of international human rights law and international humanitarian law in many regions of Ukraine and in the Russian Federation. Many of those amount to war crimes." Statement by Erik Møse, Chair of the Independent International Commission of Inquiry on Ukraine, to the General Assembly Third Committee, New York, October 25, 2023. https://www.ohchr.org/en/statements/2023/10/statement-erik-mose-chair-independent-international-commission-inquiry-ukraine; Also see: Report of the Independent International Commission of Inquiry on Ukraine. Human Rights Council, A/HRC/55/66, March 18, 2024. https://www.ohchr.org/sites/default/files/documents/hrbodies/hrcouncil/coiukraine/a-hrc-55-66-aev.pdf; Report of the Independent International Commission of Inquiry on Ukraine, Human Rights Council, A/78/540, October 19, 2023. https://www.ohchr.org/sites/default/files/documents/hrbodies/hrcouncil/coiukraine/A-78-540-En.pdf; Report of the Independent International Commission of Inquiry on Ukraine to the Human Rights Council. Human Rights Council, A/HRC/52/62, September 25, 2023. https://documents.un.org/doc/undoc/gen/g23/049/73/pdf/g2304973.pdf?token=kwW053snSExCOGGyRs&fe=true; Report of the OSCE Moscow Mechanism's mission of experts entitled "Report on Violations of International Humanitarian and Human Rights Law, War Crimes and Crimes Against Humanity Committed in Ukraine Since 24 February 2022." April 13, 2022. https://www.osce.org/files/f/documents/f/a/515868_0.pdf; A. Haque, "An Unlawful War," *AJIL Unbound*116 (2022): 155–9. doi:10.1017/aju.2022.23; Grignon J. International Law and the War in Ukraine. Institut Montaigne, https://www.institutmontaigne.org/en/expressions/international-law-and-war-ukraine

6 M. Holder, "Russia's Invasion Aims to Erase Ukrainian Cultural Identity." Atlantic Council, 2024. https://www.atlanticcouncil.org/blogs/ukrainealert/russias-invasion-aims-to-erase-ukrainian-cultural-identity/; L. Gerntholtz, "Ukrainian Culture Under Attack: Erasure of Ukrainian Culture in Russia's War Against Ukraine." PEN America, https://pen.org/report/ukrainian-culture-under-attack/.

7 The international armed conflict caused by the aggression of the Russian Federation against Ukraine began no later than February 20, 2014, with the occupation of Crimea. This qualification is of a legal nature, based on Common Article 2 of the Geneva Conventions of August 12, 1949, and is not in doubt. Russia's full-scale invasion of Ukraine on February 24, 2022, was the next stage of this single international armed conflict and a continuation of Russia's aggression against Ukraine.

8 Commissioner draws attention to Crimean Tatars' struggle for human rights. Report, April 18, 2023, https://www.coe.int/en/web/kyiv/-/commissioner-draws-attention-to-crimean-tatars-struggle-for-human-rights; Annexation of Crimea breaches international law. Global Affairs Canada, Statement, July 28, 2018, https://www.canada.ca/en/global-affairs/news/2018/07/annexation-of-crimea-breaches-international-law.html; K. Busol, "Crimea's Occupation Exemplifies the Threat of Attacks on Cultural Heritage," *Chatham House*, August 26, 2021, https://www.chathamhouse.org/2020/02/crimeas-occupation-exemplifies-threat-attacks-cultural-heritage.

9 Irvin-Erickson D. Raphaël Lemkin, Genocide, Colonialism, Famine, and Ukraine. East/West: Journal of Ukrainian Studies, Volume VIII, No. 1, 2021, P. 196, 199.

10 Російська агресія проти України: культурна спадщина, неоімперіалізм і міжнародне право [Russian Aggression against Ukraine: Cultural Heritage, Neo-imperialism and International Law] / Аблялімова-Чийгоз Е.Н., Бусол К.І., Коваль Д.О., Яшний Д.В. Кримський інститут стратегічних досліджень, 2023, https://ciss.org.ua/files/site/page_file/tfilee105fec62c46a58e1f59c3512c6e1363.pdf.

11 Російська агресія проти України: культурна спадщина, неоімперіалізм і міжнародне право [Russian Aggression against Ukraine: Cultural Heritage, Neo-imperialism and International Law] / Аблялімова-Чийгоз Е.Н., Бусол К.І., Коваль Д.О., Яшний Д.В. Кримський інститут стратегічних досліджень, 2023, https://ciss.org.ua/files/site/page_file/tfilee105fec62c46a58e1f59c3512c6e1363.pdf.

12 States parties and signatories, ICRC, https://ihl-databases.icrc.org/en/ihl-treaties/hague-conv-iv-1907/state-parties?activeTab=default. In 2015, Ukraine notified the government of the Netherlands that it considers itself bound by the 1907 Convention. The ICRC website gives the date of Ukraine's accession to the Convention as May 29, 2015. However, in our opinion, Ukraine is a party to the Convention by way of succession from the date on which it became binding on the USSR, that is, from November 27, 1909.

13 States parties and signatories, ICRC, https://ihl-databases.icrc.org/en/ihl-treaties/gciv-1949/state-parties?activeTab=default.

14 States parties and signatories, ICRC, https://ihl-databases.icrc.org/en/ihl-treaties/hague-conv-1954/state-parties?activeTab=default.

15 States parties and signatories, ICRC, https://ihl-databases.icrc.org/en/ihl-treaties/hague-prot-1954/state-parties?activeTab=default.

16 States parties and signatories, ICRC, https://ihl-databases.icrc.org/en/ihl-treaties/api-1977/state-parties?activeTab=default.

17 States parties and signatories, ICRC, https://ihl-databases.icrc.org/en/ihl-treaties/hague-prot-1999/state-parties?activeTab=default. Ukraine acceded to this Protocol in 2020 and has been a Party since June 30, 2020.

18 Дмитро Коваль: В ім'я мистецтва: міжнародно-правовий контекстуальний аналіз захисту культурних цінностей у зв'язку зі збройним конфліктом [In the Name of Art: International Legal Contextual Analysis of the Protection of Cultural Property in the Context of Armed Conflict]. (Одеса: Фенікс, 2016), С. 108.

19 States parties and signatories, ICRC, https://ihl-databases.icrc.org/en/ihl-treaties/hague-prot-1999/state-parties?activeTab=default.

20 States Parties, UNESCO, https://www.unesco.org/en/legal-affairs/convention-concerning-protection-world-cultural-and-natural-heritage#item-1.

21 States Parties, UNESCO, https://www.unesco.org/en/legal-affairs/convention-safeguarding-intangible-cultural-heritage.

22 States Parties, UNESCO, https://www.unesco.org/en/legal-affairs/convention-means-prohibiting-and-preventing-illicit-import-export-and-transfer-ownership-cultural.

23 States Parties, UNESCO, https://www.unesco.org/en/legal-affairs/convention-safeguarding-intangible-cultural-heritage.

24 Заява Верховної Ради України до Міжнародного кримінального суду про визнання Україною юрисдикції міжнародного кримінального суду щодо скоєння злочинів проти людяності вищими посадовими особами держави, які призвели до особливо тяжких наслідків та масового вбивства українських

громадян під час мирних акцій протестів у період з 21 листопада 2013 року по 22 лютого 2014 року від 25 лютого 2014 року № 790-VII [Declaration of the Verkhovna Rada of Ukraine to the International Criminal Court on the Recognition by Ukraine of the Jurisdiction of the International Criminal Court over Crimes against Humanity Committed by High-Level State Officials, Resulting in Particularly Grave Consequences and Massacres of Ukrainian Citizens During Peaceful Protests Between 21 November 2013 and 22 February 2014, 25 February 2014, No. 790-VII] / Відомості Верховної Ради України. 2014. № 13. Ст. 230, https://zakon.rada.gov.ua/laws/show/790-18#Text.

25 On April 9, 2014, the Embassy of Ukraine in the Kingdom of the Netherlands requested the Registrar of the ICC to recognise the jurisdiction of the ICC on the basis of the Declaration of the Verkhovna Rada of Ukraine to the International Criminal Court on the Recognition by Ukraine of the Jurisdiction of the International Criminal Court over Crimes against Humanity Committed by Senior State Officials, which resulted in Particularly Grave Consequences and Massacres of Ukrainian Citizens during Peaceful Protests between November 21, 2013, and February 22, 2014. Declaration by Ukraine lodged under Article 12(3) of the Rome Statute, April 9, 2014 № 61219/673/384. *International Criminal Court*. https://www.icc-cpi.int/sites/default/files/declarationRecognitionJuristiction09-04-2014.pdf; on April 17, 2014, the Acting Minister of Foreign Affairs of Ukraine, A. Deshchytsia, submitted to the Registrar a note of recognition of the jurisdiction of the ICC in connection with the above-mentioned resolution of the Parliament of Ukraine. Note Verbale of the Acting Minister for Foreign Affairs of Ukraine, Mr. Andrii Deshchytsia, April 17, 2014, № 72/35-620-1134. *International Criminal Court*, https://www.icc-cpi.int/sites/default/files/itemsDocuments/997/UkraineMFAdocument16-04-2014.pdf; On September 8, 2015, the Minister of Foreign Affairs of Ukraine, P. Klimkin, submitted to the ICC Registrar a declaration on the recognition of the jurisdiction of the ICC pursuant to Art. 12(3) of the Rome Statute, submitted in accordance with the Resolution of the Verkhovna Rada of Ukraine "On the Declaration of the Verkhovna Rada of Ukraine 'on the Recognition by Ukraine of the Jurisdiction of the International Criminal Court over the Commitment of Crimes against Humanity and War Crimes by Senior Officials of the Russian Federation and Leaders of the Terrorist Organizations 'DPR' and 'LPR', which resulted in Particularly Grave Consequences and Mass Murder of Ukrainian Citizens." Declaration by Ukraine lodged under Article 12(3) of the Rome Statute, September 8, 2015. *International Criminal Court*, https://www.icc-cpi.int/sites/default/files/iccdocs/other/Ukraine_Art_12-3_declaration_08015.pdf.

26 Situation in Ukraine. ICC-01/22. Investigation, https://www.icc-cpi.int/situations/ukraine.

27 Верховна Рада України ратифікувала Римський статут Міжнародного кримінального суду та поправки до нього [The Verkhovna Rada of Ukraine ratified the Rome Statute of the International Criminal Court and its amendments]. Прес-служба Апарату Верховної Ради України. Опубліковано 21 серпня 2024, о 17:04, https://www.rada.gov.ua/news/razom/252711.html.

28 Follow-up to decisions and resolutions adopted by the Executive Board and the General Conference at their previous sessions, part I: Programme issues, E.

Follow-up of the situation in the Autonomous Republic of Crimea (Ukraine), https://unesdoc.unesco.org/ark:/48223/pf0000378910.

29 Application of the International Convention for the Suppression of the Financing of Terrorism and of the International Convention on the Elimination of All Forms of Racial Discrimination (Ukraine v. Russian Federation). Judgment of January 31, 2024, International Court of Justice, https://www.icj-cij.org/sites/default/files/case-related/166/166-20240131-jud-01-00-en.pdf.

30 "Ukraine's Cultural Heritage in Crimea: Damage and Destruction," Profile, 2021, https://rchr.org.ua/analytics/informaczijnyj-oglyad-kulturna-spadshhyna-ukrayiny-v-krymu-poshkodzhennya-ta-znyshhennya/.

31 Стан об'єктів культурної спадщини в окупованому Криму (2014–2019) [The State of Cultural Heritage Sites in the Occupied Crimea (2014–2019)] / Аблялімова Е. Н., Яшний Д. В.; за участю Андреюк Є.С., к.ю.н. Бусол К.І., к.ю.н.Коваль Д.О., Левада М. Є.; картографія - Енвер Чашли, https://ppu.gov.ua/wp-content/uploads/2020/03/Stan-kulturnoyi-spadshhyny-Krymu.pdf.

32 Follow-up to decisions and resolutions adopted by the Executive Board and the General Conference at their previous sessions, part I: Programme issues, E. Follow-up of the situation in the Autonomous Republic of Crimea (Ukraine), https://unesdoc.unesco.org/ark:/48223/pf0000378910.

33 Анексована спадщина: скільки культурних скарбів у Криму привласнила Росія? [Annexed Heritage: How Many Cultural Treasures in Crimea Were Appropriated by Russia?], http://www.ucipr.org.ua/ua/?option=com_content&view=article&id=36:ane.

34 O. Ohredko, "What History is Taught to Crimean Children under the Occupation," "Almenda"; Civic Education Center, 2016, https://almenda.org/yaku-istoriyu-vikladayut-krimskim-dityam-v-okupaci%d1%97/.

35 Follow-up to decisions and resolutions adopted by the Executive Board and the General Conference at their previous sessions, part I: Programme issues, E. Follow-up of the situation in the Autonomous Republic of Crimea (Ukraine), https://unesdoc.unesco.org/ark:/48223/pf0000378910.

36 Since April 2014, these separate territories of the Donetsk and Luhansk regions of Ukraine have been under the control of illegal armed formations under the general control of the Russian Federation, and therefore, since the end of April 2014 at the latest, there has been an actual situation of effective control of the Russian Federation (through its proxies), over these Ukrainian territories, that is, its occupation. T. Korotkyi and N. Hendel, *The Legal Status of the Donetsk and Luhansk "Peoples' Republics" // The Use of Force against Ukraine and International Law* (Jus ad Bellum, Jus in Bello, Jus post Bellum: T.M.C. Asser Press, 2018), 145–71.

37 *Міцні обійми Пушкіна: культурна політика росіян на тимчасово окупованих територіях України* [Pushkin's Strong Embrace: The Cultural Policy of Russians in the Temporarily Occupied Territories of Ukraine] (Громадська мережа Опора, 2024), 5–46, https://www.oporaua.org/viyna/doslidzhennya-micni-obiymi-pushkina-kul-turna-politika-rosiyan-na-timchasovo-okupovanih-teritoriyah-ukrayini-25110.

38 Ті, що пережили пекло: свідчення жертв про місця незаконних ув'язнень на Донбасі [Those Who Survived Hell: Testimonies of Victims About Places of Illegal Detention in Donbas] / Коаліція громадських організацій та ініціатив "Справедливість заради миру на Донбасі". Бєлоусов Ю.Л., Кориневич А.О.,

Мартиненко О.А., Матвійчук О.В., Павліченко О.М., Роменський Я.В., Швець С.П.; за редакцією авторів (Київ: ЦП Компринт, 2015), 84 с.; "2020 Country Reports on Human Rights Practices: Ukraine," U.S. Department of State. Bureau of Democracy, Human Rights, and Labor, March 30, 2021, https://www.state.gov/reports/2020-country-reports-on-human-rights-practices/ukraine/.

39 Военнопленные и гражданские заложники Донбасса: в поисках эффективного механизма освобождения [Prisoners of War and Civilian Hostages of Donbass: In Search of an Effective Mechanism of Liberation]. Катриченко Т., 2019, С 10.

40 According to the Report of the Office of the UN High Commissioner for Human Rights for November 16, 2019–February 15, 2020, intimidation, torture, and ill-treatment were used in "Isolation" (there were so-called "press cells" where detainees were intimidated or beaten by cellmates, threatening sexual violence; facts of torture with the use of electric current; rape: eleven of the interviewed detainees were subjected to executions; of the thirty-nine detainees interviewed by OHCHR, thirty were at some stage in Isolation, where they spent between one and 20.5 months, with an average of eight months. See: Report on the human rights situation in Ukraine November 16, 2019 to February 15, 2020, https://www.ohchr.org/sites/default/files/Documents/Countries/UA/29thReportUkraine_EN.pdf.

41 Яку історію викладають кримським дітям в окупації [What history is being taught to Crimean children under occupation]. Охредько О. ЦПГ Альменда, 2016, https://almenda.org/yaku-istoriyu-vikladayut-krimskim-dityam-v-okupaci%d1%97/.

42 Ті, що пережили пекло: свідчення жертв про місця незаконних ув'язнень на Донбасі [Those Who Survived Hell: Testimonies of Victims About Places of Illegal Detention in Donbas]. Коаліція громадських організацій та ініціатив «Справедливість заради миру на Донбасі». Бєлоусов Ю.Л., Кориневич А.О., Мартиненко О.А., Матвійчук О.В., Павліченко О.М., Роменський Я.В., Швець С.П.; за редакцією авторів (Київ: ЦП Компринт, 2015), 84 с.

43 Проголошення "ДНР" і "ЛНР" і право народів на самовизначення: ілюзорний суверенітет чи суверенітет ілюзій [Proclamation of the "DNR" and "LPR" and the Right of Peoples to Self-determination: Illusory Sovereignty or Sovereignty of Illusions]. Т. Р. Короткий, О. О. Мережко, Е. А. Плешко. Українська Революція гідності, агресія РФ і міжнародне право (Київ: К.І.С., 2014), С. 685–717.

44 Міцні обійми Пушкіна: культурна політика росіян на тимчасово окупованих територіях України [Pushkin's Strong Embrace: The Cultural Policy of Russians in the Temporarily Occupied Territories of Ukraine. Public Support] (Громадська мережа Опора, 2024), С. 5–46, https://www.oporaua.org/viyna/doslidzhennya-micni-obiymi-pushkina-kul-turna-politika-rosiyan-na-timchasovo-okupovanih-teritoriyah-ukrayini-25110.

45 Короткий Т. Виклики та загрози для культурної спадщини України в умовах агресії рф проти України [Challenges and Threats to the Cultural Heritage of Ukraine in the Conditions of Russian Aggression against Ukraine]. Т. Короткий, Я. Савченко, Н. Хендель. Український часопис міжнародного права: наук.-практ (журн, 2022), № 4. С. 54–65.

46 Міцні обійми Пушкіна: культурна політика росіян на тимчасово окупованих територіях України [Pushkin's Strong Embrace: The Cultural Policy of Russians

in the Temporarily Occupied Territories of Ukraine. Public Support]. Громадська мережа Опора. 2024. С. 5–46, https://www.oporaua.org/viyna/doslidzhennya-micni-obiymi-pushkina-kul-turna-politika-rosiyan-na-timchasovo-okupovanih-teritoriyah-ukrayini-25110.

47 "Countering the Erasure of Cultural Identity in Ukraine," May 31, 2024, https://pace.coe.int/en/news/9491/countering-the-erasure-of-cultural-identity-in-ukraine-.

48 "Cultural Genocide: Who is Introducing Russian Education into Ukraine's Occupied Territories and How," IMI, https://rososvita.imi.org.ua/.

49 School education: a hidden weapon of the Russian Federation against Ukraine. Study "School Education: A Hidden Weapon of the Russian Federation against Ukraine," N. Vaskivska, K. Korniienko, D. Pidporna, M. Petrovets (Kyiv, 2023), p. 94, https://rchr.org.ua/wp-content/uploads/2024/02/study-school-education-a-hidden-weapon-of-the-russian-federation-against-ukraine.pdf; «Культурна спецоперація», або як росія використовує свою культуру у війні проти України. ["Cultural Special Operation," or How Russia Uses Its Culture in the War against Ukraine], РЦПЛ, https://rchr.org.ua/analytics/kulturna-speczoperacziya-abo-yak-rosiya-vikoristovuye-svoyu-kulturu-u-vijni-proti-ukrayini/; Russia has developed and is sponsoring four schemes for the "denazification" of education in Ukraine—study by IMI. June 1, 2023, https://imi.org.ua/en/news/russia-has-developed-and-is-sponsoring-four-schemes-for-the-denazification-of-education-in-ukraine-i53283; The Russian system of destroying the identity of children in the temporary occupied territories (TOT). Almenda, https://almenda.org/en/rosijska-sistema-znishhennya-identichnosti-ukrainskix-ditej-na-tot-sxema/; Expert conclusions of the study "Textbooks and War: Educational Literature in the Russian Federation as a Tool for Destroying the Identity of Ukrainians," Almenda, September 1, 2023, https://almenda.org/doslidzhennya-pidruchnik-i-vijna-navchalna-literatura-rf-na-okupovanij-teritorii-yak-instrument-znishhennya-identichnosti-ukrainciv/.

50 "Russian Neo-imperialism: Sources, Genesis and Consequences for the Countries of South East Europe," Policy Paper, June 2018, https://www.kas.de/documents/252038/253252/7_dokument_dok_pdf_53135_1.pdf/639ae0e6-8d84-e2ed-fe60-89c665cb1462?version=1.0&t=8.

51 In an interview and in his article, V. Putin emphasizes that "Ukrainians and Russians are basically one people." See: Прямая линия с Владимиром Путиным [Direct line with Vladimir Putin]. Президент России, June 30, 2021, http://www.kremlin.ru/events/president/news/65973; Статья Владимира Путина "Об историческом единстве русских и украинцев" [Vladimir Putin's Article "On the Historical Unity of Russians and Ukrainians"]. Президент России, July 12, 2021, http://www.kremlin.ru/events/president/news/66181. Back in 2008, in his speeches, Putin denied the existence of Ukraine as a separate state. See: Путин – Бушу: "Украина - это не государство" [Putin – Bush: "Ukraine is Not a State"], Українська правда, April 7, 2008, https://www.pravda.com.ua/rus/news/2008/04/7/4437118/; It is more detailed already in the "historical description". Див.: Статья Владимира Путина "Об историческом единстве русских и украинцев" [Vladimir Putin's Article "On the Historical Unity of Russians and Ukrainians"]. Президент России, July 12, 2021, http://www.kremlin.ru/events/president/news/66181.

52 In 2020, the joint efforts of the so-called "L/DPR" and the Russian Federation created the "Russian Donbass" doctrine. Снопок О. Народ Донбасу і культурна зброя росіян [The People of Donbas and the Cultural Weapon of the Russians]. Збруч, https://zbruc.eu/node/118174.

53 "Investigation into the Involvement of the Russian Military in the Murder of Writer Volodymyr Vakulenko," Truth Hounds, 2024, https://truth-hounds.org/en/cases/investigation-into-the-involvement-of-the-russian-military-in-the-murder-of-writer-volodymyr-vakulenko/.

54 Воєнні злочини в Україні: музеї та нематеріальна культурна спадщина під прицілом : звіт за результатами моніторингу ймовірних воєнних злочинів, вчинених проти музеїв та нематеріальної культурної спадщини України під час повномасштабного вторгнення російської федерації в Україну [War Crimes in Ukraine: Museums and Intangible Cultural Heritage under the Crosshairs: A Report Based on the Results of Monitoring of Alleged War Crimes Committed against Museums and Intangible Cultural Heritage of Ukraine during the Full-scale Invasion of the Russian Federation in Ukraine]. Ю. Гончаренко, С. Дяченко, Р. Єделєв, Т. Короткий, І. Назарчук, М. Пашковський, Я. Савченко, Н. Хендель, М. Ющенко; ГО «Фонд підтримки фундаментальних досліджень (Одеса: Фенікс, 2023), С. 27–32.

55 As of May 22, 2024, UNESCO has confirmed damage to 375 sites since February 24, 2022—137 religious sites, 172 buildings of historical and/or artistic interest, thirty-one museums, twenty monuments, fourteen libraries, one archive. Damaged cultural sites in Ukraine verified by UNESCO, https://www.unesco.org/en/articles/damaged-cultural-sites-ukraine-verified-unesco?hub=66116.

56 Expert conclusions of the study "Textbooks and War: Educational Literature in the Russian Federation as a Tool for Destroying the Identity of Ukrainians," Almenda, September 1, 2023, https://almenda.org/en/doslidzhennya-pidruchnik-i-vijna-navchalna-literatura-rf-na-okupovanij-teritorii-yak-instrument-znishhennya-identichnosti-ukrainciv/; The resume of the analytical review "Six+ Grave Violations Committed against Children: Challenges and Consequences of 9 Months of the Russian-Ukrainian War in 2022," Almenda, 2024, https://almenda.org/en/rezyume-analitichnogo-oglyadu-shist-serjoznix-porushen-proti-ditej-vikliki-ta-naslidki-9-misyaciv-rosijsko-ukrainskoi-vijni-2022/; Digest (January–March 2024). "«Universal Soldier», or Education as the Weapon of Russia In the Occupied South of Ukraine," Almenda, 2024, https://almenda.org/en/dajdzhest-sichen-berezen-2024-universalnij-soldat/

57 Report on violations and abuses of international humanitarian and human rights law, war crimes and crimes against humanity, related to the forcible transfer and/or deportation of Ukrainian children to the Russian Federation: ODIHR.GAL/37/23/Rev.1/Corr.1* May 4, 2023, https://www.osce.org/files/f/documents/7/7/542751_1.pdf.

58 Проєкт "Листівки з України" розповість про зруйновані об'єкті культурної спадщини [The "Postcards from Ukraine" Project Will Talk about Destroyed Objects of Cultural Heritage], *Sostav.ua*, https://sostav.ua/publication/pro-kt-list-vki-z-ukra-ni-rozpov-st-pro-zrujnovan-ob-kt-kulturno-spadshchini-91894.html.

59 Через російську агресію в Україні постраждало 1062 пам'ятки культурної спадщини. Міністерство культури і інформаційної політики України [Due

to Russian Aggression in Ukraine, 1,062 Monuments of Cultural Heritage Were Damaged. Ministry of Culture and Information Policy of Ukraine], May 6, 2024, https://mcip.gov.ua/news/cherez-rosijsku-agresiyu-v-ukrayini-postrazhdalo-1062-pamyatky-kulturnoyi-spadshhyny/.

60 1938 об'єктів культурної інфраструктури зазнали пошкоджень чи руйнувань через російську агресію [1,938 Objects of Cultural Infrastructure Were Damaged or Destroyed Due to Russian Aggression]. Міністерство культури та інформаційної політики України, February 5, 2024, https://mcip.gov.ua/news/1938-obyektiv-kulturnoyi-infrastruktury-zaznaly-poshkodzhen-chy-rujnuvan-cherez-rosijsku-agresiyu/.

61 У результаті обстрілу харківської друкарні знищено понад 50 тис книжок: постраждали як мінімум 3 видавництва [As a Result of the Shelling of the Kharkiv Printing House, More than 50,000 Books Were Destroyed: Atleast 3 Publishing Houses Were Affected] / Володимир Тунік-Фриз. Економічна правда, https://www.epravda.com.ua/news/2024/05/24/714182/.

62 https://t.me/vivat_publishing/3990; Книги видавництва Vivat [books of the publishing house "Vivat"], https://vivat.com.ua/vydavnytstva/vivat/.

63 Семерин Х. Видавництва й бібліотеки України під час війни: втрати, виклики, дерусифікація [Semeryn H. Publishing Houses and Libraries of Ukraine during the War: Losses, Challenges, De-Russification]. Фонд «Демократичні ініціативи» імені Ілька Кучеріва, November 11, 2022, https://dif.org.ua/article/vidavnitstva-y-biblioteki-ukraini-pid-chas-viyni-vtrati-vikliki-derusifikatsiya.

64 У результаті обстрілу харківської друкарні знищено понад 50 тис книжок: постраждали як мінімум 3 видавництва [As a Result of the Shelling of the Kharkiv Printing House, More than 50,000 Books Were Destroyed: Atleast 3 Publishing Houses Were Affected] / Володимир Тунік-Фриз. Економічна правда, https://www.epravda.com.ua/news/2024/05/24/714182/.

65 According to human rights groups, Russia's security services routinely monitored prayers at mosques for any mention that Crimea remained part of Ukraine. Russia's security forces also monitored mosques for anti-Russia sentiment and as a means of recruiting police informants, whose secret testimony was used in trials of alleged Hizbut-Tahrir members. All congregations of Jehovah's Witnesses were banned as an "extremist organization." "2023 Country Reports on Human Rights Practices: Ukraine," U.S. Department of State, https://www.state.gov/reports/2023-country-reports-on-human-rights-practices/ukraine/russia-occupied-areas/.

66 "Since Russia launched its full-scale invasion of Ukraine on February 24, 2022, its military has dismantled religious life and stifled religious diversity throughout other parts of Ukraine. On the frontlines of the war, Russian artillery and military forces frequently damaged and destroyed religious buildings and other sites and killed or injured those sheltering or worshiping in these places. In areas under Russian control, de-facto authorities have abducted and tortured religious leaders and enforced the same repressive Russian legal mechanisms that were instituted in Crimea and Donbas. Furthermore, official Russian state discourse justifying and supporting the war has frequently resorted to rhetoric demonizing Jews, distorting the Holocaust, denigrating 'non-traditional' religious groups and the LGBTQI+ community, and characterizing Russia's unprovoked war of aggression in Ukraine as justified based on religion." Issue update: russia's religious freedom violations in

Ukraine. United States Commission on International Religious Freedom, July 2023, https://www.uscirf.gov/sites/default/files/2023-07/2023%20Russias%20Religious%20Freedom%20Violations%20in%20Ukraine%20Issue%20Update_07.05.2023.pdf.

67 Russia-led forces in the occupied areas continued to implement "laws" requiring all religious organizations except the Ukrainian Orthodox Church to undergo "state religious expert evaluations" and reregister with them. "2023 Country Reports on Human Rights Practices: Ukraine," U.S. Department of State, https://www.state.gov/reports/2023-country-reports-on-human-rights-practices/ukraine/russia-occupied-areas/.

68 The report includes data from 2023. Data for 2024 were obtained from project participants (Basauri Zyuzina A.M., Leshchynskyi A., Nikiforov K., Pidhorna L., Sevastianiv U., Fenno I., Khalikov R.). "Релігія в огні": звіт за результатами моніторингу фактів пошкодження та руйнування релігійних споруд внаслідок широкомасштабного російського воєнного вторгнення в Україну (24 лютого 2022 року - 24 лютого 2023 року) ["Religion on FIR": Report on the Results of Monitoring the Damage and Destruction of Religious Buildings as a Result of the Large-scale Russian Military Invasion of Ukraine (February 24, 2022–February 24, 2023)]. Київ, 2023.

69 Звіт про прямі збитки інфраструктури від руйнувань внаслідок військової агресії Росії проти України станом на початок 2024 року [Report on Direct Damage to Infrastructure from Destruction as a Result of Russia's Military Aggression against Ukraine as of the Beginning of 2024], Квітень, 2024, p. c. 10, https://kse.ua/wp-content/uploads/2024/04/01.01.24_Damages_Report.pdf.

70 "Iryna Mudra: Any Damage to Cultural Property is a Damage to the Cultural Heritage of All Humanity," Ministry of Justice of Ukraine, March 1, 2024, https://www.kmu.gov.ua/en/news/iryna-mudra-bud-iaka-shkoda-kulturnii-spadshchyni-ie-zbytkom-kulturnii-spadshchyni-vsoho-liudstva.

71 "Damaged Cultural Sites in Ukraine Verified by UNESCO," UNESCO, February 7, 2024, https://www.unesco.org/en/articles/damaged-cultural-sites-ukraine-verified-unesco?hub=66116.

72 "Ukraine: UNESCO Estimates the Damage to Culture and Tourism after 2 Years of War at $3.5 Billion," UNESCO, February 14, 2024, https://www.unesco.org/en/articles/ukraine-unesco-estimates-damage-culture-and-tourism-after-2-years-war-35-billion.

73 Воєнні злочини в Україні: музеї та нематеріальна культурна спадщина під прицілом: звіт за результатами моніторингу ймовірних воєнних злочинів, вчинених проти музеїв та нематеріальної культурної спадщини України під час повномасштабного вторгнення російської федерації в Україну [War Crimes in Ukraine: Museums and Intangible Cultural Heritage Targeted: Monitoring Report on Alleged War Crimes Committed Against Museums and Intangible Cultural Heritage of Ukraine during the Russian Federation's Full-Scale Invasion of Ukraine] / Ю. Гончаренко, С. Дяченко, Р. Єделєв, Т. Короткий, І. Назарчук, М. Пашковський, Я. Савченко, Н. Хендель, М. Ющенко; ГО "Фонд підтримки фундаментальних досліджень" (Одеса: Фенікс, 2023), С. 45–63.

74 Application of the International convention for the suppression of the financing of terrorism and of the international convention on the elimination of all forms of

racial discrimination (Ukraine v. Russian Federation): Judgment January 31, 2024, ICJ, https://www.icj-cij.org/sites/default/files/case-related/166/166-20240131-jud-01-00-en.pdf.

75 Application of the International convention for the suppression of the financing of terrorism and of the international convention on the elimination of all forms of racial discrimination (Ukraine v. Russian Federation): Judgment January 31, 2024, ICJ, https://www.icj-cij.org/sites/default/files/case-related/166/166-20240131-jud-01-00-en.pdf.

76 Бюро демократичних інститутів та прав людини розкриває серйозні порушення прав людини та МГП в Україні [The Bureau of Democratic Institutions and Human Rights Reveals Serious Violations of Human Rights and IHL in Ukraine]. Звіт Ініціативи з моніторингу від 12 грудня 2023 р. п. 23. Бюро ОБСЄ з демократичних інститутів і прав людини, https://www.osce.org/files/f/documents/a/4/561457.pdf.

77 Воєнні злочини в Україні: музеї та нематеріальна культурна спадщина під прицілом: звіт за результатами моніторингу ймовірних воєнних злочинів, вчинених проти музеїв та нематеріальної культурної спадщини України під час повномасштабного вторгнення російської федерації в Україну [War Crimes in Ukraine: Museums and Intangible Cultural Heritage Targeted: Monitoring Report on Alleged War Crimes Committed Against Museums and Intangible Cultural Heritage of Ukraine during the Russian Federation's Full-Scale Invasion of Ukraine] / Ю. Гончаренко, С. Дяченко, Р. Єделєв, Т. Короткий, І. Назарчук, М. Пашковський, Я. Савченко, Н. Хендель, М. Ющенко; ГО "Фонд підтримки фундаментальних досліджень" (Одеса: Фенікс, 2023), – С. 88–106.

78 Шиян О. Під час ракетного обстрілу Одеси пошкоджено 29 пам'яток архітектури [During the Missile Attack on Odessa, 29 Architectural Monuments Were Damaged], *Zaxid.net.*, July 24, 2023, https://zaxid.net/pid_chas_raketnogo_obstrilu_odesu_poshkodzheno_29_pamyatok_arhitekturi_n1567886; Telegram – канал Міністра культури та інформаційної політики 2020–2023 рр. Олександра Ткаченка [Channel of the Minister of Culture and Information Policy 2020–2023 Oleksandr Tkachenko], "Tkachenko.UA," July 20, 2023, 13:45. https://t.me/otkachenkokyiv/3936.

79 Facebook – сторінка «Одеський літературний музей» ["Odesa Literary Museum" page], https://www.facebook.com/litmuzodessa/ posts/pfbid0bvbiVfe3ANQH7Cd7NtrZF6H9oQcmQDmZpSiRGLWD3zc3sQbNCzeYZvffgPDq396wl?locale=ru_RU; Від нічної атаки російських ракет 20 липня постраждав Одеський літературний музей [The Odesa Literary Museum Was Damaged by the Night Attack of Russian Missiles on July 20], *Офіційний сайт Одеського літературного музею,* https://museum-literature.odessa.ua/project/vid-nichnoyi-ataki-rosijskih-raket-20-lipnya-postrazhdav-odeskij-literaturnij-muzej/.

80 Facebook – сторінка "Міністерство культури та інформаційної політики України" [page "Ministry of Culture and Information Policy of Ukraine"], https://www.facebook.com/MCIPUkraine/posts/591919169758974?ref=embed_post.

81 Пономаренко О. В Одеському археологічному музеї обвалилася стеля після атак РФ [In the Odesa Archaeological Museum, the Ceiling Collapsed after the Attacks of the Russian Federation], *Суспільне. Новини*, September 6, 2023, https://suspilne.media/566957-v-odeskomu-arheologicnomu-muzeiobvalilasa-

stela-pisla-atak-rf/.82 РФ вдарила по Будинку вчених в Одесі: наслідки обстрілу [The Russian Federation Struck the House of Scientists in Odesa: The Consequences of the Shelling], Фоторепортаж. *Еспресо,* July 25, 2023, https://espreso.tv/rf-vdarila-po-budinku-vchenikh-v-odesi-naslidki-obstrilu-fotoreportazh.

83 "Odesa: UNESCO Strongly Condemns Attack on World Heritage Property," UNESCO, July 21, 2023, https://www.unesco.org/en/articles/odesa-unesco-strongly-condemns-attack-world-heritage-propert; "UNESCO Presents Preliminary Results of Its Mission to Odesa," UNESCO, August 8, 2023, https://www.unesco.org/en/articles/unesco-presents-preliminary-results-its-mission-odesa; Бюро демократичних інститутів та прав людини розкриває серйозні порушення прав людини та МГП в Україні [The Bureau of Democratic Institutions and Human Rights Reveals Serious Violations of Human Rights and IHL in Ukraine]. Звіт Ініціативи з моніторингу від 12 грудня 2023 р. п. 23. Бюро ОБСЄ з демократичних інститутів і прав людини, https://www.osce.org/files/f/documents/a/4/561457.pdf.

84 Воєнні злочини в Україні: музеї та нематеріальна культурна спадщина під прицілом: звіт за результатами моніторингу ймовірних воєнних злочинів, вчинених проти музеїв та нематеріальної культурної спадщини України під час повномасштабного вторгнення російської федерації в Україну [War Crimes in Ukraine: Museums and Intangible Cultural Heritage Targeted: Monitoring Report on Alleged War Crimes Committed Against Museums and Intangible Cultural Heritage of Ukraine during the Russian Federation's Full-Scale Invasion of Ukraine]. Ю. Гончаренко, С. Дяченко, Р. Єделєв, Т. Короткий, І. Назарчук, М. Пашковський, Я. Савченко, Н. Хендель, М. Ющенко; ГО "Фонд підтримки фундаментальних досліджень" (Одеса: Фенікс, 2023), С. 107–19.

85 Воєнні злочини в Україні: музеї та нематеріальна культурна спадщина під прицілом: звіт за результатами моніторингу ймовірних воєнних злочинів, вчинених проти музеїв та нематеріальної культурної спадщини України під час повномасштабного вторгнення російської федерації в Україну [War Crimes in Ukraine: Museums and Intangible Cultural Heritage Targeted: Monitoring Report on Alleged War Crimes Committed Against Museums and Intangible Cultural Heritage of Ukraine during the Russian Federation's Full-Scale Invasion of Ukraine]. Ю. Гончаренко, С. Дяченко, Р. Єделєв, Т. Короткий, І. Назарчук, М. Пашковський, Я. Савченко, Н. Хендель, М. Ющенко; ГО "Фонд підтримки фундаментальних досліджень" (Одеса: Фенікс, 2023), С. 120–2.

86 Воєнні злочини в Україні: музеї та нематеріальна культурна спадщина під прицілом: звіт за результатами моніторингу ймовірних воєнних злочинів, вчинених проти музеїв та нематеріальної культурної спадщини України під час повномасштабного вторгнення російської федерації в Україну [War Crimes in Ukraine: Museums and Intangible Cultural Heritage Targeted: Monitoring Report on Alleged War Crimes Committed Against Museums and Intangible Cultural Heritage of Ukraine during the Russian Federation's Full-Scale Invasion of Ukraine]. Ю. Гончаренко, С. Дяченко, Р. Єделєв, Т. Короткий, І. Назарчук, М. Пашковський, Я. Савченко, Н. Хендель, М. Ющенко; ГО "Фонд підтримки фундаментальних досліджень" (Одеса: Фенікс, 2023), С. 123–8.

87 "Ukraine and USA strategize new way to cooperate in investigating russian crimes against cultural heritage. Ministry of Culture and Information Policy of Ukraine, February 19, 2024, https://www.kmu.gov.ua/en/news/ssha-ta-ukraina-rozrobliat-stratehiiu-spivpratsi-shchodo-rozsliduvannia-zlochyniv-rf-proty-kulturnoi-spadshchyny.

88 Воєнні злочини в Україні: музеї та нематеріальна культурна спадщина під прицілом: звіт за результатами моніторингу ймовірних воєнних злочинів, вчинених проти музеїв та нематеріальної культурної спадщини України під час повномасштабного вторгнення російської федерації в Україну [War Crimes in Ukraine: Museums and Intangible Cultural Heritage Targeted: Monitoring Report on Alleged War Crimes Committed Against Museums and Intangible Cultural Heritage of Ukraine during the Russian Federation's Full-Scale Invasion of Ukraine]. Ю. Гончаренко, С. Дяченко, Р. Єделєв, Т. Короткий, І. Назарчук, М. Пашковський, Я. Савченко, Н. Хендель, М. Ющенко; ГО «Фонд підтримки фундаментальних досліджень (Одеса: Фенікс, 2023), С. 129.

89 Воєнні злочини в Україні: музеї та нематеріальна культурна спадщина під прицілом: звіт за результатами моніторингу ймовірних воєнних злочинів, вчинених проти музеїв та нематеріальної культурної спадщини України під час повномасштабного вторгнення російської федерації в Україну [War Crimes in Ukraine: Museums and Intangible Cultural Heritage Targeted: Monitoring Report on Alleged War Crimes Committed Against Museums and Intangible Cultural Heritage of Ukraine during the Russian Federation's Full-Scale Invasion of Ukraine]. Ю. Гончаренко, С. Дяченко, Р. Єделєв, Т. Короткий, І. Назарчук, М. Пашковський, Я. Савченко, Н. Хендель, М. Ющенко; ГО "Фонд підтримки фундаментальних досліджень" (Одеса: Фенікс, 2023), С. 129–53.

90 Воєнні злочини в Україні: музеї та нематеріальна культурна спадщина під прицілом: звіт за результатами моніторингу ймовірних воєнних злочинів, вчинених проти музеїв та нематеріальної культурної спадщини України під час повномасштабного вторгнення російської федерації в Україну [War Crimes in Ukraine: Museums and Intangible Cultural Heritage Targeted: Monitoring Report on Alleged War Crimes Committed Against Museums and Intangible Cultural Heritage of Ukraine during the Russian Federation's Full-Scale Invasion of Ukraine]. Ю. Гончаренко, С. Дяченко, Р. Єделєв, Т. Короткий, І. Назарчук, М. Пашковський, Я. Савченко, Н. Хендель, М. Ющенко; ГО "Фонд підтримки фундаментальних досліджень" (Одеса: Фенікс, 2023), С. 129–53.

91 Воєнні злочини в Україні: музеї та нематеріальна культурна спадщина під прицілом: звіт за результатами моніторингу ймовірних воєнних злочинів, вчинених проти музеїв та нематеріальної культурної спадщини України під час повномасштабного вторгнення російської федерації в Україну [War Crimes in Ukraine: Museums and Intangible Cultural Heritage Targeted: Monitoring Report on Alleged War Crimes Committed Against Museums and Intangible Cultural Heritage of Ukraine during the Russian Federation's Full-Scale Invasion of Ukraine]. Ю. Гончаренко, С. Дяченко, Р. Єделєв, Т. Короткий, І. Назарчук, М. Пашковський, Я. Савченко, Н. Хендель, М. Ющенко; ГО "Фонд підтримки фундаментальних досліджень" (Одеса: Фенікс, 2023), С. 130.

92 ГУР МО України. (2022, 24 березня). Окупаційні війська вилучають та знищують українську літературу та підручники історії [The Occupying

Forces Seize and Destroy Ukrainian Literature and History Textbooks]. Головне управління розвідки М-ва оборони України : офіц. сайт, https://gur.gov.ua/content/okupatsiini-viiska-vyluchaiut-ta-znyshchuiut-ukrainsku-literaturu-ta-pidruchnyky-istorii.html.

93 Occupation authorities imposed Russian as the instructional language in educational institutions of all levels. They forced Ukrainian citizens to enroll their children in schools and preschool facilities that followed the Russian curriculum. Children were taught by teachers and educators from the Russian Federation. If parents did not agree, the occupation administration threatened to remove children from families and place them in boarding schools, where they could be wrongfully adopted by Russian citizens. The occupation administration imposed a curriculum that included a "patriotic education program" and initial military training for schoolchildren. "2023 Country Reports on Human Rights Practices: Ukraine," U.S. Department of State, https://www.state.gov/reports/2023-country-reports-on-human-rights-practices/ukraine/russia-occupied-areas/.

94 Коли звільнимо Крим – що далі: як відновлювати зв'язки з півостровом через систему освіти [When We Liberate Crimea – What's Next: How to Restore Ties with the Peninsula through the Education System], 2024, https://nus.org.ua/articles/koly-zvilnymo-krym-shho-dali-yak-vidnovlyuvaty-zv-yazky-z-pivostrovom-cherezsystemu-osvity/.

95 About the Statement of the Verkhovna Rada of Ukraine "On the Russian Federation Committing Genocide in Ukraine": Постанова Верховної Ради України від 14.04.2022 № 2188-IX, https://zakon.rada.gov.ua/laws/show/2188-20#Text.

96 Article 438 of the Criminal Code of Ukraine is a blanket norm of law. The qualification of criminal violations under this article takes place with the application of the norms of treaties on international humanitarian law.

97 Повідомлення про підозру та повістки про виклик Панченка І.О. на 10.06.2024, 11.06.2024, 12.06.2024 (українською та переклад російською) [Suspicion Notices and Summonses for Panchenko I.O. on 10.06.2024, 11.06.2024, 12.06.2024 (in Ukrainian and translated into Russian)], Офіс Генерального Прокурора, https://www.gp.gov.ua/ua/posts/povidomlennya-pro-pidozru-ta-povistki-pro-viklik-panchenka-i-o-na-10-06-2024-11-06-2024-12-06-2024-ukrayinskoyu-ta-pereklad-rosijskoyu.

98 У Львові пройшли семінари щодо злочинів проти культурної спадщини [Seminars on Crimes against Cultural Heritage Were Held in Lviv], European Union Advisory Mission for Civilian Security Sector Reform Ukraine, червня 6, 2024, https://www.euam-ukraine.eu/ua/news/lviv-hosted-workshops-on-crimes-against-cultural-heritage/.

99 В Тренінговому центрі прокурорів України проведено тренінг "Воєнні злочини проти культурної спадщини України (культурні цінності, музеї, нематеріальна культурна спадщина) особливості кваліфікації та доказування" [The Training Center of Prosecutors of Ukraine Held the Training "War Crimes against the Cultural Heritage of Ukraine (Cultural Values, Museums, Intangible Cultural Heritage) Qualification and Proof Features"], https://www.facebook.com/fundamentalresearchfund/posts/pfbid0kDxofdQxpLSLKgWnKG2dqybxESFEPG7TwZreb3uD1CXoq68diC3tepwm4aT4rJRKl?__cft__[0]=AZXzSSNt9jYOOEhivS4Tk3j4Bk9mov1rNPXrDybxwH3_

hLvPflFbunr4V48QW7FWOieevYt6kK97jy3ILOTWWVsAa6OkNqR9scvydHI0_UIonghyUBdgFAhpYb2gGLkTKWT6sXpBH5--K7S5C-RcybQ_UYcdAYReYpxlYYm4Ba8Q93G3QfP231hCX8MXE7Gwll3p-eU8a98n01-zyWblHxg4&__tn__=%2CO%2CP-R.

100 "Ukraine and USA Strategize New Way to Cooperate in Investigating Russian Crimes against Cultural Heritage," Ministry of Culture and Information Policy of Ukraine, February 19, 2024, https://www.kmu.gov.ua/en/news/ssha-ta-ukraina-rozrobliat-stratehiiu-spivpratsi-shchodo-rozsliduvannia-zlochyniv-rf-proty-kulturnoi-spadshchyny.

101 Окупована релігія: Україна передала до МКС докази вчинення РФ у Криму злочинів проти людства [Occupied Religion: Ukraine Submitted Evidence of Crimes against Humanity by the Russian Federation in Crimea to the International Criminal Court]. Прокуратура Автономної Республіки Крим та міста Севастополя, березня 5, 2024, https://ark.gp.gov.ua/ua/news.html?_m=publications&_t=rec&id=354819&fp=60; Прокуратура АРК передала Міжнародному кримінальному суду нові свідчення злочинів РФ у Криму [The Prosecutor's Office of the Autonomous Republic of Crimea Handed the International Criminal Court New Evidence of Crimes Committed by the Russian Federation in Crimea], Крим. Реалії, березня 6, 2024, https://ua.krymr.com/a/news-prokuratura-ark-sud-oon-zlochyny-rf-krym/32849939.html.

102 Declaration on the protection of cultural heritage in Ukraine. "Committee for the Protection of Cultural Property in the Event of Armed Conflict, 2nd Extraordinary," Paris, March 18, 2022, https://unesdoc.unesco.org/ark:/48223/pf0000380949.

103 "Odesa: UNESCO Strongly Condemns Attack on World Heritage Property," UNESCO, July 21, 2023, https://www.unesco.org/en/articles/odesa-unesco-strongly-condemns-attack-world-heritage-propert; "UNESCO Presents Preliminary Results of Its Mission to Odesa," UNESCO, August 8, 2023, https://www.unesco.org/en/articles/unesco-presents-preliminary-results-its-mission-odesa

104 "Damaged Cultural Sites in Ukraine Verified by UNESCO," UNESCO, February 7, 2024, https://www.unesco.org/en/articles/damaged-cultural-sites-ukraine-verified-unesco?hub=66.

105 "Ukraine: UNESCO Supports Odesa's Heritage and Cultural Life," August 30, 2022, https://www.unesco.org/en/articles/ukraine-unesco-supports-odesas-heritage-and-cultural-life.

106 "World Heritage Committee 2023," UNESCO, https://www.unesco.org/en/world-heritage/committee-2023.

107 "Endangered Heritage in Ukraine: UNESCO Reinforces Protective Measures," UNESCO, https://www.unesco.org/en/articles/endangered-heritage-ukraine-unesco-reinforces-protective-measures.

108 Росія боїться культури України? На засіданні Ради безпеки ООН озвучили дані ЮНЕСКО [Is Russia Afraid of Ukrainian Culture? At a Meeting of the UN Security Council, UNESCO's Data Were Announced], *Радіо Свобода*, https://www.radiosvoboda.org/a/kulturna-spadshchyna-viyna-yunesko/31946538.html.

109 На засіданні Радбезу ООН обговорили знищення Росією культурної спадщини України [Russia's Destruction of Ukraine's Cultural Heritage Was Discussed at the UN Security Council Meeting], http://surl.li/txigq.

110 Звіт про порушення міжнародного гуманітарного права та прав людини, воєнні злочини та злочини проти людяності, вчинені в Україні, починаючи з 24 лютого 2022 року (неоф. перекл.) [Report on Violations of International Humanitarian Law and Human Rights, War Crimes and Crimes against Humanity Committed in Ukraine, Starting from February 24, 2022 (unofficial translation)]. *Організація з безпеки та співробітництва в Європі. Бюро з демократичних інститутів і прав людини*, https://www.osce.org/files/f/documents/5/2/517815.pdf;
Звіт про порушення міжнародного гуманітарного права та прав людини, воєнні злочини та злочини проти людяності, вчинені в Україні (1 квітня - 25 червня 2022 року). (неоф. перекл.) [Report on violations of international humanitarian law and human rights, war crimes and crimes against humanity committed in Ukraine (April 1–June 25, 2022). (unofficial translation)]. *Організація з безпеки та співробітництва в Європі. Бюро з демократичних інститутів і прав людини*, https://www.osce.org/uk/odihr/523811.

111 Звіт про порушення міжнародного гуманітарного права та прав людини, воєнні злочини та злочини проти людяності, вчинені в Україні, починаючи з 24 лютого 2022 року (неоф. перекл.) [Report on violations of international humanitarian law and human rights, war crimes and crimes against humanity committed in Ukraine (April 1–June 25, 2022). (unofficial translation)]. *Організація з безпеки та співробітництва в Європі. Бюро з демократичних інститутів і прав людини*, https://www.osce.org/files/f/documents/5/2/517815.pdf.

112 "UNESCO to Continue Help Ukraine Preserve and Protect Cultural Heritage," https://www.kmu.gov.ua/en/news/yunesko-prodovzhyt-dopomohu-ukraini-zadlia-zberezhennia-i-zakhystu-kulturnoi-spadshchyny.

113 Currently, eight objects are included in the list of world heritage from Ukraine: Kyiv: Saint-Sophia Cathedral and Related Monastic Buildings, Kyiv-Pechersk Lavra; Lviv—the Ensemble of the Historic Centre; Struve Geodetic Arc; Ancient and Primeval Beech Forests of the Carpathians and Other Regions of Europe; Residence of Bukovinian and Dalmatian Metropolitans; Ancient City of Tauric Chersonese and its Chora; Wooden *Tserkvas* of the Carpathian Region in Poland and Ukraine; The Historic Centre of Odesa. Three objects are included in the property inscribed on the List of World Heritage in Danger: Kyiv: Saint-Sophia Cathedral and Related Monastic Buildings, Kyiv-Pechersk Lavra; Lviv—the Ensemble of the Historic Centre; The Historic Centre of Odesa. World Heritage List https://whc.unesco.org/en/list/. There are sixteen objects in the preliminary list, https://whc.unesco.org/en/statesparties/ua/.

114 Воєнні злочини в Україні: музеї та нематеріальна культурна спадщина під прицілом: звіт за результатами моніторингу ймовірних воєнних злочинів, вчинених проти музеїв та нематеріальної культурної спадщини України під час повномасштабного вторгнення російської федерації в Україну [War Crimes in Ukraine: Museums and Intangible Cultural Heritage Targeted: Monitoring Report on Alleged War Crimes Committed Against Museums and Intangible Cultural Heritage of Ukraine during the Russian Federation's Full-Scale Invasion of Ukraine] / Ю. Гончаренко, С. Дяченко, Р. Єделєв, Т. Короткий, І. Назарчук,

М. Пашковський, Я. Савченко, Н. Хендель, М. Ющенко; ГО «Фонд підтримки фундаментальних досліджень. – Одеса : Фенікс, 2023. – С. 156.

115 "Ukraine: 20 Cultural Properties Receive Enhanced Protection by UNESCO's Second Protocol to the 1954 Hague Convention," UNESCO, https://www.unesco.org/en/articles/ukraine-20-cultural-properties-receive-enhanced-protection-unescos-second-protocol-1954-hague.

116 "Cultural Property under Enhanced Protection Ukraine," UNESCO, January 5, 2024, https://www.unesco.org/en/culture/cultural-property-under-enhanced-protection.

117 Угода між Україною та Латвійською Республікою про довгострокову підтримку та безпекові зобов'язання [Agreement between Ukraine and the Republic of Latvia on Long-term Support and Security Obligations], https://www.president.gov.ua/news/ugoda-mizh-ukrayinoyu-ta-latvijskoyu-respublikoyu-pro-dovgos-90189.

118 Угода про співробітництво у сфері безпеки між Україною та Канадою від 24 лютого 2024 року [Agreement on Cooperation in the Field of Security between Ukraine and Canada Dated February 24, 2024], https://www.president.gov.ua/news/ugoda-pro-spivrobitnictvo-u-sferi-bezpeki-mizh-ukrayinoyu-ta-89233.

119 Угода про співробітництво у сфері безпеки між Україною та Нідерландами від 1 березня 2024 року [Agreement on Cooperation in the Field of Security between Ukraine and the Netherlands Dated March 1, 2024], https://www.president.gov.ua/news/ugoda-pro-spivrobitnictvo-u-sferi-bezpeki-mizh-ukrayinoyu-ta-89461.

120 Проект Закону про внесення змін до Закону України "Про національну безпеку України" щодо збереження культурної спадщини України та національної пам'яті [Draft Law on Amendments to the Law of Ukraine "On National Security of Ukraine" on the Preservation of the Cultural Heritage of Ukraine and National Memory], https://itd.rada.gov.ua/billInfo/Bills/Card/41472.

121 Iryna Mudra: Any damage to cultural property is a damage to the cultural heritage of all humanity. Ministry of Justice of Ukraine, posted March 1, 2024, https://www.kmu.gov.ua/en/news/iryna-mudra-bud-iaka-shkoda-kulturnii-spadshchyni-ie-zbytkom-kulturnii-spadshchyni-vsoho-liudstva.

122 "Delta" is the information and communication system "Delta Integration Platform of the Armed Forces of Ukraine," https://delta.mil.gov.ua/wiki/info/#delta_1.

123 Гюндуз Мамедов, Віталій Титич. Як зменшити наслідки війни для культурної спадщини: можуть допомогти ЗСУ [How to Reduce the Impact of War on Cultural Heritage: The Ukrainian Armed Forces Can Help], 8 січня 2024 року. Дзеркало тижня, https://zn.ua/ukr/war/jak-zmenshiti-naslidki-vijni-dlja-kulturnoji-spadshchini-mozhut-dopomohti-zsu.html.

124 Державний реєстр нерухомих пам'яток України [State Register of Immovable Monuments of Ukraine], https://e-pamiatka.gov.ua/.

125 Reconstruction with attention to cultural monuments: Launch of the electronic system of accounting for immovable objects of cultural heritage ePamyatka. Урядовий портал. 1 грудня 2023 року, http://surl.li/uknqw.

126 Denys Shmyhal: All cultural heritage sites affected by russian aggression will be included in a special state register to determine the amount of compensation from Russia. Communications Department of the Secretariat of the CMU, posted February 29, 2024, https://www.kmu.gov.ua/en/news/denys-shmyhal-usi

-postrazhdali-vnaslidok-rosiiskoi-ahresii-obiekty-kulturnoi-spadshchyny-vnesut-do-spetsialnoho-derzhreiestru-dlia-vyznachennia-rozmiriv-kompensatsii-vid-rf.

127 Вільнюський заклик до дій: 30 країн приєднались до плану відновлення культурного сектору України [Vilnius Call to Action: 30 Countries Have Joined the Plan to Restore Ukraine's Cultural Sector], https://mcip.gov.ua/news/vilnyuskyj-zaklyk-do-dij-30-krayin-pryyednalys-do-planu-vidnovlennya-kulturnogo-sektoru-ukrayiny/.

128 Механізми захисту та реституції культурних цінностей у контексті міжнародного збройного конфлікту між РФ і Україною [Mechanisms of Protection and Restitution of Cultural Values in the Context of the International Armed Conflict between the Russian Federation and Ukraine]. Аналітичний звіт. Коаліції "Україна. П'ята ранку." 2023.

129 Порядок визначення шкоди та збитків, завданих Україні внаслідок збройної агресії Російської Федерації [The procedure for determining damage and losses caused to Ukraine as a result of the armed aggression of the Russian Federation]. Затверджено постановою Кабінету Міністрів України від 20 березня 2022. р. № 326. https://zakon.rada.gov.ua/laws/show/326-2022-%D0%BF#Text.

130 Furtherance of remedy and reparation for aggression against Ukraine. United Nations General Assembly Resolution A/RES/ES-11/5, November 14, 2022, https://rd4u.coe.int/documents/358068/372244/A_RES_ES-11_5.pdf/079afc90-b392-a0ab-43ad-41409c7e8aa4?t=1708702069853.

131 Резолюція Комітету міністрів Ради Європи CM/Res(2023)3 про встановлення Розширеної часткової угоди про Реєстр збитків, завданих агресією Російської Федерації проти України (12 травня 2023 року зі змінами від 27 вересня 2023 року [Resolution of the Committees of Ministers of the Council of Europe CM/Res(2023)3 on the establishment of the Expanded Partial Agreement on the Register of Damages Caused by the Aggression of the Russian Federation against Ukraine (May 12, 2023 with amendments dated September 27, 2023].

132 In September 2023, the president of Ukraine, Volodymyr Zelenskyi, during a working visit to the United States, took part in the ceremony of the return of the specified cultural values, illegally exported from the temporarily occupied territories of Ukraine: in his presence, the Minister of Internal Security of the United States, Alejandro Mayorkas, and Ms. Ambassador of Ukraine to the United States, Oksana Markarova, signed the corresponding certificate of transfer of cultural values. США повернули Україні скіфські мечі та половецьку шаблю, які росіяни вивезли з окупованих територій [The USA Returned to Ukraine the Scythian Swords and the Polovtsian Saber, Which the Russians Took from the Occupied Territories] /Ярослав Герасименко, Hromadske, March 11, 2023, https://hromadske.ua/posts/ssha-povernuli-ukrayini-skifski-mechi-tapolovecki-shabli-yaki-rosiyani-vivezli-z-okupovanih-teritorij; США повернули Україні скіфські мечі та половецьку шаблю, які вивезли окупанти [The USA Returned to Ukraine the Scythian Swords and the Polovtsian Saber, Which Were Taken Away by the Occupiers] / Олена Барсукова Українська Правда, March 12, 2023, https://life.pravda.com.ua/society/2023/03/12/253302/; США передали Україні артефакти, викрадені росіянами з тимчасово окупованих територій [[The USA Handed Over to Ukraine the Artifacts Stolen by the Russians from the Temporarily Occupied Territories] / Суспільне Новини, September 22, 2023, https://suspilne.media/577871

-ssa-peredali-ukraini-artefakti-vikradeni-rosianami-z-timcasovookupovanih-teritorij/; Нацзаповідник "Києво-Печерська лавра" отримав на зберігання артефакти, викрадені з окупованих територій [National Reserve "Kyiv-Pechersk Lavra" Received Artifacts Stolen from the Occupied Territories] / Суспільне Новини, October 20, 2023, https://suspilne.media/kyiv/598417-naczapovidnik-kievo-pecerska-lavra-otrimav-na-zberiganna-artefakti-vikradeni-z-okupovanih-teritorij/#:~:text=У%20п'ятницю%2C%2020%20жовтня,яну%20сокиру%20—%20виявили%20за%20кордоном.

133 США повернули Україні скіфські мечі та половецьку шаблю, які росіяни вивезли з окупованих територій [The USA Returned to Ukraine the Scythian Swords and the Polovtsian Saber, Which the Russians Took from the Occupied Territories] /Ярослав Герасименко, Hromadske, March 11, 2023, https://hromadske.ua/posts/ssha-povernuli-ukrayini-skifski-mechi-tapolovecki-shabli-yaki-rosiyani-vivezli-z-okupovanih-teritorij; США повернули Україні скіфські мечі та половецьку шаблю, які вивезли окупанти [The USA Returned to Ukraine the Scythian Swords and the Polovtsian Saber, Which Were Taken Away by the Occupiers] / Олена Барсукова Українська Правда, March 12, 2023, https://life.pravda.com.ua/society/2023/03/12/253302/; США передали Україні артефакти, викрадені росіянами з тимчасово окупованих територій [The USA Handed Over to Ukraine the Artifacts Stolen by the Russians from the Temporarily Occupied Territories] / Суспільне Новини, September 22, 2023, https://suspilne.media/577871-ssa-peredali-ukraini-artefakti-vikradeni-rosianami-z-timcasovookupovanih-teritorij/; Нацзаповідник "Києво-Печерська лавра" отримав на зберігання артефакти, викрадені з окупованих територій [National Reserve "Kyiv-Pechersk Lavra" Received Artifacts Stolen from the Occupied Territories] / Суспільне Новини, October 20, 2023, https://suspilne.media/kyiv/598417-naczapovidnik-kievo-pecerska-lavra-otrimav-na-zberiganna-artefakti-vikradeni-z-okupovanih-teritorij/#:~:text=У%20п'ятницю%2C%2020%20жовтня,яну%20сокиру%20—%20виявили%20за%20кордоном.

134 Para. 3.32.3. of the Judgement of the Court of Appeal of Amsterdam, October 26, 2021, https://uitspraken.rechtspraak.nl/details?id=ECLI:NL:GHAMS:2021:3201.

135 M. is located in the territory of Ukraine occupied by the Russian Federation, so his data are not disclosed for security reasons.

136 All-Ukrainian competition of student works "Human rights and children's rights in conditions of war," held by the Ukrainian Helsinki Union for Human Rights in partnership with the Ministry of Education and Science of Ukraine in 2024, https://osvita-omr.gov.ua/vseukrainskyj-konkurs-uchnivskykh-robit-prava-liudyny-ta-prava-dytyny-v-umovakh-vijny/.

137 M., the laureate of the All-Ukrainian competition of student works "Human rights and children's rights in conditions of war."

Selected Bibliography

Jiri, Toman. *The Protection of Cultural Property in the Event of Armed Conflict* (Dartmouth Publishing Company: Legal Monographs and Treatises, Brookfield, 1996).

Noelle, Higgins. *The Protection of Cultural Heritage During Armed Conflict. The Changing Paradigms* (New York: Routledge, Taylor & Francis Group, 2020).

Sayapin, Sergey and Evhen Tsybulenko (eds.). "The Use of Force Against Ukraine and International Law: Jus ad Bellum, Jus in Bello, Jus Post-Bellum." *East/West* 8, no. 2 (2021): 353–7.

Гончаренко Юлія, Дяченко Сергій, Єделєв Роман, Короткий Тимур, Назарчук Ірина, Пашковський Микола, Савченко Ярослава, Хендель Наталія, Ющенко Маргарита: Воєнні злочини в Україні: музеї та нематеріальна культурна спадщина під прицілом: звіт за результатами моніторингу ймовірних воєнних злочинів, вчинених проти музеїв та нематеріальної культурної спадщини України під час повномасштабного вторгнення російської федерації в Україну [War Crimes in Ukraine: Museums and Intangible Cultural Heritage Targeted: Monitoring Report on Alleged War Crimes Committed Against Museums and Intangible Cultural Heritage of Ukraine during the Russian Federation's Full-Scale Invasion of Ukraine] (ГО "Фонд підтримки фундаментальних досліджень." Одеса: Фенікс, 2023).

Коваль Дмитро: В ім'я мистецтва: міжнародно-правовий контекстуальний аналіз захисту культурних цінностей у зв'язку зі збройним конфліктом [In the Name of Art: International Legal Contextual Analysis of the Protection of Cultural Property in the Context of Armed Conflict]. (Одеса: Фенікс, 2016).

Українська Революція гідності, агресія РФ і міжнародне право [The Ukrainian Revolution of Dignity, Russian Aggression and International Law] (Київ: К.І.С., 2014).

23

Russia's War of Aggression against Ukraine and the Crime of Aggression*

Claus Kreß

The following starting points of this analysis should not be controversial: In 2014, in Crimea, the Russian Federation began to violate the prohibition of the use of force to the detriment of Ukraine. On 24 February 2022, Russia escalated its course of action into a full-scale war of aggression, which is ongoing unabated at the time of writing. Russia's conduct *vis-à-vis* Ukraine thus constitutes a continuing act of aggression which, by its character, gravity and scale constitutes a manifest violation of the Charter of the United Nations.[1] Hereby, Russia has been fulfilling the state conduct element of the international consensus definition of the crime of aggression,[2] enshrined in Article 8 *bis* of the ICC Statute as a result of the diplomatic breakthrough at the first Review Conference on the ICC Statute, held in Kampala in the summer of 2010.[3] As consequence of their role in Russia's aggression, President Putin and some other members of the Russian leadership are under suspicion of having been committing the crime of aggression.[4]

Yet, the ICC cannot presently exercise its jurisdiction over this crime.[5] For, pursuant to Articles 15 *bis* and 15 *ter* of the ICC Statute,[6] crimes of aggression arising out of an act of aggression committed by or against a non-state-party remain beyond the Court's reach, unless the UN Security Council refers the relevant situation to the ICC. In the situation of Ukraine, the ICC's exercise of jurisdiction over the crime of aggression would thus be dependent on a UN Security Council referral. But at least for as long as President Putin holds power, Russia would subject such a draft resolution to the same kind of abusive veto as it did with the Council's draft resolution of February 2022[7] which included a condemnation of Russia's aggression against Ukraine.

A Gap in the International Legal Architecture

To some, this state of affairs is not worrisome: One should be content, so they think, that the ICC can exercise its jurisdiction in Ukraine over genocide, crimes against humanity and war crimes. If seen in that light, the present situation regarding the crime of aggression, is a luxury problem[8] at best. In this essay, however, it is submitted that Russia's aggression against Ukraine has shed a bright light on a gap in the existing international legal architecture with respect to the crime of aggression. In order to make this point, it is not necessary to embrace the well-known statement in the Nuremberg Judgment that waging a crime of aggression is the "supreme international crime."[9] Instead, the following argument starts from the premise that the crime of aggression is not necessarily more heinous than genocide, crimes against humanity or war crimes committed systematically and on a large scale. The following argument does therefore not in any way belittle the enormous significance of the ongoing ICC investigation led by Prosecutor Khan which in 2023 resulted in an arrest warrant of historic importance against President Putin and his commissioner for children's rights Lvova-Belova.[10] Instead, the argument is premised simply on the assertion that the crime of aggression is no less significant than the other crimes and that there may be occasions where it is crucial to prosecute the crime of aggression. It is submitted that Russia's war of aggression against Ukraine is such an occasion.

Certainly, the war of aggression against Ukraine violates that state's sovereignty and territorial integrity as well as the right of self-determination of the Ukrainian people.[11] And certainly, Russia's war of aggression has opened the floodgate, at a minimum, for the commission of horrendous war crimes.[12] But crucially, the legal wrong entailed in Russia's aggression does not end there: It includes all the infringements of fundamental rights of Ukrainians which Russia has caused without violating the international law of armed conflict. The law of international armed conflict provides not only the soldiers of the victim state, but also the soldiers fighting on the side of the aggressor state, with the liberty to kill enemy combatants.[13] The aggressor is also at liberty, under the law of armed conflict, to accept the possibility of unavoidable, non-excessive civilian deaths or injuries as a result of attacks directed against military objects. Countless losses of such kind have been inflicted upon Ukrainians by the Russian aggressor[14] and none of those amount to war crimes, crimes against humanity, or genocide. Only by prosecuting the crime of aggression can Russia's leadership be held criminally responsible for that vast part of the war's violence.

In more general terms, Frédéric Mégret has made the point that, for humanitarian reasons, the law on the conduct of hostilities "launders" a very significant part of the violence in war which means that "war represents a monstrous exception to the notion that all human beings have an inalienable right to life, security, bodily and psychological integrity, freedom of movement etc."[15] Only the crime of aggression ensures the individual criminal responsibility of the leadership of the aggressor state for opening the floodgate to this monstrous exception. For this reason, it is deeply misleading to divide the four crimes under international law into three atrocity crimes on the one hand and the crime of aggression on the other. On the contrary, the crime of aggression is as much an atrocity crime as the other international crimes. The prohibition of aggression does not only protect the rather abstract value of state sovereignty, but also very concrete fundamental human rights of potentially countless human beings, who may suffer and die in a war of aggression.

All this is under threat when the international legal prohibition of aggression is at risk of erosion.[16] This is why a "negative precedent" regarding the crime of aggression

– that is a failure to institute proceedings for that crime – in connection with Russia's aggression against Ukraine, far from being a luxury problem, would be fundamentally detrimental to the international legal order. Robert Jackson, the U.S. chief prosecutor at Nuremberg, had identified the danger of norm erosion after Germany's wars of aggression in all clarity. Hence, Jackson saw the acute need to activate what we would today call the expressive function of international criminal law. In his opening speech in Nuremberg, Jackson made the following pronouncement:

> The ultimate step in avoiding periodic wars, which are inevitable in a system of international lawlessness, is to make statesmen responsible to law. And let me make clear that while this is first applied against German aggressors, the law includes, and if it is to serve a useful purpose it must condemn, aggression by other nations, including those which sit here now in judgment.[17]

The pronouncement of this Nuremberg promise constitutes a shining moment of true United States leadership in international criminal justice.[18] Jackson's promise remains at the core of Nuremberg's legacy. In view of Russia's war of aggression against Ukraine, it should resonate more loudly and strongly than ever since the entry into force of the UN Charter.

The Politics Behind the Gap

The question is why aggression had experienced "a decline from the leading and central crime at Nuremberg and Tokyo to one that only barely made it into the Rome Statute"[19] and why we are left with a gap in the international legal architecture concerning this crime even after the activation of the Kampala amendments.

One important reason is that the prohibition of the use of force soon turned out to be surrounded by a grey area of genuine legal uncertainty which is reflective of deep-seated policy differences among states.[20] This made it a real challenge to generalize the precedents of Nuremberg and Tokyo. This challenge had been foreshadowed by Britain's Foreign Minister Austen Chamberlain in 1927 when he informed the House of Commons of his view that a definition of aggression would amount to "a trap to the innocent."[21] But after lengthy negotiations at the global level, including States Parties to the ICC Statute and Non-State Parties alike, a definition of the crime of aggression was agreed upon at the Kampala Review Conference and enshrined in Article 8 *bis* ICC Statute. This definition contains the so-called threshold clause, which requires an act of aggression by a state, which "by its character, gravity and scale constitutes a manifest violation of the Charter of the United Nations." This requirement makes it plain that the preference of a significant number of delegations, to progressively develop the meaning of the state conduct element of the crime so as to align it with the prohibition of the use of force in its most rigorous understanding, has not prevailed. To the contrary, the formulation of Article 8 *bis* is as modest as the definition of a crime under international law should be and, accordingly, it stays clear of the above-mentioned grey area of genuine legal uncertainty. Instead, it allows for an interpretation in conformity with existing customary international law, as it should be the case with respect to a crime under international law.[22] China's Kampala representative Zhou Lulu has thus rightly observed that "the threshold clause reflects customary international law and distinguishes appropriately between illegal international acts and international crimes."[23]

This suggests that there is another part of the truth to the fact that the governments of those nations that sat in judgment in Nuremberg have in the meantime turned away from the daunting task of delivering on their Nuremberg promise. As it has recently been written in relation to the United States: "We fight war crimes, but have forgotten the crime of war."[24] When it comes to the question of independent legal scrutiny of the decision to use military force, not only the Soviet Union and now Russia, but also the three Western powers that sat in judgment in Nuremberg have adopted a position of resistance that has aptly been called sovereigntist.[25] None other than Benjamin B. Ferencz has described this sovereigntist mindset in the following way:

> The vital ingredient that was really lacking was the political will of a few major powers that persisted in their refusal to accept rational international controls over the use of military force.[26]

In the course of the negotiations, this lack of political will was mostly veiled by legal arguments. The two most important arguments, neither of which is convincing, were the assertion of a Security Council monopoly on the initiation of proceedings for the crime of aggression, and the treatment of the crime of aggression like a new crime in the ICC Statute for the purposes of setting out the conditions for the ICC's exercise of jurisdiction over it.[27] As the Coalition for International Criminal Justice recalled in a statement of April 2023:

> The majority of State Parties from Africa, Latin America and Europe opposed this position. Nevertheless, the Kampala Conference ultimately gave way to the debilitating conditions regarding the crime of aggression, although they were undoubtedly understood as being driven by self-interest of larger powers.[28]

The sidelining of the crime of aggression by the major powers during the ICC negotiations was significantly facilitated by the stance that an important part of the international human rights movement had long taken regarding the question of war. By and large, this movement had accepted the idea that the killing by an aggressor during the conduct of hostilities is no violation of human rights and not the business of human rights organizations if in conformity with the permissive rules of the law of international armed conflict. In addition, organizations with a moral authority as important as Amnesty International and Human Rights Watch had adopted the policy not to comment on the conformity of military action with the *ius contra bellum*. Instead of fully recognizing that aggression opens the floodgate to a monstrous exception to fundamental human rights irrespective of the commission of war crimes, the international human rights movement had come to see aggression primarily as an offense against state sovereignty as such.[29] This paved the way for a mindset that scholars would later conceptualize through a narrow notion of atrocity crime that embraces genocide, crimes against humanity and war crimes, but excludes the crime of aggression.[30]

When international criminal justice experienced its revival in the 1990s, this approach took a firm hold in much of the non-governmental discourse community and this had tangible consequences: While civil society played a decisive role in the creation of the ICC Statute, it did not exert sufficient public pressure to remind the major powers of Jackson's Nuremberg promise.[31] And in the meantime, France, Great Britain and the U.S., and quite a few other states, happily embraced the concept of atrocity crime as a most welcome rhetorical device to continue sidelining the crime of aggression. As a result, even after the activation of the ICC's jurisdiction over the crime of aggression as from 17 July 2018[32] the prevailing concern was to humanize war rather than to outlaw it. Here are five examples that reflect this persistently prevailing mindset:

In 2019, Turkey conducted its massive military operation "Peace Spring" in Syria: Although there was a very serious possibility that this use of force fulfilled the state conduct element of the crime of aggression, this crime was not a salient issue in the discourse among governments.[33] Second, in 2021, the European Union chose to simply ignore that crime on the day of international criminal justice. High Representative Borrell stated as follows:

> Every 17th of July we commemorate the historic adoption of the Rome Statute of the International Criminal Court in 1998, as an important moment to reflect on the importance of fighting impunity and bringing justice to the victims of the most serious crimes: genocide, war crimes and crimes against humanity[34] – full stop.

Third, in May 2022, the European Union adopted an amendment of its Regulation on Eurojust.

This amendment extended Eurojust's scope of action with respect to genocide, crimes against humanity and war crimes. The crime of aggression, however, was left out.[35] Fourth, in August 2022, the International Law Commission adopted, on first reading, its Draft Articles on immunity of state officials from foreign criminal jurisdiction. Its draft article 7 recognizes the non-applicability of functional immunity in proceedings for genocide, crimes against humanity and war crimes, but not in those for the crime of aggression.[36] And fifth, most governments, apart from the Ukrainian, kept silent about the crime of aggression even for months after the UN General Assembly had properly characterized Russia's unlawful use of force against Ukraine as an aggression. In view of all this, it was difficult, even in the summer of 2022, to disagree with the assessment that "aggression belongs to, but is hanging by a thread in the firmament of international offences"[37].

The Renewed Focus on the Crime of Aggression

In the meantime, however, the picture has begun to change: Already in 2018, the UN Human Rights Committee laid an important doctrinal ground for such a change. In its General Comment 36, it stated: "State Parties engaged in acts of aggression as defined in international law resulting in deprivation of life, violate *ipso facto* article 6 of the Covenant."[38] The significance of this statement can hardly be overstated: Hereby, the Human Rights Committee has rightly claimed a space for the human rights conscience to address by its own distinct normative voice all the war violence inflicted by an aggressor state.[39]

After 24 February 2022, Philippe Sands was the first to raise the issue of the crime of aggression in public: "Why not create a dedicated international criminal tribunal to investigate Putin and his acolytes for the crime of aggression?," he asked, and he recalled: "After all, it was a Soviet jurist, Aaron Trainin, who did much of the legwork to bring crimes against peace into international law." "Let Putin reap the legacy of Nuremberg," so Sands concluded.[40] His call, which was taken up soon thereafter at a meeting at Chatham House,[41] resonated powerfully with the victims of Russia's aggression and was immediately embraced by the head of Ukraine's diplomacy. After all, Dmytro Kuleba, now Ukraine's Minister of Foreign Affairs and an international lawyer, had written a paper at the National University of Kviv on the Declaration of St James, of January 1942, a catalyst for Nuremberg.[42] Leading voices of Ukraine's civil society soon lent their emphatic support, among them Oleksandra Matviychuk from the Centre for Civil Liberties, one of the recipients of the Nobel Peace Prize.[43]

Soon thereafter, parliamentarians worldwide began to raise their voices. One Parliamentary Assembly after the other (and, notably, also Parliamentarians for Global Action[44]) addressed the issue of the crime of aggression.[45] The culmination of this series of public pronouncements was Resolution 2482 of the Council of Europe's Parliamentary Assembly.[46] This resolution, adopted by unanimity, demands that the Russian and Belarusian political and military leaders concerned "should be identified and prosecuted for the crime of aggression."[47] The Assembly cited General Comment 36 of the UN Human Rights Committee and stated as follows: "Without their decision to wage this war of aggression against Ukraine, the atrocities that flow from it as well as all the destruction, death and damage resulting from lawful acts of war would not have occurred."[48] In its report of August 2023, the UN Independent International Commission of Inquiry on Ukraine also devoted an elaborate and important passage to the crime of aggression[49] and recognized that the international criminal justice response to Russia's war of aggression against Ukraine must include accountability for crimes of aggression. The Commission states as follows:

> Should the investigations result in trials against lead perpetrators based on genocide, crimes against humanity or war crimes, it may be argued that evidence relating to acts of aggression can be taken into account during the judicial proceedings, both as context of the crimes and as an aggravating circumstance. (. . .) However, this course of action will not fully reflect the gravity of the crime

> of aggression as such, which is a separate crime, different from the three other crimes. No other existing international court can adjudicate allegations of the crime of aggression in the current context of Ukraine. [50]

As of lately, there also seems to be a growing interest in ensuring accountability for the crime of aggression within the NGO Coalition for the ICC. The Open Society Justice Initiative, for example, has been an active participant in the debate for quite some while.[51]

This "renewed focus on the crime of aggression," as ICC Prosecutor Khan has called it,[52] was powerful enough to spill over to the governmental level. Liechtenstein and the Baltic States took the lead[53] and subsequently more and more governments took up the issue of the crime of aggression. In October of 2022, the UN General Assembly for the first time explicitly mentioned the activation of the ICC's jurisdiction over the crime of aggression.[54] Only a little later, the European Council declared that the prosecution of the crime of aggression is of concern to the international community as a whole.[55] In February of 2023, the European Council followed suit and endorsed the setting up of the International Center for the Prosecution of the Crime of Aggression[56] against Ukraine.[57] And in March of 2023, the U.S. has added its voice to the growing chorus. In an address delivered in Washington, Ambassador-at-Large for Global Criminal Justice Beth van Schaack recalled the United States' "leading role in prosecuting the crime of aggression at Nuremberg." She recognized that this is "a critical moment in history" and she confirmed that "there are compelling reasons for why the crime of aggression must be prosecuted."[58] With the U.S. appearance on the public scene, it had become abundantly clear that the new momentum concerning the crime of aggression had an effect even on the attitude of some of those governments that had for decades adopted a position of sovereigntist resistance. In that regard, however, the key question remains whether one is witnessing a genuine change of position, one that truly embraces Jackson's call for a consistent, non-selective application the Nuremberg precedent on crimes against peace.

Reform Paths

The Most Principled Path: Amending the ICC Statute

As a matter of principle, the best way to close the existing gap would be to do it directly in the ICC Statute as proposed, most notably, by Prosecutor Khan.[59] The ICC, the only permanent international criminal court – and one with a credible universal orientation – is the most legitimate judicial institution to deliver on Nuremberg's fundamental promise.[60] It has been asked whether the principle of retroactivity in criminal law could stand in the way of eliminating limitations on the Court's exercise of jurisdiction over the crime of aggression with retroactive effect to Russia's war aggression against Ukraine.[61] But the principle only concerns the substantive criminal law[62] and the conduct of the relevant Russian leaders in question was criminalized under customary international law long before 2014. Yet, the necessary reform of the ICC Statute raises a number of legal and policy issues[63] and at the time of writing it seems that decision-makers do not regard an amendment of the ICC Statute as fast enough a solution to the immediate challenge: the war of aggression against Ukraine.

A Special Tribunal for the Crime of Aggression Against Ukraine

Therefore, considerable attention has been given and continues to be given to the establishment of a Special Tribunal for the Crime of Aggression against Ukraine.[64] The idea had first been put forward in a statement which was published after the above-mentioned Chatham House meeting and which has been signed by a significant number of international experts and personalities.[65] In the meantime, the process has been taken over by governments: At the time of writing, no less than 40 states have joined a so-called Core Group in support of Ukraine's call for the establishment of such a tribunal which builds the forum of an ongoing inter-governmental conversation conducted behind closed doors.

On Two Policy Objections

It is worth addressing two arguments which challenge the very idea of a special tribunal. The first argument is that a special tribunal could weaken the ICC. But there are weighty considerations speaking against that concern: The ICC would continue to carry out its important work with respect to allegations of war crimes, crimes against humanity and genocide. A special tribunal would do no more than to complement this work with respect to the crime of aggression.[66] The special tribunal would serve precisely the same overarching goal as the ICC, that is to ensure the most comprehensive accountability possible for crimes under international law. Experienced practitioners have long suggested ways, such as the establishment of a liaison office, to allow the ICC and a special tribunal to coordinate their work and to thereby create useful synergies instead of causing friction.[67] Again, the ICC is the most important pillar of the existing global system for the prosecution of crimes under international law. But the work of the ICC will invariably need to be complemented by additional judicial activity.[68] Which kind of additional activity will differ in each situation. As Judges Higgins, Kooijmans, and Buergenthal, wrote in their memorable separate opinion in the ICJ's 2002 Arrest Warrant Case:

> The international consensus that the perpetrators of international crimes should not go unpunished is being advanced by a flexible strategy in which newly established international criminal tribunals, treaty obligations and national courts all have their part to play.[69]

The second counter-argument is that proceedings before a special tribunal for the situation of Ukraine would constitute selective justice.[70] This argument is central: Selectivity in international criminal justice undermines its legitimacy. Selectivity must therefore be reduced. With respect to the special tribunal, the argument of selectivity has been made with respect both to the past and to the future. It carries far lesser weight with respect to the past. Most regrettably, there were indeed a number of serious violations of the prohibition of the use of force in the past where investigations into possible crimes of aggression would have been warranted: Iraq's use of force against Kuwait in 1990, Uganda's use of force against the Democratic Republic of Congo as from September 1998, the use of force by the United States and United Kingdom-led Coalition of the Willing against Iraq in 2003 and Turkey's use of force in Syria in 2019. Yet, at every historic turning point in the history of international criminal justice so far, decision-makers were faced with past failures. Had those failures of the past posed an insurmountable obstacle to taking action for the future, there would have been neither Nuremberg and Tokyo, nor the International Tribunals for the former Yugoslavia (ICTY) and Rwanda (ICTR), nor the ICC. Failures of the past with respect to the crime of aggression should therefore not prevent decision-makers from doing the right thing today for the future. And even less so in view of Russia's aggression against Ukraine, which, taking all relevant factors into account, constitutes a violation of the prohibition of the use of force of unprecedented seriousness.

The issue of selectivity weighs heavily, however, if one looks to the future. Today, Russia's leadership benefits from jurisdictional constraints that have resulted not only from its own preferences, but, as mentioned above, also from the sovereigntist resistance of three major Western powers to a principled jurisdictional regime in the ICC Statute. This begs a burning question of legitimacy: Is the creation of a special tribunal for the war of aggression against Ukraine perhaps meant by those powers to remain an event as isolated as Nuremberg and Tokyo have remained to date? But asking this question should not be the end of the matter. It should rather embolden governments to show true leadership. If they decide to establish a special tribunal, they should conceive of it as an imperfect instrument of transition, as a stepping stone towards a genuine embrace of Nuremberg's promise through a more principled jurisdictional regime in the ICC Statute. Such an effect would certainly not be without precedent. It may suffice to remember how the ICTY and the ICTR, both special international criminal tribunals, helped prepare the ground for the ICC's jurisdiction over genocide, crimes against humanity and war crimes.[71] Germany's Foreign Minister Annalena Baerbock publicly recognized the need for principled action in her important speech delivered at the Hague Academy of International Law in January 2023. Minister Baerbock was as sensitive to the question of selectivity in international criminal justice as one should be. But she did not rule out a special tribunal for the war of aggression against Ukraine. Instead, she suggested that the establishment of such a tribunal should be the first track of a two-track strategy. The second and more time-consuming track would have to be, she said, the amendment of the ICC Statute with respect to the crime of aggression.[72] While, as already mentioned above, it would be preferable, to solve the problem on the single-track approach of amending the ICC Statute, Minister Baerbock's proposed two track-approach nevertheless constitutes a principled path. The following statement of the UN Independent International Commission of Inquiry on Ukraine gently points in the same direction:

> A process aimed at amending the Rome Statute in parallel with the setting up (sic!) a new tribunal would demonstrate that the current conflict in Ukraine has shown "the jurisdictional gap" in the International Criminal Court Statute and that the international community is now seeking to fill it, based on a two-pronged approach.[73]

On the Question of Format

In April 2023, the Foreign Ministers of the G7 came forward in favor of an internationalized Ukrainian tribunal as their format of choice: "We support," they said, "the creation of an internationalized tribunal based in Ukraine's judicial system."[74] Almost at the same time, thirteen European and non-European states issued a joint statement in favor of an international tribunal.[75] The latter is in line with the unanimous call of the Parliamentary Assembly of the Council of Europe.[76] In the abstract, none of the two formats is inherently superior to the other and the choice must rather be made in light of the circumstances and needs of the given situation. In her Washington address, Ambassador van Schaack gave essentially two reasons why the U.S. favors a tribunal based in Ukraine's judicial system. She said that such a court would provide the "clearest path to establishing a new Tribunal, maximizing our chances of achieving meaningful accountability."[77] None of these arguments is, however, convincing.[78] In fact, both of them are rather astonishing.

First of all, creating an internationalized tribunal in Ukraine's legal system is by no means the clearest path available. On the contrary, it remains unclear to date, what precisely the international elements of a Ukrainian tribunal should be. The only thing that is reasonably clear is that the internationalization of a Ukrainian tribunal would have to be meaningful. Otherwise, such a tribunal would become an all too easy target of charges of politicization. However, a meaningful internationalization of a Ukrainian tribunal would require this state to change its constitution.[79] Even if somehow practicable despite the imposition of martial law, this approach would cost a lot of precious time in a situation where time is of the essence. This is one important reason why Ukraine does not favor the option of an internationalized Ukrainian tribunal.[80] It is rather odd to speak of a "clearest path" under such circumstances. At the time of writing, consideration is being given within the Core Group to the question whether the constitutional challenge that the original proposal faces can be overcome by a transfer of Ukraine's most important proceedings[81] for the crime of aggression to one recipient state[82] or to a group of recipient states. Such state(s) could then establish a multinational tribunal for the purpose of conducting the proceedings thus received. At this stage, too little is known outside the Core Group to offer a considered opinion about the viability of such a model. But the fact alone, that the conversation on such a model is ongoing at the time of writing, suggests that the path leading to such a solution is not particularly straight-forward either.

Moreover, an internationalized Ukrainian tribunal, in whatever form, does not maximize the chances for meaningful accountability: First, accountability will be all the more meaningful, both for the Ukrainians and for the defense of the essence of the international legal order, the more comprehensively it reaches up to those allegedly most responsible including those forming the Russian troika. Yet, the Judgment of the International Court of Justice (ICJ) in the Arrest Warrant Case and the relevant *obiter dictum* therein,[83] the judgment rendered by the Special Court for Sierra Leone in the case against Charles Taylor,[84] the judgment issued by the ICC in the case against Al-Bashir,[85] which was followed in the ICC's decision on the arrest warrant against Putin,[86] as well as Draft Article 3 on immunity of state officials from foreign criminal jurisdiction, as adopted in 2022 on first reading by the ILC,[87] make it more likely that the judges of a future special tribunal will pierce the veil of personal immunities[88] with respect to members of the Russian troika before a genuinely international criminal court than before an internationalized Ukrainian tribunal.[89]

In addition, the ILC's above-mentioned[90] exclusion of the crime of aggression from the list of crimes in Draft Article 7 of its immunity project, as adopted on first reading, adds to the risk that judges of a tribunal based in Ukraine's legal system might also grant functional immunity.[91] This would reduce the chances for "meaningful accountability" to close to zero because the great majority of the suspects will be Russian officials who acted in that capacity. In that context, it is striking how strongly the United States has rejected Draft Article 7 in its most recent statement *vis-à-vis* the ILC[92] and how firmly France has, at the same occasion, opposed the inclusion of the crime of aggression in the list of crimes contained in this Draft Article.[93] It remains a mystery, how these positions can be reconciled with the view of those same two states that an internationalized Ukrainian special tribunal constitutes the preferable format and maximizes the chances for "meaningful accountability."[94]

The question of "meaningful accountability" has yet another dimension, and here again a genuinely international solution offers a clear advantage: As was pointed out above, the crime of aggression, because of its distinct history, today only "hangs by a thread in the firmament of international crimes."[95] Hence, at this historic juncture, the strongest possible message is needed to confirm that the crime of aggression is a crime under international law as much as genocide, crimes against humanity and war crimes. Yet, the establishment of an internationalized Ukrainian tribunal would fail to send out a message of such a strength: The institutional design would not clearly convey the international character of the crime of aggression and would emphasize Ukraine's national interest in prosecuting it as the immediate victim rather than that of the international community as a whole. Hence, to heed Ukraine's call for the establishment of a truly international tribunal for the crime of aggression would not only be a welcome deference to this country's democratic choice and, notably, to a demand voiced by a group of courageous Russian dissident international criminal and human right lawyers.[96] It would also be the most plausible way to translate into institutional design what the G7 states themselves have explicitly recognized: that proceedings for the crime of aggression are in the interest of the international community as a whole.[97]

While severable options have been put forward in that respect,[98] the preferable path to establish a truly international tribunal would be to set it up on the basis of an agreement between the UN and Ukraine, negotiated on behalf of the UN by its Secretary-General and at the request of the General Assembly.[99] Doubts have been expressed about the power of the General Assembly to get involved. These doubts are however ill-founded:[100] In its 1962 Advisory Opinion in "Certain Expenses," the ICJ has set out the functions and powers conferred on the General Assembly to exercise its secondary responsibility for the maintenance of international peace and security, taking into account both the text of the UN Charter and the practice subsequent to its adoption including that under the "Uniting for Peace" umbrella.[101] The Court explicitly recognized that those functions and powers are not confined to the making of recommendations and that they are not merely hortatory. The Court found that only coercive action is within the exclusive realm of the Security Council.[102] But the request to the UN Secretary-General to conclude an agreement with a state on the establishment of an international tribunal for the exercise of jurisdiction over crimes under international law does not involve coercive action. That was confirmed by no lesser body than the Security Council itself in relation to the establishment of the Special Court for Sierra Leone. For in that case, the Council acted under Chapter VI, rather than Chapter VII, when it requested the Secretary-General to conclude the relevant agreement with Sierra Leone to establish a special international criminal tribunal exercising jurisdiction over crimes under international law.[103] It is difficult to avoid the impression that one is once again confronted with the old strategy of conceiling a lack of political will behind a veil of legal doubt. By way of historical comparison, it is interesting to recall that in 1946 the intended precedent on crimes against peace did involve a strong element of novelty. But then, Sir Hartley Shawcross, the British Chief Prosecutor, confidently exclaimed: "If this be an innovation, it is an innovation which we are prepared to defend and justify."[104]

The second argument against an international tribunal refers to an alleged skepticism among those states that are often, but somewhat simplistically, grouped together under the umbrella term "Global South." Because of this skepticism, so the argument goes, the necessary majority in the UN General Assembly is unlikely to emerge. At first sight, this argument sounds benign because it indicates a concern for the position of states belonging to the "Global South." But suspicion sets in when this argument is advanced by major powers from the "Global North," and this before a serious and sincere engagement with the "Global South" on the issue in question has taken place. This author is not in a position to speak on behalf of anybody in the "Global South." But he may perhaps be allowed to make the following five observations: First, many states from the "Global South" were driving forces for the inclusion of the crime of aggression in the ICC Statute in Rome.[105] Subsequently, a majority of those states supported the activation of the ICC's jurisdiction over the crime of aggression on the basis of a stronger and more principled jurisdictional regime in Kampala. This suggests that at least most of the states in question are, as a matter of principle, favorably disposed to the international adjudication of the crime of aggression. For example, after the Kampala Review Conference two leading Brazilian negotiators stated as follows:

> The Brazilian delegation strongly advocated for the need to define the crime of aggression. This position reflects Brazil's long-standing commitment to international law and, specifically, to the primacy of multilateral rules on the use

> of force. The adoption of the definition of the crime of aggression strengthens the Court, fulfils an obligation undertaken by the world community in Rome in 1998 and helps ensure a more just, safe and equitable international order.[106]

Against this background, it is far from obvious why the establishment of a special international tribunal should be in the interest of the "Global North" only. Second, it is not at all far-fetched to see Ukraine's resistance against Russia's aggression and its embrace of international law in support of its cause through a(n Eastern European) post-colonial lens, not altogether different from the one often adopted within the "Global South."[107] Third, on 23 February 2023, 141 UN member states recognized the need to ensure accountability for the most serious crimes under international law committed on the territory of Ukraine.[108] Fourth, among the thirteen states that issued a joint statement in support of an international criminal tribunal there are three states from the "Global South."[109] Fifth, eminent personalities from the "Global South," such as the former ICC President Eboe Osuji[110] and the former ICTY Chief prosecutor Richard Goldstone,[111] have voiced their support for the establishment of an international tribunal. It is also noteworthy in that context that the former UN Secretary-General Ban-Ki Moon has voiced a strong preference for establishing an international tribunal at the request of the UN General Assembly.[112] Taken together, all this is to suggest that negative speculations regarding the position of the "Global South," when put forward by the G7, might well have been calculated to preempt a serious and sincere engagement with the states concerned on the question of the establishment of a special international criminal tribunal.

The most plausible explanation for this avoidance strategy might be that an earnest engagement with the "Global South" about the establishment of a special tribunal would have had to include a credible answer to the question, formulated above, as to how those who now plead for the establishment of such a tribunal for the war of aggression against Ukraine intend to deal with similar aggressions in the future. Those thirteen states that have issued the joint statement in support of the establishment of a special international criminal tribunal have given the right answer: They have reaffirmed "their commitment to harmonize the jurisdiction of the Rome Statute over its four crimes in order to allow the International Criminal Court to prosecute the crime of aggression in similar future situations."[113] However, the same commitment by the G7 is conspicuously missing. This suggests that the support of some G7 states for the establishment of a special tribunal remains overshadowed by a cloud of illegitimacy.

A Look Ahead

It is currently impossible to predict the outcome of the inter-governmental conversation over the establishment of a Special Tribunal for the Crime of Aggression against Ukraine. Whether or not such a tribunal will eventually become a reality, states Parties to the ICC are urgently called upon to close the gap in the international legal architecture against aggression within the ICC Statute.

In that regard, it is encouraging to note that a Group of Friends, favorably disposed to working toward such a principled solution, was formed last year, and that a first elaborate text proposal has been submitted by a group of independent experts for consideration by the Group of Friends.[114] It is imperative that European states which, at the time of writing, form the large majority of this group reach out to states from the other world regions to reinvigorate their interest in the subject-matter. This will require a dedicated diplomatic effort, given the disappointment caused to many of those states in the course of the negotiations before and in Kampala and later in New York that have resulted in the legal regime currently governing the ICC's exercise of jurisdiction over the crime of aggression. This disappointment is apparent from the statement that one of South Africa's leading delegates made after Kampala:

> The major weakness is, of course, the fact that (. . .) Non-State Parties (. . .) will be able to commit aggression with a sense of impunity, and this reflection of realpolitik may result in a very slow process of ratification and acceptance.[115]

Yet, the issue at stake is of such a significance for the future world order that it is worth every effort: This is a moment in time, when the prohibition of aggression is at risk of erosion and when tensions between different world regions are being strongly felt. At such a juncture, it would be particularly welcome to send out the message that in today's multipolar world dedicated co-operation across the "Global North" and the "Global South" is not only possible, but also capable of reconsolidating the international legal order at its core. A cross-regional diplomatic effort, yielding the harmonization of the conditions, under which the ICC may exercise its jurisdiction over all four crimes under international, would send out precisely this message.

Ultimately, an important responsibility will also lie with France, Great Britain, and the United States: After the Second World War, they, together with the Soviet Union, set the foundational precedent for the crime of aggression at Nuremberg. Lately, however, they have insisted most strongly, from inside the Rome Statute system and from the outside, on the imposition of legal restraints that debilitate the Court's exercise of jurisdiction over the crime of aggression and that cannot be characterized as anything other than as the embodiment of a double-standard in the existing international legal architecture. May it be recalled that the U.S. Ambassador van Schaack has observed that Russia's war of aggression against Ukraine has brought the world to a "critical moment in history."[116] The Ambassador is right, but it would be worth recognizing that such a moment calls for true leadership not only on the military front, but also in the field of international criminal justice.[117] The three major powers in question would rise to the critical moment in history that the world is facing, if they were to overcome their long-standing sovereigntist resistance to a principled jurisdictional regime for the crime of aggression in the ICC Statute.

Notes

* The text builds on and updates the Second Nuremberg Academy Lecture, held by the author on 4 May 2023 in Courtroom 600 of the Nuremberg Palace of Justice, https://www.nurembergacademy.org/events/nuremberg-academy-lecture-2023/. The author wishes to thank Fiona Abken for excellent research assistance and Astrid Reisinger Coracini and Sergey Vasiliev for several helpful suggestions for improving a draft version of this essay.

1 On the legal issues related to the prohibition of the use of force, see the chapter by Masahiko Asada in this volume; see also Claus Kreß, *The Ukraine War and the Prohibition of the Use of Force in International Law* (2022); see also James Green, Christian Henderson, and Tom Ruys, "Russia's Attackon Ukraine and the *ius ad bellum*," 9 *Journal on the Use of Force and International Law* (2022), pp. 4–30.

2 Claus Kreß, "The State Conduct Element," in C. Kreß and S. Barriga (eds.), *The Crime of Aggression: A Commentary*, vol. 1 (2017), pp. 412–564.

3 Stefan Barriga, "Negotiating the Amendments on the Crime of Aggression," in S. Barriga and C. Kreß (eds.), *The Travaux Préparatoires of the Crime of Aggression* (2011), pp. 3–57.

4 For two early "Model Indictments," see Open Society Justice Initiative, *Model Indictment for the Crime of Aggression Committed against Ukraine* (May 2022); Ryan Goodman and Rebecca Hamilton, "Model Indictment for Crime of Aggression against Ukraine: Prosecutor v. Vladimir Putin," *Just Security*, March 14, 2022, https://www.justsecurity.org/80669/model-indictment-of-the-crime-of-aggression-against-ukraine-vladimir-putin/. This essay's focus is on Russia's aggression, but Belarus' active territorial involvement in this aggression must be mentioned as well because it also gives rise to the suspicion of the commission of crimes of aggression; for an international legal analysis of the conduct of the Belarussian state, see Alexander Wentker and Claus Kreß, "L'assistance d'États Tiers dans la Guerre d'Ukraine au Regard du Droit International," 68 *Annuaire Français de Droit International* (2022), p. 173, 180.

5 Statement of ICC Prosecutor, Karim A. A. Khan QC, on the Situation on Ukraine, https://www.icc-cpi.int/news/statement-icc-prosecutor-karim-aa-khan-qc-situation-ukraine-i-have-been-closely-following.

6 Carrie McDougall, *The Crime of Aggression under the Rome Statute of the International Criminal Court* (2nd ed., 2021), pp. 258–352.

7 UN Doc. S/2022/155, 25.2.2022.

8 Former Judge at the ICTY Wolfgang Schomburg spoke of a "luxury problem" at a conference hold in February 2023 in Berlin; for a report on this conference, see Maurice Niccolò Uhlig, *Berliner Anwaltblatt* (June 2023), p. 229.

9 "International Military Tribunal (Nuremberg), October 1, 1946," 41 *American Journal of International Law* (1947), p. 172, 186.

10 ICC Press Release, March 17, 2023, https://www.icc-cpi.int/news/situation-ukraine-icc-judges-issue-arrest-warrants-against-vladimir-vladimirovich-putin-and#:~:text=Today%2C%2017%20March%202023%2C%20Pre,Ms%20Maria%20Alekseyevna%20Lvova%2DBelova; for a first analysis, see Sergey Vasiliev, "The International Criminal Court Goes All in: What Now?," *EJIL:Talk!*, March 20, 2023, https://www.ejiltalk.org/the-international-criminal-court-goes-all-in-what-now/.

11 On those protected values, see Kreß, note 2, pp. 419–20.
12 In that respect, see only the reports of the Independent International Commission of Inquiry on Ukraine, as established by the UN Human Rights Council on March 4, 2022, https://www.ohchr.org/en/hr-bodies/hrc/iicihr-ukraine/index.
13 For a recent criticism of this position, see Chile Eboe Osuji, "Military Necessity and Aggression," 65 *German Yearbook of International Law* (2022), pp. 11–36.
14 On some of those losses, see the August 2023 report by the Independent International Commission of Inquiry on Ukraine, UN Doc A/HCR/52/CRP.4, August 29, 2023, paras. 44–49, https://www.ohchr.org/sites/default/files/2023-08/A_HRC_52_CRP.4_En%20%28003%29.pdf.
15 Frédéric Mégret, "What is the Specific Evil of Aggression?," in Kreß and Barriga, note 2, vol. 2, p. 1398, pp. 1420–4, 1432.
16 On this risk, see Kreß, note 1, pp. 9–11.
17 Opening Speech by the Chief Prosecutor of the United States, reprinted in *Trial of Major German War Criminals by the International Military Tribunal Sitting at Nuremberg Germany* (William S. Hein & Co., 2001), p. 45.
18 Claus Kreß, "A Plea for True U.S. Leadership in International Criminal Justice," *Articles of War*, May 7, 2021, https://lieber.westpoint.edu/plea-true-u-s-leadership-international-criminal-justice/.
19 Mégret, note 15, p. 1399.
20 Claus Kreß, "On the Principle of Non-Use of Force in Current International Law," *Just Security*, September 30, 2019, https://www.justsecurity.org/66372/on-the-principle-of-non-use-of-force-in-current-international-law/.
21 House of Commons, *Hansard* (24.11.1927), col. 2105.
22 For a detailed account, see Kreß, note 2, pp. 526–36.
23 Zhou Lulu, "China," in Kreß/Barriga, note 2, p. 1131, 1133. Russia's Kampala delegates Gennady Kuzmin and Igor Panin also even voiced explicit agreement with the definition enshrined in Article 8 *bis*: "Russia is satisfied with the outcome of the Review Conference with regard to the definition of the crime of aggression"; in Kreß and Barriga, note 2, p. 1264.
24 Samuel Moyn, *Humane: How the United States Abandoned War and Reinvented War* (2021), p. 9.
25 Gerry Simpson, "Stop Calling it Aggression: War as Crime," 61 *Current Legal Problems* (2008), p. 191, 219.
26 Benjamin B. Ferencz, "The Long Journey to Kampala: A Personal Memoir," in Kreß and Barrriga, note 2, p. 1501, 1512.
27 Claus Kreß and Leonie von Holtzendorff, "The Kampala Compromise on the Crime of Aggression," 8 *Journal of International Criminal Justice* (2010), pp. 1179–217.
28 Coalition for International Criminal Justice, "States Parties Should Strengthen the ICC's Ability to Prosecute Aggression," CICJ Statement No. 3 (April 27, 2023), p. 1, https://cicj.eu/statement-3/.
29 Mégret, note 15, pp. 1424–8.
30 For an influential essay, see David Scheffer, "Genocide and Atrocity Crimes," 1 *Genocide Studies and Prevention* (2006), pp. 229–50.
31 Noah Weisbord, "Civil Society," in Kreß and Barriga, note 2, pp. 1310–55.
32 Claus Kreß, "On the Activation of ICC Jurisdiction over the Crime of Aggression," 16 *Journal of International Criminal Justice* (2018), pp. 1–18.

33 Claus Kreß, "A Collective Failure to Prevent Turkey's Operation 'Peace Spring' and NATO's Silence on International Law," *EJIL:Talk!*, 14.10.2019, https://www.ejiltalk.org/a-collective-failure-to-prevent-turkeys-operation-peace-spring-and-natos-silence-on-international-law/.

34 European Union, "Day of International Criminal Justice: Declaration by the High Representative Josep Borrell on behalf of the European Union," Press Release, July 16, 2021, https://www.consilium.europa.eu/en/press/press-releases/2021/07/16/day-of-international-criminal-justice-declaration-by-the-high-representative-josep-borrell-on-behalf-of-the-european-union/.

35 Regulation (EU) 2022/838 of the European Parliament and of the Council of 30.5.2022, *Official Journal of the European Union*, May 31, 2022, L 148/4, Art. 1.

36 Report of the International Law Commission, Seventy-third session (April 18–June 3 and July 4–August 5, 2022), UN Doc A/77/10, p. 191 (para. 68).

37 Mégret, note 15, p. 1399.

38 UN Human Rights Committee, "General Comment No. 36, Article 6: Right to Life"; UN Doc CCPR/C/GC/36, 30.10.2018, para. 70.

39 Claus Kreß, "A Reply to Judge Eboe-Osuji," 65 *German Yearbook of International Law* (2022), p. 37, 47–51.

40 Philippe Sands, "Putin's Use of Military Force is a Crime of Aggression," *Financial Times,* February 28, 2022. Soviet scholar Aron Trainin had coined the term "crimes against peace," that is the name under which the crime of aggression entered the international scene in Nuremberg; on the Soviet Union's contribution to the Nuremberg trial, see Francine Hirsch, *Soviet Judgment at Nuremberg. A New History of the International Military Tribunal after World War II* (2020).

41 For references, see Independent International Commission of Inquiry, note 14, p. 156 (paras. 928–9).

42 The author is grateful to Judge Mykola Gnatovskyy for sharing this information with him.

43 See, e.g., "The Appeal of Human Rights Defender Oleksandra Matviischuk to the Secretary-General of the United Nations," September 28, 2022, op. para. 3, https://ccl.org.ua/en/claims/the-appeal-of-human-rights-defender-oleksandra-matviichuk-to-the-secretary-general-of-the-united-nations/.

44 12th Consultative Assembly of Parliamentarians on the International Criminal Court and the Rule of Law (CAP-ICC), 43rd Annual Forum of Parliamentarians for Global Action, "Plan of Action on the Universality and Effectiveness of, and Political Support for, the Rome Statute System against Impunity," November 4–5, 2022 (National Congress of Argentina, Buenos Aires), https://www.pgaction.org/pdf/2022/buenos-aires-poa-2022-en.pdf.

45 For an exhaustive list of references, see Independent International Commission of Inquiry, note 14, p. 155 (para. 926 (note 625).

46 Parliamentary Assembly of the Council of Europe, "Legal and Human Rights Aspects of the Russian Federation's Aggression against Ukraine," Resolution 2842 (2023), January 26, 2023, https://pace.coe.int/en/files/31620/html.

47 Ibid., para. 4.

48 Ibid.

49 Independent International Commission of Inquiry, note 14, pp. 155–60 (paras. 922–46).

50 Ibid., p. 155 (paras. 924–5).
51 See above in note 4.
52 Karim A. A. Khan, Prosecutor of the International Criminal Court, Statement made on 5 December 2022 at the opening plenary of the 21st session of the Assembly of States Parties, para. 21, https://asp.icc-cpi.int/sites/asp/files/2022-12/ASP21-STMT-PROS-ENG.pdf.
53 For references, see Independent International Commission of Inquiry, note 14, p. 155 (para. 926, note 625); see also Gabija Grigaitė-Daugirdė, "The Lithuanian Case for an International Special Tribunal for the Crime of Aggression Against Ukraine," *Just Security,* June 1, 2023, https://www.justsecurity.org/86766/the-lithuanian-case-for-an-international-special-tribunal-for-the-crime-of-aggression-against-ukraine/.
54 UN Doc A/77/L.7, 26.10.2022, para. 25.
55 European Council Meeting (15.12.2022) – Conclusions, EUCO 34/22, CO EUR 29, CONCL 7, para. 8, https://www.consilium.europa.eu/media/60872/2022-12-15-euco-conclusions-en.pdf.
56 For the website of the ICPA, see https://www.eurojust.europa.eu/international-centre-for-the-prosecution-of-the-crime-of-aggression-against-ukraine.
57 Special Meeting of the European Council (9.2.2023) – Conclusions, EUCO 1/23, CO EUR 1, CONCL 1, para. 4, https://data.consilium.europa.eu/doc/document/ST-1-2023-INIT/en/pdf.
58 Ambassador Beth van Schaack's Remarks on the U.S. Proposal to Prosecute Russian Crimes of Aggression (27.3.2023), https://www.state.gov/ambassador-van-schaacks-remarks/.
59 Khan, note 52: "When we recognize that there is a gap in that architecture, in my view, we should try to address it through the Rome Statute (. . .)." For the same view, see Claus Kress/Stephan Hobe/Angelika Nussberger, "The Ukraine War and the Crime of Aggression: How to Fill the Gaps in the International Legal System," *Just Security*, January 23, 2023, https://www.justsecurity.org/84783/the-ukraine-war-and-the-crime-of-aggression-how-to-fill-the-gaps-in-the-international-legal-system/.
60 Independent International Commission of Inquiry, note 14, p. 155 (para. 923).
61 Independent International Commission of Inquiry, note 14, p. 158 (para. 938).
62 Claus Kreß, "Nulla poena nullum crimen sine lege," in A. Peters (ed.), *Max Planck Enclycopedia of Public International Law*, para. 20 (February 2010), https://opil.ouplaw.com/display/10.1093/law:epil/9780199231690/law-9780199231690-e854.
63 Astrid Reisinger-Coracini, "Is Amending the Rome Statute the Panacea Against Perceived Selectivity and Impunity for the Crime of Aggression Against Ukraine?," *Just Security*, March 21, 2023, https://www.justsecurity.org/85593/is-amending-the-rome-statute-the-panacea-against-perceived-selectivity-and-impunity-for-the-crime-of-aggression-committed-against-ukraine/; Fiona Abken and Paulina Rob, "Amending the Amendment: In Search of an Adequate Procedure for a Revision of the Jurisdictional Regime for the Crime of Aggression in the Rome Statute," *EJIL:Talk!*, January 13, 2023, https://www.ejiltalk.org/amending-the-amendment-in-search-of-an-adequate-procedure-for-a-revision-of-the-jurisdictional-regime-for-the-crime-of-aggression-in-the-rome-statute/.
64 For scholarly contributions, see Advisory Committee on Public International Law, *Challenges in Prosecuting the Crime of Aggression: Jurisdiction and Immunities*, Advisory Report No. 40 (September 12, 2022), https://www.advisorycommitt

eeinternationallaw.nl/publications/advisory-reports/2022/09/12/challenges-in-prosecuting-the-crime-of-aggression-jurisdiction-and-immunities; Kai Ambos, "A Ukraine Special Tribunal with Legitimacy Problems?," *Verfassungsblog,* January 1, 2023, https://verfassungsblog.de/a-ukraine-special-tribunal-with-legitimacy-problems/; Gleb Bogush and Sergei Golubok, "Why the World Needs a Special Tribunal to Prosecute Russia's Aggression Against Ukraine," *The Moscow Times,* June 26, 2023, https://www.themoscowtimes.com/2023/06/23/why-the-world-needs-a-special-tribunal-to-prosecute-russias-aggression-against-ukraine-a81606; Annegret Hartig, "Ein Aggressionstribunal für die Ukraine?," *Deutsche Richterzeitung* (2022), pp. 368–71; Olivier Corten and Vaios Koutroulis, "Tribunal for the Crime of Aggression against Ukraine – A Legal Assessment," In-depth Analysis Requested by the DROI Subcommittee of the European Parliament (December 2022), https://www.europarl.europa.eu/RegData/etudes/IDAN/2022/702574/EXPO_IDA(2022)702574_EN.pdf; Tom Dannenbaum, "A Special Tribunal for the Crime of Aggression?," 20 *Journal of International Criminal Justice* (2022), pp. 859–73; Oona Hathaway, "A Crime in Search of a Court," *Foreign Affairs,* May 19, 2022; Kevin Jon Heller, "Options for Prosecuting Russian Aggression Against Ukraine, A Critical Analysis," 26 *Journal of Genocide Research* (2022), pp. 1–24; Patryk Labuda, "Countering Imperialism in International Law: Examining the Special Tribunal for Aggression against Ukraine Through a Post-Colonial Eastern European Lens," 49 *Yale Journal of International Law* (2023) (forthcoming); Flavia Lattanzi, "Quale tribunale per I crimini russi in Ucrainia? Le proposte di Lattanzi," *Formiche.ne t,* February 20, 2023; Carrie McDougall, "The Imperative of Prosecuting Crimes of Aggression Against Ukraine," 28 *Journal of Conflict & Security Law* (2023), pp. 208–30; Anne Peters and Robert Spendel, "Ein Sondertribunal zur Aggression gegen die Ukraine? Ja.," *Vereinte Nationen* (2023), p. 74; Carmen Queseda Alcalá, "El Crimen del Agresión contra Ucrania, un Crimen Cierto, con Enjuiciamiento Incierto," 46 *Revista Electrónica de Estudios Internacioanles* (2023); Jennifer Trahan, "The Need for an International Criminal on the Crime of Aggression Regarding the Situation in Ukraine," 46 *Fordham International Law Journal* (2023), pp. 671–90.

65 Statement Calling for the Creation of a Special Tribunal for the Punishment of the Crime of Aggression Against Ukraine, https://gordonandsarahbrown.com/wp-content/uploads/2022/03/Combined-Statement-and-Declaration.pdf.

66 Independent International Commission of Inquiry, note 14, p. 158 (para. 937).

67 Astrid Reisinger Coracini, "The Case for Creating a Special Tribunal to Prosecute the Crime of Aggression Against Ukraine (Part II): Jurisdiction and Composition," *Just Security,* September 23, 2022, https://www.justsecurity.org/83201/tribunal-crime-of-aggression-part-two/; David Scheffer, "Forging a Cooperative Relationship Between International Criminal Court and a Special Tribunal for the Crime of Aggression Against Ukraine," *Just Security,* October 25, 2022, https://www.justsecurity.org/83757/forging-a-cooperative-relationship-between-intl-crim-court-and-a-special-tribunal-for-russian-aggression-against-ukraine/; Carrie McDougall, "The Proposed Special Tribunal for Crimes of Aggression Against Ukraine Should be Viewed as an Accountability Partner, Not a Competitor: Should the Tribunal be established, the ICC Should Cooperate With It to the Greatest Extent Possible," *ICC Forum,* September 13, 2023, https://iccforum.com/decentralized-accountability#McDougall; for the specific legal issue of double jeopardy, see

Gaiane Nuridzhanian and Carrie McDougall, "On Double Jeopardy, the ICC, and the Special Tribunal for the Crime of Aggression," *Just Security*, January 18, 2024, https://www.justsecurity.org/91314/on-double-jeopardy-the-icc-and-the-special-tribunal-for-the-crime-of-aggression/.

68 Independent International Commission of Inquiry, note 14, p. 158–9 (para. 940).

69 ICJ, Case Concerning the Arrest Warrant of April 11, 2000 (Democratic Republic of the Congo v. Belgium), Judgment of February 14, 2002, Joint Separate Opinion of Judges Higgins, Koijmans and Buergenthal, *I.C.J. Reports* 2002, p. 63, 78 (para.51).

70 Luis Moreno Ocampo, "Ending Selective Justice for the International Crime of Aggression," *Just Security*, January 31, 2023, https://www.justsecurity.org/84949/ending-selective-justice-for-the-international-crime-of-aggression/.

71 Claus Kreß, "The International Criminal Court as a Turning Point in the History of International Criminal Justice," in A. Cassese (ed.), *The Oxford Companion of International Criminal Justice* (2009), pp. 143–59.

72 Speech by Federal Foreign Minister Annalena Baerbock in The Hague, "Strengthening International Law in Times of Crisis," January 16, 2023, https://www.auswaertiges-amt.de/en/newsroom/news/strengthening-international-law-in-times-of-crisis/2573492.

73 Independent International Commission of Inquiry, note 14, p. 159 (para. 940).

74 G7 Japan 2023, Foreign Minister's Communiqué (April 18, .2023) Karuizawa, Nagano, https://www.mofa.go.jp/files/100492731.pdf.

75 Joint Statement by Belgium, Costa Rica, Czech Republik, Estonia, Guatemala, Latvia, Liechtenstein, Lithuania, Luxemburg, Marshall Islands, North-Macedonia, and Poland on the accountability for the crime of aggression committed on the territory of Ukraine (April 17, 2023), https://un.mfa.ee/joint-statement-on-the-accountability-for-the-crime-of-aggression-committed-on-the-territory-of-ukraine/.

76 Parliamentary Assembly of the Council of Europe, note 46, para. 6.

77 Ambassador Beth van Schaack's Remarks, note 58.

78 For two further critical analyses of the U.S. position, see Rebecca Hamilton, "An Assessment of the United States' New Position on an Aggression Tribunal for Ukraine," *Just Security,* March 29, 2023, https://asp.icc-cpi.int/sites/asp/files/2022-12/ASP21-STMT-PROS-ENG.pdf.; Jennifer Trahan, "Don't be Fooled by U.S. Smoke and Mirrors on the Crime of Aggression. Weak Proposals Carry the Risk of Weak Results," *Just Security,* April 14, 2023, https://www.justsecurity.org/85986/dont-be-fooled-by-u-s-smoke-and-mirrors-on-the-crime-of-aggression/.

79 Alexander Komarov and Oona Hathaway, "Ukraine's Constitutional Constraints: How Achieve Accountability for the Crime of Aggression?," *Just Security,* April 5, 2022, https://www.justsecurity.org/80958/ukraines-constitutional-constraints-how-to-achieve-accountability-for-the-crime-of-aggression/.

80 In January 2024, President Zelenskyy has reiterated his call for a "Special International Tribunal for the Crime of Aggression against Ukraine"; Joint Statement by the President of the Republic of Lithuania, H. E. Mr Gitanas Nauseda, and the President of Ukraine, H.E. Mr Volodymyr Zelenskyy, January 10, 2024, https://www.president.gov.ua/en/news/spilna-zayava-prezidenta-ukrayini-volodimira-zelenskogo-i-pr-88193; perhaps the clearest pronouncement of President Zelenskyy's against an internationalized Ukrainian tribunal can be found

in "The Speech by Volodymyr Zelenskyy to Representatives of the Public, Political and Expert Circles of the Kingdom of the Netherlands and International Institutions Based in The Hague" (May 4, 2023), https://www.president.gov.ua/en/news/promova-prezidenta-ukrayini-volodimira-zelenskogo-u-generaln-74001. In this speech President Zelenskyy states: "But only one institution is capable of responding to the original crime: the crime of aggression. A Tribunal! Not something hybrid that can formally close the topic . . . Not some compromise that will allow politicians to say that the case is allegedly done . . . But a true, full-fledged tribunal. True and full justice."

81 The transfer of criminal proceedings has received a detailed international treaty regulation in The European Convention on the Transfer of Proceedings in Criminal Matters of May 15, 1972, *European Treaty Series* No 73.

82 For a more recent example, see Art. 5 (2) and Art. 6 of the Agreement between the Kingdom of the Netherlands and Ukraine on International Legal Cooperation regarding Crimes connected with the Downing of Malaysia Airlines Flight MH on July 17, 2014; https://www.eerstekamer.nl/behandeling/20170707/verdrag_tussen_het_koninkrijk_der/document3/f=/vkmvd36xqxwj.pdf.

83 ICJ, *Case Concerning the Arrest Warrant of 11 April 2000 (Democratic Republic of the Congo v. Belgium)*, Judgment of February 14, 2002, p. 3, 24 (para. 58), 25 (para. 61).

84 SCSL, *Prosecutor v. Charles Ghankay Taylor, Decision on Immunity from Jurisdiction*, May 31, 2004, SCSL-2003-01-I, para. 52.

85 ICC, *Prosecutor v. Omar Hassan Ahmad Al Bashir, Judgement in the Jordan Referral re Al- Bashir Appeal*, ICC-02/05-01/09 OA 2, May 6, 2019, para. 114 in conjunction with para. 2.

86 For the reference, see note 10.

87 Report of the International Law Commission, note 36, p. 190 (para. 68).

88 On the concept of personal immunity in international law, see Claus Kreß, "Art. 98," in K. Ambos (ed.), *Rome Statute of the International Criminal Court: Article-by-Article Commentary* (4th ed., 2022), pp. 2626–7 (para. 84).

89 The topic of personal immunities is perhaps the single most intricate legal issue in connection with the conversation about the establishment of a special tribunal. This question cannot receive a detailed treatment within the limited space of this essay. The two central questions are, first, whether there exists at all an exception from the customary international personal immunity in proceedings for crimes under international law, and, second, if such an exception exists, whether it exists in all international criminal proceedings, only in certain international proceedings or in certain international and also exceptionally in national criminal proceedings. The relevant scholarly literature on these questions has been rapidly growing in parallel to the inter-governmental discourse. Apart from the pieces mentioned in note 64, see, above all, Rosanne van Alebeek, Larissa van den Herik, and Cedric Ryngaert, "Prosecuting Russian Officials for the Crime of Aggression: What about Immunities?," 4 *European Convention of Human Rights Law Review* (2023), pp. 115–32; Open Society Justice Initiative, *Immunities and a Special Tribunal for the Crime of Aggression against Ukraine* (February 2023), https://www.justiceinitiative.org/publications/immunities-and-a-special-tribunal-for-the-crime-of-aggression-against-ukraine; André de Hoogh, "Personal Immunities Redux Before a Special Tribunal for Prosecuting Russian Crimes of Aggression: Resistance is Futile,"

EJIL:Talk!, January 5, 2024, https://www.ejiltalk.org/personal-immunities-redux-before-a-special-tribunal-for-prosecuting-russian-crimes-of-aggression-resistance-is-futile/; Chile Eboe-Osuji, "International Law Rejects Immunity for International Crimes – Full Stop," 21 *Journal of International Criminal Justice* (2023), pp. 461–85; Astrid Reisinger Coracini and Jennifer Trahan, "Special Tribunal to Prosecute the Crime of Aggression Against Ukraine (Part IV): On the Non-Applicability of Personal Immunities," *Just Security*, November 8, 2022), https://www.justsecurity.org/84017/the-case-for-creating-a-special-tribunal-to-prosecute-the-crime-of-aggression-committed-against-ukraine-part-vi-on-the-non-applicability-of-personal-immunities/; for this author's position, see Kreß, note 88, pp. 2639-2653 (paras. 114–30).

90 See above text accompanying note 35.

91 On the concept of functional immunity in international law, see Kreß, note 88, p. 2601 (para. 22).

92 Comments from the United States on the International Law Commission's Draft Articles on Criminal Immunity of States Officials As Adopted by the Commission in 2022 on First Reading, pp. 9–10, https://legal.un.org/ilc/sessions/75/pdfs/english/iso_us.pdf.

93 Commentaires et observations de la République Française relatifs aux projets d'articles de la Commission de Droit International sur « l'immunité de juridiction pénale étrangère des représentants de l'État », para. 36, https://legal.un.org/ilc/sessions/75/pdfs/french/iso_france.pdf.

94 For Ukraine's detailed explanation as to why functional immunity does not apply in proceedings for crimes under international law, including those for the crime of aggression, see Comments and observations of Ukraine in relation to Draft Article 7 of the Draft Articles on Immunity of State officials from foreign criminal jurisdiction, https://legal.un.org/ilc/sessions/75/pdfs/english/iso_ukraine.pdf; for the concurring position of this author, see Kreß, note 88, pp. 2601–26 (paras. 23–83).

95 See above text accompanying note 37.

96 Gleb Bogush and Sergey Vasiliev, "Russian International and Human Rights Lawyers' Statement on Accountability," *Just Security*, June 12, 2023, https://www.justsecurity.org/86911/the-brussels-declaration-russian-international-and-human-rights-lawyers-statement-on-accountability/.

97 Of course, there are means to internationalize a tribunal anchored in the Ukrainian system in a manner that would move the expressive force of such a tribunal closer in the desirable direction: Those include an explicit reference of the crime's international character and its definition in Art. 8 *bis* of the ICC Statute, strong international features in terms of its prosecution service and the composition of the benches, and ideally also an endorsement of the tribunals' establishment by the UN General Assembly.

98 For a reference to the "London-model" underlying the Nuremberg International Military Tribunal, see the statement referred to in note 65; on regional alternatives, see Corten and Koutroulis, note 64, pp. 18–9.

99 The preference for an involvement of the UN General Assembly in the establishment of the special tribunal was voiced by the group of States referred to above in note 75; the model is set out in greater detail in "Yale Club Round Table: A Special Tribunal

for the Crime of Aggression Recommended by the UN General Assembly?" (June 22, 2022), Annex to the letter dated 12 August 2022 from the representatives of Latvia, Liechtenstein, and Ukraine, to the United Nations addressed to the Secretary-General; UN Doc A/ES-11/7-S/2022/616, 17.7.2022; Ukraine Task Force of the Global Accountability Network, *Proposal for a Resolution by the United Nations General Assembly and Accompanying Proposal for a Statute of a Special Tribunal for the Crime of Aggression* (September 7, 2022).

100 For two succinct analyses, see Hans Corell, "A Special Tribunal for Ukraine – The Role for the U.N. General Assembly," *Just Security*, February 14, 2023, https://www.justsecurity.org/85116/a-special-tribunal-for-ukraine-on-the-crime-of-aggression-the-role-of-the-u-n-general-assembly/; Oona Hathaway, Maggie Mills, and Heather Zimmerman, "The Legal Authority to Create a Special Tribunal for the Crime of Aggression Upon the Request of the UN General Assembly, *Just Security*, May 5, 2023, https://www.justsecurity.org/86450/the-legal-authority-to-create-a-special-tribunal-to-try-the-crime-of-aggression-upon-the-request-of-the-un-general-assembly/; for a detailed analysis, see Carsten Stahn, "From 'United for Peace' to 'United for Justice': Reflections of the Power of the United Nations General Assembly to Create Criminal Tribunals or to Make Referrals to the ICC," 55 *Case Western Reserve Journal of International Law* (2023), pp. 251–86.

101 UN Doc A/RES/377 (V)), 3.11.1950; in that respect, see, in particular, Corell, note 99.

102 ICJ, *Certain Expenses of the United Nations (Article 17, Paragraph 2, of the United Nations Charter)*, Advisory Opinion of 20 July 1962, I.C.J. Reports 1962, p. 151, 163.

103 UN Doc S/RES/1315 (2000), 14.8.2000, in particular op. para.

104 Sir Hartley Shawcross, *Nuremberg Trial Proceedings*, vol. 3, Twelfth Day, Tuesday, 4 December 1945, Morning Session http://avalon.law.yale.edu/imt/12-04-45.asp.

105 Namira Negm, "Egypt," in Kreß and Barriga, note 2, p. 1300–1.

106 Marcel Biato and Marcelo Böhlke, "Brazil," in Kreß and Barriga, note 2, p. 1117, 1129–30.

107 For an elaborate exposition of this point, see Labuda, note 64; for such a regional perspective, see also Patrycja Grzebyk, "Crime of Aggression Against Ukraine: The Role of Regional Customary Law," 21 *Journal of International Criminal Justice* (2023), pp. 435–59.

108 UN Doc A/RES/ES-11/6, 2.3.2023, op. para. 9.

109 For the list of States, see note 75.

110 Chile Eboe-Osuji, "Letter to Editor: On So-Called Selectivity and a Tribunal for Aggression Against Ukraine," *Just Security*, February 10, 2023, https://www.justsecurity.org/85060/letter-to-editor-on-so-called-selectivity-and-a-tribunal-for-aggression-in-ukraine/.

111 Note 65.

112 Ban Ki-moon, "The Path to International Tribunal on Aggression against Ukraine Must Run through UNGA," *The Djakarta Post*, April 20, 2023, https://www.thejakartapost.com/opinion/2023/04/20/the-path-to-international-tribunal-on-aggression-in-ukraine-must-run-through-unga.html.

113 Note 75.

114 For an introduction of this proposal, which was worked out under the auspices of the Global Institute for the Crime of Aggression (https://crimeofaggression

.info), see Jennifer Trahan, "Amending the Kampala Amendments: A Proposal to Harmonize the ICC's Jurisdiction," *Opinio Iuris*, October 2, 2023, https://opiniojuris.org/2023/10/02/amending-the-kampala-amendments-a-proposal-to-harmonize-the-iccs-jurisdiction/; for an overview over the options, see Astrid Reisinger Coracini, "One Regime to Rule Them All. Harmonizing the Exercise of Jurisdiction over Crimes Within the Jurisdiction of the International Criminal Law," in C. Stahn (ed.), *The International Criminal Court in its Third Decade: Reflecting on Law and Practices* (2023), pp. 527–61.

115 André Stemmet, "South Africa," in Kreß and Barriga, note 2, p. 1271, 1282.

116 Ambassador Beth van Schaack, note 58.

117 Kreß, note 18.

Selected Bibliography

Asada, Masahiko and Dai Tamada (eds.), *The War in Ukraine and International Law* (Springer Nature, 2024).

Barriga, Stefan, "Negotiating the Amendments on the Crime of Aggression," in S. Barriga and C. Kreß (eds.), *The Travaux Préparatoires of the Crime of Aggression* (2011), pp. 3–57.

Green, James, Christian Henderson and Tom Ruys, "Russia's Attack on Ukraine and the ius ad bellum," 9 *Journal on the Use of Force and International Law* (2022), pp. 4–30.

Kreß, Claus, "The International Criminal Court as a Turning Point in the History of International Criminal Justice," in A. Cassese (ed.), *The Oxford Companion of International Criminal Justice* (2009), pp. 143–59.

Kreß, Claus and Leonie von Holtzendorff, "The Kampala Compromise on the Crime of Aggression," 8 *Journal of International Criminal Justice* (2010), pp. 1179–217.

Myon, Samuel, *Humane: How the United States Abandoned Peace and Reinvented War* (Farrar, Straus, and Giroux, 2021).

24

Tasks, Challenges, and Significance of Documentation in a Full-Scale War

Oleksandra Matviichuk

In February 2014, Russia launched a war against Ukraine that was accompanied by numerous international crimes and violations of human rights. At that time, the Revolution of Dignity had just ended, during which millions of people peacefully protested the pro-Russian government's halting of the European integration process.[1] With the authoritarian and corrupt regime overthrown, there was a chance for the country to become democratic. To stop Ukraine on the democratic path, Russia occupied Crimea and parts of the Donetsk and Luhansk regions in 2014, and eight years later, Russia launched a full-scale invasion.

Since February 24, 2022, an unprecedented number of new war crimes and other international crimes have been on record across the country.[2] Russian troops destroy residential buildings, churches, museums, schools, and hospitals.[3] They shoot people in evacuation corridors[4] and torture them in places of detention in Russia and occupied territories.[5] Ukrainian children are being forcibly taken to Russia for re-education to erase their Ukrainian identity.[6] Ukrainian language and culture is banned.[7] They are kidnapping, robbing, raping, and killing in the occupied territories.[8] And all modern international peace and security are powerless to prevent.

Russia is practicing war crimes and crimes against humanity as a method of waging war. This is a deliberate policy. By inflicting pain on the civilian population, Russia wants to break the resistance and occupy the country. The Russian military is practicing the same "war crimes playbook" that was used in Chechnya, Moldova, Georgia, Mali, Syria, and Libya.[9] And they have never been punished for doing so. The lack of accountability for international crimes around the world is ingrained in the mentality of the Russian military, as confirmed by the UN Commission of Inquiry on Ukraine. They believe they can do whatever they want.[10]

Ukraine's law enforcement agencies are overwhelmed. At the same time, the International Criminal Court, international and national human rights organizations, and missions with mandates from the UN, the Organization for Security and Co-operation in Europe (OSCE), the Council of Europe, and the European Union are at work in the country.

We are witnessing in real time the atrocities of one of the most documented wars in human history. There are several reasons behind this.

First, documentation and assistance to victims are actively undertaken by civil society organizations, both domestic and foreign. Several dozen civil society organizations have joined forces to create a national network of local documentarians. They work throughout the country, including in the occupied territories. They have developed a standard methodology and assigned responsibilities to account for every criminal incident, regardless of whether it has occurred in a large city or the smallest town in the region. As of June 2024, the "Tribunal for Putin" initiative has documented more than 75,000 alleged episodes of international crimes. Civil society's work is shared with official national and international institutions investigating various aspects of Russia's armed aggression.

Second, the work of gathering information that may point to the commission of international crimes takes place in real time. In the past, the collection of evidence and the reconstruction of the picture of events often occurred after the end of the armed conflict. As a result, much information was lost on the ground, the memories of victims and witnesses were erased, and evidence that would be admissible in court was destroyed. Ukraine has been working on documenting international crimes since the war began. The first mobile group of the Center for Civil Liberties went to Crimea at the end of February 2014. Already in the first phase of the Russian aggression in 2014–21, there were gradual changes in the national architecture of investigative bodies: The Prosecutor General's Office of the Autonomous Republic of Crimea was reopened, a war department was created in the Prosecutor General's Office, and in 2022 a unit to deal with sexual violence in armed conflicts was created.

Third, new technologies for documentation, communication, transmission, and information storage are widely used. They create opportunities to document crimes that human rights defenders could not have imagined fifteen years ago. Even ordinary people can access various digital tools: Google Maps helps determine location, Google Lens searches the web for images like photos, checks metadata to decide where and when a video was first posted, and more. Moreover, it is possible to reconstruct events and identify war criminals without being on the ground, as the work of organizations such as Bellingcat convincingly demonstrates. Using secure methods of communicating, storing, and transmitting data, it is possible to obtain information about events that occurred in the territories occupied by Russia and even in the territory of the Russian Federation itself.

Fourth, support from the international community to enhance the capacity of national systems to investigate and prosecute international crimes following international standards, in particular Article 14 of the International Covenant on Civil and Political Rights and Article 6 of the European Convention on Human Rights, has taken a variety of forms, including logistical support, training events, and expert advice. Simultaneously, the most successful and effective format of international assistance has been hands-on, on-the-ground support to national investigators. This includes establishing joint investigative teams involving national investigators, prosecutors, lawyers, human rights defenders, researchers, and international experts working in other conflict zones and international or hybrid criminal tribunals.

Documenting international crimes committed during armed conflict serves several purposes, including the following ones.

Establishment of Justice

War turns people into figures. The number of international crimes is growing so fast that it is simply impossible to keep up with all the stories. Thus, documentarians do not merely record Geneva or Hague Convention violations. They give people their names again.

The story of Illia, a ten-year-old boy from Mariupol, is a case in point.[11] Russian troops refused to allow the International Committee of the Red Cross to open the Green Corridor and evacuate civilians when they stormed the city. So, Illia and his mother Nataliia, like thousands of other residents, hid in their basements to avoid getting hit by Russian shells. They melted snow to get water and built fires to at least cook something to eat. When supplies ran out, the mother and boy were forced out of the basement and came under Russian fire. The mother was shot in the head, and the boy was wounded in the legs. With her last strength, the mother dragged her son to her friend's apartment. There was no medical care at that time. Russia destroyed Mariupol's maternity hospital, hospitals, and medical infrastructure. So, they just hugged on the couch in the friends' apartment. They stayed there for several hours. This little boy told the documentarians how his mother had died and how she cooled down right there in his arms.

Humans are no figures. Regardless of who they are, their social status, the type of crime and brutality they have suffered, and the interest of the media or international organizations in their fate, it is essential to ensure justice for all people. Because everybody's life counts.

Affirmation of Truth

War has economic, cyber, informational, and value dimensions in addition to the military dimension. War is also about the minds and hearts of people, including those not directly involved in armed conflict. This is why it is important—and especially difficult in times of information wars—to provide the international community, from politicians to ordinary citizens, with information about an accurate picture of events. Authoritarian regimes devote vast resources to dominating social media, creating fake news to distort reality, inciting hatred through propaganda, and achieving other military-industrial objectives.

Putin directly says that Ukrainians are one people with Russians and that the Ukrainian people do not exist, just as the Ukrainian language and culture do not exist.[12] Documentarians have recorded how these words became a terrible reality throughout the ten years of this war. Russian troops attempted to physically destroy Ukrainian leadership in the occupied territories: mayors, journalists, environmentalists, business people, writers, musicians, teachers, and priests.[13] They are deliberately destroying Ukrainian cultural heritage by confiscating and burning Ukrainian books, as well as looting and removing cultural artifacts from Ukrainian museums.[14] They are forcibly deporting thousands of Ukrainian children to Russia to erase their identity and re-educate them as Russians.[15]

Providing a realistic picture of the scale of the tragedy unfolding during an armed conflict allows international organizations and foreign governments to make more informed and timely decisions about helping civilians, conducting urgent humanitarian interventions, assisting the state subjected to armed aggression, imposing sanctions to reduce the aggressor's economic capacity to finance the continuing war, etc.

Historical Memory Preservation

Communicative memory of the past lives in society for three generations, and only what is discovered, understood, and recorded remains. Therefore, for the work of national archives, museum exhibitions, artistic understanding of the experience, etc., even information and testimonies that do not have legal relevance to serve as evidence in court hearings will still be important. Those who fail to learn history's lessons are condemned to repeat them.

The twentieth century brought with it two devastating world wars, terrible colonial wars, millions of deaths, and the total dehumanization of human beings, symbolized by the Holocaust and the Nazi concentration camps. The horrific lessons of the past forced us to take decisive action. Responsibility for the past was redefined in the slogan "Never Again." Leaders created the UN system and signed international covenants. A unified European project began with the Schuman Declaration. The idea that every human being is free and equal in dignity and rights became the new humanism of the post-war period.

However, the Soviet totalitarian regime was never condemned or punished for the Gulag, the mass deportations of the indigenous peoples of the Caucasus and Crimea, forced collectivization, the executions of hundreds of thousands of people based on the infamous "Troika" verdicts, the artificial famine of the Holodomor genocide, the erasure of identity and destruction of national cultures. All these atrocities have been left without any historical rethinking or legal assessment. It is not surprising that on this day, Russia says the exact opposite—"We can do it again"—when the world remembers the end of the Second World War with the slogan "Never again." And Russia is doing it again.

Documenting with the Latest Technology

The episode with the defenders of the Azovstal plant in Mariupol is remembered by many people who followed the course of Russia's war against Ukraine. People from different countries watched almost live as the Russians bombed the plant in besieged Mariupol, which was defended by the Ukrainian military and where about a thousand civilians were hiding underground during the two months of the full-scale invasion.[16]

Using technology that allowed them to access the Internet even in such conditions, those around them began recording videos and holding press conferences. They demanded the opening of a humanitarian corridor by international organizations and the rescue of civilians and wounded people. And then, even from afar, people started to feel like participating in what happened.

This example shows that war's offline and digital dimensions are completely intertwined. Even during the Russian occupation of Crimea, human rights activists did not have this kind of war coverage and a set of digital technologies for documentation.

We will start with digital tools that ordinary people use for very different purposes, including ones other than the documentation of war crimes. These include Google Maps for locating objects, Google Lens for finding similar photos online, metadata checking resources, fake news resources for checking where and when a video was first posted, resources for checking if and where data from your email has been leaked, various types of VPNs to avoid blocking of sources on the Internet, and so on.[17]

It also includes simple searches and even social media searches. Documentarians and investigative journalists have used Russian social media to find and identify perpetrators of documented war crimes.[18]

Databases are used to store and work with the information that has been collected. Databases such as MEMEX, IDOC, UWAZI, etc., are self-generated or created for documentation purposes. A database that allows simple analysis of all episodes recorded by the "Tribunal for Putin" initiative. If a prisoner mentions a specific name of the person who tortured him, a series of databases will allow the analysts to find other episodes in which this person also appears and link them to each other.

An arsenal of digital tools is being developed that allows for the analysis of the information collected. For example, the International Federation of Human Rights filed a petition with the International Criminal Court alleging a crime against humanity in the form of persecution by Russian propagandists.[19] Experts selected several hundred statements for the submission. In the past, it would have taken years to simply listen to the publicly available broadcasts. Now, some programs direct researchers to specific video fragments using search criteria.

Ukraine employs specific platforms for reporting war crimes, such as chatbots. At different stages of the war, there were a number of state and public chatbots for reporting war crimes.[20]

Information about war crimes is collected through state services. Most Ukrainian citizens with smartphones have access to the state program "Diia," which is a convenient place to store passports, driver's licenses, and other documents. Today, information about property damage caused by the war can be submitted to the International Register of Damages, established by the Council of Europe, through this state application right from your phone.[21]

It is worth mentioning that there are several digital tools that allow everyone to participate in the documentation process. For example, the IWitness app, which an ordinary person in Ukraine-controlled territory can download to his or her phone to send photos or videos containing information about war crimes to the project team managing the database and cooperating with the International Criminal Court. Finally, using this portal at https://otplink.icc-cpi.int/submission, anyone can directly report a documented international crime to the Office of the Prosecutor of the International Criminal Court.

Satellite imagery and other digital tools that are less accessible to human rights organizations can be mentioned separately. But it is already clear that over the years, technology has made it much more efficient to collect, store, search, verify, and process vast amounts of information about war crimes.

The success of this work depends on an effective response to some challenges, as documenting international crimes is only the first step in investigating and prosecuting perpetrators.

Legal System Capacity

Within weeks of the full-blown 2022 Russian invasion, it became clear that the national legal system could not handle such a huge workload. By June 2024, more than 130,000 cases of war crimes and other crimes related to armed aggression were under investigation by the Prosecutor's Office of Ukraine.[22] This number of cases would be a challenge for the world's most developed criminal justice system. Most cases will remain the responsibility of national investigative and judicial authorities, as the International Criminal Court will limit its investigations to a few selected cases. It is, therefore, important to find ways to enhance the capacity of national legal systems to effectively respond to victims' demands for justice. This requires changing the national architecture of investigative and judicial bodies and incorporating an international element into national investigations and trials.

The inadequacies of national legislation significantly complicate the situation. For example, as of June 2024, the Criminal Code of Ukraine does not provide for liability for crimes against humanity. Not all war crimes are covered by Article 438 of the criminal code.[23] Also, all forms of command responsibility, not only for direct orders to commit an international crime but also for intentional failure to prevent or punish it, are not provided for in the Criminal Code of Ukraine. Despite having amended the Criminal Procedure Code of Ukraine to facilitate cooperation with the International Criminal Court, some procedural problems remain unresolved. On the Independence Day of Ukraine on August 24, 2024, Ukrainian President Zelenskyy symbolically signed the law previously adopted by the Ukrainian Parliament to ratify the Rome Statute of the International Criminal Court (ICC) and its Kampala amendments on the crime of aggression. The formal deposit of Ukraine's instrument of ratification will be made in due course. Once effective, Ukraine's ratification would give the ICC jurisdiction over the crime of aggression going back to July 17, 2018. However, due to the carve-out of nationals of non-state parties under Article 15bis (5) of the Rome Statute, the ICC would not be able to exercise jurisdiction over Russian nationals for the crime of aggression committed against Ukraine. Additionally, Ukraine has invoked Article 124 of the Rome Statute to exempt its nationals from the ICC's jurisdiction over war crimes for a period of seven years, while it is unclear whether such a selective use of Article 124 is allowed by the Rome Statute.

The national legal system cannot overcome the immunities enjoyed under international law by the highest officials of another state (the "troika" of the head of state, head of government, and head of the foreign ministry). Therefore, a special court for the crime of aggression against Ukraine should be established since the International Criminal Court cannot exercise its jurisdiction over the crime of aggression in connection with Russia's war against Ukraine. At the same time, the States Parties to the Rome Statute should review the "Kampala Consensus" and expand the legal capacity of the International Criminal Court to ensure equal punishment for all cases of aggression.[24]

It is worth mentioning the shortcomings of the international peace and security system that allow a veto-wielding state in the UN Security Council to launch and conduct wars of aggression without fear of being punished for violating the Organization's Charter. This is evident in Russia's flagrant disregard for the interim measures ordered by the International Court of Justice in March 2022 in the case brought by Ukraine against Russia.[25] The decision obliged the Russian leadership to immediately cease hostilities and withdraw Russian troops from the territory of Ukraine. Still, Russia has failed to do either of these things for over two years.

International humanitarian law, which does not consider the modern technological nature of warfare, needs to be improved, and its instruments for protecting civilians need to be expanded. Another example is that of genocide. Unfortunately, the definition of this crime in international law is relatively narrow. For example, it is not necessary to commit one of the five acts listed in Article 2 of the UN Convention on the Prevention and Punishment of the Crime of Genocide to realize genocidal intent and destroy, in whole or in part, a group protected by the Convention. Sooner or later, the protected group will disappear if its identity is forcibly destroyed in the occupied territories. The international community is gradually accepting this more nuanced interpretation of the crime of genocide. For example, the Parliamentary Assembly of the Council of Europe adopted a resolution on combating cultural eradication, including as a component of the genocide crime, on Ukraine's initiative in June 2024. International tribunals should broaden their perspective accordingly and take more account of policies such as erasing identities when determining genocidal intent and acts.

Psycho-emotional Stress

Documentarian work involves constant contact with traumatizing information, contact with survivors of international crimes or victims of international crimes, and work in dangerous situations in the vicinity of war zones, including bombings and airstrikes, with the risk of their repetition.

The documentarians are concerned that they have to account for increasing numbers of crimes, even though they present the results of their documentation to international and national institutions. The feasibility of all their work is questioned when they realize the ineffectiveness of existing legal instruments during a full-scale war to help people here and now.

Working with pain will inevitably cause burnout. It increases the risk of physical exhaustion, the onset and development of chronic and other diseases, and the deterioration of mental health.

There are no sociological studies to rely on. Still, based on observation, it is clear that there is a substantial turnover of people working in the field of documenting civil society. Some people change the nature of their work forever or leave the human rights sector altogether after only a few years or even months of work.

"We gathered testimony from people who survived Russian imprisonment. They told us about being beaten, raped, tortured with electric shocks, starved and denied medical care. At that point, I had a sense of loss about the purpose of this work. Because I knew that at the very moment in which I was recording the words of another survivor, the same horrors were taking place in dozens of illegal detention centers in the occupied territories, and I was powerless to stop them."

In light of this, it seems important to include regular work with a psychotherapist in the safety protocols of documentarians when circumstances allow. It is also essential to teach people the tools of basic psychological support for themselves and other colleagues in a crisis or emotionally challenging situation.

Peace and Justice Are in False Opposition

Politics continues to dominate international law. In light of that reality, the international community is not rushing to take decisive legal action.

If humanity is to prevent wars in the future, the international community will have to consider those who are now the initiators of wars. For all the atrocities that the documentarians have chronicled are the result of a decision by the leadership to launch an aggressive war. Yet there are only two precedents in human history: the Nuremberg and Tokyo Tribunals. They did punish the war criminals of the Nazis and their allies, but only after the fall of the Nazi regime. Although the "Court of the Victors" was essential in establishing law and justice, the international community must go further. We need to change the way the world deals with these crimes. Justice cannot be a function of the manner and timing of the end of the war. We are, after all, living in a new century.

Justice is often at odds with peace. People in Ukraine want peace above all. But peace will not come if the country that is being attacked lays down its arms or if it stops looking for justice. It is occupation, then, not peace. Occupation is the same war, just in a different form. As real-time documentation shows, occupation is not just changing the national flag from one to another. Russian occupation means forced disappearances, rapes, mass deportations, torture in basements, forced adoption of children, erasing Ukrainian identity, filtration camps, and mass graves.

Without justice, a lasting peace that provides freedom from fear and a long-term perspective is impossible. Unpunished evil grows. Gross violations of human rights require a response from the world. There will always be politicians who will persuade us to forget about justice, ostensibly to save lives. But neither justice nor lives will be saved if we agree.

For example, on August 21, 2013, chemical weapons were used by the government of Syria in the suburbs of Damascus. Government forces fired missiles filled with the nerve agent sarin, into the civilian population. More than 1,700 people were injured, including many children. The international community's intervention was inevitable, as the use of chemical weapons had previously been declared a red line. But when it happened, politicians compromised. The Syrian government became a member of the Chemical Weapons Convention to destroy all of its existing stockpiles of chemical weapons, including sarin. Thus, Russia became the guarantor for this to happen.

Notwithstanding that international experts had collected and presented evidence of at least four new chemical attacks against civilians. Russia vetoed the extension of the mandate of the Joint Investigative Mechanism of the United Nations and the Organization for the Prohibition of Chemical Weapons in the Security Council.[26]

Documenting to Ensure Justice

People understand justice differently. For some, justice means seeing the perpetrators of crimes behind bars. For others, justice means being compensated; only then will a person feel satisfied. For some, justice is the opportunity to know the truth about what happened to someone they love. And yet, for others, justice means being heard and receiving official recognition that what has happened is immoral and unlawful.

Documentation addresses these needs and is the foundation of a comprehensive equity strategy. However, documentation alone will not be the solution unless further steps are taken to develop and implement the strategy.

Justice is often linked only to the past and/or the future. With the past, it is essentially about making right what has already been done. In the future, it means warning that similar actions will be punished going forward. In the here and now, however, justice has the potential to strategically alter reality. If, in the face of decisive action by the international community, at least part of the Russian military has doubts that it will be able to escape responsibility this time, that doubt will have a chilling effect on gross human rights violations by the Russians or anyone else. And this will make it possible to save thousands and thousands of lives since we are talking about an ongoing full-scale war.

Notes

1 Mykola Riabchuk and Andrej Lushnycky, "Ukraine's Third Attempt," in *Ukraine after the Euromaidan: Challenges and hopes,* Viktor Stepanenko and Yaroslav Pylynskyi eds. (Bern: Peter Lang 2015), 50.

2 UN News, "Human Rights Council: Russia responsible for 'widespread death and destruction' in Ukraine," *UN News*, February 27, 2023. https://news.un.org/en/story/2023/02/1133927.

3 The colossal destruction of residential buildings: David Medzerian, "Animated Maps Reveal Shocking Level of Devastation in Ukraine," *USC Today*, February 26, 2024. https://today.usc.edu/ukraine-devastation-cutting-through-the-fog-of-war-from-hundreds-of-miles-away/; David Lewis, "Domicide: The Mass Destruction of Homes Should Be a Crime Against Humanity - MIT Faculty Newsletter," *MIT Faculty Newsletter*, March 9, 2024. https://fnl.mit.edu/january-march-2024/domicide-the-mass-destruction-of-homes-should-be-a-crime-against-humanity/; Alexander Khrebet, "Governor: Russia's War Destroys Over 100,000 Residential Buildings in Donetsk Oblast," *The Kyiv Independent*, April 19, 2024. https://kyivindependent.com/governor-russias-war-destroys-over-100-000-residential-buildings-in-donetsk-oblast/. Ruining of churches and cultural sites: Jack Hunter, "In Pictures: The Ukrainian Religious Sites Ruined by Fighting," *BBC*, March 30, 2022. https://www.bbc.com/news/world-europe-60933862; John Hall, "Law Professor Witnesses Attack on Ukrainian Culture," *Chapman Newsroom*, March 1, 2024. https://news.chapman.edu/2024/03/01/law-professor-witnesses-attack-on-ukrainian-culture/; Ian Kuijt, Pavlo Shydlovskyi, and William Donaruma, "Spotlighting War's Cultural Destruction in Ukraine," *SAPIENS*, April 9, 2024. https://www.sapiens.org/archaeology/ukraine-cultural-heritage-war-destruction/; Center for Strategic and International Studies, et al., "Russia's Religious Persecution and Misinformation in Ukraine," *Transcript*, February 29, 2024. https://csis-website-prod.s3.amazonaws.com/s3fs-public/2024-03/240229_Yelenskyi_Ukraine_Persecution.pdf?VersionId=tAVLyntVgKz4Zsx DMG8jejImbPJ72ljX. Schools are also affected: Human Rights Watch, "Tanks on the Playground: Attacks on Schools and Military Use of Schools in Ukraine," 2023; Amnesty International, "Ukraine: Children's Education Is One More Casualty of Russian Aggression - Amnesty International," December 11, 2023. https://www.amnesty.org/en/documents/eur50/7508/2023/en/; UNICEF, "Widespread Learning Loss among Ukraine's Children, as Students Enter Fourth Year of Disruption to Education – UNICEF," August 29, 2023. https://www.unicef.org/eca/press-releases/widespread-learning-loss-among-ukraines-children-students-enter-fourth-year. And devastation of hospitals and healthcare system: Diane Cole, "Russia's 226 Attacks on Healthcare Targets in Ukraine Are Part of a Larger Pattern," *NPR*, May 24, 2022. https://www.npr.org/sections/goatsandsoda/2022/03/16/1086982186/russias-strike-on-ukraine-maternity-hospital-is-part-of-a-terrible-wartime-tradi; Physicians for Human Rights, "Destruction and Devastation: One Year of Russia's Assault on Ukraine's Health Care System," February 2023; UN Meeting Coverage "Russian Federation's Attack on Ukrainian Children's Hospital 'Not Only a War Crime' but 'Far Beyond the Limits of Humanity', Medical Director Tells Security Council | Meetings Coverage and Press Releases," July 9, 2024. https://press.un.org/en/2024/sc15761.doc.htm; Vitaly Mikula, "Ne Til'ky «Okhmatdyt»: Rosiyany Atakuvaly Shchonaymenshe 1800 Medzakladiv Pid Chas Viyny," *Slidstvo.info*, July 19, 2024. https://www.slidstvo.info/news/ne-tilky-okhmatdyt-rosiiany-atakuvaly-shchonaymenshe-1800-medzakladiv-pid-chas-viyny/

4 Ben Kesslen, "Russians Booby-trap 'Safe Corridor' in Ukraine With Landmines: Report," *New York Post*, March 7, 2022. https://nypost.com/2022/03/07/russians

-plant-landmines-in-ukraine-safe-corridor-report/; The Economist, "How Russia Uses Humanitarian Corridors and Ceasefires as Tools of War," *The Economist*, March 30, 2022. https://www.economist.com/the-economist-explains/2022/03/30/how-russia-uses-humanitarian-corridors-and-ceasefires-as-tools-of-war.

5 HRMMU, Anastasiia Honcharuk, and Office of the High Commissioner for Human Rights, "Report on the Human Rights Situation in Ukraine: December 1, 2023–February 29, 2024," March 26, 2024. https://www.ohchr.org/sites/default/files/documents/countries/ukraine/2024/report-human-rights-situation-ukraine-1-dec-2023-29-feb-2024.pdf; Office of the United Nations High Commissioner for Human Rights, "Report on the Treatment of Prisoners of War and Persons Hors De Combat in the Context of the Armed Attack by the Russian Federation Against Ukraine: February 24, 2022–February 23, 2023," March 24, 2023. https://www.ohchr.org/sites/default/files/2023-10/23-03-24-ukraine-thematic-report-pows-en.pdf; OSCE ODIHR, "Third Interim Report on Reported Violations of International Humanitarian Law and International Human Rights Law in Ukraine," July 17, 2023. https://www.osce.org/files/f/documents/5/2/548629_0.pdf.

6 Kaveh Khoshnood, Nathaniel A. Raymond, and Caitlin N. Howarth et al., "Belarus› Collaboration with Russia in the Systematic Deportation of Ukraine's Children" (New Haven, CT: Humanitarian Research Lab at Yale School of Public Health, November 2023); Kaveh Khoshnood, Nathaniel A. Raymond, and Caitlin N. Howarth et al., "Russia's Systematic Program for the Re-education and Adoption of Ukraine's Children" (New Haven, CT: Humanitarian Research Lab at Yale School of Public Health, February 2023), 14; Tbilisi, U.S. Embassy. "Russia's 'Re-education Camps' Hold Thousands of Ukraine's Children, Report Says - U.S. Embassy in Georgia," U.S. Embassy in Georgia, February 27, 2023. https://ge.usembassy.gov/russias-re-education-camps-hold-thousands-of-ukraines-children-report-says/.

7 Ayad Akhtar, "Ukrainian Culture Under Attack: Erasure of Ukrainian Culture in Russia's War Against Ukraine," PEN America and PEN Ukraine, 2022. https://pen.org/wp-content/uploads/2022/12/Ukraine-Culture-Under-Attack-12-20-22.pdf; Amnesty International, "Russia/Ukraine: A Decade of Suppressing non-Russian Identities in Occupied Crimea," March 18, 2024. https://www.amnesty.org/en/latest/news/2024/03/russia-ukraine-a-decade-of-suppressing-non-russian-identities-in-occupied-crimea/; Nina Shea, "Russia Is Persecuting Christian Churches in Occupied Ukraine," Hudson Institute, July 10, 2024. https://www.hudson.org/religious-freedom/russia-persecuting-christian-churches-occupied-ukraine-nina-shea.

8 Human Rights Council, "Report of the Independent International Commission of Inquiry on Ukraine," Fifty-Second Session, A/HRC/52/62, March 15, 2023; Human Rights Watch, "Ukraine: Apparent War Crimes in Russia-Controlled Areas," October 11, 2022. https://www.hrw.org/news/2022/04/03/ukraine-apparent-war-crimes-russia-controlled-areas; United States Department of State, "Ukraine—Russia-occupied Areas - United States Department of State," April 22, 2024. https://www.state.gov/reports/2023-country-reports-on-human-rights-practices/ukraine/russia-occupied-areas/.

9 Amnesty International, "Syrian and Russian Forces Targeting Hospitals as a Strategy of War," *Amnesty International*, August 8, 2022. https://www.amnesty.org/en/latest/press-release/2016/03/syrian-and-russian-forces-targeting-hospitals-as-a-strategy-of

-war/; Paul M. Carter, "Understanding Russia's Interest in Conflict Zones" (Special Report no. 469, Washington, DC: United States Institute of Peace, July 2020); Marek Górka, "The Wagner Group as a Tool of Russian Hybrid Warfare," *Polish Political Science Yearbook* 52, no. 2 (2023): 83–98. https://doi.org/10.15804/ppsy202324; Human Rights Watch, "Russian Atrocities in Chechnya Detailed," *Human Rights Watch*, October 28, 2020. https://www.hrw.org/news/2000/06/01/russian-atrocities-chechnya-detailed; Christopher Marsh, "Putin's Playbook: The Development of Russian Tactics, Operations, and Strategy from Chechnya to Ukraine" (Washington, DC: National Defense University's College of International Security Affairs, October 2023).

10 Human Rights Council, "Conference Room Paper of the Independent International Commission of Inquiry on Ukraine," Fifty-Second Session, A/HRC/52/CRP, August 29, 2023, ¶¶ 46–47.

11 Ohmatdyt National Specialized Children's Hospital, "The Story of Little Illya From Mariupol: The Mother of a 10-year-old Boy Died in His Arms, and the Child Was Taken to the Territory Not Controlled by Ukraine," Ministry of Health of Ukraine, May 22, 2022. https://ohmatdyt.com.ua/en/the-story-of-little-illya-from-mariupol-the-mother-of-a-10-year-old-boy-died-in-his-arms-and-the-child-was-taken-to-the-territory-not-controlled-by-ukraine/.

12 Vladimir Putin, "Article by Vladimir Putin "on the Historical Unity of Russians and Ukrainians," July 12, 2021; Ukrainian Research Institute at Harvard University, "Contextualizing Putin's 'on the Historical Unity of Russians and Ukrainians,'" Ukrainian Research Institute at Harvard University, August 2, 2021. https://huri.harvard.edu/news/putin-historical-unity.

13 Joanna Kakissis et al., "She Saved the Diary of a Ukrainian Writer Killed by Russia. Then She Was Killed, Too," *NPR*, July 15, 2023, https://www.npr.org/2023/07/15/1187498040/russia-ukraine-war-writers-killed; Dinara Khalilova, "These Ukrainian Artists, Writers Were Killed by Russia's War," *The Kyiv Independent*, October 31, 2023. https://kyivindependent.com/these-ukrainian-artists-writers-were-killed-by-russias-war/; RSF: Reporters Without Borders, "Russians Use Abduction, Hostage-taking to Threaten Ukrainian Journalists in Occupied Zones," *RSF*, September 8, 2024. https://rsf.org/en/russians-use-abduction-hostage-taking-threaten-ukrainian-journalists-occupied-zones; Ukrainian World Congress, "Russians Kill Zaporizhzhia Musicians Right After Concert to Benefit Ukraine's Armed Forces," August 11, 2023. https://www.ukrainianworldcongress.org/russians-kill-zaporizhzhia-musicians-right-after-concert-to-benefit-ukraines-armed-forces/.

14 Timothy Bella and Julian Duplain, "Russian Troops Looted Art Museums in Mariupol, City Council Says," *The Washington Post*, April 30, 2022. https://www.washingtonpost.com/world/2022/04/30/ukraine-russia-art-mariupol/; Martha Holder, "Russia's Invasion Aims to Erase Ukrainian Cultural Identity," *Atlantic Council*, January 4, 2024. https://www.atlanticcouncil.org/blogs/ukrainealert/russias-invasion-aims-to-erase-ukrainian-cultural-identity/; Human Rights Watch, "Ukraine: Russians Pillage Kherson Cultural Institutions," *Human Rights Watch*, December 20, 2022. https://www.hrw.org/news/2022/12/20/ukraine-russians-pillage-kherson-cultural-institutions.

15 Anastasiia Herasymchuk and Vladyslav Havrylov, "Russian-Style 'Re-Education': Ukrainian Children Are Cut off From Their Roots," UkraineWorld, October 15, 2023. https://ukraineworld.org/en/articles/analysis/re-education-ukrainian-children;

Alla Hurska, "Russia Converts Ukrainian Children Into Enemies," *Eurasia Daily Monitor* 21, no. 36 (March 2024). https://jamestown.org/program/russia-converts-ukrainian-children-into-enemies/.

16 Liz Cookman, "The Inside Story of the Siege of Azovstal," *The Economist*, September 23, 2022. https://www.economist.com/1843/2022/09/23/the-inside-story-of-the-siege-of-azovstal; Ukrainian Research Institute at Harvard University, "Mariupol's Last Stand: Inside Azovstal," Ukrainian Research Institute at Harvard University, n.d. https://huri.harvard.edu/mariupols-last-stand-inside-azovstal.

17 Human Rights Watch and SITU Research and Truth Hounds Investigation, "Beneath the Rubble: Documenting Devastation and Loss in Mariupol," Human Rights Watch, May 15, 2024. https://www.hrw.org/feature/russia-ukraine-war-mariupol; Alison Killing and Christopher Miller, "FT Investigation Finds Ukrainian Children on Russian Adoption Sites," *Financial Times*, June 12, 2024. https://www.ft.com/content/2d0013d2-a407-449f-b1e2-3d14fe65188f.

18 Yousur Al-Hlou et al., "Caught on Camera, Traced by Phone: The Russian Military Unit That Killed Dozens in Bucha," *The New York Times*, December 22, 2022. https://www.nytimes.com/2022/12/22/video/russia-ukraine-bucha-massacre-takeaways.html; Karina Bugaichenko, "'Storming Cities and Houses Is Our Element': Who Is Destroying Vovchansk and Killing Civilians," *Slidstvo.info*, June 8, 2024. https://www.slidstvo.info/english-stories/storming-cities-and-houses-is-our-element-who-is-destroying-vovchansk-and-killing-civilians/; Clothilde Goujard, "Digital Detectives Scour Ukraine Social Media for Evidence of Russian War Crimes," *POLITICO*, March 8, 2022. https://www.politico.eu/article/activists-ukraine-social-media-evidence-russia-war-crimes/.

19 FIDH, Kharkiv Human Rights Protection Group, Center for Civil Liberties, "Communication Submitted Under Article 15 of the Rome Statute of the International Criminal Court: Situation in Ukraine: Hate Speech as the Crime Against Humanity of Persecution," FIDH, June 2024. https://www.fidh.org/IMG/pdf/article_15_communication_on_hate_speech_as_the_crime_against_humanity_of_persecution_in_the_situation_of_ukraine.pdf.

20 Vera Bergengruen, "How Ukraine Is Crowdsourcing Digital Evidence of War Crimes," *TIME*, April 18, 2022. https://time.com/6166781/ukraine-crowdsourcing-war-crimes/; Oksana Bokalo, "Chatbots Gathering Evidence About Russian War Crimes?. . .," Uacrisis.org, March 25, 2022. https://uacrisis.org/uk/chat-boty-yaki-zibrayut-dokazy-pro-zlochyny-rosijskyh-vijsk-v-ukrayini; Zaporizhzhia Regional State Administration, "News / SBU Collects Facts About War Crimes of the Russian Federation: Chatbot and "Hotline" are in Operation," Zaporizhzhia Regional State Administration, August 3, 2023. https://www.zoda.gov.ua/news/66433/sbu-zbiraje-fakti-pro-vojenni-zlochini-rf-dijut-chat-bot-ta-garyacha-liniji.html.

21 Register of Damage for Ukraine, "SUBMIT a CLAIM – Register of Damage for Ukraine – Register of Damages Instance," n.d. https://rd4u.coe.int/en/submit-a-claim.

22 Office of the Prosecutor General, n.d. https://gp.gov.ua.

23 Shevchuk, A. V., "Violation of Laws and Customs of War (Article 438 of the Criminal Code of Ukraine), Committed on Behalf of and in the Interests of the Russian Federation: Problems of Criminal Legal Response," *Uzhhorod National University Herald Series Law* 2, no. 81 (April 8, 2024): 372–77. https://doi.org/10

.24144/2307-3322.2024.81.2.58; Truth Hounds, "Sources of Interpretation of Article 438 of the Criminal Code of Ukraine," *Truth Hounds*, September 22, 2023. https://truth-hounds.org/en/cases/sources-of-interpretation-of-article-438-of-the-criminal-code-of-ukraine/.

24 Tom Ruys, "Defining the Crime of Aggression: The Kampala Consensus," *The Military Law and the Law of War Review* 49, no. 1–2 (December 1, 2010): 95–136. https://doi.org/10.4337/mllwr.2010.1-2.06;
ChristianWenaweser, "Reaching the Kampala Compromise on Aggression: The Chair's Perspective," *Leiden Journal of International Law* 23, no. 4 (November 22, 2010): 883–87. https://doi.org/10.1017/s0922156510000439.

25 International Court of Justice, "Allegations of Genocide Under the Convention on the Prevention and Punishment of the Crime of Genocide - (Ukraine v. Russian Federation)," ICJ CR 2022/5, 2022. https://www.icj-cij.org/public/files/case-related/182/182-20220307-ORA-01-00-BI.pdf.

26 Human Rights Watch, "Attacks on Ghouta: Analysis of Alleged Use of Chemical Weapons in Syria," *Human Rights Watch*, September 2013; UN Meetings Coverage and Press Releases, "Security Council Fails to Renew Mandate of Joint Investigative Mechanism on Chemical Weapons Use in Syria, as Permanent Member Casts Veto," C/13040, October 24, 2017. https://press.un.org/en/2017/sc13040.doc.htm; UN Security Council, "Seventh Report of the Organisation for the Prohibition of Chemical Weapons-United Nations Joint Investigative Mechanism (S/2017/904) - Syrian Arab Republic," November 6, 2017.

Selected Bibliography

Bennetts, Marc, "Kyiv, Voice of the Kremlin Once Backed Ukraine and Western Values" (2024) available at https://www.thetimes.com/world/russia-ukraine-war/article/voice-of-the-kremlin-once-backed-ukraine-and-western-values-j6p8h6zxx.

d'istria, Thomas, "This is Where it All Began.' Ten Years after the Maidan Uprising, Ukrainians Face the Test of War" (2024) available at https://www.lemonde.fr/en/international/article/2024/02/18/this-is-where-it-all-began-ten-years-after-the-maidan-uprising-ukrainians-face-the-test-of-war_6537612_4.html.

Matviichuk, Oleksandra, "Euroviews. Russia's War in Ukraine Has Been Knocking on Your Door, Too" (2024) available at https://www.euronews.com/2024/02/24/russias-war-in-ukraine-has-been-knocking-on-your-door-too.

Mirovalev, Mansur A., "Tribunal for Putin' from a Nobel Prize-winning Ukrainian Rights Defender" (2024) available at https://www.aljazeera.com/features/2024/7/15/a-tribunal-for-putin-from-a-nobel-prize-winning-ukrainian-rights-defender.

Stern, David L., "As the U.S. Rushes to Send Military Aid, Ukrainians Applaud Lobbying Efforts" (2024) available at https://www.washingtonpost.com/world/2024/04/29/ukraine-lobbying-military-aid-war.

The Telegraph, 'Russia Must Lose to Stop World War 111'| Ukraine: The Latest Anniversary Special in Kyiv" (2024) available at https://www.youtube.com/watch?v=LutJ6UwFvAg.

Part 8

Reflections

25

The Nuremberg Principles

A Unique Legal Inheritance

Viviane E. Dittrich and Kiran Mohandas Menon[1]

The formulation of the Nuremberg Principles following the Nuremberg trial was anchored in a period that saw the formation of a new rules-based international order. The formulation process reflected an opportunity to elaborate and better understand the contours of key foundational norms and procedures underpinning this new order. The process was perhaps also a test case for exploring the possibilities of how the United Nations (UN) could encourage the progressive development and codification of international law as envisioned by the UN Charter. Such development was accompanied by solid albeit variable member state engagement, which was also essential for fortifying a nascent and fragile new institution. References to Nuremberg and the Nuremberg legacy remain ubiquitous. In a nutshell, notwithstanding shortcomings, criticisms and challenges today: "The outstanding significance of the Nuremberg Trials for modern international criminal law is evident in the lasting relevance of legal proceedings addressing wrongs committed, and in the effective force of a rules-based international order to the present day."[2] Eighty years on since the end of the Second World War and the opening of the Nuremberg trial, the rules-based international order is being attacked and eroded. International law is ignored or blatantly disregarded in unprecedented ways and the rule of law is facing widespread and deliberate attacks on a global scale.

References to Nuremberg and the Nuremberg legacy remain ubiquitous. In a nutshell, notwithstanding shortcomings, criticisms and challenges today: "The outstanding significance of the Nuremberg Trials for modern international criminal law is evident in the lasting relevance of legal proceedings addressing wrongs committed, and in the effective force of a rules-based international order to the present day."

This brief chapter assesses the historical and contemporary relevance of the Nuremberg Principles for the development of international criminal law as well as the foundational narratives that continue to define its purposes and prospects. The first section sketches the historical context of the formulation of the Nuremberg Principles, particularly concerning state engagement with this process. The second section traces how various courts and tribunals have featured the seven Nuremberg Principles in landmark proceedings that have contributed to changing the contours of international criminal law's norms. The final section turns to the Nuremberg Principles in contemporary discourse by looking at how they continue to be invoked in light of modern developments and the broader Nuremberg legacy.

An Incomplete and Sacred Representation

Primo Levi once wrote of being "intimately satisfied" by the conduct of the Nuremberg trial, describing it as having led to a "symbolic, incomplete, tendentious, sacred representation."[3] Levi's eloquent and imposing reflection can perhaps be extended to the enduring resonance of the Nuremberg Principles. Upon proposing the formulation of these principles, Francis Biddle, the primary US judge at the International Military Tribunal (IMT)[4] was highly aware of the volatilities that defined the era. Biddle called for the "scope and incidence" of the key legal postulations of the Nuremberg Charter and for judgment to be made "more precise."[5] He believed that this additional step would help secure the Nuremberg precedent and legacy.[6] Further, Biddle opined that such principles would be integral to ensure the suitable and gradual growth of substantive international criminal law. This objective required careful and delicate handling of an increasingly vulnerable international order influenced by a budding Cold War.

A nascent UN was considered as an authoritative forum for pursuing the formulation of the principles of international law recognized in the Nuremberg Charter and judgment. Article 13 of the UN Charter would allow the UN to undertake this task as the provision empowered the UN General Assembly to initiate processes "encouraging the progressive development of international law and its codification."[7] Trygve Lie, the first Secretary-General of the UN, had prominently called for these principles to be made a permanent part of international law:

> In the interest of peace and in order to protect mankind against future wars, it will be of decisive significance to have the principles which were implied in the Nürnberg trials, and according to which the German war criminals were sentenced, made a permanent part of the body of international law as quickly as possible. . . . From now on the instigators of new wars must know that there exist both law and punishment for their crimes. Here we have a high inspiration to go forward and begin the task of working toward a revitalized system of international law.[8]

Initiating such a process under the aegis of the UN indeed lent an extra layer of legitimacy to the Nuremberg precedent, especially at a time when questions surrounded the *ex post facto* nature of the Nuremberg judgment's legal character.[9] This can be deduced from Hersch Lauterpacht's response to the General Assembly resolution that certain enactments from the Nuremberg Charter and judgment had now taken "a significance transcending the occasion which gave rise to them."[10] The Nuremberg Principles had started taking on a new and singular character, complementing the charter and the judgment of the IMT.

The formulation process further reflected a moment when many states had identified an opportunity and a need to revive the Nuremberg judgment or respond to it. Francis Biddle had viewed the formulation process as necessary to ensure that the IMT's foundational postulations would be "significant" and not "ephemeral."[11] Some states echoed Biddle's views and thus backed the formulation process, designed to distill the key legal postulations that arose from the IMT's charter and judgment. Others identified the General Assembly as the forum best suited to respond to the limitations of the Nuremberg judgment. The exclusion of the crime of genocide in the judgment had evoked both consternation and indignation among some member states.[12] The formulation of the Nuremberg Principles demonstrated an important international consensus on fundamental norms and universal ambition.[13]

In the case of the Nuremberg Principles, no less than two resolutions passed during the first and second sessions of the UN General Assembly dealt with their formulation. In the immediate aftermath of the Nuremberg trial, Resolution 95(I) of December 11, 1946, affirmed the "Principles of International Law Recognized in the Charter of the Nürnberg Tribunal and in the Judgment of the Tribunal." Nearly a year later, Resolution 177(II) of November 21, 1947, entrusted the formulation of the Nuremberg Principles to the newly established International Law Commission. These resolutions have been portrayed as examples of the General Assembly adopting "resolutions declaring what it finds to be an existing rule of international law."[14]

Another resolution that closely interacted with the formulation process overlapping in time is Resolution 96(I) of December 11, 1946, which originated the Genocide Convention. Such assertions were based on the General Assembly's inclusive and multilateral forum, which ostensibly allowed it to uniquely reflect a consensus by a majority of nations on what they determined to be existing law. This delicate reality was of great importance at a time when the UN was seen as a potent forum for expressions concerning the anti-colonial movement.[15] For many states, engagement with these General Assembly resolutions provided an avenue to exhort changes to an international legal order that they perceived to be *hitherto* dominated by a small number of powerful states. Within the General Assembly, these differing positions were influenced by varying circumstances. Bert Röling, formerly a judge at the Tokyo Tribunal, explained these varying positions as being influenced by how different states discerned "societal forces, power relations, prevailing interests, and existing values."[16] In this context, it was clear that a discordance of views endured regarding the actual value and effect of the General Assembly's resolutions. Of particular interest in this context was the legal character and binding nature of resolutions of the UN General Assembly.[17] However, these pronouncements reflected a rare and acute period of opportunity to reinforce international law's norms and procedures before that momentum crumbled with the onset of the Cold War.

In Biddle's 1962 memoir, he recollects his rationale for pushing for formulating the Nuremberg Principles.[18] He describes the political state of affairs immediately after the closure of the trial as being defined by a "state of mutual international distrust."[19] Despite this, he surmised that "the most fruitful approach would be to push the procedural codification and to allow substantive law, already largely defined and accepted in the Nürnberg judgment, to grow empirically, from case to case."[20] Biddle knew that a lack of political will would hinder the formulation process. This, in turn, would make creating any sort of enforcement mechanism for the principles impossible. However, he still saw value in letting the "professors and the experts having a whack at it, clearing the way for political statesmen when they are ready, rather cautiously, to begin to act."[21] He was hopeful that a draft code for international criminal law would eventually follow a re-affirmation of the Nuremberg Principles by the UN.

It is noteworthy that the Nuremberg Principles were never formally adopted by the UN. The inability to create an international court or any form of enforcement for these principles made some contemporary experts weary of the formulation process. Vespasian Pella, an early proponent for establishing an international criminal court, worried whether an opportunity was being missed for establishing such an institution.[22] However, it is clear that the formulation of the principles was not seen as a standalone initiative. The actual formulation of each of the principles, along with their drafting history is telling, yet it is beyond the scope of this chapter. The essence of the formulation process and the form of these principles was an acknowledgment that international criminal law does not occupy a state of permanence, and its growth and survival require careful attention and refinement. The principles thus reflected what might be seen as a "symbolic, incomplete, tendentious, sacred representation", to borrow from Primo Levi, of the aspirations of international criminal law. Today, they can serve as a lens through which this law's modern origins,[23] development,[24] and systemic and structural myopias[25] may be observed. As courts traced normative and historical trajectories, the principles have become a veritable reference point for elaborating on sources of history, context, and authority.

Accompanying Landmark Jurisprudence

As international criminal law grew "empirically, from case to case," as Biddle had put it, the Nuremberg Principles featured in landmark jurisprudence. Their influence can be seen in the statutes and jurisprudence of various international criminal tribunals and regional human rights courts. The Nuremberg Principles have featured in proceedings at the International Criminal Court (ICC) as well as the *ad hoc* criminal tribunals and hybrid courts. This includes the International Criminal Tribunal for the former Yugoslavia (ICTY), International Criminal Tribunal for Rwanda (ICTR), Dili District Court Special Panel for Serious Crimes, Special Court for Sierra Leone (SCSL), and Extraordinary Chambers in the Courts of Cambodia (ECCC).[26] Also, the principles have appeared in other courts such as the International Court of Justice, European Court of Human Rights (ECtHR), and Inter-American Court of Human Rights (IACtHR).[27] It is worth tracing briefly where and how courts have referenced the principles.

Principle I was rather evocatively featured in the trial of Duško Tadić, the first defendant to stand trial before the ICTY. Tadić had challenged the legality of the tribunal, its subject matter jurisdiction, and the primacy over national courts that UN

Security Council Resolution 827 had designated to the Tribunal.[28] Noting that "[t]he principle of individual responsibility and punishment for crimes under international law recognized at Nuremberg is the cornerstone of international criminal law." The Trial Chamber relied on literature describing what became Nuremberg Principle I as the "enduring legacy of the Nuremberg Charter and Judgement."[29] Antonio Cassese, the first president of the ICTY, would later state that *Tadić* was the "most important case" he ever sat on, which also presented an opportunity to the tribunal to remove the "unacceptable distinction between internal and international as far as war crimes are concerned."[30] The decision's impact would shift the contours of how international criminal law was to be operationalized.

Principle II was highlighted in the trial of Ieng Sary held before the ECCC, which dealt with the responsibility of a former foreign minister of the Khmer Rouge regime.[31] The lawyers for the defendant argued that "genocide did not exist in Cambodian law and that liability for genocide was not accessible to Ieng Sary at the relevant time."[32] The ECCC dismissed this notion and held that the position of domestic law on the subject was irrelevant for triggering responsibility under international law. The Chamber relied on *inter alia* Nuremberg Principle II as it arrived at such a decision to dismiss Sary's appeal to close the proceedings.[33] While the trial proceeded despite a pardon that Sary had received decades earlier from the Cambodian King, a verdict was not reached due to the accused's untimely death.

Principle III and the question of immunity received great attention in the trial of Charles Taylor, former president of Liberia, who became the first head of state to be convicted by an international criminal tribunal for "planning, aiding and abetting war crimes and crimes against humanity."[34] Taylor had been indicted by the SCSL while he was still in office. While deliberating on the law's postulations amid contentions on immunity, the Appeals Chamber declared that no head of state immunity existed under international law. In doing so, the Chamber invoked Nuremberg Principle III to declare how this position had been entrenched in customary international law: "As long ago as 12 December 1950 when the General Assembly accepted this formulation of the principle of international law by the International Law Commission, that principle became firmly established."[35] The Taylor trial advanced the possibilities of international criminal law in matters beyond those relating to immunity. Valerie Oosterveld, for example, has written on how the Taylor trial was able to "confirm, expand, and clarify international criminal law on gender-based crimes."[36]

About questions of immunity, the case of the former Sudanese President Omar Al-Bashir is of particular significance. After a series of processes played out in various judicial, political, and diplomatic fora, the ICC Appeals Chamber held that there existed no immunity for heads of state accused of international crimes under customary international law in relation to an international court. In referring to how such a position had developed and specifically on how the ICTY and ICTR statutes had treated immunity, the Appeals Chamber stated that "both Statutes include provisions similar to Principle III of the Nuremberg Principles."[37]

Principle IV was brought forth in *K.-H. W. v. Germany*,[38] a 2001 proceeding held before the ECtHR. The case dealt with former leaders of the German Democratic

Republic who had been prosecuted for ordering the killing of individuals attempting to flee the country. In this proceeding, a former soldier who had been convicted in Germany approached the ECtHR, claiming the violation of the principle of *nullum crimen sine lege* as "the act on account of which he had been charged did not constitute an offence under the criminal law of the GDR."[39] Nuremberg Principle IV heavily featured in the court's tracing of the relevant normative histories as it dismissed the applicant's argument and upheld his conviction.[40]

The inclusion of Principle V had led to some disagreement during the formulation of the principles. Some ILC members viewed this principle as beyond the aim of the formulation process, which was about "imposing punishment."[41] The majority of the commission disagreed, and the right to a fair trial was found to be rightful, as was the fifth Nuremberg Principle. Since then, jurisprudence has considered the contours of what this right means in practice. Various elements have been identified and elaborated in relation to access to evidence and financial resources, as well as considerations in relation to language, cooperation, and length of procedures. Yvonne McDermott has highlighted that international criminal law "ought to act as a beacon of fairness for domestic legal systems," and courts have aspired to fulfill such a function.[42] In *Nikolić*, the ICTY Trial Chamber connected the "accused's right to a fair trial to the Tribunal's role in promoting human rights and respect for the rule of law."[43] The ICTR has also dealt with themes relating to the "duty to ensure the fundamental fairness of the trial" in multiple proceedings.[44] Despite this, challenges persist in this area of international proceedings, with the defense often still struggling for resources and procedural concerns where it faces "the danger of losing itself between national and international law."[45]

Principle VI(a) has not hitherto featured in jurisprudence. Despite the conception of the crime of aggression as crimes against peace at the time by the IMT and the International Military Tribunal for the Far East, also known as the Tokyo Tribunal,[46] efforts to build an international architecture to confront aggression lay dormant for decades. That changed to some extent with the onset of the "Kampala Compromise," which Claus Kress and Leonie von Holtzendorff hail as "a milestone in the development of international law" despite the "flaws and the complexities of the ultimate compromise."[47] However, the ICC's jurisdiction concerning this crime remains limited and lacking. How the Nuremberg legacy can be revived in this regard is today timely and amplified, especially after the Russian full-scale invasion of Ukraine in 2022. Decades after the IMT pronounced that "waging a war of aggression constitutes the supreme international crime"[48] international efforts are accelerating to further international prosecutions for aggression.

As for the other parts of Principle VI, a prominent case involves *Kordić & Čerkez*,[49] in which the ICTY Appeals Chamber ruled that the crime of "the wanton destruction of cities, towns or villages, or devastation not justified by military necessity" was "a violation of the laws and customs of war recognized by Article 3(b) of the Statute."[50] By way of elaboration, the chamber highlighted how this crime formed part of Article 6(b) of the Nuremberg Charter, which in turn was restated by Nuremberg Principle VI(b). That foundation was among the factors that determined for the ICTY that such a crime was part of customary law at the time it was allegedly committed.[51] In another highly prominent proceeding before the ICTY, the decision on preliminary motions in the case of Slobodan Milošević was handed down by the ICTY Trial Chamber in 2001.[52] Milošević was the first sitting head of state to be charged with war crimes. While deliberating on the status of the crime of deportation of a civilian population, the Trial Chamber elicited Nuremberg Principle VI(c).[53] The importance of Principle VI(c) for codifying murder as a crime against humanity was also emphasized in *Almonacid-Arellano et al v. Chile*.[54] In this case, the IACtHR, the court declared that serious violations of the Geneva Conventions and other international treaty obligations would not be "susceptible" to amnesties.[55] The judgment's interpretation of the control of conventionality principle has proved influential and contentious.[56]

Principle VII was cited in the first-ever international trial on genocide, the prosecution of Jean-Paul Akayesu before the ICTR. Principle VII was relied on by the Trial Chamber while tracing the origin and applicability of the crime of incitement to genocide and complicity in relation to international crimes.[57] *Akayesu* saw the "first international conviction of an individual for genocide" and, to some degree, clarified, if not extended, the scope of the crime.[58] The judgment remains further notable for recognizing the concept of genocidal rape and for its attention to gender-specific crimes showing a "sensitivity to gender-specific violence that, to date, has been absent from previous international judgments."[59]

In short, the Nuremberg Principles have been featured in international and national proceedings along with the Nuremberg Charter and judgment. Nuremberg was a turning point for what Justice Robert Jackson described as the "power of the precedent."[60] It challenged age-old notions of the creation of international law as the exclusive realm of nation-states and their vested and (often) insidious interests. The trial brought the judiciary to the forefront as a "legitimate enabler of international law."[61] This role, preserved by the courts and tribunals, along with related notions of judicial creativity, has been hugely influential in the subsequent development of international criminal law.[62] As briefly sketched above, the contribution of the Nuremberg Principles to this growth and development of international criminal law's procedural and operational contours has been noteworthy, even if perhaps understated and uneven.

Contemporary Challenges and Public Discourse

When assessing Nuremberg retrospectively, Justice Jackson already predicted that the trial's value would "depend less on how faithfully it interpreted the past" but rather how "accurately it forecasted the future."[63] He posited that "strife and suspicion" would lead to "new aggressions" with nations not "yet ready to receive and abide" by the law that was laid down at Nuremberg.[64] As Europe once again experiences the waging of a war of aggression, renewed attention to interpretations and reinterpretations of 'Nuremberg' is warranted. References to the Nuremberg trials and Nuremberg Principles, and often Nuremberg *tout court* as shorthand, remain potently present in public discourse. A cursory glance reveals the battle over the control of interpreting what is portrayed as the Nuremberg legacy. Indeed, as observed elsewhere, the legacy formation of international criminal tribunals remains ongoing and involves a multiplicity of actors and legacy constructions, that is how legacies are received, commemorated, and continuously constructed and re-constructed.[65] Legacy planning and legacy building has become an institutionalized endeavour at the *ad hoc* tribunals as well as the hybrid courts. The Nuremberg legacy, or Nuremberg legacies in the plural, to be more precise, continue unfolding.

The invocation of 'Nuremberg' has been omnipresent in initiatives aspiring to confront the Russian aggression against Ukraine. Less than a month following the invasion of Ukraine calls restoring to the symbolic power of Nuremberg came to dominate headlines. A campaign referred to as Justice for Ukraine, prominently initiated by Philippe Sands with the support of 140 legal experts and led by two former UK prime ministers, called for the creation of a "Nuremberg-style tribunal."[66] Ukraine's President Volodymyr Zelensky referred to the need for a "Nuremberg-like trial" at the UN Security Council.[67] For Ukraine, Kateryna Busol has noted that the "Nuremberg model is more about catalyzing a powerful reverberation of a particular message rather than procedural particularities."[68] On May 13, 2022, the European Parliament passed a motion calling for the establishment of a special *ad hoc* international criminal tribunal in order to prosecute the ongoing crime of aggression in Ukraine.[69] The preamble of the resolution explicitly mentioned the "Nuremberg Principles developed by the International Law Commission" as a definitive standard determining what constitutes war crimes. Scholars and practitioners have continued to deliberate on institutional design, including its potential composition and procedural and substantial framework.[70] Since early 2023, an internationalized tribunal rooted in the Ukrainian legal system has garnered wide policy support and a considerable alignment of international actors.[71] This movement culminated in the widely acclaimed agreement on May 9, 2025, by the Council of Europe and the Ukrainian government along with the "representatives of an international coalition of states" in relation to the establishment of a Special Tribunal for the Crime of Aggression against Ukraine".[72]

The symbolism of Nuremberg is regularly reinforced and resorted to in this context. A prominent example is a special field hearing by the US Commission on Security and Cooperation in Europe (Helsinki Commission), in cooperation with the Nuremberg Academy, held in Courtroom 600, the historic place of the Nuremberg trials, on February 20, 2024. The hearing entitled "Holding Russia Accountable for its War Crimes against Ukraine: Lessons from Nuremberg" engaged with leading experts on the best international and domestic avenues and approaches to ensure accountability for the Russian aggression against Ukraine and international crimes committed. In this context, Beth van Schaack, then US Ambassador-at-large for Global Criminal Justice, directly appealed to "the legacy of Nuremberg and the promise of the Nuremberg Principles":

> Just as the Allies at the end of the Second World War advanced the imperative of justice and ushered in a new era of accountability for the worst imaginable crimes, it falls on all of us to ensure that the legacy of Nuremberg and the promise of the Nuremberg Principles are not merely history.[73]

However, in a remarkable reinterpretation, Nuremberg has also been invoked to justify the aggression. Francine Hirsch has written about Russian leaders' weaponization of Nuremberg, emphasizing how this serves as "a reminder of how history and the law can be manipulated to serve almost any end."[74] There is great irony and incongruity in a totalitarian state using its self-proclaimed role as a "guardian of the Nuremberg trial"[75] in furthering a crime that was conceived and ingrained in the legal architecture by the IMT's charter and judgment. This is a poignant example of how different actors engage in competing or conflicting legacy constructions or re-constructions, shifting over time and serving current agendas and political interests and attempts to construe or restore meaning. Another example is the reinterpretation and public rewriting of the conflict and roles played by Ukraine and Russia by US President Donald Trump in spring 2025.

Propelled by the present-day Russian aggression, this is a moment of reckoning for the discourse surrounding the crime of aggression. By extension, the various narratives that are part of this discourse also continue to call upon and reassess what is seen as the Nuremberg legacy. Former Nuremberg prosecutor Henry King observed, "The area of international law where Nuremberg's legacy is more cloudy is aggressive war" and also cautioned that "a glaring gap in our inheritance from Nuremberg that must be corrected if peace and security are to be the order of the day."[76] In this context, the ostensible limitations placed on the ICC despite the "Kampala compromise" also become relevant. The importance of drawing the right lessons from the negotiations featured in the review conference calls for renewed attention. Prosecuting aggression is relatively new territory for international criminal justice. In relation to Jackson's prognosis on Nuremberg's forecasting of the future, it is seen as necessary that any progress made in this regard empowers the international criminal justice project as a whole. Any accountability efforts elucidate the imperative to consider and rethink prevention.

The Nuremberg Declaration on the Crime of Aggression, based on expert consultations in 2023, is also a response to the need for reinforcing the relevant international architecture and calls for "the implementation of the Nuremberg Principles everywhere at any time and in particular now with regards to Ukraine."[77] The declaration is particularly resonant considering the ever-increasing "need to align the ICC's jurisdiction over the crime of aggression with its jurisdiction over genocide, crimes against humanity and war crimes."[78] The declaration has become particularly timely with the special session of the Assembly of States Parties to the Rome Statute which will be held in July 2025.[79] Reaching an agreement to harmonise the ICC's jurisdiction on aggression with the other crimes would be a worthy tribute to the architects of the Nuremberg trials and principles.

The symbolic power of the Nuremberg Principles endures. There is no doubt that critical assessments and re-assessments of historic and foundational moments like the holding of the Nuremberg trials and the formulation of the Nuremberg Principles continue to be pertinent and necessary.[80] As David Luban observed in his seminal assessment of the legacies of Nuremberg, even Nuremberg's failures have much to teach us.[81] International criminal law has fortunately attended to some of the principles' omissions; jurisprudence, normative developments, and institutional practices have addressed *inter alia* genocide, sexual and gender-based violence, children's rights, victims' participation, and reparations—all of which constitute elements that were not established when the principles were formulated. As seen in the above section, the principles have been featured in jurisprudence where courts have addressed and rectified certain historical myopias accordingly. However, limitations endure with the law fighting to keep up with the changing and asymmetrical nature of modern warfare.

In conclusion, the attention that Nuremberg attracts and commands in public discourse is pervasive. Concerning the law's continuous development, the Nuremberg Principles remain today a valuable tool for introspection in international criminal justice. Certainly, the Nuremberg Principles are a product of their time. The weight and symbolic importance, albeit uneven implementation, of the Nuremberg Principles can be seen in how the broader Nuremberg legacy is routinely resorted to and regularly revived by scholars and practitioners, first and foremost, taking new forms and shapes while being absorbed into different discourses. What is certain is that the Nuremberg Principles are the most concrete and tangible legal inheritance of the Nuremberg trials.

Notes

1 Views expressed in this chapter do not necessarily reflect the views of the International Nuremberg Principles Academy.
2 Viviane Dittrich, "The Nuremberg Trials: The Foundation of Modern International Criminal Law," *"That four great nations" 75 Years Nuremberg Trial* (Publication Series the Nuremberg Municipal Museums), ed. Thomas Eser (Nuremberg: Michael Imhof Verlag, 2002) 47.
3 Cit in The Registry, International Court of Justice, Nuremberg Trial Archives, The International Court of Justice: Custodian of the Archives of the International Military Tribunal at Nuremberg, (2018), 19.
4 The Department of State Bulletin, vol. 15, 954.
5 The Department of State Bulletin, vol. 15, 954.
6 Viviane E. Dittrich, "Legacies in the Making: Assessing the Institutionalized Legacy Endeavour of the Special Court for Sierra Leone", in The Sierra Leone Special Court and Its Legacy: The Impact for Africa and International Criminal Law, ed. Charles C. Jalloh (Cambridge: Cambridge University Press, 2014), 663–91.
7 U.N. Charter, art. 13.
8 U.N. Secretary-General, *The Charter and Judgment of the Nürnberg Tribunal: History and Analysis*, U.N. Doc. A/CN.4/5 (1949), 11.
9 Hans Kelsen, "Will the Judgment in the Nuremberg Trial Constitute a Precedent in International Law?," *The International Law Quarterly* 1, no. 2 (1947): 153; Herbert Wechsler, "The Issues of the Nuremberg Trial," *Political Science Quarterly* 62, no. 1 (1947): 25.
10 Hersch Lauterpacht, "The Subjects of the Law of Nations," *Law Quarterly Review* 64, no. 1 (1948): 105.
11 The Department of State Bulletin, vol. 15 (1946): 954.
12 William A. Schabas, "Origins of the Genocide Convention: From Nuremberg to Paris," *Case Western Reserve Journal of International Law* 40 (2007): 35–55.

13 Viviane Dittrich and Natacha Bracq, "Passé et présent des principes de Nuremberg", *Déliberée* 19, no.2 (2023): 6-11.
14 Sloan, "The Binding Force of a Recommendation of the General Assembly of the United Nations": 25. Also see United Nations General Assembly Resolution 95 (I) of 11 December 1946, Affirmation of the Principles of International Law Recognized by the Charter of the Nuremberg Tribunal (December 11, 1946), https://legal.un.org/avl/pdf/h/ga_95-I/ga_95-I_ph_e.pdf and United Nations General Assembly Resolution 96 (I) of 11 December 1946, The Crime of Genocide (December 11, 1946), https://documents.un.org/doc/resolution/gen/nr0/033/47/pdf/nr003347.pdf?token=giFS6rOoAs4ObS6VF5&fe=true
15 See Swapna Kona Naidu, "We Were Once Colonized: Nehru, India, and Afro-Asianism at the United Nations," in *How Democracy Survives: Global Challenges in the Anthropocene*, eds. Michael Holme and R. S. Deese (Oxford: Routledge, 2023), 29–42.
16 Bert Röling and Antonio Cassese, *The Tokyo Trial and Beyond: Reflections of a Peacemonger* (Cambridge: Polity, 1994), 134.
17 F. Blaine Sloan, "The Binding Force of a Recommendation of the General Assembly of the United Nations," *British Yearbook of International Law* 25,1–33 (1948).
18 Francis Biddle, *In Brief Authority* (London: Bloomsbury Academic, 1976), 478.
19 Biddle, *In Brief Authority*, 478.
20 Biddle, *In Brief Authority*, 478.
21 Biddle, *In Brief Authority*, 478.
22 Vespasian V. Pella, "Towards an International Criminal Court," *The American Journal of International Law* 44, (1950): 37–68.
23 See Henry King Jr., "Commentary: The Modern Relevance of the Nuremberg Principles," *Boston College Third World Law Journal* 17, no. 2 (1997): 279–84.
24 See e.g. Philippe Kirsch, "Applying the Principles of Nuremberg in the International Criminal Court," *Washington University Global Studies Law Review* 6, no. 3 (2007): 501–9; Leila Sadat Wexler, "The Interpretation of the Nuremberg Principles by the French Court of Cassation: From Touvier to Barbie and Back Again," *Columbia Journal of Transnational Law* 32, no. 2 (1994): 289.
25 See Diane Marie Amann, "Portraits of Women at Nuremberg," *Impunity Watch Annual Review* 1 (2010–2011): 1–14; Benjamin B. Ferencz, "The Nuremberg Principles and the Gulf War," *St. John's Law Review* 66, no. 3 (1992): 711–32.
26 See International Nuremberg Principles Academy, "Resource Collection on the Nuremberg Principles," October 2020, https://www.nurembergacademy.org/fileadmin/media/pdf/projects/Resource_Collection_on_the_Nurembeg_Principles.pdf.
27 See International Nuremberg Principles Academy, "Resource Collection on the Nuremberg Principles," October 2020.
28 Christopher Greenwood, "International Humanitarian Law and the Tadic Case," *European Journal of International Law* 7, no. 2 (1996): 265–83.
29 Prosecutor v. Tadić, Case No. IT-94-1-T, Opinion and Judgement, 665 (International Criminal Tribunal for the Former Yugoslavia, May 7, 1997).
30 Cit. in Joseph Weiler, "Nino in His Own Words," *EJIL Talk*.
31 Seth Mydans, "Ieng Sary, Former Official of Khmer Rouge, Dies at 87," *The New York Times*, March 14, 2013, https://www.nytimes.com/2013/03/15/world/asia/ieng-sary-khmer-rouge-leader-tied-to-genocide-dies-at-87.html.
32 Mydans, "Ieng Sary, Former Official of Khmer Rouge, Dies at 87."

33 Co-Prosecutors v. Ieng Sary, Case File No. 002/19-09-2007-ECCC/OCIJ (PTC75), Decision on Ieng Sary's Appeal Against Closing Order (Extraordinary Chambers in the Courts of Cambodia April 11, 2011).

34 "UN Officials Welcome Court's Guilty Verdict in Charles Taylor Trial," *U.N. News*, April 26, 2012, https://news.un.org/en/story/2012/04/409542. For a wider appraisal of the court's functioning and legacy, see Charles C. Jalloh (ed.), The *Sierra Leone Special Court and its Legacy: The Impact for Africa and International Criminal Law* (Cambridge: Cambridge University Press, 2013).

35 Prosecutor v. Taylor, Case No. SCSL-03-01, Decision on Immunity from Jurisdiction (Special Court for Sierra Leone, May 31, 2004), https://docs.rscsl.org/document/SCSL-03-01-0059.

36 Valerie Oosterveld, "Gender and the Charles Taylor Case at the Special Court for Sierra Leone," *William & Mary Journal of Women and the Law* 19, no. 1 (2012): 10.

37 Prosecutor v. Al-Bashir, ICC-02/05-01/09 OA2, Appeals Chamber, Judgment in the Jordan Referral re Al-Bashir Appeal, 107 (International Criminal Court, May 6, 2019).

38 K.-H. W. v. Germany, App. No. 37201/97, Judgement (March 22, 2001), https://hudoc.echr.coe.int/eng?i=001-59352.

39 K.-H. W. v. Germany, App. No. 37201/97, Judgement.

40 K.-H. W. v. Germany, App. No. 37201/97, Judgement.

41 David S. Koller, "The Nuremberg Legacy in the Historical Development of International Criminal Law," in *Historical Origins of International Criminal Law: Volume 1*, eds. Morten Bergsmo, Cheah Wui Ling, and Yi Ping (Brussels: Torkel Opsahl Academic EPublisher, 2014), 573.

42 Yvonne McDermott, "The Right to a Fair Trial in International Criminal Law" (Irish Centre for Human Rights, School of Law, National University of Ireland, Galway, 2013).

43 As seen in McDermott, "The Right to a Fair Trial in International Criminal Law," 59.

44 As seen in McDermott, "The Right to a Fair Trial in International Criminal Law," 95.

45 Christoph Safferling, "The Rights and Interests of the Defence in the Pre-Trial Phase," *Journal of International Criminal Justice* 9, no. 3 (July 1, 2011): 651.

46 For an appraisal of the Tokyo Tribunal's legacies, see Viviane E. Dittrich, Kerstin von Lingen, Philipp Osten, and Jolana Makraiova, eds., *The Tokyo Tribunal: Perspectives on Law, History and Memory* (Brussels: Torkel Opsahl Academic EPublisher, 2020).

47 Claus Kreß and Leonie von Holtzendorff, "The Kampala Compromise on the Crime of Aggression," *Journal of International Criminal Justice* 8, no. 5 (2010): 1217.

48 France et al. v. Göring (Hermann) et al., Judgment and Sentence, (1946) (International Military Tribunal), 203.

49 Prosecutor v. Kordić & Čerkez, Case No. IT-95-14/2-A, Appeals Chamber, Judgement (International Criminal Tribunal for the Former Yugoslavia December 17, 2004).

50 Prosecutor v. Kordić & Čerkez, Case No. IT-95-14/2-A, Appeals Chamber, Judgement. 76.

51 Prosecutor v. Kordić & Čerkez, Case No. IT-95-14/2-A, Appeals Chamber, Judgement. 76.

52 Prosecutor v. Milošević, Case No. IT-02-54, Decision on Preliminary Motions (International Criminal Tribunal for the Former Yugoslavia November 8, 2001).

53 Prosecutor v. Milošević, Case No. IT-02-54, Decision on Preliminary Motions, para 49.

54 Almonacid Arellano et al. v. Chile, Preliminary Objections, Merits, Reparations and Costs, Judgement, Inter-American Court of Human Rights (ser. C) No. 154, 90, 98 et seq. (Sept. 26, 2006).

55 Almonacid Arellano et al. v. Chile, Preliminary Objections, Merits, Reparations and Costs, Judgement.

56 Néstor Pedro Sagüés, "Obligaciones Internacionales y Control de Convencionalidad," *Estudios Constitucionales* 8, no. 1 (2010): 117–36.

57 The Prosecutor v. Jean-Paul Akayesu, Judgment (International Criminal Tribunal for Rwanda September 2, 1998); https://docs.rscsl.org/document/SCSL-03-01-0059. The Principle is explicitly featured in para 526.

58 Jose E. Alvarez, "Lessons from the Akayesu Judgment," *ILSA Journal of International & Comparative Law* 5, no. 2 (1999): 359.

59 Alvarez, "Lessons from the Akayesu Judgment," 359.

60 See "Justice Jackson's Final Report to the President Concerning the Nurnberg War Crimes Trial," *Temple Law Quarterly* 19 (1946): 342. Justice Jackson was paraphrasing a statement from another renowned Justice of the US Supreme Court, Justice Benjamin Cardozo.

61 Guénaël Mettraux, "Judicial Inheritance: The Value and Significance of the Nuremberg Trial to Contemporary War Crimes Tribunals," in *Perspectives on the Nuremberg Trial*, ed. Guénaël Mettraux (Oxford: Oxford University Press, 2008), 601.

62 See Shane Darcy and Joseph Powderly eds., *Judicial Creativity at the International Criminal Tribunals* (Oxford: Oxford University Press, 2010).

63 Robert H. Jackson, "Nuremberg in Retrospect: Legal Answer to International Lawlessness," in *Perspectives on the Nuremberg Trial*, ed. Guénaël Mettraux (Oxford: Oxford University Press, 2008), 371.

64 Jackson, "Nuremberg in Retrospect: Legal Answer to International Lawlessness," 371.

65 For more detailed accounts of legacy formation and the first systematic examination of the institutional creation of legacies, see e.g. Viviane E. Dittrich, "Legacies in the Making at the ICTY", in *Legacies of the International Criminal Tribunal for the Former Yugoslavia: A Multidisciplinary Approach*, eds. Carsten Stahn, Carmel Agius, Serge Brammertz, and Colleeen Rohan (Oxford: Oxford University Press, 2020), 83–111; Viviane E. Dittrich, "Legacies in the Making: Assessing the Institutionalized Legacy Endeavour of the Special Court for Sierra Leone", in *The Sierra Leone Special Court and Its Legacy: The Impact for Africa and International Criminal Law,* ed. Charles C. Jalloh (Cambridge: Cambridge University Press, 2014), 663–91.

66 Christopher Schuetze and Victoria Kim, "In The Hague, Zelensky Renews Call to Prosecute Russian War Crimes," *The New York Times*, May 4, 2023, https://www.nytimes.com/2023/05/04/world/europe/zelensky-ukraine-hague-netherlands.html.

67 "Speech by the President of Ukraine at a meeting of the UN Security Council," Official Website of the President of Ukraine, April 5, 2022, https://www.president.gov.ua/en/news/vistup-prezidenta-ukrayini-na-zasidanni-radi-bezpeki-oon-74121.

68 Kateryna Busol, "Russia's Aggression against Ukraine and the Idealised Symbolism of Nuremberg," *EJIL: Talk*, June 16, 2022, https://www.ejiltalk.org/21022-2.

69 European Parliament, "Motion for a Resolution on the fight against impunity for war crimes in Ukraine", May 13, 2022, https://www.europarl.europa.eu/doceo/document/B-9-2022-0282_EN.html.

70 See Tom Dannenbaum, "A Special Tribunal for the Crime of Aggression?," *Journal of International Criminal Justice* 20, no. 4 (September 2022): 859–73.

71 At the conference entitled "The Nuremberg Principles: The Contemporary Challenges," convened in Washington, DC on March 29, 2023, to discuss the applicability of the Nuremberg Principles, which inspired the creation of this edited volume, Beth van Schaack announced US support for this accountability model.

72 European Commission, "International coalition agrees on the establishment of the Special Tribunal for the Crime of Aggression against Ukraine" May 9, 2025.

73 Beth van Schaack, Remarks to the Helsinki Commission, February 20, 2024, https://www.state.gov/remarks-to-the-helsinki-commission-holding-russia-accountable-for-war-crimes-against-ukraine-lessons-from-nuremberg/.

74 Hirsch, "Why Ukraine and Russia Both Look to the Nuremberg Trials," *TIME, https://time.com/6181464/ukraine-war-crimes-nuremberg/*.

75 Busol, "Russia's Aggression against Ukraine and the Idealised Symbolism of Nuremberg."

76 Henry T. King Jr., "Without Nuremberg, What?," *Washington University Global Studies Law Review* 6, no. 3 (2007) :655.

77 International Nuremberg Principles Academy, "Nuremberg Declaration on the Crime of Aggression," May 8, 2023.

78 Global Institute for the Prevention of Aggression, "The Urgent Need to Align the ICC's Jurisdiction over the Crime of Aggression with the Court's Jurisdiction over its Other Core Crimes," July 17, 2024.

79 Assembly of States Parties to the Rome Statute, "Special session on the review of the amendments on the crime of aggression", April 4, 2025.

80 For a recent collection for a recent collection including 70 perspectives by scholars and practitioners by scholars and practitioners on the Nuremberg Principles, see Viviane E. Dittrich, ed., *The Nuremberg Principles at 70 - 70 Perspectives*, forthcoming.

81 David Luban, "The Legacies of Nuremberg," *Social Research* 54, no. 4 (1987): 779–829.

Selected Bibliography

Amann, Diane Marie. "Portraits of Women at Nuremberg." *Impunity Watch Annual Review* 1, no. 1 (2010–2011): 1–14.

Biddle, Francis. *In Brief Authority*. Longdon: Bloomsbury Academic, 1976.

Dittrich, Viviane E., Kerstin von Lingen, Philipp Osten, and Jolana Makraiova, eds. *The Tokyo Tribunal: Perspectives on Law, History and Memory*. Brussels: Torkel Opsahl Academic EPublisher, 2020.

Jalloh, Charles C., ed., *The Sierra Leone Special Court and its Legacy: The Impact for Africa and International Criminal Law*. Cambridge: Cambridge University Press, 2013.

Mettraux, Guénaël, ed. *Perspectives on the Nuremberg Trial*. Oxford: Oxford University Press, 2008.

Dittrich, Viviane E., ed., The Nuremberg Principles at 70 - 70 Perspectives, forthcoming.

U.N. Secretary-General, *The Charter and Judgment of the Nürnberg Tribunal: History and Analysis*, U.N. Doc. A/CN.4/5 (1949).https://digitallibrary.un.org/record/160809?ln=en&v=pdf

26

How the Ukraine Situation Is Testing the International Criminal Court

Leila Nadya Sadat and Jack Hueseman

It has been more than two years since the Russian Federation invaded Ukraine in 2022 and a decade since its annexation of Crimea. During this time, Ukraine has sought to use international law to combat Russia's attacks on its territorial integrity, its sovereignty, and its political independence, with some limited degree of success. Indeed, in Spring 2022, Ukraine's Ambassador to the United States observed that her country had made a "civilizational choice" to put its faith in international law and institutions.[1] Ukraine has brought cases against the Russian Federation to the International Court of Justice,[2] the International Tribunal for the Law of the Sea,[3] the Permanent Court of Arbitration,[4] and the European Court of Human Rights.[5] It has addressed the Security Council on several occasions[6] and, when that failed due to Russian vetoes, obtained resolutions in the General Assembly condemning the invasion and emphasizing the need to investigate and prosecute serious crimes under international law.[7]

Most importantly, for this Chapter, Ukraine accepted the jurisdiction of the International Criminal Court ("ICC") in two declarations, allowing the Court to begin an examination of the situation to ascertain whether war crimes, crimes against humanity, or genocide (but not the crime of aggression, as discussed below) had been committed on its territory. The first declaration addressed the period from November 13, 2013, to February 22, 2014.[8] The second expanded the ICC's temporal jurisdiction to any time after February 20, 2014.[9] In 2019 and again in 2020, ICC Prosecutor Fatou Bensouda concluded that there was a "reasonable basis" to find that war crimes and crimes against humanity had been committed in Crimea and Eastern Ukraine.[10] However, she noted that given the operational limits of her office, as well as the difficulties imposed by the COVID-19 pandemic, she would consult with her successor before moving forward with an investigation.[11]

No further actions were taken, at least publicly, by Prosecutor Bensouda's successor, Karim A.A. Khan, until Russia invaded Ukraine in 2022. On February 28, 2022, Prosecutor Khan announced that the Office of the Prosecutor (OTP) would open an investigation into the Situation in Ukraine after concluding that there was a "reasonable basis to believe that both war crimes and crimes against humanity have been committed in Ukraine."[12] He then immediately invited states to refer the situation to him to avoid the need for Pre-Trial Chamber approval of the investigation,[13] and an unprecedented forty-three states obliged.[14] Since that time, the ICC has issued six public arrest warrants against top Russian officials, including Russia's President, Vladimir Putin.[15] The Court has also received additional funds for the Ukraine investigation,[16] and states seconded personnel to assist in its undertaking.[17] Even the United States supported the ICC's investigation,[18] which was a refreshing change from the bellicose rhetoric and sanctions imposed by former President Trump's administration just two years earlier.[19] Some of the funds donated supported the Court as a whole, and some seconded personnel are working on other situations,[20] but the general perception has been that the Ukraine situation has been a game changer for the Court, energizing the Court itself and causing states to rally around it in a new and important way.

There was a flurry of excitement when Prosecutor Khan began issuing arrest warrants in the Ukraine situation, even though he cannot bring charges for the crime of aggression due to jurisdictional limitations of the Kampala amendments.[21] That said, the war is ongoing, and the arrest warrants remain unenforced at this time. Although it is not unusual for international arrest warrants to be outstanding for extended periods of time, especially against leaders able to insulate themselves from the proceedings,[22] concern remains about the eventual success of the ICC's intervention and Ukraine's legal strategy more generally. As of this writing, Russia controls nearly 20 percent of Ukraine's territory.[23] While at least 50,000 Russian soldiers have died since 2022,[24] Ukraine has also suffered heavy losses. As of the end of May 2024, the Office of the High Commission of Human Rights ("OHCHR") recorded 11,126 civilian deaths caused by the Russian Federation's war against Ukraine, although it believes that the actual number may be considerably higher.[25] Millions have been displaced,[26] children have been kidnapped,[27] and nearly every city in the East has been destroyed.[28]

While it is too soon to declare that the ICC's intervention has been ineffective or useless, right now the Putin regime appears to have the upper hand. The ICC's slow reaction to the annexation of Crimea and the conflict in Eastern Ukraine may have given President Putin a feeling of impunity as he planned the 2022 invasion. Moreover, Russia has gone on the offensive since the issuance of the arrest warrants: the Russian Federation is suspected of being behind a major hacking of the ICC's computer systems, has attempted espionage at the Court,[29] and has opened its own criminal cases against the ICC Prosecutor and three judges of the Court.[30]

Efforts to fund assistance for Ukraine using the interest on frozen Russian assets,[31] as well as endeavors to create a new tribunal to prosecute Russian leaders for the crime of aggression,[32] demonstrate the creativity of international lawyers faced with obstacles to direct enforcement. A recent peace conference attended by 100 states was a positive step forward. However, Russia was not invited, China did not attend, and several countries from the Global South declined to sign the joint communique in the absence of Russia's exclusion from the conference.[33]

Yet there remains room for optimism. Although Ukraine's resort to international law and institutions has not produced immediate results, the long-term application of international law, including international criminal law, may make a real difference in the ultimate outcome of the conflict and the ability of the international legal system to withstand Russia's aggression and commission of international crimes. For this to happen, however, the ICC must overcome many challenges.

To begin with, there are real questions about the untested provisions of the Rome Statute in the Ukraine situation. The ICC has not previously adjudicated cases of international armed conflict between states engaged in aerial bombardment and siege warfare. Thus, it lacks well-established precedents to apply as it enters legally uncharted waters, although, as will be explained in Part IIIA, the precedents from the *ad hoc* international criminal tribunals may prove useful. Second, neither Ukraine nor the Russian Federation has ratified the Rome Statute, and thus the ICC's jurisdiction remains limited, which poses a particular problem with respect to the crime of aggression and enforcement of the Court's arrest warrants. Third, the conflict involves a powerful Permanent Member of the UN Security Council that has used its status as a global power to attack the ICC and more generally resist the application of international law. Finally, the West's stirring enthusiasm for the ICC's intervention in the Ukraine situation, as opposed to its often-tepid support for other situations, has exposed the Court's lack of universality and given rise to credible allegations of double standards in the application of international criminal law, which could undermine both the long- and short-term effectiveness of the ICC. This was evidenced by recent US attacks on the Court prompted by the Prosecutor's application for arrest warrants for Israeli (and Hamas) leaders in the Palestine Situation,[34] and the United Kingdom's recent challenge to the jurisdiction of the ICC over Israelis in the Palestine Situation (while presumably accepting the Court's jurisdiction over Hamas).[35] Although the United Kingdom ultimately dropped its challenge to jurisdiction, its initial filing led to 60 different submissions on the question of jurisdiction by states, scholars, and NGOs as of this writing,[36] consideration of which is likely to delay the proceedings considerably.

For the ICC to succeed in Ukraine, it must overcome Russian intransigence, uncertain and sometimes challenging legal precedents, and attacks on the Court from both state and non-state parties. If the arrest warrants issued to date are seen as merely symbolic, and if the Court is unable to implement them in a reasonable period, or at least to apprehend some suspects in the Ukraine situation, the ICC's future is precarious. It will lose the support of the West if it fails in Ukraine. If it succeeds in Ukraine and fails in Palestine, however, or in many of the other pressing situations now under investigation or examination, it may retain the support of Western states but will lose the support of African and Latin American states, which comprise a large number of its 124 States Parties. For this reason, states and non-state Parties must realize that to succeed in Ukraine, the Court and its Prosecutor must also bring cases without fear or favor in the other situations currently before it.[37]

Background of the Conflict and Its Signature Crimes

The Russian Invasions of Ukraine

The Annexation of Crimea in 2014: In February and March 2014, Ukraine's Russia-leaning President Viktor Yanukovych was forced from power during the Maidan

Revolution. During this period, the Russian Federation invaded and annexed the Crimean Peninsula,[38] and pro-Russia armed separatists took control of Donetsk and Luhansk,[39] two eastern provinces of Ukraine.[40] Russia declared Yanukovych's ouster to be an illegal coup,[41] describing it as "carried out by 'Russophobes and neo-Nazis'" which "justified Russia's efforts to protect Crimea's population."[42] The Russian Federation also argued that it was a necessary response to NATO's eastward expansion, which threatened its security.[43] However, as has been well-documented, the invasion was meant to punish Ukraine for supporting Western values and threatening Russian influence in a former Soviet territory[44] and to bolster Putin's dreams of restoring Russia's empire.[45]

More than 3,000 civilians died in the conflict between 2014 and 2020, during which Russia persistently used heavy military weaponry in populated civilian areas.[46] Ukraine filed declarations in 2014 and in 2015 under Article 12(3) of the ICC Statute, accepting the Court's jurisdiction for war crimes and crimes against humanity committed on its territory.[47] Although the Russian Federation formally incorporated Crimea into its territory[48] and has exercised effective control over it since then,[49] the United Nations General Assembly,[50] the ICC Prosecutor, and the European Court of Human Rights have determined that Crimea is occupied territory.[51] Under international law, territory cannot be acquired by annexation, and states are required not to recognize the effects of an illegal annexation.[52]

The 2022 Military Invasion: Eight years after invading Crimea, on February 21, 2022, Russian Federation President Vladimir Putin formally recognized the independence of the so-called Donetsk People's Republic and the Luhansk People's Republic, two separatist-controlled territories in Ukraine.[53] Three days later, on February 24, 2022, the Russian Federation invaded and attacked other parts of Ukraine.[54] As Russia shelled Ukrainian cities, President Putin appeared on television to formally announce the commencement of a "special military operation" that would "demilitarize" Ukraine.[55] According to Putin, the invasion was a humanitarian effort to save ethnic Russians from "genocide" by Ukraine and thwart Ukraine from acquiring nuclear weapons.[56] The invasion was the subject of a special session of the Security Council on February 25, 2022, which attempted to adopt a resolution condemning the attack and demanding Russia's withdrawal from Ukrainian territory.[57] The Resolution was never adopted, however, as the Russian Federation vetoed it. Instead, the General Assembly met under the Uniting for Peace Resolution[58] to deplore Russia's aggression and demand it withdraw its military forces from Ukraine.[59]

Signature Crimes

Russia's attacks on Ukraine represent a textbook example of a war of aggression[60] and have been marked by the widespread commission of international crimes. These "signature crimes" evince characteristics typical of specific criminals or a particular *modus operandi*. The conduct of the war in Ukraine exhibits many of the features seen in prior Russian military interventions, including Chechnya, Georgia, and Syria,[61] including a tendency to wage unrestricted warfare to destroy cities and target civilians and civilian infrastructure.[62]

Russia's campaign in Ukraine has been marked by indiscriminate attacks on civilians and a disregard for international humanitarian law (IHL).[63] The Report of the United Nations Human Rights Council-mandated Independent International Commission of Inquiry on Ukraine ("CoI") has documented attacks on thousands of residential buildings and educational institutions,[64] as well as more than 600 medical facilities.[65] Moreover, even when the Russian Federation has attacked military targets, it has done so using indiscriminate methods of warfare.[66] The CoI report identified four types of weapons used in indiscriminate attacks: unguided bombs, long-range anti-ship missiles, cluster munitions, and multiple-launch rocket systems.[67] In February 2023, the OHCHR stated that the Russian Federation's frequent use of these weapons in populated areas caused 90.3 percent of civilian casualties.[68]

The attack on Mariupol[69] is a tragic example of the Russian Federation's indiscriminate methods and disregard for civilians. By mid-May 2022, Russia had damaged 93 percent of the 477 multi-story apartment buildings in the central part of the city, all nineteen hospital campuses city-wide, and eighty-six of eighty-nine educational facilities.[70] Witnesses reported "constant" and "never-ending" bombardment of civilian objects.[71]

In total, 15,555 structures were reportedly affected, with 831 destroyed and nearly 6,000 severely damaged.[72] "It was hell," according to witnesses.[73] Indeed, the Russian Federation "reserved its cruelest for Mariupol"[74] from the beginning of the war. On March 16, 2022, just three weeks after the special military operation began, the Russian Federation bombed a maternity hospital in Mariupol.[75] One week later, despite significant markings with the word "CHILDREN" in Russian, the Russian Federation bombed the Donetsk Academic Regional Drama Theater, where hundreds of civilians were sheltering.[76]

As the attack on Mariupol continued, the Russian Federation cut off the city's power, heating, water, communications, and emergency services.[77] No one knows how many people died in Mariupol.[78] The Russian Federation deported many survivors to Russia,[79] and those who remain in Mariupol now live under Russian occupation.[80] Mariupol today bears no resemblance to the "vivacious port city" it once was.[81]

Russian Federation forces have also targeted Ukraine's civilian population with executions, torture, and sexual violence.[82] In the first few months after the special military operation began, the UN Commission of Inquiry confirmed the executions of sixty-eight Ukrainian civilians in the Chernihiv, Kharkiv, Kyiv, and Sumy regions.[83] The executions were worst in Bucha, which the Russian Federation forces left littered with dozens of bodies,[84] only two of whom appeared to be members of the military.[85] Residents said the Russians "shot everything,"[86] and many of the dead were shot in the head with their hands tied behind their backs.[87] In addition to executions and torture[88]—for example, beatings and electrocution—investigators are uncovering sexual violence "in every place that Russia occupied."[89]

The Russian Federation also targeted the civilian population by attacking Ukraine's electrical grid. In October 2022, Russian forces significantly increased attacks on energy-related infrastructure in Ukraine, targeting sub-stations that distribute electricity to homes and leaving millions without access to electricity, heat, and water during winter.[90] Russia also recklessly endangered civilians and the environment during its takeover of the Zaporizhzhia Nuclear Power Plant in southeastern Ukraine.[91] When Russia first took control of the power plant shortly after the invasion, 11,000 individuals worked there.[92] That number has dwindled to 3,000, and allegations of torture by Russian officials have been levied by the remaining employees.[93] The Russian military is also operating weapons and military equipment in close proximity to nuclear materials, heightening the risk of disaster not only for Ukraine but for much of Europe, and potentially involving the commission of environmental crimes under Article 8(2)(b)(iv) of the Statute.[94]

Even with the issuance of new arrest warrants in 2024, Russian attacks have continued unabated. On July 8, 2024, Russian forces destroyed Ukraine's largest children's hospital in one of its most devastating assaults on Kyiv.[95] Experts identified the weapons used in the attack as Russian Kh-101 cruise missiles and have observed that the use of these weapons, with their controlled and likely pre-programmed trajectories, indicates that Russia deliberately targeted the hospital.[96] The World Health Organization has documented 1,682 attacks on healthcare in Ukraine,[97] as Russia repeatedly conducts "double-tap" strikes on first responders.[98] The Russian Federation presided over the Security Council during July 2024, and its ambassador not only denied responsibility for the Kyiv hospital strike but contended that Ukraine had bombed the hospital. Speaking in his national capacity, Russia's ambassador stated that "if this had been a Russian strike, there would have been nothing left of the building and all the children would have been killed and not wounded."[99]

As of this writing, the ICC Prosecutor has made six arrest warrants public in the Ukraine situation. The first two warrants, issued on March 17, 2023, targeted Russia's unlawful deportation of Ukrainian children to Russia. The second two warrants were issued on March 5, 2024, against Sergei Ivanovich Kobylash and Viktor Nikolayevich Sokolov, two top Russian military commanders. The third set of warrants were issued on June 25, 2024, against Sergei Kuzhugetovich Shoigu, Russian Minister of Defense, and Valery Vasilyevich Gerasimov, Chief of the General Staff of the Russian Armed Forces. The 2024 warrants charge the four accused with the war crimes of directing attacks at civilian objects under article 8(2)(b)(ii) of the Statute[100] and causing excessive incidental harm to civilians or damage to civilian objects under article 8(2)(b)(iv).[101] They are also charged with the crime against humanity of inhumane acts under Article 7(1)(k), predicated upon the "alleged campaign of strikes," which are alleged to have caused great suffering and/or serious injury to the body or to mental or physical health.[102] This is a particularly interesting use of the "other inhumane acts" provision of Article 7 of the Rome Statute on crimes against humanity.

The allegations against the six individuals publicly charged in the Ukraine situation present novel charges and complex legal questions at the ICC. The following section explores how the ICC might approach the crimes charged. It leaves aside the first warrants, which address offenses against children, and focuses on the charges relating to the airstrike campaign and siege warfare.

The Challenge of the Ukraine Situation for the ICC

Legally Uncharted Waters

Sources of Law

One challenge the ICC faces in prosecuting the Russian Federation's crimes in Ukraine is a lack of precedent with respect to interstate conflict and warfare tactics such as aerial bombardment, siege warfare, and terror. Thus far, the ICC has focused chiefly on conflicts between organized armed groups or on crimes committed by non-state actors within a state. This is true of the situations in the Central African Republic, the Democratic Republic of the Congo, Mali, and Uganda. There have been allegations of crimes committed by state forces in the situations of Côte d'Ivoire, Kenya, Libya, Palestine, and Sudan, but no final judgments have been rendered in these situations. To date, none of the Court's judgments have addressed interstate conflict using modern weaponry, including aerial bombardment campaigns. These cases can be extremely challenging given the difficulties of evidence collection, linking higher-ups with the conduct of hostilities in the field, and distinguishing legitimate military actions from indiscriminate bombing campaigns or attacks directed against civilians.

Under Article 21 of the Rome Statute, which sets out the Court's applicable law, the Court may look to the case law of other international criminal courts and tribunals, assuming they are consistent with the ICC Statute. Article 21(1)(a) requires the Court to look first to its Statute and the Elements of Crimes. In the absence of specific guidance from the Statute and the Elements of Crimes, however, it is to apply in second place "applicable treaties and the principles and rules of international law, including the established principles of international law of armed conflict."[103] This allows—indeed requires—the ICC to apply the customary international law of armed conflict when considering and interpreting the war crimes provisions of the Rome Statute. Likewise, the Elements of Crimes instruct the Court to interpret the Statute within the established framework of the international law of armed conflict.[104] This includes, *inter alia*, the 1949 Geneva Conventions, their Additional Protocols, the 1907 Hague Convention, and customary international law. The Russian Federation is a party to the Geneva Conventions and the 1907 Hague Convention.[105] The Soviet Union ratified Additional Protocols I and II; however, in 2019, Vladimir Putin revoked Russia's adherence to Protocol I.[106] Ukraine is a party to each of those treaties. That said, the provisions of Protocol I largely reflect customary international law.

A rich source of customary international law in the context of armed conflict is the jurisprudence of the *ad hoc* international criminal tribunals, including the International Criminal Tribunal for the former Yugoslavia ("ICTY"), the International Criminal Tribunal for Rwanda, the Special Court for Sierra Leone, and the Extraordinary Chambers in the Courts of Cambodia.[107] The Court has typically relied heavily on the jurisprudence of the *ad hoc* international criminal tribunals in developing and interpreting the Rome Statute,[108] although some Chambers have cautioned against doing so from time to time.[109] Because the war in Ukraine has been conducted in many ways like the war in the former Yugoslavia, the jurisprudence of the ICTY may be useful as an interpretative source at the ICC in the Ukraine context, even given some of the textual differences between the ICTY Statute and the Rome Statute. This is particularly true as regards the 2024 warrants, which address attacks on civilians and civilian objects.

The ICTY Statute had two war crimes provisions: Article 2 covering grave breaches of the Geneva Conventions of 1949, and a broader provision, Article 3 ("violations of the laws or customs of war"), which included provisions of the 1907 Hague Convention and served as a "residual clause" to ensure that no serious violation of international humanitarian law remained outside the ICTY's jurisdiction.[110] Article 5 covered crimes against humanity arising out of widespread or systematic attacks directed against civilian populations.[111] Several cases applying these provisions are discussed briefly below.

Of Siege Warfare and Aerial Bombardment

The Siege of Sarajevo: During the Bosnian War, Bosnian Serb forces besieged Sarajevo as part of an ethnic cleansing campaign targeting Bosnian Muslims and Croats. Like Mariupol, Sarajevo was a strategically located city and an "important political, cultural, industrial, and commercial centre."[112] The siege lasted from April 1992 to November 1995 and included heavy shelling in civilian areas.[113] The resulting harm to civilians was immense. Attacks on civilians were so widespread that one soldier "said he felt more secure at the frontline than elsewhere in Sarajevo because 'fire was opened less often' at the confrontation lines."[114] Residents appearing before the ICTY testified that no areas were safe and that civilians were targeted everywhere,[115] with a "constant fear of death."[116] The "unrelenting violence" devastated the city.[117]

The ICTY convicted several individuals on charges relating to the siege of Sarajevo, including Commander Stanislav Galić, Commander Dragomir Milošević, Commander Ratko Mladić, and Bosnian-Serb President Radovan Karadžić, finding that the perpetrators had carried out a widespread and systematic campaign of sniping and shelling in Sarajevo.[118] Convictions resulted both for attacks directed against the civilian population or against civilians not taking direct part in hostilities (along the lines of ICC Statute arts. 8(2)(b)(ii) and. 8(2)(b)(iv)), and for crimes against humanity or as the war crime of terror. These cases may prove instructive as the ICC addresses the cases against Kobylash, Sokolov, Gerasimov, and Shoigu, and are discussed briefly below.

Stanislav Galić: Galić was a commander in the Bosnian-Serb Army from 1992 to 1994[119] in charge of the Siege of Sarajevo.[120] The ICTY charged Galić with war crimes under Article 3[121] of the ICTY Statute and crimes against humanity under Article 5[122] of the ICTY Statute.

The indictment against Galić included seven charges. He was successfully convicted of four, including murder and inhumane acts as a crime against humanity as a result of sniping, artillery, and mortar attacks upon civilian areas and the civilian population of Sarajevo, which caused civilian deaths and civilian suffering and injury.[123] The war crimes charges were based on Article 51(2) of Additional Protocol I and Article 13(2) of Additional Protocol II to the Geneva Conventions, representing conventional and customary international law.[124] The Trial Chamber found that the attacks on civilians qualified as grave breaches of Additional Protocol I.[125] Galić was also convicted of violating the laws or customs of war by unlawfully inflicting terror upon civilians.[126] These acts were also found to constitute the crimes against humanity of murder and other inhumane acts (the latter covered the non-fatal injuries inflicted in the course of the attacks on civilians).[127]

When determining whether Galić bore individual criminal responsibility for the siege of Sarajevo, the Trial Chamber considered his knowledge of the crimes and his effective control over the perpetrators. The Trial Chamber noted that Galić had been present on the battlefield[128] and had "personally observed the situation in the field."[129] UN representatives had also personally delivered complaints to Galić and his subordinates,[130] and there was "evidence that the SRK was put on notice via the media coverage."[131] Finally, because artillery was a "key asset" of the SRK,[132] the Tribunal found it "inconceivable" that the SRK "would allow its gunners to fire according to their own volition, without the knowledge of the hierarchy."[133]

The Tribunal also found that Galić had effective control over his soldiers because of the SRK's "normal military command and control" structure[134] and Galić's "material ability to prosecute and punish" soldiers that disobeyed orders or committed criminal acts.[135] Yet despite this knowledge and control, Galić failed to take "reasonable measures to prosecute and punish perpetrators of crimes against civilians,"[136] demonstrating "a deliberate intent to let the situation pervade and continue"[137] and engaging his superior responsibility. The Trial Chamber determined that Galić was responsible for the commission of the crimes because they revealed a striking pattern and were committed in a widespread fashion and over a long period of time,[138] leading to the inference "that the criminal acts were not sporadic acts of soldiers out of control but were carried out pursuant to a deliberate campaign of attacking civilians, which must have emanated from a higher authority or at least had its approval."[139]

Dragomir Milošević: Milošević succeeded Galić as commander of the SRK and was convicted of similar crimes.[140] Like Galić, Milošević was found to be aware that crimes were being committed under his command,[141] and the troops committing those crimes were under his effective control.[142] The Trial Chamber found that, because the crimes were "not single incidents or sporadic occurrences," but constituted a pattern, Milošević was guilty of ordering and planning the shelling of Sarajevo's civilian population.[143] Although Milošević did not devise the strategy on his own, he "was able to implement the greater strategy in a manner he saw fit" and "decided on the deployment of weapons, . . . on the placement of artillery batteries and movement of modified air bomb launchers." On appeal, Miloševič argued that the Trial Chamber erred by failing to consider certain areas as "military zones," even when those areas contained civilians.[144] The Appeals Chamber rejected this challenge, finding that "the population in certain urban areas within the confrontation lines retained its civilian status."[145] Moreover, "the Trial Chamber engaged in a case-by-case analysis of the character of the objective and modalities of the attack in order to establish whether the civilian population . . . [was] unlawfully targeted."[146]

Ratko Mladić: Mladić commanded the Army of Republika Srpska and issued orders to the SRK. During his command, he monitored operations in Sarajevo.[147] He was convicted of the crimes of terror, unlawful attacks on civilians, and murder for his role in personally directing the bombardment of Sarajevo and ordering the SRK to cut utilities supplying Sarajevo.[148] He was convicted of participating in several related joint criminal enterprises, both as a matter of direct responsibility and as a superior for knowing or having reason to know that crimes were about to be committed or had been committed by forces under his effective control and failing to prevent the crimes or punish the perpetrators. He was one of the first individuals indicted by the ICTY in 1995 but was not arrested until 2011.[149]

Radovan Karadžić: Karadžić was president of the Republika Srpska and the supreme commander of its armed forces.[150] Like Mladić, he was indicted in 1995 but not arrested until 2008.[151] The ICTY convicted Karadžić of murder, terror, and unlawful attacks on civilians for his involvement in the siege of Sarajevo. The Trial Chamber found the existence of a common plan to be "the only reasonable conclusion" that could be drawn from the longevity of the siege and the high number of civilian casualties.[152] It concluded that had the targeting of civilians not been part of the SRK's plan, it "would not have persisted unabated for so long."[153] Karadžić significantly contributed to the plan by:

> (i) his continuous support of [General Ratko] Mladić, who was central in the implementation of the Sarajevo JCE; (ii) his direct involvement in the military matters in and around Sarajevo at the planning and operational levels; (iii) his knowledge of the attacks on civilians in Sarajevo and of indiscriminate or disproportionate SRK fire, together with his persistent denials and deflections of any SRK responsibility; (iv) his failure to prevent the shelling and the sniping of civilians and to punish those responsible, despite being at the apex of control over the VRS and SRK; (v) his support for and promotion of the SRK commanders and units while aware of their involvement in the campaign of sniping and shelling of civilians; and (vi) his modulation of that campaign in accordance with his political goals.[154]

The Shelling of Zagreb: Zagreb is another example of an artillery attack that resulted in individual criminal responsibility. In May 1995, Croatian-Serb forces repeatedly shelled Zagreb.[155] This shelling killed seven people and injured more than 200.[156] Shelled locations included a school, a theater, and a children's hospital.[157] Milan Martić ordered the shelling,[158] which Croatian-Serb forces conducted with Orkan rockets. Orkan rockets are non-guided projectiles used to target soldiers and armored vehicles and containing a cluster warhead with 288 "bomblets" or twenty-four anti-tank shells.[159] They are released approximately 800–1,000 meters in the air and explode upon impact.[160] The range of error is about 1,000 meters.[161] These were found to be an indiscriminate weapon by the Trial Chamber because they were incapable of hitting specific targets.[162]

The ICTY convicted Martić of murder and attacks on civilians for the shelling of Zagreb.[163] Because of the SRK's methods—specifically the use of the indiscriminate Orkan rockets—the Tribunal found that the presence of legitimate military targets in Zagreb was irrelevant.[164] Moreover, it found that the effects of these methods were well known to those ordering the attack.[165]

Application to the ICC: War Crimes: Although the ICTY Statute and the Rome Statute differ, the Rome Statute defines a war crime as a serious violation of the laws and customs applicable in international armed conflict,[166] including intentionally directing attacks against the civilian population,[167] intentionally directing attacks against civilian objects,[168] and "intentionally launching an attack in the knowledge that it will cause loss of life or injury to civilians or damage to civilian objects . . . which would be clearly excessive in relation to the concrete and direct overall military advantage anticipated."[169] These provisions of the Statute reflect the principle of distinction in international humanitarian law ("IHL"), which requires the parties to a conflict to distinguish between the civilian population and enemy combatants and between civilian and military objects.[170] This principle is codified in Articles 48 and 51 of Additional Protocol I and reflected in customary international law.[171]

The Rome Statute instructs the ICC to apply applicable treaties and the principles and rules of international law, including the established principles of IHL.[172] Just as the ICTY applied the Geneva Conventions to the commanders responsible for the destruction in Sarajevo, so too should the ICC apply them to the Russian commanders to assist the Court "in the interpretation of the relevant provisions of the Rome Statute."[173]

The four high-ranking Russian commanders indicted by the ICC have been accused of the war crimes of directing attacks at civilian objects and causing excessive harm to civilians and civilian objects. Kobylash and Sokolov are accused of bearing responsibility for missile strikes carried out by Russian armed forces against Ukraine's electric infrastructure from at least October 10, 2022, to March 9, 2023, including strikes against electric power plants and substations. Shoigu and Gerasimov are charged with the same offenses. The crimes are undoubtedly serious, and the accused are high-ranking. According to one source, "Russia's attacks on Ukraine's power plants during the winter of 2022–2023 left 12 million people with limited or no access to energy and severely damaged Ukraine's health care system."[174] The crimes resemble the sniping and shelling campaign against Sarajevo. As with the siege and shelling of Sarajevo, the centralized command structure of the Russian military[175] and the extensive documentation[176] of harm to civilians in Ukraine mean that knowledge of the pattern is undeniable to Russian commanders. Russia has leveled cities, targeted hospitals, tortured and executed civilians, and cut off civilians from basic necessities such as electricity. This is evidence of a systemic plan or practice. Indeed, the relationship of the four accused to each other is not dissimilar to the ICTY quartet of Galić, Milošević, Mladić, and Karadžić. That said, while the success of the prosecutions in the ICTY should give ICC Prosecutors some confidence, there are nonetheless differences between the ICTY and Rome Statutes that will make obtaining convictions at the ICC potentially more difficult.

First, the ICC does not use the doctrine of joint criminal enterprise ("JCE"), which allowed ICTY Prosecutors to link individuals to specific crimes so long as they substantially contributed to their commission through their commission in a joint criminal enterprise,[177] not unlike conspiracy law in the United States. The ICC, however, has thus far rejected the doctrine of JCE and instead interpreted Article 25 of its Statute in a complex, controversial, and novel manner, relying upon the German notion of "control of the crime" to link higher-ups to those perpetrating crimes on the ground.[178] This has made convictions at the ICC difficult unless the accused are shown to have direct knowledge of and, in some cases, participation in the crimes on the ground.[179]

ICC Prosecutors are undoubtedly aware of this issue, including the head of the Ukraine Pillar in the Office of the Prosecutor ("OTP"), Brenda Hollis, who was a highly successful Prosecutor at the ICTY, as well as at other international criminal tribunals.[180] This may be why they have not yet levied charges of war crimes involving the conduct of hostilities against President Vladimir Putin, where it might be more challenging to establish the linkage between specific offenses and the President himself. Instead, they have directed them at Kobylash, a Lt. General in the Russian Armed Forces, who was the commander of the long-range aviation of the Aerospace Force during the campaign against Ukraine's energy infrastructure, and Sokolov, an Admiral in the Russian Navy who commanded the Black Sea Fleet at the time of the attacks.[181] Shoigu was the Russian Federation's Minister of Defense at the time of the alleged conduct, and Gerasimov was the Chief of the General Staff of the Armed Forces of the Russian Federation and First Deputy Minister of Defense during the relevant time period. As noted above, this is remarkably similar to the charging pattern at the ICTY.

All four accused have been charged under Article 25(3)(a) as co-perpetrators who committed the acts jointly and/or through others; under 25(3)(b) with ordering the commission of the crimes; and under Article 28 with failure to exercise proper control over forces under their command. To convict the accused under 25(3)(a) either as direct or indirect co-perpetrators is a challenging task, requiring that the Prosecutor establish the existence of a common plan and an intent to commit the crimes (among other elements).[182] As top commanders, the charge of "ordering" others to commit the attacks is a sensible one but must still be proven, meaning that the chain of command and evidence of actual orders will need to be established. Finally, regarding command responsibility, the Prosecutor will need to show that the accused had effective control over the operations and committed the relevant offenses with intent and knowledge, case law which remains undeveloped at the ICC.[183]

Finally, under Article 8(2)(b)(iv), the attack on the electrical infrastructure must be found to have been "intentionally launched" "in the knowledge" that the attack would cause incidental loss of life or injury to civilians or damage to civilian objects that is *clearly excessive in relation to the concrete and direct overall military advantage anticipated.* This latter proviso can be tricky to establish for "dual use" objects (like power grids) that have both military and civilian uses, as the Final Report to the Prosecutor on the NATO Bombing Campaign makes clear.[184] Under Article 52 of Protocol I, military objectives are those which make an effective contribution to military action and whose destruction offers a definite military advantage.[185] Dual-use objects, like power plants and power grids, must be examined on a case-by-case basis,[186] but in cases of doubt, an object that is "normally dedicated to civilian purposes" must be considered as such.[187] That said, because power grids can be regarded as military objectives, it will have to be shown that the strikes were "clearly excessive" in relation to the concrete and overall military advantage anticipated. This is a more demanding proviso than customary international law or the standard at the ICTY.[188]

Finally, the *Galić* case makes an important contribution in finding that shelling and aerial bombardment of civilian infrastructure can be criminalized as the war crime of inflicting terror on the civilian population. The Appeals Chamber in *Galić* found that the crime of acts and threats of violence, the primary purpose of which is to spread terror among the civilian population, is a crime under customary international law and enshrined in Article 51(2) of Additional Protocol I and Article 13(2) of Additional Protocol II.[189] While this would seem relevant to the Ukraine situation, the ICC Prosecutor did not charge any of the four high-ranking Russian officers with the crime of terror, perhaps because Article 22 of the Rome Statute forbids the creation of crimes by analogy and the Rome Statute does not include a specific offense regarding the crime of terror.[190] Instead, they accused the defendant of committing other inhumane acts as a crime against humanity, which is discussed below:

Application to the ICC: Crimes Against Humanity: The ICC Prosecutors have also charged the attacks on civilians and civilian infrastructure as crimes against humanity of other inhumane acts. The Rome Statute provides that murder and other inhumane acts of a similar character intentionally causing great suffering are crimes against humanity when committed as part of a widespread or systematic attack directed against any civilian population.[191] For the crime against humanity of inhumane acts, the acts must be of a similar character to any other act referred to in Article 7(1) of the Rome Statute, considering the nature and gravity of the act.[192]

At the ICTY, the crime against humanity of inhumane acts served as a residual clause for serious crimes that were not otherwise enumerated in Article 5 of the ICTY Statute.[193] The specific elements were (1) an act or omission of similar seriousness to the other acts enumerated in Article 5; (2) the act or omission caused serious mental or physical suffering or injury or constituted a serious attack on human dignity; and (3) the act or omission was performed intentionally by the accused, or by a person or persons for whose acts and omissions the accused bears criminal responsibility.[194]

At the ICC, the elements of the crime against humanity of inhumane acts the ICC are (1) great suffering or serious injury to bodily or mental or physical health by means of an inhumane act; (2) such act was of a character similar to any other act referred to in Article 7(1); (3) the perpetrator was aware of the factual circumstances establishing the character of the act; (4) the conduct was committed as part of a widespread or systematic attack directed against the civilian population; and (5) the perpetrator knew that the conduct was part of or intended the conduct to be part of a widespread or systematic attack directed against a civilian population.[195] The Trial Chamber must consider all the factual circumstances, including the nature of the act, the context, the circumstances of the victim, and the physical, mental, and moral effects on the victim.[196]

While there is not yet extensive jurisprudence on Article 8 (war crimes) at the ICC, given the generally conservative reading of the Statute to date (with some notable exceptions), it is likely that to be successful, the war crimes charges will require the Prosecutor to identify specific unlawful attacks rather than allege the illegality of the overall bombing and siege campaign against Ukraine. In contrast, the crime against humanity of other inhumane acts may be a vehicle for the Prosecutor to charge Russians for a widespread and systematic campaign of aerial bombardment directed at civilian objects in Ukraine. This may offer a way to "get from the specific incident at the micro level" to the unlawful campaign at the macro level, as William Fenrick has pointed out.[197] As in *Galić*, where the tribunal found that it "would be impossible to treat each incident of killing as a separate murder case,"[198] here too the Russian campaign has been so widespread and devastating that it would seemingly be appropriate to pursue a theory of crimes against humanity in order to prosecute the campaign as a whole. Indeed, rather than proceed attack by attack—and allow the Russians to claim that each attack involved military objectives—in a case involving widespread attacks on hospitals, residential areas, and power grids that caused extensive loss of life and other harm to the civilian population, the Court could look at the totality of the campaign and the overall damage incurred. Some ICC judges have voiced objections to such an approach regarding crimes against humanity, suggesting that an "incident by incident" rather than a holistic approach should be employed, but it is unclear how widespread (or appropriate) this view is.

The Non-State Party Problem

Neither the Russian Federation nor Ukraine is a State Party to the Rome Statute. However, Article 12(3) of the Rome Statute permits states to accept the ICC's jurisdiction on an ad hoc basis,[199] and, as noted earlier, Ukraine did so in two Article 12(3) declarations lodged with the Court in 2014 and 2015. The Russian Federation has not consented to the ICC's jurisdiction, but it is well-established that the ICC may exercise jurisdiction over crimes committed on the territory of a state that has accepted the jurisdiction of the ICC by the nationals of other states.[200] Indeed, the ICC has had several preliminary examinations, investigations, and trials that involve the commission of ICC crimes by non-state party nationals on the territory of States Parties, including in the Democratic Republic of the Congo, South Korea, Georgia, Bangladesh, and Palestine.[201] As the ICC Prosecutor has observed on prior occasions, the basis of such conferred jurisdiction is not novel, as it was the basis for establishing the Nuremberg Tribunal.[202] Indeed, as Professor Sadat has written elsewhere:

> The Court . . . enforces the *ius puniendi* of the international community with respect to the core crimes falling within its jurisdiction.[203] This competence is not derived from or transferred by each individual State's national jurisdiction but is, rather, a function of their collective action at the international level, representing, in other

> words, a form of "collective conferral." The ICC has the powers conferred upon it by States Parties to the Rome Statute, as well as those inherent to its function as an international court.[204]

While the United States originally took that position that the ICC could not legally exercise jurisdiction over non-state party nationals without the consent of their national state,[205] it abandoned this objection in the case of Ukraine, eager to see President Putin and his regime in the dock.[206] This was a surprising development because just two years prior, the United States had sanctioned the ICC Prosecutor and a high-ranking member of her staff based upon their request in the Afghanistan situation to investigate allegations of torture committed by US persons in Afghanistan.[207] While the sanctions were lifted by the Biden administration in 2021, in repudiating the Executive Order, President Biden continued to maintain US objections to ICC jurisdiction "over personnel of such non-state parties as the United States and its allies absent their consent or referral by the United Nations Security Council."[208] While the United States appears to have completely reversed its prior position in the Ukraine case, some scholars continue to maintain a more limited view of the Court's jurisdiction, arguing that because the Russian Federation is not a party to the Rome Statute, Putin remains immune from criminal prosecution as a head of state as Russia has not waived his immunity.[209] Although the Appeals Chamber's judgment in the *Al Bashir* decision at the Court seems to have definitely decided the question as regards the ICC,[210] because that case involved a Security Council referral to the Court rather than a State Party referral, arguments are still advanced, and not only by the Russian Federation, that Putin is immune.

Russia's Superpower Status

The ICC has also been seriously challenged by the Russian Federation's status as a global power. The Court is a relatively fragile institution. It has no police force of its own and is dependent upon member states' protection and cooperation. Conversely, the Russian Federation exercises substantial global influence through its permanent membership (and veto power) in the UN Security Council, its cyber and nuclear capabilities, and its ability to evade sanctions. The Russian Federation's veto power has enabled it to block any action by the Security Council relating to Ukraine,[211] including referring the Ukraine situation to the ICC Prosecutor under Chapter VII of the UN Charter.[212]

The Russian Federation has also targeted the ICC and its personnel. After the Pre-Trial Chamber issued its warrants of arrest for Putin and Lvova-Belova, the Russian Federation opened criminal investigations into the ICC Prosecutor and three ICC Judges.[213] Two months later, it announced indictments *in absentia* for Prosecutor Khan and Judge Rosario Salvatore Aitala for "preparing to attack a representative of a foreign country enjoying international protection in order to complicate international relations."[214] Additionally, in September 2023, the ICC experienced a serious cyber security incident, which it "interpreted as a serious attempt to undermine the Court's mandate."[215] Although the ICC has not confirmed who was behind the attack, the evidence "indicates a targeted and sophisticated attack with the objective of espionage."[216] Given the Russian Federation's history of sophisticated cyber warfare,[217] the ICC's ongoing investigation into the Russian Federation, and its previous attempts at infiltrating the ICC,[218] experts have speculated that it is likely that the Russian Federation played a role in the attack.

In addition, the Russian Federation's ability to evade financial sanctions enables it to continue funding its war in Ukraine. At the outset of the full-scale invasion in February 2022, many Western states imposed sanctions on the Russian Federation's economy meant to hinder its ability to wage a long war. Most experts believed such measures would significantly impact the Russian Federation,[219] but much of the world has declined to participate,[220] and Russia's economy has remained resilient.[221] Although Russia's supply of artillery may be shrinking,[222] its economic resilience provides all the more reason for Western states to continue funding Ukraine. Moreover, and alarmingly, when faced with threats, the Russian Federation continuously reminds the world of its stockpile of nuclear weapons.[223]

Global South, Global North: The Problem of Double Standards

The apparent commitment of Western powers to ensure that justice is meted out to Russian President Vladimir Putin and members of his cabinet and military struck many observers as inconsistent with the disinterest many of the same states had shown regarding ICC investigations involving less favored victims.[224] Patryk Labuda has referred to the recent enthusiasm for the ICC among Western nations as a "Ukraine moment" for the Court, noting that more than twenty governments pledged assistance, including through financial contributions and seconded personnel;[225] the OTP sent its most significant deployment in a single situation to collect evidence; and parallel national investigations were undertaken and international evidence gathering mechanisms were established. Yet this enthusiasm was largely absent among African states and much of the Global South,[226] and the efforts of US and UK scholars to create a Special Tribunal for the Crime of Aggression[227] to try Putin and a handful of others was seen as particularly irksome given that the ICC's inability to do so was largely a result of US pressure exerted at Kampala to ensure that ICC non-state party nationals could never be tried for the crime of aggression without the consent of their national state unless the Security Council referred the situation to the Court. Indeed, given the long-standing jurisdictional objections by the United States to the exercise of jurisdiction over the nationals of non-state parties without consent, the US enthusiasm for ICC arrest warrants directed at Russian nationals seems hypocritical.

Yet one can also argue that if it took the Ukraine situation to finally convince the United States to abandon its attacks on the Court and its longstanding arguments, this would be a welcome development. In addition, the enthusiasm for prosecutions in the Ukraine situation at least laid to rest the concern that the ICC was only "targeting Africa"[228] and evoked the possibility that the justice meted out by the Court could be more universally applicable. Moreover, Ukrainians have often been disparaged within

Europe as less "European" than their brethren in the West, and they are and have been the victims of atrocities warranting a robust response.

More troubling has been the efforts by some states, including ICC States Parties, to support the ICC's intervention in Ukraine as regards Russian nationals but oppose it with respect to Israeli nationals. This became particularly apparent in the wake of the October 7 Hamas attacks in Israel and the ensuing war in Gaza. Palestine had sought the protection of the ICC for many years before the October 7 attacks (as Ukraine had done following the annexation of Crimea in 2014) but without success. Initially rebuffed by Prosecutor Luis Moreno Ocampo, Palestine sought and received recognition as a "non-member observer state" of the UN General Assembly in 2012 under GA Resolution 67/19.[229] On January 2, 2015, Palestine acceded to the Rome Statute,[230] and in 2018, asked the Prosecutor to "investigate, in accordance with the temporal jurisdiction of the Court, past, ongoing and future crimes within the Court's jurisdiction committed in all parts of the territory of the State of Palestine,"[231] referencing alleged crimes committed by Israeli nationals.[232]

Prosecutor Bensouda found that there was a "reasonable basis" to believe that war crimes had been committed by the Israeli Defense Forces, Hamas, and Palestinian armed groups under the war crimes provisions of the Statute in Article 8 and opened an investigation.[233] She then applied to the Court for a preliminary ruling on jurisdiction, seeking confirmation that the "territory" over which the Court may "exercise its jurisdiction under article 12(2)(a) comprises the Occupied Palestinian Territory, that is, the West Bank, including East Jerusalem, and Gaza."[234] In 2021, a majority of the Pre-Trial Chamber found that it could not "review the outcome of the accession procedure" whereby Palestine acceded to the Rome Statute[235] and that Palestine was therefore a "State Party" to the Statute, whose territory was referenced by article 12(2)(a) of the Statute, without prejudice to matters of international law not within the Court's jurisdiction, including the nature of Palestine's present or future borders.[236] A handful of ICC States Parties had objected to jurisdiction in the case, and Israeli officials opined that any ICC investigation of its nationals represented "undiluted antisemitism."[237] As the situation in Palestine continued to deteriorate, in Gaza and the West Bank, civil society organizations in 2022 and 2023 frequently contacted the ICC and requested that the Prosecutor speak out when violence erupted and hasten the ICC's investigation. The Prosecutor declined to do so in a particularly tense exchange during the annual meeting of the ICC Assembly of States Parties in 2022.

Following the October 7 attack and Israel's response, the Court faced an existential challenge. Given the speed with which the ICC had acted in the Ukraine situation, the same alacrity was expected for the war in Gaza. Prosecutor Khan's full-throated condemnation of the Hamas attack, unaccompanied by a similarly harsh response to Israel's military operations, as well as his inability to enter Gaza to investigate (because Israel would not allow him to do so at the outset, although later apparently an offer was made to provide some access to the territory),[238] led to concerns about his independence.[239] Seven additional states referred the Palestine situation to the Prosecutor for investigation, and Belgium offered 5 million Euros in financial support,[240] placing additional pressure on the Prosecutor to act. The largest regional group at the ICC is the African group, which had been frustrated by the ICC's focus on Africa and threatened a mass withdrawal from the Statute some years ago. It was also relatively unenthusiastic about the Court's "Ukraine moment." The perception of double standards in Gaza reignited this concern and threatened to undermine the legitimacy and future effectiveness of the Court.

In the midst of much speculation, on May 20, 2024, the Prosecutor announced that he had applied for five arrest warrants: two for Israelis (Prime Minister Binyamin Netanyahu and Defense Minister Yoav Gallant) and three for Hamas leaders.[241] US officials thereupon threatened the Court with sanctions (again),[242] and the United Kingdom filed a challenge to the jurisdiction of the Court based upon the Oslo Accords.[243] Although the United Kingdom declined to file a submission, thereby withdrawing its objection as a practical matter, the decision of the Pre-Trial Chamber to permit states and others to make observations regarding jurisdiction in the case has led to a flood of submissions, which is likely to delay the proceedings. Moreover, as a legal matter, Article 19 of the Statute does not permit challenges to jurisdiction by the United Kingdom in the case, meaning that the Pre-Trial Chamber allowed the United Kingdom to do through the backdoor of Rule 103 what the Statute[244] and the Court's jurisprudence in the Afghanistan situation do not permit. The disingenuousness of the UK challenge is stunning: managing to craft a theory that would allow the Court to prosecute members of Hamas (as Palestinian) but not Israelis due to the effect of the Oslo Accords. This challenge to the ICC's jurisdiction was followed by a German intervention arguing that the case is inadmissible because the question of complementarity cannot be decided during an ongoing armed attack.[245] Dozens more *amici* followed. Given that the six warrants in the Ukraine situation—like the warrants in the Israel/Hamas conflict—have been issued during an ongoing armed conflict, the effort to misshape legal doctrine to permit ICC actions against Russians but not Israelis undermines the legitimacy of the Court and its ability to command universal acceptance for its work.

Conclusion

The ICC's intervention in the Ukraine situation in 2022 represented a watershed moment for international justice. The Russian Federation's invasion caused states to rally behind the Court, which was revitalized with enthusiastic support, financial resources, and additional staff. Even the United States, which has historically been antagonistic to the ICC—and especially its exercise of jurisdiction over the nationals of non-state parties—relented, amending its legal position and softening its objections.[246] But as the war has dragged on, enthusiasm has waned. Meanwhile, the Russian Federation has continued its bombing campaign and aggression toward Ukraine apace. Although Ukraine has thus far defended most of its territory; it has not yet secured its future.[247]

As this Chapter has identified, there are internal and external challenges to the success of the Ukraine situation at the Court. Some result from the non-cooperation of non-state parties, including the Russian Federation, which has attacked the Court and its personnel and refused to surrender the accused. That does not mean that the Court's arrest warrants have been without any effect: They have effectively confined Vladimir Putin and the other indictees to the Russian Federation and its close allies, preventing them from traveling abroad more broadly[248] and potentially eroding their standing at home. Additionally, the ICC Prosecutor can convene hearings to confirm the charges against them *in absentia*, as he has done in the *Kony* case,[249] which may subject them to additional pressure and publicly air the allegations against them.

Perhaps the most significant set of challenges to the Ukraine situation at the Court, however, is not Russian intransigence but difficulties applying the Rome Statute and the problematic legal arguments now being proffered by some state and non-state parties to immunize Israeli officials and their actions in Gaza, while allowing the Court to prosecute Palestinians, including members of Hamas. In other words, double standards.

The conflicts in both Ukraine and Gaza involve aerial bombardment, siege warfare, and allegations of serious war crimes and crimes against humanity. The ICTY successfully prosecuted individuals for similar crimes committed during the war in the former Yugoslavia, but the ICC has a more difficult Statute to apply and little precedent to use, which makes its task more difficult. Likewise, while the Court's jurisdiction over the Ukraine and Palestine situations is clear, it has nonetheless been challenged by the perpetrators, in the case of Ukraine, and by Western states protective of Israel (as of this writing, including Germany, the United Kingdom, and the United States) in the situation in Palestine. Ironically, the "delegation" theory that the United Kingdom is relying upon to advance its objections in the Palestine situation would ensure the immunity of Vladimir Putin, just as limitations embedded in the Statute's regime regarding the crime of aggression introduced by the United States and the United Kingdom at Kampala have left the Court unable to prosecute the "supreme international crime"[250] regarding Russia's invasion of Ukraine. Likewise, arguments made by many US and Israeli military lawyers in the situation in Gaza are not consistent with the jurisprudence of the ICTY in cases involving the siege and bombardment of Sarajevo. Yet this jurisprudence will be vital to any possible successes of the OTP in the Ukraine situation. Indeed, what Western champions of justice for Ukraine have failed to recognize is that the success of the Ukraine and Palestine cases are inextricably linked and juridically tied together.

The situation in Palestine tests whether the ICC's "Ukraine moment" represented a universal cry for justice or was merely a cynical effort to best a formidable adversary. Just as the Russian Federation threatens Ukraine's political independence and territorial integrity, attacks on the ICC and ill-founded arguments undermining its jurisdiction and the interpretation of its Statute undermine the rule of law and the fabric of the international legal system. Bending the law of the Court to the will of the powerful will, ultimately, destroy the Court. The ICC can only succeed if it pursues justice "without fear or favor," applying the same legal principles to all accused in situations involving weak and powerful states alike.[251] If it is unable to do so, its credibility and effectiveness will be diminished.

Addendum to Sadat & Hueseman

This chapter was finalized for publication in August 2024, at a time when the Biden administration was strongly supportive of Ukraine, but Ukraine was facing significant challenges as the war dragged on. As the chapter will be published in September 2025, it is important to note that although the legal principles governing the conflict remain the same, the geopolitical situation has changed significantly. Under President Biden's administration, the United States strongly supported holding Vladimir Putin and other high-ranking Russian officials responsible for international crimes. However, the US abruptly reversed course under the second Trump administration, with President Trump suggesting that he is interested in ending the war no matter the terms and accepting Russia's revisionist (and false) explanation for the invasion. This was evidenced by the Oval Office meeting on February 28, 2025 between President Trump, Vice President Vance, and President Zelensky, during which President Trump and Vice President Vance not only berated President Zelensky for refusing to "thank" the United States, but blamed Ukraine for starting the war (which was started by Russia's invasion first of Crimea, and then of Eastern Ukraine). Thanks to the chaos generated by the US about face, Russia has continued to bombard Ukrainian cities, including residential areas and hospitals, and President Vladimir Putin appears unrepentant in the manner in which he has prosecuted this aggressive war.

Moreover, the United States appears to be reversing course with respect to holding Russian officials accountable for atrocities committed during the war, as well as the crime of aggression. Apparently copying the Putin playbook, just as Russia indicted the Prosecutor and several judges, Trump has sanctioned the ICC Prosecutor and four ICC judges—ostensibly because of their participation in the Afghanistan and Palestine situations. The sanctions have a broader impact however, as they undermine the ICC and the principles of accountability it stands for, including the impossibility of asserting head of state immunity. The Europeans have stood up a Special Tribunal for the crime of Aggression for Ukraine but have unfortunately undermined its effectiveness by providing Putin with immunity so long as he remains in office, as it preserves so-called "troika" immunity for heads of state, heads of government, and foreign ministers. It is thus to be wondered if Vladmir Putin will ever be held accountable at all.

Despite this geopolitical turbulence, although Ukraine has at times appeared to be "losing" the war, its June 1, 2025 "Spider's Web" operation destroyed several significant Russian military assets and demonstrated that it retains a strong ability to resist Russia's onslaught, which it continues to escalate. Thus, it is unclear that a negotiated end to war is near.

Notes

1 Oksana Markarova, keynote address, American Society of International Law Annual Meeting, April 14, 2022, Washington, DC, 2:40:00, https://perma.cc/EU5K-U4T5.

2 Application of International Convention for Suppression of Financing of Terrorism and of International Convention on Elimination of All Forms of Racial Discrimination (Ukraine v. Russian Federation), Case Overview, https://perma.cc/NTT2-SZ53; Allegations of Genocide Under Convention on Prevention and Punishment of Crime of Genocide (Ukraine v. Russian Federation), Case Overview, https://perma.cc/JJJ4-RKVZ.

3 Detention of Three Ukrainian Naval Vessels (Ukraine v. Russian Federation), Case No. 26, Case Overview, https://perma.cc/8XNQ-SH6G.

4 Detention of Ukrainian Naval Vessels and Servicemen (Ukraine v. Russian Federation), Case Overview, https://perma.cc/N25U-BTD9; Coastal State Rights in the Black Sea, Sea of Azov, and Kerch Strait (Ukraine v. Russian Federation), Case Overview, https://perma.cc/H398-9CXN.

5 Interstate Applications, Respondent State Russia, https://www.echr.coe.int/inter-state-applications?filter_category_3475244=1224862.

6 For example, see Permanent Representative of Ukraine to the United Nations, "Letter dated 28 February 2014 from the Permanent Representative of Ukraine to the United Nations addressed to the President of the Security Council," S/2014/136, February 28, 2014, https://perma.cc/V5AP-7CMW; Security Council, "Russian Federation Announces 'Special Military Operation' in Ukraine as Security Council Meets in Eleventh-Hour Effort to Avoid Full-Scale Conflict," U.N. Press Release SC/14803, February 23, 2022, https://perma.cc/VKV9-Q64B.

7 For example, see U.N. General Assembly, Resolution A/RES/ES-11/1, "Aggression Against Ukraine" (March 2, 2022), https://perma.cc/7MWV-2Z32; U.N. General Assembly, Resolution A/RES/ES-11/6, "Principles of the Charter of the United Nations Underlying a Comprehensive, Just and Lasting Peace in Ukraine (February 23, 2023), https://perma.cc/A2TG-Y9BU.

8 Letter from Embassy of Ukraine to Registrar of the International Criminal Court, April 9, 2014, https://perma.cc/T3F6-LZ4W.

9 Letter from Paylo Klimkin, Minister for Foreign Affairs of Ukraine, to Herman von Hebel, Registrar, International Criminal Court, September 8, 2015, https://perma.cc/4SWA-Q2LE.

10 Office of the Prosecutor, *Report on Preliminary Examination Activities (2019)* (The Hague: International Criminal Court, 2019), ¶¶ 267, 272–3, 279–80, https://perma.cc/PE9H-XAJN; Office of the Prosecutor, *Report on Preliminary Examination Activities (2020)* (The Hague: International Criminal Court, 2020), ¶¶ 277–81, https://perma.cc/B6T9-HYLT.

11 Office of the Prosecutor, *Report on Preliminary Examination Activities (2020)*, ¶ 299.

12 International Criminal Court, "Statement of ICC Prosecutor, Karim A.A. Khan QC on the Situation in Ukraine: 'I Have Decided to Proceed with Opening an Investigation.,'" February 28, 2022, https://perma.cc/5XR4-NB4F.

13 International Criminal Court, "Statement of ICC Prosecutor, Karim A.A. Khan QC, on the Situation in Ukraine: 'I have Decided to Proceed with Opening an Investigation.,'" February 28, 2022, https://perma.cc/A4JD-MDR3; see Giorgi Nakashidze, "Uniting for Justice: Group Referrals to the International Criminal Court," *Opinio Juris*, March 25, 2022, https://perma.cc/855R-97AV.

14 "Situation in Ukraine," International Criminal Court, accessed June 25, 2024, https://perma.cc/X6QN-CF83.

15 In addition to Putin, the additional five arrest warrants concern Maria Aleksyevna Lvova-Belova, the Russian commissioner for Children's Rights; lieutenant general Sergei Ivanovich Kobylash, the commander of Russia's Long-Range Aviation of the Aerospace Force; Admiral Viktor Nikolayevich Sokolov, the commander of Russia's Black Sea Fleet; Sergei Kuzhugetovich Shoigu, the Russian Minister of Defense; and Valery Vasilyevich Gerasimov, the chief of the General Staff of the Russian Armed Forces. International Criminal Court, "Situation in Ukraine: ICC Judges Issue Arrest Warrants Against Vladimir Vladimirovich Putin and Maria Alekseyevna Lvova-Belova," March 17, 2023, https://perma.cc/HTJ5-GRMF; International Criminal Court, "Situation in Ukraine: ICC Judges Issue Arrest Warrants Against Sergei Ivanovich Kobylash and Viktor Nikolayevich Sokolov," March 5, 2024, https://perma.cc/46VC-D3AB; International Criminal Court, "Situation in Ukraine: ICC Judges Issue Arrest Warrants Against Sergei Kuzhugetovich Shoigu and Valery Vasilyevich Gerasimov," June 25, 2024, https://perma.cc/CL9V-VJG5. It is likely that other warrants have been issued but remain under seal.

16 Patryk I. Labuda, "Beyond Rhetoric: Interrogating the Eurocentric Critique of International Criminal Law's Selectivity in the Wake of the 2022 Ukraine Invasion," *Leiden Journal of International Law* 36, no. 4 (2023): 1095, 1098; International Criminal Court, "Statement of ICC Prosecutor, Karim A.A. Khan QC: Contributions and Support from States Parties Will Accelerate Action Across Our Investigations," March 28, 2022, https://perma.cc/FE44-QR7P.

17 Labuda, "Beyond Rhetoric," 1098; International Criminal Court, "Statement of ICC Prosecutor, Karim A.A. Khan QC: Contributions and Support from States Parties Will Accelerate Action Across Our Investigations."

18 For example, see United States Department of State, "Ambassador Van Schaack's Remarks on the U.S. Proposal to Prosecute Russian Crimes of Aggression," March 27, 2023, https://perma.cc/J39Q-8WG8 ("The ICC occupies an important place in the ecosystem of international justice, and the United States supports the investigation by the ICC Prosecutor, who received an unprecedented referral of the situation in Ukraine by 43 States Parties last year."); United States Senate, Resolution 531, 117th Congress, ¶ 2 (2022), https://perma.cc/99ZT-T5QK ("[T]he Senate . . . encourages member states to petition the ICC and the ICJ to authorize any and all pending investigations into war crimes and crimes against humanity committed by the Russian Armed Forces and their proxies and President Putin's military commanders, at the direction of President Vladimir Putin[.]").

19 "US Sanctions on the International Criminal Court," *Human Rights Watch*, December 14, 2020, https://perma.cc/LK6E-J397.

20 Ryan Goodman, "How to Best Fund the International Criminal Court," *Just Security*, May 27, 2022, https://www.justsecurity.org/81676/how-best-to-fund-the-international-criminal-court/.

21 Because unlike the other crimes, the Statute explicitly limits jurisdiction over the crime of aggression to crimes committed by the nationals of States Parties. Rome Statute of the International Criminal Court art. 15*bis*, July 1, 2002, 2187 U.N.T.S. 3, https://perma.cc/H3CJ-7WD8.

22 For example, see Iva Vukušić, "Later Rather Than Sooner: Time and Its Effects on the Karadžić and Mladić Trials," *International Criminal Law Review* 22 (2022): 189;

Eric Stover, Victor Peskin, and Alexa Koenig, "Radovan Karadzic and the (Very) Long Arc of Justice," *Foreign Policy*, March 24, 2016, https://perma.cc/NB59-8RJW.

23 "Is Ukraine Losing the War Against Russia?," *Economist*, February 21, 2024, https://perma.cc/6HAA-E9CR.

24 Olga Ivshina, Becky Dale, and Kirstie Brewer, "Russia's Meat Grinder Soldiers - 50,000 Confirmed Dead," *BBC*, April 17, 2024, https://perma.cc/M7WS-GN2A.

25 OHCHR, "Ukraine: Protection of Civilians in Armed Conflict: May 2024 Update," June 7, 2024, https://perma.cc/3DHL-MQ5P.

26 "Operational Data Portal: Ukraine Refugee Situation," UNHCR, accessed June 25, 2024, https://perma.cc/CMD4-DWQH.

27 For an in-depth discussion on the crime of child taking, see Diane Marie Amann, "Child-Taking," *Michigan Journal of International Law* 45, no. 3 (2024): 305.

28 Marco Hernandez et al., "What Ukraine Has Lost," *New York Times*, June 3, 2024, https://perma.cc/LGX9-276W.

29 Claire Moses, "The Dutch Intelligence Service Says It Prevented a Russian Spy from Infiltrating the International Criminal Court," *New York Times*, June 17, 2022, https://perma.cc/7PU8-76GQ.

30 "Russia Indicts ICC Prosecutor, Judge Who Issued War Crimes Warrant for Putin," *Associated Press*, May 21, 2023, https://perma.cc/CX3F-K75Z.

31 See Janet L. Yellen, "A New Way to Make Russia's Assets Pay for Ukraine's Defense and Rebuilding," *New York Times*, June 13, 2024, https://perma.cc/U4WG-39CG; Harold Hongju Koh, "Past Time to Liquidate Russian Assets, *Just Security*, March 5, 2024, https://perma.cc/WB2E-XJ5U.

32 For further discussion, see Gaiane Nuridzhanian, "International Enough? A Council of Europe Special Tribunal for the Crime of Aggression," *Just Security*, June 3, 2024, https://perma.cc/HT3C-68LD; Patrick Butchard, *Conflict in Ukraine: A Special Tribunal on the Crime of Aggression* (research briefing, House of Commons Library, London, February 2024), https://perma.cc/MR6V-SLS8.

33 Veronika Melkozerova, "Russia's Ghost Loomed over Ukraine Peace Summit," *Politico*, June 16, 2024, https://perma.cc/2CYW-4EBH; "Ukraine Peace Summit: Why Some Countries Refused To Sign the Plan," *Al Jazeera*, June 17, 2024, https://perma.cc/CG3Z-QVNM.

34 Robert Jimison, "House Votes to Impose Sanctions on I.C.C. Officials over Israel Prosecution," *New York Times*, June 4, 2024, https://perma.cc/N2WF-C7AD; Michael D. Shear, "Biden and Blinken Accuse I.C.C. Prosecutor of Falsely Equating Israel and Hamas," *New York Times*, May 20, 2024, https://perma.cc/B95B-67L3.

35 Situation in Palestine, Case No. ICC-01/18, Request by the United Kingdom for Leave to Submit Written Observations Pursuant to Rule 103 (June 10, 2024), https://perma.cc/2XLY-2H67; Adil Ahmad Haque, "The International Criminal Court's Jurisdiction in Palestine and the 'Oslo Accords Issue,'" *Just Security*, July 9, 2024, https://perma.cc/Z6VU-LKT4. The United Kingdom changed its position after a new Labour government was installed, but its application started an avalanche of submissions to the Court by individuals, NGOs, and States on the question of jurisdiction in the Palestine situation.

36 "Court Records and Transcripts: Observations," International Criminal Court, accessed August 12, 2024, https://www.icc-cpi.int/documents?f%5B0%5D=court

_record_document_type%3A48&f%5B1%5D=court_record_situation_name %3A786.

37 Leila Nadya Sadat, "'Justice Without Fear or Favour?' The Uncertain Future of the International Criminal Court," in Alexander Heinze and Viviane E. Dittrich, eds., *The Past, Present and Future of the International Criminal Court* (Brussels: Torkel Opsahl Academic EPublisher, 2021), 121.

38 Office of the Prosecutor, *Report on Preliminary Examination Activities (2020)*, ¶¶ 272–3. At this time, Ukraine was marred by violent protests concerning Yanukovych's refusal in 2013 to sign an association agreement with the European Union. Ibid., ¶ 272.

39 Office of the Prosecutor, *Report on Preliminary Examination Activities (2020)*, ¶ 274.

40 *Report on Preliminary Examination Activities (2020)*, ¶¶ 273, 275.

41 Becky Sullivan, "Russia's at War with Ukraine. Here's How We Got Here," *NPR*, February 24, 2022, https://perma.cc/PEY5-AQPP.

42 Steven Lee Myers and Ellen Barry, "Putin Reclaims Crimea for Russia and Bitterly Denounces the West," *New York Times*, March 18, 2021, https://perma.cc/J4QP -A9W3.

43 Daniel Treisman, "Why Putin Took Crimea," *Foreign Affairs*, April 18, 2016, https://perma.cc/362V-PZAB. On March 16, 2014, nearly 97 percent of Crimean voters voted for secession from Ukraine in a referendum, but the UNGA declared the referendum invalid. U.N. General Assembly, Resolution 68/262, "Territorial Integrity of Ukraine," A/RES/68/262, ¶ 5 (April 1, 2014), https://perma.cc/UU9S -ZX9P.

44 For further background, see Vladimir Putin, "On the Historical Unity of Russians and Ukrainians," *Kremlin*, July 12, 2021, https://perma.cc/F9DD-N4Q2; Fiona Hill and Angela Stent, "The World Putin Wants," *Foreign Affairs*, August 25, 2022, https://perma.cc/CTJ5-XUFH; Andrew E. Kramer, "For Many Ukrainians, It's Been a 10-Year War, Not a 2-Year One," *New York Times*, February 23, 2024, https://perma .cc/V9XB-5SRA.

45 Cristina Florea, "Putin's Perilous Imperial Dream," *Foreign Affairs*, May 10, 2022, https://perma.cc/S7BV-QEGL.

46 *Report on Preliminary Examination Activities (2020)*, ¶¶ 276.

47 Letter from Embassy of Ukraine to Registrar of the International Criminal Court, April 9, 2014; Letter from Paylo Klimkin, Minister for Foreign Affairs of Ukraine, to Herman von Hebel, Registrar, International Criminal Court, September 8, 2015.

48 Kremlin, "Agreement on the Accession of the Republic of Crimea to the Russian Federation Signed," March 18, 2014, https://perma.cc/5LZR-D82G.

49 Office of the Prosecutor, *Report on Preliminary Examination Activities (2020)*, ¶ 274.

50 A/RES/68/262, ¶ 6.

51 Office of the Prosecutor, *Report on Preliminary Examination Activities (2020)*, ¶¶ 277–9; Ukraine v. Russia (re Crimea), App. Nos. 20958/14 & 38334/18, ¶ 918 (June 25, 2024), https://perma.cc/MS2M-GVWA. One day after the Report on Preliminary Examination Activities was released, Putin withdrew the Russian Federation's signature from the Rome Statute. Max Seddon, "Russia Withdraws from International Criminal Court," *Financial Times*, November 16, 2016, https://perma.cc/MJ9B-LDNR.

52 U.N. Charter, art. 2, ¶ 4; see Juergen Bering, "The Prohibition on Annexation: Lessons from Crimea," *New York University Journal of International Law and Politics*

49, no. 3 (2017): 747; Lauri Mälksoo, "The Annexation of Crimea and Balance of Power in International Law," *European Journal of International Law* 30, no. 1 (2019): 303.

53 Decree No. 71, On the Recognition of the Donetsk People's Republic (Russian Federation) (February 21, 2022), https://perma.cc/72QP-J2HA.

54 "Russia Invades Ukraine," *Economist*, February 24, 2022, https://perma.cc/2FUC-5FBR; Paul Murray, "Troops and Military Vehicles Have Entered Ukraine From Belarus," *CNN*, February 24, 2022, https://perma.cc/HE2U-BKLH.

55 Max Fisher, "Putin's Case for War, Annotated," *New York Times*, February 24, 2022, https://perma.cc/AP9J-3MV2.

56 Permanent Representative of the Russian Federation to the United Nations, "Letter dated February 24, 2022 from the Permanent Representative of the Russian Federation to the United Nations addressed to the Secretary-General," S/2022/154, February 24, 2022, 5, https://perma.cc/KGC9-TZRW; *Allegations of Genocide* (Ukraine v. Russian Federation), March 16, 2022 Order on Provisional Measures, ¶¶ 39–41.

57 Security Council, "Security Council Fails to Adopt Draft Resolution on Ending Ukraine Crisis, as Russian Federation Wields Veto," U.N. Press Release SC/14808, February 25, 2022, https://perma.cc/X68B-SXFY.

58 U.N. General Assembly, Resolution 377(V), "Uniting for Peace," November 3, 1950, https://perma.cc/X29M-5B4E.

59 A/RES/ES-11/1.

60 U.N. General Assembly, Resolution 3314 (XXIX), "Definition of Aggression," December 14, 1974, https://perma.cc/5XK6-9U6H; see Ralph Janik, "Putin's War Against Ukraine: Mocking International Law," *EJIL:Talk!*, February 28, 2022, https://perma.cc/F3KY-BTLE; Claus Kreß, *The Ukraine War and the Prohibition of the Use of Force in International Law* (Brussels: Torkel Opsahl Academic EPublisher, 2022), https://perma.cc/326Z-679L.

61 Janine di Giovanni, "Putin's Gruesome Playbook," *Foreign Policy*, April 18, 2022, https://perma.cc/ALJ6-SYVN; Mona Yacoubian, "How Russia May Reprise Its Syrian Playbook in Ukraine, *United States Institute of Peace*, March 30, 2022, https://perma.cc/CN25-R997.

62 Mark Galeotti, "Putin Is Playing by Grozny Rules in Aleppo," *Foreign Policy*, September 29, 2016, https://perma.cc/A7TA-5DGU.

63 See Protocol Additional to the Geneva Conventions of 12 August 1949, and Relating to the Protection of Victims of International Armed Conflicts art. 52, June 8, 1977, 1125 U.N.T.S. 3, https://perma.cc/W7YC-XGAX.

64 Human Rights Council, Resolution 52/62, Report of the Independent International Commission of Inquiry on Ukraine, A/HRC/52/62, ¶ 26 (March 16, 2023), https://perma.cc/UK33-CQNZ; see Keith Collins et al., "Russia's Attacks on Civilian Targets Have Obliterated Everyday Life in Ukraine," *New York Times*, March 23, 2022, https://perma.cc/W6GU-Q65H.

65 Collins, "Russia's Attacks on Civilian Targets"; Constant Méheut and Daria Mitiuk, "Russia Pounds Ukrainian Cities in One of the Largest Air Attacks of the War, *New York Times*, December 29, 2023, https://perma.cc/Y9AS-NJTC.

66 Protocol I, art. 51; cf. Human Rights Council, Resolution 55/66, Report of the Independent International Commission of Inquiry on Ukraine, A/HRC/55/66, ¶ 31 (March 5, 2024), https://perma.cc/95UU-VH2P.

67 A/HRC/52/62, ¶ 30.

68 United Nations Office of the High Commissioner for Human Rights, "Türk Deplores Human Cost of Russia's War Against Ukraine as Verified Civilian Casualties for Last Year Pass 21,000," February 21, 2023, https://www.ohchr.org/en/press-releases/2023/02/turk-deplores-human-cost-russias-war-against-ukraine-verified-civilian.

69 For a deeper analysis of the attack on Mariupol, see Gerry Simpson and Richard Weir, *"Our City Was Gone": Russia's Devastation of Mariupol, Ukraine*, eds. Anagha Neelakantan and Ida Sawyer (New York: Human Rights Watch, 2024), https://perma.cc/JCE4-LGED; *20 Days in Mariupol*, directed by Mstyslav Chernov (2023).

70 Simpson and Weir, *Russia's Devastation of Mariupol*, 81.

71 A/HRC/52/62, ¶ 27.

72 A/HRC/55/66, ¶ 14.

73 A/HRC/55/66, ¶ 15.

74 "Mariupol's Outnumbered Defenders Refuse to Give In," *Economist*, April 15, 2022, https://perma.cc/SH5N-25ZV; Shaun Walker et al., "Mariupol: The Ruin of a City," *Guardian*, February 23, 2023, https://perma.cc/5V3G-GSRT; Mstyslav Chernov, "20 Days in Mariupol: The Team that Documented City's Agony," *Associated Press*, March 21, 2022, https://perma.cc/76CX-9BWR.

75 A/HRC/52/62, ¶ 33.

76 Walker et al., "Mariupol: The Ruin of a City."

77 "Hundreds of Thousands Face Catastrophe in Mariupol," *Economist*, March 21, 2022, https://perma.cc/BRH7-NVRJ; Simpson and Weir, *Russia's Devastation of Mariupol*, 26.

78 Simpson and Weir, *Russia's Devastation of Mariupol*, 2, 169.

79 "Mariupol's Last Ukrainian Defenders Begin to Surrender," *Economist*, May 17, 2022, https://perma.cc/B75B-HSTK.

80 Leon Aron, "See Occupied Mariupol, Where Dread and Suspicion Reign," *Washington Post*, May 3, 2023, https://perma.cc/F75N-MK8C.

81 Michael Schwirtz, "Evacuees from Mariupol's Steel Plant Tell of Horrors and Survival," *New York Times*, May 3, 2022, https://perma.cc/ZUY7-TX2U; Jonathan Yerushalmy, "Mariupol Before and After: Updated Google Maps Reveal Destruction in Ukraine City," *Guardian*, April 27, 2023, https://perma.cc/HQ8K-F48L.

82 A/HRC/52/62, ¶ 109.

83 A/HRC/52/62, ¶ 53.

84 Yousur Al-Hlou et al., "Caught on Camera, Traced by Phone: The Russian Military Unit that Killed Dozens in Bucha," *New York Times*, December 23, 2022, https://perma.cc/Z97L-4Z6M; Masha Froliak, Yousur Al-Hlou, and Haley Willis, "Their Final Moments: Victims of a Russian Atrocity in Bucha," *New York Times*, December 21, 2022, https://perma.cc/2FE4-RVGS; Carlotta Gall, "Bucha's Month of Terror," *New York Times*, April 11, 2022, https://perma.cc/6VKL-AYM5.

85 Gall, "Bucha's Month of Terror."

86 Gall, "Bucha's Month of Terror."

87 Gall, "Bucha's Month of Terror."

88 See A/HRC/52/62, ¶¶ 71–77; A/HRC/55/66, ¶ 80; Nick Cumming-Bruce, "'Welcome to Hell': U.N. Panel Says Russian War Crimes Are Widespread," *New York Times*, March 15, 2024, https://perma.cc/U6PH-HEG6.

89 Carlotta Gall, "'Fear Still Remains': Ukraine Finds Sexual Crimes Where Russian Troops Ruled," *New York Times*, January 5, 2023, https://perma.cc/F5PR-NSAL; A/HRC/55/66, ¶ 86; A/HRC/52/62, ¶¶ 78–85.

90 A/HRC/52/62, ¶¶ 40–43; Oona A. Hathaway et al., *Remote Assessment of Bombardment of Ukraine's Power Generation and Transmission Infrastructure, 1 October 2022 to 30 April 2023* (New Haven, CT: Humanitarian Research Lab at Yale School of Public Health and Ukraine Digital Verification Lab, 2024), 6, https://perma.cc/76TB-9W3Q; "Ukraine Prepares for Winter Again as Russia Targets Its Power Grid," *Economist*, October 2, 2023, https://perma.cc/EQ8U-XGW5.

91 A/HRC/52/62, ¶ 45; see Nataliya Gumenyuk, "A Looming Disaster at the Zaporizhzhia Nuclear Power Plant," *Atlantic*, March 6, 2024, https://perma.cc/GM8H-5MNM; "Fears About the Reactors at Zaporizhzhia Continue to Mount," *Economist*, May 18, 2023, https://perma.cc/5QHE-9QNT.

92 Gumenyuk, "A Looming Disaster."

93 Gumenyuk, "A Looming Disaster."

94 Gumenyuk, "A Looming Disaster"; Laurence Norman and Drew Hinshaw, "Explosions Near Ukraine's Giant Nuclear Plant Prompt Diplomatic Push," *Wall Street Journal*, April 29, 2023, https://www.wsj.com/articles/explosions-near-ukraines-giant-nuclear-plant-prompt-diplomatic-push-fe031af2.

95 Marc Santora and Brendan Hoffman, "Russia Strikes Children's Hospital in Deadly Barrage Across Ukraine," *New York Times*, July 8, 2024, https://perma.cc/K357-494X.

96 Santora and Hoffman, "Russia Strikes Children's Hospital." The attack on the children's hospital was just one of several across Ukraine that day, which involved X-101 cruise missile and Iskander-M ballistic missiles and resulted in at least 38 deaths and over 100 injuries.

97 World Health Organization, "Triple Risk of Harm for Ukraine's Health Transport Workers over Other Health-Care Staff, WHO Data Indicates," April 4, 2024, https://perma.cc/JXQ6-P9EB.

98 Mercedes Sapuppo and Shelby Magid, "Death Toll Climbs in Ukraine with Russia's 'Double-Tap' Strikes," *Just Security*, July 8, 2024, https://perma.cc/Q6B4-NT5B.

99 United Nations, Meetings Coverage, 9682nd Meeting (AM), "Russian Federation's Attack on Ukrainian Children's Hospital 'Not only a War Crime' but 'Far Beyond the Limits of Humanity,' Medical Director Tells Security Council," SC/15761, July 9, 2024, https://perma.cc/99T9-XN2F; Jennifer Peltz, "In a Diplomatic Quirk, Russia Chairs a UN Meeting Decrying Its Strike on a Ukraine Kids' Hospital," *Washington Post*, July 9, 2024, https://perma.cc/6PLT-YP57.

100 Rome Statute art. 8(2)(b)(ii).

101 Rome Statute art. 8(2)(b)(iv).

102 Rome Statute art. 7(1)(k).

103 Rome Statute, art. 21(1)(b); Margaret deGuzman, "Article 21, Applicable Law," in Kai Ambos, ed., *Rome Statute of the International Criminal Court, Article-by-Article Commentary* (Oxford: Beck Hart Nomos, 2022).

104 International Criminal Court, *Elements of Crimes* (The Hague: International Criminal Court, 2013), 9, https://perma.cc/8TXW-8VLD.

105 Geneva Convention (III) Relative to the Treatment of Prisoners of War, August 12, 1949, 75 U.N.T.S. 135; Geneva Convention (IV) Relative to the Protection

of Civilian Persons in Time of War, August 12, 1949, 75 U.N.T.S. 287; Hague Convention (IV) Respecting the Laws and Customs of War on Land and Its Annex: Regulations Concerning the Laws and Customs of War on Land, October 18, 1907; States Party to the Following International Humanitarian Law and Other Related Treaties as of 19-January-2024," International Committee of the Red Cross, accessed June 25, 2024, https://perma.cc/59VK-LTHZ; see Andrew Clapham, "We Need To Talk About Grave Breaches of the Geneva Conventions," *Opinio Juris*, April 25, 2023, https://perma.cc/A2Y5-5AXA.

106 "Russia's Putin Revokes Geneva Convention Protocol on War Crimes Victims," *Reuters*, October 17, 2019, https://www.reuters.com/article/world/russias-putin-revokes-geneva-convention-protocol-on-war-crimes-victims-idUSKBN1WW2J3/.

107 See Sir Christopher Greenwood, "What the ICC Can Learn from the Jurisprudence of Other Tribunals," *Harvard International Law Online Journal* 58 (Spring 2017): 71, https://perma.cc/M8MG-C5GN.

108 Prosecutor v. Katanga, Case No. ICC-01/04-01/07, Judgment Pursuant to Article 74 of the Statute, ¶ 47 (March 7, 2014), https://perma.cc/5ACS-H34H; Prosecutor v. Lubanga, Case No. ICC-01/04-01/06, Judgment Pursuant to Article 74 of the Statute, ¶ 603 (March 14, 2012), https://perma.cc/YM4L-4T3Y; deGuzman, "Article 21, Applicable Law," 1136–7.

109 Prosecutor v. Lubanga, Case No. ICC-01/04-01/06, Decision Regarding the Practices Used To Prepare and Familiarise Witnesses for Giving Testimony at Trial, ¶¶ 44–45 (November 30, 2007), https://perma.cc/6CNJ-AJ6H; see Volker Nerlich, "The Status of ICTY and ICTR Precedent in Proceedings Before the ICC," in Carsten Stahn and Göran Sluiter, eds., *The Emerging Practice of the International Criminal Court* (Leiden: Brill Nijhoff, 2010), 305, 317.

110 Galić, ICTY Case No. IT-98-29-T, ¶ 10 (quoting Prosecutor v. Tadić, ICTY Case No. IT-94-1, Decision on the Defence Motion for Interlocutory Appeal on Jurisdiction, ¶¶ 89, 91 (October 2, 1995), https://perma.cc/C98N-JF7Y).

111 Galić, ICTY Case No. IT-98-29-T, ¶ 140 (citation omitted).

112 Prosecutor v. Galić, ICTY Case No. IT-98-29-T, Judgment, ¶ 197 (December 5, 2003), https://perma.cc/E9EU-5R9R.

113 Galić, ICTY Case No. IT-98-29-T, ¶ 212.

114 Galić, ICTY Case No. IT-98-29-T, ¶ 216.

115 Galić, ICTY Case No. IT-98-29-T, ¶ 584.

116 Galić, ICTY Case No. IT-98-29-T, ¶ 584.

117 Galić, ICTY Case No. IT-98-29-T, ¶ 2; "25 Years Since the Siege of Sarajevo Ended," *Associated Press*, February 25, 2021, https://perma.cc/9M9J-KLGG.

118 Galić, ICTY Case No. IT-98-29-T, ¶ 583.

119 Galić, ICTY Case No. IT-98-29-T, ¶ 3.

120 Galić, ICTY Case No. IT-98-29-T, ¶ 609. Galić "became the implementor of a pre-existing strategy." Ibid. ¶ 610.

121 Statute of the International Criminal Tribunal for the Former Yugoslavia art. 3, May 25, 1993, https://perma.cc/X6BY-CYN8.

122 ICTY Statute art. 5.

123 Galić, ICTY Case No. IT-98-29-T, ¶ 151.

124 Galić, ICTY Case No. IT-98-29-T, ¶¶ 16, 94–95, 97, 105. Cf. Carolin Wuerzner, "Mission Impossible? Bringing Charges for the Crime of Attacking Civilians or

Civilian Objects Before the International Criminal Tribunals," *International Review of the Red Cross* 90, no. 872 (2008): 907; William J. Fenrick, "Riding the Rhino: Attempting to Develop Usable Legal Standards for Combat Activities," *Boston College International and Comparative Law Review* 30, no. 1 (2007): 111.

125 Galić, ICTY Case No. IT-98-29-T, ¶¶ 27, 108.

126 Galić, ICTY Case No. IT-98-29-T, ¶ 64. He was not convicted of the counts alleging that he had violated the laws and customs of war by attacks on civilians through sniper attacks and artillery and mortar shelling, respectively (counts 4 and 7) because the Trial Chamber found they were subsumed by Galic's conviction on count one. Ibid. ¶¶ 159–62.

127 Galić, ICTY Case No. IT-98-29-T, ¶¶ 598–9, 751–2.

128 Galić, ICTY Case No. IT-98-29-T, ¶ 618.

129 Galić, ICTY Case No. IT-98-29-T, ¶ 620.

130 Galić, ICTY Case No. IT-98-29-T, ¶¶ 667, 685.

131 Galić, ICTY Case No. IT-98-29-T, ¶ 695; cf. Kyle Chayka, "Watching the World's 'First TikTok War,'" *New Yorker*, March 3, 2022, https://perma.cc/G7J4-AUUX.

132 Galić, ICTY Case No. IT-98-29-T, ¶¶ 696–7.

133 Galić, ICTY Case No. IT-98-29-T, ¶ 699. The Court also noted that "the daily ammunition expenditure had to be recorded and be known," that "[t]hese criminal activities had to be carried out by using a vast amount of ammunition," and that the "rate of use of ammunition which would have been in excess of what was required for regular military operations . . . allow[s] the Trial Chamber to infer that the Accused knew of criminal activities by his troops." Ibid. ¶ 703.

134 Galić, ICTY Case No. IT-98-29-T, ¶ 661. This strict control applied especially to shelling activity because of the "high level of co-ordination" required. Ibid., ¶ 637.

135 Galić, ICTY Case No. IT-98-29-T, ¶ 662.

136 Galić, ICTY Case No. IT-98-29-T, ¶ 723.

137 Galić, ICTY Case No. IT-98-29-T, ¶ 722.

138 Galić, ICTY Case No. IT-98-29-T, ¶ 741.

139 Galić, ICTY Case No. IT-98-29-T, ¶ 741.

140 Prosecutor v. Miloševič, ICTY Case No. IT-98-29/1-T, Judgment, ¶ 1006 (December 12, 2007), https://perma.cc/RS8V-LP32.

141 Miloševič, ICTY Case No. IT-98-29/1-T, ¶ 845–52.

142 Miloševič, ICTY Case No. IT-98-29/1-T, ¶ 809–26.

143 Miloševič, ICTY Case No. IT-98-29/1-T, ¶ 978. Ibid., ¶ 960.

144 Prosecutor v. Miloševič, ICTY Case No. IT-98-29/1-A, Judgment, ¶ 52 (November 12, 2009), https://perma.cc/W43A-6ZZN.

145 Miloševič, ICTY Case No. IT-98-29/1-A, ¶ 56.

146 Miloševič, ICTY Case No. IT-98-29/1-A, ¶ 56.

147 Prosecutor v. Mladić, ICTY Case No. IT-09-92-T, Judgment, ¶ 4791 (November 22, 2017), https://perma.cc/254E-PDW9.

148 Mladić, ICTY Case No. IT-09-92-T, ¶ 4921.

149 Case Information, Ratko Mladić, United Nations International Residual Mechanism for Criminal Tribunals, accessed July 3, 2024, https://perma.cc/JG83-MR4P.

150 Prosecutor v. Karadžić, ICTY Case No. IT-95-5/18-T, Judgment, ¶ 2 (March 24, 2016), https://perma.cc/TC75-62V9.

151 Andrew Gardner, "Radovan Karadzić Arrested, *Politico*, July 21, 2008, https://perma.cc/9TVD-5R3V.
152 Karadžić, ICTY Case No. IT-95-5/18-T, ¶ 4650.
153 Karadžić, ICTY Case No. IT-95-5/18-T ¶ 4649
154 Karadžić, ICTY Case No. IT-95-5/18-T, ¶ 4891.
155 Prosecutor v. Martić, ICTY Case No. IT-95-11-T, Judgment, ¶¶ 303–13 (June 12, 2007), https://perma.cc/C4GU-4Q5Q.
156 Martić, ICTY Case No. IT-95-11-T, ¶¶ 308, 313.
157 Martić, ICTY Case No. IT-95-11-T, ¶¶ 305, 307, 309.
158 Martić, ICTY Case No. IT-95-11-T, ¶ 460.
159 Martić, ICTY Case No. IT-95-11-T, ¶ 462.
160 Martić, ICTY Case No. IT-95-11-T, ¶ 462.
161 Martić, ICTY Case No. IT-95-11-T, ¶ 462.
162 Martić, ICTY Case No. IT-95-11-T, ¶¶ 305, 309, 462–3.
163 Martić, ICTY Case No. IT-95-11-T, ¶ 39.
164 Martić, ICTY Case No. IT-95-11-T, ¶ 461–3. See, however, Prosecutor v. Gotovina, ICTY Case No. IT-06-90-A, Judgment, ¶ 64 (November 16, 2012), https://perma.cc/2KZP-JDZR (overturning a conviction based mainly on "the [200 meter] distance between a given impact site and one of the artillery targets").
165 Martić, ICTY Case No. IT-95-11-T, ¶ 463.
166 Rome Statute art. 8(b).
167 Rome Statute art. 8(b)(i).
168 Rome Statute, art. 8(b)(ii).
169 Rome Statute art. 8(2)(b)(iv).
170 Nils Melzer, "The Principle of Distinction Between Civilians and Combatants," in Andrew Clapham and Paola Gaeta, eds., *The Oxford Handbook of International Law in Armed Conflict* (Oxford: Oxford University Press, 2014): 296–332.
171 International Committee of the Red Cross, IHL Databases, "The Principle of Distinction Between Civilians and Combatants," accessed July 12, 2024, https://perma.cc/9GXW-JTLN.
172 Rome Statute art. 21(1)(b).
173 Lubanga, Case No. ICC-01/04-01/06, Judgment Pursuant to Article 74 of the Statute, ¶ 603.
174 Kateryna Busol et al., "The Just Security Podcast: ICC Arrest Warrants for Russian Attacks on Ukraine's Power Grid," *Just Security*, June 28, 2024, https://perma.cc/2HGX-77DN.
175 Congressional Research Service, "Russian Military Performance and Outlook," 1, March 8, 2024, https://crsreports.congress.gov/product/pdf/IF/IF12606.
176 Greg Myre, "From Drone Videos to Selfies at the Front, Ukraine Is the Most Documented War Ever," *NPR*, August 2, 2023, https://perma.cc/DLR3-HB3U.
177 See Kai Ambos, "Joint Criminal Enterprise and Command Responsibility," *Journal of International Criminal Justice* 5, no. 1 (2007): 159.
178 Leila Nadya Sadat and Jarrod M. Jolly, "Seven Canons of ICC Treaty Interpretation: Making Sense of Article 25's Rorschach Blot," *Leiden Journal of International Law* 27, no. 3 (2014): 755; Pamela J. Stephens, "Collective Criminality and Individual Responsibility: The Constraints of Interpretation," *Fordham International Law Journal* 37, no. 2 (2014): 501.

179 Carsten Stahn, *A Critical Introduction to International Criminal Law* (Cambridge: Cambridge University Press, 2019), 132–46.
180 Case Western Reserve University School of Law, "ICC Lead Investigator Discusses Putin Case at CWRU School of Law," September 5, 2023, https://perma.cc/JM2D-8SW5.
181 Janet H. Anderson, "Ukraine: 'We Could Still Expect Another ICC Arrest Warrant Soon,'" *Justice Info.Net*, March 8, 2024 (interview with Dr. Sergey Vasiliev), https://perma.cc/9WGH-BGJX.
182 Lubanga, Case No. ICC-01/04-01/06, Judgment Pursuant to Article 74 of the Statute, ¶¶ 973–5.
183 Carmel O'Sullivan, "New Court, Same Division: The *Bemba* Case as an Illustration of the Continued Confusion Regarding the Command Responsibility Doctrine," *Leiden Journal of International Law* 35, no. 3 (2022): 661.
184 "Final Report to the Prosecutor by the Committee Established to Review the NATO Bombing Campaign Against the Federal Republic of Yugoslavia," June 13, 2000, https://perma.cc/2GD6-PPMH.
185 Protocol I art. 52.
186 Mark Klamberg, *Commentary on the Law of the International Criminal Court*, 80.
187 Prosecutor v. Abu Garda, Case No. ICC-02/05-02/09, Decision on the Confirmation of Charges, n.131 (February 8, 2010), https://perma.cc/S9F8-M5CS.
188 William J. Fenrick, *Crimes in Combat: The Relationship Between Crimes Against Humanity and War Crimes* (The Hague: Guest Lecture Series of the Office of the Prosecutor, March 5, 2004), 7–8, https://perma.cc/EVR6-CXX4.
189 Prosecutor v. Galić, ICTY Case No. IT-98-29-A, Judgment, ¶ 90 (November 30, 2006), https://perma.cc/8TCT-8L6V.
190 Mark Klamberg, *Commentary on the Law of the International Criminal Court* (Brussels: Torkel Opsahl Academic EPublisher, 2017), 75, https://perma.cc/P4VG-6ZVF.
191 Rome Statute art. 7(1)(a), (k); Prosecutor v. Katanga, Case No. ICC-01/04-01/07, Decision on the Confirmation of Charges, ¶¶ 446–55 (September 30, 2008), https://perma.cc/536U-VV29.
192 Katanga, Case No. ICC-01/04-01/07, Decision on the Confirmation of Charges, ¶ 451.
193 Galić, ICTY Case No. IT-98-29-T, ¶ 152.
194 Galić, ICTY Case No. IT-98-29-T, ¶ 152.
195 Katanga, Case No. ICC-01/04-01/07, Decision on the Confirmation of Charges, ¶ 446–7; International Criminal Court, *Elements of Crimes*, 8–9.
196 Katanga, Case No. ICC-01/04-01/07, Decision on the Confirmation of Charges, ¶ 449.
197 Fenrick, *Crimes in Combat*, 8.
198 Fenrick, *Crimes in Combat*, 8.
199 "If the acceptance of a State which is not a Party to this Statute is required under paragraph 2, that State may, by declaration lodged with the Registrar, accept the exercise of jurisdiction by the Court with respect to the crime in question." Rome Statute art. 12(3).
200 Rome Statute art. 12(2)(a); see ICC-RoC46(3)-01/18-37, Decision on Prosecution's Request for Ruling on Jurisdiction Under Article 19(3) of Statute (September 6, 2018), https://perma.cc/J5TR-JXL6; Leila Nadya Sadat, "The Conferred Jurisdiction of the International Criminal Court," *Notre Dame Law Review* 99, no. 2 (2023):

549, 582–3; Jordan J. Paust, "The Reach of ICC Jurisdiction Over Non-Signatory Nationals," *Vanderbilt Journal of Transnational Law* 33, no. 1 (2000): 1.

201 Sadat, "Conferred Jurisdiction," 582–3.

202 Sadat, "Conferred Jurisdiction," 585–6.

203 Claus Kreß, "Article 98," in Kai Ambos, ed., *Rome Statute of the International Criminal Court, Article-by-Article Commentary* (Oxford: Beck Hart Nomos, 2022), 2585, 2649; Kai Ambos, "Punishment without a Sovereign: The *Ius Puniendi* Issue of International Criminal Law: A First Contribution towards a Consistent Theory of International Criminal Law," *Oxford Journal of Legal Studies* 33, no. 2 (2013): 293.

204 Dan Sarooshi, "The Powers of the United Nations International Criminal Tribunals," *Max Planck Yearbook of United Nations Law* 2 (1998): 141, 151.

205 David J. Scheffer, "The United States and the International Criminal Court," *American Journal of International Law* 93, no. 1 (1999): 12, 18; Theodor Meron, "The Court We Want," *Washington Post*, October 13, 1998, https://perma.cc/69QM-2PWV; Ruth Wedgewood, "The International Criminal Court: An American View," *European Journal International Law* 10 (1999): 93.

206 Todd Buchwald, "Unpacking New Legislation on US Support for the International Criminal Court," *Just Security*, March 9, 2023, https://perma.cc/N78U-BNDU.

207 Sadat, "Conferred Jurisdiction," 587.

208 Executive Order 14022, "Termination of Emergency with Respect to the International Criminal Court," April 1, 2021, 86 Federal Register 17895, https://perma.cc/63LX-G3AB.

209 Dapo Akande, "International Law Immunities and the International Criminal Court," *American Journal of International Law* 98, no. 3 (2004): 407, 417.

210 Prosecutor v. Al-Bashir, Case No. ICC-02/05-01/09 OA2, Judgment in the Jordan Referral re Al-Bashir Appeal (May 6, 2019), https://perma.cc/755C-8UFE.

211 For example, see Farnaz Fassihi, "Russia Vetoes a U.N. Security Council Resolution Calling on It to Withdraw from Ukraine," *New York Times*, February 25, 2022, https://perma.cc/NS9F-89D2.

212 Rome Statute, art. 13(b); U.N. Charter Ch. VII (action with respect to threats to the peace, breaches of the peace, and acts of aggression).

213 "After Arrest Warrant for Putin, Russia Opens Case Against ICC," *Al Jazeera*, March 20, 2023, https://perma.cc/8RC6-HFHV.

214 "Russia Indicts ICC Prosecutor, Judge Who Issued War Crimes Warrant for Putin," *Associated Press*, May 21, 2023, https://perma.cc/CX3F-K75Z.

215 International Criminal Court, "Measures Taken Following the Unprecedented Cyber-Attack on the ICC," October 20, 2023, https://perma.cc/3D3J-TCLX.

216 International Criminal Court, "Measures Taken Following the Unprecedented Cyber-Attack."

217 Cf. "The Cyberwar in Ukraine Is as Crucial as the Battle in the Trenches," *Economist*, March 20, 2024, https://perma.cc/9CT5-U5E2.

218 Moses, "The Dutch Intelligence Service Says It Prevented a Russian Spy from Infiltrating the International Criminal Court."

219 "Western Sanctions Will Eventually Impair Russia's Economy," *Economist*, August 24, 2022, https://perma.cc/8YKT-WSC4.

220 "Rogue Russia Threatens the World, Not Just Ukraine," *Economist*, March 14, 2024, https://perma.cc/J3DE-JEJF.

221 "Russia's Economy Once Again Defies the Doomsayers," *Economist*, March 10, 2024, https://perma.cc/6BZF-WKLF.

222 "Might Russia Run Out of Big Guns?," *Economist*, March 20, 2024, https://perma.cc/9E75-CNL3.

223 In a televised speech on February 24, 2022, Putin threatened: "No matter who tries to stand in our way or all the more so create threats for our country and our people, they must know that Russia will respond immediately, and the consequences will be such as you have never seen in your entire history. We are ready for any scenario. All necessary decisions in this regard have been taken. I hope you all hear me." "Russia Invades Ukraine." On February 27, 2022, Putin announced that Russian Federation nuclear forces were on high alert. Jeremy Shapiro, "Russia's Nuclear Alert Means NATO Must Tread Carefully," *Financial Times*, March 4, 2022, https://perma.cc/CL4C-XRX9. And in an interview with CNN on March 22, 2022, Putin's Press Secretary, Dmitry Peskov, refused to say definitively that Russia would never use nuclear weapons, stating that an "existential threat to [the Russian Federation] could be a condition for using nuclear weapons." Luke McGee and Claire Calzonetti, "Putin Spokesman Refuses to Rule Out Use of Nuclear Weapons if Russia Faced an 'Existential Threat,'" *CNN*, March 22, 2022, https://perma.cc/5957-Q7M8; cf. David E. Sanger, "New Nuclear Threats from Putin, Timed for a Moment of Anxiety," *New York Times*, February 29, 2024, https://perma.cc/WWA8-JRV6.

224 See Kai Ambos, "Ukraine and the Double Standards of the West," *Journal of International Criminal Justice* 20, no. 4 (2022): 875–92.

225 Labuda, "Beyond Rhetoric," 1098.

226 Labuda, "Beyond Rhetoric," 1098 (noting abstentions from the Global South on resolutions relating to Ukraine).

227 The Office of Gordon and Sarah Brown, "Statement Calling for the Creation of a Special Tribunal for the Punishment of the Crime of Aggression Against Ukraine," January 6, 2023, https://perma.cc/65V3-HGBQ; David Crane et al., Considerations for the Setting up of the Special Tribunal for Ukraine on the Crime of Aggression" (Ukraine Task Force of the Global Accountability Network, 2022), https://perma.cc/YR5S-U846; "Prosecuting the Crime of Aggression (Series)," *Just Security*, accessed July 12, 2024, https://perma.cc/7Z58-YJKE.

228 Labuda, "Beyond Rhetoric," 1099.

229 U.N. General Assembly, Resolution A/RES/67/19, "Status of Palestine in the United Nations" (November 12, 2012), https://perma.cc/BMP7-BDCT.

230 Palestine accepted the ICC's Jurisdiction under article 12(3) in 2014. Mahmoud Abbas, President of the State of Palestine, Declaration Accepting the Jurisdiction of the International Criminal court, December 31, 2014, https://perma.cc/EAF7-DRUB. It subsequently acceded to the Rome Statute.

231 Referral by the State of Palestine Pursuant to Articles 13(a) and 14 of the Rome Statute, May 15, 2018, https://perma.cc/V2JB-U6ZW.

232 Situation in the State of Palestine, Case No. ICC-01/08, Prosecution Request Pursuant to Article 19(3) for a Ruling on the Court's Territorial Jurisdiction in Palestine, ¶ 2 (January 22, 2020), https://perma.cc/8HPT-HR4Y; see Alain Pellet, "The Palestinian Declaration and the Jurisdiction of the International Criminal Court," *Journal of International Criminal Justice* 8, no. 4 (2010): 981; Yael Ronen, "Israel, Palestine and the ICC—Territory Uncharted but Not Unknown," *Journal*

of International Criminal Justice 12, no. 1 (2013): 979; Yuval Shany, "In Defence of Functional Interpretation of Article 12(3) of the Rome Statute," *Journal of International Criminal Justice* 8, no. 2 (2010): 329.

233 Office of the Prosecutor, Situation in Palestine: Summary of Preliminary Examination Findings, https://perma.cc/RST4-FUWD.

234 Situation in the State of Palestine, Case No. ICC-01/08, Prosecution Request Pursuant to Article 19(3) for a Ruling on the Court's Territorial Jurisdiction in Palestine, ¶ 5.

235 Situation in the State of Palestine, Case No. ICC-01/18, Decision on the "Prosecution Request Pursuant to Article 19(3) for a Ruling on the Court's Territorial Jurisdiction in Palestine," ¶ 99 (February 5, 2021), https://perma.cc/C9NL-FUQZ.

236 Situation in the State of Palestine, Case No. ICC-01/18, Decision on the "Prosecution Request Pursuant to Article 19(3) for a Ruling on the Court's Territorial Jurisdiction in Palestine," ¶¶ 104–13.

237 Peter Beaumont, "ICC Opens Investigation into War Crimes in Palestinian Territories," *Guardian*, March 3, 2021, https://perma.cc/55AW-6NZ8.

238 Anthony Deutsch, Stephanie van den Berg, and Humeyra Pamuk, "Exclusive: ICC Prosecutor Opted for Warrants over Visit to Gaza," *Reuters*, July 5, 2024, https://www.reuters.com/world/middle-east/icc-prosecutor-opted-warrants-over-visit-gaza-2024-07-05/.

239 Mat Nashed and Zena Al Tahhan, "'Alarming': Palestinians Accuse ICC Prosecutor of Bias After Israel Visit," *Al Jazeera*, December 9, 2023, https://perma.cc/DC7E-VTGE.

240 "Belgium Provides 5M Funding to Investigate War Crimes in Israel and Palestine," *Belga News Agency*, November 8, 2023, https://perma.cc/T36X-YCFM.

241 International Criminal Court, Statement of ICC Prosecutor Karim A.A. Khan KC: Applications for Arrest Warrants in the Situation in the State of Palestine, May 20, 2024, https://perma.cc/G3YN-P2J9.

242 Jimison, "House Votes to Impose Sanctions on I.C.C. Officials over Israel Prosecution"; Shear, "Biden and Blinken Accuse I.C.C. Prosecutor of Falsely Equating Israel and Hamas."

243 Situation in Palestine, Case No. ICC-01/18, Request by the United Kingdom for Leave to Submit Written Observations Pursuant to Rule 103; Haque, "The 'Oslo Accords Issue.'"

244 Situation in Palestine, Case No. ICC-01/18, Observations by the State of Palestine to the Pre-Trial Chamber I Pursuant to Rule 103 of the Rules of Procedures and Evidence (August 6, 2024), https://www.icc-cpi.int/sites/default/files/CourtRecords/0902ebd1809236d9.pdf; Situation in Palestine, Case No. ICC-01/18, Amicus Curiae Observations of Professor Adil Ahmad Haque Submitted to the "Decision on Requests for Leave to File Observations Pursuant to Rule 103 of the Rules of Procedure and Evidence" of 22 July 2024 (ICC-01-18-249) (August 6, 2024), https://www.icc-cpi.int/sites/default/files/CourtRecords/0902ebd180923d40.pdf; Situation in Palestine, Case No. ICC-01/18, Observations by Norway Pursuant to Rule 103 of the Rules of Procedure and Evidence (August 6, 2024), https://www.icc-cpi.int/sites/default/files/CourtRecords/0902ebd18091a09c.pdf; Situation in Palestine, Case No. ICC-01/18, Written Observations of Chile and Mexico Pursuant to Rule 103(1) of the Rules of Procedure and Evidence (August 6, 2024), https://www.icc-cpi.int/sites/default/files/CourtRecords/0902ebd1809233ac.pdf.

245 Situation in Palestine, Case No. ICC-01/18, Observations Pursuant to Rule 103(1) of the Rules of Procedure and Evidence, ¶ 15 (August 6, 2024), https://www.icc-cpi.int/sites/default/files/CourtRecords/0902ebd18092376e.pdf.
246 See United States Department of State, "Ambassador Van Schaack's Remarks on the U.S. Proposal to Prosecute Russian Crimes of Aggression"; United States Senate, Resolution 531, ¶ 2.
247 "House Republicans Fear Trump Too Much To Aid Ukraine," *Economist*, February 14, 2024, https://perma.cc/DD78-MWZC; "France and Germany Are at Loggerheads over Military Aid to Ukraine," *Economist*, February 29, 2024, https://perma.cc/629Q-SSZ7.
248 Marlise Simmons, Charlie Savage, and Anushka Patil, "Here's What to Know About the I.C.C.'s Arrest Warrant for Putin," *New York Times*, March 17, 2023, https://perma.cc/9JTJ-BK9T; Amanda Taub, "The I.C.C.'s Arrest Warrant for Putin Is More Than 'Just Symbolic,'" *New York Times*, March 31, 2023, https://perma.cc/FW6A-Y7LD.
249 Prosecutor v. Kony, Case No. ICC-02/04-01/05, Decision on the Prosecutor's Request to Hold a Confirmation of Charges Hearing in the Kony Case in the Suspect's Absence (November 23, 2023), https://perma.cc/R6LK-E6UL.
250 Cf. International Military Tribunal (Nuremberg), Judgement (October 1, 1946), https://perma.cc/A6DE-M5ZG.
251 Sadat, "Justice Without Fear or Favour."
Kai Ambos, "Joint Criminal Enterprise and Command Responsibility," *Journal of International Criminal Justice* 5, no. 1 (2007): 159

Selected Bibliography

Ambos, Kai, "Joint Criminal Enterprise and Command Responsibility," *Journal of International Criminal Justice* 5, no. 1 (2007): 159

Busol, Kateryna, et al., "The Just Security Podcast: ICC Arrest Warrants for Russian Attacks on Ukraine's Power Grid," *Just Security*, June 28, 2024, https://perma.cc/2HGX-77DN.

Fenrick, William J. *Crimes in Combat: The Relationship Between Crimes Against Humanity and War Crimes* (The Hague: Guest Lecture Series of the Office of the Prosecutor, March 5, 2004), 7–8, https://perma.cc/EVR6-CXX4.

Haque, Adil Ahmad, "The International Criminal Court's Jurisdiction in Palestine and the 'Oslo Accords Issue,'" *Just Security*, July 9, 2024, https://perma.cc/Z6VU-LKT4.

Kress, Claus, "Article 98," in Kai Ambos, ed., *Rome Statute of the International Criminal Court, Article-by-Article Commentary* (Oxford: Beck Hart Nomos, 2022), 2585

Labuda, Patryk I., "Beyond Rhetoric: Interrogating the Eurocentric Critique of International Criminal Law's Selectivity in the Wake of the 2022 Ukraine Invasion," *Leiden Journal of International Law* 36, no. 4 (2023): 1095

Sadat, Leila Nadya, "The Conferred Jurisdiction of the International Criminal Court," *Notre Dame Law Review* 99, no. 2 (2023): 549

Sadat, Leila Nadya, "'Justice Without Fear or Favour?' The Uncertain Future of the International Criminal Court," in Alexander Heinze and Viviane E. Dittrich, eds., *The Past, Present and Future of the International Criminal Court* (Brussels: Torkel Opsahl Academic EPublisher, 2021): 121–57.

27

From Nuremberg to Kyiv

Four Puzzles of Aggression and Accountability

David Luban

[1]This chapter explores four puzzles about the crime of aggression. First, what precisely is the evil that brings aggression into the pantheon of core crimes, alongside war crimes, crimes against humanity, and genocide? The evils of the other core crimes need little explanation—but aggression seems like a different sort of crime, a crime against states rather than against people. Second, who can be tried for the crime of aggression? Presumably, it will be the leaders who planned and launched the aggression, not the foot soldiers who carried it out. But which leaders are we talking about, and where do we draw the line? Third, under international law, apex leaders (paradigmatically, the head of state or head of government) are immune from prosecution in the courts of other states. As we will see, the International Criminal Court (ICC) has no jurisdiction over the crime of aggression committed by non-members like the Russian Federation. Does that mean the only people who can be tried for aggression are those immune from prosecution? I call this the *paradox of immunity*. The fourth puzzle is closely related to the third. An alternative to ICC and domestic-court prosecution would be creating an international aggression tribunal. Plainly, the UN Security Council will not do it because Russia and its ally China hold the veto power. Could some group of states—the EU, for example—create an international tribunal for aggression? That proposal has been on the table for two years, and under customary international law there are no immunities in international tribunals. The question is, what entitles a group of states to create a tribunal, declare it international, and grant it the power to bring a foreign sovereign to trial for aggression? How can a small group of states proclaim itself the authentic representative of the international community? The ICC makes that claim—but the ICC, at least, has 125 members from all the inhabited continents, and membership is open to all states.

In answer to these questions, I will argue for four propositions: first, that aggression is a crime against people, not against states. Second, the circle of leadership who can be held accountable for aggression is more comprehensive than some suppose. Third, and contrary to generally received opinion, there is no customary rule of immunity for the crime of aggression, and there never has been. That means that victim states are fully entitled to prosecute the leaders of a state that aggresses against them. And fourth, if there is no customary-law immunity for aggression, the only legitimacy requirement for a multilateral tribunal created by treaty is its fairness and adherence to all the principles of natural justice. All this, I argue, is entirely consistent with the Nuremberg Principles, and indeed, it is necessary to give them practical force.

The Criminalization of Aggression: A Brief Genealogy

I begin, however, four centuries before the Nuremberg Principles, with a brief genealogy.

Although theorists from Grotius on maintained that wars of aggression are unjust, they also held that the injustice of war is not for other states to adjudicate. In a system of sovereign states, no state can judge another: *par in parem non habet imperium* (equals have no dominion over equals)—a sovereign immunity rule that traces back to Dante's *De Monarchia* (1313).[2] Furthermore, with no judge enthroned above the states themselves, outsiders must be legally agnostic about the justice or injustice of wars. Furthermore, because international commerce requires that clear title to land and property be established quickly after a war, international law from the early modern period forward permitted victors to keep whatever land and loot they conquered, regardless of who the aggressor actually was.[3]

In practice, therefore, all that a prince needed to launch a war of conquest was some official grievance that required redress and could not be settled peacefully. The result, as Oona Hathaway and Scott Shapiro document, is that declarations of war routinely included a manifesto of grievances detailing the (supposed) just cause.[4] Unsurprisingly, the grievances were often mere pretexts. For example, Frederick the Great invaded Austria in 1740 over an arcane dispute about which dynasty had inherited Silesia centuries earlier. But as Frederick explained later, that was not his real motive.

> At my father's death I found all Europe at peace . . . I found myself with highly trained forces at my disposal, together with a well-filled exchequer, and I myself was possessed of a lively temperament. These were the reasons that prevailed upon me to wage war against Theresa of Austria, queen of Bohemia and Hungary. Ambition, advantage, my desire to make a name of myself—these swayed me, and war was resolved upon.[5]

The result: wars of conquest became *de facto* legitimate, as long as sovereigns pretended they were somehow just. The Berlin Conference of 1884–5 legitimized the Scramble for Africa, meaning European colonization by force. The Scramble was not described as aggression because the conquered colonies were not deemed "civilized" states—but of course aggression is exactly what it was.

Thus matters remained until the First World War blew the European system of sovereign states to smithereens. After the catastrophe, Allied statesmen and lawyers bickered over whether the German Kaiser could be tried for the crime of aggression and finally settled on a legally ambiguous compromise between criminal prosecution and impunity. The Versailles treaty stipulated that the Kaiser would be tried for a "supreme offense against international morality" (not international crime), and in the end the Allies never pressed for his extradition and never tried him.[6]

Between the world wars, the Kellogg-Briand Peace Pact committed states to abandoning war as an instrument of policy, and the Pact attracted a surprisingly large number of parties. But it failed to establish a mechanism for responding to breaches, and it did not call for criminal penalties against aggressors.

Aggression was finally criminalized after the Second World War devastated two continents. The Soviet jurist Aron Trainin proposed a new legal category, *crimes against peace*, and his proposal found its way into the Nuremberg Charter.[7] In *The Criminal Responsibility of the Hitlerites*, Trainin explains, "Peaceful relations between countries are a basic surmise [sic] of any international association. Peace is the greatest social value and therefore infringement on peace constitutes . . . the first species of international offenses."[8] He continues: "A direct and most dangerous form of infringement of peace appears to be the attack on one country by another, i.e., aggression, which explodes peace directly and presses war upon people. Aggression therefore is the most dangerous international crime."[9] The Soviet government translated Trainin's book into English in 1944 and circulated it among the other Allies.

The surviving "top Nazis" were tried before the International Military Tribunal for the Trial of Major War Criminals (the Nuremberg Tribunal, IMT for short). Its Charter adopts Trainin's phrase and defines crimes against peace as "planning, preparation, initiation or waging of a war of aggression, or a war in violation of international treaties, agreements or assurances, or participation in a common plan or conspiracy for the accomplishment of any of the foregoing" (art. 6(a)).

By its terms, the IMT was not making international law: it had jurisdiction only over Axis criminals, and the Charter was the product of only the four Allied powers. But within a few years, the UN General Assembly (UNGA) requested the International Law Commission (ILC) to identify those IMT principles that were now customary international law. These are the Nuremberg Principles[10]—and although UNGA never formally adopted them, they stand today as the standard codification. Notably, Principle VI(a) is identical to its Nuremberg Charter counterpart.

Complementing the Nuremberg definition, the UN Charter prohibits states from threatening or using force against another state's territorial integrity or political independence, "or in any other manner inconsistent with the Purposes of the United Nations" (art. 2(4))—and those Purposes include suppressing acts of aggression (art. 1(1)). The Charter empowers the Security Council to determine the existence of acts of aggression and to take steps against them (arts. 39, 53). The only exception to this ban on the unauthorized use of force is the "inherent" right of self-defense against an armed attack (art. 51). In effect, the Charter dramatically narrows the classical conception of just cause from any legitimate grievance that can only be addressed by force to the single right of self-defense.

Unfortunately, the Charter contains important ambiguities. It fails to define aggression or acts of aggression; it leaves unclear the difference between prohibited uses of force, acts of aggression, and armed attacks; and it does not define the boundaries of the inherent right of self-defense. There is an extensive legal literature, and some International Court of Justice jurisprudence, that partly fills these gaps, but it is not my purpose here to get into these technicalities.

Notably, the Charter does not say whether acts of aggression are crimes. We have seen that Nuremberg law criminalizes *wars* of aggression, but presumably an act of aggression needn't turn into a war.

The most pressing of the ambiguities was the need to define "acts of aggression" and to decide whether they are crimes. But repeated efforts in the General Assembly were thwarted by Cold War rivalries. The Great Powers, which cherish the Not-So-Great desire to use military force however they see fit, opposed efforts at a definition, or occasionally made their own proposals—which, predictably, outlawed the kind of military action their rivals engaged in but not their own.

Finally, during a period of Cold War détente, the General Assembly succeeded in crafting a definition of aggression, in UNGA Resolution 3314 (1974). It provides a non-exclusive list of seven acts of aggression, and it sternly declares that "No consideration of whatever nature, whether political, economic, military or otherwise, may serve as a justification for aggression" (art. 5). But it too left questions unanswered because it was watered down in a series of compromises. Only *wars* of aggression are crimes against peace; for lesser aggression, "there is State responsibility" (art. 5)—but with no explanation of what state responsibility means. Nor does Resolution 3314 provide for individual criminal liability. First uses of force are not aggression *per se*, merely prima facie evidence of aggression; and the Security Council can determine that a first use of force is not an act of aggression (art. 2). These limitations were all concessions to the Great Powers. In return, the "non-aligned" powers extracted the concession that dominated peoples can struggle for the right of self-determination and can receive support from other states in their struggle without these being condemned as aggression.

The most recent development is the ICC's Rome Statute. From the beginning, it included the crime of aggression in its subject-matter jurisdiction, pending a definition of the crime. That came in 2010 when the Assembly of States Parties adopted the Kampala Amendments, which defined the crime of aggression and activated the aggression clause (over strong objections by the United States). The amendments adopt the list of aggressive acts from UNGAR 3314. Like all ICC crimes, individuals can be charged. At the same time, though, Kampala severely restricted the ICC's jurisdiction over the crime of aggression. Unlike the other core crimes, the ICC has no jurisdiction over aggression committed by non-members, even if it is aggression against a member or against some other state (like Ukraine) that has given the ICC ad hoc jurisdiction. And only member states that opt into the Kampala amendments fall under its jurisdiction; to date, only one-third of ICC members have opted in.

From the standpoint of the Nuremberg Principles, the net result and the current state of international criminal law are rather disappointing. To be sure, aggressive war is widely recognized as an international crime.[11] But the first and foremost Nuremberg Principle is that "[a]ny person who commits an act which constitutes a crime under international law is responsible therefor and liable to punishment." The Kampala Amendments come nowhere near fulfilling Principle I.

Puzzle One: What Makes Aggression a Core International Crime?

International law is an inherently state-based (I will say "statist") enterprise, and it should surprise nobody that it classifies aggression as an offense against states, not against the people who live in them. That is common ground among various UNGA resolutions, the International Law Commission, and the ICC.[12] State sovereignty, which a General Assembly resolution identified as "the personality of the State,"[13] is granted a value of near-mystical proportions, and aggression against a sovereign is a kind of *lèse majesté*. (Who says so? Sovereigns, of course.)

The trouble is that sovereignty is an abstraction, and "the personality of the State" is a legal fiction. It is hard to see why an offense against an abstraction or a fiction should matter the way that genocide or war crimes matter. They involve tangible violence against human bodies and the material world; abstractions and legal fictions are, in Aldous Huxley's phrase, gaseous invertebrates.

One possible response is that sovereignty means freedom from foreign powers dictating the decisions of a state's legitimate government, and aggression (especially, but not only aggression to steal territory) takes away that freedom. The virtue of this version of statism is that the victim of aggression is something tangible. It is not an abstraction—it is the state's government. Aggression is the forcible domination of a state's government, and its exclusive power of decision-making, by a foreign state.

But this theory does not really answer the question of why aggression is a core evil. The value of a government's autonomous decision-making is only as great as the quality of its decisions. Why should exclusive governmental control over policies matter so much that interfering with it should join genocide, crimes against humanity, and war crimes in the pantheon of evils? Governments come and go, and their policy choices are not necessarily valuable except to their ruling elites. Furthermore, it is fanciful to suppose that governments with little political or economic clout make their policies on their own. With some justice, the political realist Stephen Krasner calls sovereignty a form of "organized hypocrisy," because it pretends that weak states exercise exclusive decision-making without the influence of more powerful states.[14] This is plainly untrue. Certainly, the US government, which makes extensive use of economic sanctions to influence foreign governments, thinks this is untrue.

Of course, there is a difference between sanctions and aggression. Sanctions do not involve military force; aggression does. But this is exactly the point: the evil of aggression is not the domination of another government, but the use of force to accomplish it.

A statist can try again: sovereignty matters normatively because the government represents its *people*, and aggression violates the people's right to self-determination.

This is Michael Walzer's argument in his modern classic *Just and Unjust Wars*, and he is clearly onto something that matters: the yearning for self-determination is what drives the Ukrainian people's fierce resistance to Russian aggression. But it is important to recognize that Walzer ultimately grounds the right of self-determination in individual human rights, and he explains that "[t]he real subject of my argument is not the state at all but the political community that (usually) underlies it."[15]

This shifts the ground from a statist theory of the crime of aggression to a human rights theory, focused specifically on "the rights of contemporary men and women to live as members of a historic community and to express their inherited culture through political forms worked out among themselves."[16]

Once we move from the terrain of statism to the terrain of human rights, we must ask where the individual right to live in a self-determining state ranks within the full catalog of human rights. We should take a clue from Henry Shue's definition of basic rights as those without which no other rights can be enjoyed. In Shue's sense, the two most basic rights are those to security and subsistence.[17] Self-determination is not a basic right of individuals, because members of minority communities can enjoy the full panoply of human rights without self-determination, even if many members yearn for a state of their own. Think of the Quebecois, the Catalans, and the Scottish. All have, or had, strong separatist movements, but all enjoy the robust human rights of Canada, Spain, and the United Kingdom. By contrast, Ukrainians today resist Russian aggression because they know from experience that Russian domination is the enemy of their human rights.

To understand why aggressive war is a core international crime, we should look away from statism (even in Walzer's benign form) toward the basic human right of physical security. Quite simply, the evil of aggressive war is the violence it inflicts, even when both the aggressors and defenders fight within the limits of *jus in bello*. The aggressor has unleashed the dogs of war, and the *jus in bello* merely launders the violence. This is a view that Tom Dannenbaum and Fréderic Mégret have extensively developed, and I embrace it as well.[18]

There is one complication in the view. What if there is no violence because the victim surrenders without a fight? Hitler's annexations of Austria and Czechoslovakia were almost bloodless, but even so they were clear cases of aggression. Consistent with his view that the evil of aggression is the violence it unleashes, Dannenbaum argues that although bloodless aggressions are illegal, they are not crimes. I disagree. Conquerors seldom have benign intentions toward the people they conquer. They will maintain the occupation by force, placing the occupied people in a long-term state of oppression and insecurity. And, if the occupied people resist or launch an insurrection, the blood will flow. Even after the bloodless invasion, the specter of violence hovers in the background.

So far, I have considered two theories of aggression: that it is a crime against states and that it is a crime against the basic human right of physical security. What about the original idea in the Nuremberg Principles, that it is a crime against peace? Is peace as such a value, distinct from states and security rights? I think it makes more sense to regard it through the human rights lens.

Here, we should distinguish two versions of the argument for a separate category of crimes against peace. The first is that peace as such is a basic and paramount value. The problem with the argument is that it fails to distinguish between just and unjust peace, what Mégret calls the "peace of tombs." In his famous dissent in the Tokyo Tribunal (the International Military Tribunal for the Far East, IMTFE), the Indian Judge Radhabinod Pal argued bitterly that criminalizing aggression was nothing more than an effort by the West to freeze into place an oppressive colonialist status quo. Indeed, Pal argued, oppressed peoples can fight for freedom, and surely they can accept help from outside powers without that help being defamed as aggression. Pal's passionate skepticism resonated with much of the developing world, and it is reflected in UNGA 3314's Article 7, which declares that the prohibition of aggression does not prejudice the right of "peoples under colonial and racist regimes or other forms of alien domination . . . to struggle to that end [independence and self-determination] and to seek and receive support." Notably, when Trainin defines crimes against peace, he adds in a footnote, "It is obvious, that just wars for liberation are not comprised here."[19]

There is a better argument for crimes against peace. In a world of thermonuclear bombs and conventional weapons of incomprehensible lethality, the risk of any war escalating into a war of universal devastation is high, and it poses the ultimate threat to human rights. Thus, the best way of thinking about the crimes-against-peace interpretation is to assimilate it to the human rights rationale for criminalizing aggression: the evil of aggression is the intolerable risk of lethal violence it imposes on the inhabitants of a tightly networked world.

Puzzle Two: Who Are the Criminals?

From Nuremberg on, unanimous opinion holds that aggression is a leadership crime, even though it is the foot soldiers (and sailors and pilots) who inflict the physical violence. They are simply carrying out their duties, and evaluating the *jus ad bellum* is not their responsibility. The prospect of punishing thousands of foot soldiers in the aggressor's army is absurd.

Perhaps so; but the innocence of foot soldiers is far less obvious than it seems. If a soldier *knows* that the war is aggression and not self-defense, and *knows* that aggressive war is a crime—but nevertheless deploys and kills in the course of service—why *shouldn't* he be held liable for the crime of aggression? Under Nuremberg Principle IV, "The fact that a person acted pursuant to order of his Government or of a superior does not relieve him from responsibility under international law, provided a moral choice was in fact possible to him."[20] Only extreme duress can be said to make moral choice impossible, and even then some legal systems do not allow a duress defense for murder.

To be clear, I think there are excellent reasons to amnesty the aggressor's foot soldiers, and in the post-Second World War cases the thought of prosecuting them never crossed anyone's mind, so no formal amnesty was even necessary.[21] But amnesty forgives the guilty and innocent alike, and it is entirely consistent with criminal guilt. Many soldiers who have killed in unjust wars know this intuitively, and some carry the burden of guilt with them forever in the form of moral injury.[22]

Understanding the (theoretical) liability of foot soldiers is essential for putting the leadership requirement in the crime of aggression in proper perspective. Many jurists assume that only apex leaders can be charged with the crime of aggression, and view with suspicion efforts to widen the scope of liability beyond the apex. In my view, they approach the issue from exactly the wrong end. Instead of asking what justifies a wide leadership requirement, the right question is what justifies a narrow one. Why shouldn't intermediate-level generals and admirals, industrialists contributing to the war effort, warmongering media moguls, or influential clerics preaching holy war be regarded as leaders for purposes of prosecuting the crime of aggression?

This is a live question today as Ukrainian prosecutors decide who to indict for aggression under that nation's domestic aggression statute.[23] Only apex leaders like Putin and Shoigu? Or general officers in the field? Had he lived, could they have indicted Prigozhin as well? Presumably, the Ukrainian prosecutors want to adhere to international legal doctrine even in their domestic law prosecutions (although they do not have to).

The doctrinal issue concerns the legal tests for leadership. The customary international law definition considers all those who are able to "shape or influence" the decision to pursue aggressive war to be leaders who may be prosecuted. But the Kampala amendments to the Rome Statute changed the test, or at least its wording: only those "in a position effectively to exercise control over or to direct the political or military action of a State" can be charged as principals or even accomplices to the crime of aggression.[24] Intuitively, the new wording narrows the circle of leadership: only someone granted the final say-so on a political or military action is in a position to effectively control or direct it because, by definition, those without final say-so can be overruled. But those lacking that authority can nevertheless shape or influence the decision through their advice or actions. A president's trusted advisers might be able to dissuade him from ordering an act of aggression, even if the sole final authority is the president's. So too, a field commander who explains to higher-ups why proposed acts of aggression are operationally impractical may influence policy, even though the field commander cannot control or direct the state's military policy. On this reading, the "control or direct" formula applies to fewer people than the "shape or influence" test. Scholars disagree about whether it was intended that way or whether negotiators thought the new phrasing is equivalent to the old.[25] Either way, the danger is that at least some states are likely to read the Rome Statute phrasing narrowly and regard the narrow test as the new customary international law. That would be a mistake, and inflict an unnecessary defeat on the Nuremberg Principles. It can only give aid and comfort to aggressors, because they can reassure nervous elites that they can assist the aggressive war effort with impunity.

Puzzle Three: The Paradox of Immunity

A long-standing principle of international law holds that heads of state and heads of government are immune from lawsuits and criminal prosecutions in the courts of another state (this is sometimes abbreviated as "HOS/HOG immunity"). This chapter is not the occasion to delve deeply into the theory behind immunity, which derives from the *par in parem* principle. It is a mix of medieval political theology, in which the king personifies the state, and the practical requirements of diplomacy: kings, like diplomats, need to visit other realms without being beheaded. Doctrinally, HOS/HOG immunity applies to all the head of state or government's crimes by virtue of their office, and even after their incumbency they enjoy immunity for acts of state during their reign (but not for private crimes).

The modern question is whether these immunities apply to the core international crimes, what lawyers call "*jus cogens* offenses." Under the Nuremberg Principles, they should not. The celebrated 1999 *Pinochet* decision by the UK House of Lords—which found that Chile's former president could be extradited from the United Kingdom to Spain to stand trial for torture—gave some reason for thinking that the answer might soon be no. In that decision, Lord Browne-Wilkinson explained that after Chile joined the Convention Against Torture (CAT), Pinochet regime tortures could no longer be regarded as state acts. Otherwise, "bizarre results" ensue: CAT criminalizes only official acts of torture, and if their status as state acts cloaks torturers in immunity, no one could ever be prosecuted for torture in the courts of another state. The paradox of immunity would defeat the entire point of CAT.

Unfortunately, a series of judgments by the International Court of Justice and the European Court of Human Rights pushed back against the revolution in accountability: they held that there is no *jus cogens* exception to the customary law rule of immunity.[26] Most were divided judgments with strong dissenting opinions (which I think were right), and in 2017 the International Law Commission proposed stripping away act-of-state immunity (but not HOS/HOG immunity) for half a dozen core crimes.[27] It may happen yet.

Conspicuously, though, the ILC did not include aggression on its list of crimes. The reason was overtly political: concern about the "political implications it could have for the stability of relations between States" if state leaders could be tried for aggression in the courts of another state.[28] The decision to omit aggression from the list was deeply contentious, and it led to a first-ever divided vote in the Commission.[29]

All the judicial decisions rejecting the *jus cogens* exception for core crimes reason in the same way: they assume that a robust rule of immunity exists and then announce that they can find no state practice or *opinio juris* removing it for *jus cogens* crimes. I maintain, though, that this reasoning fails in the case of aggression because *there is no customary rule of immunity for the crime of aggression*. Customary law is generally founded on state practice undertaken because the states recognize a legal obligation. (The term of art for that recognition is "*opinio juris.*") Therefore, jurists would have to find a state practice of immunizing leaders for the crime of aggression, along with an *opinio juris* that doing so is a legal obligation. Neither exists. The reason is straightforward: there was no officially recognized crime of aggression before the IMT, and the handful of post-war state prosecutions of Nazi officials for aggression all resulted in convictions, not immunity.[30] As for *opinio juris*, as late as the post-First World War effort to prosecute the Kaiser, the opinion about his immunity was deeply divided, with some leading experts denying that there was any such immunity. The British expert Sir Robert McDonnell pointed out that there was no immunity rule until the time of the Sun King, the apogee of the divine right of kings and royal absolutism—and for good reasons that ideology was long dead by the twentieth century. As for "those recent writers who use comprehensive language as to such immunity," they

> do not distinguish between the position of a Sovereign who visits or resides in a foreign country at the invitation or by the permission, express or implied, of its Sovereign, and that of a Sovereign who invades and occupies foreign territory in spite of the resistance of its Sovereign. For immunity in the latter case there seems to be no authority. [31]

The Nuremberg Principles explicitly deny that heads of state are immune from prosecution (Principle III).

In short: No state practice of immunity; no consensus in the *opinio juris*—hence, no rule of immunity for the crime of aggression.

Puzzle Four: What Makes a Tribunal International?

In fairness, it is important to note that in modern practice only international courts have codified a "no immunity" rule, and even the experts who thought the Kaiser could be tried favored an international court rather than a domestic court. Presumably, the no-immunity Nuremberg Principle is intended for international courts.

Since the Russian invasion of Ukraine, several governments have proposed a new international court to try the crime of aggression.[32] Perhaps the most concrete proposal would be a treaty among EU states, including Ukraine, to create such a tribunal. The question is whether a tribunal created by the treaty could exercise jurisdiction over Russian aggressors. What would make such a tribunal sufficiently "international"? Or, to put it another way, how many states acting together does it take to create an international tribunal? Is two enough? Plainly not; if it were, nothing would prevent Russia and Belarus from creating a faux-international tribunal to try Volodymyr Zelensky for aggression! But if not two, then how many? Are the twenty-seven states in the EU enough? What is magical about the number 27?

These questions, taken on their own terms, pose a seemingly intractable slippery-slope problem. But if I am right that there is no customary rule of immunity for the crime of aggression, there is no *legal* problem at all. (Of course tremendous political problems would still have to be overcome.) Even a single state can try an aggressor under its domestic law; therefore, Ukraine would actually have no immunity hurdle to overcome. Neither would a treaty-based international court.

But could such a regional court genuinely claim to speak for the international community? As a general matter, I think the answer is no. But the case of Russia and Ukraine is materially different: in the UN General Assembly, more than 140 states, from all regions of the world, have twice declared the invasion to be aggression and denounced it. This overwhelming condemnation provides a strong tailwind boosting the claim that an aggression tribunal is international.

The important thing, though, is that any such tribunal would have to earn its legitimacy by scrupulous fairness.[33] That would require familiar institutional safeguards, including the rule that no two judges can come from the same country; that all judges maintain the high ethical standards recently proposed by the Ethica project;[34] that the due process guarantees enshrined in the International Covenant on Civil and Political Rights are met; that proof be beyond a reasonable doubt; that adequate defense resources to establish equality of arms be provided; and that evidence be rigorously authenticated. In short, the tribunal would need to respect all the decencies of natural justice.

The aggression tribunal may never happen. In the nearly three years since the Russian invasion, the political will to create it has faded, as European politics has moved in a direction more sympathetic to Russia, and the Gaza War has displaced Ukraine from the headlines. It would not be the first time that politics has inflicted setbacks on international law. Even so, the reasons behind the criminalization of aggression have not faded in importance, and the need for a robust international criminal law against aggression remains as urgent as it was eighty years ago.

Notes

1 Distinguished University Professor, Georgetown University Law Center. The arguments in this chapter are drawn from a longer work, "The Crime of Aggression: Its Nature, the Leadership Clause, and the Paradox of Immunity," which will appear in Eliav Lieblich and Tom Dannenbaum, eds., *Elsevier Research Handbook on International Legal Theory*.

2 Yoram Dinstein, *Par in Parem Non Habet Imperium*, 1 Israel L. Rev. 407, 409 (1966).

3 Oona A. Hathaway and Scott J. Shapiro, *The Internationalists: How a Radical Plan to Outlaw War Remade the World* (New York: Simon & Schuster 2017), 23–6, 69–71. They attribute this conquerors-keepers view to Grotius, but of course it long predates him. In the *Politics* Aristotle writes that "the things conquered in war are said to belong to their conquerors" (bk. 1, ch. 6, 1255a5), indicating that "might makes right" was a conventional view in the ancient world, where conquerors enslaved those they conquered.

4 Hathaway and Shapiro, *The Internationalists*, 32–45.

5 Quoted in 1 Gerhard Ritter, The Sword and the Scepter: The Problem of Militarism in Germany, Vol. 1: The Prussian Tradition,, trans. by Heinz Norden (Miami:

University of Miami Press, 1969), 18–19 (internal quotation marks and citation omitted).

6 William A. Schabas, *The Trial of the Kaiser* (Oxford: Oxford University Press, 2018). The quote is from Article 227 of the Versailles Treaty.

7 See Francine Hirsch, *Soviet Judgment at Nuremberg* (Oxford: Oxford University Press, 2020), 7–8, 17–8, 35–8. In fact, the idea of post-war trials rather than summary executions came from the USSR, not the United States.

8 A. N. Trainin, *The Criminal Responsibility of the Hitlerites*, ed. A. Y. Vishinsky (Moscow: Legal Publishing House NKU, 1944), 47, typescript available at https://cgsc.contentdm.oclc.org/digital/collection/p4013coll8/id/2366. Trainin's second species is "offenses connected with the war," which in the London Charter were divided into war crimes and crimes against humanity.

9 Id. at 47–8.

10 International Law Commission, Principles of International Law Recognized in the Nürnberg Tribunal and in the Judgment of the Tribunal (1950).

11 Even Russia claimed self-defense, not aggression, when it invaded Ukraine. The claim was preposterous. Among Putin's justifications are (i) collective self-defense of the Donbas People's Republics, the existence of which was declared by insurrectionists just three days before the invasion (and which are not internationally recognized); (ii) individual self-defense against the supposedly existential threat posed by NATO expansion and Western cultural values ("pseudo-values . . . directly leading to degradation and degeneration . . . contrary to human nature itself," presumably referring to equal respect for gender non-conforming persons); and (iii) prevention of "genocide against the millions" of ethnic Russians in Ukraine, which is a patently absurd accusation. See *Letter dated 24 February 2022 from the Permanent Representative of the Russian Federation addressed to the Secretary General*, UNSC doc. S/2022/154. On the non-recognition of the newly conjured People's Republics, see UNGA Resolution ES-11/4, Territorial Integrity of Ukraine: defending the principles of the Charter of the United Nations, UN Doc. A/RES/ES-11/4, October 13, 2022, where 143 states voted against international recognition.

12 The General Assembly equates armed intervention with "interference or attempted threats against the personality of the State," rather than against the personalities of its inhabitants. UNGA Res. 2625 (XXV)(1970), Declaration on Principles of International Law concerning Friendly Relations and Co-operation among States in accordance with the Charter of the United Nations. The International Law Commission's *Responsibility of States for Internationally Wrongful Acts* recognizes only states and "the international community as a whole" as possible victims of internationally wrongful acts. ILC *Responsibility of States for Internationally Wrongful Acts* (2001), art. 33, 42. The Rome Statute, following the line of Resolution 3314, defines the crime of aggression as "the use of armed force against the sovereignty, territorial integrity, or political independence of a state . . .." Rome Statute, art. 8 *bis*(2).

13 UNGA Res. 2625.

14 Stephen D. Krasner, *Sovereignty: Organized Hypocrisy* (Princeton: Princeton University Press, 1999). Recently, Vladimir Putin traveled to Mongolia, which as an ICC member state was obligated to arrest him and extradite him to The Hague to stand trial for war crimes. Obviously, that was not going to happen: Mongolia is

sandwiched between Russia and its ally China—two of its five trading partners, with more than 80 percent of Mongolia's annual exports going to China.

15 Michael Walzer, *The Moral Standing of States: A Response to Four Critics*, 9 Phil. & Pub. Aff. 209, 210 (1980). Walzer insists that his statism rests on a foundation of individual rights. See *Just and Unjust Wars* (New York: Basic Books, 1977), xvi–xvii.

16 Id., 211.

17 Henry Shue, *Basic Rights: Subsistence, Affluence, and U.S. Foreign Policy* (Princeton: Princeton University Press, 2nd ed., 1996), 19–29.

18 Tom Dannenbaum, *Why Have We Criminalized Aggressive War?*, 126 Yale L.J. 1242, 1249 (2017). This article is incorporated in Dannenbaum's book *The Crime of Aggression, Humanity, and the Soldier* (Cambridge: Cambridge University Press, 2018), chapter 3. Fréderic Mégret, *What is the Specific Evil of Aggression?* in The Crime of Aggression: A Commentary, (Claus Kreß and Stefan Barriga eds., Cambridge: Cambridge University Press, 2017). I borrow the "laundering violence" metaphor from Mégret.

19 Trainin, at 47–8. He does not explain how to reconcile this exception with the claim that "peace is the greatest social value." Moreover, it will not always be obvious when a war for liberation is just—unless one assumes that all wars of liberation are just, and all forms of outside support for them are just.

20 To take a real example, in 2016 Ukraine convicted two captured Russian soldiers of aggression—only to release them in a prisoner exchange. *Ukraine finds Russian "Soldiers" Guilty of Waging War*, BBC News, April 18, 2016, https://www.bbc.com/news/world-europe-36070383. Sergey Sayapin, *A Curious Aggression Trial in Ukraine: Reflections on the* Alexandrov and Yerefeyev *Case*, J. Int'l. Crim. Justice 16(5) (2018): 1093–104.

21 See, for example, the I.G. Farben Trial, 10. The U.N. War Crimes Comm'n, Law Reports of Trials of War Criminals 37–8 (1949), where the judges justified the leadership requirement on the crime of aggression because otherwise "there could be no practical limitation on criminal responsibility that would not include, on principle, the private soldier on the battlefield . . . ." Obviously, in their eyes imposing criminal responsibility on the private soldiers would be unthinkable.

22 David Luban, *Moral Injury and Atonement*, 22 Journal of Military Ethics 214, 218 (2023).

23 Ukraine Criminal Code, art. 437. Importantly, both Russia and Belarus have also criminalized aggression, so no issue of dual criminality arises. Russian Federation Criminal Code, art. 353; Belarus Criminal Code, art. 22.

24 Rome Statute, Art. 8 *bis* (1), 25(3).

25 Kevin Jon Heller, *Retreat from Nuremberg: The Leadership Requirement in the Crime of Aggression*, 18 EJIL 477, 489 (2007) (quoting several delegations and scholars who regard the "control or direct" test as a restatement of the "shape or influence" test, not a narrowing of the circle of liability; Heller himself disagrees); Carrie McDougall, The Crime of Aggression Under the Rome Statute of the International Criminal Court (Cambridge: Cambridge University Press, 2013),182 ("key negotiators were aware of the distinction proposed and its precedent and made a conscious choice to narrow the scope of perpetrator captures"); on the other hand, Claus Kreß, one of the German negotiators, informs me that there was no such intention (personal communication). Nikola Hajdin likewise sees no narrowing in the "control or

direct" test. Hajdin, *Aggression in International Criminal Law*, 127–34 (unpublished manuscript); see also Nikola R. Hajdin, *Responsibility of Private Individuals for Complicity in a War of Aggression*, 116 AJIL 788 (2002). Yudan Tan, *The Rome Statute as Evidence of Customary International Law* (Leiden: Brill Neijhoff 2021), concludes that the Rome Statute's version of the leadership clause does not represent customary international law, because of the possibility that it narrows it. Tan, 202–46.

26 *Case Concerning the Arrest Warrant of 11 April 2000 (Democratic Republic of Congo v. Belgium)*, I.C.J. Reports 2002, p. 3; Al-Adsani v United Kingdom (App. No. 35763/97), [2001] ECHR 35763/97 21 Nov. 2001; Jones v. UK; *Arrest Warrant*; *Jurisdictional Immunities of the State (Germany v. Italy; Greece intervening)*, I.C.J. Reports 2012, p. 99 (Feb. 3, 2012). See David Luban, *European Court of Human Rights to Torture Victims: Get Lost*, Just Security (January 15, 2014), https://www.justsecurity.org/5726/echr-torture-victims-lost/ (describing the decisions as "the ugly face of counter-revolution"). The *Jones* decision poo-pooed Lord Browne-Wilkinson's argument that international crimes are not state acts because he and one other Law Lord were the only ones who made it.

27 Draft Articles on Immunity of State officials from foreign criminal jurisdiction, in Report of the International Law Commission, 73rd sess. (18 April–3 June and 4 July–5 August 2022), UNGA Supp. No. 10 (A/77/10), art. 7, at 190–91.

28 Fifth report on immunity of State officials from foreign criminal jurisdiction, by Concepción Escobar Hernández, Special Rapporteur, ILC 68th Sess., UNGA Doc. A/CN.4/701 (14 June 2016), §222, incorporated by reference in Report of the ILC, 69th Sess., UNGA Doc. A/72/10 (2017), §122.

29 Open Society Justice Initiative, Immunities and a Special Tribunal for the Crime of Aggression against Ukraine, February 2023, 23–4, https://www.justiceinitiative.org/publications/immunities-and-a-special-tribunal-for-the-crime-of-aggression-against-ukraine. Since then, many states have asked the ILC to reconsider and to add aggression to the list of crimes for which there is no immunity.

30 Best-known is the first-ever aggression prosecution—preceding the IMT: that of Arthur Greiser, deputy Gauleiter of the Warthegau. Mark A. Drumbl, *"Germans are the Lords and Poles are the Servants": The Trial of Arthur Greiser in Poland, 1946*, in The Hidden Histories of War Crimes Trials, 411 (Oxford University Press, 2013); 1949 Law Reports of Trials of War Criminals (Law Reports), The UN War Crimes Comm'n, Law Reports of Trials of War Criminals, 13 (1949) 70; Patrycja Grzebyk, *The Role of the Polish Supreme National Tribunal in the Development of Principles of International Criminal Law*, in Historical Origins of International Criminal Law, 2 Morten Bergsmo et al., eds. (Florence: Torkal Opsahl, 2014).. Other Polish convictions were Albert Forster, Josef Bühler, and Ludwig Fischer (as an accomplice); the USSR also convicted several Sachsenhausen personnel for crimes against peace. Jonathan Friedman, *The Sachsenhausen Trials: War Crimes Prosecution in the Soviet Occupation Zone and in West and East Germany* in Atrocities on Trial: Historical Perspectives on the Politics of Prosecuting War Crimes (Lincoln, NE: University of Nebraska Press, 2008) 159, 162–3 (Patricia Heberer and Jürgen Matthäus, eds., 2008).

31 First, Second, and Third Interim Reports from the Committee of Enquiry into Breaches of the Laws of War, with Appendices, First Interim Report, at 31 British National Archives, CAB\24\11. I am grateful to Bill Schabas, who kindly provided

me with a copy of this document. However, he disagrees with my views on the immunity issue.

32 European Commission, *Ukraine: Commission Present Options to Make Sure that Russia Pays for its Crimes*, https://ec.europa.eu/commission/presscorner/detail/en/ip_22_7311; Eurojust, *International Centre for the Prosecution of the Crime of Aggression Made Official at United for Justice Conference in Ukraine*, March 5, 2023, https://www.eurojust.europa.eu/news/international-centre-prosecution-crime-aggression-made-official-united-justice-conference; *Ambassador Van Schaack's Remarks on the U.S. Proposal to Prosecute Russian Crimes of Aggression* (March 27, 2023), https://www.state.gov/ambassador-van-schaacks-remarks/; Dr. Gabija Grigaitė-Daigirdė, *The Lithuanian Case for an International Special Tribunal for the Crime of Aggression Against Ukraine*, Just Security (June 1, 2023), https://www.justsecurity.org/86766/the-lithuanian-case-for-an-international-special-tribunal-for-the-crime-of-aggression-against-ukraine/. Ambassador Rein Tammsaar (Estonia), *An International Special Tribunal is the Only Viable Path to a Just and Lasting Peace in Ukraine*, Just Security, May 9, 2023, https://www.justsecurity.org/86516/an-international-special-tribunal-is-the-only-viable-path-to-a-just-and-lasting-peace-in-ukraine/.

33 So I have argued in David Luban, *Fairness to Rightness: Jurisdiction, Legality, and the Legitimacy of International Criminal Law*, in The Philosophy of International Law (Samantha Besson and John Tasioulas, eds., Oxford University Press, 2010), 569–88.

34 Ethica: Ethical Principles for International Criminal Judges (2023), https://www.nurembergacademy.org/fileadmin/user_upload/Ethica_Principles_English.pdf.

Selected Bibliography

Dannenbaum, Tom. *The Crime of Aggression, Humanity, and the Soldier*. Cambridge: Cambridge University Press, 2018.

Hathaway, Oona and Scott J. Shapiro. *The Internationalists: How a Radical Plan to Outlaw War Remade the World*. New York: Simon and Schuster, 2017.

Kreß, Claus and Steven Barriga, eds. *The Crime of Aggression: A Commentary*, 2 vols. Cambridge: Cambridge University Press, 2016.

McDougall, Carrie. *The Crime of Aggression Under the Rome Statute of the International Criminal Court*. Cambridge: Cambridge University Press, 2021.

Open Society Justice Initiative. *Immunities and a Special Tribunal for the Crime of Aggression against Ukraine*, February 2023. Available at https://www.justiceinitiative.org/publications/immunities-and-a-special-tribunal-for-the-crime-of-aggression-against-ukraine.

Trainin, A. N. *The Criminal Responsibility of the Hitlerites* (translation), ed. A. Y. Vishinsky. Moscow: Legal Publishing House NKU, 1944. Available at https://cgsc.contentdm.oclc.org/digital/collection/p4013coll8/id/2366.

Walzer, Michael. *Just and Unjust Wars: A Moral Argument With Historical Illustrations*, 5th ed. New York: Basic Books, 2015.

Concluding Remarks

Marshall J. Breger and Herbert R. Reginbogin

The contributors to this volume have addressed several important topics related to the Nuremberg Trials, particularly concerning individual criminal responsibility for conspiracy against peace, crimes against humanity, war crimes, and the waging of aggressive war. They discuss how these and other war crimes relate to the ongoing conflict in Ukraine and the Nuremberg Principles, having established the legal framework at Nuremberg to prosecute and convict the major war criminals of the European Axis powers of the Second World War. For the first time in history, high-ranking officials were held liable for committing international crimes under individual criminal responsibility. Rather than summary executions, the judicial proceedings of the Nuremberg Trials represented a legal and moral breakthrough, illustrating the triumph of the rule of law over brute force.

The world is currently witnessing horrific atrocities inflicted upon the Ukrainian population due to Russia's invasion on February 24, 2022. Some experts argue that the West and the United States bear responsibility for creating, provoking, and perpetuating the war in Ukraine while intentionally obstructing a diplomatic resolution. The ongoing situation has sparked widespread concern and discussion, outcry, and unsettling silence regarding the challenges faced by the world as Ukraine endures brutal acts of violence.

Meanwhile, the United States distances itself from a rule-based international order by remaining outside the International Criminal Court, a decision that inadvertently supports the primacy of brute force over law. This positions the United States as a benign hegemon, suggesting that the liberal ethos of a superpower can serve as an alternative to established international legal frameworks; this is the complaint of much of the global south. However, this narrative is incomplete; the United States and Europe are, in principle, aligned in their support for a rules-based order. But the reliance on brute force seen in the nineteenth century and now manifested by the Russian invasion of Ukraine poses severe threats to the definitions of international criminal and humanitarian law in the twenty-first century, thereby endangering peace, security, and justice.

The influence and legacy of the Nuremberg Principles on international law are entrenched in the rules, norms, and institutions that formed the attempt at a coherent global governance system after the Second World War. But it was only after the Cold War that a genuine global system emerged, and a clear liberal international order thrived during the subsequent unipolar decade. With no significant competitors, the liberal norms and ideals of the Cold War victors permeated global governance institutions, providing a level of coherence and vitality that was lacking during the era of Soviet-American rivalry. This order reached its full maturity during the era of hyper-globalization when liberal norms and ideals related to free markets, democracy, and human rights became embedded in and promoted by both international and non-governmental organizations in the 1990s.

Nevertheless, the rule-based international order began to decline in the early 2010s with the rise of China, the relative geopolitical decline of the United States, accelerating power shifts, the Covid-19 pandemic, and repeated financial crises corrosively undermining the institutions of global governance. And it must be recognized that the United States itself moved away from the international rules-based order in many ways; "international law" is a dirty word in many parts of Washington today. The rule-based international organizations no longer exert the same regulatory or structural influence, leaving a vacuum for the rise of multipolarity marked by fragmentation amid a surge of protectionism and the widespread weaponization of economic relations and potential trade wars. This situation recalls the interwar years when international organizations struggled with ineffectiveness and the rise of authoritarianism while the spread of democratic governance was backsliding, a sentiment captured by Italian political theorist Antonio Gramsci when he stated, "The old world is dying, and the new world struggles to be born." As Gramsci continues, we live in a "time of monsters," characterized by tension and fear, marked by tyranny against those who dissent or hold differing religious and secular beliefs.

Is the rules-based international liberal world order coming to an end? If so, what might replace it? Will heads of state, leaders, jurists, and others work to prevent the disintegration of the liberal international order unfolding before our eyes? Will it be "America Great Again?"

The chapters in this book have aimed to highlight the increasing importance of international criminal law, especially given the ineffectiveness of the United Nations Security Council. The norm against wars of aggression has been violated without sufficient outrage or punitive actions by UN member states.

Although this "time of monsters" may seem daunting, it is not entirely unexpected. The rules-based international order is simply going through its natural life cycle. Currently, the Regional Brand International Organization like the European Union and Organization for Security and Co-operation in Europe (OSCE) is in decline. Some cling to the hope that the old order can still be salvaged, but they largely ignore harsh realities and continue to narrate a myth. The economic and geopolitical foundations upon which the institutional superstructure of liberal global governance was built appears to be eroding. To meet the crises we now face, the international order must continue to evolve.

About the Editors and Contributors

About the Editors

Marshall J. Breger is Professor of Law at the Columbus School of Law, The Catholic University of America. During the George H. W. Bush administration, he served as Solicitor of Labor and the chief lawyer of the Labor Department. He is the author (with Gary Edles) of *Independent Regulatory Agencies of the United States* (2015) and co-authored *Contest and Control of the Holy Places in Jerusalem*. With Herbert Reginbogin, he edited *The Vatican and Permanent Neutrality* (2022).

Herbert Reginbogin is a Collegiate law fellow at the Catholic University of America Institute for Policy Research. He is a professor of international relations and international law. In recent years, he has taught at several institutions of higher learning on both sides of the Atlantic, including Lefke University (Cyprus), Bogazici University (Turkiye), Cag University (Turkiye), University of Potsdam, Germany, Touro Law School of New York, Kehl University am Rhein (Germany), and Istanbul Kent University Graduate School in Turkiye. Dr. Reginbogin's selected list of publications includes *The Nuremberg Trials: International Criminal Law Since 1945* with Christoph Safferling (2006), *International Notions of Neutrality* with Pascal Lottaz (2018), *Permanent Neutrality: A Model for Peace, Security, and Justice* with Lottaz (2020), *Permanent Neutrality in the Post-Cold War* along with Heintz Gaertner and Pascal Lottaz (2022), *The Vatican and Permanent Neutrality* with Marshall Breger, forthcoming *Turkiye-US Relations in the 21st Century* with Ozan Ormeci, and *Nuremberg Principles and Ukraine: Peace, Security, and Justice* with Marshall Breger. Several publications have appeared in diverse fields, from international finance to climate security and sustainability. In addition, he has worked on several high-profile litigation cases and energy security issues in the Eastern, Mediterranean, European Union, and the United States regarding international Maritime law, international refugee issues, the stabilization of the international world order, and kleptocracy. He is currently working on a new security architecture for US national security. He received his Licentiate Philosophiae/PhD from the University of Bern and a Bachelor of Arts from Whittier College.

About the Contributors

Herve Ascensio is Professor of International Law at the University of Paris 1 Panthéon-Sorbonne (Sorbonne Law School) is also the Director of the master's degree program in Global Business Law and Governance. He serves as counsel in proceedings before the International Court of Justice, as an expert before investment arbitral tribunals and national courts, and as an alternate arbitrator at the Court of Conciliation and Arbitration within the OSCE. Additionally, he is a national expert for the OSCE human dimension and served as a rapporteur on human rights in Belarus in 2023. Professor Ascensio has co-edited a treatise on international criminal law (Pedone, 2012), written a handbook on international economic law (PUF, coll. Thémis, 2020), and authored numerous publications on public international law, international criminal law, and international economic law. In January 2022, he taught a special course at the Hague Academy of International Law on the responsibility of business enterprises in international law. He is also the co-editor of the Annuaire français de droit international (French Yearbook of International Law).

Michael Bazyler is Professor of Law and the 1939 Society Law Scholar in Holocaust and Human Rights Studies at Fowler School of Law at Chapman University in California. His book *Holocaust Justice: The Battle for Restitution in America's Courts* was cited by the US Supreme Court, and *Holocaust, Genocide, and the Law* was a 2016 National Jewish Book Award winner. His current research examines the role of legal professionals during the Second World War. He has held fellowships at Yad Vashem, the US Holocaust Memorial Museum, and Harvard University.

Stephanie Bock is Professor and Chair for Criminal Law, Criminal Procedure, International Criminal Law, and Comparative Law at the Philipps-University Marburg and Director of the International Research and Documentation Centre for War Crimes Trials in Marburg, Germany. Her main research fields are international criminal law, transitional justice, comparative criminal law, feminist legal theory, and victims' rights.

Michael Bryant is Professor of History and Legal Studies at Bryant University, specializing in the impact of the Holocaust on the law, human rights, German criminal law, and international humanitarian law. He is the author of *Confronting the Good Death: Nazi Euthanasia on Trial, 1945–53*; *Eyewitness to Genocide: The Operation Reinhard Death Camp Trials, 1955–66*; *Nazi Crimes and Their Punishment, 1943–1950: A Short History with Documents* (Passages: Key Moments in History) (Hackett, 2020); *A World History of War Crimes: From Antiquity to the Present* (with Michael Bazyler, Kristen Nelson, and Sermid al-Saraf); *Comparative Law: Global Legal Traditions for the 21st Century*; and (with John Michalczyk and Susan Michalczyk) *Hitler's Mein Kampf and the Holocaust: A Prelude to Genocide.*

Aubrey Butler graduated with honors from the University of California, Los Angeles, with a Bachelor of Science in Biology. She is currently a student at Fowler School of Law at Chapman University in California, where she has received both a scholarship and the Distinguished Student Fellowship. She is also a Managing Editor of the prestigious *Chapman Law Review*. She has written extensively inside and outside the classroom with publications in the genres of both fiction and nonfiction.

Eric Chang is the founder and principal of an international dispute practice focusing on international commercial and investor-state arbitration. Eric has trained, qualified, and practiced in civil law and common law systems and jurisdictions: he is a former French *Avocat à la cour* at the Paris Bar and a member of the New York and California Bars.

In addition to his international disputes practice, Eric is an Officer in the United States Army Judge Advocate General's Corps, Reserve Component. In this role, Eric has served on three active duty mobilizations, including, most recently, a combat deployment with Combined Special Operations Joint Task Force–Levant (CSOJTF-L) in the Middle East. He currently serves as a National Security Law Attorney at the Office of the Judge Advocate General, National Security Law Division, at the Pentagon.

David Cohen is the founding co-director of the Center for Human Rights and International Justice (the Center) and WSD Handa Professor in Human Rights and International Justice at Stanford University. He is also a professor of Classical and Environmental Social Sciences at Stanford. He taught at UC Berkeley from 1981 to 2012 as the Ancker Distinguished Professor for the Humanities and the founding Director of the War Crimes Studies Center (which moved to Stanford as the Center for Human Rights and International Justice in 2013).

At the Center, Cohen has led various rule of law, human rights, international justice, and judicial reform projects in Southeast Asia/ASEAN, Bangladesh, Sierra Leone, the former Yugoslavia, Kosovo, and Rwanda. At the UN Special Court for Sierra Leone, he developed and led judicial training, trial monitoring, and research projects, including victim support and protection. From 2006 to 2008 he served as the International Law Expert Advisor for the Commission on Truth and Friendship established by the governments of Indonesia and Timor-Leste, and from 2006 to 2022 assisted the Khmer Rouge Tribunal/ECCC in Cambodia on trial monitoring, training, and community outreach programs. Since 2003, he has worked with the Supreme Court of Indonesia, the Indonesian Attorney General's Office, and the National Human Rights Commission on various capacity-building, human rights, rule of law, and judicial reform projects. Prof. Cohen has published widely in international criminal law, transitional justice, human rights, legal history, and other areas.

Viviane Dittrich is the deputy director of the International Nuremberg Principles Academy. Previously, she taught for several years at the London School of Economics and Political Science (LSE), at Royal Holloway, University of London, and Sciences Po Paris. She was a visiting fellow at the LSE Centre for International Studies, an Honorary Research Associate at Royal Holloway, and a Visiting Researcher at iCourts, Centre of Excellence for International Courts at the University of Copenhagen. Her research has appeared in several edited volumes and academic journals. Drawing on extensive field research, her work has focused on the notion of legacy and the process of legacy building at the international criminal tribunals and comparatively investigates the ICTY, ICTR, SCSL, ECCC, ICC, and IMT (Nuremberg). Dr. Dittrich has been editor of the Nuremberg Academy Series (TOAEP) and recently co-edited three volumes:

The Past, Present, and Future of the International Criminal Court (2021), *Integrity in International Justice* (2020), and *The Tokyo Tribunal: Perspectives on Law, History, and Memory* (2020). Her new book is an edited collection of 70 Years Nuremberg Principles – 70 Perspectives (forthcoming). After studying in France, England, and the United States (Wellesley College), she received an MSc in International Relations from the LSE and a master's degree from Sciences Po Paris. She holds a PhD from the LSE.

Lawrence Douglas is the James J. Grosfeld Professor in the Department of Law, Jurisprudence, and Social Thought at Amherst College. He is the author of seven books, including *The Memory of Judgment: Making Law and History in the Trials of the Holocaust* (2001) and *The Right Wrong Man: John Demjanjuk and the Last Great Nazi War Crimes Trial* (2016), a New York Times "Editor's Choice" and an inspiration for the Netflix documentary series "The Devil Next Door." In addition, Douglas has published two novels, *The Catastrophist* (2007), a Kirkus "Best Books of the Year," and *The Vices* (2011), a finalist for the National Jewish Book Prize. His commentary and essays have appeared in many venues, including *Harper's*, *The Wall Street Journal*, *The Washington Post*, *The Economist*, and *The Los Angeles Times*, and he is a regular contributor to the *Times Literary Supplement* and *The Guardian* (United States), where he is a contributing opinion writer.

He is the recipient of major fellowships from the National Endowment for the Humanities, the American Council of Learned Societies, the United States Holocaust Memorial Museum, the Institute for International Education, the Carnegie Foundation, and the American Academy Berlin.

Nataliia Hendel is a researcher at the Institute of Information, Security, and Law of the National Academy of Legal Sciences of Ukraine. She was a research fellow at the Geneva Academy of International Humanitarian Law and Human Rights (2022–2024). She is a member of the advisory board of the GROMADA project, which aims to recover Ukraine's environment. Dr. Nataliia Hendel is a member of the Ukrainian Association of International Law, a member of the European Society of International Law, and a member of the Environmental Peacebuilding Association. She is the Head of the Centre for International Humanitarian Law at the Ukrainian Association of International Law. She is an expert at the Fundamental Research Support Fund. Dr. Hendel holds an LLM and a PhD in international law. Dr. Nataliia Hendel is an expert and trainer on international humanitarian law of the Ukrainian Red Cross Society, the Training Centre for Prosecutors of Ukraine, the Higher School of Public Administration, and the Ukrainian Helsinki Human Rights Union. She is an expert in the Council of Europe Programme for Human Rights Education for Legal Professionals (HELP) working group in the "HELP for Ukraine including during wartime" to develop a course on international humanitarian law and human rights. She was a member of Ukraine's Interdepartmental Commission for Implementing International Humanitarian Law (2015–17). She is a member of the working group on protecting the natural environment from the consequences of armed conflict of the Interdepartmental

Commission on the Application and Implementation of International Humanitarian Law in Ukraine.

Gerd Hankel is Dr. jur., MA, philologist and legal scholar, studied at the Universities of Granada (Spain), Mainz and Bremen. Since 1993 Hankel has been doing freelance work for the Hamburg Institute of Social Research; since 1998 Hankel was a research fellow at the Hamburg Foundation for the Advancement of Science and Culture. Hankel's current research deals with the legal aspects of atrocity crimes in the African Great Lakes region, international humanitarian law, and human rights law.

For recent publications, see https://www.his-online.de/en/staff/person-details/person/gerd-hankel/.

Isabelle Hassfurther is a German-qualified attorney and legal advisor at the Berlin-based European Center for Constitutional and Human Rights. As a member of ECCHR's International Crimes and Accountability program, it focuses on accountability for international crimes committed in the war of aggression against Ukraine, supporting survivors through strategic legal interventions in various European jurisdictions. Isabelle Hassfurther studied politics and law with a focus on general public international law, international criminal law, and human rights in Germany, France, and the UK. She holds an LLM from the University of Cambridge with a specialization in international law. After her studies, she worked as a research and teaching associate at the Walther Schücking Institute for International Law, Kiel, where she is pursuing her PhD.

Francine Hirsch is the Alice D. Mortenson/Petrovich Distinguished Chair of Russian History at the University of Wisconsin-Madison, where she teaches courses on Soviet history, Modern European history, and the history of human rights. She received her PhD in History from Princeton University in 1998. Her first book, Emp*ire of Nations: Ethnographic Knowledge and the Making of the Soviet Union* (2005), received several awards, including the Herbert Baxter Adams Prize of the American Historical Association and the Wayne S. Vucinich Prize of the Association for Slavic, East European, and Eurasian Studies. Her second book, *Soviet Judgment at Nuremberg: A New History of the International Military Tribunal after World War II* (2020), won four book prizes, including the George Louis Beer Prize of the American Historical Association and the 2021 Certificate of Merit for a Preeminent Contribution to Creative Scholarship from the American Society for International Law. Hirsch has also published op-eds and thought pieces in *The Washington Post*, *The Boston Globe*, *The New Republic*, *Time*, *Lawfare*, Just Security, and other outlets. Her new book project investigates the history of Russian-American-German entanglement, focusing on economics, science, culture, and diplomacy.

Kristina Hook is Assistant Professor of Conflict Management at Kennesaw State University's School of Conflict Management, Peacebuilding, and Development. She is an anthropologist and scholar-practitioner specializing in genocides and mass atrocities, Ukrainian identity, and Ukraine-Russia relations, past and present. She has conducted multiple years of fieldwork across thirty-three locations in Ukraine since 2015. Dr. Hook's forthcoming book explores the 1932–3 Holodomor's enduring impact on modern Ukrainian society, including how diverse Ukrainian stakeholders interpreted this history to predict Russia's modern genocide and Ukraine's strong resistance.

She is the Principal Author of "The Russian Federation's Escalating Commission of Genocide in Ukraine: A Legal Analysis," published in July 2023 by New Lines Institute and the Raoul Wallenberg Centre for Human Rights. She received a joint PhD in Anthropology and Peace Studies from the University of Notre Dame, USA.

Jack Hueseman Jack Hueseman is an associate attorney at Thompson Coburn LLP in St. Louis, Missouri. He previously clerked at the United States District Court for the Eastern District of Missouri, following his graduation from Washington University School of Law with a Juris Doctor in 2023. During law school, he was a research assistant and teaching assistant for Professor Leila Nadya Sadat, as well as a member of the Philip C. Jessup International Law Moot Court Team, an Executive Articles Editor on the Washington University Global Studies Law Review, and President of the International Law Society.

Michael J. Kelly holds the Senator Allen A. Sekt Endowed Chair in Law at Creighton University in Omaha, Nebraska. He serves as Co-Chair of the American Bar Association's Internet Governance Task Force on the Board of Directors for both L'Association International de Droit Penal (AIDP) based in Paris and the International Scientific and Professional Advisory Council (ISPAC) of the United Nations Crime Prevention Programme based in Milan, and on the Board of Trustees of the Foundation for Natural Resources and Energy Law (FNREL) based in Denver. Professor Kelly directs the Kaiman Center for International Criminal Justice & Holocaust Studies at Creighton University.

Anton Korynevych is a Ukrainian lawyer specializing in public international law, international humanitarian law, and international criminal law. He serves as ambassador-at-large in the Ministry of Foreign Affairs of Ukraine. Dr. Korynevych is the Agent of Ukraine before the International Court of Justice in the Allegations of Genocide and was the Agent of Ukraine before the International Court of Justice in the Application of the International Convention for the Suppression of the Financing of Terrorism and of the International Convention on the Elimination of All Forms of Racial Discrimination cases (Ukraine v. Russian Federation). Dr. Korynevych is also a Co-Agent of Ukraine before the International Court of Justice in a dispute under the Convention for the Suppression of Unlawful Acts against the Safety of Civil Aviation (Canada, the Kingdom of Sweden, Ukraine, and the United Kingdom of Great Britain and Northern Ireland v. Islamic Republic of Iran). He is also the Head of the Task Force Working Group on freeze, seize, and confiscation of Russian assets within the Prosecutor General's Office of Ukraine. He holds the title of Honored lawyer of Ukraine, having served as Permanent Representative of the President of

Ukraine in the Autonomous Republic of Crimea (June 25, 2019 to April 25, 2022). He received his PhD in International Law in 2011 at Taras Shevchenko National University of Kyiv. He is an associate professor of the International Law Department of the Institute of International Relations of Taras Shevchenko National University of Kyiv and a member of the Board of Trustees of the Ukrainian Association of International Law. Dr. Korynevych is coordinating the establishment of the Special Tribunal for the Crime of Aggression against Ukraine in the Ministry of Foreign Affairs of Ukraine.

Tymur Korotkyi is a vice-president of the Ukrainian Association of International Law. He has taught international law and related subjects for over twenty-five years in Kyiv and Odesa. He is a leading researcher at the Institute of Information, Security, and Law of the National Academy of Legal Sciences of Ukraine. He is Chairman of the Fund for Fundamental Research Support. Tymur Korotkyi authored over 600 publications on various problems of international and domestic law. In partnership with the Ukrainian Helsinki Human Rights Union, he developed a course on international humanitarian law for schoolteachers. Since 2014, Professor Korotkyi has concentrated on implementing international humanitarian law as an expert, coach, and consultant. He is a member of the Interdepartmental Commission on the application and realization of norms of international humanitarian law with the Ministry of Reintegration of the Temporary Occupied Territories of Ukraine. He also serves as an advisor to the President of the Ukrainian Red Cross Society.

Vaios Koutroulis is a professor of public international law at the Faculty of Law and Criminology of the Free University of Brussels (Université libre de Bruxelles—ULB). He has published extensively on international humanitarian law and *jus contra bellum*. Vaios Koutroulis is a member of the International Humanitarian Fact-Finding Commission, the only treaty-based standing body addressing compliance with the 1949 Geneva Conventions and their first additional protocol. As a practitioner, he was a member of the legal team of Belgium in the case concerning *Questions relating to the Obligation to Prosecute or Extradite (Belgium v. Senegal)* in 2012 and the Counsel of Belgium in the recent (2024) advisory proceedings on the occupied Palestinian territory, both before the International Court of Justice.

Claus Kreß is Professor of International Law and Criminal Law. He is the Director of the Institute of International Peace and Security Law at the University of Cologne. In addition to his scholarly work, comprising more than 200 publications on the law on the use of force, the law of armed conflicts, and international criminal law, he has been a member of Germany's delegations in the negotiations regarding the International Criminal Court between 1998 and 2017. In 2019, he was appointed Judge ad hoc at the International Court of Justice in the Case of the Application of the Convention on the Prevention and Punishment of the Crime of Genocide (*The Gambia v. Myanmar*). Since 2021, he has served as the Special Adviser to the Prosecutor of the International Criminal Court on the Crime of Aggression.

David Luban is Distinguished University Professor at Georgetown University Law Center and also holds the Distinguished Chair in Ethics at the Stockdale Center for Ethical Leadership, United States Naval Academy. A philosopher by training, his research interests include legal and military ethics, international criminal law, and human rights. He is a member of the American Academy of Arts and Sciences, a distinguished fellow of the National Institute for Military Justice, and recipient of the 2022 M.C. Bassiouni Justice Award for contributions to the study of core international crimes. His 2014 book *Torture, Power, and Law* received the American Publishers Association Award for Professional and Scholarly Excellence in philosophy. Other books include *Lawyers and Justice: An Ethical Study*; *Legal Modernism*; *Legal Ethics and Human Dignity*; and the co-authored textbooks *Legal Ethics* (ninth edition) and *International and Transnational Criminal Law* (fourth edition). He has lectured in more than twenty countries, and his work has been translated into nine languages. Luban is currently completing a book on the moral and legal thought of Hannah Arendt.

Oleksandra Matviichuk is a human rights lawyer focused on Ukraine and the OSCE region issues. She leads the human rights NGO Center for Civil Liberties. It works on legislative reforms, conducts public oversight of law enforcement agencies and the judiciary, organizes educational initiatives, and implements international solidarity programs.

Since the onset of Russian aggression in Ukraine in 2014, the Center has monitored political persecution in occupied Crimea, documented war crimes and crimes against humanity in the Donbas region, and spearheaded international campaigns to secure the release of political prisoners held by Russian authorities. In response to the full-scale war beginning in February 2022, Oleksandra Matviichuk and other partners launched the Tribunal for Putin initiative to document international crimes under the Rome Statute of the International Criminal Court in all regions of Ukraine targeted by Russian attacks.

Kiran Mohandas Menon is a lawyer specializing in international criminal law, public international law, international human rights law, and transitional justice. Apart from his long association with the International Nuremberg Principles Academy (including a stint with its Founding Office), Menon has extensive international experience, having worked on international law and human rights matters in Sri Lanka, Spain, Greece, Ireland, and Germany. He taught international human rights law courses at the Irish Centre for Human Rights at the University of Galway.

Very Rev. Mitered Archpriest Mark Morozowich, a western Pennsylvania native, began doctoral studies at the Pontifical Oriental Institute in Rome after serving parochial assignments in the great Pittsburgh area. He earned his doctorate with a Summa Cum Laude as he defended his dissertation entitled: "The Holy Thursday Liturgy in Jerusalem and Constantinople from the Fourth to the Fourteenth Centuries." He began his teaching career at the Catholic University of America. He quickly became the Associate Dean for Seminary and Ministerial Programs in 2006. He was then promoted to Dean of the School of Theology and Religious Studies in 2011. From 2014 to 2015, he served the University as its Interim Provost. He then returned to lead the school as Dean until July 2023. Among his many notable activities, he raised over $23 million for the school, including establishing five fully funded chairs. He is currently the Bishop Basil H Losten Chair of Ukrainian Church Studies and the Director of the Bishop Basil H. Losten Center of Ukrainian Church Studies within the Institute of Eastern Christian Studies. His research focuses on various topics of liturgical history, from penitential practices and the liturgical year to divergent issues in Eastern Christian Mysteries. His current work focuses on the theology of the assembly in the Byzantine Eucharistic Liturgy and issues of Latinization in the eighteenth-century Ukrainian Catholic Church.

Noelle Quenivet is Professor in International Law and Director of Research and Enterprise at the Bristol Law School of the University of West of England (UK). Before that, she worked as a researcher at the Institute for International Law of Peace and Armed Conflict in Germany. She has widely published in the fields of international humanitarian law, international criminal law, and human rights law, mainly on issues relating to child soldiers, women, and sexual violence in armed conflict. Her latest book, co-authored with Windell Nortje, examines whether child soldiers can invoke duress as a defense under international criminal law.

Eli M. Rosenbaum investigated war criminals and human rights violators for nearly forty years as a prosecutor in the US Department of Justice, including sixteen years as Director of its former Office of Special Investigations. Following Russia's 2022 full-scale invasion of Ukraine, he was appointed by US attorney general Merrick B. Garland to lead the Department's War Crimes Accountability Team (WarCAT) to pursue justice on behalf of victims of Russia's atrocity crimes. Rosenbaum's awards include the Attorney General's Award for Exceptional Service (USDOJ's highest award) and Ukraine's Order of Merit, conferred by President Volodymyr Zelenskyy for the support rendered to Ukraine's pursuit of justice following Russia's 2022 invasion. He is a graduate of Harvard Law School.

Leila Nadya Sadat is the James Carr Professor of International Criminal Law and former longtime Director of the Whitney R. Harris World Law Institute at Washington University School of Law. She served as Special Adviser on Crimes Against Humanity to two International Criminal Court Prosecutors, Fatou Bensouda and Karim A.A. Khan, K.C., from 2012 to 2023. Sadat is an internationally renowned scholar with more than 170 books, articles, and essays to her name. She is the Director of the Crimes Against Humanity Initiative, a project that wrote the world's first model treaty on crimes against humanity, and continues to spearhead the treaty's adoption at the United Nations. Sadat is the current Chair of the International Law Association (American Branch) and a member of the US Council on Foreign Relations and the American Law Institute. She is currently a fellow at Yale Law School's Schell Center for International Human Rights.

Christoph Safferling studied Law in Munich and London. He received his doctoral degree at the University of Munich in 1999 and passed the bar exam in 2000. From 2006 to 2015, he was a professor at the Philipps-University of Marburg and the Director of the International Research and Documentation Center for War Crimes Trials. Since 2015, he has held the chair for criminal law, criminal procedure, and international law at the Friedrich-Alexander University Erlangen-Nuremberg and has been Director of the International Nuremberg Principles Academy since February 2023.

His main fields of research are cybercrime, IT forensics, international criminal procedural law, the mental elements of the crime, and the history of international criminal law. He is one of the principal investigators in the Graduate Training Group of the Deutsche Forschungsgemeinschaft on Cybercrime and IT-forensics and organizer of the annual "Erlanger Cybercrimetag."

Next to more than eighty articles, he is the author of *International Criminal Procedure* (2012), "Internationals Strafrecht" (2012), and is the co-author of the studies "Die Akte Rosenburg. Das Bundesministerium der Justiz und die NS-Zeit" (2016), "Staatsschutz im kalten Krieg. Die Geschichte der Bundesanwaltschaft zwischen NS-Vergangenheit, Spiegel-Affäre und RAF" (2021), and *Victims before the International Criminal Court* (2021). This year he published together with the historian Friedrich Kießling: "Der Streitfall. Wie die Demokratie nach Deutschland kam und wie wir sie neu beleben müssen" (2024).

Ulf Schmidt is Senior Professor of Modern History at the University of Hamburg, founding Director of the Centre for the Study of Health, Ethics, and Society, and a fellow of the Royal Historical Society. His research interests are in the history of modern medical ethics, warfare, and policy in twentieth-century Europe and the United States. He is the author, among others, of *Justice at Nuremberg: Leo Alexander and the Nazi Doctors' Trial* (2004); *Karl Brandt: The Nazi Doctor. Medicine and Power in the Third Reich* (2007); *Secret Science. A Century of Poison Warfare and Human Experiments* (2015); co-editor of *Propaganda and Conflict: War, Media and the Shaping of the Twentieth Century* (2019); and *Ethical Research: The Declaration of Helsinki, and the Past, Present, and Future of Human Experimentation* (2020).

Toby Simpson is Director of The Wiener Holocaust Library, the world's oldest archival and library collection relating to the Holocaust and Nazi era. He led the project "Testifying to the Truth: Eyewitnesses to the Holocaust," which has cataloged, digitized, and translated over 1,000 eyewitness accounts gathered by The Wiener Library between 1954 and 1961, which is now a popular online resource.

Dr. Simpson completed his PhD at Selwyn College, University of Cambridge, with the thesis "Criminology and Criminal Justice Reform in the German Democratic Republic and the Federal Republic of Germany, 1949–1989." He joined the Wiener Library in 2011, creating new exhibitions, tours, and event programs. Between 2011 and 2016, he curated or co-curated over a dozen exhibitions for the Library, including "Humanity After the Holocaust: The Jewish Relief Unit, 1943–1950" and "Four Thousand Lives: The Kitchener Camp Rescue." As the Library's Head of Digital, he initiated a long-term project to create an online platform to support the digitization and digital preservation of the Wiener Library's unique holdings across multiple formats, set to be published in January 2025.

Yuri Stoyanov (PhD, the Warburg Institute, University of London) is based at SOAS, University of London. Formerly a senior fellow at the Albright Institute, Jerusalem, his recent and current assignments include visiting professorships at several universities in Europe and Asia; his past assignments include Oxford, British Academy, and Wingate fellowships, and Directorship of the British Academy Kenyon Institute/British School of Archaeology in Jerusalem. He has published widely on the interaction between Zoroastrianism, Judaism, Christianity, and Islam in the ideologies of warfare and peace, sacred space, heterodoxy, and apocalypticism and their current manifestations.

His publications include English-language books such as *The Hidden Tradition in Europe* (1994), *The Other God* (2000), *Defenders and Enemies of the True Cross* (2011), *Fighting the Final Battle. Christian Ideologies of Apocalyptic Warfare* (forthcoming), chapters, articles, and anthologies of sources on Eastern Orthodox theologies of war and peace.

Index

www.ingramcontent.com/pod-product-compliance
Lightning Source LLC
Chambersburg PA
CBHW072001160925
32686CB00003B/8
9781666960761